By the same author

DRUM

THE TREASON CAGE

COMMONSENSE ABOUT AFRICA

ANATOMY OF BRITAIN

ANTHONY SAMPSON

ANATOMY
OF
BRITAIN

HODDER AND STOUGHTON

First published July 1962
Third impression 1962

PRINTED AND BOUND IN GREAT BRITAIN FOR
HODDER AND STOUGHTON LIMITED, ST. PAUL'S
HOUSE, WARWICK SQUARE, LONDON, E.C.4
BY C. TINLING AND CO., LIMITED, LIVERPOOL,
LONDON AND PRESCOT

FOR

MY MOTHER

The characteristic danger of great nations, like the Roman, or the English, which have a long history of continuous creation, is that they may at last fail from not comprehending the great institutions they have created.

Walter Bagehot (Essay on Lord Althorp)

Institutions are worth no more than the men who work them.

Amiel

Just at this moment we are suffering a national defeat comparable to any lost military campaign, and, what is more, self-inflicted.

Duke of Edinburgh, Oct. 17, 1961.

CONTENTS

Contents

Contents

Contents

INTRODUCTION

THIS is a book about the workings of Britain—who runs it and how, how they got there, and how they are changing.

I have not tried to approach it as an historian, or as a student of constitutions, but simply as an enquiring journalist. I first became interested when I returned to England after four years in Africa, and found myself curious about the slowness and complexity of Britain compared to Africa: and later, as a columnist for *The Observer*, writing often about people in prominent positions, my curiosity broadened. So I decided, rashly, to spend eighteen months exploring the ramifications of people and power, and this book is the result.

I have aimed to offer myself as an informal guide to a living museum, describing the rooms and exhibits as I found them, giving basic hard facts and frequent quotations from others, but not hesitating to add my own comments.

I have had to restrict the field. There has been no time or space to cover the broad fields of art, medicine, religion or provincial life and culture which all go to make up the character of Britain: they would need another quarter-million words. I have concentrated on the basic anatomy—the arms and legs and the main blood stream. Nor do I deal with the life of ordinary people. Basically this is a book about the managers—in government, industry, science or communication. But within those spheres I have let my curiosity wander and filled in some flesh and blood. In particular I have tried to give some picture of the metabolism of the anonymous institutions which settle our everyday lives.

My method has been fairly straightforward: I have written to about two hundred people, asking to see them, and asking what they were up to. They have, with a few exceptions, been surprisingly helpful: the more important the people, the easier, it seems, they are to see. There was no difficulty in talking to all the cabinet, senior civil servants, or chairmen of the biggest corporations. One or two said that they could not, for differing reasons, talk freely: but the only people who said they were too busy to see me were Charles Clore, Sir Hugh Fraser and Lord Cobbold.

Many people I have quoted directly, but several of the exciting conversations were off-the-record, and the information I gleaned from them is discreetly disseminated through the book. Apart from those two hundred top people, I have talked to many more in junior positions, and have tried to build up an intelligence system inside the institutions.

In the design of the book, I have begun by looking at the old ruling powers—the aristocracy, the palace, parliament and the cabinet: from there—where decisions cease to be central—I have tried to trace the fragments and splinters of power. I have toured through the old Whitehall institutions where major decisions are taken, pausing to examine the education which produces them, and bringing several threads together in the person of the Prime Minister. In the second part I turn to the financial institutions of the City of London, culminating with the massive new influence of insurance companies, and their impact on ordinary people. In the third part I look at industrial organisations, the vast, self-contained corporations and the professions that intertwine with them—scientists, accountants or advertising men—ending with the upstart and revolutionary world of television. I have given more space and attention to the newer and lesser-known institutions, particularly the great bureaucracies of Whitehall and industry. Much of the earlier chapters will be familiar to those who follow contemporary affairs, but in the later sections I cover territories which are less widely reported.

Finally, in the last part, I put forward a general view of British leaders and institutions as I found them, and how they stand in relation to Britain's current problems.

In each chapter, and particularly in the last, I try to trace not only the changing power, but the changing people. This is primarily a book about personalities, both single and corporate, and I have not hesitated to write about individuals and their idiosyncrasies. I am convinced that, in spite of the anonymity of bureaucracies, individuals are still decisive.

I have stuck firmly to Britain as it is now, avoiding historical flashbacks whenever possible, but inevitably I have found myself frequently referring to the Victorians, who invented so many of our institutions, and from time to time I have used Walter Bagehot, both as a critic with a very contemporary tang, and as a kind of yardstick for developments since.

Several themes recur in different chapters, and are brought together in the last: the impact of the new 'meritocracy' on the old aristocracy; the conflict between professionals and amateurs; the gap between prestige and power and (in Bagehot's phrase) between dignified and efficient parts; the proliferation of committees; the prevalence of sons-in-law; the obscuring of ends by means; the pressure of conformism; the difficulties of combining democracy with efficiency; the conflict between old, protected, semi-feudal values and aggressive competition and salesmanship— a contrast typified by taxis and minicabs, or Lord Kindersley and Jack Cotton. Some themes—for instance the dominance of Oxbridge and public schools in some fields—recur regularly: but they have thrown themselves up so repetitively that I do not feel that they can be ignored. Many of the themes are common to America and Europe, and many of the problems are those of all capitalist countries: but in Britain—with her continuous traditions —the contrasts are unusually vivid, in the harsh juxtaposition with the Common Market and America. I have tried to use the quotations at the heads of chapters to illuminate some of the themes.

I make no apology for being critical and sharp in my comments: there is no point, it seems to me, in inspecting institutions without a sceptical eye. A loss of dynamic and purpose, and a general bewilderment, are felt by many people, both at the top and the bottom in Britain today, including many of the two hundred I talked to, and I see no point in disguising it. Nor do I see why we should refrain from the self-criticism which marked Victorian critics or many critics in America today. I have written in a deliberately detached and analytical way, rather as a foreign correspondent reporting territories: I have tried to expose myself to the influences of each of the institutions, and then (the hardest part) to retreat, and consider them dispassionately. I have not thought it necessary to reiterate that I consider Britain the most civilised and humane country, and the happiest to live in, and I have not dwelt on the long traditions of democracy, and the tolerance and humanity of most British institutions, which Englishmen easily forget and which writing this book has brought home to me.

To cover this large canvas before its characters and situations change, to try to catch a moment of contemporary history before it moves on, I have been forced to write this book at high speed. I am well aware that I have often failed to do justice to complex institutions, but writing such a book is like painting the Forth Bridge: if I had spent longer on it, the beginning would have been rusty by the time I had reached the end. But I hope, nevertheless, that this brisk tour through the gallery of power may be of some interest to others, as it has been to me, in understanding the kind of country we live in.

My indebtedness to others is enormous. This has been a brain-picking operation on a large scale, and to all whose brains I have picked I am grateful: there is no space to thank them, and many would prefer not to be mentioned. But the people without whom the book would not have happened are Michael Davie of *The Observer*, who first encouraged me to try it; Robin Denniston of Hodders, whose collaboration and perspective, as with my first book, have been crucial; the printers, Tinlings, who have wonderfully faced the difficult task of producing a long book in a short time; Professor Asa Briggs, for his advice and encouragement; my colleague Ivan Yates for many patient and perceptive comments; my secretary Madeleine Kallay, who has had the appalling task of filing, checking, reading my writing and typing 300,000 words twice over; and the research assistants who have helped me at various stages—Ann Grant, Corinna Ascherson, Kathleen Halton, Juliet Shubart, and particularly Virginia Makins, who has seen the book through the last exhausting stage of rewriting, checking and updating, with great efficiency and perception. I have also much appreciated the help of T. J. Wardill, who drew the charts, and of my friend Len Deighton for his design of the endpapers.

I am also greatly indebted to R. L. Urwin, for his compilation of a prodigious index in the most difficult and hectic conditions, and for his help with proof-reading and advice.

We have taken great pains to corroborate facts, and the chapters have been read—though not necessarily approved—by people in the institutions concerned. But I am well aware that among roughly 50,000 facts some will inevitably have errors, and I will be grateful for any corrections.

Anatomy of Britain

PART ONE

I

ARISTOCRACY

The feudal character of the English state, now that it is getting obsolete, glares a little, in contrast with the democratic tendencies.
Ralph Waldo Emerson, 1856.

(The aristocracy) has impressed on the whole nation the sound ideal of a certain comfortable ease which is undoubtedly a useful corrective to the nerve-destroying contemporary scramble for gold.
Wilhelm Dibelius, 1922

The English aristocracy has been adroit in more than one respect. First of all it has always been involved in public affairs; it has taken the initiative in protecting its rights; it has talked a great deal about liberty. But what distinguished it from all others is the ease with which it has opened its ranks.
de Tocqueville, 1833.

In the eighteenth century, it was not difficult to answer the question: 'who rules Britain?' It was ruled by the ruling classes. More specifically, it was governed by—apart from the monarch— two great families, the descendants of the Churchills, Granvilles and Pelhams on one side, and the Stanhopes, Pitts and Grenvilles on the other. The wealth and dominance of the great British families—only about one hundred and fifty prominent people— reached its climax in the late eighteenth century. They became richer and more separate, competing in domestic splendour: palaces like Chatsworth or Belvoir Castle are their memorials.[1] Then, in the age of the French Revolution, the intrusion of industry and the growth of the towns, the aristocracy began to come to terms with the new world, and to lose its separateness. In five years from 1784, the younger Pitt increased the numbers of peers from 200 to 250.[2] In the famous if exaggerated words of Disraeli: 'He created a plebeian aristocracy and blended it with the patrician oligarchy. He made peers of second-rate squires and fat graziers. He caught them in the alleys of Lombard-street, and clutched them from the counting-houses of Cornhill.'

[1] J. H. Plumb: *Sir Robert Walpole, the Making of a Statesman*, 1956. p. 8–11.
[2] A. R. Wagner: *English Genealogy*, 1960.

3

The end of the old order—or what looked like the end—came with the first Reform Bill in 1832. Lord Bathurst cut off his pigtail —the mark of the superior courtier—and said 'Ichabod, for the glory is departed.'

But the glory was a long time departing, and the aristocracy managed to adapt themselves. 'By exercise, temperance and plebeian alliance', wrote G. M. Young of early Victorian England, 'the spindle-shanked lord of Fielding had become the ancestor of an invigorated race. They had shed their brutality and extravagance; their eccentricities were of a harmless sporting kind; they were forward in good works; they habitually had family prayers.' And they succeeded in keeping their wealth: Emerson, visiting Britain in 1856, described how the Marquess of Breadalbane could ride a hundred miles in a straight line, on his own property, and the Duke of Sutherland owned the whole of Sutherland, from sea to sea. He heard how some lords (even then) were forced to earn money showing people round their houses, and how ruined dukes were living in exile for debt: but in general he regarded the English nobles as 'high-spirited, active, educated men born to wealth and power'.[1]

Gradually, with the rise of industry, public schools, the professional civil service, death duties and Lloyd George, the old aristocracy lost its monopoly of power. The growth of the Labour Party and the big business corporations, with their new race of managers and technocrats, had little to do with aristocrats. The first world war was a greater shock to their world than the second. The great London palaces of the Whig oligarchs—Devonshire House, Lansdowne House, Holland House, Grosvenor House— which for so long were the centres of intrigue and influence—gave way to hotels and office blocks. The names remained, but the occupants were quite different. On their country estates they were forced to sell land to pay death duties, and to show the public round their houses to pay for their upkeep.

This is a popular picture of the twentieth-century aristocrat— much promoted by plays, films and aristocrats—a sad, impoverished man, living in a flat in a crumbling Tudor mansion, helping to collect half-crowns and serve the ice-cream, while the public in thousands come out of charabancs, their plastic raincoats squeaking together, to gape at armour, four-posters and tables laid for imaginary banquets.

But it is a misleading picture. In the first place, the aristocracy

[1] Emerson: *English Traits*, 1888. p. 178.

4

are, in general, much richer than they seem. With democracy has come discretion. Their London palaces and outward show have disappeared, but the countryside is still full of millionaire peers: many of them, with the boom in property, are richer now than they have ever been. Their individual wealth cannot compare with the new corporate wealth of industrial giants or insurance companies: but members of some of the oldest families are still among the richest men in Britain. Death duties, which used to eat into the large fortunes, are now nearly always circumvented by trusts and gifts.

In the second place, the British aristocracy have remained entangled with politics and power to an extent which—one suspects—Lord Bathurst would never have dreamt. Would he have guessed that, a hundred and twenty years after 1832, a Churchill would be prime minister? Would he have imagined that, in 1962, the Prime Minister, the Foreign Secretary, the Governor of the Bank of England, the Chairman of the Defence Committee, the Ambassador to Washington would all either belong, or be closely related to, the old aristocratic families?

THE ARISTOCRATIC EMBRACE

The British aristocracy has survived partly because it has never been very exclusive: it has always been ready to admit outsider sons-in-law, provided they were rich, and this has helped it to keep up with the times. There has never been a nobility as in pre-revolutionary France, where 100,000 aristocrats had a separate, privileged life of their own, provided they could show that all sixteen great-great-grandparents were aristocrats: (in 1842 an English earl's daughter married a member of the Hungarian Esterhazy family, but found life in Vienna intolerable because the experts discovered that her grandmother's father had been a banker).[1]

By Continental standards, the English aristocracy is not very aristocratic, and its history has been very mercenary. Only two families, the Ardens and the Berkeleys, can be traced to before the Norman Conquest. There is still a George Arden, a doctor at Windsor, author of *Posterior Dislocation of Both Shoulders*: and there are several Berkeleys, including Baroness Berkeley and Lennox Berkeley, the composer; a Captain Berkeley still lives at Berkeley Castle, where Edward II was murdered. A few

[1] G. W. E. Russell: *An Onlooker's Notebook*, 1902.

aristocratic families, such as the Giffards and Ferrers came over with William the Conqueror: but a large number of titles—including all the dukedoms—were killed off in the Wars of the Roses.

The first big batch of surviving peers came with the dissolution of the monasteries in 1530, which founded the persistent fortunes of the Dukes of Bedford and Devonshire, and the Marquesses of Bath. But the numbers of the peerage were doubled by James I and Charles I, who made seventy-two peers in twenty-six years: King James charged £10,000 for a barony. Another large increase came with the younger Pitt: and the new aristocrats soon became merged with the old. In the nineteenth century scores of politicians, bankers, and merchants became peers, and a vast increase came with Lloyd George, who raised over three million pounds for the Liberal Party by the sale of peerages. Another boom —without the politics—came after the last war, under Attlee (who made 98 in six years), and has continued under Macmillan. There has been a steady inflation in the proportion of peers: in medieval times there were about fourteen peers per million: now there are nineteen—not including life peers. And *over half* the peerages existing today date from 1906 or later.[1]

While new blood was coming into the aristocracy through new titles, peers introduced new blood to their families by marrying heiresses. Long before death duties, gambling, drinking and building had reduced many noble fortunes, which could only be revived by marrying money (it has even been argued that several families brought about their own extinction by marrying single heiresses—the children of less fertile marriages, who were liable themselves to be infertile). And the British aristocracy kept itself rich by the ruthless custom of primogeniture, by which the estate and the title passed only to the eldest son, and other sons had to make their own way in the army, the Church or business, or vanish into obscurity and poverty. It is still common to find a rich peer living grandly in the family mansion, and his younger brother or his dowager mother living in a three-roomed flat: before the war there was even a second sons' club founded to protest against it. The favouritism for the eldest son has kept the old estates intact: peers could never maintain their pomp if every son of a lord was a lord.

But the greatest strength of the British landed aristocracy is that they are the *only* aristocracy. There is no strong separate mercantile aristocracy as in Holland, or an intellectual aristocracy

[1] Sir Ivor Jennings: *Parliament,* 1957. p. 384.

as in France, or an urban aristocracy as in America. The life of the country squire, if not of a peer, remains the ambition of successful Englishmen, whether dons or property developers, and few intellectuals would turn down an invitation from a duke. Before the war, it looked as if intellectuals more successfully rejected aristocratic habits, knighthoods and invitations: but since the war there has been much less revolt, and the aristocrats remain masters of the 'aristocratic embrace'—hugging angry radicals, poets, or working-class novelists into their cosy world. 'Never', said the American sociologist, Edward Shils, writing on Britain, 'has an intellectual class found its society and its culture more to their liking.'[1]

THE DUKES

'The Parson knows enough who knows a Duke.'
William Cowper, 1783.

Among the peerage, dukes have always been regarded as a class by themselves. Of the twenty-seven still surviving—excluding the five royal dukes—the origins are odd. Only two, Norfolk and Somerset, go back before Charles I. Two, Bedford and Devonshire founded their fortunes on the sacking of the monasteries by Henry VIII. Four were bastard sons of Charles II—St. Albans (from Nell Gwynn), Grafton (from the Duchess of Cleveland), Richmond (from the Duchess of Portsmouth) and Buccleuch (from Lucy Walters). Only two were promoted for obvious merit as opposed to wealth—Marlborough and Wellington.

Up till the first world war, the dukes lived legendary lives— though already diminished. Many were wealthier than the King. To commoners brought up before 1914—men of the generation of Harold Macmillan, Oliver Lyttelton or Duff Cooper (who all married duke's daughters) ducal families were awesome. They had massive country estates, teams of liveried servants and dominating town houses—Grosvenor House, Norfolk House, Devonshire House: scores of London streets still bear their family names. Grosvenor House was the grandest, with a great grey colonnade along Park Lane and a courtyard behind it: inside was one of the finest picture galleries in Europe, to which the working classes were admitted on Sundays. The house was knocked down in 1930, to build Grosvenor House hotel—still with a grey colonnade in front of the hotel rooms. The new Norfolk House contains

[1] *Encounter*, April, 1955.

British Aluminium, Devonshire House has motor-car show-rooms. Only one of the ducal town houses remains—Apsley House, stranded on an island and surrounded by traffic in the middle of Hyde Park Corner; it has been turned into the Wellington Museum, but it still contains a live Duke of Wellington, devoted to the memory of his forefather, and author of his iconography, living in a large flat on the top. Once Apsley House was known as 'No. 1, London': but the present duke calls it more discreetly '149, Piccadilly'.

What sort of lives do the dukes lead today? Four live abroad—two in Africa (Montrose in Southern Rhodesia, Manchester in Kenya), where for the moment it is easier to live a ducal existence. But the other twenty-three live remarkably similar lives: nearly all went to Eton (three were there together), and several to Christ Church: half have been Guards officers. All are based in the country, and most have a flat in London. They have an average of 1·5 wives, 2·2 children, 1·7 houses and 7 titles. There are twenty-five married dukes, and thirty-eight duchesses.

Dukes are apt to be involved in royal occasions, and their daughters often become ladies of the bedchamber. They are referred to by the Queen in official documents as 'right trusty and entirely beloved cousins'; and they are supposed to be addressed as 'your grace'—which makes for conversational embarrassments. Like bishops, they are referred to by their christian name and their title—Bernard Norfolk, or Walter Buccleuch.

The dukes keep themselves to themselves. Of those in Britain, only four married (as their first duchess) a commoner, five married daughters or grand-daughters of dukes, three of marquesses, four of earls; the range of their duchesses is no broader than it was in 1900. The most remarkable case of endogamy is the Duke of Northumberland: his father was the eighth Duke, his brother was the ninth Duke, his mother was the daughter of the Duke of Richmond (who was also related to the Duke of Portland). He married the daughter of the Duke of Buccleuch (who had married the grand-daughter of the Duke of St. Albans), and his sister married the Duke of Hamilton. He is thus related to a quarter of the dukes.

Only two dukes are anywhere near broke: none are salaried employees, and most of them have succeeded in hanging on to much of their fortunes. At least half are millionaires. The Duke of Beaufort—a master of foxhounds whose car-number is MFH1—

owns 52,000 acres in Gloucestershire, an area often known as 'Beaufortshire'. The Duke of Buccleuch—the descendant of a medieval Scots chieftain—has three big houses in Scotland and the Midlands, all of them full of art treasures and closed to the public, and a flat in Grosvenor Square: he controls businesses, including a harbour, and is Chairman of the Royal Bank of Scotland. The Duke of Rutland has 18,000 acres, two big houses in the Midlands, and an art gallery. Most dukes have held on to their family collections: in 1961 the Duke of Leeds sold Goya's portrait of the Duke of Wellington for £140,000. The Dukes of Westminster, Bedford and Portland still own areas of London.

The oldest dukedom is held by Bernard Marmaduke Fitzalan-Howard, sixteenth Duke of Norfolk; his family became earls of Arundel (where they still have 15,000 acres) in 1139, and dukes in 1483. As hereditary Earl Marshal of England, the Duke is paid twenty pounds a year—a salary fixed in 1483. He is put in charge of special royal occasions, such as the Coronation and State Funerals, and his teddy-bear features, encased in heraldry, have thus become familiar on television.

But in spite of their ritualistic functions, the Norfolks remain very wealthy and shrewd: they own not only a chunk of Sussex, but part of Sheffield: and recently the duke, in a well-timed property deal, sold bits off the Strand which bear his names (Norfolk Street, Howard Street, Arundel Street).

The Norfolks have always—with temporary exceptions—been Roman Catholics, and remained so throughout the Reformation: their estate in Sussex is still a centre of Catholic activity, with a big Catholic church at Arundel and a smaller Protestant one, and the duke is surrounded by Catholic members of his family, the Fitzalan-Howards. The dukedom will pass, through a complicated succession, to a Brigadier in the Guards, Miles Fitzalan-Howard.

The number of Howards has for long been legendary. The eleventh and drunken Duke of Norfolk, according to Wraxall, in 1783 planned a dinner party in St. James' Square, to commemorate the tercentenary of the dukedom, to which every male descendant of the first duke would be invited. He discovered at least six thousand, many 'in very obscure and indigent circumstances', and gave it up. As Pope wrote:

What can ennoble sots, or slaves, or cowards?
Alas, not all the blood of all the Howards.

9

Into the discreet and sheltered world of the traditional dukes there burst in 1953 a disturbing new presence—the new Duke of Bedford, who came back from South Africa. The Russell family, of which the philosopher is a reluctant member, have always been unpredictable: the previous duke was a prominent pacifist and the family have been rich enough to indulge every kind of eccentricity: their motto is *Che Sarà Sarà*. The new duke was no exception. Faced with the problem of paying £4½ million death duties, he set about establishing himself as a new phenomenon—a showman-duke—and came into the middle of the cosmopolitan whoopee world. He pushed the financial assets of a title and estate to their legitimate conclusion, opening up his eighteenth century mansion, Woburn Abbey, with every kind of ballyhoo and side-show, including a private zoo, a park with bison and eleven kinds of deer, a playground, two million pounds' worth of pictures, a chinese dairy, and occasional nudist camps. 'I soon found to my embarrassment', he blandly explains in his autobiography, *A Silver-plated Spoon*, 'that one of the principal attractions of the house was myself'. But his embarrassment has not been over-apparent; his genial bespectacled face stares out from advertisements to attract customers: 'just a quick run on the M1'. He offers special lunch-parties for Americans to have lunch with a duke for ten pounds: and he shows no signs of disliking his duties: 'being a showman is more fun', he wrote, 'than sitting about in dignity or potting pheasants.' His surrounding publicity was heightened when he left his duchess to marry a French TV producer; and his son married a banker's beautiful daughter.

Bedford's brash exploits appalled more stately dukes who, while using and often enjoying publicity, preferred to maintain a private mystique of dukedom. 'I suspect many of my fellow peers disapprove of my behaviour and approach', remarked Bedford, 'but frankly I couldn't care less. Perhaps a little more friendliness on their part would make them more popular and more successful.' Apart from exploiting his title, Bedford has added little to the conception or influence of a duke: but in purely financial terms he has been sensationally successful. He moved Woburn Abbey quickly to the top of the 'league table' for stately homes, bringing in almost twice as many visitors as Devonshire, and three times more than Marlborough. These were the leaders among the five hundred houses that were on show in 1960, with the revenue from half-crown tickets (not including the large extra profits from trinkets, ice-cream or teas):

Duke of Bedford (Woburn).	.	431,000	£53,875
Lord Montagu (Beaulieu) .	.	289,000	£36,125
Duke of Devonshire (Chatsworth)	.	239,000	£29,875
Earl of Warwick (Warwick Castle)	.	200,000	£25,000
Duke of Marlborough (Blenheim)	.	123,000	£15,375
Marquess of Bath (Longleat)	.	112,000	£16,000
Ministry of Works (Osborne)	.	100,000	£12,500
Marquess of Salisbury (Hatfield) .	.	90,500	£11,312
Princess Royal (Harewood)	.	71,000	£8,875
Duke of Rutland (Haddon Hall) .	.	62,000	£7,750

Most of the ducal families have retreated from politics: only Buccleuch's son sits in the House of Commons. Sutherland was once Paymaster-General, Portland was once an Assistant Whip, and Norfolk was a Parliamentary Secretary—all Conservatives: but now the only duke in Whitehall is Andrew Cavendish, eleventh Duke of Devonshire. He lies in the centre of the network following page 34: his uncles include the Prime Minister and Lord Salisbury, and he is related by marriage to President Kennedy and Fred Astaire. Devonshires have been in and out of politics for four hundred years: the first Duke, who built the family seat in 1687, was once fined £30,000 for brawling at court; and other Cavendishes discovered the composition of water and founded the Cavendish laboratory at Cambridge.

The present Duke became Minister of State for Commonwealth Relations in 1961, in his uncle's government, and since then he has surprised some members of the Turf Club by bringing black men to lunch. He is a tall, gay, quite witty duke who talks fast and irreverently: he is about as near as one can get to the debonair young dukes of novelists. He moves between his house in Mayfair, his shooting lodge in Yorkshire, his house in Ireland, and Chatsworth, the colossal palace in Derbyshire with 111 bedrooms, which he moved back into in 1960, where he entertains ducally while the public mill around the lawns: even after £2½ million death duties much of the family estate is still intact. Devonshire is probably the most active of all the dukes—shooting, racing, politics, City and elaborate social life: but they remain traditional ducal activities, and the earlier Cavendish interest in science and art has subsided.

What will happen to the dukes? The last to be created, apart from royal relatives, was Westminster in 1874, who came from an old Norman family, the Grosvenors, and became one of the richest of all the Victorians, owning a quarter of central London including the whole of Belgravia (named after him), much of which—including Eaton Square—still remains in the family's hands. The present Westminster is a solitary old man who used to breed heavy-laying ducks: but his family's fortune is by far the largest of the dukes' (said to be bigger than Charles Clore's) with big estates in Canada, Australia and South Africa, as well as London. Since 1953, when the last duke died, a whole sub-department of the Inland Revenue has been engaged in collecting £20 million death duties.

Since 1874 there have been no non-royal dukes: and the fact that Churchill did not accept a dukedom suggests that no more will be made. Churchill, as it happened, very nearly *was* a duke: for the first eighteen years of his life, until his uncle had a son, he was the heir to the dukedom of Marlborough. That is one example of the danger of modern titles, for as a duke, in the House of Lords, Churchill could probably not have been prime minister. But Churchill has never taken very kindly to the aristocracy from which he sprung: and even in his old age he has preferred the company of self-made men, like Aristotle Onassis, Emery Reves and Lord Beaverbrook.

Dukedoms will never actually die out: Leeds will become extinct, and so possibly will Portland and Newcastle, but most others have plenty of potential heirs: but with their inter-marriages, their isolated estates, and their absorption with the past, they are becoming more and more cut off from the world around them. They have become more shut in on themselves, more of a close-knit tribe, than they ever were: now there are not even upstart dukes to revivify them. They have largely retreated from the world of politics and London life, back to the estates from which they came: to an extraordinary extent they have succeeded in continuing a feudal, rural, pre-industrial existence in the midst of an urban, bourgeois country. With one or two exceptions—such as the sons of the Duke of Richmond—they and their offspring have little connection with the new world of managers, bureau-cracies and industrial corporations with which most of this book will be concerned. In only one industry are they prominent—the heavy industry of horse-racing.

Dukes are often spoken of nowadays as if they were men to be pitied, debilitated by their titles, fenced-in like a tribe of aborigines. It is sometimes assumed that to be a duke is itself an all-consuming and productive profession. Thus Lord Kinross, writing in 1943:

'Twenty-six men with few of the average man's opportunities. Men who cannot rise, only descend in the social scale. Men condemned to eternal publicity, whose private lives are seldom their own. Men who may live only where their grandfathers have chosen, and where the public expects. Men hamstrung by an inherited amateur status, to whom barely a profession is open. Men born limited by the responsibilities of too large an income. Men born into a world where there is one law for the duke, and another for the poor, perpetually victims of their own class government.'[1]

But in fact the limitations on dukes' lives are very few. They are not compelled to spend their day in seventeenth-century sports. The management of their estates is nearly always successfully delegated: and in so far that they have publicity—such as attended the wedding of the Duke of Marlborough's heir to Tina Onassis —it is not always unwelcome. There is nothing to stop them taking an interest in new universities, technology, the Commonwealth or contemporary art. Their social prestige gives them, as to Prince Philip, immense opportunities for leadership and enterprise—a duke can make anything fashionable—but most have preferred to live in the world of their ancestors. Their speeches in the House of Lords give some idea of their interests: between 1955 and 1960 only eight spoke at all: Atholl spoke about salmon, game laws, leisure and pig meat; Buccleuch spoke about pests, agriculture, deer and trees; Sutherland made several speeches, half of them about deer.

PEERS AND GENTRY

Altogether in December 1961 there were 934 hereditary peers in Britain, belonging to five different orders:

> 5 Royal Dukes
> 27 Dukes
> 38 Marquesses
> 203 Earls
> 138 Viscounts
> 523 Barons.

All of them except dukes are called 'Lord': but within the peerage each order has a different aura. The younger sons and the

[1] Lord Kinross: The Dukes of England. *Life*, November 15, 1943.

daughters of dukes and marquesses are known as 'Lord John' or 'Lady Ann': but the children of viscounts or barons are merely called 'Honourable'.

Marquesses, like dukes, are becoming rarer: none has been created since the Marquess of Willingdon, the Viceroy of India, in 1936. The premier Marquess is Winchester, whose title goes back to 1551: he is the oldest peer at 99, married the daughter of a Parsee high priest, and lives in a hotel at Monte Carlo. But most of the rest date from the eighteenth and nineteenth centuries. They are noticeably less grand than dukes, though several are very wealthy—like the Marquess of Northampton (known as the 'Boxing Marquess') who moves between the oldest country house, Compton Wynyates, and his Elizabethan mansion, Castle Ashby, and owns 10,000 acres, including a valuable corner of Surrey.

New earls, too, are rare: only nine have been created since the war—an odd mixture including a wartime field-marshal (Alexander), an admiral of the fleet (Mountbatten), two ex-prime ministers and two ex-cabinet ministers. Retiring prime ministers are always offered an earldom, though since 1900 four of them (Bonar Law, MacDonald, Chamberlain and Churchill) have turned it down.

Viscounts are scarcer, but more contemporary: they are thought, for some odd reason, to be more in keeping with modern Britain, and twenty have been made since the war. Between earls and viscounts are nice distinctions: why, for instance, was Alexander made an earl and Montgomery only a viscount? (Was it anticipated that Montgomery might be more eccentric?) There are a motor-car viscount (Nuffield), two newspaper viscounts (Rothermere and Kemsley), a soap viscount (Leverhulme) and a beer viscount (Younger).

Last come the barons—much the commonest of the peers, and the most booming: half were created in this century, and 110 have been made since the war—a fifth of the total baronage, and a curious reflection on the social revolution. In the past, barons have been something of a joke: G. W. E. Russell, the nineteenth century diarist, has described how Pitt was once asked by his banker, Smith, for the privilege of driving through the horseguards: 'No,' said Pitt, 'but I can make you an Irish Peer.' Next day Mr. Smith was Lord Carrington—the ancestor of the present First Lord of the Admiralty.

A few of the baronies are very old: the premier barony is held by a young baroness who farms in Ireland, whose title goes back to 1264: and the ten oldest baronies, all medieval, still have land and fortunes. But most of them are more modern and mercantile. There are a Unilever baron, a Shell baron, a BP baron, a Rootes baron, a sugar baron (Lyle), tobacco barons (Dulverton, Sinclair), banker barons (Swaythling, Rothschild, Catto, etc.) and several whisky and brewing barons—collectively known as 'The Beerage' (Guinness have an earl, a viscount and a baron). Since Lloyd George's time the new barons have not necessarily been wealthy men, and many of them, like Lord Heyworth of Unilevers, are managers rather than entrepreneurs.

To the hereditary barons have been added since 1958 the life barons—a device for bringing new peers into the House of Lords without being burdened with their offspring.[1] When life peers were introduced, many people expected that new hereditary peers would no longer be made, but the supply has continued unabated. Nineteen life barons had been made by 1961, and five women (whose form of address is still uncertain: they were meant to be called 'Baroness', but the title has not caught on). There is no obvious difference between life peers and ordinary new peers: but the influx of life peers has had a relatively enlivening effect on the House of Lords. 'It's like the BBC and the ITA', said one peer, 'competition seems to have improved the programmes.'

But the peerage is very far from being synonymous with the aristocracy and outside the world of Lords and Honourables, there are thousands of families who have continued for centuries, living prosperously in the country—loosely known as 'the gentry': there are 2,400 pages of them in *Burke's Landed Gentry*. There is also the curious title of baronet—a kind of hereditary knight— invented by King James I to pay for the settlement of Ulster, 'so that the King's wants might be relieved out of the vanities and ambitions of the gentry'. There are now about 1,500—nearly twice the peerage, including no less than 27 Tory MPs: but their future seems shaky. The Labour Party, between 1945 and 1951, stopped making them at all—except for one each year to the Lord Mayor of London: but the Conservatives have shown a renewed fondness for them, and made 73 between 1952 and 1960.

One example of the continuing gentry is Sir William Worsley, Bart., who emerged suddenly into the limelight when his daughter married the young Duke of Kent in 1961. Sir William is part of a proud, prosperous breed, the Yorkshire squires. His family have

---

[1] Life Peers were first proposed in 1856, for distinguished men who were too poor to support the dignity of an hereditary title.

lived at Hovingham for five hundred years, and when his daughter married the Duke one genealogist calculated that she, too, had royal blood. Sir William lives in a big Palladian mansion, Hovingham Hall, surrounded by farming land, hunting and shooting. He takes part in local affairs and committees: he joined the local regiment, the Green Howards, in two world wars, and became Lord Lieutenant of the North Riding. Like other members of the gentry, the Worsleys have kept themselves separate from London. 'Their proverb is', wrote Emerson of old English families in 1856, 'that fifty miles from London a family will last a hundred years; at a hundred miles, two hundred years; and so on; but I doubt that steam, the enemy of time as well as of space, will disturb these ancient rules.' But the continuity of the gentry has survived railways, cars and planes.

The direct advantages of a peerage are few. A lord finds it easier to get servants, to run up credit, to get the best cuts of beef, to book tables at restaurants and sleepers on trains. He receives parliamentary debates free of charge, and three guineas for every day he sits in the House of Lords. On the other hand he receives hundreds of begging letters, is expected to be rich, and to open bazaars, sign letters and 'take things up' with the government.

But if he has social ambitions, the benefits are obvious. Peers are very active in professions where social prestige is important; and for any form of showmanship or salesmanship a title is invaluable. The fourth Baron Tennyson is an advertising representative; the fourth Earl of Kimberley runs a public relations firm. Lord Montagu of Beaulieu is a publicist and showman, specialising in cars and jazz. Lord Kilbracken has written *Living like a Lord* and *A Peer behind the Iron Curtain*, and Lord Kinross has written *The Century of the Common Peer*. Lord Vivian runs a Chelsea restaurant with his signature on every menu and a special wine called 'My Claret'. Lord Foley has played jazz in America with a coronet on the piano: the Duke of Argyll has signed Argyll socks.

The more confused the social structure in Britain becomes, the more attractive, it seems, is the status-symbol of a title: and the Englishman's love of a lord remains undiminished. 'Never have class divisions been so acute and anguished', Anthony Crosland has written, 'as since they were, theoretically, abolished.' It is often argued that snobbery —the 'pox Britannica' as it has been called—is most rife when classes are confused: 'Snobbery belongs rather to the situation where one class melts imperceptibly into another', wrote Sir Anthony Wagner, the Garter King of Arms, 'and where fairly free movement from one into another is possible.'

PLUTOCRACY

Americans relate all effort, all work and all of life to the dollar. Their talk is of nothing but dollars. The English seldom sit happily chatting for hours on end about pounds.

Nancy Mitford (*Noblesse Oblige*).

Interacting with the traditional Society of old families is the new Society of the self-made rich, the entertainers, the communicators, and the urban hurly-burly sometimes called café society. Writing in 1872, Bagehot quoted approvingly that there is no country where a 'poor devil of a millionaire is so ill off as in England', and said, in defence of the House of Lords, that 'the order of nobility . . . prevents the rule of wealth—the religion of gold'. 'Money alone—money *pur et simple*', he said, 'will not buy "London Society".' Ninety years later he would be much less certain. The ennobled still have a prestige different from that of the merely rich: but the impact of death duties, America, publicity-machines and gossip columns has helped to confuse the two: between peers and publicists there is a natural alliance.

Here we might briefly digress to note the numbers of the rich: the British government does not, as the Americans do, publish the names of the men with the highest salaries, thus proclaiming its plutocracy: all that is known is that 3,000 people have incomes (before tax) of over £20,000 a year, and 15,000 have incomes of over £10,000. But these figures are misleading, because they take no account of capital gains. One recent survey has thrown light on capital wealth. Lydall and Tipping, writing in the Bulletin of the Oxford Institute of Statistics in 1961, estimated that the top one per cent of British adults owned 43 per cent of total net capital —whereas in America (in 1954) the top one per cent owned only 24 per cent of personal wealth. The authors estimated that 20,000 people owned more than £100,000, and that their average holding was £250,000. (While at the bottom there are 16 million people with less than £100 each, and an average of £50.)[1]

This large number of quarter-millionaires obviously includes only a small proportion of aristocrats in the conventional sense: and with the capital gains of the last three years—when the value

[1] *The Economist*, April 29, 1961. p. 434.

of even average equities has doubled—thousands of new men have come into the six-figure class.

A hint of private wealth is provided by servants: the Ministry of Labour in 1960 recorded 30,000 men and 275,000 women in 'private domestic service'—though this includes daily helps or gardeners. According to one domestic agency there are still six hundred butlers in Britain. The *Financial Times* has estimated that their incomes vary from £7 to £15 per week—not including tips which can amount to £5 from a wealthy weekend guest: This is how they reckoned the cost of service in a well-appointed household:[1]

	£
Butler	500
Two footmen at £350	700
Odd man	250
Head housemaid	300
Two housemaids at £250	500
Cook	400
Kitchenmaid	250
Lady's-maid	300
Chauffeur (non-resident)	650
Three daily helps at £150	450
	£4,300
Keep (residents only)	2,000
	£6,300

How far, with a large class of new rich, is the old aristocracy losing ground? The 'religion of gold' has probably waned since Victorian times, when Emerson noted: 'there is no country in which so absolute homage is paid to wealth', and Taine was appalled by the ruthless money-worship. In the gossip columns— a useful if fitful pointer to public interest—the worlds of new millionaires and old aristocrats are often colliding. One frivolous example may throw some light. One night in July, 1961, the *Daily Express* gossip-columnist, William Hickey, had a main exclusive story about the £400,000 yacht built for the shipping millionaire, Basil Mavroleon. Then there arrived a photograph of a baronet, belonging to a 900-year-old family, who had ejected an intruder from his family's pew in the local church—a story which

[1] *Financial Times*, October 18, 1960.

had already appeared, without the photograph, in the previous day's papers. The *Daily Express* had no doubts: the millionaire was pushed out by the baronet.

The two worlds of aristocracy and plutocracy overlap in the 'season'—the succession of private dances and balls given between April and July, which serve as the marriage-market for richer children. In spite of the cost—the minimum for a coming-out is a thousand pounds, and a large dance at a hotel costs about £4,000 —the season has swelled since the war: in 1936 *The Times*—which acts as house magazine for the season—listed 64 private dances: in 1960 there were 108: and in the past few years there has been a bonus of autumn dances, not listed in *The Times*. The season has become an increasingly commercialised affair, with paid hostesses and elaborate publicity arrangements: and since 1959 the Queen has ceased receiving debutantes at the Palace. But the entertainment continues unabated, with a momentum of its own.

FAMILY NETWORKS

Yet with all the apparent confusion in London between plutocracy and aristocracy, and the fissiparous tendencies of modern life, titled families still remain something apart. In spite of the oddity of the modern peerage—the abuses of titles, the disreputable origins, the 'kicking upstairs'—peers remain a proud, self-contained group. Lords are still inclined to marry lords' daughters and honourables to marry honourables: and the old aristocracy has succeeded in maintaining a network of inter-marriages with political and financial powers. Their success can be seen in the tree following page 34, which shows a small sector —though politically the central sector—of the family networks. (The tree is abridged and extrapolated from the series of diagrams published by Lupton and Wilson in the *Manchester School* in 1960, in their revealing commentary on the Bank Rate Tribunal. It omits many relations who have *not* reached jobs of importance: on the other hand it omits many other inter-relationships.)

Several points can be noted in the tree: one is the continuing influence of two great eighteenth-century families—the Devonshires and Marlboroughs—whose relations still abound in politics and banking. Another is the fact that, while the sons and nephews of dukes are not often prominent—with the single exception of Sir Winston Churchill—their sons-in-law frequently are: it is not nepotism so much as *generism* which marks successful careers. It may also be noted that, while old families have their connections with banking, conservative politics, and family businesses, they have very little connection with the heads of corporations, new industries, Whitehall departments, scientists or the heads of other professions which occupy most of this book. It is likely, too, that the tree will appear less striking in five years' time, when the new generation of middle-class conservatives are more in evidence. Part of the tree is due to the idiosyncrasies of Harold Macmillan.

It would be wrong, no doubt, to see this tree as the result of a dynastic plot, whereby old families deliberately ally themselves to future prime ministers: nor is there a secret wand which dukes can wave, which puts their sons-in-law into the cabinet. At some points the tree can be misleading, since sometimes one half of a family do not speak to the other half, or are quite unaware of them: nor does it do justice to the large number of rich backwoods aristocrats, including the middle aged 'custard pie set', who do not often emerge into daylight. But the family relationships do, in general, produce social relationships: and upper-class families, much more than the middle-class, keep contact with their extended families. The importance of the tree, in fact, is not so much the power it confers, as the access and system of communication—a common background and attitude, a common language and trust, reinforced by Eton, Oxbridge and country-house life, which leads one member to prefer another. Every country has its power élite of men at the top keeping in touch with each other: but it is this other network of families which gives Britain its special situation and the contemporary fascination with the idea of 'The Establishment'. Its significance has been explained by Lord Chandos, chairman of Associated Electrical Industries (brother-in-law of the Duke of Leeds):

Chandos: Well, one of the things that people are apt to forget about the Establishment—and I am using it in the pejorative sense, very much like the Jews in finance—is the tremendous interchange of information. Somebody will ring me up and say 'What about Sir Somebody Something to be Chairman of this thing?' and I will say: 'Well, mmm, perhaps'—'all right old boy, that's all I want to know.'

Muggeridge: And this is how it works.

Chandos: Well, you see, because we've seen a certain proof of the thing, like the croupier shuffling the cards, we've seen all these people and we know that so-and-so is superficial but honest, and that so-and-so is profoundly dishonest, and that so-and-so looks over his partner's hand at bridge, and so on, and a lot of this information isn't available. You see some astonishing appointments made by political parties that haven't got this particular...

Muggeridge: Inside information about the élite?

Chandos: Well, yes.[1]

This is one view of the rôle of the 'Establishment': an alternative view is that it creates a closed, self-contained circle which favours hereditary amateurs against self-made professionals, produces 'old-boy' agreements between banks and businesses, and acts as a drag on ambition and dynamic. How far either view is justified is one of the themes of this book.

HOUSE OF LORDS

But much of the prestige of the peerage still rests on its ancient centrepiece, the House of Lords. It has a charm which few people —least of all radicals—seem able to resist. The more cut-off it becomes from everyday life, the greater its attraction for weary businessmen or politicians. On the road outside, the word 'Peers' is painted across the car-park in large white letters. At the door stands a policeman with a strong sense of occasion: 'Do you know who that was who went in?—that was the fifth Marquess of Salisbury.' Inside a tall liveried ex-guardsman, with the decorum of a Hollywood butler, directs you through the vaulted entrance hall, past a long row of elaborate gothic coat-hooks, each one labelled—beginning with H.R.H. D. Windsor (what would happen, one wonders, if he were to walk in?) progressing through other royal dukes to all the peers from L. Aberconway to M. Zetland—one of the many features of the building reminiscent of a school.

Upstairs you come to a series of high dark rooms, embellished with gothic woodwork and carved ceilings: the powerful architecture gives an atmosphere of peace and timelessness, like an eccentric but well-run country house. A life-size white marble statue of the young Queen Victoria, sitting on the Coronation chair and crowned with laurels, looks down on elderly peers sitting at

[1] Interview with Lord Chandos: Granada TV, July 25, 1960.

hexagonal tables, writing letters on gothic writing-paper. Doors lead off to long dining-rooms—one for guests, another for peers only—and to a large bar looking over the river, which serves drinks all day and sells special 'House of Lords' cigarettes. Other closed doors are simply marked 'Peers'—an embarrassing ambiguity for lady peers, for 'peers' can mean the Lords' equivalent of 'gentlemen'.

In the ante-room and passages, soft-footed attendants take messages, escort visitors, and address all peers as 'My Lord'. But in the dining-rooms a momentary sense of reality breaks in: cosy aproned waitresses are apt to talk about the telly and to call peeresses 'my dear', and serve a meal of roast beef and two veg.

Ambling between the ante-rooms are elderly men, exchanging reminiscences and comments about debates. There is an aura of contented old age—older than the oldest men's club. The rooms are full of half-remembered faces of famous men, or politicians who had dropped suddenly out of public life twenty years ago, who—how shall one put it—one had forgotten were still around. There is banter between left-wing peers and right-wing peers, and a great deal of talk about operations and ailments and nursing homes. 'You see this is a kind of hospital,' one earl explained to me, after two peers had come up to talk about their recent illnesses: 'you have to be something of an expert on operations.'

Occasionally a young man appears among the old faces— perhaps a young peer well-off enough to be independent, or one of the many young Government peers. But, as the number of life peers increases, so young faces become rarer and rarer: and the average age climbs inexorably up: in 1961 there were 8 nonagenarians and 87 octogenarians.

Leading off the main ante-room is the chamber itself—the fine flower of the Victorian romantic style. It is quite small, only eighty feet long—twice the length of a large drawing-room. Stained glass windows shed a dark red light, and rows of statues of the barons of Magna Carta—looking misleadingly like saints—look down from the walls. The hall is extravagantly ornate and reminiscent of a rich private chapel. On either side are long red-leather sofas, facing each other across the gangway with dark wood choir-stalls at the back. Between the two sides is something which looks like a huge red pouff, with a back-rest in the middle of it: this is 'the Woolsack', the traditional seat of the Lord Chancellor, stuffed with bits of wool from all over the Commonwealth. Facing the Woolsack are two men in wigs, sitting at a large old desk, full of bits of writing-paper, glue, inkpots, paper clips and an hour-glass.

At the far end, like a reredos, is an immense gilded canopy, stretching half-way up to the roof, with twenty-foot high candlesticks on either side rising from the floor like stalagmites. And in the middle of the canopy, behind bronze rails and a deep red carpet, is the throne.

Sitting on the red-leather sofas, facing each other, leaning back, whispering, putting their feet up, fumbling with papers, making notes, putting a deaf-aid (supplied by the attendant) to their ear, or simply sleeping, are the peers. On a full day—which is rare— you can see them in their groups: a group of bishops or 'Lords Spiritual' (26 of them are allowed to sit in the Lords) in white surplices; a handful of judges (9 sit in the Lords); a cluster of industrial peers—Chandos, Poole, Rootes or Knollys—a row of Government peers—Hailsham, Home, Mills; and facing them some Labour peers—Morrison, Longford, Silkin. More often there is only a handful of peers in the room and a pleasant somnolençe descends while one of them is speaking. The speakers are relaxed, prolix, delighting in the formalities—'My Lords', 'Your Lordships' House', 'The Noble Earl'.

The hours are not strenuous: the peers often sit for only three hours at a time, and never on Fridays. Nor are attendances spectacular: since peers can claim three guineas for attending, young peers have taken to looking in after work, for a sit-down and a drink: the average afternoon attendance has gone up to about 110. Only three peers are needed for a quorum. Lord Chandos did not bother to speak until seven years after becoming a peer, and other recent peers have never spoken. The record number to have attended since the war is about 350—for the debate on commercial television in 1953. 'A policy of militant abstentionism' is how one peer described his absence from a debate.

In the imposing surroundings of the Lords, it is sometimes difficult to remember how unimportant they are. (It is odd to recall, too, that the magnificent edifice was built by the Victorians in 1847, after the first Reform Act had been passed which began the eclipse of its power.) The most that the Lords can do now is to delay a bill by one year: and any 'money bill' they can delay only for a month. Their main impact comes from the few inches of space in next morning's papers.

The unimportance of the Lords derives ultimately from the discomforting fact that the prime minister can create as many peers as he wants to, and so flood the chamber with his supporters:

ever since 1712, when the Tories created twelve new peers to pass the Treaty of Utrecht, the threat has been in the background. The threat was used to pass the Reform Bill of 1832 and the Parliament Bill of 1911—when the powers of the Lords were curbed, after they had thrown out Lloyd George's budget of 1909. Actually to *carry out* the threat nowadays would be embarrassing: in 1950, if the Labour Party had wanted a majority in the Lords, it would have had to create about six hundred peers.[1] But the nightmare is real enough to bring the peers to heel.

What will happen to their Lordships' House? For years, both political parties have been worried about it: as a Second Chamber it is hopelessly unrepresentative—about ninety per cent Conservative, and much more conservative than the Conservative Party. They haven't voted against a Conservative motion since 1832. However many Labour peers are made, their sons often turn out to be Conservative. Life peers have hardly redressed the balance, for more than half of *them* are Tories.

Moreover, peers with political ambitions or other objections are increasingly reluctant to be peers at all. Wayland Young, otherwise Lord Kennet, sits in the Lords but refuses to use his title. Lord Altrincham uses his title but refuses to sit in the Lords. Lord Stansgate, otherwise Anthony Wedgwood Benn, refuses to do either and has tried to continue sitting in the House of Commons —where all his ambitions lie.

There are aspects of the Lords which are delightful—the kindliness, the clubbiness, the eccentric discussions—about prostitutes, or drunkenness, or forestry, or *Lady Chatterley's Lover:* and some debates are far from fatuous. But this extraordinary assembly of dukes, earls, marquesses, viscounts, barons, bishops and judges remains an apparently insoluble dilemma for both parties in Britain of the sixties. Few people are happy about having such an anachronistic assembly in the midst of parliament, but few people can bring themselves to advocate abolishing it. It epitomises the divorce between prestige and power which we will find elsewhere.

Sir Ivor Jennings: *The British Constitution,* 1946. p. 100.

Duke	Date of creation	Name	Education	Home Address
NORFOLK 16th	1483	Bernard Marmaduke Fitzalan-Howard	The Oratory School	Arundel Castle, Sussex.
SOMERSET 18th	1547	Percy Hamilton Seymour	Blundell's, Clare Coll., Cambridge	Maiden Bradley, Wilts.
HAMILTON and BRANDON 14th and 11th	1643	Douglas Douglas-Hamilton	Eton, Balliol	Lennoxlove, E. Lothian.
BUCCLEUCH and QUEENSBERRY 8th and 10th	1663 1684	Walter John Montagu-Douglas-Scott	Eton, Christ Church	Bowhill, Selkirk.
GRAFTON 10th	1675	Charles Alfred Euston FitzRoy	Wellington, Sandhurst	Euston Hall, Suffolk.
RICHMOND and GORDON 9th & 4th also 9th of Lennox	1675 1876	Frederick Charles Gordon-Lennox	Eton, Christ Church	Goodwood, Sussex.
BEAUFORT 10th	1682	Henry Hugh Arthur Fitzroy Somerset	Eton, Sandhurst	Badminton, Glos.
ST. ALBANS 12th	1684	Osborne de Vere Beauclerk	Eton	Newtown Anner, Tipperary.
DEVONSHIRE 11th	1694	Andrew Robert Buxton Cavendish	Eton, Trinity, Cambridge	Chatsworth, Derbyshire.

25

Duke	Date of creation	Name	Education	Home Address
BEDFORD 13th	1694	John Robert Russell	Privately	Woburn Abbey, Bedfordshire.
LEEDS 11th	1694	John Francis Godolphin Osborne	Eton, Jesus Coll, Cambridge	Melbourne House, Jersey.
ARGYLL 11th	1701	Ian Douglas Campbell	Milton, Mass., Christ Church	Inveraray Castle, Argyll.
MARLBOROUGH 10th	1702	John Albert Edward William Spencer-Churchill	Eton	Blenheim Palace, Oxford.
ATHOLL 10th	1703	George Iain Murray	Eton, Christ Church	Blair Castle, Perth.
RUTLAND 10th	1703	Charles John Robert Manners	Eton, Trinity, Cambridge	Belvoir Castle, Grantham.
MONTROSE 7th	1707	James Angus Graham	Eton, Christ Church	Derry Farm, Salisbury, S. Rhodesia.
ROXBURGHE 9th	1707	George Victor Robert John Innes-Ker	Sandhurst	Floors Castle, Kelso.
PORTLAND 7th	1716	William Arthur Henry Cavendish-Bentinck	Eton	Welbeck Woodhouse, Worksop, Notts.

26

Duke	Date of creation	Name	Education	Home Address
MANCHESTER 10th	1719	Alexander George Francis Drogo Montagu	Osborne, Dartmouth	Kapsirowa, Hoeys Bridge, Kenya.
NEWCASTLE 9th	1756	Henry Edward Hugh Pelham-Clinton-Hope	Eton, Magdalene Coll., Cambridge	Madzugatu, Salisbury, S. Rhodesia.
LEINSTER 7th	1766	Edward FitzGerald	Eton	Domaine de Pigranel Mouans Sartoux, France.
NORTHUMBERLAND 10th	1766	Hugh Algernon Percy	Eton, Oxford	Alnwick Castle, Northumberland.
WELLINGTON 7th	1814	Gerald Wellesley	Eton	Stratfield Saye House, Berks.
SUTHERLAND 5th	1833	George Granville Sutherland Leveson-Gower	Eton	House of Tongue, Sutherland.
ABERCORN 4th	1868	James Edward Hamilton	Eton, Sandhurst	Baron's Court, Tyrone, N. Ireland.
WESTMINSTER 3rd	1874	William Grosvenor		
FIFE 3rd	1900	James George Alexander Bannerman Carnegie	Gordonstoun	Elsick House, Stonehaven, Kincardine.

2

LAND

Land is about the only thing that can't fly away.
Anthony Trollope.

LAND occupies such an important place in the mind of Britain that it deserves a digression: with the increase in wealth, cars, suburbs and sport, the shortage of land is becoming agonisingly apparent.

The total area of the United Kingdom is only sixty million acres for a population of fifty-two million—only just over an acre per head: an analysis of populations per square mile is:

United Kingdom	559
United States	57
France	213
Italy	386
W. Germany	554
Holland	845
Belgium	775
Japan	509

But much of the nineteen million acres in Scotland, and the three million in Northern Ireland, are virtually uninhabitable, and can be bought for as little as a pound an acre. In 1924 Lord Leverhulme sold 56,000 acres for £500—twopence halfpenny an acre: and the huge county of Sutherland has a hundred acres per inhabitant. But 80 per cent of British land is agricultural, and it contains, apart from people:

11 million cattle
28 million sheep
6 million pigs
107 million poultry (twice as many poultry as people)
200,000 horses.[1]

[1] Agriculture in Britain, C.O.I., 1960

28

The ownership of land has changed a good deal in the last century: these were the biggest landowners in 1883:

Duke of Sutherland	1,358,000 acres
Duke of Buccleuch	460,000 „
Marquess of Breadalbane	438,000 „
Duke of Richmond	286,000 „

Today the biggest landowner, by far, is the Forestry Commission, which owns 2,475,000 acres, on which they plant more than a million trees a year: they own, in fact, almost a twentieth of Britain—though most of it is bleak and mountainous. The other richest landowners are

The Crown	292,000 acres
The Church	220,000 „

The size of the big private estates is not published: but the Duke of Sutherland, the Duke of Buccleuch and other hereditary land-owners, such as the Countess of Seafield or Lord Lovat, are still among the biggest. On a humbler level, there are now far more people who own the land they farm: in 1908 only 12 per cent of agricultural land was farmed by owner-occupiers: but since then death duties have broken up big estates, and rent controls (until 1957) were so uneconomic for landowners that they often sold off their land. Today more than 50 per cent of land is farmed by owner-occupiers.

For nine hundred years or so, the value of much of the land remained, in real money terms, about the same as it was in the Domesday survey of 1086.[1] But in the past few years the price of nearly all land has begun to rise steeply: between 1958 and 1960 the average price of small farms of under fifty acres went up by 54 per cent—from £134 to £206 an acre.[2] This jump is partly explained by the freeing of agricultural rents; but also by the sheer shortage of earth. Even the value of Scottish moors has rocketed: in 1961 the Balnagown Castle Estate of 90,000 acres was sold for £420,000—about five pounds an acre, while a next-door moor had not long before gone for less than a pound an acre.[3]

Several factors have pushed up the prices: one important one

[1] L. Dudley Stamp: *The Land of Britain*, 1946.
[2] Figures from Agricultural Economics Research Unit at Oxford.
[3] *Daily Telegraph*, September 14, 1961.

has been the fact that land which is not being developed suffers lower death duties than ordinary capital: this probably explained, for instance, the keenness of Charles Clore, the shoe-and-property millionaire, to buy two million pounds' worth of Herefordshire, which only yields $2\frac{1}{2}$ per cent. But round the urban areas the steady cause of the increase is the simple need for space.

Britain has not, like Holland, France or America, developed an urban bourgeosie which is content with a luxury flat. The fact that Britain, one of the most urbanised countries in the world, continues to takes its values and habits from the land has repercussions in many subsequent chapters. The lure of the land gives strength to the amateur ideal, and reinforces the distaste for trade: behind the most intensive urban activity there is still the vision of hedgerows, villages and a country manor. This indestructible tradition has given stability, charm and humanity to the English tradition; but at a time when the country is not being vigorously challenged, it can provide a misleading retreat. Architecture is often held to be a symbol of national attitudes; if so current building suggests that the image of the country house is now almost overpowering. For while the Victorians approached town architecture with boundless daring, building new forests of cast-iron and gigantic Gothic castles, contemporary businessmen prefer to dress up office blocks as outsize Georgian mansions full of fake antiques. While eighteenth-century aristocrats were full of architectural innovation, scarcely a dozen large private houses have been built since the war in anything approaching a contemporary style.

3

PALACE

When there is a select committee on the Queen the charm of royalty will be gone. Its mystery is its life. We must not let in daylight upon magic.

Walter Bagehot.

We invest our rulers with qualities which they do not possess and we connive at the illusion—those of us who know better—because monarchy is an illusion which works. It has a 'pragmatic sanction'.

Dr. Tom Jones, 1937.

MONARCHS

IN Europe in 1900, there were kings or emperors in Germany, Austria, Russia, Italy, Portugal and Spain. Now there are only seven monarchies (excluding the Grand Duchess of Luxembourg, the Prince of Monaco and the Prince of Liechtenstein, who has only 14,000 subjects). They are, in order of numbers of subjects:

> Queen Elizabeth of the United Kingdom
> Queen Juliana of the Netherlands
> King Baudouin of Belgium
> King Paul of Greece
> King Gustav Adolph of Sweden
> King Frederick of Denmark
> King Olaf of Norway

They are a select, endogamous profession: five of them are descendants, or married to descendants, of Queen Victoria, 'the matriarch of Europe'. Both the King of Sweden's wives have been descendants of Queen Victoria: and the King of Denmark married the daughter of the King of Sweden. The English are German, the Swedes are French, the Norwegians and Greeks are Danes. They might seem an anachronous and dwindling profession; but in fact all the monarchs are more secure than they were fifty years ago. All of them have yielded most of their traditional power to prime ministers and cabinets.

But most of the kings and queens have kept the respect of their people by diminishing not only their power, but their style and expense. Outside England, the most formal is King Baudouin, who has a big palace in Brussels and is attended by a large household and heated controversy. The Queen of Holland is probably richer than Queen Elizabeth, with an allowance of £170,000 a year; but she lives a simple life with her husband, Prince Bernhard, who is an active director of KLM, the Royal Blast Furnaces and the Netherlands Bank for National Recovery.

The others are aggressively democratic: the King of Denmark —who has a well-tattooed chest—answers his own letters and telephone, bows to his guests, conducts the royal orchestra, and has even made a film of 'a day in the life of a king' to show how ordinary he is. The King of Norway (who is in remote succession to the British Throne) studied political science at Balliol; and his father Haakon began the modernisation of kings by refusing to accept the throne in 1905 unless he was elected. The King of Sweden, an archaeologist and Fellow of the Royal Society, spent years in the civil service as a monarch-trainee. The poorest of them is probably Paul of Greece, who once worked as a mechanic with Armstrong Siddeley's in Coventry (one of the many unnoticed visitors to Britain—like Chou En-lai, who once worked in the Carlton Grill). In 1956 King Paul had to close down his Athens palace from lack of funds, and refused a rise of £40,000 a year because of political opposition.

But the British monarchy is in a class by itself: and in the past fifty years it has become increasingly cut off from the rest. Edward VII, when thrones were shaky, was touchy about monarchic solidarity: 'I cannot be indifferent to the assassination of a member of my profession,' he said when he refused to recognise the Serbian régime after the murder of King Alexander: 'We should be obliged to shut up our businesses if we, the Kings, were to consider the assassination of Kings as of no consequence at all.' But nowadays—though assassinations are of course disapproved of— there is a less close fellow-feeling. British courtiers are apt to talk with contempt about 'those bicycling kings' (it is a measure of the sanctity of the British monarchy that the thought of a sovereign on a bicycle, or even on a bus, is regarded as inherently laughable). And the coolness between monarchs was reflected by the lack of 'foreign royals' (as the palace calls them) at Princess Margaret's wedding.

Only in Britain is there still a monarchy on the grand and sanctified scale, supported by religious processions, courtiers, mass adulation and above all by a full-blown titled aristocracy. In its blend of showmanship, religion, diplomacy and occasional public hysteria, the monarchy remains an important part of the national character.

At the head of this unique institution is Her Most Excellent Majesty Elizabeth the Second, by the Grace of God, of the United Kingdom of Great Britain and Northern Ireland and of Her other Realms and Territories Queen, Head of the Commonwealth, Defender of the Faith, Sovereign of the British Orders of Knighthood. The Queen is the fortieth monarch since the Norman Conquest, descended among others from Charlemagne, Egbert King of Wessex, Rodrigo the Cid and the Emperor Barbarossa.

BLOOD ROYAL

At this point we might digress to look at the question of royal blood, which has attracted so much mystique in the past. The ancestors of the Queen are a mixture of German, Greek, and English: the English side is much less exclusive than the Continental—among the Queen Mother's sixty-four great-great-great-grandparents have been two dukes, a director of the East India Company, a banker, three clergymen (one related to George Washington), the landlord of the George Inn at Stamford, a London toyman and a London plumber.[1]

After twelve centuries or so, royal blood has been scattered through Britain: the genealogist the Marquis of Ruvigny estimated about 100,000 living descendants of Edward III in 1911. The most concentrated area of descendants of early kings, extraordinarily enough, is probably Pitcairn Island in the Pacific. This happened because Fletcher Christian, the chief mutineer of the Bounty, was descended from Edward I. He and his accomplices took refuge on Pitcairn, together with eleven Tahitian women; and their descendants—many of them called Christian—survive on the island.

With all this royal fecundity, and with Queen Victoria's grandchildren spread over Europe, it is surprising how small the actual British royal family remains. All younger sons of kings are made dukes, and their sons and descendants continue as dukes (though they drop 'His Royal Highness' after two generations). With so many large families, one might expect scores of royal dukes. But it seems that younger sons of kings have a habit of leaving the

[1] A. R. Wagner, *English Genealogy.* p. 198.

country or just dying out: apart from bastards' families, only the Dukedoms of Gloucester and Kent survive.

THE QUEEN'S YEAR

The outward life of the Queen is bound by a routine which has hardly changed from year to year—Christmas at Sandringham, Easter at Windsor, August and September at Balmoral, most of the rest of the year at Buckingham Palace or abroad. The royal excursions to Ascot and Edinburgh have become a fixed part of the calendar, as certain as spring and autumn. This is the sum of the official engagements of the Queen, as listed in the Court Circular between May 1960 and May 1961:

The Queen gave about 240 audiences

    of these 22 were to the Prime Minister,
           20 to other Ministers,
           23 to Commonwealth PMs,
           60 to British diplomats, governors and high commissioners,
           26 to foreign diplomats,
           12 to generals, admirals, air marshals,
           6 to judges and bishops,
           4 to civil servants.

She held 13 Councils,
           6 Investitures,
           3 Garden parties,
           5 Receptions and Evening parties,
           2 State Banquets for visiting royalty,
           4 Dinner parties,
           8 Lunches,
           10 small lunches after audiences.
              (And other informal lunches and dinners not listed in the Court Circular.)

She went to 13 Lunches (mainly on visits),
           4 Dinners (at embassies, etc.),
           5 Receptions,
           14 Exhibitions, films, theatres, sporting events.

She spent 5 weeks at Windsor,
           9 weeks at Balmoral,

4 weeks at Sandringham,
1 week in Edinburgh,
3 days in Wales,
1 week in Shetland and the Outer islands,
4 days in Copenhagen,
6 weeks in India,
4 days at Ascot,
2 days at Epsom,
1 day at a horse show.
> (Apart from unofficial visits to Goodwood, Badminton and other equestrian events.)

She took part in 2 State Visits (Nepal and Thailand),
1 Opening of Parliament,
1 Trooping the Colour,
1 Cenotaph service.

She visited 11 Schools, Colleges, Universities,
3 Factories,
11 Other institutions.

Attended 10 Military functions.
Opened 8 Buildings.
Launched 1 ship.
Unveiled 9 Plaques.

It is a settled routine. On royal tours it can become exhausting: but it has large compensations—including three months' holiday (apart from the interruptions of cabinet boxes) at Balmoral and Sandringham.

Behind the official routine, the Queen's own life remains remarkably well concealed. She is known to be shy, conscientious and painstaking: as an employer she is fair, kind, but exacting. She likes formality: at Balmoral, for instance, she arranged for the footmen to be put back into livery. Her pleasures are characteristic of the orthodox landed aristocracy: she likes the country, horse-racing, deer-stalking, corgis, riding and playing the piano. She enjoys the Crazy Gang, 'Oliver!', 'The Bride Comes Back', or Gilbert and Sullivan. Of her homes, her favourite—as was Queen Victoria's—is Balmoral, the huge grey granite Victorian castle in Scotland, with pepper-pot turrets and a great square keep which has a persistent fascination for British royalty. It is a bizarre and isolated place, surrounded by grouse-moors, full of antlers, tartan chairs, and flock wallpaper embossed with 'VR'. It is here, for nine weeks every year, that the Queen retreats from the public—working in the morning, walking, riding or deer-stalking in the afternoon, watching television, playing scrabble or party games in the evenings.

The Queen's circle of personal friends all come from the same landed background: among them are Lord Rupert Nevill, brother of the Marquess of Abergavenny; the Dukes of Beaufort and Nor-folk; Gavin Astor, chairman of *The Times*; Lord Euston, son of the Duke of Grafton. Sometimes the Queen and Prince Philip spend weekends with them, but since they must be accompanied by a dresser, a valet, a chauffeur and one or two detectives, the numbers of hosts are limited; entertaining the Queen is not as difficult as in the first Queen Elizabeth's day—when the Queen's visit could almost ruin a nobleman—but it is still a large commitment; and the Queen, realising this, usually prefers to be host rather than guest.

The Queen's life has many ordeals but there is no sign that she has difficulty in the central rôle—being royal. As a young child she was brought up in the aura of 'Grandpa England': and since the age of ten, when her uncle abdicated and it was clear that she would be Queen, her education, her attitudes, and the attitudes of her friends have revolved round the awesome fact. Both the Queen and her sister have become used to the fact that in any social situation their will can dominate. In spite of the intrusion of democracy, the votes of parliament and the pressures of the populace, the world of the palace remains something quite separate from the world of Whitehall, or Westminster: and that world revolves firmly round the personality of the Queen.

However much one discusses the monarchy as an institution, it remains primarily a *person*. 'You can't separate the private and public functions of the Queen,' said one court official, 'that's the main difference between a monarchy and a republic. In a republic you know that the President's life is arranged by the state, and that eventually he'll retire back to his own home. But what most impresses the visitors to Windsor or the royal yacht is the feeling that they're in a private home—that it's part of a family life.'

Dashing in and out of this private and settled world, taking off from the palace garden in a helicopter, is the restless figure of Prince Philip, Duke of Edinburgh, who married Princess Elizabeth in 1947. The Duke, like Prince Albert, has strong ideas about the rôle of a consort. He has been strongly influenced by his formidable uncle, Earl Mountbatten; and he has tried to identify himself with the future rather than the past, and particularly with science, industry and technology. He writes his own speeches, has published two books of them, and appears on television. He has described himself as 'one of the most governed people you could hope to meet', but he has managed to establish a place for himself as a free-booting critic. He has cultivated the art of what he calls 'dontopedalogy'—opening his mouth and putting his foot in it. While narrowly avoiding partisan politics, he has aired views on Anglo-German unity, national service, the VIPs' lounge at London Airport, the rear-lights on lorries, or the fitness of Canadians.

But most of all, he has courageously set himself up as the chief critic of British complacency, and has said things which no cabinet minister would dare, or bother, to say. His calculated bricks have increased with the years, and among his statements in the past six years have been:

> It's no good shutting your eyes and saying 'British is best' three times a day after meals and expect it to be so. We have to work for it by constantly criticising and improving.
>
> *(April, 1956).*

> The frustrations of a pettifogging bureaucracy or the slow poison of bad industrial relations are not so obvious . . .
>
> *(June, 1958).*

> If anyone has a new idea in this country, there are twice as many people who advocate putting a man with a red flag in front of it.
>
> *(February, 1960).*

> Just at this moment we are suffering a national defeat comparable to any lost military campaign, and, what is more, self-inflicted . . .
> The bastions of the smug and the stick-in-the-mud can only be toppled by persistent undermining . . .
> Gentlemen, I think it is about time we pulled our fingers out . . .
>
> *(October, 1961).*

This last speech had the expected reaction: a few days later Mr. R. S. Redmond, chairman of the North Western Export Club, complained that the speech was very damaging, and that 'the world was being given a distorted picture of British industry'.

The Duke has added his own circuit to the traditional royal routine, and has rushed round Britain with a determination and drive which has exhausted his staff: these were his year's official engagements between May, 1960 and May, 1961—apart from the Queen's events, where he was usually present:

He went to 28 lunches,
24 dinners,
10 receptions, etc.,
15 exhibitions, films, games.

Made a 4-day tour of Canada and the U.S. (and other short trips in Europe).

Attended 20 meetings of various societies (mainly scientific and technical).

Visited 7 factories,
3 schools, etc.,
5 regiments, etc.,
3 scientific establishments,
6 boys' clubs,
13 other institutions.

Opened 12 institutions (including 5 recreation grounds, all at once on TV).

Unveiled 3 plaques.

But while the Duke has made vigorous forays into the world of science and industry, he has not succeeded in appreciably changing the character of the court itself, and between the Duke's competitive pep-talks and the traditional aura of the palace, there remains a large discrepancy.

THE ANATOMY OF FAIRYLAND

'It is a great mistake to make government too dull.'
Lord Attlee, 1952.

To the unique glory of royalty has been added, since Victorian times, unique wealth: exemption from death duties has heightened the fairyland. Even after the first world war there were still people, like Lord Derby or the Duke of Devonshire, who were richer than the King. Buckingham Palace, though the biggest, was only one of many great town houses, and the dukes and parvenu millionaires could rival royal entertainment. In two world wars taxation cut down all other palaces, and diminished the great country estates. But the Sovereign's allowance remained exempt from his tax commissioners, and his land and palaces remained the sole relic of the old order, with Buckingham Palace at the centre. There it stands, between Victoria station and Hyde Park Corner, over-looked by office blocks and surrounded by traffic, a symbol of fantasy in an age of commerce. It has six hundred rooms and half-a-mile of corridors cleaned by two hundred cleaners, forty-five acres of garden kept up by nine gardeners, and a lake of five acres, big enough to contain the whole of Grosvenor Square. There are three hundred clocks, wound by the royal clock-winder, fifty TV sets (exempt from licence) maintained by the royal electricians.

The isolation of the palace has transformed the social rôle of the monarch. 'Before it was like a pyramid,' explained one courtier, 'now it is more like a bumpy plain, with an island in the middle.' Sitting on this island, the palace has become much more aware of being watched and judged: royal lunches and garden parties acquire a unique significance and every new guest is interpreted as a national gesture.

Life in Buckingham Palace, it is true, is not as grand as it looks. The front rooms are uninhabited except on a few state occasions: only the first floor of the north wing, looking over Constitution Hill, provides the actual living quarters of the Queen, with the royal nursery above, and the administrative offices below. At the door are not gold-braided flunkeys, but tall men in a kind of blue battle-dress, with 'E II R' on the front. The offices have dictating machines and intercoms, with a row of names and one in red, saying 'The Queen'. Most of the extraordinary collection of people called the 'Queen's Household'—such as the Master of the Horse, Gold Stick, the High Almoner, or the Mistress of the Robes —are not to be seen wandering through the corridors: they are unpaid, and very part-time, and normally only emerge from mufti for royal processsions or coronations. The full-time house-hold—apart from servants and grooms—amount to only sixty people: and in Buckingham Palace, apart from the Queen's own lunch-table, only about fifteen people—private secretaries, privy purse people, equerries or press officers—sit down to lunch.

But still the courtiers are sufficiently formidable to maintain a sense of a court, isolated from the outside world, and to act as cushions between royalty and reality—small change, time-tables or awkward encounters. There is a team of three equerries (to rhyme with ferries) seconded from the services who work in fort-

39

nightly shifts, and act as royal ADC's: there are ladies-in-waiting who accompany the Queen everywhere, avoiding difficulties, answering telephones, picking up handkerchiefs, arranging payments in shops (the Queen never carries money). On royal tours a large secretariat prepares every inch of the ground, measures the rooms, works out time-tables—to ensure that the monarchy shall maintain smoothness and dignity. 'It is', as one court observer remarked, 'the Rolls Royce of monarchies.' Courtiers remain a very distinct profession, often handed down from father to son, and with a sense of vocation acquired as a child: even accountants or grooms acquire a special stateliness in the service of royalty.

The most important job in the palace is the Private Secretary to the Queen: for he is the main link between the monarch and the world outside. 'It is he more than anyone else who creates for the Sovereign the background of the régime.'[1] Sir Michael Adeane, the present chief secretary, might seem the quintessence of the professional courtier: his grandfather, Lord Stamfordham, was private secretary to King George V and Adeane himself began his royal service at the age of thirteen, as a page of honour to King George V. He took a first at Cambridge and has been a keen wild-fowler. He is a neat, white-haired man, with old-fashioned courtesy, who arrives at Buckingham Palace every morning from his flat in St. James's Palace. But he is essentially a realist in his approach to the monarchy: he does not, like many courtiers, regard himself as part of the mystery, and he talks shrewdly about his problems. In the changes in the monarch's rôle since the war—particularly in the handling of the Commonwealth—Adeane has played an important part.

But when royalty comes into touch with ordinary life, it is nearly always royalty which wins: when Prince Philip married the Queen, he ceased to be a Naval Lieutenant and became, with a wave of the wand, an Admiral of the Fleet, Field Marshal, Marshal of the RAF. (In the monarchy, as in business, there is still no substitute for marrying the boss's daughter.) When Anthony Armstrong-Jones married Princess Margaret he ceased to be a photographer, and became Earl of Snowdon and bird-cage designer. (At the wedding there was even a suggestion that the whole profession of photography had been ennobled: 'With the marriage of Mr. Armstrong-Jones', said one brochure, 'photography as a fine art may be said to have come of age.') When

[1] Sir John Wheeler-Bennett: *King George VI*. Appendix B.

Prince Charles went to Cheam School, it was not Prince Charles who became ordinary in the public's eye, but Cheam which became magical.

Even the royal food and equipment acquires its own splendour: the words 'By Appointment', together with a royal crest, adorn over 1,000 firms, all listed in the *London Gazette*: they include the royal dog food (supplied by Clark and Sons), the royal mushrooms (Aylesbury Mushrooms Ltd.), the royal sparking plugs (Lodge Plugs), the royal turtle soup (John Lusty Ltd.) and the royal marmalade (Frank Cooper's), the royal kippers (John Curtis) and the royal bagpipes (Lawne Ltd.).

Between this fairyland palace and the practical world there is an effective psychological moat, and a drawbridge which is only let down on special occasions. The palace has succeeded in maintaining not only wealth and dignity but also secrecy. There is not so much secrecy that the public eventually loses interest: the palace is far from unaware of publicity, and the Queen reads nearly all the papers every day. But there is enough hidden to stimulate intense public curiosity, and not only in England but in America or Germany (where a royal picture-cover can still increase a magazine's circulation by 50,000 copies). The palace's chief press officer, Commander Colville, is not a journalist, but an ex-naval officer, a courtier and son of a courtier. He is angrily criticised by the press for withholding information: the Queen has never held a press conference, and on royal tours the Queen and the Duke rarely meet the journalists who follow them round. But this inaccessibility is the essence of the royal magic: in spite of the hundreds of journalists who have hunted for royal stories, no one yet knows how life is led in the royal palaces, what private views the Queen holds, what she says to her visiting statesmen. Visitors to the palace maintain that embarrassed discretion that is the special mark of the courtier.

The remoteness of the Queen is enhanced by her *entourage*: most of her time is spent with people who, from the public's point of view, are in a half-and-half world between royalty and ordinariness. Most of the guests at Windsor or Balmoral have titles, and dukes, particularly racing dukes, provide the foothills to royalty. The monarchy, it is true, is not the undisputed centre of the aristocracy, and since Charles II's time the monarch has ceased to be the acknowledged head of London Society (in so far as that exists). But the monarch and the aristocracy for their prestige are mutually interdependent. The aristocracy would not be the

41

same without a pinnacle and a mystery at the top: and the palace would not have the same mystery if it were surrounded by misters.

Certainly the Queen gives no impression of unhappy isolation. Viewed from the outside, seeing this island of royalty surrounded by ordinariness, preserved as a deliberate symbol, a kind of living flag, by calculating parliaments, one might imagine that to be a British monarch was an unbearably lonely profession—like a caged lion in a field of rabbits. But this is not, apparently, how it strikes the visitor to Buckingham Palace. There it is the visitor who is isolated, coming into a world with apparently limitless ramifications. When, from time to time, the Queen and Prince Philip give informal lunch parties to meet cricketers, actors or businessmen, it is not so much they who seem to be glimpsing the world outside as the visitors who are glimpsing the world *inside*.

The problem of how to keep the fairyland under control has caused some worry to the palace. Already before the war, the monarchy had taken over a quasi-religious position. 'In the middle of the last century,' wrote Kingsley Martin in 1937, 'it needed courage to break the religious taboo, to doubt the literal truth of the first chapter of Genesis, or question the scientific basis for belief in the virgin birth. The throne on the other hand was frankly criticised in the newspapers and on the platform. In the twentieth century the situation is exactly reversed.'[1]

But after the war, with the end of emergency secrecy, the royal wedding, and the royal baby, public excitement began to reach alarming proportions: and with the Coronation in 1953, public adoration seemed to have got out of control—like a captive balloon that had broken loose from its moorings. Ever since then the public frenzy has continued, watched by some palace officials with growing bewilderment, and an uneasy feeling that the balloon might eventually hit something and explode.

But how to regulate the mystery presents difficult problems: for palace people are aware that once you touch the trappings of monarchy, like opening an Egyptian tomb, the inside is liable to crumble. At the Coronation there were discussions as to whether the procession should be adapted to include Commonwealth leaders: but eventually it was felt that the actual meaning of the procession was anyway so doubtful that to change it could be tricky. Likewise the fact that the Queen is head of the Church of England and yet (when she crosses the border) attends the

[1] Kingsley Martin: *The Magic of Monarchy*, 1937. p. 9.

Church of Scotland does not bear too much theological inspection, and is best left as a mystery. The basic dilemma of the palace is that, because of the mystery, the public expects far more to be happening inside the palace than actually does: and the public frenzy brings with it the danger of terrible bathos.

THE COST OF THE QUEEN

The total cost of this apparatus is hotly debated. There are even some—for instance Sir Charles Petrie—who insist that the monarchy makes a profit. This argument assumes that the Queen is the real owner of the Crown Lands of which the revenue, since the time of George III, has been handed over to the state. The Crown is the second biggest landowner in Britain, with 180,000 acres in England, 105,000 in Scotland, and valuable city properties, including Regent's Park, Carlton House Terrace, and chunks of Pall Mall, Piccadilly, Holborn and Kensington. The Crown also has such items as income from wrecks, whales and sturgeons, the excise on beer, cider and wine licences, and treasure troves. All these properties, from whales to terraces, are run by the Crown Commissioners in Whitehall, under a shrewd financier Sir Malcolm Trustram Eve: their profit, which after tax and expenses amounts to about £1½ million a year, is handed to the Exchequer. This income, it is argued, more than makes up for the Queen's salary. But usually the Crown Lands are regarded as belonging to the state: and by any calculation the monarchy is an expensive affair.

The sovereign's salary is fixed by parliament at the beginning of the reign. Queen Elizabeth's allowance amounts to £475,000 a year—which has hardly changed since George V's time, and is worth only a third as much: but when it was increased in 1952, it was described by Emrys Hughes, MP, as 'the largest wage claim of the century'. It is made up by:

	£
Her Majesty's Privy Purse	60,000
Salaries of Household	185,000
Expenses of Household	121,800
Royal Bounty, alms and special services	13,200
Supplementary provision (to allow for inflation, Duchess of Kent, Princess Alexandra, etc.)	95,000
	£475,000

On top of this, separate allowances are voted by parliament for a few other members of the Royal Family:

	£
Queen Elizabeth the Queen Mother	70,000
Duke of Edinburgh	40,000
Duke of Gloucester	35,000
Princess Margaret, Countess of Snowdon	15,000
Princess Royal	6,000
	£166,000

There are also the Duchies of Cornwall and Lancaster—the only bits of Crown Land which were not given up by George III. The income from this, which amounts to about £90,000 a year, belongs to the Prince of Wales: until he is eighteen, most of it is paid back to the Exchequer, but after that he will have the whole amount, together with an allowance of £10,000.

But the actual upkeep of the Royal Palaces, including Buckingham Palace, Windsor Castle and Holyroodhouse is paid for by that dreary patron, the Ministry of Works: between them they cost £668,000 in 1960. The cost of the Queen's Flight—four Herons, two helicopters and a Chipmunk, all painted fluorescent red and with eighty people to look after them—is paid for by the RAF. The cost of royal tours is borne by the host governments in the Commonwealth countries. The cost of the royal trains, royal postage, royal telegrams (which have precedence) and telephone calls, all fall on the state. The most obviously extravagant royal perquisite is the yacht *Britannia*, paid for by the Navy: it cost £2 million to build, and its crew of 250 cost about £200,000 a year. Altogether the cost to the state of the monarchy is probably not less than two million pounds a year—roughly as much as the Annual Arts Council grant, or as much as Omo and Daz spend on advertising.

On top of this, the Queen has her private fortune, a source of interminable speculation. Queen Victoria was said to have left at least £2 million, from savings and gifts (she was given half-a-million by an old miser called John Nield in 1852): and since then the fortune has probably increased. King George V is said to have left a million pounds to each of his four sons: and Queen Mary left £406,000—though to *whom* it was left is not known. One American magazine reckoned that the Queen is the third richest woman in the world. In addition to her capital, the Queen

44

owns the finest art collection in the world, amassed by Henry VIII, George I, George IV, etc., including more than 5,000 paintings, and an unparalleled collection of French and Italian drawings. The Queen also personally owns Sandringham and Balmoral (when Edward VIII abdicated, George VI had to buy them from him). And there is the fabulous royal jewellery, the royal stamp collection, valued at over a million pounds, and the royal racehorses, which yield a profit.

But it is doubtful whether the Queen has much scope for saving. There are some very expensive items not allowed for by parliament —including the Duke of Windsor: and other royal relations need financial help. In an age of affluence with full employment, the archaic trappings of royalty have been increasingly expensive to maintain: salaries of grooms and footmen, for instance, have risen steeply: the number of horses in the royal mews dwindled from 86 in 1937 to 30 in 1959: the cost of the fodder went up from two to three thousand pounds. And the Queen has a number of incidental expenses—including such oddments as the salary of the Poet Laureate (£99), and a present of £3 to each set of triplets.

THE POWERS OF THE QUEEN

'A monarch is a kind of referee, although the occasions when he or she has to blow the whistle are nowadays very few.'

Lord Attlee.

The constitutional impotence of the Queen is well enough known. In theory, as Bagehot pointed out, if a bill was passed for the execution of the Queen, the Queen would have to sign it.

The actual political influence of the monarch is difficult to assess. The Queen retains one important attribute of power— information. All cabinet minutes and cabinet papers go in a red box to Buckingham Palace: atomic secrets, correspondence with presidents, budget plans, all make their way to the Queen, whether she is at Balmoral, Windsor, or in Africa: Whitehall goes to tremendous pains to keep the sovereign in the news: the Queen is, on this basis, the best informed person in Britain.

And every Tuesday night, when the Queen is in London, the Prime Minister goes round to Buckingham Palace for a talk with the Queen. The relationship has gradually changed: when Chatham was Prime Minister, according to one witness he bowed so low that you could see his great nose between his knees. When Gladstone went to see Queen Victoria, he remained standing up.

Now the Prime Minister is allowed to sit down and have a cigarette.

In the past thirty years the meetings between the monarch and the ministers have become much more formalised. The political associations of King George V were often private and personal: he wrote long letters to Haig, supporting him against Lloyd George —an intervention that might not have seemed so odd then as it does now. But now the meetings with ministers are deliberately arranged at fixed and stated times. Lord Attlee has described the kind of conversation he had with George VI:

> It would have been quite natural for George VI to say to me: 'How is Mannie hitting it off with the French generals?' or 'Well, Nye seems to be getting the doctors in line'. I, on the other hand, might have said to the King: 'The Old Man was really rather naughty in the House about India.'[1]

George VI, on his side, was touchy about being kept informed. In America, after long and frank conversations with Roosevelt, he complained: 'Why don't my ministers talk to me as the President did tonight?'[2]

There is nothing to stop a monarch trying to influence his prime minister. According to King George VI, when Attlee came to see him in 1945, after the Labour victory:

> I asked him whom he would make Foreign Secretary, and he suggested Dr. Hugh Dalton. I disagreed with him, and said that Foreign Affairs were the most important subject of the moment, and I hoped he would make Mr. Bevin take it. He said he would . . .'[3]

In theory, the Queen's area of patronage is large: in particular, as Head of the Church of England, she can recommend bishops. The Queen takes an interest in the Church, sees all bishops when they are appointed, and often has them to preach at Windsor. But in fact nearly all episcopal appointments come from the prime minister, after consulting the Archbishop of Canterbury.

The most important residual powers of the sovereign are the right to dissolve parliament, and to choose a prime minister. The

---

[1] *The Observer*, August 23, 1959.
[2] Sir John Wheeler-Bennett: *King George VI*. p. 389.
[3] Wheeler-Bennett. p. 638. Attlee, on the other hand, denies that he was influenced by the King in choosing Bevin.

first has hardly been exercised in modern times: Attlee has said that the dissolution in 1951 was influenced by the King's anxiety and ill-health: but it was mainly due to the narrow majority and the vulnerability of the Labour cabinet.

Twice in the last twenty-five years has the choice of prime minister been in question. The first was in 1940, when the King made it clear that, if he had been given the choice, he would have chosen Lord Halifax.[1] The second was in 1957, when Sir Anthony Eden resigned. It is still sometimes thought that the Queen's choice depended on three men who she visibly consulted—Eden, Churchill, Salisbury: but in fact, as we shall see, her choice of Macmillan depended on the careful sounding-out of the Tory Party, the cabinet and the Lords, made by the Chief Whip and the Lord Chancellor.

The influence of the Queen on her prime ministers is still largely unknown: with Churchill, as a young queen confronting a grand old man, she was said to be shy and awed: she did not pretend to be more informed than she was. Eden was not very communicative, and did not talk freely about his large problems. Macmillan is known to respect her sharpness of mind and retentive memory, and keeps her scrupulously well-informed. What seems certain is that her influence will grow with age; already at thirty-six she has seen three prime ministers: after another thirty years she will probably have dealt with ten or twelve, and will have outlived nearly all presidents and kings. Alone of the Heads of State, she will remember Churchill, Khrushchev and Eisenhower. She will not, doubtless, be as intimidating or interfering a monarch as Queen Victoria: ('No, Mr. Bannerman,' said Victoria to Campbell-Bannerman about an army scheme towards the end of her reign: 'Lord Palmerston proposed exactly the same thing in '52 and Lord Palmerston was wrong.')[2]. But the balance of awe will be on the Queen's side.

There remains another important rôle—the most guarded of all: and that is her rôle as a super-diplomat—a last weapon of secret diplomacy, and a 'sweetener' for difficult diplomatic situations. Being above parties and politics, the Queen can attract a trust above that of politicians; and royalty, even behind the iron curtain, still has a special diplomatic value. The extent of royal

---

[1] Wheeler-Bennett. p. 444. But in Iain Macleod's biography of Chamberlain, Lord Halifax is shown as unwilling to accept the premiership, if it was offered him, ostensibly because of the problem of being a prime minister in the House of Lords.

[2] Quoted in Sir Charles Petrie: *The Modern British Monarchy*, 1961.

diplomacy will only emerge in fifty years' time: but occasionally there is a hint of the Queen's usefulness. One example was the sudden arrival of Major Gagarin in July, 1961, which took the British Government by surprise. Only an unknown civil servant was at the airport to meet him, and the press was in an uproar over his neglect. The Foreign Office made anxious arrangements: a Rolls Royce called 'YG 1' was quickly produced; ministers were mobilised, a reception was improvised, the Prime Minister arranged a lunch. And, as the ultimate weapon, the Government contacted the palace to enquire whether the Queen would agree to . . . It would be wrong to assume that the Queen, in such matters, is no more than a civil servant: the palace has views of its own about Russian visitors. At the time of Khrushchev and Bulganin's visit to England, the most they were allowed was tea at Windsor Castle: no photograph was allowed of the Queen with the Russians.

The mention of Gagarin was met with that stiff silence and delay for which courtiers are renowned. The Queen's programme was full, and to entertain Gagarin was most inconvenient: but it so happened that an informal lunch had already been planned for the Friday, with a mixture of guests including Bud Flanagan of the Crazy Gang, the Governor of Holloway Prison, Sir John Hunt and Lord Mountbatten: and an invitation was quickly extended to Gagarin. What made things worse was that the Russians insisted on Gagarin's entourage also coming, and the palace announced that 'the lunch is for people the Queen wants to meet, and not, as has been suggested, for a group of people the Queen thought Major Gagarin would like to meet'. But eventually the strange lunch party took place, with Bud Flanagan cracking jokes with the cosmonaut and asking the waiters what the food cost, and the royal corgis running round everyone's feet.

THE AURA OF MONARCHY

The main importance of the palace is not its political, but its social influence. It is fashionable to regard the palace as a pleasant irrelevance in British life, a convenient side-show for the masses. But any institution which attracts such vast publicity and bemusement must influence its audience.

There is much to be said for the British device of presenting a façade of a mystic monarchy, surrounded by bearskins, dukes and Gold Sticks, behind which the real machinery of government can function quietly and unnoticed. 'Royalty', said Bagehot, 'is a Government in which the attention of the nation is concentrated on one person doing interesting things. A Republic is a Government in which that attention is divided between many, who are all doing uninteresting things.' During a time of social upheaval, such as the Victorian, an apparently unchanging head can give a sense of stability: and to separate pomp from power makes a safeguard against political megalomania or dictatorship.

But when there is no great social change, and the country is inclined to escape from harsh facts, a mysterious monarchy can easily become a refuge for foggy ideas. Among the more old-fashioned areas of British life, a blurred image of Buckingham Palace often lies in the background. That recurring theme: 'it may seem odd to you, but it *works*', which crops up in British institutions, from Lloyd's to the House of Lords and the election of bishops, has its prototype in the mystery of the monarchy. Businessmen with feudal pretensions; arrogant Guards officers; jingo speakers at Conservative conferences; pompous ambassadors; young blimps (a far less pleasant species than old ones); parliamentarians talking about bogus mystique—all these invoke the palace in support of their mystery. While Britain is having to make the painful transition from imperial splendour to competitive trading, the palace represents in most people's minds a feudal, uncompetitive haven of 'it's not *done*'.

For much of this, it is unfair to blame the palace. Many of the pretensions spring from deeper causes than the monarchy: and Prince Philip himself has said: 'If we are to recover prosperity we shall have to find ways of emancipating energy and enterprise from the frustrating control of timid ignoramuses.' Nor is it fair to expect the royal family to change their private pleasures to suit public education—to abandon the Doncaster races for the Edinburgh Festival, to move from the Crazy Gang to Covent Garden, to spend weekends with industrialists and scientists rather than landed aristocrats.

In one very important respect the monarchy *has* personified change—in the Commonwealth. Ever since Nehru and Cripps invented the ingenious new formula of 'Head of the Commonwealth' for the Queen's role in republican India, the monarchy has kept abreast of a changing situation. The monarchy has ceased to be indivisible—as it was by pre-war doctrines—and has become something divisible and different for each Commonwealth country: its divisibility can produce embarrassments—as appeared

49

before the visit to Ghana in 1961: but it has impressively typified Britain's new relationships.

But inside Britain the changes have been much less spectacular: and the monarchy, like other old institutions, has a heavy drag of tradition and protocol. Bold schemes—like a project that was discussed for rebuilding Sandringham in gay modern style—are defeated by inertia: and even the informal lunch parties for unorthodox guests have recently dwindled. In spite of Prince Philip's excursions, the Court Circular is still preoccupied with audiences with minor ambassadors, judges, bishops or governors—representing the traditional nineteenth-century powers: the palace still gives a powerful impression of being detached from the world of science and trade. The discrepancy between outward show and inner realities reaches its picturesque climax in royal processions, where cabinet ministers come well at the back, squeezed between the Vice-Chamberlain of Her Majesty's Household and viscounts' eldest sons. (Only in 1902 was the prime minister promoted to a place after the archbishops: till then he had to follow after the sons of peers he himself had created.) And this outward show has curious echoes: even *Whitaker's Almanack*, that important organ of public instruction, has sixteen pages about the monarchy, and thirty-five pages of peers and orders, including a page of octogenarian peers: but if you look up Unilevers or ICI in the index, you will find nothing.

It is often assumed that the monarchy must stand for no-change —that it is there, like Stonehenge, with the encrustations of centuries. But the monarchy, if it is to be useful, cannot be just a question of Gold Sticks and Black Rods: it must be a living institution, closely related to its country. No doubt there are elements which have long since become fossilised: to put the Chairman of the Coal Board or the Head of the Civil Service at the head of a royal parade would merely spoil the procession. But in many of the conflicts that appear in this book—between old schools and new, old universities and new, classicists and scientists, public service and trade, old regiments and new corps, the royal magic hangs always over the old. The Victorians were practical and ruthless in their use of the monarchy: they used honours to glorify their new civil service, and made the Queen the focal point of their Empire. But since the nineteenth century the monarchy has become much less associated with the present, and more with the past.

4

PARLIAMENT

You have not a perception of the first elements in this matter till
you know that government by a *club* is a standing wonder.
Walter Bagehot, 1872.

It's taken us nine hundred years to create our democratic and
parliamentary system, and when you look at it, my God!
Lord Chandos (TV interview), *1960.*

SINCE the eighteenth century the heirs to the powers of the
monarch and the House of Lords have been the members of the
House of Commons. In theory these 630 have sovereignty:
they can pass laws, summon anyone to give evidence, cross-
examine civil servants and reprimand editors. The judges are
waiting to interpret their laws, and the civil servants are waiting
to administer them.

And yet over the past fifty years, the members have been aware
of their powers mysteriously oozing away. In all European
countries, the complaint has been the same. In Britain, with its
magnificent parliamentary tradition, and its miniature West-
minsters exported to Ghana, Singapore or Australia, complete
with maces, wigs and copies of Erskine May, the realisation of the
decline of parliamentary power has been particularly painful and
disturbing. The current fashion for belittling parliament does no
service to democracy: it is, after all, the only democratic instrument yet devised. But the British parliament has been slow to come
to terms with new problems and bureaucracies, and it has long ago
acquired a life and momentum of its own.

It is the sense of a club which is the most obvious feature of the
Commons. In spite of its range, from earls' sons to engine-drivers
from all over the country, it retains unity and compactness. The
chamber, only sixty-eight feet long, cannot seat all members at
once: the public and the press in the steep galleries can sometimes
outnumber the members by ten to one. But the parliamentarians
continue their ritual—dawdling in from the lobby, bowing to the
Speaker, exchanging whispers, and speaking as if they were
addressing, not a nation but a room. The members, though

mostly very ordinary people, assume the heightened manner of a club—the affectation of an older, more confident generation.

Members love talking about 'The House' as if it were a person —moody, headstrong and feminine. 'The House won't stand being lectured, you know', said one of them, 'she hates to be treated like a fool.' 'The House of Commons', said one Victorian sage, 'has more sense than any one in it.' The building itself has an over-powering atmosphere for any new member: this is how one recent MP, Mark Bonham-Carter, described it when first coming into it:

'It's just like being back as a new boy at public school—with its ritual and rules, and also its background of convention, which breeds a sense of anxiety and inferiority in people who don't know the rules. Even the smell—the smell of damp stone stairways—is like a school. All you have of your own is a locker—just like a school locker. You don't know where you're allowed to go, and where not—you're always afraid you may be breaking some rule, or wandering into the Speaker's house by mistake. In the smoking room, you're afraid to sit down in case you're in somebody's special chair. The only place where you can work is in the library: and even there you daren't ask the man for a book, because you don't know whether he's a librarian or an old member. In the chamber, you don't know where you're supposed to be sitting, and whether you're allowed to walk over and talk to somebody. It's just like a public school: and that's why Labour MPs are overawed by it— because they feel that only the Tory MPs know what a public school is like.'

The New Palace of Westminster (as it is called) has 100 staircases, 2 miles of corridors, 13 quadrangles, 130 statues, averaging seven feet high, and 1,100 rooms (including one for BBC television, another for ITV). 26 policemen and 32 doorkeepers (who act as chuckers-out) guard the doors: 251 people, including 60 cleaners, look after the upkeep: the maintenance and house-keeping of the Commons costs £270,000 a year, and fuel alone costs £47,000. Three-quarters of a million tourists a year pass through: but most of the palace is closed to the public. No debate has ever been televised: and if a photograph is taken anywhere in the palace, the film is destroyed (only Lord Brabazon has admitted secretly taking a photograph—of Neville Chamberlain's last speech in 1940[1]).

The mystique of the House is deliberately maintained by what

[1] *The Times*, October 13, 1961.

Sir Ivor Jennings calls 'The Importance of Being Ancient'. The royal opening of parliament every October, the procession led by Black Rod, the antique methods of beginning and ending the day, all bolster the impression that parliament has a meaning quite apart from its functions; the House is never happier than when debating the exact position of the mace. The day begins with the words 'Speaker in the Chair' being shouted through the lobbies: and the Speaker, who is the centre of the ritual, sits down on an Australian-made throne at one end of the House, wearing a full-bottomed wig.

The present Speaker, Sir Harry Hylton-Foster, began like all Speakers as an ordinary MP. The son of a barrister, he became a barrister and later solicitor-general: he had married the daughter of a previous Speaker, Lord Ruffside: (even in the tiny profession of Speakership—there have only been 15 since 1800—a son-in-law tradition has apparently begun). 'All Speakers are highly successful,' wrote Lord Rosebery, 'all Speakers are deeply regretted and are generally announced to be irreplaceable. But a Speaker is soon found, and found, almost invariably, among the mediocrities of the House.' But the Speaker is carefully removed from his fellow-members: he lives in a gothic house inside the Palace of Westminster, earns £5,000 a year, gives occasional discreet tea-parties, but remains strictly aloof from politics, and will eventually retire with a viscounty.

The Speaker maintains the rules. He insists that members call each other 'honourable members', bow to him on entering and leaving, address all their speeches to him. He stops them using 'grossly insulting' language: Speakers in the past have forbidden the words villain, hypocrite, murderer, insulting dog, swine, pecksniffian cant, cheat, stool-pigeon and bastards.

MEMBERS OF PARLIAMENT

Politics is perhaps the only profession for which no preparation is thought necessary.

Robert Louis Stevenson.

To be a member of parliament is an odd profession, with very odd hours. The House sits for only thirty-six weeks a year, with a break for two-and-a-half months from August till mid-October. It sits from 2.30 p.m. to 10.30 (or later) from Mondays to Thursdays, and from 11 a.m. to 4.30 on Fridays (which can often be cut). When parliament is sitting, an MP is ruled by the clanging sound of the division bell, demanding him to vote. Often at 9.45, a frequent time for divisions, MPs rush from their dinner parties to the House. Wealthier members favour houses in the 'division bell district', just behind parliament—Barton, Cowley or Lord North Streets—within five minutes of parliament. They have bells fixed in their houses, and you can see them all dashing out into their cars. In the session 1960–1 there were 268 divisions: and unless MPs were 'paired' or excused by their whips, each one demanded their presence.

Since the war, being an MP has become a much more professional business, which can be seen by the way they use the palace. Far more members, according to the serjeant-at-arms, now use the House as an office in the mornings: usually between two and three hundred, either in committees or dealing with letters. Fewer members use the dining-room, which serves meals at hotel hours, and more take meals when they can in the cafeteria or tea-room, which are always open during debates (if everyone wants tea at once, as in the 1960 filibuster, women members have to help out). Then there is the consumption of alcohol: parliament being a Royal Palace is exempt from licensing laws, and has bars open all afternoon, with wide scope for drunkenness. Before the war, drunk members laughing or even speaking in the chamber were not unknown. There are still a few notoriously bibulous members: but intoxication is generally agreed to be rarer.[1]

The presence of more members in the House does not necessarily make them more useful. 'A whole day can agreeably disappear', wrote a former MP, Nigel Nicolson, 'in answering a few constituency letters in the morning while attending a standing committee with only a quarter ear open to the debate, listening to Questions and Ministerial Statements from 2.30 to 4 p.m., looking in on two party committees in the evening, entertaining a couple of visiting Americans to drinks on the terrace, and then gossiping in the smoking room until it is time for bed.'[2] But though much time is wasted, it is nowadays harder for members to stay away from the House without comment.

At the same time, members are spending more time in their constituencies: this is the dark side of a member's life—sitting in a dingy local office once a week, seeing constituents about anything from housing to drainage. The average MP receives eighty letters a week from constituents, and spends £100 a year on letters and

---

[1] Peter G. Richards, *Honourable Members*, 1959. p. 89.
[2] Nigel Nicolson: *People and Parliament*, 1958. p. 64–65.

telegrams. While members have become less grand in Westminster, with less scope for deciding the future of the world, they have become more useful in their constituencies, and closer to their local parties.

MP's have their own lope, their own handshake, their own jokes, their own way of saying to visitors, 'can you find your way out?' They belong to the 'best club in Europe'; they know it and the club dominates their lives, and also those of their wives. 'I hope you're going to write something about the St. Stephen's Widows', said Lord Kilmuir. Few MPs can stop being political, and their wives have to marry both them and their politics. Parliament remains a very nocturnal affair, and this cuts off politicians and their wives still further from ordinary people. 'King Louis Philippe once said to me', said Disraeli, 'that he attributed the great success of the English in political life to their talking politics after dinner.'[1]

But while MPs are becoming increasingly professional, they do not have professional rewards. Their salary is £1,750, of which officially £750 is allowed for expenses: but nearly a third of the members, it transpired in 1961, spend their whole salary on expenses.[2] It was not till 1911, when Lloyd George proposed £400 a year, that members were paid at all: it went up to £600 in 1937, to £1,000 in 1945, and to £1,750 in 1957. In addition members are allowed free first-class travel to and from their constituency, with accident insurance; free telephone calls from the palace to the rest of London, but not further; and a daily ration of 24 large sheets and 24 small sheets of House of Commons writing paper, with envelopes.

The salary is obviously inadequate—most of all for the Opposition leaders who have to spend their whole time in politics with no additional income (except the Leader who has an additional £1,250 a year). Many members have to scrounge what they can from journalism, lecturing or broadcasting, or representing organisations: some have had to send their wives out to work. Before the war—according to a doctor who was a whip at the time —several Labour MPs actually fainted from undernourishment.[3] While some members can hardly afford to be in parliament, others can hardly afford *not* to be: pension schemes are inadequate, and several elderly trade union members hang on to their seats, because they have saved nothing on which to live afterwards.

[1] Banquet at Glasgow. November 19, 1873.
[2] *See* reply by Sir Edward Boyle, March 24, 1961.
[3] *Honourable Members*, p. 238.

The plight of British MPs is shared by parliamentarians in most Western countries except America. These were the remunerations in a few countries in 1953:

United States:	£4,450 plus £5,625 for secretarial expenses, etc.
Canada:	£1,450 plus £725 for expenses.
South Africa:	£1,400 plus secretarial expenses.
France:	£1,600 plus £535 for lodging and secretarial expenses.
Holland:	£680–£860.
Denmark:	£647–£987.
India:	£3 a day during session.[1]

The idea behind low salaries is to stop politics becoming purely professional. 'Few would support the idea', said a select committee of 1954, 'of a House of Commons composed principally of full-time politicians in the sense of men and women cut off from any practical share in the work of the nation.' But as politics become full-time, the small salaries restrict increasingly the range of members; they must either be subsidised by a trade union or other organisation, or have private means, or have jobs which allow time off. Thus many of the most able people are simply unable to consider standing for parliament.

The range of members might seem impressive—from five earls' sons to thirty-four miners; from the 'Father of the House', Sir Winston Churchill (who first came into the House in 1900), to Paul Channon, aged twenty-seven, who entered in 1959. Members include twenty-five women (three less than in 1958), twelve doctors and dentists, seven architects, eight railway clerks and twelve dons. In theory anyone can become a member of parliament, except for aliens, minors, non-dissenting clergy, lunatics, judges, civil servants, peers, bankrupts, felons and candidates found guilty of corrupt practices at elections: the last time a member went to prison was in 1954. But in fact the range of members is not wide.

These were the leading occupations in 1959:

Conservative:	72 Barristers,
	38 Farmers,
	37 Soldiers, sailors, airmen,
	26 Journalists and publicists,
	113 Businessmen.

[1] Report from the Select Committee on Members' Expenses, 1954.

Labour: 36 Teachers,
              34 Miners,
              27 Barristers,
              25 Journalists and publicists.[1]

The figures can be misleading: many barristers have long ceased to practise, and 'farmers' can mean anything from a large land-owner to a retired businessman. But they point to the lopsidedness of the House. Nearly a sixth are barristers and a quite dispropor-tionate number, because of the early pensions, are retired officers (only three Socialists). 282 members in the 1959 parliament had business directorships, compared to 269 in the previous parliament: three-fifths of the Conservatives have directorships. (The record is held by Sir Cyril Black, a former Mayor of Wimbledon, with 61 directorships.) But there were fewer chairmen and managing directors—191 compared to 213.[2]

The education of members, too, is untypical. In 1959 73 Conservative MPs and three Socialists had been to Eton. 104 Conservatives and 34 Socialists were from Oxford: 79 Conserva-tives and 12 Socialists from Cambridge. Oxford and Cambridge provided more than a third of the House, and other universities only a seventh.[3]

Changes since the war have been slow but significant. Men with private means have decreased, and professional men have gone up from about 45 per cent before the war, to 50 per cent since. While the average age of Conservatives has remained around 48, average Socialists have become more aged, rising from 50 in 1945, to 52 in 1951, to 55 in 1959: in 1959 there were 33 septuagenarian Labour MPs and only 8 Tories: though recently there have been signs of the oldest Socialists retiring. The number of professional 'communicators' in parliament has strikingly increased: to the familiar journalist-politicians have been added a new race of TV-politicians, including such well-known faces as Christopher Chataway, Geoffrey Johnson Smith and Christopher Mayhew: and there has been an inrush of public-relations and advertising politicians, who find parliament convenient: over twenty members had public-relations director-ships in 1961, compared to only seven in 1958. Nobody can be very happy about this.

[1] David Butler and Richard Rose: *The British General Election of 1959.* p. 127.
[2] *The Business Background of Members of Parliament,* Parliamentary Profiles, 1961
[3] Butler and Rose. p. 128.

Politics is now more wrapped up in itself, and there is less time for an outside career. It is far harder to combine a first-class bar practice with serious politics, or to be (as Macmillan was before the war) a publisher in the mornings and a politician in the evenings. 'The position is not, as used to be', wrote Sir Ivor Jennings in 1957, 'that a minority of full-time employees (including self-employed) could afford to be part-time politicians: it is that full-time politicians have to become part-time employees in order to live.'[1]

With these snags, is parliament still attracting first-class men? At first sight the dedication is impressive: there are many more members who take politics seriously, reading White Papers, attending committees, nursing constituencies, than before the war. The lazy Tory squires and the retired trade unionists are going out fast.

But parliament no longer attracts the very ablest men—with the intellectual calibre of Butler or Maudling (both from the diminished private-income class) or of Gaitskell or Wilson (both thrown up by the more compulsive pre-war movement). Members are the cabinets of the future: and looking round the benches on both sides of the House, one cannot be very hopeful about future cabinets. (This, it is true, has been the complaint for the last hundred years.) 'While the general level of ability is higher', wrote Lord Attlee in 1957, 'there are fewer members of distinction in other walks of life . . .'[2] Top barristers or top businessmen can no longer combine two careers: and the odd make-up of parliament tends to produce odd cabinets. There are very few managers, administrators, engineers or scientists in the House: and at a time when the cabinet has to run giant businesses—railways, airways, scientific research or roads—MPs are being selected for totally different qualities. 'They're chosen because they're good at talking, not *doing*', as one cabinet minister put it: 'It's very difficult to find people who can actually *run* things.'

PARLIAMENT AND PRESS

As parliament becomes less sure of her importance so, like a waning film star, she becomes more anxious about both her privileges and her publicity. Up till the eighteenth century the press was barred from debates: the *Gentleman's Magazine*—the first to

[1] Sir Ivor Jennings: *Parliament*, 1957 p. 57.
[2] *The Times*, April 11. 1957

report parliament—employed a memory-man, Guthrie, who memorised speeches and then had them put into classical English by Dr. Samuel Johnson.[1] But today the reporting of parliament has affected parliament itself. Official reports are a major operation: four super-speed shorthand reporters, working in twenty-minutes shifts, take down the debates, helped by eight typists (who then allow members to improve their grammar on the typescript). The reports are rushed to the parliamentary presses across the river, where eighty people print 2,300 copies, finishing them by 2.30 in the morning—in time to be delivered to MPs for breakfast. Publicity, once scorned, is now courted: big speeches are made early in the day in order to get into the papers,[2] and many members intervene with a wary eye on the press. If parliament eventually agrees to be televised, the dangers of publicity-seeking will be greater: on the other hand parliament may retrieve some of the public interest which has moved over to television studio debates.

LOBBYING

If we had some way of measuring political power, we could possibly demonstrate that at the present time pressure groups are more powerful in Britain than in the United States.

Professor Samuel Beer.

One sign of the dwindling importance of parliament is in the activities of their 'lobbies'—the unseen pressure groups, pointed at the sources of power. The process of lobbying is a basic part of the mechanism of power, and it might be expected to centre on parliament. At first sight, the attention paid by the lobbies to Westminster has never been greater. Their number and scope have swelled in the past fifty years: 'their day to day activities', wrote Professor Finer, a prominent lobby-watcher, 'pervade every sphere of domestic policy, every day, every way, at every nook and cranny of government.'[3] 'In no other country', wrote Robert McKenzie, 'are the great sectional interests . . . brought more intimately into consultation in the process of decision-making in government and political parties.'[4] Pressure groups have come to be regarded as a respectable and even necessary instrument of

[1] Francis Williams: *Dangerous Estate*, 1957. p. 38.
[2] Sir Ivor Jennings: *Parliament*. p. 165.
[3] S. E. Finer: *Anonymous Empire*, 1958.
[4] Politics of Pressure. *The Observer*, May 14, 1961.

democracy, so that 'if an organised group does not exist, the government helps to invent it'.[1]

The pressure groups range from the hundreds of charitable societies, from the National Society for Promoting the Welfare of the Feeble-minded, to the National Farmers Union, the most pervasive of all, with 200,000 members, representing nine-tenths of all farmers. Several organisations arrange for MPs to represent their views in parliament, and probably half the members—including trade unionists—represent some group. The National Sheep Breeders of Great Britain, the Royal Society for the Protection of Birds, the Association of Drainage Authorities, all have their spokesman.

Every member of parliament is constantly assailed by sectional interests. 'In each day's mail he can safely rely on being pursued by at least 15 different causes, campaigns, companies and cliques. Books, circulars, newsletters, pamphlets and holograph letters all plugging an identical theme pour each morning through his letterbox.'[2]

Certain pressure campaigns have had a spectacular effect in parliament: one was the campaign for commercial TV in 1953—which we will observe later. More recent has been the campaign by the Central African Federation. Late in 1959 Sir Roy Welensky became increasingly worried by British hostility to Federation, and his government engaged the public relations firm of 'Voice and Vision'—a subsidiary of Colman Prentis and Varley, the Conservative Party's advertising agents. Voice and Vision launched an expensive campaign, including advertisements in radical weeklies proclaiming 'Good News from Africa': and they offered free trips to Africa to a careful selection of members of parliament from both sides. The MPs were flown out for ten days, escorted by a public relations adviser, A. J. McWhinnie, rushed round to showpieces of the Federation, and taken to see Government leaders and selected Africans. Many MPs returned to London with very changed views about white settlers, and the campaign has had a visible effect on Conservative attitudes. Its success has worried not only left-wing critics but some Conservative leaders, including Iain Macleod.

But the truth is that the biggest business interests do not bother much about MPs and few of the big corporations now maintain their own MPs in the House. They have seen where decisive

[1] Allen Potter: *Organised Groups in British National Politics*, 1961. p. 32.
[2] *The Times*, July 17, 1961.

power lies, and so they now deal directly with cabinet ministers or civil servants: even the trade unions, with their vast representation in the Commons, often prefer to deal direct with Whitehall.[1] Industrial lobbying may be open—through organised deputations or statements, or covert—through casual social occasions. It is typical of Britain, compared to America, that important lobbying is done over lunches or drinks in clubs or homes. 'It's so much easier here', a senior manager in one big corporation told me: 'we don't have to organise great formal expeditions, as in Washington. Whitehall is only two tube stations away: we have a permanent secretary to lunch from time to time.'

The chairman of ICI, Paul Chambers, does not need to stir up members of parliament to push Britain into the Common Market: he is on friendly terms with most of the cabinet and many senior civil servants, and can urge his views there, where they are listened to with respect. The more civil servants who go into industry, the easier such informal pressure becomes. In fact, pressure to make someone do something they don't want to do becomes in the end a sort of like-mindedness in which it may not be clear who is the persuader and who the persuaded. Most important lobbying—on trade agreements taxes, Budgets, or building sites—is done before Bills ever reach Westminster. MPs may feel tormented or flattered by the lobbies in parliament: but they are well aware that the most important pressures by-pass them altogether.

PARLIAMENT'S POWER

What clearly is in train, however, is a rapid trend towards the exaltation of the executive (both cabinet ministers and civil servants) at the expense of the House of Commons.

The Economist, August, 1960.

Two main forces have weakened the importance of parliament. First, the leaders of political parties have decided on issues beforehand. 'Parliamentary government has already very largely perished', wrote one former MP, Christopher Hollis: 'the member is the obedient servant of the party machine. He tramps into the division lobby voting for or against he knows not what upon subjects which as a general rule no opinion save that of the specialist is of the least value.'[2]

'With the single exception of the overthrow of the Chamberlain

[1] J. D. Stewart: *British Pressure Groups*, 1958.
[2] Christopher Hollis: *Can Parliament Survive?* 1949. p. 64.

government in the supreme crisis of 1940', wrote *The Economist* (which has inherited from Bagehot the rôle of chief critic of the constitution) 'the great deterrent function that once made Parliament an occasional unmaker of ministries has diminished into a small deterrent function of regular parliamentary fuss.'

Members are kept firmly in check by the whips—the party policemen, known for their mixture of jolliness and toughness. The Government chief whip—at present Martin Redmayne—is also Patronage Secretary, with the Prime Minister's ear and so influential in promotion and honours. The combination is devastating. The government backbencher has less scope than the opposition for expressing his personality: 'The whips do not want speeches but votes. The Ministers regard an oration in their praise or defence as only one degree less tiresome than an attack.'[1]

'Backbenchers are much less independent than they were before the war,' one former Conservative whip told me: 'They don't seem to have the same independence and resources that they used to have. Even when our majority was only seventeen, they never made use of the fact that the tail could wag the dog. Recently there's been no equivalent of the strong Tory backbenchers before the war. Perhaps they were emotionally drained after Suez.' There have been some apparent spectacular successes for small groups of backbenchers—for instance Commercial TV or the support of Katanga: but both these were backed by pressures outside parliament.

The other main force which has defeated parliament has been the sheer size and complexity of government affairs. What is basically a club of talkative amateurs has been faced with discussing a machine which, among other things, controls nearly half Britain's investment. Like indignant shareholders, MPs have tried to supervise the ministries and industries which, in theory, they own. They set up committees to cross-examine civil servants and managers, and they ask fierce questions about late trains and bad coal. Sometimes their interventions have been successful: but the intricacy of administration has usually defeated them, and most parliamentarians are much more interested in debates than in the less glamorous, but more influential, committees.

The newspapers have continued to look up to parliament as the maker of policy. The fluctuations of parliamentary reputations, the gossip in the lobbies, the rhetorical performances, are analysed,

---

[1] *See* Winston Churchill: *Lord Randolph Churchill*, new ed. 1951. p. 60, quoted in R. R. James: *An Introduction to the House of Commons*, 1961.

and the 'feeling of the House' is lovingly recorded—bored by Selwyn Lloyd or Henry Brooke, delighted by Emrys Hughes. But parliamentary reputations bear little relation to reputations in Whitehall; and while parliament goes on applauding its orators, a new race of manager-politicians (often far from eloquent but very able), like Marples or Lloyd, is emerging. 'Administrator-ministers', wrote *The Economist*, 'are being permitted to treat the House of Commons as little better than a nuisance.'[1]

The rate of diminishment in the power of parliament is often exaggerated: even in the nineteenth century MPs had little influence on policy: they sat for half the year, and debated recondite subjects at length—in 1928 parliament could devote 21 hours to the prayer-book. It is not so much that the influence of MPs has declined, as that the scope of the cabinet and the civil service has grown. The huge industrial and social areas of state control have outgrown parliament: the central power has become fragmented, and the big ministries and corporations, which occupy following chapters, have fitful connections with Westminster.

But the most drastic by-pass of parliament has been the most important of all post-war issues—the question of joining the Common Market. When the Treaty of Rome was prepared in 1957, none of the European parliaments were able to discuss it in detail: the Treaty itself had been drafted by delegates from each country, who spent several months with their civil servants, negotiating and working out the complicated technical questions of tariffs, capital movement, agriculture. The Treaty was then put forward to the parliaments virtually as a *fait accompli*, to be either rejected or ratified as a whole. The arrangements were far too technical to be left to ordinary parliamentarians: faced with a take-it-or-leave-it proposition, they reluctantly took it.

With Britain, the same process seems likely. The arguments throughout the beginning of 1961 went on, not in parliament, but in the inner rooms of the Treasury, and inside the cabinet. The country was gradually prepared for the news by leaks in the press, a speech by Lord Home in Chicago, and odd hints from cabinet ministers. It was not until July 31st that the Prime Minister made an official statement to the Commons, announcing that 'after long and careful consideration, Her Majesty's Government have come to the conclusion that it would be right for Britain to make application under Article 237 . . .'

[1] 'House in Decline': *The Economist*, August 20, 1960.

Two days later parliament had its first chance to debate the Common Market: and pent-up indignation broke out. While some members congratulated each other on their speeches and the historic debate, many suspected that the real discussions had passed out of their hands, and that the Common Market foreshadowed a new diminution of their powers: that perhaps it presaged the effectual end of Western parliamentary rule.

'The sovereignty of parliament and the rule of law', said Sir Derek Walker-Smith, a former minister, 'are for us the twin pillars of our Constitution and our way of life. For the Six, parliament has its roots less deep; and perhaps the institution is held in less high regard than with us.'

'I am afraid', said William Blyton, a Labour MP, 'that parliament will be manoeuvred into a position in which it will have no option but to consent to our joining it.'

'We are facing in the long run the giving up of the independence and identity of this country in order to merge it with Europe,' said Sir Lynn Ungoed-Thomas: 'There may be a case for that, but it is clearly a case which should be proved to the hilt . . .'

'Frankly,' said Harold Wilson, 'until we know what terms we can get, anyone who can claim to understand, see this issue in simple black and white terms in or out, is either a charlatan or a simpleton.'

Mr. Bellenger, a Labour member, complained that no copies of the Treaty of Rome had been made available to members. Mr. Turton, a Conservative, complained that 'Britain is tonight being dragged kicking and screaming into the Common Market in the arms of her American financial nurse'. Mr. Shinwell, the former Labour cabinet minister, said 'I wonder what this place will be like during the next ten years. There will not be 630 honourable members. There will be no need for more than 150 or so. It will be like a parish council.'

'It is a well-known technique—the softening-up process,' complained Sir Robert Grimston, a Tory baronet: 'The House is told: "You have not got to agree to it now; you just say 'Let us have talks'." That goes on a bit, and a little later on the Government say: "This has turned out rather differently from what we thought. It is a very serious matter." A three-line whip is put on, and they go still further.'

'The real decision as to whether this country is to go into the Common Market', complained Michael Foot, 'will be made tonight.'

The main question, approving the beginning of negotiations, was passed by 313 to 5—the only noes being Anthony Fell, Michael Foot, Emrys Hughes, Konni Zilliacus and S. O. Davies: and a few weeks later negotiations began, in Brussels, with a team of civil servants headed by Edward Heath. The eventual outcome—whether parliament will become a parish council, or be out-manoeuvred, or find a new dynamic—is not yet certain. But what seems clear is that the important discussions and decisions about the Common Market will be largely taken by specialists and bureaucrats: and that in a new and closer Europe, our own parliament, the parliaments of the Common Market countries, and the Common Market parliament itself will all lose their power to the commissions and standing committees which will operate the market. It seems clear that if parliament is to help surveillance over these great new administrative machines, and maintain its role as the watchdog of democracy, it will have to revise its old amateur debating procedures, and rely much more heavily on expert examinations and committees; and that its historic amateur, club-like character must suffer a change.

5

CLUBS

I'm not going to pay good money to join a club that lets in people like me.

Groucho Marx.

That the Athenaeum should be at its full strength of about 1,700 must augur well for Britain's future.

The Tatler, 1961.

THE club is a pervading image among British institutions. Parliament is a club, and when they discuss the Commonwealth or the Common Market members always like to talk in terms of clubs. The Conservative Party has always been bound up with a small group of clubs. The Whitehall bureaucracies all have club-like ideas of corporate solidarity: and the London clubs are themselves an intrinsic part of the life of Whitehall. 'No formal arrangements of committees or staffs', wrote Professor Beer of Harvard, discussing the Treasury, 'could quite free the British Government of its dependence upon the common rooms and lunch tables of the clubs of Pall Mall.' Before we penetrate further into Whitehall or the professions, therefore, we should look, by way of a sidelight, into the insides of London clubs—where I found myself frequently in the course of this enquiry.

Viewed from the outside, the clubs have an air of infinite mystery. Every lunch time, the taxis and government Humbers draw up outside the palazzi of Pall Mall, and bowlers and umbrellas disappear through the great stone doorways, acknowledged by reverent porters. Through the big windows you see men reading *The Times*, hailing each other, exchanging surreptitious conversation with special clubman's gestures—the pat on the shoulder, the grip on the forearm, the steering from the back. When an hour-and-a-half later they all emerge again, they have the look of having changed the world. To Americans, used to snatching a sandwich at their desks, the London clubs seem to suggest a special alchemy.

Clubs are an unchallenged English invention: the Empire was built round clubs, and they remain one of our most successful exports: the authentic gloom of Pall Mall is almost outdone by the morbid staircase of the Rand Club in Johannesburg, the dim ante-rooms of the Century Club in New York, or even the Hunting Club in Rome. In Karachi, Delhi, Durban or tropical Africa, the grim exclusiveness of the English club successfully defies the gaiety of local life, and they have even penetrated to Scotland. The point of a club is not who it lets in, but who it keeps out. The club is based on two ancient British ideas—the segregation of classes, and the segregation of sexes: and they remain insistent on keeping people out, long after they have stopped wanting to come in. At their best, clubs are still havens of disinterested friendliness where professions mingle. At their worst, they are havens of humbug.

After the war the London clubs, like so many institutions, seemed on the verge of collapse: the tables were half empty, the entrance fees were high, it was hard to find staffs to maintain the palazzi. Some clubs, like the Marlborough, sold up their sites and shared the (large) profits between members: others amalgamated—like the Bath and the Conservative clubs, now vulgarly known as the Lava-Tory. But as prosperity returned and expense-accounts mounted, so clubland came back into its own: businessmen, solicitors, advertising men, salesmen, all found clubs an ideal field for operation, and the buildings, rich with associations of Regency gamblers and Victorian giants, were an invaluable status-symbol. And the clubs, like successful flirts, have maintained an aura of exclusiveness while welcoming almost any new member. Very few clubs, in fact, have a waiting-list and only a few have black balls: but all of them convey an atmosphere full of the dread of rejection.

The mystique of clubs has been encouraged by Harold Macmillan, who belongs to five clubs (the Carlton, Turf, Pratts, the Beefsteak and Bucks) and frequents all of them. (This is far from the record: Lord Mountbatten belongs to sixteen.) Eden and Churchill are not clubmen—though Churchill did found his own. Attlee in the war used to dine night after night at the Oxford and Cambridge (an extraordinary portrait of him, sitting at one end of a big desk, hangs in the dining-room): but he was not a gregarious clubman. Macmillan is thoroughly clubbable, with the right voice, the right walk, the right job: and as he disappears into the Beefsteak or Pratts or Bucks it is hard to believe that something isn't going to happen there.

And the clubs have kept their buildings: they occupy some of the finest architecture in the most coveted sites in London, including some of the last surviving town houses: and it is hard to believe that people entering such splendid places are not equally splendid. The Naval and Military—the 'In-and-Out'—occupies Lord Palmerston's old house in Piccadilly. The Turf Club, down the road in Piccadilly—a half-empty club, containing dukes, seascapes and racing results—has a site said to be worth a quarter of a million: members, having calculated that their share would come to £600, are reluctant to elect more members. A few clubs have been knocked down: the Royal Thames Yacht Club in Knightsbridge sold its old building, in return for two floors of a new one: but Pall Mall and St. James Street, the heart of clubland remain solid with club buildings. And one or two shrewd old clubs, like Brooks's, have been given large compensation for *not* being knocked down.

What does the influence of clubs amount to? Like most things in Britain, they are not what they seem: in the first place, many of them are very unsociable. Clubs can be firmly divided into those where you are expected to talk to your neighbour and those where you are not. The big anonymous clubs favoured by the civil service—the Oxford and Cambridge, United University, or the Union—are places to get away from people, not to meet them. They are deliberate extensions of Oxbridge; the United University Club, for instance, refuses to admit members from London University (United *against* Universities might be a more appropriate name). They have huge libraries with deep and solitary armchairs; and they have book-rests on the lunch-tables where under-secretaries can devour cold pie and *The Times* undisturbed. When Sir Norman Brook goes into the bar of the Oxford and Cambridge, there is no hush of recognition or surge of lobbying: no one even seems to recognise him. The most hotel-like club is the Royal Automobile, founded by hearty motoring men in 1897, which had three dining-rooms, twelve thousand members and a swimming pool once much frequented by Bernard Shaw. No one at the RAC appears to know anyone else, except in a small and boisterous bar upstairs, full of seasoned drinkers.

But other big clubs, while leaving scope for solitude, provide a useful venue for intrigue. Two of the most active are the Reform and the Travellers, next to each other in Pall Mall—the haunt of the Treasury and the Foreign Office respectively. Membership qualifications for both are equally stringent: for the Reform you must subscribe to the Reform Bill of 1832: for the Travellers you must have travelled at least *five hundred* miles from London (though the entry marked 'travel' in the candidates book offers scope for showing-off).

The Travellers was founded in 1819 with the support of the Duke of Wellington, whose portraits clutter the walls. It is very conscious of its dignity: it has a special hand-rail on the staircase, put up to help Talleyrand up the stairs. It has tall West Indian waiters and menus with a silhouette of Ulysses, though the actual *food* is not exciting. Diplomats, with their careful arrogance, set the tone. Usually the Foreign Office is well represented on the club committee; and so misbehaviour in the club is a double disaster. A few friendly men are crammed into an underground bar: but the chandeliered dining-room and coffee-room are full of supercilious second secretaries. The contrast in clubs becomes apparent in the summer holidays, when they share each other's premises: the Garrick, where members *are* expected to speak to each other, shares with the Travellers, where conversation with someone you don't know is virtually forbidden. 'I always know when the Garrick's shut,' said one veteran traveller: 'you hear laughter in the bar of the Travellers.'

The Reform next door (from which Phileas Fogg went Around the World in Eighty Days) is architecturally flabbergasting. It has a huge indoor courtyard with orange pillars and economists standing ominously drinking sherry—as if waiting for the news of a crash—while others look down from tables on the balcony. The Reform was built by Barry, in the Italian style, with a kitchen the size of a ball-room—where the famous chef Soyer, author of a standard work on 'Gastronomic Regeneration' presided over a steam-operated kitchen. Gastronomic reform is still a feature of the club, but other radical instincts have deserted it. The Reform is the temple of *laissez-faire*: it is here that Treasury men agree about the difficulties of change, and where the Economists' Tuesday Club reject thoughts of planning. It was in a private room at the Reform, too, that a group of shrewd lobbyists—Norman Collins, Robert Renwick, Lord Bessborough—successfully plotted commercial television.

But the most august of the big clubs, of course, is the Athenæum, with its big stucco building, behind the gold goddess Athene, facing the United Service Club (The Senior) in Waterloo Place.

It is, in many respects, the most unsociable and uncomfortable of all: 'Where all the arts and sciences are understood', said

G. W. E. Russell in 1906, 'except gastronomy': and of its cavernous dining-room the same could still be said. Even outside the Silence Room, which is the real heart of the club, a sense of solitude prevails. Old men wander alone up and down the broad staircase: (they always walk up the *right-hand* staircase, one scientific member pointed out: they have to change the carpets round from time to time to wear both down equally).

The Athenæum retains an atmosphere of bleak and uncompromising wisdom: a bust of Charles Darwin broods over the hall, and the Greek letters Alpha Theta Eta evoke intimidating memories. Moreover there is always a cluster of bishops, and the club is never without episcopal activity on a Trollopean scale (Trollope himself used to write his novels in the long drawing-room, before breakfast, and it was there that he was persuaded to kill off Mrs. Proudie).

But the Athenæum, for all its dignity, is not above intrigue: members have complained that they could hardly hear themselves talk above the noise of lobbying—particularly for university grants: the Athenæum is the favourite meeting place for vice-chancellors. It is also a centre for a very unclubbable breed—the scientists (the Royal Society Dining Club assemble there) who use it as a base for manoeuvre and fund-raising. 'The last war was run by the Athenæum on one side, with the scientists and civil servants, and the Senior on the other, with the admirals and generals': one scientist explained, 'since they all talked very loudly, it wasn't difficult to discover what was going on.'

A more sociable and arrogant group are the eighteenth-century clubs, with their elegant façades down St. James's Street. The most sedate is Boodle's, with its big bow window, from which one eighteenth-century duke used to enjoy watching 'the damn'd people get wet'. Boodle's was originally known as the 'Savoir Vivre', famous for orgiastic feasts: but it is now very demure, with a hard core of old country members who can be seen snoozing in the window. Brooks's on the other side of the street, founded in 1764, and frequented by Charles James Fox, was the scene of reckless gambling by the Whig aristocrats in Regency times: George Drummond, of Drummonds bank, only gambled once: he lost £20,000 to Beau Brummel and had to resign from the bank. It is now mainly Conservative and much less reckless; but it keeps a certain style, and boasts the best hall-porter in London. Bored-looking men stand in front of a blazing fire. The most arrogant club, of course, is White's, the traditional haunt of idle Tories: but that is so much part of the character of the Tory Party that it belongs, together with the Carlton, to that chapter.

In a special class are the cultural clubs, all somewhat confused between a Victorian past and a commercial present. The most ponderous is the Garrick, founded in 1831 in memory of the actor, with a gaudy array of Zoffany portraits up the staircase. Their early members included Trollope, Lord John Russell, Gilbert and Sullivan, Dickens and Thackeray—who quarrelled there, later to be reconciled on the staircase of the Athenæum: Thackeray adored 'the little G 'and called it 'the dearest place in the world': but nowadays the Garrick, though it still has actors, is full of lawyers, editors and businessmen.

Less pompous is the Savile, which tries to steer a middle course between gravity and bohemianism. 'There are other places', says the history of the Savile (with a dig at the Savage with which it resents confusion) 'where the self-conscious eccentrics and aggressively Bohemian types can circulate and deviate with more approval.' The Savile is unpretentious and not rich: 'Oh yes, the Savile Club,' said Oscar Wilde, 'a real republic of letters, not a sovereign among 'em.' Their motto is 'sodalitas convivium'—but occasionally the *convivium* gets in the way of the *sodalitas*—as when a few years ago one member lifted up a former Lord Chancellor and dumped him on the mantelpiece.

The hard core of the Savile are publishers, authors, actors and broadcasters: Ralph Richardson, Compton Mackenzie and Professor Jimmy Edwards are among its more obvious inmates, and C. P. Snow—an inveterate clubman—an archetypal member. Around the bar there is booksy chat and the atmosphere of a literary salon—of reputations being made and broken, of 'what do you think of G's new thing?'

The Arts Club in Dover Street has had a sadder transformation: it was founded in 1863, for Art, Literature and Science: it has a pleasant new building, with flock wallpaper, portraits of artists and a few men with beards: but it is now also concerned with the art of advertising and the science of public relations, and from the bar can be heard the braying sound of admen on the move.

The least reticent of the artistic clubs is the Savage, which occupies a faded Regency house in Carlton House Terrace. It is an extrovert place, full of cartoons of famous men with big heads, and jungle fantasies about 'Brother Savages' wearing straw skirts and shaking spears. There are no bowlers and few umbrellas: instead, lots of friendly comedian artists and actors, dumping large cases in the hall and striding into a small, overcrowded drinking den: the club is noisy with theatrical patter—'yes, he's a sweetie—and quite a good actor too'. The Savage is aggressively sociable—not to be seen talking to someone provokes comment: its most surprising Brother Savage is the stern octogenarian former Lord Chief Justice, Lord Goddard.

A more likely setting for secret influence might seem to be the smaller clubs, of the kind frequented by the Prime Minister. The most exotic is Pratt's, in two basement rooms in St. James's; it began its existence in 1841 as the kitchen of the Duke of Beaufort's steward, called Pratt, which became the Duke's dive. It still has a large kitchen dresser, and its small rooms are full of stuffed fishes, birds, bric-a-brac and members of the Government. Another unexpected place is Buck's in a plain Georgian house in Mayfair, founded just after the first world war as a reunion club by Captain Buckmaster, who still owns it. It serves a champagne cocktail called 'Buck's Fizz', oysters and mutton chops, and retains a faint air of rakishness.

Or there is the Beefsteak, at the top of a dingy staircase off Leicester Square, opposite a strip-tease joint. The Beefsteak is very sociable, and generates remarkable dialogues. Members have to sit wherever the waiters (all called Charles) put them on the single long table, and they like to tell the story how before the war the police, seeing old men emerging happily every evening, assumed it was a brothel and began watching the club: one night they raided it, and found four men sitting round the long table. The conversation went something like this:

'And who might you be?' asked the policeman of one old gentleman.

'I am the Lord Chancellor.'

'Aha! And you, sir?'

'The Archbishop of Canterbury.'

'Oh yes! And the next?'

'I am the Governor of the Bank of England.'

'And I suppose', said the policeman to the fourth, 'that you're the Prime Minister.'

'As a matter of fact I am,' said Arthur Balfour.

Now only the Prime Minister and the Governor are members, together with the Home Secretary, three dukes, Osbert Lancaster,

Sir Malcolm Sargent and three hundred others: but many of the junior members like me are too frightened to actually go there.

The most select clubs of all have no premises at all. The most famous is 'The Club', the traditional top people's dining-club, which included such men as Balfour, John Buchan, and Geoffrey Dawson, and now includes the Prime Minister, T. S. Eliot and J. C. Masterman: and 'The Other Club', which was founded by F. E. Smith and Winston Churchill in 1911, as a rival body of political bounders. Smith himself wrote the constitution, which states that 'the names of the executive committee shall be wrapped in impenetrable mystery'. Since then the outsiders have become the insiders, and The Other Club is now the more active: it still meets every other Thursday during the parliamentary session, at a private room in the Savoy, and its members include Lord Boothby, Lord Shawcross and—once again—the Prime Minister. Originally there were an equal number of Liberal and Conservative members, who could be paired in parliament: but the rise of socialism has unbalanced it, and there are hardly any Labour members.

But clubland altogether is unrepresentative: a few names recur again and again, while the huge area of socialists, managers, scientists and technologists hardly appear at all. The Labour Party has always been pubbable rather than clubbable: there is no left-wing equivalent to the Carlton or White's: and even a Liberal club like Brooks's has ended up largely Conservative. 'Clubland is as Conservative as the sea is salt,' wrote G. W. E. Russell in 1906: and the ineluctable conservatism—both social and political—continues: English clubs progress in the opposite direction to African night-clubs: they begin by being disreputable, full of wild actors and poets drinking into the night: and end up with cautious lawyers toying with cold beef and *rosé*, reminiscing about the wild old days.

Is the future still being settled among port and cigars in club chairs? Can membership confer a sliver of power? Perhaps there are still a few moments of intrigue when clubs are important. But while the reminiscences ramble on in Pall Mall, the future is being decided in the Cabinet Office canteen, in the directors' dining-room in ICI, or between the TV tycoons at large lunches at the Savoy.

Two major invasions have troubled clubland since the war. The first has been business, which is anathema to the amateur spirit of clubs: many clubs actually forbid members to produce business documents. But while clubs admitted more and more businessmen, the appearance of amateurism has become hard to keep up: and even in White's—traditionally the enemy of trade—the *Financial Times* and Sir Miles Thomas can be seen.

But a more serious revolution has been the intrusion of women. The most formidable weapon of women has been to found their *own* clubs—the Ladies' Alpine Club, the Women's Press Club, or the Sesame Club, for women explorers and pioneers. One by one the men's clubs have given way, either by inaugurating a ladies' night, or a ladies' annexe (often a converted billiard-room)—but never by introducing lady *members*. Women are kept carefully segregated. At the Reform, 'LADIES may be entertained for DINNER on FRIDAYS and for LUNCH and DINNER on SATURDAY in the East End of the Coffee Room'. At the Senior the Admirals objected fiercely for years before the billards room was finally converted for ladies in 1921. At the Savile, women are admitted once a year. The arrangement of Ladies' annexes arouses fundamental controversy, for it raises the problem of the club's *image*, and all clubs are very image-conscious. Should clubs try to adapt their style to welcome women, or should they remain defiantly masculine? The clubs have reacted to the problem in different ways, but the favourite solution is the 'Ladies' Annexe'—a phrase which speaks volumes—where the club can present a different image without interfering with its old one.

In all clubs, perhaps, there is an element of imposture. Everyone, as he ushers his guest through those mahogany doors, becomes a slightly less real person, talks a bit louder, shakes hands a bit more heartily. The Arts Club has admen pretending to be artists. The Garrick has lawyers pretending to be actors, or vice-versa. White's has ordinary men pretending to be eccentric. The Travellers is a Foreign Office canteen pretending to be an amateurs' drawing-room. Only the Athenæum is completely *sui generis*—there the bishops are being bishops, the professors are professors, the eccentrics are eccentric, and the dull, distinguished men sit in their deep leather chairs in the silence room, where no one can disturb them. And they hold to themselves the secret of setting themselves, ostentatiously, at ease, and leaving their interlocutors puzzled, embarrassed, gratified but obscurely discomfited.

Can clubs withstand the pressures of democracy *and* women? At lunch time they seem confident enough: but it is in the evenings, when the wife and family beckon, that the loyalty of clubmen is tested: and it is then that the crumbling of clubs is revealed. A few fiercely masculine clubs, like White's, succeed in drinking and gambling till late into the night. But in most clubs, only a handful of bachelors, grass widowers or visitors inhabit the cavernous rooms. No doubt clubs will survive a long time, with their myths, their sites and the convenience: but the old misogynist zeal, which built the Empire and kept wives in their place—that has gone.

6

CONSERVATIVES

'Damn your principles! Stick to your party.'
Disraeli to Bulwer Lytton.

EVERY autumn the two main political parties hold their conferences at seaside resorts, after the summer guests have left.
Sometimes both parties choose the same resort, for successive
weeks. One week there is the Labour party. The lounge of the
main hotel is full of jollity, with large comfortable men sitting in
braces; the bar is packed with talkative intellectuals, full of witty
disloyalties. Outside the conference hall are salesmen for every
kind of cranky organisation. Inside the hall are many of the trade
unionists who met a month before at their congress, now diluted
with other Labour elements—the middle-class intellectuals, or the
intense young radicals, and girls are in trousers and duffels.

The proceedings bear the marks of the origin of the Labour
party—non-conformism and Marxism: speeches, addressed to
'Comrade Chairman', are full of time-honoured phrases—'count-
less millions yet unborn', 'brotherhood of man', or 'commanding
heights'. The conference ends with singing the 'Red Flag', sung
with visible embarrassment by the intellectuals:

> The people's flag is deepest red
> It's shrouded oft our martyrs dead.
> And ere their limbs grew stiff and cold
> Their heart's blood dyed its every fold . . .
>
> With heads uncovered swear we all
> To bear it onward till we fall.
> Come dungeon dark or gallows grim
> This song shall be our parting hymn.

The next week the main hotel is suddenly full of dinner-jackets
and large hats. The girls are dressed as if for a weekend in the
country. Solid North Country businessmen and tireless Tory
women talk in the foyer: when one of the great men of the party
comes through, the crowd edges respectfully away, murmuring
loyal noises.

In the conference hall the bearded cranks have all disappeared: instead there is a Conservative bookstall, full of dark-blue pamphlets. Well-tailored young men and trim, two-piece girls eagerly greet visitors. A huge union jack is draped across the dais: speeches refer to 'Her Majesty's Government' or 'Her Majesty's ministers'. The impression that the Queen belongs to the Conservatives is overpowering. Speakers begin 'Mr Chairman, Sir, My Lords, Ladies and Gentlemen', and have their own private idioms: 'worthy of our calling', 'I count myself fortunate', 'ever-increasing standard of living', 'you all know what *that* means'. The whole conference has a background of ritual and organ music. At many constituency meetings the Conservatives still sing the old imperial hymn:

> Land of hope and glory
> Mother of the Free.
> How can we extol thee
> Who are born of thee?
> Wider still and wider
> Shall thy bounds be set.
> God who made thee mighty
> Make thee mightier yet.

Passing from one conference to the other, one might well imagine that Britain was still unmendably split into two nations. But the contrast can be misleading. Both conferences have inherited archaic trappings from the pre-war world. In both parties delegates are more extreme than MPs, and the MPs more extreme than the leaders—so that the two sides sometimes nearly meet at the top. For both sides, however committed their supporters, are preoccupied with one question—survival: to gain votes, they have to appeal to the mass of middling people who roam in the no-man's land and wouldn't be seen dead in a conference.

THE CONSERVATIVES

'It was the biggest change in a hundred years', said Lord Poole, who was one of the architects of the Conservative re-building after the war, 'between those who were anxious to put the clock back as far as possible to the pre-war world and those who preferred the post-war. Intellectually, we captured the party.' The actual change in leaders was not as abrupt as some have made out. Tory leaders have always been a mixture of landed grandees and middle-class men: at the top, there are now as many aristocrats as before the war. But behind the privilege, something different has emerged and the actual power structure of the party has undergone a basic change.

Most importantly the influence of wealthy families and business interests has given way to the professional politicians, and the party machine. The Maxwell Fyfe Report of 1948 forbade Conservative candidates to contribute more than £100 to election expenses—making it harder for rich families to dominate constituencies, and increasing the power of the central office. There are still many places, like Southend, where voters remain loyal to old dynasties, and peers' sons still abound in the House. But the war swept away shoals of squires, and brought a new catch of middle-class politicians with political expertise but without landed connections.

The most gruesome assembly of old Tories remains White's Club in St. James' Street with its proud tradition of philistinism, gambling and drinking. Before the Reform Bill of 1832 (according to Lord Russell's Recollections) one peer at White's, who owned several pocket boroughs, nominated one of the waiters, called Robert Mackreth, for a seat in the Commons, which he duly occupied. And the club still likes to defy democracy—as when, in 1950, Aneurin Bevan was kicked in the hall. In Regency times White's boasted two-thirds of the 'upper ten thousand': it would not admit anyone who had made his money through trade. It still maintains the atmosphere of ungainful employment: on a hot summer afternoon loud men can be seen warming themselves in front of a roaring fire, or watching the racing results on the ticker-tape. It keeps its own schoolboy language—about hols, prep, brekkers or 'being on our side'. The arrogance still fascinates the Tory Party, and the prospect of White's back-benchers howling for blood can still intimidate a cabinet minister. But its political importance nowadays is slight, and many senior Tories, including the last three prime ministers, have remained aloof from it: the more serious meeting-place is the Carlton Club, which provides full-length portraits of Tory prime ministers but a less terrifying atmosphere.

The old Tory tradition had grandeur as well as arrogance. At their best, the landed aristocrats were independent, courageous and outspoken: the three great pre-war opponents of appeasement —Churchill, Eden and Salisbury—all came from such backgrounds, and were able to defy their constituents and their party. The two most severe Tory critics in the Commons, Lord Hinchingbrooke and Lord Lambton, are both heirs to earldoms and fortunes. But the most eminent survivor of this old independence is Lord Salisbury, head of the House of Cecil. The conflict between this legendary figure, confident, convinced and deeply conservative, and the new phenomenon of Iain Macleod, shrewd, and adaptable, sums up the struggle of the old world against the new, and the eclipse of the old.

LORD SALISBURY

Cecils don't give a damn—and that makes a lot of difference.
Lord Attlee.

Robert Arthur James Gascoyne-Cecil, fifth Marquess of Salisbury, strokes a tidy moustache under his long 'Cecilian nose', and intertwines his thin fingers. Like his brother Lord David Cecil—who is a Professor of English at Oxford—he walks in a vague, slanting way, and talks with a faint lisp and a slightly cracked voice, which becomes higher as he talks faster, with old pronounciations like '*lorst*' and '*acrorss*'.

He moves between three homes—the family's old Tudor estate at Cranborne in Dorset (looked after by his son Lord Cranborne), a secluded town house in Chelsea, and Hatfield, the great cupolaed Jacobean mansion outside London which has been the home of the Cecils since 1607. The Cecils are one of the most potent symbols, outside the monarchy, of Britain's continuity: the first great Cecil, Lord Burghley (thought to be the original of Shakespeare's Polonius), was Secretary of State to Queen Elizabeth for forty years. His son advised James I, and built Hatfield. Then, for two centuries, the Cecils fell out of politics. But the second Marquess of Salisbury brought the railway to Hatfield, diverted the Great North Road for his greater convenience, and married a rich brewer's daughter, Miss Gascoyne, who brought money and brains; and from them came the third Marquess—the bearded Victorian prime minister. From then on Cecils proliferated. The Prime Minister's nephew, Arthur Balfour, became Prime Minister, and his four sons all became prominent between the wars (one in the League of Nations, one as Provost of Eton, one as cabinet minister and one as Bishop of Exeter).

The present Marquess, grandson of the Prime Minister, has watched the steady diminution of territorial powers. As a child at Hatfield, before the first war, he saw the old ducal world still largely untouched. His cousin was prime minister: his father was in the cabinet. His variegated uncles, known as the 'Harlequin Set'—were all in evidence. But after the first war the Cecils, like many old families, felt their fortunes threatened, and the future Marquess went to work in the City for eight years, to learn about money: he only drifted into parliament at thirty-six—for the local seat of South Dorset—where he soon showed his independence. He resigned from Chamberlain's Government over appeasement, was brought back during the war by Churchill, and was one of the few men who were prepared to stand up to him.

In the Conservative Government of 1951 Salisbury was regarded as the elder statesman—aloof, unambitious, high-principled. When in 1957 the Queen asked Harold Macmillan to become prime minister, the public at large pictured Salisbury (who married Macmillan's wife's cousin) as 'the king-maker', exerting unseen power, as the Cecils had done four hundred years before. However, in the retreat from Suez, Macmillan followed policies which the Marquess increasingly disliked. Several times he threatened to resign. At last, when Archbishop Makarios was released from exile, he *did* resign—protesting that the release was 'neither timely nor wise'. The idea of a Tory Government without a Cecil was unthinkable: yet nothing happened, the Government continued with scarcely a tremor.

The climax came over Africa. Salisbury had old connections with Rhodesia: its capital had been named after his grandfather (the whole country had nearly been called 'Cecilia' after him and Rhodes); Salisbury's lifetime (as he told me) had corresponded roughly to the time the white man had settled in Africa and as a young man he had been stirred by the pioneers. He owned lands in Rhodesia, and after he had resigned from the cabinet, he became a director of the ultra-conservative British South Africa Company. He watched the British concessions in Kenya and Rhodesia with growing indignation: he is not a die-hard: he likes to talk about conservatism being 'intelligent opportunism' and quotes his grandfather on the need to 'feel your way forward'. He insists that his objections are on matters of degree, not of principle. But he thought, quite simply, that the Government were going too fast.

At last, in March, 1961, he broke out. In a debate on Central Africa in the House of Lords, Lord Salisbury rose quietly from the red benches and to the astonishment of his peers launched a stinging personal attack on the Colonial Secretary, Iain Macleod.

'He has adopted a most unhappy and entirely wrong approach. He has been too clever by half . . . It almost seems to me as if the Colonial Secretary, when he abandoned the sphere of bridge for the sphere of politics, brought his bridge technique with him.' He accused Macleod of being 'rather unscrupulous'; of deliberately setting out to outwit his opponents, and producing a 'miasma of distrust' between the white settlers and Britain; he wound up with a moving plea for 'these little communities, including wives and children, scattered about among primitive people'.

A ferocious two-day debate followed: the traditional courtesies about the 'Noble Marquess' only sharpened the edge. Lord Salisbury was backed up by Lord Robins, a fellow-director of the British South Africa Company, and by the Duke of Montrose, who had flown specially over from Rhodesia, and who obscurely linked African affairs with the Jameson Raid and *Lady Chatterley's Lover*. But the Government peers—as well as the left-wing peers—moved in with solid and unfeigned indignation, and with the passionate zeal of the newly converted. The Lord Chancellor himself rose from the Woolsack, saying 'who touches my brother touches me'; he described Salisbury's speech as 'the bitterest attack that I have known on a Minister in my 26 years in parliament'. 'The noble and learned Viscount can abuse me as much as he likes', replied Salisbury, 'I will not withdraw it.'

The Archbishop of Canterbury tried to act as mediator and calm the peers, but the storm was quickly revived by Lord Hailsham, the irascible Leader of the House of Lords. After briefly reminiscing about how he had been bitten at Eton by the Duke of Montrose, he moved into an attack on Salisbury, so bitter that the Earl of Arran, Salisbury's cousin, walked out. 'Hailsham looked like a vegetarian who had just had his first meal of meat', as one peer described it. 'If I had to choose between marquesses I prefer the Queensbury rules to the Cecil rules', said Hailsham, 'because the Queensberry rules at least prescribe that it is unfair to hit below the belt.' Lord Salisbury politely replied to Hailsham's 'speech of extreme violence': 'If he is the guardian of his conscience, so am I the guardian of mine; and my conscience is clear.'

'It wasn't really about Africa,' one peer said afterwards: 'it was pure class warfare—the upper-class peers against the middle-class peers.' But it was not only a conflict between classes, and between old and new Conservatives: it was a conflict between a generation strong enough to stand up to its enemies, and one preoccupied with solidarity and survival, and uncertain exactly who might be friend and who foe.

Conservatives anxiously waited for Salisbury's supporters to muster. Two days later, when the Hertford Conservative Association held their annual meeting, the Marquess was not in the chair: the next day he announced his resignation from the two Hatfield Conservative Associations: 'A member of the Salisbury family', the secretary said sadly, 'has been our president as long as we can remember.' And two days later Salisbury resigned from two more associations.

But no rumpus followed. Salisbury's cousin, Lord Selborne, aged 73, resigned from the East Hampshire Conservatives: Lord Forester, aged 60, stopped his subscription to the Ludlow and Wrekin Association. But even Lord Balniel, the local Conservative member for Hertford, who is Salisbury's nephew, stood up for the Government: and the Tory party survived almost unscathed. The legend of the Cecils has never been quite the same since.

In the meantime Iain Macleod advanced steadily. Six months later he was appointed Leader of the House of Commons and Chairman of the Conservative Party: and his arrival in this central position marked a new stage in the refurbishing of Conservatism.

IAIN MACLEOD

Macleod is a mysterious new kind of Tory, detached from traditional background. He is shortish, rather bald, with dark, impersonal eyes: he is unobtrusively dressed, though he blossoms out into double-breasted waistcoats. He lives in a modest Chelsea flat, with his wife—a parson's daughter—and two grown-up children, Diane and Torquil. He watches television, spends weekends in London, and works a lot in bed. He has no large hinterland of learning and culture. He entertains a good deal, without pomp, and his wife does the cooking. He has only a small circle of old friends, including Nigel Fisher, a Tory MP. He enjoys celebrating and pulling out corks, but he never seems to let himself go. He appears a rather solitary person. But he is self-contained and at peace with himself; he likes going for long walks to 'renew himself to himself'. In some respects he appears a pure professional, a Nixonish politician: but he has a strange layer of romanticism, half real, half assumed. His Conservative career has been full of difficult manoeuvres and compromises, and the real value of his ideals will probably only emerge—as has happened with Eden and Macmillan—if and when he becomes prime minister.

He comes from tough Scots stock: his father, a doctor who emigrated from the Western Isles to Yorkshire, sent his son to an exacting Scots public school, Fettes. Macleod went on to Cambridge where bridge became his passion, and afterwards had a brief and desultory career in business—appropriately in the playing-card firm of De La Rue. It was the war which shook up his career: he was wounded, rose to be a Major, took part in the D-day landings, and after the war went into Tory politics. He joined R. A. Butler's research staff. In 1950 he was elected to parliament and founded the 'One Nation' group of new Conservatives and in 1952 had his crucial stroke of luck, when Aneurin Bevan intervened in a debate on the health service, and gave Macleod the chance to show his form. Soon after that, Churchill made him Minister of Health—a sudden promotion—and he rose to be Minister of Labour and then to the hottest seat of all— Colonies, which he occupied perilously but without disaster for two years.

In all his jobs Macleod has shown an astonishingly agile mind. He has a memory which almost equals Macaulay's (he is distantly related to Macaulay): he can recite lists of thirty-year old Olympic results and Derby winners without any strain: and he is able to prepare and memorise speeches and then come out with apparently extempore witticisms. He is a master of any kind of political manoeuvre. He is cool, calculating but not unemotional. In his two years dealing with Africans he was genuinely sympathetic: 'I believe in the brotherhood of man,' he said quite simply at the 1961 party conference. The disabilities of his wife, who had polio, and his own pain with fibrositis, have given him experience of suffering, which Africans such as Kaunda and Banda appreciated. He was stimulated by the social change implicit in Africa, not depressed by it, as Salisbury was.

Macleod often shows signs of being restive with Conservatives: he talks with witty dislike of the 'Deep South'—the right-wing strongholds along the south coast—and he likes to depict himself not as a Conservative—a word which he dislikes—but as a romantic Tory, of the Disraelian kind. He is very aware of his Highland blood, and has even written a romantic play about the Hebrides. He sometimes talks of himself as being too left for his party, and as Colonial Secretary he was in the firing-line from the right. But his position was not as exposed as it looked: he has growing support from younger Conservatives, and he is well aware of the dangers of 'being right too soon'; on the major issues such as Africa and the Common Market—to which he was a late convert— he is prepared to wait until he has enough support. He knows that he lacks the nostalgic appeal of Macmillan or Eden, and that if he is to lead his party he must never appear to be jostling them.

RAB

Richard Austen Butler, Macleod's main rival for the future Conservative leadership, represents a yet more ambiguous aspect of the Conservative party: for thirty years he has been defending all sorts of different Tory policies. He is not a typical Tory—he is essentially an intellectual—but he accurately represents that broad slice of his party which, without being excited by social change, knows when to give in to it. He has been an appeaser both in the good and the bad sense. He has appeased Hitler and Franco, but also Gandhi: and there have been moments—in education during the war, or in his stand against flogging—when he has been ahead of his party. But cautious ambiguity has been his consistent feature: and this has stood in his road to the top job.

In his background he stands between the landed and the bourgeois strands of his party. He comes from academic-administrator stock: father and uncle were both Indian provincial governors; he was brought up in a Governor's mansion; wanted to be Viceroy of India. His father later became Master of Pembroke, Cambridge, and other Butlers—a large clan—have been scattered through the universities. Rab likes to murmur—like so many other Tories—about Scots ancestry, and his beginnings were donnish and modest. But ever since he married an heiress, Sydney Courtauld, he has been a wealthy man: he has a house in Westminster, full of Impressionist paintings, a big house in Essex, and a manse on the Island of Mull. Yet he has not become the complete landed squire, and his self-critical side remains strong. This cleavage has heightened his ambiguity. He moves in stately circles: but he loves to encourage young men to attack 'the Establishment'. He is careful in parliament about homosexuals and flogging, but privately encourages agitation for reform.

The years have increased his reputation for evasion: in the same sentence he can suggest that he is both against the Common Market and for it. There is a favourite parliamentary story of how Rab, if asked the time, would congratulate the honourable member on his question, discuss different measurements of time, heartily endorse the importance of timekeeping, but fail to actually give the answer. But he apparently enjoys such parodies, and seems sometimes to be caricaturing himself.

His manner conveys an agreeable unconvincingness. He wags his finger incessantly but without fervour: he uses didactic phrases with blinks and nods of the head: 'I must tell you that . . .' 'I can assure you . . .' 'You see? You see?'

He can come out with statements of extraordinary silliness, with a smell of the common-room about them: 'We have lived too long on old port and over-ripe pheasant,' he remarked in a crisis, and during the economic crisis in 1961 he suddenly recited a little ditty—

> Nations earn their right to rise
> By service and by sacrifice

—which turned out to have been composed by his uncle, for Rab's own birth. Part of his political weakness may stem from an obstinate niceness of character. A large part of him remains happy and frank, and delightfully indiscreet: he does not have the cold mask of Macmillan, and he is said—very credibly—to be happiest on all fours, barking away with children. At the Treasury he was well known for his imagination—eccentric but endearing. Once when a long memorandum came to him about the British Lion Film Corporation, discussing the details of the Government subsidy, he simply put a red ring round the word 'lion' pointing to the word in the margin—*Grrr*.

But he lives politics to the finger-tips. He has been in half the ministries in Whitehall. He came into the Government as long ago as 1932, as a brilliant young don, when Churchill was blustering on the side-lines and Gaitskell was lecturing to workers. His greatest achievement was probably in the years out of office, when he took over with Lord Woolton the reconstruction of the Tory party; he built up his team of 'Rab's boys'—the young unknown ex-soldiers, such as Macleod, Maudling, Powell, Maude and Alport, who helped to present an up-to-date party, with slogans like 'property-owning democracy'. He was rewarded with the job of Chancellor of the Exchequer, which he held for four years: he seemed set fair to become eventually leader of the party. But during this time his wife, who had inspired him politically as well as personally, died; he showed signs of losing his grip; and he was moved by Eden to the nebulous functions of Lord Privy Seal. He was distrusted, too, by the right-wing for being too liberal, too evasive, and he lacked the reassuring, old-fashioned appeal of his more obscure rival, Macmillan: in the planning of Suez he was kept out of the inner cabinet, but was not politically strong—or brave—enough to attack it. When Eden resigned, nearly everyone, except Randolph Churchill, forecast Rab for PM. When the Queen called Macmillan, Rab faced the ultimate disappointment —amounting almost to public humiliation.

Between Rab and Macmillan a barbed state of co-existence prevailed, with Rab clearly resenting the Prime Minister's histrionic airs. Rab married again, and as Home Secretary seemed to recover his form. But in the meantime 'Rab's boys', whom he had brought to the front, were pushing ahead: and as Macmillan stayed on, so Rab's position seemed increasingly threatened by younger men.

Many Conservative leaders are more liberal than their party: Macleod has partly overcome the difficulty by a romantic public image, and identification with youth. But Rab has fallen into the habit of being elaborately Conservative in public, and liberal and rebellious in private: and this perpetual ambiguity has weakened his standing on both fronts.

NEW TORIES

Macleod is one of five middle-class, middle-way, middle-aged Conservatives who—though rivals—talk about themselves as 'we', and see themselves as the apostles of the new conservatism: Thorneycroft, Maudling, Heath and Powell are the others.

Peter Thorneycroft, at the Ministry of Aviation, is the most old-style—Eton, regular army, married to an Italian countess. His bland manner conceals great ability and tough principles— which led him to resign from the Chancellorship in 1957, in protest against Macmillan's too-soft policies. Since then he has had to work his way up again.

Reginald Maudling is sometimes described as the cleverest man in the cabinet; he is certainly one of the most likeable—beaming behind large glasses, he smokes fat cigars at the Colonial Office, with his legs up on his desk. He is lazy and happy, but also compassionate, and can be stirred into vigorous action by outrage. Nor is he as *laissez-faire* as he sounds. But he seems to lack the drive or the ruthlessness for power politics. When he was in charge of Common Market talks in 1958, his heart was never fully in it. But at the Colonial Office he has shown signs of being more uncompromisingly liberal than Macleod.

The most obviously professional New Tory is Ted Heath—a kind of officer-politician, who has moved briskly up from the ranks, into the heart of the party. He has a boyish face, grey hair and a sudden, disconcerting smile. Bachelor, plays the organ, conducts a choir at Ramsgate, was once news editor of the *Church Times*. He is a rare thing—a grammar-school Tory leader: son of a master-builder, went to Oxford, then army and politics. He went into parliament in 1951, rose quickly to become Chief Whip, and Macmillan's confidant: then to Ministry of Labour and the Foreign Office, where he is leading the negotiations for the Common Market. Heath is well-liked, hard-working, with the right mixture of toughness and tact: in the Common Market negotiations he has shown unexpected mastery and finesse.

The most courageous of the five is Enoch Powell, the pale, ascetic ex-professor of Greek, who once shared a flat with Iain Macleod. Powell is unmistakable: he has piercing eyes and a discomforting gaze, which breaks through suddenly into alarming laughter. He is one of those straightforward people who go round parties saying 'and what do you do?' He respects bold, plain-speaking people, and has romantic ideas about strength, which emerge in his early poems:

> I only love the strong and bold
> The flashing eye, the reddening cheek.

His background is exotic—Birmingham non-conformist, grammar-school and Cambridge, with a brilliant Greek career: he taught Greek in Cambridge and Australia, became a Brigadier in the war, joined 'Rab's boys', and went into parliament. The arrival of his sharp and uncompromising mind has fluttered the party, for Powell, for all his hexameters, is a fierce believer in old-fashioned free enterprise: he admires Clore as well as Herodotus, and looks back with nostalgia to the old days before monopolies and nationalisation. His determination to take 'free enterprise' literally has embarrassed many protective Tories, who look with distress at take-overs: but in the new European Britain, his doctrines may find more favour.

Alongside these new men there are still many Conservative leaders from a more privileged tradition; the Earl of Home; Churchill's two sons-in-law, Sandys and Soames; Macmillan's son-in-law, Julian Amery; wealthy, unexciting men like Sir David Eccles or John Hare; and the extraordinary periphery of peers with ancient titles who form a kind of guard of honour to Macmillan's ministry—the Marquess of Lansdowne, the Earl of Perth, the Earl of Dundee, Lord Carrington, or Lord Waldegrave. There is still a bevy of dull, solid men with country estates, who provide a kind of cargo to all Tory cabinets.

There are also people who, while not politically strong, are efficient managers of departments. Men like Selwyn Lloyd or Henry Brooke can empty the benches in parliament, and bore Tory conferences to distraction: but in the corridors of Whitehall they enjoy solid and well-earned repute. These manager-politicians include self-made men with business background—most notably Reginald Bevins, the Postmaster-General, and that curious phenomenon Ernest Marples—who will crop up later, invading nationalised industries. None of these men are very welcome at conferences: few people know, or care much, about their views on high policy. But they are the managing directors of Whitehall, and we will encounter them in the departments where they belong. Parliament is better at throwing up talkers than doers, but these men run counter to this rule.

Who are the future Conservative leaders? There is still a wide range of backbenchers, from landowners to TV announcers: there is still a flow of young fogeys, drenched in tradition and reverence. But the most thoughtful collection is the 'Bow Group', who supplied ten MPs in the 1959 election. The Bow Group does not have a corporate policy. It is a think-box for the party, like the Fabians on the left, and its views range from die-hard to radical: but it has an ambience of its own. The Bow Groupers are nearly all young professional men—barristers, executives, journalists or advertising men, with an earnest, professional attitude to politics. There is a story of a girl who joined them, thinking they were the 'Beau Group', and was disappointed to find them dull and not very sexy. They are studious and carefully pedestrian—compared to the more equestrian postures of pre-war young Tories. They write long, well-printed pamphlets full of accurate figures and cautious suggestions, and they give sober parties in Kensington and Chelsea. They have an active social conscience, shown in their campaigns for the World Refugee Year and Old-people-for-Christmas. Occasionally they have shown signs of tentative rebellion: and their first chairman, James Lemkin, had an important influence in stirring up interest in

Central Africa. But the Bow Groupers have been embraced by the Conservative party machine and praised by the Prime Minister, and with age they have become more conformist.

There remain some radical pockets within the Conservatives. A surprising one is Sir Edward Boyle, the young Financial Secretary to the Treasury. Boyle has a nineteenth-century look to him: he is a huge, rubicund baronet who wears formal clothes, and talks with unconcealed learning, assuming others to be equally learned. He walks like a bear, with a formidable shuffle, and he has the broad interests and leisureliness of a cultivated squire. But, behind this Victorian appearance, he is one of the most radically-minded men: he was one of only two members of the Government to resign over Suez, and he has an interest in social change and education, a dislike of Conservative snobbery, and a belief in the purposive rôle of government, which is rare in his party.

Who really runs the Conservative party? The question is carefully shrouded in mystery: 'Loyalty,' said Lord Kilmuir, 'is the Tory's secret weapon': and the paraphernalia of conferences encourages the belief in mystic leadership from above. The Leader only appears at the end of the conference week, as a *deus ex machina*, greeted with organ music and thunderous applause, and three-quarters of the speeches are in praise of the leadership. There is still a vast discrepancy at a Conservative conference between the platform and the hall. Down below are hundreds of housewives, shopkeepers, accountants and even trade unionists: while up on the platform are peers, rentiers, professional men and gentry. 'The Tory party is run by about five people', said one leading Tory: 'and they all treat their followers with disdain: they're mostly Etonians, and Eton is good for disdain.'

The disdainful tradition is still strong. The party still gives the impression of being ruled by a few men over port in a club: in the inner ring of the party are still landed gentry—such as Major John Morrison, chairman of the Conservative Members' Committee and laird of the Scottish island of Islay; or Lord Stuart, Macmillan's wife's brother-in-law and Chairman of the Scottish Conservatives. The air of mystery and reverence in the party, together with the popular myth of 'the Establishment', is a great help in the constituency organisations, where party workers assume that they will be part of an inner circle of gentry and CMGs. But behind this ostensible feudalism, the party is much more sensitive to its voters than it pretends. In spite of the apparently impregnable position of its leader, he is always liable to face sudden mutiny from his party—a mutiny all the more alarming and unprepared for because of the outward obedience. Since Disraeli, three Tory leaders have been driven off the bridge—Balfour, Austen and Neville Chamberlain, and nearly Baldwin.[1]

And behind the disdain, the Conservatives are well aware of the electors: ever since the Maxwell Fyfe report, they have cleared the lines between voters and leaders; and the power has moved towards the glossy, well-managed headquarters of the Conservative Central Office. It is no accident that most of the new leaders —Macleod, Maudling, Powell—should have come to parliament via the party machine.[2]

MACLEOD'S BRITAIN

How far can the Conservative party, so full of associations of empire, ritual and aristocracy, come to terms with the new challenges to Britain, needing dynamism, brashness and mobility? I asked Macleod:

Macleod: The Conservative party has always tried as best it can to adapt itself. We don't believe in establishing the 'Clause 4 mentality' as part of our thinking. We're prepared to take all the new problems of the nuclear age and the Common Market and the rest as they come, and not try to solve them in the context of something that one of our leaders laid down half a century ago.

Sampson: Do you think that the Conservative party will succeed in breaking away from its class associations?

Macleod: I'm generally not very conscious of these class associations. They're no doubt there, because the Conservative party is associated, and always has been, with the land and with property. But I've always defined property in much wider terms than this. I define it nowadays in terms, not only of estates, but in terms of cars, and houses, the holding of shares, and even refrigerators and washing machines. And this is a form of property which is spreading very fast indeed, and whose owners are becoming, as I think we've seen for some time, increasingly Conservative. Now this is the reason why against all the prognostications of the psephologists and all the other eggheads like myself, we swept the new towns in 1959. Now this is very

[1] Robert McKenzie: *British Political Parties*, 1955. p. 66.
[2] *See* Henry Fairlie: Ten Years of Tory Rule. *Time and Tide*, October 12, 1961.

strange indeed. You would have thought that here is a community of people, obviously not connected with privilege or with inherited wealth, most of them with young families and their way to make in the world, and you would think that here, if anywhere, the Labour and Liberal and radical philosophies would make a great appeal. In fact it is the Conservative philosophy that made an appeal there, because I think the modern Conservative appeal has, within it, a great deal of the radical.

Sampson: A lot of people feel that Britain has been in the doldrums for some time, with nostalgia in her attitudes. Do you see any signs of a break-through into a new kind of Britain with an eye on the future?

Macleod: Yes, I do very much. You see, I think it's very difficult for people in Britain, and this certainly includes myself, to accept the fact that we aren't now the power we once were. Most of us, even people like myself in their forties, remember the day when at school a third or a quarter of the map was coloured red, and you did get some sort of consolation for being in this bright little, tight little island, and all the old jingo phrases, because of the very vastness of the empire, of which Britain was not only the head but the owner. Now all that is changing. It's a very exciting thing that it does change. To me, it's a magnificent thought that the people who go out from here to, shall we say, Tanganyika, will be going as nurses and technicians and engineers and doctors and the rest of it. I think this is a very good exchange for going as administrators. But the big new event that is happening, of course, is the coming-together of Europe. And I would think that—this is certainly true of myself—Conservative people see in Europe, not quite a compensation for a lost empire, that sounds altogether too dreamy, but a way in which in terms of 1962 we can still play a leading and dynamic part amongst the nations. We've always been able to do it before; I believe this is our opportunity to do it again. Now whether we're going to succeed or not, I don't know yet. But I think it is here that we will show whether we are or are not really prepared to go into the cold waters of 1962.

Sampson: But how far are we managing to adjust ourselves to being a trading nation with all the aggressive and salesman's aspects that are involved?

Macleod: Nothing like as swiftly as one would like to see it, but I think this is partly because we haven't had as much direct and stimulating competition as I'm certain we would have if, for example, we became members of the Common Market.

Sampson: Doesn't the traditional solemnity of British institutions make it harder for us to adjust ourselves to the salesman's attitude?

Macleod: I wouldn't have thought so. You could make some sort of argument, purely on paper, against the French in the same sort of way, but they don't seem to have been inhibited in the economic progress they've made in recent years because of their devotion to, and here and there their adherence to, the memories of the past.

Sampson: How far is the Conservative party still dominated by the idea of conservatism?

Macleod: Quite a lot, and yet not necessarily very devotedly. You can probably get the best answer in the second pamphlet of the 'One Nation' group that I founded. Our first was 'One Nation'. The second was called 'Change Is Our Ally'. Now, it was a very good production but it's a better title, and this, I believe, is true: we don't change just because we want to change, but we do change if we can think of a better way of doing it; we aren't inhibited from change because of the patterns of the past.

Sampson: Do you think Britain is more 'one nation' than it was at that time?

Macleod: Oh yes, much, much, much more. It is largely because of what is called 'The Affluent Society' (I dislike the term very much, it sounds like a sort of illness). In fact, the affluent society really means that people have money and property, and the more money and property they have, the more we become one nation. This is, of course, speaking purely in the material sense.

Sampson: The sense of crusade and vigorous mission that Britain seemed to have in Disraeli's time, do you think that is going to return to us in new situations?

Macleod: I think it may well do. If you talk to audiences of predominantly young people at schools, or university, or union meetings you find that they're not really occupied in the least with the immensely important matters of living in this country, even like education and the health service and housing; the really young people are concerned with the wider fields. This is why World Refugee Year struck such an excellent chord. And then again, if you take something like voluntary service overseas: each of these people have given a part of their lives deliberately in service to some other country. Now this has always been a particular theme of mine; that as we become 'one nation' in this country, we should try to become 'one world': that we should stretch out our hands particularly to the Commonwealth, but also to all the underdeveloped countries. And I think that there is an immense amount of idealism in young people today, more than I can ever remember. I'm sure that it's connected with the sheer vastness of the issues. You see, when you've really got into this position that nuclear power exists, and young people don't really know what to do about it: some people protest and march or sit down. Other people do rather more positive things about it—they give a form of service—and I have an idea that it's partly because all these appalling forms of knowledge have come to mankind, that you are getting a response of idealism from youth which, provided one understands it, can be of great service to many countries.

7

OPPOSITION

LABOUR

Let us not forget that we can never go farther than we can persuade at least half of the people to go.

Hugh Gaitskell, October 3, 1961.

THE Labour party, like all European socialist groups, has experienced the painful change from being a passionate 'movement', united against a straightforward enemy, to becoming a major political party, involved in divisions and compromises. It has watched Russia, its old ally, become the arch-enemy, and the old bogey America become the crucial ally: nationalisation, which was once a shining Utopia, has become fogged with disillusion: and in the meantime the Conservatives have crept up windward, and left Labour sagging. 'No one who has observed the Party since 1951', wrote Anthony Crosland in 1956, 'furiously searching for its lost soul, can have failed to sense a mood of deep bewilderment.'

There have been rows about the Defence budget, health service charges, nationalisation, the H-bomb and NATO. The motives and arguments have been varied and muddled. But the underlying division has been between those who have inherited a fiery, doctrinaire attitude from pre-war socialism, and those who are determined to produce an up-to-date, moderate party capable of winning power. For a long time the two sides gathered round the two contrasting personalities of Hugh Gaitskell and Aneurin Bevan: then, for the past three years, the left has centred round the strident person of Frank Cousins. There is always a danger of describing Labour politics too much in terms of personalities: the men in the end rise or fall by their policies and by their votes. But the duel between Cousins and Gaitskell, though only one part of Labour's predicament, accurately embodies two warring elements.

FRANK COUSINS

Cousins is a dramatic example of the impact of a single personality on politics. His rise has been extraordinarily swift. Early in 1956 he was one of the sixteen group secretaries of the Transport and General Workers' Union, unheard of in the Labour party. Then he was elected secretary of his union—the largest in the western world—and armed with a million votes[1] set out to dominate the conference and challenge the Labour leadership. Within three years he had split the party in two, and nearly destroyed it.

He is a tall, erect man, with swept-back grey hair, a long stride, and a beak-like nose between heavy spectacles. He has none of the easy-going, phlegmatic approach of most union leaders: he is proud, temperamental, capable of swift changes from charm to prickly suspicion. He is the brusquest man (apart from Sir David Eccles) that I encountered in my tour. He is a powerful speaker, capable of swaying an audience—with a clipped, tense way of talking, and a ground swell of constant indignation. He lives simply in a bungalow near Epsom, with a small garden where he digs and mows, with his wife Nancy—herself a left-wing Socialist and a powerful support to her husband: at all his big speeches she can be seen watching him intently from the gallery.

Cousins comes from the hard old school of union leaders. He was brought up in Doncaster, one of ten children of a miner, went into the coal-pit at fourteen, and later became a driver: 'I was one of the new young men who drove motor vehicles.' He argued in the transport cafés and saw at close quarters the hunger and unemployment of the depression. He has described in a television interview with John Freeman the incident that most stood out in his mind:

> I happened to be in a transport café on the Great North Road, when a young couple came in, with a child in a nearly broken down pram. They were walking from Shields—Shields was one of the places that was hit in the slump, Mr Freeman, as you will remember. They were walking from there to London, because the man understood he could get a job in London. They came into the café and sat down, and they fetched a baby's feeding bottle out, and it had water in it. They fed the baby with water, and then lifted the kiddy's dress up—it was a small baby—and it had a newspaper nappy on. They took this off, and wiped the baby's bottom with it and then they picked up another newspaper and put that on for a fresh nappy. I think if ever I felt a resentment against the system it was on that occasion. I thought somebody ought to do something about it.[2]

[1] *See* page 556.
[2] *The Listener*, October 26, 1961.

He began reading Socialist writers, and his young wife encouraged him to militancy: 'We did a lot of our early hand-holding in front of political meetings.' Before the war, he became a full-time organiser for the lorry-drivers—still one of the most militant groups in Britain. After the war he moved to the headquarters of the Transport and General Workers, and came sharply up against Arthur Deakin, who infuriated him with his right-wing anti-Communist views (though Cousins himself has never been a Communist). Many trade unionists were softened by the post-war Labour Government, but Cousins kept his militancy, with new outlets. And so, when he strode on to the General Council of the TUC in 1956, with his million votes, he changed electrically the atmosphere of the council-hall. A swing was in fact already occurring in several unions, towards the rejection of Britain's H-bomb and more wholesale policies of nationalisation. But Cousins gave the impression of having provoked a crisis single-handed. In his attitude to the bomb and to NATO, Cousins often appeared to be muddled and equivocal: but in this he echoed many of his followers. His indignant oratory appealed to that large slice of the party who felt that they had been cheated of their Utopia by the post-war compromisers, and that Britain's peacemaking rôle had been sacrificed to the Atlantic alliance.

HUGH GAITSKELL

The trouble about Mr Gaitskell is that he is going through all the motions of being a Government when he isn't a Government.
Harold Macmillan, January, 1959.

Cousins thus came into immediate conflict with the leader, Hugh Todd Naylor Gaitskell, who was trying to steer his party to a more moderate policy of public ownership, and urged the retention of American bases. To their political differences was added a personal conflict, between the ex-lorry driver and the ex-don, two years his junior.

But Gaitskell cannot be easily typed as a don: he is a man full of paradoxes. He talks in a clear-cut way, with a precise donnish voice, from a mouth which neatly opens and shuts: his speeches sometimes have the plaintive sound of a teacher chiding a backward pupil. But behind the appearance of the 'desiccated calculating machine', which so infuriates his rivals, he is deeply emotional, and his faults come from too much blood, not too little.

He is relaxed and gregarious, with an extraordinary capacity for enjoyment and no political pomp. He has, like President Kennedy, a talent for listening which is almost unknown among politicians. At parties—which he loves—he can often be seen in a jaunty suit and a shiny tie, waltzing dreamily on the dance floor. His friends, who call him Gaiters or Hugh, treat him loyally but casually, and he never likes to be thought square.

His circle is large and surprising: he can be seen at Belgravia lunch-parties, at night clubs, at the celebrations of café society, or—more rarely—at trade union socials: he has never found it easy to adapt his social pleasures to political expediency. He lives in an ample house in Hampstead, with a dynamic Socialist wife and two grown-up daughters. He entertains widely and well, with cosmopolitan scope: Gaitskell dinner-parties can include tycoons, Tory peers and American intellectuals. He talks about almost anything, travels widely and forgets nothing. In his gaiety, his freedom, his apparent rootlessness, he seems more like an American egghead; he loves America, and gets on very well with Kennedy's dons. He is certainly, on the English scene, a new kind of man.

Gaitskell comes from a sedate pro-consular family—like Butler's, but less august: his father, who came from Cumberland, was an Indian Civil Servant and married the daughter of a Consul-General in Shanghai. Hugh's elder brother went to the Sudan, and one of his sisters is now Lady Ashton, wife of a Tory MP. Gaitskell's early career was not brilliant: he was not a scholar at Winchester or New College, and not outstanding among his college contemporaries (who included Richard Crossman, Frank Pakenham, Douglas Jay, William Hayter and Edmund Compton —now Auditor-General). It was not till the general strike, which broke on his Oxford career, that he was jolted into politics: he took a union card and distributed the *British Worker*, while others were strike-breaking. From then on he took socialism very seriously: he was shocked by the cruelty and muddle of capitalism, though he never embraced Marx. He studied under G. D. H. Cole, took a first in Modern Greats, and then went to lecture to coal-miners in Nottingham. From there he moved to London University. He stood unsuccessfully for parliament, wrote books which were not published; he was quite active in Fabian circles, but he made no obvious mark on the party.

His first real fulfilment was in the war, when he joined the civil service and was taken up by Hugh Dalton, at the Ministry of Economic Warfare. Gaitskell enjoyed the rational, civilised world of Whitehall, and still talks of it with nostalgia: he had a patient, persistent approach to problems, and a clear way of arguing. But when in 1945 he stood successfully for parliament, he was still an unknown young man, and not much of a speaker. Yet he had the administrative qualities which Attlee needed, and his rise was sudden. By 1950—at the age of forty-four—he was Chancellor of the Exchequer.

A year later he was out of office, and his hardest time was to come. For five years the party was split between him and Aneurin Bevan, who had resigned because Gaitskell had imposed charges on the health service. Bevan had all the fire and eloquence, and the romantic proletarian background: but Gaitskell was a shrewder politician, and persuaded the big unions to back him. When Atlee retired in 1955, the Labour Party discovered, rather to their surprise, that in the midst of the radical hullabaloo this quiet man had become their leader.

But Gaitskell has mastered the arts of political organisation. He succeeded in healing the breach with Bevan, and set about producing a unified, moderate party without extremes of nationalisation or non-alignment. And then, just when the party seemed to be recovering its balance, there emerged the uncompromising shape of Frank Cousins. Between the two men, from the start, there was visible friction. Cousins disliked the sweet reasonableness of Gaitskell, his habit of patronising talks, his use of the party machine, and his apparent lack of emotion. Gaitskell did not disguise his contempt for Cousins' emotionalism, and made no attempt to patch up this quarrel.

The conflict reached its climax at the Labour party's conference at Scarborough in October, 1960. Cousins, with large union support, renewed his attack on Gaitskell's defence policy: 'If the two mad groups want to have a go at each other', he said: 'we want no part of them . . . Is Britain really going to tie itself to an organisation where the complete control of policy is in the hands of General Norstad?' Gaitskell, in a reply of rare passion, defended the NATO agreement: 'I know there are people who would like to see the Americans out. But they were glad enough to see them in 1942. There are some of us', he ended, 'who will fight and fight and fight again to bring back sanity and honesty and dignity, so that our party—with its great past—may retain its glory and its greatness.'

Cousins' motion, rejecting any defence policy based on nuclear weapons, won by 3,282,000 votes to 3,239,000. But Gaitskell stood firm to his policy, and in the subsequent months his supporters set about trying to swing the unions round to a more moderate policy. Cousins' power showed signs of waning, and by the 1961 conference the mood had changed: when Cousins got up to propose, once more, the rejection of nuclear weapons, he was met with jeers and shouts, and his motion was defeated by 4,309,000 to 1,891,000—a fair comment on the fickleness of block votes. Gaitskell's victory was far from complete: another motion, condemning the Polaris bases in Britain, was passed with a million majority: and Cousins' supporters said that *they*, this time, would 'fight and fight and fight again'. But Gaitskell's position was far more secure: 'Last year our task was to save the party' he said, 'this year it is to save the nation.' On the question of public ownership, Gaitskell put his emphasis not on nationalisation, but on bringing dynamic planning and social change:

'How can Britain look to other people if it continues to stagnate economically? Visitors will still come and praise the behaviour of our policemen and will say half-pityingly and half-affectionately, that we are an easy-going, kindly, tolerant people with a great and glorious past whose only trouble is that they are stuck to it. They will no longer come to Britain for ideas about the future but only to study history. They will see that, somehow, the British have lost out, lost their dynamic, are sunk in complacency, are far too snobbish, and have carried on a pattern of social relationships that is disappearing elsewhere in the world.'

LABOUR INTELLECTUALS

Gaitskell is only one example of a modern phenomenon—the don-politician. He is one of the group of intellectuals, nearly all Oxford economists, who left the universities for the Labour party. Oxford high tables provided the same kind of common background for new Socialists as White's Club provides for old Tories.

Hovering round Gaitskell are the group of sociable intellectual Labour MPs known as the 'Hampstead Set'—the most prominent of whom are Patrick Gordon Walker, Douglas Jay, Anthony Crosland and Roy Jenkins: most of them took firsts in Economics at Oxford. Their ambience is lively, cultured and wide-ranging, interested in music and art as well as politics, and more urban then their Tory equivalents, a world roughly represented by *Encounter*. From time to time they have gathered at Gaitskell's house for cocktails and politics: all of them are 'revisionists', determined to give the party a less proletarian, more middle-class look, closer to the Democrats in America. 'We must now all learn to be middle-class', wrote Anthony Crosland in the *Future of Socialism*. 'We must learn to be gay, to appreciate the arts, to burn down the Victorian prejudices.' But Gaitskell's gregarious-ness, and the 'Hampstead Set' give a misleading impression: for Gaitskell, in spite of his sociability, is a solitary thinker, who does not exchange confidences with his friends. At heart he keeps himself, like Macleod, very much to himself.

Other intellectuals are even less close to the leader. Denis Healey, for instance, the Shadow Foreign Secretary, is very much a lone wolf—more austere than the others and at odds with Gaitskell over the Common Market which he dislikes. The rogue elephant among intellectuals is Richard Crossman, whose begin-nings make an illuminating contrast with his leader's: he is the same age as Gaitskell, was at the same school and college, was also a don, and became a Labour MP at the same time. But his career was much flashier, and hardly touched Gaitskell's: at Winchester Crossman was a brilliant scholar and sportsman, while Gaitskell was unobtrusive and late in developing; at New College, Crossman went about with Auden and Spender, while Gaitskell went in for politics and ballroom dancing. Crossman lectured brilliantly at Oxford and wrote a book called *Plato Today*, while Gaitskell lectured on economics at London and wrote *Money and Everyday Life*. In parliament, Crossman joined forces with Bevan, and soon clashed with Gaitskell over nationalisation and defence. While Gaitskell climbed quietly up the ladder, Crossman remained where he was, full of exciting ideas, defying discipline. He has never found a steady place for himself in the party, but he remains an important intellectual influence, with a passionate awareness of the rôle of the West in the cold war.

LABOUR TROIKA

Since the death of Bevan in 1960, three men have stood out in the Labour party—Hugh Gaitskell, Harold Wilson and George Brown.

James Harold Wilson is an intellectual, but of a different stamp to Gaitskell—ten years younger, and for many years a boy wonder: in 1947 he became President of the Board of Trade at the age of only thirty-one—the youngest cabinet minister in this century (Churchill was in the cabinet at 34, Malcolm MacDonald at 35). Now he looks older than his forty-six years: he is portly, with greying hair, a slow and solemn walk and—as his special political mascot—a curved pipe, which he puffs between epigrams. He talks drily, with an astonishing memory for details and a Yorkshire accent.

Wilson is proud of his more humble stock. His father—a friendly Yorkshireman who listens to his son at Labour conferences—was a works chemist. Wilson made his way through grammar school to Oxford, where he *too* took a first in Economics, and became a lecturer, described as the 'cleverest man in Oxford'. His socialism, like Gaitskell's, came both from personal outrage and an economist's logic: but he was more obviously politically ambitious, without Gaitskell's more rigid convictions. He went into parliament in 1945, and the arrival of this confident young minister— who insisted on discussing ideas with junior civil servants—caused ructions in the higher reaches of Whitehall.

In the years out of office, Wilson and his pipe became increasingly enigmatic. He first aligned himself with Bevan, and then joined the Gaitskell camp, but without obvious loyalty. He lives quietly in North London, with his wife—a parson's daughter—and two young sons. Wilson remained carefully non-committal, and seemed to be biding his time. His calculating caution became legendary: when Gaitskell made his speech to 'fight, fight and fight again', Wilson was markedly detached. 'If the Labour party ends this week facing two directions', wrote the *New Left Review*, 'it is certain that the figure of Mr Wilson will be there, at the end of both of them.' Later Wilson stood unsuccessfully against Gaitskell as Leader of the parliamentary party.

GEORGE BROWN

George Alfred Brown, deputy Labour leader, represents the third and most crucial ingredient of the party. He comes from the solid working-class core: his father was a lorry-driver, he was born in Peabody Buildings in Southwark, and he had the self-made beginnings which are now at a premium in Labour politics. He became an organiser for the Transport and General Workers Union (in left-wing politics, unions often take the place families take in Conservative circles in providing a political stable). He was on the right of the left, and first made his name, just before the war, by attacking Sir Stafford Cripps at a Labour conference. After the war he joined the rush into parliament, when he was only thirty-one, became known as the 'boy orator' and was soon noticed: by 1951 he was Minister of Works. Since then he has become steadily more important to his party: and in 1960 he succeeded Bevan as deputy-leader.

Brown is a friendly man with bushy eyebrows and a round, podgy face. He lives simply in a small suburban villa, and married a keen Socialist: his brother is a local Labour candidate. He calls everyone 'brother', and has even been known to address a party gathering as 'brothers and sisters'. He has a reputation for plain speech and political courage: he is in the blunt, bull-necked mould of his early hero, Ernest Bevin. His most famous encounter was with Khrushchev on his visit in 1956, at a dinner given by the Labour party: Khrushchev, talking about the war, said 'you threw the Germans at our throat' and Brown muttered 'May God forgive you'—which began an angry argument, ending with Krushchev saying that if he was in Britain he would support the Tories. 'I react emotionally not intellectually,' Brown has said, and he is sometimes considered unpredictable and temperamental. But in the past year he has worked closely with Gaitskell, and their alliance is the linchpin which keeps the party wheel in place.

NEW SOCIALISTS

The two main streams of Labour—university men and trade unionists—still flow: but the division is less clear-cut than before the war. There are fewer young intellectuals, and some trade unionists win university scholarships, and go into parliament younger: an example is Reg Prentice—again from the T & GW stable—who won a scholarship to the London School of Economics and went into parliament in 1957, at thirty-three.

Much of the young leadership is made up by the 'Oxbridge Gaitskellites'—the middle-way, middle-class socialists. They came into the party with less fire, less sense of outrage, than the pre-war converts: many took to the left after 1945, when the Labour party was already established. It is not always easy to differentiate the Oxbridge Gaitskellites, sipping whisky in Kensington, from the Bow Groupers; or to detect what mysterious force has pulled one group to the left, the other to the right. There are radicals and reactionaries on both sides, and the words left and right often seem to lose their meaning. But under their moderation, the Gaitskellites still have a rooted dislike for upper-class attitudes, and even though they arrange to send their sons to public schools, they have a more fervent belief in the need for social change.

After sixty years the Labour party is beginning to evolve its own dynasties and traditions: Anthony Wedgwood Benn, Roy Jenkins and Anthony Greenwood, are all sons of Socialist MPs: and among the very young Socialists, family groups seem to be taking shape. The son of one ex-Labour MP, Hilary Marquand, has married the daughter of another, Elwyn Jones: the son of Douglas Jay has married the daughter of James Callaghan. Young Gaitskells and young Pakenhams remain in a Socialist set, and some schools (most notably the North London Collegiate girls' school at Edgware) seem to acquire a Socialist tradition. But there is little sign of the Labour party acquiring the dynastic continuity of the Conservatives or Liberals, and the bulk of the leadership comes from new blood, impelled into socialism by idealism or some personal experience.

Round the outer fringes of the Labour party is the jumble of personalities, pressure-groups, factions, and magazines which make up the left wing of the party. They include such exotic figures as Ian Mikardo, the loud, square leader of the 'Victory for Socialism' group; Konni Zilliacus, the Finnish-Swedish pamphleteer; Sydney Silverman, the small, bearded lawyer from Liverpool; or the group of fiery young radicals centring on the *New Left Review*, an intellectual quarterly which attacks NATO, the Common Market and Gaitskell. The most vocal of the radicals is Michael Foot—a stooping, haggard-looking man, with swept-back hair who on the platform always manages to appear in the last paroxysms of rage—though off-stage he is charming and kindly.

To counteract these left-wing cliques, the moderate element in the Labour party in mid-1960 organised its own group, the Campaign for Democratic Socialism, founded by a young Fabian, Bill Rodgers. It was the CDS who by persistent lobbying helped in reversing some of the trade union votes in 1961. Another moderating influence is the Fabian Society which, though officially non-partisan, has a bias towards moderation, realism: its secretary, Shirley Williams, is one of the most European-minded of the young politicians. Between the two wings of the party the friction throughout 1961 became more severe; and after Cousins' defeat in October, it seemed quite likely that the left would split off altogether.

WHO RUNS LABOUR?

The Labour party does not have the same façade of loyalty and leader-worship as the Conservatives: the frictions between its components are more obvious, and paraded in broad daylight every autumn. But a certain discreet confusion nevertheless surrounds the eventual decisions: and the Labour party like the Conservatives is not quite what it seems. Its outward decisions do not altogether correspond to results.

First comes the Trade Union Congress, early in September (as we will see in Chapter 35) which propounds its own resolutions. Next, a month later, comes the Labour Party Conference, where trade unionists are joined by delegates from constituencies: this conference elects the National Executive of twenty-eight people—twelve from trade unions, seven from the constituency parties. The constituency votes act as a kind of popularity poll, led by well-known and left-wing figures. At the top of the poll in 1961 were Barbara Castle, Anthony Greenwood, Harold Wilson and Tom Driberg.

A month later the Parliamentary Labour Party—consisting entirely of Labour MPs—meets to elect twelve members of their 'shadow cabinet', which reveals a very different order: in 1961 the top votes went to Harold Wilson (175), Sir Frank Soskice (174), Douglas Houghton (169) and Denis Healey (161).

The National Executive and the Shadow Cabinet coexist painfully. Their conflict arises from the origins of the party: for when it was founded in 1900, the Labour party was little more than the 'political arm' of the Trade Union Congress, with small prospect of power. But as the movement swelled, grew into a parliamentary party and eventually gained office, so inevitably the actual legislators became the centre of power. The frictions have been exacerbated by Cousins' attacks, and still threaten to sever the link between the TUC and the Labour party.[1] In theory the parliamentary party is supposed to be responsible to the annual conference and its executive: but in practice the Shadow Cabinet has successfully remained independent. 'By a continuous process of flattery', wrote one Labour critic,[2] 'delegates to Conference are persuaded that they are the ultimate wielders of sovereignty; while simultaneously the leadership is working to ensure that they are never in a position to wield it.'

The chairmanship of the Labour Party Executive rotates every year, and is thus much less influential than the Tory chairmanship; this gives more importance to the general secretary at

---

[1] *See* page 557.
[2] Ivan Yates: Power in the Labour Party, *Political Quarterly*, July, 1960. p. 308.

Transport House, the party headquarters, who runs the machine. The new secretary, Len Williams, appointed in 1962, is a party worker who took over from his boss, Morgan Phillips, who had held the job for eighteen years. But in the changeover the executive have discreetly given more power to the modest-sounding position of 'chairman of the organisation sub-committee', occupied by the deputy leader, George Brown—bringing Labour closer to the Tory organisation, with the party machine in the charge of a key politician.

LIBERALS

> The thing I can't stand about Liberals is the way they take swipes at everybody.
>
> *Iain Macleod, 1961.*

The unhappy position of the Labour party, torn between left and right, between the past and the future, has been made worse by the apparent resurgence of the old Liberal party. Since 1922, when the coalition headed by Lloyd George broke up, the Liberals gradually dwindled, eclipsed by the new forces of Labour. But in the fifties they showed new signs of life and the Liberal candidates at the 1959 election had a special panache: they included several television personalities, such as Ludovic Kennedy, Robin Day, John Arlott, and Jeremy Thorpe—an extrovert young barrister who wore a brown bowler—and their leader Jo Grimond toured Britain in a helicopter.

Grimond is a convincing leader for a revivified party. He is tall and handsome, with a shock of grey hair which falls over his face as he becomes excited: he addresses mass meetings with a boyish, school-prefect manner, full of enthusiasm for the future and get-up-and-go. His career has been impeccably Liberal: the son of a Fifeshire laird, he went to Eton and Balliol, and married the daughter of Lady Violet Bonham Carter, the formidable high-priestess of Liberalism. Grimond thus came into the midst of the Liberal establishment, which includes Lady Violet's son Mark, the most intellectual of the Liberals, and Frank Byers, a business-man and former chairman of the party.

In 1959 the Liberals won only 5.9 per cent of the votes, and returned six members to parliament. But in by-elections since, they have made spectacular inroads on Tory votes. Their policies are often vague—except concerning the Common Market, which they have consistently supported. But the Liberals have the advantage of being less cluttered by the class totems of the other two parties: they are not associated either with Rolls Royces and grouse-moors, or with cloth caps and the Red Flag. And although their leaders are mostly from well-to-do families, the Liberals have an appeal to the new young people of indeterminate class who find both Tory and Labour myths equally tedious—people who belong to the new classless Americanised world of Wimpy bars, coffee-bars, television, minimotors, pre-packaged food, ice-skating, Marks and Spencers, Vespas and airport lounges.

The future of the Liberals is still a huge question mark: if the Labour party finally splits and sheds its left wing, Gaitskell and Grimond may find themselves with a great deal in common, and may coalesce—which is the secret hope of several Liberal leaders. On the other hand the Common Market, which Liberals support but which Labour is undecided about, may eventually produce a quite new alignment.

THE PENDULUM

Is Britain settling down into a one-party nation? Since 1959, when the Labour party lost for the third time in succession, the left has had nightmares of permanent eclipse—as in France, Italy or Canada. The chart opposite shows the swings of the pendulum since 1868.

During the 130 years since the Reform Bill there has been a fairly equal swing between left and right: but in the years since 1884—which marked the beginning of universal household suffrage—the right has predominated. 'In the course of the 75 years up to 1959', wrote Richard Crossman, 'there have been only two left-wing governments with outright majorities, the Liberal Government elected after the Boer War and the Labour Government elected after World War II. Moreover, within five years each of these left-wing governments had lost most of its popular support.'[1]

Group	% of popula-tion	Con. %	Lab. %	Other %
Solid middle class	15	85	10	5
Lower (non-manual) middle class	20	70	25	5
Upper (manual) working class	30	35	60	5
Solid working class	35	30	65	5

[1] *Labour in the Affluent Society*, Fabian Society, 1960.

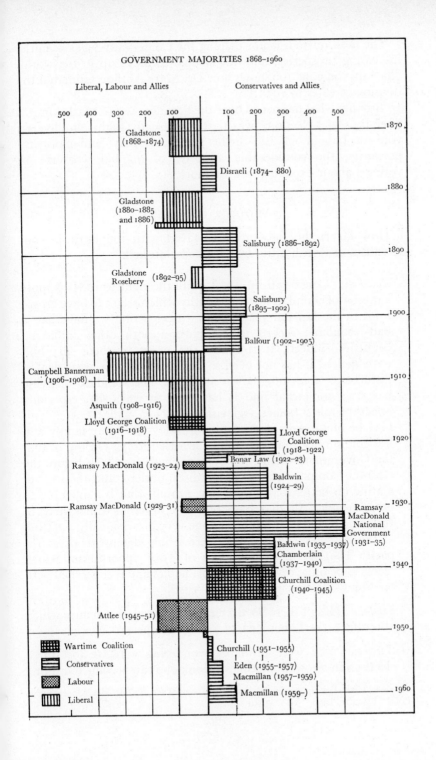

GOVERNMENT MAJORITIES 1868–1960

Liberal, Labour and Allies   Conservatives and Allies

500   400   300   200   100   100   200   300   400   500

1870

Gladstone
(1868–1874)

Disraeli (1874– 880)

1880

Gladstone
(1880–1885
and 1886)

Salisbury (1886–1892)

1890

Gladstone
Rosebery   (1892–95)

Salisbury
(1895–1902)

1900

Balfour (1902–1905)

Campbell Bannerman
(1906–1908)

1910

Asquith (1908–1916)
Lloyd George Coalition
(1916–1918)

Lloyd George
Coalition
(1918–1922)

1920

Bonar Law (1922–23)

Ramsay MacDonald (1923–24)

Baldwin
(1924–29)

Ramsay MacDonald (1929–31)

Ramsay
MacDonald
National
Government
(1931–35)

1930

Baldwin (1935–1937)
Chamberlain
(1937–1940)

1940

Churchill Coalition
(1940–1945)

Attlee (1945–51)

1950

▥ Wartime Coalition
▤ Conservatives
▨ Labour
▥ Liberal

Churchill (1951–1955)

Eden (1955–1957)
Macmillan (1957–1959)

Macmillan (1959–)

1960

The most obvious factor helping the Conservatives has been the increasing prosperity, allowing people to move up in the world. The table on page 106 shows how Dr. Mark Abrams estimated the division of votes in 1958:[1]

'Broadly what happened over the decades', wrote Mark Abrams after the 1959 election, 'was that the already slight middle-class vote for Labour fell still further; and, secondly, and more importantly, the considerable minority of manual workers not voting Labour expanded a little more.'[1]

How far is the Labour party faced with the intrinsic conservatism of British attitudes? I asked Gaitskell.

Gaitskell: 'Conservatism' is not quite the right word. It is more a matter of complacency and apathy which seems to have grown a lot in the last ten years. During that period we have had a bad economic record in comparison with other industrial countries—indeed, it is really the worst of them all; but, nevertheless, it has not been so bad as to cause a great deal of disturbance and indignation at home. The standard of living has risen somewhat and it has risen in ways that especially affect people's homes—television, kitchen gadgets, etc. This may be one reason why people nowadays are more family and less community conscious than they used to be. On top of that the Government deliberately encouraged, especially before the election, complacency, a materialistic outlook and the idea of getting on better for yourself never mind what is happening to other people. All that has created a different atmosphere in Britain. Of course, it has been done very professionally—getting at the subconscious as if you were selling detergents or toothpaste. That is the consequence of Tory opportunism which seems to be quite divorced from principles and is concerned with one thing—to stay in power at all costs.

Sampson: Hasn't there been a change in the class structure which also affects the Labour party and its prospects?

Gaitskell: You were probably wondering why we lost three elections in a row. Sometimes I think one can become too subtle

[1] *From* 'Class Distinction in Britain', *The Future of the Welfare State,* Conservative Political Centre, 1958.

and sophisticated in trying to find explanations for this. The main reason for our 1955 and 1959 defeats is surely that people were, as I have said, better off, and that the Tory propaganda was very effective. Governments in most countries in this last decade, whether of the Right or the Left, have found it pretty easy to stay in power.

At the same time, I agree that there have also been important changes in the class structure which have certain political consequences. Technical change has produced more white collar and fewer manual labour jobs, both within each firm and as between different industries; and, of course, the broadening of the educational ladder—although it still leaves us a long way short of equal educational opportunity—has made movements from one class to another easier. But notice that I use the phrase 'from one class to another'. For these changes have not produced a classless society. Far from it. They have produced a larger middle class and great fluidity.

The new social pattern, together with the other developments I mentioned in answer to your first question, have certainly created problems for the Labour party. In the old days we were up against the general acceptance of class status—what I call the 'touch your cap' snobbery. That is gradually disappearing, but at the same time there is more of what I call the 'keeping up with the Joneses' snobbery. I mean by that people wondering all the time whether they can do better for themselves alone—looking up to those who are just a bit above them and looking down on those just a bit below them. I believe this is all linked with the reduction in community consciousness of which I have just spoken.

It is not that Labour is a working class party, that there is now a smaller working class and that there are now, therefore, fewer Labour votes. That is a great over-simplification. We have never had all the working class votes and we have always had quite a number of middle class ones. And, in spite of the last three elections, don't forget that there are still far more Labour voters than before the war and far more Labour members of parliament, except for the 1929-1931 period when a good many seats were won on three-cornered contests.

Nevertheless—as compared with, say, ten years ago—a combination of great fluidity and a more self-regarding and less community conscious attitude has made difficulties for us, even though the changes are marginal.

Sampson: How far is this different from the situation in the rest of Europe?

Gaitskell: Well, I think the changing social pattern is causing concern to most Labour parties in the world. But those Labour parties which have been in power have the immense advantage of a period of full employment, and they have remained in power largely because of that. The Swedes and the Norwegians, for instance, and the Danes all say the changing class structure is something which they are a bit bothered about, but it's not as serious as it is for us; and perhaps in Scandinavia you also have so much less snobbery, a more classless atmosphere, which is a help to them. In Germany, I would say they were up against very much the same problem as us. Of course, they've moved right away from Marxism to a policy which is well to the right of that of the Labour party here. In Italy and France it's different because there you have large Communist parties, and the Labour parties themselves are rather different in character from ours.

Sampson: To what extent is the lack of dynamic in industry linked with the actual managerial structure of family firms and the social traditions in industry?

Gaitskell: It is difficult to generalise about family firms. No doubt some are inefficient because the management remains in the one family, but it is by no means true in all cases. And anyway are there fewer family firms in France or Italy or Germany? 'Social tradition' is, I would guess, far more the villain of the piece, if you mean the kind of snobbery I have been talking about. And, personally, I think the public school system and the influence it has must carry quite a bit of the blame. You have a set of social values, encouraged by the public schools, that it is really not done to be too professional, that what wins renown and social repute is not whether you sold a large number of motor-cars to the United States but what sort of handicap you've got at golf. It is an attitude which often still looks upon industry as something inferior to the professions or the civil service or even finance. It is a nineteenth-century hangover, as it were, which the public schools preserve and I think this is a bad thing. Here is one example. Foreign languages. If you meet a German or an Italian or a Scandinavian you usually find them speaking pretty good English simply as

a result of what they have learnt at school. It is exceedingly rare
to find an Englishman who can speak German or French
simply because of what he learnt at school. And, of course,
more generally, British sales representatives too frequently
assume that everybody else speaks English. This in turn, of
course, goes back to the idea that we are more important than
foreigners and that therefore they should learn our language
while we do not have to learn theirs. And it is mixed up too
with the old idea that although we have to shoulder the
white man's burden, we do not have to go out and work for our
trade in quite the same way as other people.

8

PRESS

Burke said there were Three Estates in Parliament; but in the
Reporters' Gallery yonder, there sat a *Fourth Estate* more important far
than they all.

Carlyle.

Were it left to me to decide whether we should have a government
without newspapers or newspapers without a government, I should
not hesitate for a moment to prefer the latter.

Thomas Jefferson, 1787.[1]

SINCE the long fight for the freedom of the press in the eighteenth
century, the importance of newspapers as the Fourth Estate,
informing and reflecting public opinion, has become unquestioned.
The need for independent journalists, free comment and access to
information, are agreed by all politicians and administrators. But
during the twentieth century several new forces have threatened
this independence. Of these, the most spectacular and dangerous
is the commercialisation of and concentration of newspapers, which
reaches its most extreme form in Britain.

The British press has the biggest circulations in the Western
world. The four-and-a-half million copies of the *Daily Mirror* and
the seven million copies of the *News of the World* have no equal in
America or Europe, and Britain is so compact and homogeneous
that the same newspapers can arrive on the same morning from
Land's End to John O' Groats. Britain has 114 daily papers compared to 1,745 in America, 130 in France, 473 in West Germany.
And the British (although total circulations have fallen by about
9 per cent since 1950), still read more newspapers per head than
any other people: they read nearly twice as many newspapers as
the Americans[2] (though American papers are fatter), and only the
Swedes approach the British consumption.

Four vast newspaper groups now share most of the British
popular press between them. These are the four groups of morning

[1] Quoted by Sir William Haley: *The Formation of Public Opinion.* Haldane Memorial
Lecture, 1958.

[2] 573 newspapers sold per 1,000 population, compared to 327 in America. (*The
Economist*, September 9, 1961, p. 960).

newspapers with their chairmen or owners, and circulations at the
end of 1961 (this list does not do justice to Roy Thomson, who
controls not only the national *Sunday Times*, but fourteen provincial dailies, Scottish TV and about eighty other newspapers in
North America and Africa):

	Daily		Sunday
Daily Mirror Newspapers (Cecil King)			
Mirror	4,561,876	*S. Pictorial*	5,306,246
Herald	1,394,919	*People*	5,450,727
Associated Newspapers (Lord Rothermere)			
Mail	2,610,487		
Sketch	981,698		
Beaverbrook Newspapers (Lord Beaverbrook)			
Express	4,328,524	*S. Express*	4,457,528
Telegraph Newspapers (Michael Berry)			
Telegraph	1,248,961	*S. Telegraph*	700,000

Other dailies:

The Times (Gavin Astor)	253,441
The Guardian (Laurence Scott)	245,056
Financial Times (Lord Robbins)	132,928

Other Sundays:

News of the World (Sir W. Emsley Carr)	6,643,287
Sunday Times (Roy Thomson)	994,459
The Observer (The Observer Trust)	725,835
Reynolds News (Co-operative Press)	310,369

This concentration has caused both the opportunity and the
crisis of British journalism: for it has put newspapers into the
class of heavy industry, on the scale of steelworks and ship-
yards, and it has led to intense and still growing commercialisation, which has reached a new climax in the past four years. Up
till January, 1957, for eighteen years, a truce existed: newsprint
was rationed by the Government, and papers agreed to compete
not in size, but only in circulation. The smaller papers survived
on the advertisements which the bigger ones had to reject. Then
newsprint became free, just at the time when commercial television
was becoming successful. The top papers in each field—the *Express*,
Mirror, *Times* and *Telegraph*—became fatter with advertising,
while the bottom papers, like the *Herald* and *Chronicle*, became

thinner. In 1960 and 1961 one of the nine national dailies and three of the national Sundays collapsed: and two more dailies and one more Sunday lost money heavily. The harsh competition induced a wave of mergers and take-overs, and the concentration of papers—many of them linked with television companies—settled round the four big groups.

This is not the first time that Britain has seen newspaper concentration. In the early nineteenth century *The Times* had a circulation four times as big as all other London papers, and in 1923 the first Lord Rothermere owned fourteen newspapers. Newspaper empires can still rise and fall with surprising speed; but the capital investment involved in newspapers today is far larger than before the war, and the restrictions of printing trade unions and the requirements of advertisers make the task of a newcomer much harder. The present trend is still towards greater concentration.

The impact of the brute strength of big business on the old organs of free speech presents capitalism with an awkward dilemma. Many Western countries face a newspaper crisis: in America dependence on advertising is still greater—(the Sunday edition of the *New York Times* touched 490 pages, in 12 sections in October, 1961); in Italy most newspapers are subsidised by political parties or industrialists. In Australia or South Africa a weak and commercialised press is unable to stand up to a strong government.

While free enterprise may have produced good cars, refrigerators and aircraft, it is much more doubtful whether it has produced good newspapers: yet government intervention strikes (in theory) at the heart of free expression. In Britain this dilemma has come abruptly to the forefront: and the mergers and take-overs of the past three years have produced an unparalleled situation, precipitated by two gigantic entrepreneurs, Cecil King and Roy Thomson. The events which produced it were so bizarre and illuminating that they must be briefly recorded.

CECIL KING

The only job I ever wanted was chairman of the *Daily Mirror*.
And here I am.   *Cecil King to Jocelyn Stevens, 1961.*

The most spectacular result of the mergers has been the supremacy of Cecil Harmsworth King, Chairman of the *Daily Mirror*. He controls only four national newspapers—the *Daily Mirror*, the *Sunday Pictorial*, the *Daily Herald* and the *People:* but between them —according to his own calculation—they have 38 per cent of the national daily circulation and over 40 per cent of the Sunday sales. His group also owns the six leading women's magazines, two hundred other magazines, a nine per cent holding in Associated-Television, immense paper mills, and *Debrett's Peerage*. It is the largest publishing house in the free world, with assets approaching £100 million—much larger than Cunard or Whitbreads. It was the extent of King's power which precipitated the setting up of a Royal Commission on the Press in 1961.

Cecil King is a large, rumpled man of six foot four with a brusque, dominating manner: he is one of those tycoons who deal with correspondence by returning letters with comments scribbled at the bottom. He lives simply among fine furniture and silver, in a house in Chelsea: he finds people difficult and usually goes to bed at ten. He works on the ninth floor of the red glass *Daily Mirror* cliff in Holborn, looking over St. Paul's: when it was finished in 1961, at the cost of £9½ million, King described it as 'the finest newspaper building in the world, a Taj Mahal'—forgetting perhaps that the Taj Mahal is a tomb. The Mirror building is noted for the nice gradation of status in its offices: editors, for instance, have felt under their carpets, while directors have rubber underlay, cocktail cabinets and TV sets. Cecil King has a dining-room, a kitchen, bathroom and an open-grate fireplace.[1]

The most important fact about Cecil King is his uncle, Alfred Harmsworth, Lord Northcliffe—who invented modern journalism, founded *Answers*, bought *The Times* and *The Observer*, and died of megalomania. Lord Northcliffe's dominating personality still haunts two Fleet Street groups—the *Daily Mail* group of his nephew Lord Rothermere, and the *Daily Mirror* group of Cecil King.

King was brought up in the shadow of his uncle, his mother's brother, who was then at the height of his eccentric power; but his father, an Irish Professor of Oriental Languages, was a much milder man. From these two strains, the brash and ruthless Harmsworths and the cultured, public-spirited Kings, came the curious paradox of Cecil King. He is inhibited, cultivated, educated at Winchester and Christ Church: but he is also ruthless, rebellious and fascinated by popular newspapers. He sometimes gives

---

[1] *Time and Tide*, January 20, 1961.

E   115

the impression of an intellectual pretending to be Northcliffe: but there is nothing assumed about his ambition. By the time he was twenty-five he was working for the *Daily Mirror*, then owned by Northcliffe's brother, the first Lord Rothermere; he became director three years later. In spite of his fastidious tastes and personal shyness, he loved the rebellious vulgarity of the tabloid, defying everyone—even Churchill in the war: and he was one of the team who helped to push the circulation of the *Mirror* in twenty years from 800,000 to 4½ million—'the largest daily sale on earth'. By a mixture of nepotism, ability and drive—he owns only four per cent of the shares—he increased his power in the *Mirror*: by 1951, after a classic boardroom struggle, he ousted the chairman, Harry Bartholomew, and achieved his life's ambition.

With the *Mirror*'s profits behind him, King looked round for new empires: he acquired a share in television, bought papers in Scotland, and then, unpredictably, bought another part of Lord Northcliffe's old empire, a jumbled group of magazines called Amalgamated Press. This set off a chain reaction. It was a profitable but difficult new empire, and King soon found himself involved in a hectic magazine war. He moved into the musty magazine offices which had been undisturbed for twenty years, sacked editors, shut down magazines, had all the vans painted light blue, renamed the group Fleetway, and advertised massively against his rival magazine group, Odhams, who also owned the *Daily Herald* and the *People*. Then, in January, 1961, came the flash-point. Odhams, fearing that King in his difficulties would try to take them over, took fright and tried secretly to merge with Roy Thomson, the other expanding tycoon. King, furious, immediately issued a counter bid, far more attractive than Thomson's proposals, to the Odhams shareholders. A week later, to the astonishment of parliament, the Prime Minister and most of all Odhams, King was in control of the biggest newspaper empire in British history. It had happened, by the irony of big business logic, not because King had been successful with newspapers, but because he had been in difficulties with magazines.

But what does King do with his power? His personal opinions are well known, if erratic: he regards himself as leftish, but not a Socialist: his relationship with Gaitskell is fitful, and in his impish rebellion he is closer, for instance, to Malcolm Muggeridge. He is genuinely concerned with defending the underdogs and exposing

injustice, and has a streak of great personal kindness. He dislikes
Eton, *The Times*, titles, pomposity and humbug in high places,
and he loves attacking the Establishment and displaying
rebellious views—all of which fits well with the image of the
Mirror. At a lunch given by the National Press Club in Washington
in 1961, he astonished American reporters by suddenly accusing
American politicians of living in the nineteenth century, attacking
American journalism for its lack of new ideas and its 'soggy
verbiage' and talking about the 'weary old men of Europe . . .
from Adenauer to Macmillan'.

But the actual impact of King's personality on his papers is
small and his public outbursts give the impression more of letting
off steam than of being part of a large design. When politics
interfere with circulation, circulation always wins. When, after
1959, readers seemed less keen on Labour, the *Mirror* became
much less political, and dropped its old slogan 'Forward with
the People'. When King acquired, as part of the Odhams
deal, the only other left-wing daily, the *Herald*—now known
familiarly as 'King's Cross'—it happened by accident: 'When I
opened the £38 million package I found the *Herald* there', he
told American reporters; 'if anybody wants the *Daily Herald*,
which was losing a million pounds a year, I would be delighted
to get rid of it.'

The contrast between King and his uncle is poignant. Northcliffe loved his political campaigns, joined Lloyd George's war-
time government, and bought *The Times* to extend his influence.
His policies were wild, often ineffectual and eventually crazy: but
he sold papers to influence people, and sometimes succeeded. King
is fascinated not by the politics, but by the business of newspapers.
He loves his financial powers, and ability to outwit others: 'I am
already', he said, 'the most powerful publisher in the world.'[1] But
his political power is hedged in by the financial pressures: unlike
his uncle he is circumscribed by shareholders, and he cannot
afford to offend his twenty million readers. The contrast between
Northcliffe and his nephew in one generation typifies the change,
which recurs often in this book, from the old-style tycoon—rich,
autocratic and politically ambitious—to the new-style boss,
controlling a vaster corporate wealth, but bound round by
managers and shareholders, and governed by the rises and falls of
circulation. It is the difference between those who used their

[1] Interview with Jocelyn Stevens. *The Queen*, March 15, 1961.

power as a means to further their own ends, and those to whom the exercise of power is itself an end.

ROY THOMSON

A more sudden intrusion has been that of the small Canadian, Roy Thomson, proprietor, among nearly a hundred papers, of the *Moose-Jaw Times Herald*, of Saskatchewan, and the *Sunday Times* of London. For Thomson has not only become, in eight years since he first arrived in Scotland, the second biggest newspaper proprietor in the country. He also represents, more forcibly than General Motors or IBM, the impact of traditional North American business attitudes on a sleepy British situation.

The features of 'Uncle Roy', as he is known in Fleet Street, have become very familiar: his benign face beams out—each year more benignly—from the reports of the Thomson Organisation. He has a salesman's bonhomie: he is shortish, well-groomed, with a round bland head and a broad mouth which seems fixed in a satisfied smile. He conforms almost exactly to an Englishman's old-fashioned picture of an American. He has a vigorous handshake, calls everyone by his Christian name, mixes easily, jokes, teases and banters, likes to greet recruits with 'you make a dollar for me, I make a dollar for you'. Above all, he talks incessantly, enthusiastically and unashamedly about money. He has a paperweight made of imitation sovereigns, with a folksy slogan on it. It is his commercialism which makes him at the same time so simple, and so baffling.

Thomson's success story is well known. His boyhood as a poor barber's son in Toronto, his peddling of radio sets as a young man in the slump, his beginnings with radio stations in mining camps, his first shaky newspaper in Ontario, all this, so very remote from most British experience, moulded his simple, dynamic philosophy. By 1953, by shrewd costing and mass-produced journalism, he had built up a chain of thirty newspapers, nearly all small ones, from Florida to Ontario.

When he was fifty-nine he took a bold step: he came over to Edinburgh and bought, with the backing of the Royal Bank of Canada, its morning paper *The Scotsman*. He was a widower, and, it seemed, needed something to occupy his mind: and he had a nostalgic affection for Scotland, where his great-grandfather came from. He came to live in Edinburgh, but stayed aloof from its straight-laced social life. Soon afterwards, commercial television was launched, and his ownership of a newspaper gave him the right to apply for the Scottish station. Thomson had a simple rule in assessing business potentials: what works in America will work in Britain. While knowing Scotsmen were shaking their heads over the risks, Thomson, with the help of his paper, bought over 80 per cent of the shares in Scottish Television: it was, as he said later, 'a licence to print your own money'.

Television made him a multi-millionaire, and opened up great new horizons. Only six years after he had bought *The Scotsman*, the ageing Lord Kemsley, proprietor of the *Sunday Times* and twenty-three provincial papers, began to tire of his property. Kemsley, who had worked his way up from poverty like Thomson, had become interested—as the British so often do in late middle age—in prestige and politics more than in profits. He ran his papers with the help of four sons, in a gentlemanly way, with strictly Conservative politics and editorials about the Royal family in italics. He was driven in his Rolls to the office every morning, where he presided over dignified conferences and stately luncheons: at his country house there was a ticker-tape in the hall, and the butler brought in important news on a tray.

Thomson, remembering American precedents, and advised by his very shrewd banker Siegmund Warburg (whose help he freely acknowledges), saw the potential of the Kemsley empire. He bought it quickly for what looked like a very high price, and moved his headquarters to London. Then he found himself for the first time in his life in the big time, at the centre of politics and prestige. Kemsley House, a big half-empty building in the Gray's Inn Road, became Thomson House, and the beaming Canadian strode into the office with zest. He was now running, not a chain of small-town dailies, but a cultural, political weekly which could make authors and flutter Cabinets. His arrival in Gray's Inn Road was the most startling event since Northcliffe walked into *The Times*. He walked through the building shaking hands, gave cocktail parties for the staff and told jolly stories to the printers. The exotic literary contributors dreaded the prospect of being costed, but they had no need to worry: Thomson was well aware of the importance, as he put it, of 'salaried eccentrics'.

But he applied to the group the same process of 'consolidation and reorganisation' which he had learnt in the mining camps of Canada. He toured the provinces, fired a few managers and promoted others, increased advertising rates, established strict budgets, and scrutinised everything from wrapping paper to Scotch Tape. He imported a team of aggressive businessmen from

Scotland and the provinces: and men who had been leading quiet uncompetitive lives became suddenly activated with profit mindedness. He bought £2 million worth of printing machinery, and Thomson House rose up to seven storeys. He expanded the *Sunday Times* into a great supermarket paper, added a supplement and hired the Queen's brother-in-law. He even ventured to the perilous field of Africa; he bought half a Nigerian paper; together with the young Aga Khan he built up an East African chain, producing Swahili papers for the Kikuyu and Luo; and later bought a group of dingy weeklies in Central Africa. He works relentlessly, flying round the world, and never relaxing into the Riviera life of Rothermere and Beaverbrook. By the end of his first year the profits of the group had already been increased by 32 per cent.

What in all this frenzied activity had been Thomson's driving motive? He is not, like King, troubled by shareholders: he is in absolute control of his empire, and now personally a very rich man. Yet he has constantly said that he has no political interests. 'Newspaper publication and television', he said in his 1961 report, 'appeal to me as the most fascinating forms of business enterprise. I do not regard them as instruments for securing or wielding personal power.'

Journalists were at first disinclined to believe him. It seemed extraordinary that given such a powerful political weapon as the *Sunday Times*, he should not wish to wield it. But he has been visibly bored by politics: at one weekly conference, when his editor was explaining a detailed political point, he opened a parcel on his desk, containing a large collection of penknives, and began talking about the pleasures of knife-collecting. Although Thomson has clearly enjoyed mixing with politicians, from Gaitskell to Macmillan, and staying in Tory country-houses, he refuses to commit his papers to any one party. He insists on parading both Socialist and Conservative views in the *Sunday Times*, and has said repeatedly that he would like to own a Labour paper. If—as many suspect—he hopes for a title, he is going about it in a novel way.

Thomson has only one obvious political aim, which is to give the majority of his readers what they want. In America, he has a paper in the South supporting segregation, and others in the North attacking it. He likes to boast of the independence of his editors, but insists that they must be second-in-command to the managers. 'It is not true,' he said at a conference at New Delhi in 1961, 'as some say, that I use editors as mere tools of management

—editors should thank their stars I shield them from the worries of business.' But the supremacy of management makes it inevitable that editors with unpopular views will be threatened, and Thomson's speech provoked worried replies. 'Is it a good thing for a man to have the power to sack a hundred editors?' asked Lord Burnham of the *Telegraph:* 'I think not.'[1]

BEAVERBROOK

I run the paper purely for the purpose of making propaganda, and with no other motive.

Lord Beaverbrook to the Press Commission, 1948.

The attitudes to power of King and Thomson are in complete contrast to those of Max Lord Beaverbrook who, in the sense of personally dominating his newspapers, is the Last Tycoon of Fleet Street. Like his friend Churchill, Beaverbrook has the larger-than-life quality of a man who has risen out of the nineteenth century: he seems to pre-date the world of committees, managers, shareholders, and readership surveys. As a young Canadian millionaire, he bought the *Daily Express* for £17,000 in 1916, and ever since then he has moulded its journalism, its politics, and its staff. As a journalist and a businessman, Beaverbrook has been staggeringly successful. In its mixture of entertainment, slanted news and violent comment the *Daily Express* has proved irresistible to the British public: it has presented a star-spangled fantasy-world to brighten suburban homes. The black glass building of the *Daily Express*, with its hectic, theatrical atmosphere, however much it is hated, has had a dominating influence on the techniques of British journalism.

For forty years Lord Beaverbrook has had no office in the building: he does not appear in the list of directors, and holds no official title. But he remains in sole control, and his personality lurks behind every page, defying the managerial revolution. From his villa in the South of France, his house in Canada, his flat off Piccadilly, or his estate in Surrey, he rings up every day. His biblical Canadian phrases echo through the editorials—'Be sure', 'Praise this man', 'Not so', 'Let us rejoice'. He takes delight in appointing left-wing journalists and bending them to his right-wing views, and his eccentric interests and vendettas are all faithfully reflected in his papers—the denigration of Lord Mountbatten,

[1] *The Guardian*, November 4, 1961.

the glorification of New Brunswick, and above all, the praise of Empire Free Trade.

What does this agitation amount to? Unquestionably the *Daily Express* has had a strong social influence—encouraging British complacency and escapism, playing down depressing realities and evoking bygone glories. It has a sizeable nuisance-value, and no minister would gladly cross its path. But the lack of political influence of the *Daily Express*—with all its propaganda and cunning—is a standing tribute to its readers. The victims of its vendettas, including Lord Mountbatten, Prince Philip and Harold Macmillan, have all gone from strength to strength: and when in 1961 Lord Beaverbrook launched a ferocious campaign against the Common Market, many who were also against it were afraid that this would finally ruin their cause.

POSH PAPERS

The wheels of big business have involved the highbrow as well as the popular papers. The most striking case has been with the two old Sunday 'posh papers', *The Observer* and the *Sunday Times*. Before the war their combined circulations were less than half-a-million: they had tiny, gentlemanly staffs and a few literary contributors who sent in long articles from the country. St. John Irvine might write 3,000 words about the theatre, and J. L. Garvin would cover a whole page with advice to the Government, sent in by Rolls Royce, on the political situation (J. B. Morton talked about 'grazing on the Southern slopes of a Garvin article'): they were both more like estates than competitive business organisations. The war, the rise in the school-leaving age, and the expansion of universities have changed all that: their combined circulations are now nearly two million, and both have become far fatter, more competitive, and richer. But they have also become much more dependent on advertising, with all its attendant dangers: more than three-quarters of the revenue of the *Sunday Times* now comes from advertisements.

Equally spectacular has been the advance of the *Daily Telegraph*, controlled by a branch of the Berry family—the surviving part of the empire of the Berry Brothers which until 1937 had the biggest concentration in Fleet Street. The *Telegraph* has a simple formula: it looks like *The Times*, but is cheaper and less demanding. It has unwavering Conservative views, letters from angry colonels in Tunbridge Wells, columns of Births, Deaths and Marriages. It reports murder trials in a detailed and stately way, and it has the largest quantity of news of any daily paper. Compared to the *Express*, which is hip and glittering, the *Telegraph* is square and flat. But the *Telegraph* strikes a chord in the growing managerial middle-class: and its rise is an important clue to the social pattern of Britain. The *Telegraph*'s circulation has doubled since 1937, and in 1961 it extended its territory by introducing a Sunday edition. Many people, including Cecil King, forecast that the *Telegraph* formula of copious news would fail at weekends, with associations of relaxation and magazines: but the *Sunday Telegraph* has established itself with a circulation of 700,000—thus increasing the competition for the rich weekend market.

THE TIMES

Even *The Times* has changed. For a hundred and eighty years *The Times* has lived in a sheltered world of its own. Northcliffe, who owned it for fifteen years, could not bend it to his will: he was baffled by the 'black friars'—as he called its stately leader-writers —and talked of writing over its door 'abandon scope all ye who enter here'. After Northcliffe died it was bought for £1½ million by J. J. Astor, now Lord Astor of Hever. Its circulation, which in 1800 was bigger than all other newspapers combined, is now one of the smallest—260,000 a day, or hardly more than a twentieth of the *Daily Mirror*'s. But it gives the impression of being read by everyone that matters: its editorials suggest an intimate correspondence with the Government: its letters constitute a private debating-chamber, and its social columns provide a House Magazine for Society ('Countess Attlee has lost her engagement book', said an entry on September 29, 1961: 'she would be obliged if those with whom she has engagements would communicate with her').

The Times is so sedate that it is often regarded, like Eton or Buckingham Palace, as strictly non-commercial—an impression strengthened by the existence of five impeccable Trustees—the Lord Chief Justice, the Warden of All Souls, the President of the Royal Society, the President of the Institute of Chartered Accountants and the Governor of the Bank of England. But the sole object of the Trustees is to ensure that *The Times* does not fall 'into unworthy hands'[1] a duty which has not so far been onerous. *The Times* has to pay its way like any other newspaper: even its nine-

---

[1] *See* History of *The Times*, Vol. IV, Part II, 1952, p. 790.

teenth century supremacy was due as much to its steam-printing press as to its journalism: and today, with the *Guardian* overtaking and the *Telegraph* imitating and undercutting, its position is increasingly challenged. *The Times* still regards itself as the only 'journal of record'—the only paper which puts information, however dull, above everything else. But its less confident position was revealed by its £150,000 advertising campaign, with the slogan 'Top People read *The Times*'—a statement which would have seemed platitudinous thirty years ago.

The Times' monopoly of top people is now being further threatened by the growth of *The Guardian*. Before the war the *Manchester Guardian*, as it then was, sold only 48,000 copies a day—equivalent to half-a-year's increase for the *Daily Express*: but in the past two years it has dropped its prefix, printed in London as well as Manchester, and increased its circulation to over a quarter of a million, nearly overtopping *The Times*: and under a very independent Glaswegian editor, Alastair Hetherington, it has strengthened the old reputation for 'robust North Country commonsense'. *The Times* insists that no other paper approaches its coverage and reliability: but the contest between *The Times* and *The Guardian* is likely to become increasingly vigorous—with the dangers as well as the benefits of competitive journalism.

However, the most important feature of *The Times* is not its circulation but its political influence: and here the change has been striking. Before the war, Geoffrey Dawson, who edited *The Times* (with a four-year gap) for twenty-nine years, moved in the heart of Conservative politics. Baldwin, Chamberlain and Halifax were his close personal friends, and at All Souls, Cliveden and other country-house weekends he talked incessantly about diplomatic policy, pressing always the importance of appeasing Hitler. That closed, compact circle, revealed in memoirs of pre-war politicians, has done much to cultivate the idea of 'The Establishment' among the next generation—one of the many examples of the history of one generation providing the myths for the next. Dawson appropriated to himself the job of Foreign Editor of *The Times*, cut and trimmed the despatches of his European correspondents, and preferred to take the advice of his Government friends: in one terrible, self-revealing phrase he described his editorial approach to the Germans:

'I did my utmost, night after night, to keep out of the paper anything that might hurt their susceptibilities.'[1]

[1] *See Times History*, Vol. IV, Part II, p. 907.

The pre-war rôle of *The Times*, with its deliberate suppression of news, caused a deep trauma in Printing House Square since the war, and *The Times'* own history—a remarkable piece of corporate psycho-analysis—mercilessly exposes the faults of the paper.

The present editor, Sir William John Haley, shows a total change from the Dawson tradition. He is a self-made, retiring man who regards himself above all as a professional journalist. He is very self-contained, with an impersonal gaze and an intimidating habit of resting his teeth on his fingers. He talks long and precisely about the rôle of journalism, with self-generating enthusiasm. He has had a romantic success story: the son of a Yorkshire clerk, who died when he was two years old, he was brought up in the Channel Islands and left school—a bookish, introverted boy—at the age of sixteen. He went to sea as a wireless operator, found a job on a Jersey newspaper, and then reached *The Times* as telephonist. At the switchboard he thought out a scheme for saving continental calls and was sent to Brussels to work it—in the meantime having married the Foreign Editor's secretary. But *The Times* offered no chance of writing, so Haley moved to the *Manchester Evening News* as a reporter, and then as sub-editor. He had self-discipline and ambition rare in journalists, and eight years later he had become Managing Editor at the age of twenty-nine. He was not much interested in editorial policy: his pre-occupations were accurate news, making the paper pay, and writing book reviews—which he still enjoys more than almost anything.

In journalism he became a figure of legendary and alarming efficiency: he was made joint-managing director of the *Manchester Guardian*, and undertook negotiations for Reuters. He was asked—through Brendan Bracken—to join the BBC, which was in one of its periodic states of muddle, as Editor-in-Chief; six months later he became its Director-General at only forty-three. He ruled the corporation with firmness and austere idealism: he admired Lord Reith, extended popular education, and invented the Third Programme.

After eight years' broadcasting, he was asked to become Editor of *The Times:* the man who had refused to promote him thirty years before was still there. He made gradual, unspectacular changes: he moved out of the Editor's traditional gloomy room into a more cheerful place. He introduced a women's page and wrote his own booksy column under the name 'Oliver Edwards'. He insisted on professional reporters who knew shorthand, rather than the retired diplomats or generals or the old-style amateur 'Men from the Times'. He did not mix much with cabinet ministers, and he did not get on well with Harold Macmillan—his dead opposite in character: he preferred quiet evenings at home to political pow-wows. Of his predecessors—whose miniatures hang above his desk—it is Barnes, who rescued *The Times* from the Government's embrace in the 1820's, and dined off tripe in his office, whom Haley most admires.

An extraordinary glimpse of the distance between *The Times* and the Government appeared on the morning of June 1, 1959. The main news item in *The Times* announced:

PRIME MINISTER'S PLANS
FOR MR. SELWYN LLOYD

EASING STRAIN OF OFFICE

POSSIBLE TRANSFER STILL
SEVERAL MONTHS AHEAD

From our Political Correspondent

'We may safely accept that Mr. Macmillan has lately taken Mr. Selwyn Lloyd's arm in a paternal grip, led him to one side, and spoken from the heart. Call it the personal advice a leader offers to a favoured lieutenant, or call it the first unmistakable hint about the Prime Minister's intentions if he is summoned to form another Ministry after the general election—it makes no difference. What matters is that Mr. Macmillan has let Mr. Lloyd know that at the Foreign Office, in these troubled times, enough is enough.'

The effect was electric. At that very moment Selwyn Lloyd was negotiating in Geneva, and the European press, assuming as usual that *The Times* was the official voice of the Government, was agog with excitement. The Prime Minister had to make a statement in the House denying any such notion, and sent a reassuring telegram to Selwyn Lloyd. Political commentators were full of every kind of interpretation: Randolph Churchill explained that it was either a plot by Mr. Butler to get rid of Mr. Lloyd, or a warning to Lloyd to adopt a more appeasing line towards Russia.

But the actual circumstances were less exciting. What had happened, it transpired, was that Haley, inspecting the next day's paper on Sunday night—always a bad night for news—found the headlines unusually dull: and had remembered his political correspondent's story on a more obscure page, in a weekly gossipy column called 'In and Out of Politics'. The story was based on one of the inconclusive, mildly indiscreet conversations which Macmillan enjoys having with journalists. In its usual position, with a light heading and a whimsical title, the article would have caused no more stir than other similar speculative political articles. But proclaimed on the main news page, alongside hard world news, the speculation had the look of urgent information, with a strong sense of purpose.

Selwyn Lloyd stayed at the Foreign Office for another year, and *The Times'* prestige took a knock. In Dawson's day it could never have happened, for the Editor would certainly have had it confirmed with the Prime Minister. But the fact that *The Times* can now make such a blunder is at least a reassuring sign that it is no longer in the bosom of the Government. There are still many relics of *The Times'* special position, including its adulatory attitude to public figures, its ambiguous and cloaked editorials. *The Times* still believes in giving the Government, wherever possible, the benefit of the doubt, and its long sentences and formal typography persuade readers that it is written, not by young men just down from Oxford, but by sages in Whitehall. But the affair of Selwyn Lloyd showed that *The Times* is now no more, and no less, than a newspaper.

JOURNALISTS

> Your connection with any newspaper would be a disgrace and a degradation. I would rather sell gin to poor people and poison them that way.
>
> *Sir Walter Scott to Lockhart, 1829.*

> You cannot hope to bribe or twist
> Thank God, a British journalist:
> But seeing what the man will do
> Unbribed, there's no occasion to.
>
> *Humbert Wolfe.*

Caught unhappily in the commercial cogs are the journalists—over fifteen thousand of them in the National Union of Journalists and thousands more outside it—more journalists in Britain than solicitors. British journalists are aware of being less respected than Americans; there is no British equivalent to the American journalist-pundit—Reston, Lippmann, or the Alsops, and a successful British journalist will usually like to think of himself as something else—a writer, a diplomat or a politician. American newspapers helped to create their democracy, spreading news from coast to coast—in a country without traditional social networks, journalism was crucial—but in Britain, the secretive ruling classes in the eighteenth century had no love of journalism, and it began as an eavesdropping profession, where even parliamentary reports had to be smuggled out. In spite of such eminent journalists as Churchill, Milner or Dickens, journalism has never quite recovered from this backdoor feeling. Cabinet secrecy, which has become almost complete since the first world war, has made it hard for newspapers to drive a wedge into politics: compare the Cuban fiasco in Washington in 1961, when cabinet disagreements were immediately leaked to the press, with the Suez crisis of 1956, whose inner history remains to this day largely a secret.

Part of the difficulty of British journalists comes from its concentration: journalism has lacked the greatest safeguard of professional standards—a multiplicity of clients. The pressure of profits and the shortage of space make press lords unwilling to employ good reporters for the sake of prestige, and the business of reporting—which is often inevitably dull—has become more and more mixed with entertainment and comment. The contrast with America is not as unfavourable as Americans make out: transatlantic reporters, because of cheap newsprint and copious advertisements, have room to be dull, and their turgid prose is often unread and unreadable: like provincial dons, they lose touch with their audience. But journalists in Britain have never had the cosy sense of profession which Americans enjoy. In America journalism is apt to be regarded as an extension of history: in Britain, as an extension of conversation.

On the other hand, British papers can be more vocal, and more varied in their views, than American. At the time of the Quemoy crisis in 1958, or the Castro affair in Cuba in 1961, there was not the same sense of fierce public debate in the American press as arose over Suez in 1956 or even Immigration in 1961. There is no American equivalent to the national controversies in *The Times* letter-columns; and even though the British popular papers may be often opportunist and absurd, they can occasionally produce an uproar which can change the Government's mind. Every journalist has his own view of the power of the press: my own impression is that the British Government often takes newspapers more seriously than the journalists do.

Broadcasting has added to the problems of journalism. Before the war, radio had already usurped some of the news-providing side of papers, and had pushed them towards magazines: and during the war the prestige of the nine o'clock news, as the voice of the government, put it above all newspapers. Since then television has broken that monopoly, and there are some (including Sir William Haley) who believe that this gives journalism a new opportunity as a serious medium. But television has infected much of journalism with its hectic aggressiveness: jet planes and TV cameras between them have made news seem more like a series of sudden and disconnected crises and shows. Special correspondents rush from Cuba to Berlin to Ghana, discovering crises, plots and disasters, and then moving hurriedly on. Television, too, has broken down some of the old anonymity of journalism, and has tended to drag journalists, not reluctantly, into show business.

Another unpleasant intruder has been the subterranean machinery of public relations, creating its own fake news, organising airlifts of journalists, stimulating bogus controversies and presenting prefabricated images—most extremely in fashion, where news is entirely invented by the publicity machine. But the machinery has also penetrated to industry and politics, where the façade of handouts and pre-arranged news often bears little relation to what actually happened.[1]

The financial operations in the press over the past three years have been so bizarre, so like the juggling with other industrial investments, that it is sometimes difficult to remember that these properties are supposed to be the basic instruments of democracy. In spite of all the other elements mixed with them—entertainment, comment and advertising—newspapers remain the principal channels of communication, and if readers do not obtain their facts from them, they are unlikely to find them elsewhere. There are some who believe that the press has already become so mixed with absurdities that its further commercialisation is hardly worth worrying about. But for those who still have hopes for the press as a moulder of public opinion, the position is certainly alarming.

Probably the most serious effect of commercialisation is its swamping of minority views. The fewer and more competitive the papers, the less any one paper will be liable to embrace an

[1] *See* Chapter 37.

unpopular view, at the risk of losing readers and advertising: at the present pace no paper, not even *The Times*, can be oblivious to its circulation graph. Every paper must strive after the majority of readers in its own field, and this necessity is enormously enhanced by the demands of advertisers.

Advertising has not influenced journalism in the direct, corrupt way that many people forecast: advertisers have not, except in a few angry moments such as at the time of Suez, tried to bring pressure on to editorial opinion. But it has had more indirect, and equally dangerous effects: it has in the first place compelled journalists, without bribing or twisting, to play in with the uncritical world of advertisements, beginning in the relatively harmless world of fashion and travel but spreading imperceptibly to other areas. When for instance one journalist consistently recommended readers to buy clothes at Marks and Spencers, the more expensive shops quietly withdrew their advertising from that paper. If a journalist adopts a critical attitude to a company, their prestige advertisements will be withdrawn, and no newspaper can survive a cut of 25 per cent in its advertising. But more serious is the effect of advertising in pressing towards mass markets: advertisers are not much interested in the diversities of opinion, they are only interested in the main income groups—A, B, C, D, and the papers which lead in each group are quite adequate. Advertising, which itself exists to build up mass markets, has forced journalism to do the same.

But it is not only commercialism which limits the journalists' scope. It is the increasing difficulty, as the bureaucracies take over from parliament, of finding anything out. While parliament remains a convenient outward show, full of drama, intrigue and gossip, vast areas of government remain quite unpenetrated by journalism. In the civil service and the big corporations, protection from publicity is a sacred principle, and arguments are perpetually put forward to explain why making issues public will make matters worse. 'The mumbo-jumbo words *sub judice*', wrote Sir William Haley, 'are applied to all kinds of proceedings which are not in the remotest way legal, in order to stifle opinion about them'. Bureaucrats, by their rule, prefer, in Haley's words, to 'cloak their proceedings and present accomplished facts only'.[1]

Over the last forty years the blanket of secrecy round Government affairs has become much more impenetrable: the difference

[1] Sir W. J. Haley: *The Formation of Public Opinion*. Haldane Memorial Lecture, 1958.

is in the immense tightening-up of the Government machine. The Whitehall bureaucracies which we encounter later in this book have learnt to suppress all unofficial news, to channel their information through a single well-disciplined official, and specialist journalists are dependent on that official's goodwill for their sources. Every day a Foreign Office spokesman sees the diplomatic correspondents of the daily press—adjusting his information to the acceptability of the paper, with plenty of news for *The Times* and very little for the *Worker*. If a paper offends against Foreign Office rules, and publishes embarrassing information, the co-operation of the Foreign Office will be quietly withdrawn: correspondents find it harder to maintain an aggressive fact-finding attitude, and become sucked into the diplomatic machine.

All bureaucracies are secretive, but the British civil service, with its self-contained corporate tradition is more successfully secretive: and in the great contemporary debates within Whitehall—about the Common Market, the future of the fighting services, or economic planning—it is becoming increasingly difficult for journalists to discover the issues before the decisions are actually reached.

9

CABINET

The most curious point about the Cabinet is that so little is known about it.

Walter Bagehot.

There can be no friendship between the five top men in a cabinet.
Lloyd George.

THE most important job of the political parties is to provide cabinet ministers. For whatever parliament may do, it is on these twenty men that the week-to-week running of the country depends: and as the state becomes increasingly involved in industry, planning and monetary control, so the area of cabinet decisions becomes larger. The cabinet has no legal existence, beyond the powers of the ministers of the Crown. It is merely a committee, whose very existence was originally secret, formed from the majority party in the House, to carry out the business of government. Yet it is in theory the crucial joint on which power ultimately rests. In Bagehot's words: 'A Cabinet is a combining committee—a hyphen which joins, a buckle which fastens, the legislative part of the State to the Executive part of the State'. But in the following century the buckle has had to join a far greater area of execution.

When an MP is appointed to the government, the post office engineers arrive at his home to install a green 'scrambler' telephone, which can only be unscrambled by other ministers and senior civil servants. He is provided, too, with a big red leather-covered box with a royal crest and 'ER' on top, (which no spy, incidentally, could fail to notice) to carry state papers. The red boxes and green telephones mark the secret, self-contained world of government to which nearly every member of parliament aspires.

A government consists altogether of about seventy politicians —about a ninth of the members of parliament—including such unlikely people as the Solicitor-General for Scotland and five junior Lords of the Treasury. There are six 'Ministers of State' (a title created by Churchill during the war) each under a major cabinet minister. There are also nine ministers who, although heads of important departments, including Pensions, Health and Power, are not in the cabinet. But it is the cabinet which forms the heart of decisions, and between the cabinet and the rest is a great divide. Non-cabinet ministers are occasionally invited to the cabinet room to discuss their own topics, but the ordeal is alarming. This is how one former cabinet minister, Patrick Gordon Walker, described it:

> You are invited to attend at a stated hour when your business is expected to be reached—your appearance is nearly always premature; though occasionally, if the cabinet goes on unexpectedly fast, you may have to rush over from your office on a suddon summons. Usually you have to wait outside the cabinet room, alone in the ante-chamber, which is the only place I know bleaker than a dentist's waiting room. When the Secretary calls you in, you enter a cabinet in full swing; you find an empty chair where you can; hurriedly open your papers; and, at the prime minister's invitation, embark on an exposition of your case. When the point is settled, you rise and leave the cabinet to get on with its remaining business.[1]

It is in the cabinet that the strands of democracy, in theory, meet. Ministers have to run their ministries, attend cabinet and cabinet committees, report to parliament when necessary, and answer privately the complaints of MPs and of their own individual electors. They are company chairmen, barristers and public relations officers all rolled into one, and if not many of them are good at all three, that is not altogether surprising. For this they earn £5,000 a year, together with an official car, parties and travel. They earn £2,000 less than the permanent secretaries who work under them, and £3,000 less than judges: and they have no pension when they retire.

The cabinet meets in a long white room at the back of 10, Downing Street, with awkward pillars in the middle, looking out on to a garden. Ministers leave their hats and coats on a rack outside, labelled 'Lord Chancellor', 'Paymaster-General', etc., and sit down in front of green baize, pens and paper: the prime minister—who also uses the room as his office—sits in the middle, facing the garden. The prime minister opens the meeting, and ministers address their remarks to him, referring with careful

On being a Cabinet Minister. *Encounter*, April, 1956.

impersonality to their colleagues: 'I can't quite agree with the Lord Privy Seal...'

The agenda for the cabinet is short and brisk—the final result of a long process of distillation by the retorts of the civil service. It contains usually only about seven or eight points: one is always the Foreign Secretary's report, and another concerns government business in parliament. The remaining matters are usually brought up either by the prime minister, or by two ministers who have failed to agree. Discussion in cabinet is brief, and speech-making strongly discouraged. 'Democracy means government by discussion but it is only effective if you can stop people talking,' said Lord Attlee.[1] The performance of ministers in cabinet is often quite different to their performance in parliament, or in public: Sir David Eccles, for instance, is said to be brisk and impressive in cabinet, and Selwyn Lloyd is reported to be confident and concise. A number of ministers, one gathers, hardly ever speak in cabinet at all, and one or two have been suspected of sleeping.

There are no rules about how to run a cabinet, and each prime minister has his own method. 'Harold's a very good prime minister as far as taking cabinet goes', one minister said: 'he takes it slowly, lets everyone have his say, and if they don't agree he doesn't mind calling an extra meeting to come back to it. But as he grows older he thinks about fewer things—he's now mainly occupied with the Common Market, the cold war and the Atlantic Alliance. But he can turn his mind to detailed things, like pensions, if he has to.' It is the prime minister's job to sum up discussions at the end, moulding the cabinet's view into one. Discussions hardly ever come to a vote: if there is disagreement, they return to the subject, giving and taking until either a majority view takes shape, or—in extremity—a minister resigns.

'The job of a prime minister', Lord Attlee has said, 'is to get the general feeling—collect the voices. And then, when everything reasonable has been said, to get on with the job and say, "Well, I think the decision of the cabinet is this, that or the other. Any objections?" Usually there aren't.'[2]

Cabinet ministers are overworked, underpaid, and deprived of most of the ordinary pleasures of life. Yet very few willingly give up their burden. What keeps them there (I felt more strongly after talking to them) is not so much the love of power—many of them

[1] *The Times*, April 11, 1957.
[2] Francis Williams: *A Prime Minister Remembers*. 1961. p. 81.

seem to have no clear idea what they want with it—but simply the love of being at the heart of information and events: as Iain Macleod has put it:

> I think the main attraction for me at least, and I believe this would be true of most politicians, is of being at the centre of the web, not just of having power, although I think that is part of the make-up of most politicians, but in the end, in every decision of importance that affects this country, the threads of those decisions run into the cabinet room.[1]

Probably only four or five of them have serious ambitions to be prime minister—in many respects a more agreeable and manageable job than running a department. With many of the others, the fear of losing power is probably as great a motive force as the desire to gain it, and it is this which helps to make resigning so difficult, and so rare: inside the cabinet room, a minister is caught up in the stream of events, sure of his importance as part of a team, and linked to the network of reassuring officials. Outside, he is alone: and the loneliness of a would-be resigner is terrible. To quote Macleod again:

> Sometimes it's on something that events can't necessarily prove whether you're right or wrong: it's a matter of judgment ... you come more and more into yourself. You withdraw more and more really from your friends, and then you think it out yourself in the watches of the night, and then you come to whatever conclusion you may have to.

However exhausting or compromising the job, having it is less agonising than losing it. Patrick Gordon Walker has described the experience of *not* being a cabinet minister:

> From being at the very heart of affairs and among the few dozen best-informed men in the world, faithfully served day and night, he suddenly reverts to obscurity. The invitations which a short time before had seemed to flow in embarrassing numbers, thin to a trickle. Workmen arrive to remove the direct line which linked him to his Private Office and by which he could control a great Department of State.[2]

[1] Interview with Malcolm Muggeridge. Granada TV, October 16, 1961.
[2] *Encounter*, April, 1956.

CABINET-MAKING

Duchess of Omnium: 'You Ministers go on shuffling the old cards
till they are so worn out that one can hardly tell the pips on them.'
The Prime Minister: 'I am one of the dirty old cards myself.'
Trollope: The Prime Minister.

The prime minister in cabinet is officially no more than 'primus inter pares'—just one member of a committee. But in fact, apart from his political advantage, he has a strong hand. He is chairman of the committee: he appoints it, summons it, guides it, and can eventually dissolve it. Cabinet-making is probably the most important part of a prime minister's job: but the scope is not perhaps as great as might appear from outside. Political rivals cannot easily be demoted, discontented followers must be pacified: left and right must be balanced: the heads of the most important departments cannot be constantly changed: and the number of first-class men in parliament does not give unlimited choice. Cabinet reshuffles are apt to be acclaimed by the press either for their cunning or their aptness: if a man is put into a job which is manifestly unsuitable—like putting Butler, an old critic of the Common Market, in charge of the Common Market committee— it is acclaimed as a shrewd political manoeuvre: the fact that Duncan Sandys, a keen European, was put into the Commonwealth Relations Office, was held to be an act of brilliant foresight. In fact, the press seems inclined to overestimate the government's cunning; cabinet reshuffling, like so much else, is often more a question of expediency than planning, and prime ministers, like the Duke of Omnium, are well aware of being themselves part of the pack.

But a cabinet remains very much the expression of a prime minister's personality—not least in the case of Harold Macmillan. He can introduce peers (like Lord Home), and if necessary make peers (like Lord Mills): he can bring in ballast (like Christopher Soames) and he can—up to a point—demote his rivals (like Lord Hailsham).

This was the cabinet in April, 1962, with their ages:

Prime Minister	Harold Macmillan (68)
Foreign Secretary	The Earl of Home (58)
Chancellor of the Exchequer	Selwyn Lloyd (57)
Minister for Science	Viscount Hailsham (54)
Lord Chancellor	Viscount Kilmuir (61)

Home Secretary and Central Africa Office	R. A. Butler (59)
Commonwealth Relations	Duncan Sandys (54)
Colonial Secretary	Reginald Maudling (45)
Secretary of State for Scotland	John Maclay (56)
Minister of Labour	John Hare (51)
Lord Privy Seal (Foreign Office)	Edward Heath (45)
President of the Board of Trade	Frederick Erroll (47)
Chief Secretary of Treasury	Henry Brooke (59)
Minister of Housing	Charles Hill (58)
Leader of the House of Commons and Chairman of the Conservative Party	Iain Macleod (48)
Minister of Agriculture	Christopher Soames (41)
Minister of Education	Sir David Eccles (57)
Minister of Transport	Ernest Marples (54)
Minister of Aviation	Peter Thorneycroft (54)
Paymaster-General	Lord Mills (72)
Minister of Defence	Harold Watkinson (52)

Surveying this list, it is difficult to imagine them as the pick of parliament, or even of the party, and some of the reasons for their being appointed are complex and odd. At the top are a few men of obviously first-class ability, but in the lower ranks are several mysterious mediocrities. The youngest, Christopher Soames, is not obviously the most brilliant, and the most recent recruit, Frederick Erroll, a hard-working ex-engineer, was almost unheard of in parliament. Once appointed to cabinet, ministers are liable to stay there unless they resign or seriously misbehave: but of the twenty-one, only four were in the Cabinet in 1951.

Most prime ministers like to have a kind of ballast in their cabinet: this is how Atlee described it:

'You've got to have a certain number of solid people whom no one would think particularly brilliant, but who between conflicting opinions can act as middlemen, give you the ordinary man's point of view . . . You remember little George Tomlinson. I can remember a thing coming up which looked like a good scheme, all worked out by the civil service. But I wasn't quite sure how it would go down with the ordinary people so I said "Minister of Education, what do you know of this." "Well", says George, "it sounds all right, but I've been trying to persuade my wife of it for the last three weeks and I can't persuade her".[1]

Much of the running of cabinet depends on five men at the top —Macmillan, Home, Butler, Macleod and Lloyd—and many of the junior ministers only speak on their own departmental matters. Three members have special positions: Lord Mills, the Paymaster-General is perhaps the only personal friend of the Prime Minister. Lord Kilmuir, as Lord Chancellor, is more detached from the political fray than the rest, and acts as a kind of patient mediator. Lord Hailsham occupies the important position (previously occupied by Lord Salisbury) as the man who speaks his mind, and is not afraid of, even perhaps enjoys, annoying the Prime Minister. There are not many close friends in the cabinet, and departmental differences accentuate personal rivalries. The Ministers of Education, Defence and Labour are in constant friction with the Treasury, and the Commonwealth Relations and Colonial Offices are usually at loggerheads.

A few patterns emerge in the composition of the cabinet: six were at Eton, five of them at the same time: four were at Balliol, and three at Trinity, Cambridge. Two were at Fettes (Macleod and Lloyd), two at Winchester together (Eccles and Maclay), two at Marlborough together (Brooke and Butler). None are women: the only three woman cabinet ministers have been Margaret Bondfield, Minister of Labour, Ellen Wilkinson and Florence Horsbrugh, both Ministers of Education. Four are sons of peers, three others married daughters of peers or Churchill, two are self-made, the rest are middle-class. Two (Mills and Marples) have been accountants, two (Watkinson and Erroll) have been engineers. But most of the senior ones belong to the old amateur traditions of government: Lord Hailsham knows nothing about science, and Reginald Maudling had not been to Africa until two months before he became Colonial Secretary. One (Heath) is a bachelor, and five have been divorced. The cabinet as a whole, though younger than Attlee's, was older than Chamberlain's: this is how it compared with the 1937 cabinet, which also had twenty-one members—but which included three Labour ministers:

[1] *A Prime Minister Remembers.* p. 81.

	1961	1937
Non-public school	4	2
Etonians	6	8
Oxford	9	11
Cambridge	6	2
Non-university	5	5
Average age	54	52
Sons or sons-in-law of peers	5	9
Lawyers	5	8

The cabinet, most people agree, is too big. It has fluctuated over twenty years between fifteen and twenty-two: but since the eighteenth century—as Professor Parkinson has duly noted—it has steadily got bigger. It is much bigger than the American cabinet of ten, though about the same size as the French, German or Italian. Several pressures have blown it up: one has been the need to satisfy groups, by embracing symbolic ministers—such as the Secretary of State for Scotland, the Minister of Labour (to placate the trade unions) or the Minister of Agriculture (to pacify farmers). Another difficulty is that parliament refuses to take non-cabinet ministers seriously, so that departments with heavy pressure of work, the Foreign Office and the Treasury, have to have two in the cabinet. But also there are personal and political pressures: once a man reaches the cabinet, it is painful and danger-ous to demote him. (It is a situation echoed in business, where the size of boards has likewise swelled. ICI has twenty-two directors, and Unilever has eighteen. Both are inclined to use their board-rooms as partly honorific affairs, leaving the real planning to a triumvirate.) Big cabinets lead inevitably to formality, and any meeting of twenty has severe limitations. 'The cabinet's a very good jury', one minister said: 'but it's no good at drafting, which is half the battle: that all has to be done beforehand.'

Inside a big cabinet there nearly always develops an 'inner cabinet'—the small group of ministers who are consulted by the prime minister beforehand and who prepare and guide the decisions. Most Prime Ministers have had one: Churchill's was open and obvious like a court; Atlee operated in a more imper-sonal, green-telephone way; Macmillan's is not very finite, but roughly embraces Home, Lloyd, Butler and Macleod. It is between these that formulae are discussed and compromises reached, so that in full cabinet the main political powers will be in agreement.

The most potent of all recent 'inner cabinets' was Sir Anthony

Eden's in the months before Suez: and the power of this cabal has since raised serious doubts as to the effectiveness of the full cabinet. Eden's group consisted of Macmillan, Lloyd, Hailsham and Antony Head: it was among these that the preparations for the Suez invasion were made, while others like Butler were kept ignorant. Another forty-five years must elapse before the full story emerges: but it is clear that the inner cabinet was able virtually to present cabinet with a *fait accompli*, before they had time to object. 'It seemed to make nonsense of the cabinet', said one former permanent secretary: 'I still don't understand how it could have happened.'

CABINET NETWORK

Behind the full meetings of cabinet, which only occupy about four hours a week, lies the mechanism known as 'the cabinet network', centring on the cabinet office. The office was established by Lloyd George in 1916, to provide a secretariat for cabinet meetings: before then no record was kept, and two ministers would often embarrassingly interpret the same decision in opposite ways. 'The cabinet', wrote Lord Hankey, 'often had the haziest notions of what its decisions were'. Lord Hartington's private secretary wrote to Gladstone's PS in 1882: 'My chief has told me to ask you what the devil was decided, for he be damned if he knows.'[1] After the war the cabinet office became permanent, under Sir Maurice Hankey, who was its secretary for nineteen years—under Lloyd George, Bonar Law, MacDonald, Baldwin and Chamberlain. Lord Hankey (as he now is) is eighty-five, has lived to see his old office grow into the centre of the Whitehall machine.

There have only been three Secretaries of the cabinet— Hankey, Bridges and Brook. Sir Norman Brook, who has held the position since 1946, will appear later under his other hat, as Head of the Civil Service; but in cabinet he is responsible for the organisational nexus behind cabinet decisions. 'Cabinet papers' are kept circulating by messengers with red boxes, giving details of matters which one minister wants to bring up, and providing a secret newspaper for Whitehall, including a daily report on Foreign Affairs: a box goes each day to the Queen. From the cabinet papers the Prime Minister, with the help of Brook, compiles the cabinet agenda, which is itself an important instrument of policy, playing up some issues and ignoring others.

[1] Lord Hankey: *Diplomacy by Conference.* 1946. pp. 53–67.

In the cabinet network, too, is the ring of 'cabinet committees', which are offshoots of the full meetings: they are in theory so secret that no one outside the office is supposed to know which are sitting, when and about what. They are appointed by the prime minister (though they do not necessarily include him) for getting particular things done; they include the Defence Committee, the Home Affairs Committee, the Common Market Committee, and a Future Legislation Committee. They have the same powers as the cabinet itself, though crucial questions are always passed to the full cabinet. But the more unmanageable the full cabinet, the more important the committees: and gradually they have taken over a large part of the business of government. Small committees inevitably supersede large ones.

The summoning and briefing of all these committees falls on the cabinet secretariat. It is a machine of legendary speed, and its few rooms in the Treasury building are the flywheel of government. Over the years the cabinet office has moved closer metaphorically to 10, Downing Street, helped by the closeness of Sir Norman Brook and Harold Macmillan: and some people feel that the cabinet office has become too much the centre of all information, and that its influence gives too much power to civil servants. The civil servants insist that they do no more than co-ordinate complex departments: 'All we do', said one man in the cabinet office, 'is to try to collect people together, to get things *done*. Somebody's got to do it.' But (as we have already observed, and as we shall see again) in the modern pattern of government co-ordination is a large part of power, and the gap between policy and execution is a large one: the decision, for instance, whether to make South Africa's exclusion from the Commonwealth a gesture or a reality, has rested largely with civil servants—who chose the latter.

The most crucial job of the secretariat is the translation of cabinet decisions into action. Brook or his deputy sit at every cabinet meeting, and it is their cabinet minutes which are the frail but effective paperchain between the green table and the departments of state. 'I used to check up to make sure that cabinet decisions were carried out', said Rab Butler: 'but I soon realised it wasn't necessary. The civil servants come out of their caves like hungry animals and gobble them up.' (What happens inside the caves we will see in subsequent chapters.)

The cabinet secretary miraculously transmutes the rambling arguments into a neat summary of conclusions, with all the art of the de-personalised civil servant. First-person speeches are changed into *oratio obliqua*, angry arguments are transformed into mild disagreements, doubt and muddle become dignified imponderables: and two hours of disjointed discussion is boiled down to a few coherent paragraphs. 'It takes a bit of the personality out of politics', said one cabinet minister: 'when Quintin loses his temper, it appears in the minutes as "Lord Hailsham voiced dissent".' The cabinet minutes are the process by which the arguments of twenty-one men with twenty-one views are distilled into a collective government, with an apparently solid front of policy.

THE BUCKLE

It is easy to explain how the cabinet, in theory, is as the buckle which joins the two parts of the State, and the core of collective responsibility. But after exploring Whitehall and talking to ministers, I feel like others less confident about the theory. Many people might imagine that the cabinet sat down twice a week and said to each other 'What shall we do next?' But one has the disturbing impression that the cabinet are so busy having things done *to* them that they are more often saying, 'How do we get out of this one?' And between the cabinet's policies and its actual execution intervenes the huge area of national and international pressures, conflicting forces, and the nebulous influence which will appear elsewhere in this book, which can only be described as Muddle.

In Victorian times, when parliament sat for half a year, and the government had no hand in industry, the cabinet could have collective discussions about prisons, post offices and foreign policies. But since the first world war the area has spectacularly increased to the point that public investment is now 42% of the whole, and the government has a finger in nearly every industry. As a result of the pressure, as early as 1931 Sir Maurice Hankey drafted a memorandum, saying that ministers should only bring points out to the cabinet after they had been thrashed out with the departments concerned: and since then the cabinet has become more involved in particular disputes and less in general problems. In June, 1961 for instance the cabinet was repeatedly concerned with Northern Rhodesia, not so much because of a passionate collective interest in African welfare, but because Iain Macleod and Duncan Sandys could not agree.

The sheer pressure of work on a minister, rushing between

parliament, his department and cabinet, has strained the buckle apart. There has always been a prejudice against having a 'Minister of Thought', who could sit back and survey long-term problems, and a cabinet minister usually lacks influence if he is detached from a department. But the resulting pressure on individuals has worried most prime ministers since the war: Macmillan's solution of 'double-banking' in the heaviest ministries —the Foreign Office and Treasury—helps to relieve the burden, but increases the scope for friction and muddle. When a problem falls between two or three departments—as most serious problems do—their discussion often goes by default: and some of the most disastrous cabinet decisions seem to have arisen as much from lack of discussion as from positive folly. The contemptible Immigration Bill of 1961, which fell between the two stools of the Home Office and Colonial Office, at a time when the Colonial Office was changing hands, happened more as a gradual concession to right-wing pressure than as a carefully thought-out cabinet decision. The slowness to come to terms with the Common Market in 1959 and 1960 was not least because few ministers had time to think about it. The one technically most concerned with it, Reginald Maudling, was not very interested, and the 'Europeans' in cabinet, such as Sandys and Heath, were too busy with their own departments: and it was left to the Prime Minister, as we shall note later, to come slowly towards the Common Market idea, and push the cabinet into it.

The underlying principle of the cabinet, as of all the committees which spread out from it, is that of 'collective responsibility': and this apparent solidarity distinguishes the British government, for instance, from the American—in spite of the fact that American ministers are not elected representatives. 'While in Britain cabinet ministers must support a common policy', wrote Lord Attlee, 'in America these subordinates of the chief executive are apt to speak with a diversity of voices.' From the outside, the appearance of unanimity, with the help of rigid cabinet secrecy, is fairly well kept up. But how collective the responsibility really is, is very doubtful. As ministers become more absorbed in their departments, fighting each other for money, the dividing line between their individual departmental responsibility and their collective governmental responsibility becomes very blurred. Sir Ivor Jennings, the constitutional authority, believes that, as departments become more complex and cabinets busier, so the scope for individual ministers within their departments inevitably becomes greater; and a new minister can impose a new policy without much cabinet consultation: he has observed how they nowadays refer less to 'Her Majesty's Government' in their speeches, and more to 'I'. When Iain Macleod took over the Colonial Office from Alan Lennox-Boyd in 1959, although the cabinet had in the meantime become more aware of the change in Africa, a good deal of the change of policy was certainly due to the change of man. Likewise when Enoch Powell took over the Ministry of Health in 1960—outside the cabinet—he was able to make drastic doctrinal changes without much trouble. The pressure of time in the cabinet makes it easier for ministers to run their departments without interference: 'It's probably true that as the civil service becomes more complex,' said one minister, 'so ministers become more independent: on the whole the cabinet's prejudice is to let the minister do what he wants with his department.' Many of the ministers are running departments with investments much bigger and more complex than any private company: and for most of their time they are managing directors absorbed in their separate business, which we will see in later chapters.

But while ministers are left more to themselves, their areas of business have overlapped more and more: and the government has become increasingly involved in investment and planning on a national scale. It is difficult, whatever your political doctrine, to think about railways without also thinking about airlines, fuel and industrial growth: and the government finds itself no longer running a group of separate businesses, but one large investment company in which one business affects all the others. With the current new wave of planning and attempts at wage restraints, this necessity becomes more apparent: and government requires not a group of separate managing directors, meeting to discuss disagreements, but a single board of directors, with time to make plans for the future. But the ministers are so pressed with work and absorbed in departments, that the opportunities for correlation are few. Gordon Walker remarked how, in the Labour Government, the pressure of meetings set 'a strict upper limit upon the extent of democratic planning.' A recent dramatic example of the lack of co-ordination emerged in November, 1961, when the Ministry of Power permitted a pay increase for electricity workers just at a time when the Treasury were urging the pay 'pause'. As Lord Plowden tactfully put it, in his report on government expenditure: 'There should be an improvement in arrangements to enable ministers to discharge their collective responsibility for the oversight of public expenditure as a whole.'[1] In other words, the cabinet must try to work together.

At a time when Britain needs more than ever before a governing committee with time to plan and look ahead, the cabinet is caught between the exacting treadmills of parliament and departments. Most ministers—not least the Prime Minister—agree that the system is strained, and that the jobs of managing director, parliamentarian and cabinet minister are becoming more incompatible: but what the outcome will be is very uncertain. There may be more Marpleses, who run their departments without much care for parliament, or more Millses, to serve as ministers of thought: there may even be businessmen brought straight into the government on the American pattern, and made Life Peers to give them a seat in the Lords. But whatever happens, it seems that the buckle is being pulled apart, and that the traditional system of combining parliamentary accountability with collective responsibility is splitting at the centre.

Cmd. 1432 of 1961. p. 12.

10

LAW

> For my part I must own that I wish the country to be governed by law, but not by lawyers.
>
> *Edmund Burke.*

> The characteristic conservatism of lawyers—a conservatism which is not so much self-interested as ill-informed.
>
> *Sir Alexander Carr-Saunders*[1]

Two further traditional powers are interlocked with the history of Britain—the Law and the Church. Both take a large place in pageantry; judges and bishops sit in the House of Lords, join in processions, are honoured with ancient titles and are received by the Queen. Both reached a climax of fame and splendour in Victorian times. Both judges and bishops have been intensely conservative and resistant to change—as their votes in the House of Lords, from the Reform Bill onwards, showed. Many have become diverted by the workings of their profession, rather than its ultimate ends, and have found themselves increasingly out of touch with the movements of contemporary Britain. In both professions there is a loving attachment to the phrase, 'It may seem odd to you, but it works'.

The Law is the most striking example of a profession which has become trapped in its conservatism and mystique. Its proud independence and remoteness have given it magnificent strength as a bastion of liberty and justice; but have also made it very unsusceptible to pressures of change. The Victorian prestige of the law is expressed in the Royal Courts of Justice, built in 1880 by the architect G. E. Street, when the legal profession was at its height. A broad doorway leads into a fake-medieval hall, like a stripped cathedral, adorned with big black-letter notices announcing 'Lord Chief Justice's Court', or 'Wash and Brush Up'. Ordinary dark-suited men carrying red bags walk into a room by the entrance, and emerge a few minutes later solemnly wearing horse-hair wigs and flowing gowns.

The 1880s were the heyday of private property: lawyers were

[1] *The Professions*, 1933. p. 53–4.

the advisers and protectors of the rich men's estates and the law courts were their battleground. And, with the rush of reforming legislation between 1830 and 1880, the great Victorian lawyers had been interlocked with politics: they could argue in court in the morning, and in parliament in the afternoon. But in the past eighty years the pattern of the rest of the country has changed, and left the lawyers behind. Rich individuals have been replaced by the big business corporations, trade unions, insurance companies and civil service departments, and the immense new area of state administration has crept up on the old powers of the law. Eighty per cent of the common law cases fought in the courts are now about compensation for accidents—factories and motor-cars —usually fought by one institution against another, for instance, a trade union against an insurance company. The joint-stock companies do not have the same need of lawyers as rich men had: they use lawyers in time of trouble, like doctors, rather than as close advisers. The whole territory of taxation, which had enveloped both corporations and individuals, has been largely neglected by lawyers (who proverbially have never been good at sums) and annexed by the new profession of accountants.[1] There is still no part of a lawyer's examination which requires him to be able to read a balance sheet.

While lawyers have gone on preparing title deeds in Victorian offices, filled with black tin boxes and stiff paper, a whole new world has grown up outside them. While accountants have multiplied, the number of lawyers has fallen in sixty years from about one in 1,400 to one in 2,000, and there are now three times as many accountants as lawyers. The change has worried many attorneys. 'We must retain in a world of changing customs and changing values our position as men of affairs,' wrote Sir Leslie Peppiatt, a recent President of the Law Society: 'men (and women, too) to whom our clients will turn for help in their problems. Do not let us force them to seek this help from their accountants or bankers.' Recently there have been signs of an attempt by the law to make itself more attractive to the public, on whom ultimately it depends.

British lawyers do not have the same influence as their American counterparts, who play an important rôle in big business decisions. A few eminent British barristers like Lord Shawcross and Lord Monckton have left the bar for business, but practising barristers are not allowed to hold working directorships. The American

[1] *See* Chapter 29.

lawyers, sometimes at the cost of professional standards, have become much more adaptable, embracing the world of tax and finance, and often taking over the running of companies.

Nor do the British courts have the same obvious impact as in countries with a written constitution, and a court to interpret it (though ironically it is Britain which has *exported* more written constitutions than any country). The Supreme Court of America can visibly affect the lives of ordinary men, and can openly contradict the government: the names of its nine members are constantly in the headlines. But the decisions of British courts, gradually establishing precedents and rights, do not challenge the government; and few ordinary people know the names of the nine Law Lords. Compared to America or the Continent, the Law in Britain is less closely related to society and its problems. At the time of Blackstone's commentaries—in 1787—the Law was regarded as revealing the pattern of society, and lawyers the great interpreters and prophets.[1] Today, it is the economists and the historians who interpret society: while the lawyers—at least in the public's view—are relegated to the position of long-stop rather than wicket-keeper.

The conservatism of English lawyers is reinforced by their strict division into solicitors and barristers—found only in South Africa, New South Wales and Great Britain. Only solicitors are allowed to deal directly with the public. There are 17,000 of them and they perform all the routine business: but when they have to take a case to the central courts, they must employ a barrister to plead—much as a GP employs a specialist to operate. The two sides—the wigged and the unwigged—are kept severely apart: solicitors cannot have lunch in the barristers' Inns of Court, and barristers must never be seen at the solicitors' Law Society.

The system has its advantages. For solicitors it is a special form of subcontracting which often makes for lower total costs. It provides a group of specialists, none tied to a particular firm, all individualists and carrying only minimal overheads, all skilled in pleading and so providing a fairly smooth system of trial. But the division, and the traditions that have grown round it, have produced a web of archaic restrictive practices designed unashamedly to maintain the employment of lawyers. A client, having engaged a barrister, cannot even talk to him except in the presence of his solicitor: in court, he has to employ both solicitor

[1] *See* Asa Briggs: *The Age of Improvement*, 1959, p. 89.

and barrister together. If a client wants to employ a barrister on another circuit, he has to pay both that barrister *and* a special 'circuit fee' of fifty guineas. If a client wants to employ a Queen's Counsel or senior barrister, he must also employ—at two-thirds the QC's fee—a junior barrister as well. The bar often seems designed more to maintain full employment for lawyers than to meet the needs of clients. But if it wasn't that the public needed them there would be no lawyers.

SOLICITORS

The old 'family solicitor' was designed as the adviser to prosperous middle-class clients: he worked in an office which closely resembled a Victorian gentleman's study, and he regarded himself strictly as a legal adviser as a doctor was a medical adviser: he shrunk, like a good professional man, from giving general opinions. But with the complexities of modern business affairs, people—both companies and individuals—look more and more for opinions: they need not merely an occasional adviser, but an agent, to take charge of their affairs, and to advise on policy as well as procedure. 'It is because he is rarely qualified to give such policy advice', wrote Professor L. C. B. Gower of London University, 'that the lawyer is losing more and more work to the accountant and the banker'.[1]

A new kind of lawyer's office is emerging. A third of the solicitors are still practising alone: but large partnerships—up to the maximum of nineteen partners allowed by law—have grown up to deal with a specialist age. Four large ones dominate the City of London, with stately Dickensian titles which—like the big auditors or bankers—have become stamps of respectability. They are, in order of size:

> Slaughter and May
> Linklater and Paines
> Freshfields
> Allen and Overy

The new kind of lawyer is a more adaptable and positive person: he is staking his claim in the new corporate world, and prepared to deal with any business, including tax, pensions and hire purchase, that his client might have. The new rôle is reflected in the Law Society—the great stone building in Chancery Lane, which serves as a solicitors' lunch-club and their professional

[1] Quoted by Michael Birks: *Gentlemen of the Law*, 1960, p. 281.

headquarters. The Law Society prides itself on go-ahead methods, and gradually it is coaxing its members into more up-to-date habits, with the help of efficiency experts, a cinema room, a photo-copying machine, and a large information service.

In the new situation, solicitors often have more scope than barristers. They are more adaptable, and they often make more money: and able barristers now often change over to being solicitors—instead of the other way round. Solicitors are far better educated than they were: in 1922 17 per cent were graduates; in 1960, 60 per cent.[1] But solicitors remain the 'junior branch of the profession': most of the mystique and prestige of the law settles on barristers, only a barrister can reach the top of the profession —a judgeship.

BARRISTERS

There are only about 1,900 practising barristers—only one-ninth of the solicitors—and they have diminished by 75 in the past seven years:[2] the whole profession could be shipped off on one voyage of the *Queen Mary*. Half the barristers in Britain work in an area of London half-a-mile across, in one of the four Inns of Court. There they enjoy a remote life of their own. At lunch they sit at long wooden benches in big hammer beam halls, like the halls of a public school or an Oxbridge college. They work, in groups of six or more in 'chambers', approached by stone steps, with their names proclaimed in elegant eighteenth-century lettering. The Inns have their own elaborate snobberies and peck-order. The oldest and richest is the Inner Temple, alongside a round Saxon church, which has produced the largest number of judges. Next to it, the Middle Temple is less exclusive, though frequently visited by the Queen Mother. Across the road, Lincoln's Inn is almost entirely frequented by Chancery lawyers: while Gray's Inn, the newest of them, is known for its numbers of provincial barristers.

The Inns, like Oxbridge colleges, have very large powers: they are responsible for admissions and discipline, and have refused to delegate real power to the Bar Council. They are a 'survival of medieval republican oligarchy, the last to be found in Europe'.[3] They have large endowments in land, but no one knows the extent of their wealth since, unlike most institutions, they are exempted from publishing their accounts. They are ruled by Benchers—a

[1] *The Times*, November 14, 1961.
[2] Though in 1961 there was a slight increase of 16.
[3] Sir Frederick Pollock: *Essays in the Law*, 1922.

self-perpetuating group of senior lawyers, who sit at a high table at one end of the hall, and run the Inn: to be elected a Bencher brings a barrister into the heart of the small society of the Bar. The Benchers are among the most die-hard and self-centred groups in the country, and the Inns of Court find it difficult to come to terms with each other, let alone with the public. Even the Attorney-General, Sir Reginald Manningham-Buller, after trying to reform legal education to allow interchange between barristers and solicitors, remarked on 'the archaic and time-wasting procedure' of consulting the Inns: 'there seems in the circumstances little prospect of getting the agreement of all four Inns in the near future to a proposal which the Bar Council on behalf of the Bar has advocated since 1907'.[1] The Inns are among the most absurd anachronisms in Britain, and their selfishness has done real harm: for instance, their reluctance to make decent arrangements for colonial students, who stream into the Bar[2] has contributed to the embittered and anti-British attitudes of many African and Indian barristers.

But the most striking characteristic of barristers is not so much their corporate life, as their loneliness. In an age of organisation men they remain individuals—which gives to the profession both its charm and its hazards. By their own decree, barristers cannot, as doctors or solicitors do, share their risks with anyone else. If they make money, they make it only for themselves, and if they fall ill they have no one to take their place. Barristers have the self-indulgent and idiosyncratic appearance of men who work by themselves, with none of the sameness of bureaucrats. They include a high proportion of bachelors or half-bachelors, and a surprising proportion of private incomes: barristers are apt to be shambling, bulging figures, looking rather obsolete in their penguin outfits, and (as one of them put it) the wrong shape for the twentieth century.

Living, as some of them do, a quarter of their life in the court-room, they have an odd mixture of scholarship and showmanship. There is an old fellow-feeling between the Bar and the stage, and at the Garrick Club, which they share, it is hard to tell them apart. Sir Patrick Hastings had only two interests—the Law and acting—and Lord Devlin, one of the present Law Lords, has a brother who is an equally distinguished actor. But in the past thirty years the barristers have had to come to terms with a more humdrum age,

[1] *The Times*, July 11, 1961.
[2] *See* Lord Denning's Report of January, 1961.

and histrionics have been at a discount. They are more likely to be recounting the details of a factory accident to a sceptical judge, than passionately urging the virtues of a client to a weeping jury. The decline of juries has discouraged acting, and full-throated advocates have found themselves without their audience. In 1933 36 per cent of common law cases were tried by jury: today less than 3 per cent have juries.

Like the army or the air force, the Bar has had much of the glamour taken out of it—and some of its profits too. Today there are perhaps ten barristers earning over £20,000; but the average earnings of the practising barrister are said to be only £1,000 a year, though recently the increase of legal aid has revived the profession. Taxation has made the Bar less popular, and judgeships more desirable. Today, a judge's salary of £8,000 with pension is worth more than most successful barristers' practices, and ambitious young barristers are much more inclined to look to the bench as their ultimate aim.

JUDGES

There is a certain discrepancy between the public picture of judges, influenced by their wigs and majesty, as men of acknowledged wisdom, picked from a very competitive profession—and the actual situation. In fact the judges as a whole are not a spectacular *élite*. Out of fewer than 2,000 barristers, 76 judges are appointed, together with 67 county court judges—a ratio of about fifteen barristers to one judge: and barristers themselves are a much less carefully selected profession than, for instance, administrative civil servants. Allowing for the fair proportion of impossible barristers, and a large number who don't want to be judges or who go into parliament or business, it is not too difficult for a hardworking man to be some kind of judge by the age of fifty. Every profession likes to appear more competitive than it is; but judges, who are thicker on the ground than admirals or bishops, have been unusually successful. While the senior judges are mostly men of exceptional intellect, the inflation among junior ones, and the resulting quality, has caused some criticism, even from *The Times*[1]: and the fact that a judge must be chosen from the ranks of barristers, at a time when many solicitors are more able, has been repeatedly criticised. The appointment of judges has never had the same radical reorganisation which the civil service underwent in the 1870's.

[1] *The Times*, November 2, 1961.

Nor do judges necessarily have a wide experience to furnish their wisdom: while they give their views on morals, criminology and politics, their actual experience outside the law is usually small. They rarely visit prisons to which they sentence criminals: their own lives revolve round medieval institutions: and their preoccupation has been with the interpretation of the law, rather than its making. As Lord Devlin has said:

> The judges of England have rarely been original thinkers or great jurists. Many have been craftsmen rather than creators. They have needed the stuff of morals to be supplied to them so that out of it they could fashion the law.[1]

More than any other group, judges are detached from everyday life. For two hundred and twenty-five days in the year, they sit in their wigs from 10.30 to 4.15, listening to barristers arguing abstruse points of law. Their presence is deliberately surrounded with pomp, to emphasise the majesty of the law, and even in their private lives they are expected to remain fairly remote. Judges are not seen in pubs and cafés: their usual habitat is their cavernous office in the Law Courts, the high table of an Inn of Court, the Reform, the Garrick or the Oxford and Cambridge, a house in the country and a London flat. Much more than American or continental judges the British bench has grown up detached from society and social developments. They have regarded the new sciences of psychology and sociology with scepticism and many judges have prided themselves on their ignorance of everyday life. (Before the war the comedian George Robey was once cross-examined by Sir Patrick Hastings, in front of Mr. Justice Darling: 'Who *is* Mr. Robey?' asked Darling. Sir Patrick quickly replied: 'The Darling of the Music Halls, My Lord.')

Judges are not as dispassionate as they appear: two have even been divorced, three have sat as members of parliament, and several have strong and known political views. But some young barristers feel that their pomp is excessive—making trials increasingly unrealistic and deferential—and complain that the majesty of the law becomes muddled with the majesty of the judges. I asked Lord Devlin about this: 'I don't think it's very serious,' he said: 'of course judges are bound to be a bit behind the times: you can't expect men with an average age of sixty to be as up-to-date as undergraduates. But I don't think the majesty of the law gets in the way of justice.'

[1] Quoted by Ludovic Kennedy: 'The Legal Barbarians'. *Spectator*, September 15, 1961.

But judges have always enjoyed airing their views on general matters, with all the authority of their bench. Sir James Cassels, who retired in 1961, was one of the wittiest: he once described the House of Commons as 'six hundred men all thinking a great deal of themselves and very little of each other'. Sir Charles Harman, with his moustache and eyeglass, is well known for a fund of classical knowledge and his opinion that 'outside London the bath is still the exception, not the rule'. The most Victorian judge is the seventy-nine-year-old Sir Malcom Hilbery, who walks to court in a silk hat and morning coat: he persistently advocates more flogging, and objects to the use of new-fangled words like bus ('I deprecate the use of these ordinary, perhaps slang phrases' —1952). Could judges hold forth with such confidence if they were not shrouded with a wig and robes?

Judges come from a small and conservative section of the community—and their section is not growing much larger. Of the forty-two judges who list their education in *Who's Who*, seven came from Christ Church, Oxford, six from Trinity, Cambridge, and only one from a Redbrick university. Winchester produced five, Rugby four, Eton three: eleven came from grammar schools. Judges, like barristers, have become less eccentric; and shouting judges, sarcastic judges, sleeping judges, bullying judges are dwindling. Since 1959 parliament has fixed an age limit for new judges of seventy-five. 'Judges talk less nowadays, and listen more,' Lord Devlin said to me: 'they don't often doze off. Manners are much better than they used to be, on both sides.'

The change in the manners of judges is typified by the Lord Chief Justice of England, Lord Parker of Waddington. He is head of the Queen's Bench Division, which deals with all common law and criminal cases. He can sit in any court, from the Queen's Bench to the House of Lords: he can decide which judge hears which case, he can make bold public statements, and he has the ear of the Government. But most days he can be seen in his own large green room in the Law Courts, with brass chandeliers and velvet curtains, sitting with two of his colleagues in red robes and flapping white tabs, in front of a carved lion and unicorn.

Lord Parker is in keeping with the sequestered tradition of the British Law. He is the son of a famous judge (he wears his father's old wig), took a double first in science at Cambridge, and has a nephew who is a QC. He began as a barrister for commercial cases, became a Treasury counsel and was appointed a judge at the age of fifty: he became Lord Chief Justice in 1958. He belongs to the non-histrionic school of judges, in contrast to his opinionated predecessor, Lord Goddard. Parker is unobtrusive and patient: he has not, as Goddard did, made known his political views, and he belongs to a more single-minded generation. He farms in the country, and is an expert on the genetics of cattle. When he was elevated, it was assumed that he would be much more lenient than his predecessor, and scores of convicted men appealed to his court, hoping for diminished sentences. But Parker soon dashed these hopes. He embarked on a tour of America in which he strongly advocated flogging, and back in London made speeches urging sterner sentences: he astonished the Bar by passing a record sentence of 42 years on George Blake, convicted of spying. And when the flood of appeals came up to him, he and his colleagues later began actually *increasing* the sentences.

The progress of a judge is circuitous, and marked by an archaic confusion of titles. Every judge must begin as a barrister: after ten years or more he may become a Queen's Counsel, known as John Smith, QC, entitled to higher fees and the assistance of a junior. From there he may be appointed one of the 67 county court judges, when he will become known as Judge Smith, with a salary of £4,400 a year. Alternatively, a QC may be chosen for the High Court, where he becomes known as 'The Hon. Mr. Justice Smith', or 'Smith, J.', or 'Sir John Smith' (acquiring a knighthood automatically), and sits in red robes, earning £8,000 a year. From there he may become one of eleven judges in the Appeal Court, where he will wear black robes, become a privy councillor, and be known (although he is not a Lord) as 'Lord Justice Smith', 'Smith, L. J.', or 'the Right Honourable Sir John Smith'. Finally, he may become one of the nine Law Lords, who are life peers, sitting in the House of Lords, earning £9,000 a year, and known as 'the Right Honourable Lord Smith'.

Each court has a different atmosphere: as Lord Asquith of Bishopstone described it: 'A trial judge should be quick, courteous and wrong. That is not to say that the Court of Appeal should be slow, rude and right, for that would be usurping the function of the House of Lords.'[1]

The Law Lords are the supreme judiciary of Great Britain: (the Scottish courts have a separate hierarchy of judges, but one

[1] Quoted in *Law as Literature*, edited by Louis Blom Cooper, 1961.

or two Scots judges sit in the House of Lords.) They are a very homogeneous group, and they can often be seen lunching together at a special table at the House of Lords. Of the nine English ones no fewer than three went to New College, Oxford; none of them are under sixty, but their excessive questioning can easily demoralise barristers. Several have made a name in other spheres, as Government sages, including Lord Radcliffe, who wrote a constitution for Cyprus and analysed the Bank of England, and Lord Devlin, who wrote a devastating report on Nyasaland in 1959. Their sittings are undramatic and impressive; a group of five men, not in wigs and robes but in plain grey suits, sit in the chamber of the House, listening to the intricate arguments of counsel, which have by now reached a rarified plane. They have about forty appeals a year, sitting a hundred days.

What are the qualities of a successful judge? 'Ability isn't the most important thing,' Lord Devlin told me: 'In most cases the facts aren't really very difficult to get at: no, the most important thing for a judge is—curiously enough—judgment. It's not so very different from the qualities of a successful businessman or civil servant. I'm always struck by how alike men in high positions seem to be. It's rather like seeing a lot of different parts of the stage, and finding that they're all Gerald du Maurier in the end.'

THE LORD CHANCELLOR

At the top of the intricate legal pyramid is the ancient and confusing position of Lord High Chancellor. For the Lord Chancellor (as usually abbreviated) combines three quite separate functions: he is the head of the legal profession and senior judge—selecting judges, Queen's Counsel, the 16,000 Justices of the Peace, and 35,000 members of tribunals, and presiding (if he wishes) over the hearings of the Law Lords. He is also Speaker of the House of Lords, sitting on the Woolsack. He is also a member of the cabinet, and the government's chief legal adviser. He is the only man who combines the powers of the cabinet, the judiciary and the executive: he helps to make the laws, to carry them out, and to interpret them.[1] His post is the most ancient one in the government, centuries older than the prime minister's, dating back to the medieval court, when the Lord Chancellor was the 'Keeper of the King's Conscience': and this seniority is still reflected by his salary of £12,000 a year, the highest in the

[1] The negation of Montesquieu's theory of the separation of powers.

government and £2,000 more than the prime minister's: at formal dinners or royal processions he walks in front of the prime minister. He lives in a Victorian house inside the Palace of Westminster, above a special 'Lord Chancellor's Courtyard' adjoining the House of Lords, and he works in a long high room overlooking the Thames, with heavy Gothic lamps hanging from the ceiling, and a tapestry at one end. In these surroundings it is a surprise to find an amiable Scotsman in a dark grey suit, more like a politician than a judge, discussing frankly the problems of his job.

The career of David Maxwell Fyfe, first Viscount Kilmuir, is typical of the old interweaving of law with politics. Educated at Edinburgh and Balliol, he practised as a barrister in Liverpool with two other political lawyers, Selwyn Lloyd and Hartley Shawcross, and married a Liverpool girl—the sister of the actor Rex Harrison. With Lloyd and Shawcross, he moved to London, and again shared their chambers. He became an MP and during the war was appointed Solicitor-General—the junior of the government's three law officers. After the war he was tireless in Conservative party affairs, producing among other things the 'Maxwell Fyfe Report'[1] on the organisation of the Tory party. He became Home Secretary in the 1951 Government, and three years later Lord Chancellor. He has described how he reached the job: 'You remember in musical chairs that two things had to coincide, the stopping of the music and being opposite a chair. For those who want office, the office must be vacated and the candidate must be ripe. For the lucky law officer of the Crown, the chair was the Woolsack which was empty when the political music stopped.'[2]

'The Lord Chancellor's main job,' Kilmuir told me, 'is to be responsible for seeing that the machinery of law and administration is in working order. Because he's well placed to do this, public opinion accepts the anomaly of his three different powers. The rest of the cabinet looks to the Lord Chancellor to see that criticisms of the law are not unheeded: that justice is neither denied nor delayed; and that the law is moulded to the changing needs of society'.

'I've tried to improve the law on two main principles. The first is that the courts must meet the public need: the one basis of democracy, in the end, is that a man can say with confidence either

[1] *See* page 78.
[2] *See* The Lawyer-Statesman: speech reprinted in the American Bar Association Journal, November, 1954.

that "I'll sue you" or "Sue me and be damned"—the machinery of the law must make this possible. The second is that the law must be within easy reach of everyone. There's an old jibe that "The Courts of Justice, like the Ritz Hotel, are open to rich and poor alike": I've tried to get rid of that jibe and to see that legal aid is extended to all the regular courts.

'The law has to protect the individual in the modern state. Often the state *must* infringe the rights of individuals, for good causes like building schools or roads. But the individual must have a fair opportunity of stating his objection, and fair compensation. Inevitably there's a conflict between the interest of the state and the interest of private property: and the state has to be able to act with reasonable speed. In 1958 we set up a council as a watchdog on tribunals. But there's still much to be improved, and I'm earnestly seeking further improvements.'

THE LAW AND POLITICS

The House of Commons doesn't like lawyers.
Hazlitt.

Lord Kilmuir told me how, when he first came to the House of Commons, Sir John Simon said to him: 'Remember that you have just been elected to the one legislative assembly in the world where lawyers as such are not popular. You will be hailed with almost perennial suspicion as the "Honourable and Learned Member".' Lawyers have excelled in politics, but not often reached the peak. The last career barrister to become prime minister was Asquith: the last (and only) solicitor was Lloyd George. The only law officer who ever became prime minister was Spencer Perceval in 1809, and he was shot dead two years later.

But nevertheless lawyers—more than any other profession—have gravitated to politics, and barristers make up a sixth of the House of Commons. For successful barristers politics has been a natural climax; and they have been able to combine a lucrative practice with a successful political career: the careers helped each other, and QCs and judges in the past have been often chosen for partly political reasons.

It is doubtful whether this close connection can continue. Both careers are more specialised and professional: to maintain a successful bar practice while sitting on the back benches is much more difficult, and first-class barristers are more inclined to keep out of parliament: 'All of us' said one QC, 'are much more in grooves than we were'. This grooviness will make it difficult to find future Lord Chancellors who can be both politicians and judges, and this ancient intertwined job may have to be disentangled.

But while the Law has become a much more self-contained profession, split off from politics, it still likes to cling to its old authority and prestige, rather than to interest itself in the exciting new developments of society. The Law, more than any other profession, is imprisoned in its own myths and shibboleths, and while the benchers preserve their traditions, and the solicitors tie up their thick paper in pink tape, their protected world has become increasingly irrelevant to the great corporate world outside.

11

CHURCHES

Kenneth Harris: Can the Church change the economic order?

Dr Coggan: It can always be a gadfly in the conscience of those who make the economic order, and I think that is its main function.[1]

The trouble with the Church of England is that in its old age it's got religion.

Anon.

LIKE the Law, the Church is part of the ancient fabric of the country. It is not within the scope of this book, which is concerned with temporal powers, to examine the character of the Churches, or to discuss the decline of religion. Yet the Churches of England and Scotland, since their establishment, have been too intertwined with the State to be left out, and the minorities have helped to mould the social structure of the country. In the course of its involvement, the Anglican Church, like the Law, has often been distracted by means rather than ends: its leaders have often become more interested in their archaic trappings than in their contemporary functions; and the public fame of the Archbishop reaches its climax in the astonishing medieval ceremony of the Coronation. The more obvious oddities, such as the appointments of bishops, the presenting of livings and the parochial system are justified with the same kind of argument 'it's odd but it works' which might be heard in the Inns of Court. The fact that the system is of no value unless it builds up the religious life of the country may be forgotten, as barristers are apt to forget that their sole justification is to serve the ends of justice.

LAMBETH

Every ten years, three hundred bishops of the Anglican Churches converge on London for the Lambeth Conference, not only from Britain, but from all over the world. At the opening, they gather at a garden party at Lambeth Palace to meet their spiritual head,

[1] 'Three Archbishops', ATV June 11, 1961.

the Archbishop of Canterbury. Wandering by the trees and marquees in their purple robes and gaiters, they present a magnificent spectacle. There are bishops from Korea, South Western Brazil, Ceylon, Japan, and even from Wales. There are Oriental bishops with exotic crosses; there is an Arab bishop, from Jordan and Syria; and there are ninety American bishops—outnumbering the English by two to one—looking more like businessmen. (There is even an American, Bishop Bayne, on the staff at Lambeth.) They all possess the same bonhomie, rubbing their palms together, reminiscing and stretching out welcoming hands. To the splendour of their appearance is added the splendour of their names, which give a Damon Runyon sound to them—Donald the Arctic, Edward Barbados, Kenneth Matabeleland, Victor Rangoon. They enjoy the extravagance and welcome each other across the lawn: 'Good Heavens, here comes Bombay!'

Most of the overseas bishops have only a loose relationship with the English Church: Canterbury is given special spiritual prestige, but exercises no authority. The six bishops in Wales and the seven bishops in Scotland have their own jurisdiction and autonomy. Out of the three hundred bishops, only forty-three are in England, under the jurisdiction of the Archbishops of Canterbury and York; and it is they who form the core of that puzzling institution, the Established Church of England.

The extraordinary origins of the Anglican Church still set its character and determine its relations with the State—ever since the break with Rome in 1534, when Henry VIII assumed the title of 'Supreme Head of the Church of England'. In theory, the Church exchanged its independence for a close moral influence on the sovereign and the government—including twenty-six seats for bishops in the House of Lords and the right of the Archbishop to crown the sovereign. It has never exerted a radical influence. Throughout the eighteenth and nineteenth centuries, it remained closely identified with the aristocracy and Conservatism. The Anglican Church supported the persecution of dissenting Churches and Roman Catholics: only since 1829 have Catholic priests been allowed to live within five miles of towns, and only since 1871 have dissenters been allowed to teach at Oxford and Cambridge. The sovereign and the lord chancellor must both be Anglicans, but the prime minister can now be of any religion: Lloyd George was a Welsh dissenter, Ramsay MacDonald and Campbell-Bannerman were both Scottish Presbyterians, and Neville Chamberlain was a Unitarian. It is the prime minister, as adviser to the sovereign, who

appoints the bishops[1], (with the help of a special patronage secretary at 10, Downing Street, sometimes known as the 'bishop-
spotter').

The Church of England is not actually *owned* or subsidised by
the State. Its income comes (apart from the offerings of the
faithful) from its own land and capital—though the Ecclesiastical
Commissioners who administer it are appointed by the Crown.
The Church is one of the biggest proprietors in the country: their
total assets are more than £230 million—a third of ICI's—providing an income of over £16 million a year: they own 223,000
acres of land, third only to the Forestry Commission and the
Crown. The money is looked after by a team of three commissioners, headed by Sir Malcolm Trustram Eve, the same man who
handles the crown lands. Over half their assets (£128 million)
are now in stock exchange securities, and since 1948 they have
moved most of that out of government stock into industrial
shares, to the delight of the stock exchange. They have also
co-operated with Jack Cotton, Charles Clore and other property
financiers to develop their more valuable properties in the centre
of cities; but the Commissioners still refuse to invest in drink,
gambling or armaments.

BISHOPS

The splendour and wealth of bishops has diminished in the past
fifty years. In the nineteenth century the discrepancy between
the bench and the clergy was grotesque. In 1906 the average
income of a parson was about £150, while the Archbishop of
Canterbury had £15,000 a year. The incomes of bishops and deans
are among the very few which have *not* gone up over the past
century, as this table suggests:

	1871	1954
Permanent Secretary, Board of Trade	£1,500	£4,500
Town Clerk, Liverpool	£2,000	£5,000
Professor of Moral Philosophy, Edinburgh	£502	£2,100
Dean of Durham	£3,000	£3,000[2]

Most of the forty-three bishops today earn £2,500 or less—

---

[1] Unless he is a Roman Catholic: but there has not yet been a Catholic premier.
[2] Abridged from R. K. Kelsall: *Higher Civil Servants in Britain.* 1955. p. 183.

together with a house and garden (the total upkeep of bishops' gardens cost £28,000 p.a.). The Archbishop's salary is £7,500 — together with two fine houses in London and Canterbury: the first Archbishop Temple, at the end of the nineteenth century, sold the country estate of the Archbishop of Canterbury, believing it wrong for the primate to be associated with landed wealth.

The bishops in England are much more unobtrusive than they were: they inhabit their antique palaces without pomp or splendour, and often without gaiters. They are still addressed as 'My Lord', and archbishops, like dukes, are called 'Your Grace': but they come from the same kind of Oxbridge stock as judges or top civil servants, and nowadays a good deal of their time, like permanent secretaries', is spent in committees. Three-quarters of the bishops went to public schools, and all but three went to Oxford and Cambridge, mostly Cambridge: two of the others were at Trinity College, Dublin. Half the bishops are sons of clergymen, only one is the son of a bishop, and only one is an old Etonian. Eight have been Oxford or Cambridge dons. But there is still a muscular tradition: Lichfield, Gloucester and Chester all rowed in their university boat, Exeter played hockey for the West of England, Portsmouth was a Rugger blue, and Norwich was an explorer-geologist in Iceland and the Antarctic.

Among theologians probably the most eminent bishop is Robert Mortimer, Bishop of Exeter, a handsome grey-haired former Regius Professor at Oxford, who is the Church's main authority on gambling, sex and moral problems. The most prominent administrator is Robert Stopford of London, a lively, extrovert man with bushy eyebrows, who organised the 1958 Lambeth Conference; he has been a housemaster at Oundle School, Chaplain to the Queen and is keen on amateur theatricals. Most bishops keep out of politics, but a few display opinions, including William Manchester, a former civil servant from Northern Ireland, who talks often against the H-bomb and capital punishment, and several show a weakness for showmanship: the bearded Bishop of Birmingham, for instance, has a car called SOB 1. The most politically voluble is Mervyn Southwark, an elegant bachelor well-known for left-wing views and dramatic sermons, who has written articles in the *Evening Standard* (like Dean Inge, 'from being a pillar of the Church, he became a column in the Standard'). He seems to have made the classic episcopal transformation from poacher to gamekeeper.

On most contemporary political issues, including capital

punishment, the bishops have till recently been divided. At the time of Suez Bishop Mortimer of Exeter and Bishop Harland of Durham wrote to *The Times* in defence of the Government; Bell of Chichester, Greer of Manchester and Martin of Liverpool attacked the invasion; Ramsey said in the Lords that a Christian could equally conscientiously support or reject the Suez policy. But Dr Fisher, then Archbishop of Canterbury, though he made an ambiguous speech in the Lords, went to Downing Street to express his concern.

One man who combines learning with administration is Donald Coggan, Archbishop of York. He was the son of a business-man, and after leaving Oxford he became a don, a curate, and later Professor of the New Testament in Toronto. He is an evangelical bishop, and is particularly concerned with preaching and the Bible. Known as a friendly, unpompous man, he is also a skilful mimic—mimicry and story-telling are favourite ecclesiastical pastimes—and one of his favourite imitations is of the Archbishop of Canterbury. Christina Foyle—who runs the Foyle's literary luncheons—is a connoisseur of speeches, and has reported that bishops make the wittiest speeches but lawyers make the best ones.

But some of the most testing bishoprics are abroad, in the East and Africa—where Christianity is on the way out. One of the most dynamic is Joost de Blank, Archbishop of Cape Town, a short, bald tycoon, working tirelessly in a large house in the Cape. As the head of the Anglican Church in South Africa he has been in the midst of the racial conflict. Some thought he might have succeeded Dr Fisher as Archbishop of Canterbury.

One bishop, more than any other, has become associated with politics—though more by accident than design: he is Trevor Huddleston, Bishop of Masasi in Tanganyika. Huddleston's tall and gentle presence has made a unique mark on Africa. Though still regarded as a political priest, he is primarily a pastor, impelled by a warm, simple approach to people: and only reluctantly did he become involved in politics. He came from a distinguished Anglo-Catholic family, and after Oxford entered the monastery at Mirfield—a stark old mill-owner's mansion, with a stone chapel on top of a grey hill in Yorkshire. From there he was sent out to Johannesburg and over twelve years became steadily more deeply involved in African rights, at a time when the Anglican Church was slow to commit itself. 'It has been the teaching of the Church through the centuries,' he said at the time of the Defiance Campaign in 1953, 'that when government degenerates into tyranny, laws cease to be binding on its subjects.' He was recalled from South Africa by his Superior in 1955, spent five years in Mirfield and London, and then, to his relief and delight, was appointed Bishop in Tanganyika. In Africa and London, Huddleston has come to stand for a radicalism and simplicity of religion which becomes lost in the intricacies of the Anglican Church at home.

CLERGY

What bishops like best in their clergy is a dropping-down-deadness of manner.

Sydney Smith, 1859.

The contrast between bishops and clergy is less sharp than it was, but still striking. The average salary of a clergyman is still only £800 a year—less than a steelworker's—and his pension after the age of seventy is £300 a year. The poverty of clergymen is proverbial: there are a few wealthy town parishes where priests can live in style, and in some fashionable London churches the Easter offering can amount to £300. But most parsons are poor, and some have to subsist on as little as £600 a year—less than the wage of a bus-driver.

At the end of 1959 there were 18,969 clergymen in the Church of England, and about 18,000 churches. But the distribution among the population is uneven: 'I'll tell you what's wrong with the Church,' said a man at the Information Office: 'the people are all in the towns, and the clergy are all in the country.' In some country parishes there is one parson to 250 people, whereas some towns have only one to 15,000. But the total numbers of parsons have fallen steadily since 1900, when it reached a peak of 23,670: since then old clergymen have died, fewer and fewer young ones have come forward, and the average age has gone up from 49 in 1901 to 56 in 1960. Parishes have doubled-up, and curates have dwindled. Even since 1948 the numbers of clergymen have fallen by 1,500: but recently there have been signs of an upturn, and in 1960 more clergymen were ordained than in any year since before the first world war.

The Victorian idea of having 'a gentleman in every parish' is being dropped. In the nineteenth century a large proportion of parsons were parsons' sons, or the younger sons of the gentry: the large country rectories which still remain next to country

churches are the reminders of their wealth, and from the parson-
ages have come an extraordinary high proportion of distinguished
people—including Addison, Swift, Goldsmith, Wesley, Coleridge,
Sterne, Crabbe, the Brontës, Kingsley, Tennyson, Samuel Butler,
Nelson and Rhodes. But the contemporary clergyman is less part of
society than his forebears, and less certainly a part of the small-
town community—with the solicitor, bank manager, doctor or
magistrate: parsons are more apt to be eccentric, independent
men, who find in their parish and church a retreat from the world,
and the isolation of the Church increases this tendency.

The placing of clergy remains a curiously feudal affair: over
half the 12,000 livings are still in the gift of private patrons—
including trusts. Lord Salisbury, for instance, has seven livings in
his gift, and the Duke of Norfolk has five—though being a Roman
Catholic he is not allowed to exercise his choice. It is still possible
to buy an 'advowson'—as the patronage of a living is called—
though there are now fewer on the market. Of the remaining
6,000, 800 livings are appointed by universities and colleges,
who give preference to old college men. Another 850 are under the
Crown and its officers, and only the remaining 5,000 are directly
under the diocesan bishops. Some clergy defend the system of
patronage on the grounds that it provides variety of choice, and
avoids 'one opinion': but private livings are gradually falling into
disuse, and passing to the bishops.

Apart from 18,000 clergymen there are immense numbers of
people engaged in Church activities—including (at the end of
1958)

    101,330 Sunday school teachers
      5,971 Licensed readers
    279,398 Members of Church youth organisations
     24,898 Organists
    254,204 Choristers
     12,608 Parishes with church magazines.[1]

How many Englishmen are active members of the Church of
England? More than sixty per cent are baptised, but only thirty
per cent are confirmed, and only eight per cent go to Easter
Communion. Over half the marriages in England are in Anglican
churches: but the proportion of Anglican marriages has fallen
steadily since 1840[2]—when it was as high as ninety per cent—while
the number of civil marriages and Roman Catholic marriages has

[1] *Facts and Figures about the Church of England.* Church Information Office, 1959.
[2] Though the 1957 figures were the same as in 1952.

gone up. But for Easter Communion the numbers have begun to rise since 1947—when they reached their lowest figure of five per cent. Since the war there has been an increase in the congregations in suburbs and new towns—where churchgoing seems to be becoming part of the social pattern, as in America. But it does not appear that the Church exercises any more power through its parishes than it does through its synods and bishops. It does, however, appear that the Church is a less discredited institution now than it was before the war.

CANTUAR

At the head of the Church of England is the Most Reverend Michael Ramsey—the hundredth Archbishop of Canterbury and Primate of All England since St. Augustine, the Roman missionary, was appointed in AD 597. Since his appointment in 1961, Ramsey's unmistakable presence has suddenly loomed out from television and newspapers. He is a big man, with a venerable medieval look, tufts of white hair and big eyebrows, which wobble up and down in a friendly way while he listens. To meet, he gives an immediate impression of unworldliness and compassion. He could not, like other bishops, be mistaken for a businessman or a headmaster: he sits back in his chair, encased in purple, listening intently and nodding with frequent mmms, and talking in a simple biblical language—'right glad', 'mark that', 'be sure of that'. He is much less vague than he seems: he takes a close interest in other people's problems, has a good memory for names, and is not unaware of Church politics. But he is, unlike his predecessor Dr Fisher, primarily a theologian and a pastor; he lives more at Canterbury than Lambeth, is driven in an Austin Princess, and spends his holidays with his wife (they have no children) in a small village pub in Devon, chatting and walking. Under him the Church of England may not obviously become a greater force in the land, but is quite likely to become more religious—with possible consequences which no one can predict.

Ramsey's career has been academic and rarefied: his father was a Congregationalist Cambridge don and his brother, who died very young, was a brilliant Cambridge philosopher and mathematician writing standard works on Hydrodynamics. At Cambridge Ramsey changed from classics to theology, took a first, and became a Liberal President of the Union—just before Selwyn Lloyd. He was ordained, took to teaching at Lincoln Theological

College and, after a brief interval in a parish, became professor of divinity, first at Durham, then at Cambridge. Then came the bishopric of Durham and the Archbishopric of York.

When Dr Fisher was due to retire, there was great uncertainty about his successor: Fisher himself was thought to favour the Bishop of Peterborough, or Dr Coggan, then Bishop of Bradford. Some people regarded Ramsey as too much a pure theologian, and too High Church, and too ineffectual for the big job, with its heavy administrative burden. But others insisted that he alone had the necessary theological toughness and preoccupation with religion, and after a long period of consultation with the clergy, the Prime Minister decided in favour of Ramsey.

Ramsey approached his job with caution: 'We are here as a Church to represent Christ crucified and the compassion of Christ crucified before the world', he said in a television interview, 'and because that is so, it may be the will of God that our Church should have its heart broken, and perhaps the heart of the Archbishop broken with it, just because we are here to represent Christ and Christ's compassion. But if that were to happen it wouldn't mean that we were heading for the world's misery but quite likely pointing the way to the deepest joy.'[1]

How great is the influence of the Church on the government? All the most prominent men in the present cabinet are regular churchgoers: Harold Macmillan reads the lesson in his village church; Lord Home, R. A. Butler, Lord Hailsham, Henry Brooke (who owns the copyright of 'Silent Night') and Ted Heath (an excellent organist) are all active churchmen. But their contact with the Church is largely at parish level, on Sundays only: and the relationship between Archbishop and Prime Minister is much less obviously significant than it was in the days of Cosmo Lang and Stanley Baldwin.

CHURCH OF SCOTLAND

In remarkable contrast to the Church of England is its neighbour, the Church of Scotland, and the co-existence of these two disparate bodies is one of the oddest features of the kingdom: when the Queen comes to Edinburgh every year, she becomes suddenly Scottish, and head of a Church which is Calvinist, Presbyterian and hostile to bishops.

Every June the Church of Scotland meets for an annual assembly, when about 1,400 commissioners gather to debate Scottish

[1] 'Three Archbishops', ATV June 4, 1961.

and world affairs. The membership is impressive: 1,300,000 Scotsmen are communicant members, out of 3,500,000 adults—compared to only 2,000,000 communicants in the whole of the Church of England. The Assembly comes near to taking the place of a Scottish parliament, and is often regarded as the 'Voice of Scotland': 'It is (said the *Glasgow Bulletin* in 1948) 'perhaps the nearest thing to Parliament that we have had since 1707'. The splendour which surrounds Assembly Week, some Scotsmen suggest, is a substitute for the gap left by the departure of a Scots king and a Scots parliament.

The General Assembly is much more politically outspoken than the Convocations or Church Assembly in England, and it does not confine itself to Scottish affairs. Their most angry debates in recent years have been over Nyasaland—which is a kind of African Scotland, full of tough Scottish priests and teachers, and Scots-speaking Africans—and many Presbyterian ministers have emerged to champion Nyasa rights. The most persistent of them has been the Very Reverend George Macleod, a former Moderator who was the founder of the Iona Community (where he lives in the summer).

NONCONFORMISTS

The influence of dissenters, on the other hand, has weakened since the beginning of the century—when the number of nonconformist marriages reached its peak of about fourteen per cent, and nonconformity was optimistic and strong: the Liberal party of 1906 was said to be the first since the time of Charles II with most of its members non-Anglican. Since then, some of the impetus of the Chapel has waned, in striking contrast to America; partly this has come from the general decline of working-class zeal, and partly from the tendency for nonconformist families, once they become prosperous, to turn to Anglicanism: 'The coach and pair,' says the old Victorian saw, 'does not pass the church door for more than two generations.' There are prominent Methodists in business, including Lord Mackintosh, the toffee-maker, and Lord Rank, the film magnate; but there is no real Methodist aristocracy.[1]

The fact that the old rift between Church and Chapel is less deep than it was has obvious benefits, but the dissenting Churches had a radicalism and fervour which did much to break into British

[1] *See* D. W. Brogan: *The English People*, 1943. p. 122.

complacency, and which is much less apparent today. Now the Free Churches are apt to be as conformist as the Church of England, and have lost much of their hold on significant developments. But the nonconformist conscience remains a powerful force, and has moulded men as different as Sir Oliver Franks, Lord Woolton, Lord Rank and Sir Ivan Stedeford.

These are some of the sects, with their membership in 1960:

Methodists:	5,200 Ministers	1,104,500 Members & Probationers
Baptists:	2,100 pastors and deacon- esses	317,700 Members
Congregationalists:	1,800 Ministers	211,300 Members
Presbyterian Church of Wales:	816 Ministers and preachers	201,068 Adherents
Congregational Union of Scotland:	167 Ministers	34,000 Members
Independent Methodists:	310 Ministers	8,500 Members
Wesleyan Reform Union:	25 Ministers	6,100 Members

ROMAN CATHOLICS

A recurring British topic is the idea that Roman Catholics are taking over key sectors of British life—usually the Foreign Office, the BBC, *The Times*, and the House of Lords.

About one in ten of the population of Britain is Catholic. The great majority are working class, from poor Irish immigrants; many are upper class, but there is no great middle class core of Catholicism. (Upper class Catholics are said to talk about mass to rhyme with *pass*, middle class rhyme it with *lass*, working class rhyme it with *fuss*.) The social superiority of Catholics has been emphasised by the novels of the two great Catholic novelists, Evelyn Waugh and Graham Greene ('I'm sure between them they're responsible for the idea that Catholicism is a snob religion,' said one Catholic). But the aristocratic Catholic families do have a social exclusiveness of their own, and spend a great deal of time in each other's homes. Some of them, such as the Duke of Norfolk, have remained Catholic ever since the Reformation, under considerable persecution, which has given a tradition of close-knit, protective loyalty: and there are pockets of England, such as the Arundel Estate, Stonor near Henley, Mells in Somerset, or parts of Lancashire, which have a strong Catholic territorial influence. To the old Catholic families have been added the many Victorian converts, and the twentieth-century Catholic intellectual converts, such as Edith Sitwell, Alec Guinness and Lord Longford.

Catholics favour certain professions: the army, for instance— 'there's a tradition of fighting in the Church, and it's a way, if you're a minority, of proving your patriotism.'[1] Medicine is becoming less popular, partly because of the prohibition of contraception, which could make a GP's life difficult. Some good Catholics often avoid politics, because they are afraid of a conflict of loyalties, but they hold their own in parliament, with eleven Labour MPs and thirteen Tories: there are only two junior ministers in the present Government—Hugh Fraser and Lord Perth.

But the numbers of Catholics are increasing. The proportion of Catholic marriages has risen steadily since 1910, from 4 per cent to 11 per cent: and all children of Catholic marriages must be brought up in the Catholic faith. The increase has come partly from conversion—about 15,000 people are converted every year with the help, among other things, of an Enquiry Centre, a well-organised advertising campaign, and twenty-one leaflets about the Pope, sin, confession, etc.

The Catholic Enquiry Centre reported in 1961 that since it began in 1954

108,000 people have applied for the course,
100,000 took the course,
  7,300 were received.

The total of converts to Catholicism were

1954	..	11,920
1955	..	13,291
1956	..	14,770
1957	..	14,581
1958	..	14,363
1959	..	15,794[2]

[1] *See* Ampleforth and Downside Schools, p. 260.

[2] On the other hand in 1958, 3,771 Roman Catholics were received into the Church of England, according to *Facts and Figures*, 1962.

But the numbers are also increased by the tendency for Catholic families to be larger than Protestant ones. And when Protestants marry Catholics, they have Catholic children: in this way a number of old aristocratic families—for instance the families of the Duke of Rutland and the Earls Ferrers and Dalhousie, who have all married Catholics—will become Catholic in the future. Eleven peerages have become Catholic since 1900 and another twelve are expected to do so in the next generation.

Among peers, novelists and labourers, Catholics are prominent, but there is no sign of any disproportionate influence in the seats of power. In Whitehall or politics their representation is slight: and although many Catholics have used their influence in favour of the Common Market, it was a Catholic Tory MP, Anthony Fell, who was the first to attack the Prime Minister for selling out the Commonwealth.

With its different traditions and somewhat introverted outlook it is not easy to find one man to speak interestingly on the state of the Church in England. Bishops tend, as one of them put it recently, to sit on the fence with both ears to the ground. Archbishops are reluctant to go beyond generalities.

Many people in the Church regard Dr Max Warren, the general secretary to the largest missionary society, the CMS, as the most outstanding figure in the contemporary Church and the one most worth listening to. He is reported to have turned down several offers of higher office: he writes, thinks, travels, speaks tirelessly. Small, friendly and Irish he is very closely involved in most missionary and ecumenical activities. The Church and the world, is entering a new Dark Age, he says. We are living in a society which has dropped Christianity, and this challenges the Christians who are left to re-examine their basis of belief. This thinking, in small groups throughout the world, may eventually spread through that intransigent figure 'the-man-in-the-pew' to re-create in time a true national Church. Our declining international situation now lays us more open to outside influences, in religion as in politics; stewardship, for instance, the planned giving of money and talents to the Church, which is now an accepted fact of modern Church life, began in America and was adopted throughout Australia and New Zealand before it took root in England. Britain's entry into the Common Market could well in time re-shape the religious life of the country.

What of the Church in AD 2000? There may well be union,

he suggested, with Methodists and Presbyterians. Such reunion need not be any impediment to a *rapprochement* with the Church of Rome, which is now thinking much more realistically about the unity of christendom. In such matters as sacramental theology there are great areas of common ground between theologians of all Christian persuasions. There is the problem of relating total loyalty to the Church of Christ with lesser loyalty to particular traditions. Lesser loyalties should not be obliterated for they are great witnesses to truth.

On reform Dr Warren feels that a proper synodical government in the Church is the first essential. The convocations of Canterbury and York will in their present form have to go, and speedily. Reforming developments move slower than we could wish, but they *are* moving, and the signs are that they will move faster as the true rôle of Britain in the world today is accepted by the Church as well as by the country at large. Experiments in lay training, and team ministries will grow; the Church must be ready and willing to make mistakes and learn from them.

Dr Warren had none of the facile optimism of the popular preacher, or indeed of the professional ecumenicist. He fully realises the low state of the Church's contemporary image, the difficulty of communicating new religious insights to existing churchgoers, the materialistic mood of the country. There is no religious revival, he says. But out of the Dark Age into which we are entering, out of our decline as a world power, out of a situation in which traditional Christianity has been rejected by society, may grow a new self-knowledge and a new religious impulse.

12

SCHOOLS

Look out Gentlemen, the Schoolmaster is abroad!
Lord Brougham.

WITH the Church, we have reached the last of the traditional estates which have moulded the character of Britain, and which are entrenched in its history. Most of the rest of this book will be concerned with new institutions and professions—the bureaucrats, managers, scientists or financiers who make up the modern powers. But before we turn to the great bureaucracies of White-hall, it is important to look at the institutions which supply their material—the schools and universities. For it is education which provides the main instrument of social change and mobility: in so far that the managers of Britain are changing, or not changing, it is here that the ingredients will be found.

In the midst of the last war, most people imagined that the post-war educational system would be turned upside down. The Fleming Committee of 1944, with members of unimpeachable respectability, emphasised how the war, to which 'all classes of society have contributed without distinction of origin' had increased the impatience with the exclusiveness of fee-paying public schools, and remarked that 'it may almost be said that nothing could have been better devised to perpetuate them (social distinctions) than this educational development'. They recommended that a minimum of 25 per cent of public schoolboys, in the first place, should be chosen from primary schools and educated free of charge. When the Education Act was passed in 1944, giving greater opportunities for clever boys to go to grammar school and thence to university, many people assumed that the expensive public schools would wither away from lack of funds from overtaxed parents. But the revolution, of course, never happened: and the changes were blurred and confused. The Fleming proposals were quietly abandoned—partly because responsibility for financing them was shifted from the central government to local councils; partly because public schools took boys at a later age (13), and insisted on Latin or Greek; and partly because of heavy opposition from grammar schools. Middle-class parents, including left-wing ones, saved to send their sons to fee-paying schools, helped by the system of tax-free 'covenants', and industrialists subsidised the public schools with laboratories and scholarships. The most extraordinary result of the war—which no headmaster would have predicted in 1941—was that the public schools—133 of them, many of which before the war had been close to bankruptcy—emerged stronger than ever before, with over 20 per cent more pupils.[1]

ETON

> Mr. Attlee had three Old Etonians in his cabinet. I have six. Things are twice as good under the Conservatives.
>
> *Harold Macmillan, 1959.*

And since the war, the most celebrated of all schools, the College of the Blessed Mary of Eton, has emerged with more stability and prestige than ever. The supremacy of Eton is not old: in the seventeenth century it was Westminster, under Dr Busby, which set the pace, and in the early nineteenth century it was Rugby. Even fifty years ago Harrow was, in social terms, almost co-equal with Eton, acceptable enough to educate Winston Churchill and Jawaharlal Nehru, and to include five members of Baldwin's Cabinet ('One of my first thoughts', wrote Baldwin in a famous passage, 'was that it should be a government of which Harrow should not be ashamed.'). But during this century Eton has become established as the unique symbol not so much of expensiveness (in 1961 it cost little more than Oundle or Harrow, and Millfield in Somerset, not in the Headmasters' Conference, was more expensive at £585 a year) but of social exclusiveness. Already the word Eton has cropped up several times in this book, and it will crop up again in diplomacy, banking, insurance and industry; it is impossible to avoid it. Eton has educated 6 out of 21 in the Cabinet, and 18 out of the 26 dukes. It has produced Humphrey Lyttelton, Aldous Huxley, Lord Dalton and Lord Longford. It induces in its pupils a relaxed confidence in dealing with the world and the near-certainty of a good job, which scions of other public schools observe with envy.

Ever since its foundation by King Henry VI in 1440, Eton has been closer to the Crown than other schools, and this has backed

[1] Estimated by Headmasters' Conference.

up its authority. The Provost, who is a kind of chairman of governors, is still appointed by the Crown, and other governors are elected by Oxford, Cambridge, the Royal Society, and the Lord Chief Justice. Eton is thought to be the richest of the schools,[1] with medieval endowments which pay for the upkeep of the seventy scholars, the choir school and the ancient buildings.

The Eton school buildings are scattered round the gothic pin-nacled chapel—an early edition of King's College Chapel at Cambridge (founded by the same king, for the same kind of boys). Through the courtyards and across the street surge boys of all sizes—the small ones in big white Eton collars and short black Eton jackets, like picture-book scholars, the big ones with butterfly ties and morning coats. A few stride like peacocks through the streets, wearing bright damask waistcoats, spongebag trousers and a look of unassailable arrogance. These are the twenty members of 'Pop', the schoolboys' club which provides special monitors for the school, with powers of beating and fining.[2] Pop is the youngest of the many self-perpetuating oligarchies which we will find in this book. It was founded in 1811, has included Lord Home, Lord Hailsham, Lord Altrincham and Ian Fleming among its members, but not Harold Macmillan or the Duke of Kent.

Past the Eton chapel, through a courtyard, and up a medieval staircase, is a long blue-carpeted corridor, covered with pictures of monarchs and prime ministers, with a row of gothic doors along one side. Behind one of the doors, with a big brass plate saying 'Headmaster' in florid copper-plate, is Robert Birley, Headmaster of Eton for the past twelve years. Birley is a tall, friendly man of 58, wrapped in a black cassock, with two white tabs flapping from his collar. He has straggly white hair, a humorous Margaret Rutherford chin, a quick, precise way of speech: but he is unexpectedly shy. His career is fairly typical of a senior headmaster. He was the son of an Indian civil servant, went to school at Rugby, and took a first in history at Balliol, whose high intellectual tradition moulded his standards. He taught at Eton and Charterhouse, helped to organise education in post-war Germany, and then went to rule Eton. He took part in the Fleming Report of 1944 which, together with other mildly radical statements (he is even suspected of having refused a knighthood), earned him the Eton nickname of 'Red Robert'.

[1] Though its endowments amount to far less than a third of its income, as has been suggested (*see*, *Whose Public School?*, Bow Group, 1957).

[2] *See* 'What Pop means to Eton," by Peter Fleming. *The Times*, October 25, 1961.

Birley talked to me about the importance of Eton keeping up with the modern world—and specially with science. He has tried to break down the division between the 'two cultures' of science and the arts, and to make sure that boys do not leave school being 'scientifically illiterate': he pointed with pride to the number of the cleverest Eton boys reading science. 'Our ambition is to have the head of Harwell research station an Old Etonian, who learnt Greek at Eton, and reads the lesson at Harwell parish church.' Etonians, he said, are still going into the Foreign Office, the civil service, the merchant banks and politics in much the same proportion as before. 'It's a very political school, you know . . . The boys have a sense of service and political responsibility here which is fairly rare—and hardly known in American schools.' After the war Birley had worked devotedly under Ernest Bevin in the Foreign Office, and when he left for Eton, Bevin said: 'Birley, keep on sending us your boys: we can't get along without them.'

It is important to distinguish between the influence of Eton on careers and the influence of the families that send boys there. The Etonians in the cabinet and in merchant banks are more remarkable for their ancestry than for their Etonianism. Much more than other schools, Eton is full of the sons of prominent men: 60 per cent of Etonians (Birley told me) have Old Etonian fathers: and the proportion is still rising. Eton's contribution to social change is thus strictly limited and even its rôle of turning a plutocracy into an aristocracy is dwindling. As Eton's position grows more unique, so it becomes a more tribal school.

Eton is very far from being an intellectual place: its boys are chosen not for intelligence, but in a quaint and personal way by the individual housemasters. The teaching is personal but not intensive, and its record (see page 191) is not outstanding. The seventy 'King's Scholars' at Eton, some of whom are entirely supported by scholarships, are kept in a separate hot-house, and the other boys, Oppidans, are apt to regard the 'tugs' as eccentric and rather beyond the pale: the seven hundred or so ex-scholars of Eton show a mixture of ambition and literariness: and although seventeen Old Etonians have been prime ministers, only two—Walpole and Macmillan—have been King's Scholars. But former Eton scholars include

Lord Keynes	John Lehmann
George Orwell	Julian Slade

Cyril Connolly   Sir Henry Willink
Harold Macmillan   Julian Huxley
Sir John Maud   Aldous Huxley
Andrew Sinclair   Lord Hailsham

But they are far from typical Etonians, and Eton is proud not so much of its scholastic achievements as of its breadth of interest, and its capacity to produce not only prime ministers but happy eccentrics of all kinds, giving more emphasis to self-expression than to ambition.

WINCHESTER

> Eton and Winchester sometimes seem to be conspiracies rather than
> educational establishments.
>
> *Anthony Hartley.*

One public school above others *does* produce an intellectual cream: Winchester. It is the oldest, founded by William of Wykeham, Bishop of Winchester, in 1394—as 'a perpetual college of poor scholars clerks', with the contentious motto 'Manners Makyth Man'. For the last century Wykehamists have had a unique reputation for cleverness and public service. Winchester's entrance examination is the stiffest, and it produces nearly twice as many university scholarships, in proportion to its numbers, as any other public school (see page 191). Its headmaster, Sir Desmond Lee, is the son of a clergyman, a rigorous philosopher, and editor of Aristotle and Plato. About 80 per cent of Wykehamists (I was told) go on to universities, and 70 per cent to Oxford and Cambridge—compared to Eton's 33 per cent. Winchester is a much less dynastic school than Eton, and only about 30 per cent of its boys are sons of Wykehamists. While Eton provides a separate study for each boy (the only school to do so) Winchester has a mass of boys in the same room—which is sometimes thought to explain the eccentricity of Etonians on the one hand and the conformism of Wykehamists on the other.

Winchester has produced boys ranging from Cecil King and Hugh Gaitskell to Sir David Eccles: but Wykehamists often have a common denominator of tough ambition and single-mindedness. They are sometimes depicted, in the warfare between public schools, as smug and dedicated bores.

Broad of Church and broad of mind
Broad before and broad behind
A keen ecclesiologist
A rather dirty Wykehamist.[1]

Like Eton, Winchester has its hot-house of scholars, but they are apt to become men of a more single-minded stamp than Old Etonian scholars—including:

Richard Crossman
John Sparrow
Norman Crump
Lord Simonds
Anthony Asquith
William Empson
Arnold Toynbee
Sir William Hayter

Prof. Nowell-Smith
Prof. Andrewes
Prof. Driver
Prof. Macartney
Prof. Seton Watson
Prof. Champernowne
Dr. A. L. P. Norrington

PUBLIC SCHOOLS

At an early age the system divorces a small section of the community from the main stream of national life.

Lord Balniel.[2]

Officially, a 'public school' is a school whose headmaster belongs to a group of about two hundred, known as the 'Headmasters Conference', which includes sixty-four grammar schools: but usually a public school is taken to mean one which is independently financed—that is, the other 133. They vary from old medieval foundations to a bevy of schools founded in the 'twenties. But a small number have had a quite disproportionate influence, and in this book only about twenty schools appear regularly. Below are the nine schools which were singled out by the Clarendon Commission of 1861–4, as 'significant of the position that a few schools had gained in the public eye'.[3] Since then a few old schools have risen in prestige, and a few new ones, like Stowe (1923) and Gordonstoun (1934), have become prominent: but the 'Clarendon Schools', a hundred years later, remain among the most impor-

[1] John Betjeman: *Mount Zion*, John Murray, 1932.
[2] *Twentieth Century*, May 1960, p. 428.
[3] *See* Fleming Report, p. 34.

tant,[1] and in public schools there is no real substitute for antiquity and tradition.

(*December* 1961)	*Fees*	*No. of boys*	*Headmaster*	*Date of foundation*
Charterhouse	£450	650	B. W. M. Young	1611
Eton	490	1,189	Robert Birley	1440
Harrow	462	658	R. L. James	1571
Merchant Taylors	339	600	H. Elder	1561
Rugby	459	700	Walter Hamilton	1567
St. Paul's	339	671	A. N. Gilkes	1509
Shrewsbury	420	550	J. M. Peterson	1552
Westminster	462	407	J. D. Carleton	1561
Winchester	453	525	Sir Desmond Lee	1394

The 5 per cent who go to public schools has no real parallel in other countries. In 1942 the Fleming Committee were told that out of 830 bishops, deans, judges, stipendiary magistrates, highly paid home civil servants, Indian civil servants, governors of Dominions and directors of banks and railways companies, 76 per cent came from public schools, and of those, 48 per cent came from twelve major public schools.[2]

Public schools are distinguished from the rest not only by their cost, but by their segregation. Of these nine, only two, St. Paul's and Merchant Taylors are mainly for day-boys: most public school boys spend nine months a year, for five years, in the exclusive company of other boys. The drastic weaning and intensely introverted society thus created provide an experience from which many public school boys never recover—as appears for instance in the horrific reminiscences of *John Bull's Schooldays*:[3] and the boarding system has been blamed for most faults of public school boys—their excessive respect for authority, their obsession with tradition, their prolonged adolescence. And the separateness has been prolonged by the 'prep schools' which have grown up to prepare boys for them, often from the ages of 7 to 13—thus deepening the groove and making it harder for primary schoolboys to change over.

In the Victorian ethos it was by uprooting boys from their parents, and forging them into a tough society, that imperial leaders were created. Many Victorian schools were built round

[1] R. K. Kelsall: *Higher Civil Servants in Britain*, 1955. p. 119, etc.
[2] Fleming Report, p. 54.
[3] *John Bull's Schooldays*: edited by Brian Inglis, 1961.

imperial service, or the army: the 'Imperial Service College', now merged with Haileybury, was founded to provide recruits for the East India Company. In Britain itself, the segregated world of public schools crops up in all kinds of institutions: a boy can pass from Eton to the Guards to Oxford to the Middle Temple to parliament, and still remain the same male world of leather armchairs, teak tables, and nicknames. They need never deal closely with other kinds of people, and some never do, with consequences which are to be found scattered through this book.

Since the war the public schools have become slowly aware that there is no longer an empire out to which to send their boys. They have become less philistine and brutal, and art is no longer regarded as pansy: they have become more conscious of industry and trade. But no one visiting a public school can fail to be struck by the continuity of these isolated communities: they roll on with their Latin jokes, their founders' prayers, their fags and private languages, still perpetuating vestigial aspects of a Victorian world. Only half the public schoolboys are sons of public schoolboys: as Chesterton put it, 'the public schools aren't for the sons of gentlemen, they're for the fathers of gentlemen'. But, in the words of *The Times*, 'once the boys get to the schools the insidious element of accent unifies them all'.[1] The public schools remain, as they were designed by the Victorians, a device by which the new rich can become absorbed with the old rich, and the sons of tradesmen can be removed from the taint of trade. But in contemporary Britain the demand is for the reverse. What is needed is to turn the sons of gentlemen into businessmen: the sons of amateurs into professionals.

The isolation of the public schools is enhanced by their rulers, the headmasters. These are awesome and formidable men, whom no ex-public school boy can recollect in tranquillity; wielding immense power, maintaining exact if sometimes irrelevant standards. They are figures of massive integrity and moral uprightness: a divorced headmaster is unimaginable. Their way of life combines monasticism with worldly ambition. They are insulated against the outside world, living in the midst of the country, surrounded by inferiors, both masters and boys. Most of the major headmasters are sons of schoolmasters, clergymen or civil servants, and several are the sons or brothers of headmasters. Groves of Dulwich is the son-in-law of a former headmaster of Dulwich, whose son is headmaster of Haileybury. An extraordinary number

[1] 'The Public Schools are not Static': *The Times*, September 25, 1961.

have won the Porson Greek Prize at Cambridge, and among the top ones only Groves of Dulwich has been scientists.

They include heroic and unusual men: Anthony Chenevix Trench, the gay young headmaster of Bradfield, translated Housman into Latin while working as a prisoner on the Death Railway: Brian Young of Charterhouse has been not only a brilliant Greek scholar, but a footballer and clarinet player: Canon Shirley of King's School, Canterbury, with the help of unparalleled public relations techniques, has built up his school from a handful of boys to 660. It is now one of the leading schools in the country. But the headmasters, whatever their virtues, are not closely linked with contemporary Britain: their attitude to their schools is protective, and their interest in reform tends to dwindle as the prospect of a Labour government dwindles. Every year they meet at the Headmasters Conference, to discuss syllabuses, examinations or applications from would-be public schools. Occasionally a motion for a reform is introduced, but never successfully. Birley remains worried about the future of the public schools. 'We must not let public schools become too far out of alignment with the social developments of the country,' he said in April 1961. At the 1961 Conference he introduced a mild motion, expressing the hope that a national scheme might be introduced for subsidising poorer boys at public schools. What happened then, behind the closed doors of the Conference, seems to have been a conflict between two kinds of snobbery: Birley's motion was opposed not only by the old ostrich-headmasters, who resented any intrusion into their privileged world; but also by the major grammar school headmasters, led by the veteran Claydon of Maidstone, who resented the idea of public schools creaming off their cleverer boys, and being subsidised by the state while keeping their independence. The motion was rejected, and the headmasters instead 'reaffirmed belief in the value of independent schools'.[1] The conflict between the two school groups has produced a deadlock in which neither dare change.

THE STREAMS OF SCHOOLS

With their long waiting lists, the support of industry, and the continued demand for the 'public school accent', the independent schools might appear entirely secure. But in fact their future is still uncertain. Their difficulty comes from the fact that since the

[1] *The Times*, October 3, 1961.

war the importance of a university degree—and particularly an Oxford or Cambridge degree—has been growing: while at the same time the Oxford and Cambridge colleges have gradually become more concerned with the ability and intelligence of boys, and less with their fathers and schools. This has given a new opportunity for the 95 per cent of boys who do not go to public school.

The education of the non-public school boy, as every parent knows, begins with one decisive selection at the age of eleven—the sorting-machine for producing Britain's élite. Most countries in Europe, including France, Germany and Russia, select their clever boys at this age: among major Western countries, only America can afford to avoid this segregation, and to keep all their children together, without a special élite, until sixteen or eighteen. The importance of eleven was described by the Hadow report in 1926:

> 'There is a tide which begins to rise in the veins of youth at the age of eleven or twelve. It is called by the name of adolescence. If that tide can be taken at the flood, and a new voyage begun in the strength and along the flow of its current, we think that it will move on to fortune. We therefore propose that all children should be transferred, at the age of eleven or twelve, from the junior or primary school.'

After eleven, the clever children go to the 'grammar schools', in roughly the same way that French boys go on to *lycées* and *collèges classiques*, and German boys to *gymnasium*. The less clever boys go to 'secondary modern schools', where most of them will leave at fifteen to go to work (the word 'modern', both here and in the French *collèges modernes*, is a curious euphemism for 'less clever'): while a few go to 'secondary technical schools', where they learn more from lathes and workshops and less from books and grammar. It is these three streams which are referred to as the 'Tripartite System': the chart overleaf shows their progress, alongside the separate public school stream.

The most striking feature of the map is the abrupt end for most children at fifteen—the official leaving age. In America, 75 per cent of children are still at school at seventeen: in Britain, only 12 per cent are. It is true that since the war more children are staying on voluntarily than had been expected, represented by the trickles on the map (the phenomenon known to school-

STREAMS OF SCHOOLING

Boys in England and Wales with percentages of total age group (Jan. 1960)

Ages	8–11	12	13	14	15	16	17	18+

Preparatory

Public and other independent

5% 6% 6% 6% 6% 4% 3%

35% of Public School boys go to Universities

17% 18% 13·5% 18% 14% 9·5%

Grammar

27% of Grammar School boys go to Universities

60% 58·5% 56% 8·5% 1% 0·1%

Secondary Modern

Primary 95%

Comprehensive and other Secondary

12% 12% 12% 3·5% 1·5% 0·4%

Technical

2·5% 3·5% 4·5% 4% 1·5% 0·4%

(Copyright)

teachers as 'Trend'). But the great proportion of children are sent out to work at fifteen. Most of Europe is as ill-educated as Britain: in France, from 1967 onwards, the leaving age will be pushed up from fourteen to sixteen.[1] In West Germany, Holland and Italy, it is fourteen. The recommendation of Sir Geoffrey Crowther's committee of thirty in 1959—one of the most radical documents of the decade—was that the leaving age should be raised to sixteen by the late nineteen-sixties, which would cost an extra £134 million a year (compared with £580 million a year spent on dwellings, or £1,319 on plant and machinery).[2] The proportion of Britain's national income spent on education—about 2.8 per cent[3]—has hardly increased over the last twenty years. But Sir Geoffrey's proposal was turned down flat by the Government in 1960. The effect of an established Conservative Government and the new success of the public schools has been to distract governmental and parliamentary attention from state education and the educational needs of the great majority of the population.

For the purposes of this book, the most significant tributary is the stream of grammar school boys, and the thin river on the top right-hand corner of boys going from grammar schools to universities: for it is this breakthrough which is beginning to change Britain's élite. The grammar schools provide what has come to be known as the 'meritocracy'—the new caste of men owing nothing to family influence or money, sifted out by intelligence tests, separated from the rest, and groomed for positions of influence. Every country produces its class of meritocrats, but in Britain, where the idea of a segregated group goes deep, fortified by the predominance of Oxford and Cambridge, the emergence of this new class is more dramatic.

MERITOCRATS AND ARISTOCRATS

The impact of the meritocracy of clever boys from humble homes on the public-school aristocracy provides a sharp juxtaposition: and its repercussions will pop up at various stages of this book.

This brain-race is not of course new: it goes back at least a

---

[1] Crowther Report, p. 492.

[2] Crowther, p. 58.

[3] Excluding 'social' rather than 'educational' costs. *See* John Vaizey: *The Costs of Education*, 1958.

century, to when the civil service introduced competitive examinations: T. H. S. Escott, writing a book about England in the eighteen eighties, lamented the shortcomings of the 'competition wallahs' who were replacing young aristocrats in the Indian Civil Service. But the intrusion of those wallahs, disconcerting though it seemed at the time, was limited to university men and therefore, almost necessarily, public school men: only after the first world war was there a large flow of grammar school boys (such as Frank Lee and Norman Brook) to Oxford and Cambridge, and thence to the civil service. The new post-war meritocracy can come from any class of British life, and nearly half of the sixth-form boys in grammar schools are now the sons of manual workers.[1]

The implications of the meritocracy, with its ruthless selectivity, have caused many educationalists to be worried. One nightmare of the future is contained in the brilliant essay by Dr. Michael Young, 'The Rise of the Meritocracy', purporting to have been written in the year 2033, and describing the gradual extension of sifting and segregation, denying all opportunity to the rest—who eventually, goaded by the constant reminders of their inferiority, rise in angry revolt.

The pressure of competition forces nearly all schools to segregate their cleverest children. *The Times* commented in 1961 that:

'It is remarkable that the great movement towards educational equality initiated by Locke and Rousseau should at the end, faced with the demands of scientifically based industry, threaten to produce a hierarchical society which, though status in it would depend on educational parchments, would have some resemblance to that of the Middle Ages. There will not even be the satisfaction of being able to claim that a man's place is at least the reward of his own merit, for the experts in examinations agree that proficiency in them is owed partly to inherited intelligence and partly to family environment, and both endowments are as fortuitous as noble birth.'[2]

COMPREHENSIVES

The eleven-plus is a familiar British bogey. At that age three-quarters of the children are firmly and finally classified as less intelligent than the rest, and sent into the broad stream of

[1] Crowther, p. 230.
[2] *The Times*, April 6, 1961.

secondary modern schools. It is a stream sometimes called by teachers the 'submerged three-quarters', and once in it, it is very difficult to escape. Only one out of five of the modern schools provide courses to the General Certificate of Education—the GCE, equivalent to the French Baccalaureat or the German Abitur—which is the key to further education.

The finality of this day of judgment is under heavy attack from teachers and parents. 'Once it is agreed', wrote Crowther in his report, 'as more and more people are coming to believe, that it is wrong to label children for all time at eleven, the attempt to give mutually exclusive labels to the schools to which they go at that age will have to be abandoned.'[1]

It was to avoid these labels, and to mix the streams, that the most spectacular of the post-war experiments were invented—the comprehensive schools. The comprehensives were designed after the war to contain all kinds of children under one roof. But they were *not*, as in America, to be all in one stream: the comprehensives have their own 'grammar school' classes, leading on to university, and their own technical and modern classes. The importance of comprehensives is that they allow children to change streams after eleven, and also to mix out of class with other children cleverer or stupider than themselves.

The comprehensive schools, together with other variations, are growing rapidly. Crowther estimated that by 1965 11 per cent of the children will be at 'secondary schools which provide for all levels', as opposed to only 2 per cent in 1956. But in spite of their obvious advantages, the comprehensive schools remain hotly criticised: because they are big, described as 'factories' or 'sausage machines': and, more important, because they run against the grammar school idea of segregating an élite.

The first and most famous of them, founded in 1954, is Kidbrooke, a school for 2,200 girls at Blackheath. Its architecture expresses both the idealism and the size of the concept, and the atmosphere of a brave new world of schooling. It is a huge triangle of buildings of brick and glass and cedar-wood, with a low copper-covered hall in the middle of it, big enough to hold all two thousand girls at prayers every morning. Inside there are rows of glassy, brightly painted classrooms, including a room of typing girls, a room of dressmakers, a row of model kitchens, a pottery, a model flat, laboratories, libraries and three gymnasia. It certainly has some of the appearance of mass-production: there

---

[1] Crowther, p. 23.

are long rows of pegs, numbered from 1 to 2,200, two thousand steel chairs in the hall, two thousand girls dressed in identical light grey skirts. The school timetable, showing the criss-crossing of fifty different classes, looks like a Continental railway timetable. But it shows the freedom, as well as the intimidation, of bigness: it is clear at Kidbrooke, as is far from clear at most British schools, that you can study almost anything, and find any kind of girl. And the school is split up into smaller units: there are eight different houses (Dolphin, Salamander, Unicorn, etc.), which cut across classes and ages, and a huge range of unacademic activities, like an orchestra, an Old Vic Club, rounders or fashion shows.

Behind a yellow door in the entrance hall is a light office more like a sitting-room—with a loud-speaker, a microphone, and a mass of charts and timetables—inhabited by the headmistress. Miss Green, who founded the school, is now regarded as one of Britain's most important educationalists. She herself went to Wellingborough High School in the midlands, took a first-class degree at Westfield College, London. She has, from the beginning, been heart-and-soul behind the idea of comprehensives. She is a relaxed, undominating administrator, with rimless glasses, neat greying hair, and a neat grey suit which matches the girls'.

When Kidbrooke started there was an acrimonious quarrel with the local grammar school at Eltham, which Kidbrooke was intended to replace. The Eltham girls, and still more their parents, hated the idea of mixing with the *hoi polloi*: eventually the grammar school was allowed to continue, while Kidbrooke built up their own senior classes. The jealousy of Eltham towards Kidbrooke was symptomatic of the way most grammar schools regarded comprehensives, which challenged the idea of keeping all clever children *socially* separate, and the class-consciousness that often lingers round grammar schools. Although the comprehensives were invented by a coalition government, they have become firmly associated with Socialism and egalitarianism. In fact, both kinds of school believe in special courses for clever children, and neither are pre-occupied with rich men's children. But there remains a strong political prejudice against comprehensive schools. 'I wish', said Miss Green, 'that we could keep politics out of it.'

But while the comprehensives are at odds with the grammar schools, they have much more friendly relations with the public schools—partly because they are not in serious competition; and partly because the public schools are themselves like comprehensives, including both stupid and clever. On her side, Miss Green is a strong supporter of public schools. 'They set us a standard of teaching, which we wouldn't otherwise have', she said: 'and they set a pattern of eccentricity, too, which is useful'.

It is too early yet to assess properly the comprehensive schools: the first clever boys and girls who joined at eleven are only now leaving school. But it is clear that in their main purpose, of allowing children to change streams after eleven, they are succeeding: and many more children stay on after fifteen than at modern schools. Miss Green has a chart showing, like a bumps race at Cambridge, the children moving up and down between streams in the years after eleven: in one form, four out of thirty girls went up from the bottom to the top stream at the age of fifteen.

The numbers of comprehensives will certainly grow much further: but the decisions rest with the local authorities, whose ideas and funds vary enormously. There are still many critics who believe that comprehensive schools are too egalitarian for Britain, and that the country must have a young élite of clever boys, trained in hard, tough schools on their own.

GRAMMAR SCHOOLS

The production of the meritocracy is the job of the grammar schools. There are over fourteen hundred of them, divided between the 'direct grant' schools which, because of their special history and standards,[1] are financed directly by the Ministry of Education: and the other 'maintained' schools which are financed (and often interfered with) by the local county councils. The 'direct grant' are regarded as the pick of the grammar schools, and they include many of the oldest, largest and most successful. A handful have an outstanding record, including Bradford, Bristol, Manchester, Birkenhead, Dulwich (London), Newcastle, King Edward's, Birmingham: each is in the middle of a large conurbation, with a big 'catchment area'—as their recruiting territory is gruesomely called.

The biggest and most famous, with 1,400 boys, is Manchester Grammar School, a low brick building outside the city, surrounded by playing fields. 'MGS' has become a by-word at Oxford and Cambridge for scholarship and success. There is nothing very new about the success of Old Mancunians: their alumni have included Lord Woolton; the editor of the *Daily Herald*

[1] They must, for instance, have at least 60 boys in the sixth form.

(John Beavan); the chairman and vice-chairman of Marks and Spencer (Sir Simon Marks and Israel Sieff—who are brothers-in-law); the playwright Robert Bolt; four Labour MPs, a bishop and an ambassador. But since the war, the success of MGS at the universities has been more widely spread. 75 per cent of their boys go on to university, 25 per cent ot Oxbridge. Out of one group of sixty who joined the school in 1946, 30 per cent became scientists, 10 per cent lawyers, 10 per cent teachers, and 8 per cent accountants. Among public schools there is an idea that the clever Old Mancunians 'fizzle out': in fact many of them go into the large world of provincial industry and technology, away from metropolitan glitter, but with large and important jobs.

The man most closely associated with MGS has been Lord James of Rusholme, who was High Master for sixteen years, until he became Vice-Chancellor of York University in 1962. Lord James has become one of the prophets of the 'meritocracy' (though he did not coin the word). He was a scientist from Oxford, who taught at Winchester until he became High Master at only thirty-six. He is a vigorous, articulate administrator: and he has insistently championed the grammar schools and attacked the comprehensives.

'This place exists as the spearhead of social mobility', he told me: 'ten per cent of the boys are sons of manual workers, and we probably have a wider social cross-section than anywhere in the Western world. But the change is blurred by the question of families: as you equalise opportunity, family background becomes more important—to take advantage of the opportunity.

'One may be worried by the idea of a "meritocracy"—but what's the alternative? If you want to have equality of opportunity, you inevitably have a meritocracy: but you can mitigate the dangers, by producing essentially *humane* meritocrats. The grammar schools must have their own *noblesse oblige*—but in order to have that, they have to *know* that they are a new kind of aristocracy—as Etonians know it.'

Between the big grammar schools and the public schools there is a mounting competition, centring on the entrance examinations to Oxford and Cambridge. 'The grammar schools realised quite suddenly', said Birley, 'about three or four years ago that they could get as many boys into Oxford and Cambridge as were clever enough, and that made things far more competitive. Ten years ago half the boys at Eton went to Oxford and Cambridge: now it's only a third.' 'They are giving us a terrific run for our money,' one public school headmaster told me: 'I've been trying to get my head boy a place at Oxford for the last few months.' The grammar schools on their side are becoming more confident of their potential. 'I think we've got the Establishment on the run,' said one leading headmaster.

An index of the relative success of the grammar schools is provided by the awards of scholarships to Oxford and Cambridge every July. Because of the intense competitiveness which it encourages, some schoolmasters say the list should never be published: but it does give some indication of a school's intellectual status. This list shows the schools which won most scholarships and exhibitions to Oxford and Cambridge in the five years covering 1957 to 1961, together with the number of boys, and the number of scholarships per thousand boys:

	Scholarships and Exhibs.	No. of Boys (1960)	Scholarships per 1,000[1]
Manchester Grammar School	140	1,390	10·1
Dulwich	128	1,340	9·6
Winchester	102	526	19·4
St. Paul's	79	705	11·2
Bradford Grammar School	73	1,050	6·9
Rugby	72	700	10·3
Bristol Grammar School	72	1,139	6·3
King's, Canterbury	72	661	10·9
Marlborough	65	807	8·0
Downside	62	518	12
Christ's Hospital	58	834	6·9
Eton	56	1,196	4·7
King Edward's, Birmingham	55	685	8·1
King's College School, Wimbledon	54	595	9·1
King Edward VII, Sheffield	53	784	7·2
Shrewsbury	51	550	9·3
Ampleforth	49	667	7·3
Latymer Upper	48	1,050	4·7
Clifton	46	676	6·8
Charterhouse	45	660	6·9
City of London	44	880	5·0

The most successful scholarship-winners do not necessarily correspond to the most celebrated public schools, and alongside the famous public schools are grammar schools, such as

[1] This does not give an exact comparison, since the range of age-groups varies widely between schools.

Wyggeston and Latymer Upper, which few public schoolboys will have heard of. Out of the total number of 963 unrestricted awards to Oxbridge in 1959–60, 447 went to public schools, and 467 went to grammar schools. (The list omits the 'restricted awards' which are available to only one school: in the case of Winchester and Westminster this adds considerably to the total.)

TEACHERS

It might appear that the 60,000 public school boys, not rigorously selected for intelligence, could not compete against the 700,000 grammar schoolboys, seeded beforehand. But several factors blur the position. Firstly, only a few grammar schools are attuned to Oxbridge examinations: the others have been in the habit of sending boys to provincial universities, and continue to do so. Secondly, parents of grammar school boys are often less ambitious for their sons. Thirdly, public schools have succeeded in attracting the best teachers, partly by their higher status, partly by offering about 25 per cent higher salaries: and while the grammar schools have an average of seventeen boys to a teacher, public schools have an average of thirteen.[1] Teaching, together with better equipment and more ambitious parents, have so far enabled public schools to maintain their lead.

The future of the grammar schools depends on the future of the teachers: as since the war Britain has become more concerned with education, so teachers have become more evident and militant. There are 320,000 of them in England and Wales, of whom more than half are women. They are the biggest profession of all—if they can be regarded as a profession: they range from village schoolma'ams teaching six-year-olds to university graduates (though those comprise only 22 per cent of the profession). British teachers are less sure of their place in society than Americans or French—which partly derives from the murky roots of British schools, and partly perhaps from their social segregation at training colleges. Today teachers are relatively better paid than before the war; according to the 'Burnham Scale' they earn anything from £520 to £2,400 a year (for a major grammar school headmaster). But the prizes for a headmaster are small compared to leaders in other professions.

In the highest rungs of grammar school teaching, the standard of recruits is lower than it used to be. The 'golden age' of recruit-

[1] But this ratio is misleading: grammar schools include boys between 11 and 13, who naturally have 1-year classes.

ment[1] was in the slump of the thirties, which induced a high proportion of first-class minds to go into teaching. But since the war the competition for first-class graduates, notably from industry, has been much stronger, and the recruitment of teachers has passed (in Crowther's expression) into an 'ice age'. All through the teaching profession there is a serious shortage (made worse by the habit of girl-teachers getting married earlier than was reckoned). Already the size of a class in a modern school can be as large as forty or even fifty. On the grammar school front, the success of pupils closely depends on the quality and number of teachers. So long as public schools can outbid them with salaries—and parents can afford to carry the extra cost—they will have the edge over grammar schools: as soon as the public schools' salaries are outbid, their future will be threatened.

PUBLIC V GRAMMAR

The outcome of the competition between public and grammar school boys is still very uncertain. But it seems likely that grammar schools will creep steadily up over the next ten years. Already in the new centres of power (which appear later in this book) non-public school boys dominate: half the permanent secretaries in the civil service, including the three senior men in the Treasury, come from grammar schools, and so do most of the prominent accountants, engineers and scientists. None of the heads of the very big industries come from boarding schools:

British Transport Commission	Dr Beeching	Maidstone Grammar
National Coal Board	Lord Robens	Council School
Central Electricity Generating Board	Sir Christopher Hinton	Chippenham Grammar
ICI	Paul Chambers	City of London College
Unilever	George Cole	Raffles (Singapore)
Joint Secretaries of Treasury	{ Sir Norman Brook	Wolverhampton Grammar
	{ Sir Frank Lee	Brentwood

The public schools, on the other hand, remain more prominent in the old professions—in diplomacy, the Bar and the bench, the

[1] *See* Crowther, p. 234.

army and navy, Conservative politics and above all in the City of London—and also in occupations which involve salesmanship and 'face-to-face communication'—such as advertising and public relations—where the public school accent and manner are very marketable. The demand for major public schools, which provide intensive teaching and university places, is not very surprising. What is odder is the popularity of the minor public schools: only 35 per cent of the total public school boys go on to universities. But the lesser public schools allow the sons of well-to-do parents to escape from the 'eleven plus' and to grow up with confidence. It is these schools which help to provide the well-dressed, well-spoken 'public school proletariat' in the army, the City or farming.

The future of the major public schools, however, is inextricably mixed up with the entrance examinations to Oxford and Cambridge, whose difficult requirements reverberate through every sixth-form classroom. The complicated grafting of public schools on to colleges, of prep. schools on to public schools, has produced over the decades a tangled thicket of roots, branches and trunks which daunts all but the most ardent reformers.

13

UNIVERSITIES

For the first time in recorded history the survival of the country depends upon the universities.

Dr. Vivian Bowden.

More and more we must live by our wits.
Sir Geoffrey Crowther.

THE spiky barrier between public and grammar schools is followed by further divisions, whose implications are larger—the division between graduates and non-graduates; and between Oxford and Cambridge, and the Rest.

The fewness of Britain's universities has become notorious. In 1901 Ramsay Muir observed that Britain had fewer universities per head than any other civilised country in Europe except Turkey. In 1957 UNESCO showed that this situation had hardly improved: out of twenty-eight countries, Britain was fourth from the bottom—better only than Ireland, Turkey and Norway: this was the number of university students per million of population in leading countries:

USA	16,670
USSR	10,060
Argentine	7,100
France	3,880
W. Germany	3,000
Britain	1,815
Turkey	1,780

Four per cent of British schoolchildren go on to universities compared to 30 per cent in America, and there are fewer British undergraduates than Negro undergraduates in America. It can be argued that British teacher-training and technical colleges are equivalent to universities, but even if both those are included, only 8 per cent have higher education. For a country so rich, for so long, this weakness is astonishing. The Victorians, while they revolutionalised schooling, seldom regarded universities as a national necessity: the industrial revolution and the expansion of trade and empire had happened without any help from universities, and the supply of cheap labour and materials kept Britain supreme. While Germany quickly realised that technical education was the key to economic expansion, Britain somehow evaded this truth: the results are apparent elsewhere in this book, and in British plumbing, telephones, or railways. For the whole interwar period the university population hardly increased: even the postwar expansion, which resulted in one much-heralded but skimped new university at Keele, now seems ridiculously small.

At last, there are signs of unprecedented change. Since 1945, while the Empire was disappearing, universities have gradually loomed larger. The energy and missionary zeal which had been devoted to colonies slowly began to turn towards improving Britain itself. 'The New Empires', said Sir Winston Churchill, 'are the Empires of the Mind.' Between 1960 and 1970 there will be seven new universities and one new College of Advanced Technology. The university population in 1959 was double that of 1939, and by 1970 it is expected to increase by another 70 per cent. The annual government spending on universities is expected to rise from £80 million to £130 million in 1970,[1] but if the demands for expansion are to be met, far more than this will be needed.

This stretching is causing strains and groans. For the old British universities have been preoccupied with their own values, and detest the idea that universities should be an expanding national investment producing practical results. The anti-expansionist attitude has been summed up simply and surprisingly by Kingsley Amis: 'More Means Worse': or by John Wain: 'There's a natural ceiling in the population who are able to profit by academic education, and I think we've reached that ceiling.'

The expansionist party on their side insist that the stretching has not gone far enough. Sir Geoffrey Crowther insists that 20 per cent of young people should have some form of further education. Visualising Britain's position in the technology of the twenty-first century, he has asked: 'Can we conceive that it will be adequately run by a generation of whom only one in twenty-five will have reached even a first degree? Is this not, in fact, a formula for national decline?'

Over the last century the idea has slowly grown that Britain's survival depends on higher education. 'University competition between states', said Joseph Chamberlain, 'is as potent as competition in building battleships' but parliament did not show the same

[1] *See The Times*, June 12, 1961.

interest in dons as in battleships, and even now MPs do not often debate education. The universities, on their side, have resisted this 'menace of the practical', and have always been able, by their powerful alchemy, to make useful subjects rarefied. Noel Annan at Cambridge described to me how after the war the Government had been worried by the lack of experts on the Middle and Far East, where Britain had important interests: the Scarbrough Report recommended giving the universities money to teach the languages and culture of the countries there. 'What happened? The universities created posts in Egyptology, Sanskrit, Mandarin Chinese and Middle Persian—apart from London they seem to be uninterested in teaching modern languages or culture.'

The demand for degrees has hugely increased since the war, and with the growth of big corporations, the break-up of family firms, and the need for professional managers, 'graduatisation' has spread through industry and even into parts of the City. An Arts degree is no longer regarded as an agreeable cultivation before starting serious work, but more as a vital qualification for the higher rungs of government and industry. In another twenty years, it seems likely that the graduate population in Britain will correspond much more closely to the managerial elite.[1]

OXBRIDGE

The primary influence of Oxford and Cambridge is to make the vast majority of its young men, contrary to the tendencies natural to the early twenties, conservative.

Wilhelm Dibelius, 1929.

It's terribly difficult for anyone to get out of the Oxford-Cambridge feeling: like class itself in Britain, it's the last thing we let go after our clothes, I think.

Richard Hoggart, 1960.[2]

Oxford and Cambridge are the last medieval islands, all right for first-class people. But their security is harmful to second-class people— it makes them insular and gaga.

Bertrand Russell

For seven hundred years two universities dominated British education, and today they dominate more than ever, with a fame enhanced by their isolation, and their sheer hypnotic

[1] *See* 'The Élite of Tomorrow' by Dr. Mark Abrams, *The Observer*, September 4, 1960.
[2] Quoted in 'Pressure at Eighteen-plus' by Michael Young, *The Listener*, June 2, 1960.

beauty. Like dukes, Oxford and Cambridge preserve an antique way of life in the midst of the twentieth century, and the dreaming spires legend is supported by tourists, the Ford Foundation, conventions of chartered accountants and international fame. Oxford and Cambridge have provided 87 per cent of permanent secretaries, 72 per cent of the cabinet, nearly 40 per cent of members of parliament, and 71 per cent of the vice-chancellors of other universities. In 1959 Oxford and Cambridge provided all but one of the successful candidates (by examination and interview) for the Senior Civil Service and Foreign Service. The 18,000 students of Oxbridge make up, from the outside, at least, one of the most élite élites in the world. Less than one per cent of Britain's population go to Oxbridge but, once there, they are wooed by industry and government. A BA (Oxon) or BA (Cantab.) is quite different from an ordinary BA. Sir Alexander Carr-Saunders told me that when he was invited to sit in on interviews for the civil service, he found 'everyone on the board was prejudiced in favour of the Redbrick candidates: yet they always ended up by choosing Oxbridge men. You see, they speak the *same language*'.

Oxford is different from Cambridge. Oxford is older, more worldly, more philosophical, classical and theological (eight professors of theology and one of engineering) and with a flair for self-congratulation and public relations ('It may be, after all', wrote one editor-don, John Hale, 'that Oxford's prominence in the press is due less to the inherent fascination of the place for the public, than to the efficiency of the local news gathering services').[1] Cambridge is more isolated, more theatrical, more scientific: five of the heads of Cambridge colleges are scientists; only one in Oxford. Cambridge has a more self-contained intellectual élite, with the tradition of intermarried Huxleys, Darwins, Keyneses, Wedgwoods, and is less obsessed with London. But compared to the others, these two stone cities with their quadrangles, cloisters, damp staircases and punts are uncannily alike. Like the monarchy, they are a fairyland in the heart of Britain: but more successfully than the monarchy they have avoided criticism—by casting their spell on their alumni and would-be alumni, particularly in the mass media and politics. (*Whitaker's Almanack*, for instance, lists every Oxbridge professor including the Vigfussan Professor of Icelandic Literature and Antiquities, but no Redbrick ones.)

Oxbridge is only in session for half the year, and the universities

[1] *Oxford Magazine*, March 2, 1961.

adjourn for four months in the summer—a relic from medieval times, when scholars had to bring in the harvest. Dr. Vivian Bowden of Manchester has remarked on the appallingly low 'plant utilisation factor', reckoning that their buildings are only used for 125 days a year. Sir Geoffrey Crowther, in a celebrated attack, has suggested that dons could do twice the work for (if necessary) twice the pay, working a shift system with two universities using each set of buildings.[1]

Slowly the population of Oxford and Cambridge has been changing. In the nineteenth century it was a mixture of some boys who were poor and clever, and others who were rich and idle. The pattern was already changing before the war, when the (Conservative) Government gave more grants to poorer boys. But since the war, government grants enormously increased, and now over 80 per cent of university students are paid for by the state. And at the same time, brains have come increasingly into demand. Not surprisingly, therefore, the competition to become part of the Oxbridge élite has steadily grown. Colleges now have from five to ten candidates for every one place. The Oxford and Cambridge examinations have become the great challenge to the schools, distorting their syllabus for three or four years before. The most intense battle is among girls. Only since the 1870's have women been admitted, and the eight women's colleges constitute only 12 per cent of the Oxbridge population, so that competition to reach them is fierce: at St. Anne's, Oxford, only 10 per cent of the candidates are chosen—mainly on the results of the written examination.

Ostensibly, the amenities of Oxbridge are now wide open to the meritocracy, but in fact the proportion of grammar school boys has not spectacularly increased. In 1957 it was calculated that 45 per cent of Oxford undergraduates and 55 per cent of Cambridge undergraduates came from public schools. No previous figures are available, but the change since before the war is not (at Cambridge, at least) very striking: and in fact (because of the expansion of places) *more* public school boys are going to Oxbridge than in the 'thirties. Comparatively few grammar schools so far are straining to get their boys into Oxbridge. 'I'm surprised how few grammar schools are really trying to get their boys into Cambridge,' said Sir Eric Ashby, the most radical of the Cambridge heads of houses, who moved from Belfast to

[1] *See The Times*, December 10, 1960.

become Master of Clare in 1959: 'It's part of an old tribal pattern: many grammar schools would rather send their boys to a provincial university, which they know, rather than risk being turned down by Oxbridge. We don't get anything like as many grammar school boys applying as we'd like: we only awarded two-thirds of our scholarships in 1960. Cambridge is still regarded as a finishing school for a small set of schools.'

The quasi-aristocratic atmosphere of Oxbridge remains remarkably unchanged by post-war pressures. Much of the attraction depends on the individual teaching, the range of lectures, the sense of being an international centre, exposed to some of the best minds in the world. But much, too, depends on the social climate—the unchanging calendar of boat-races, college balls and summer frolics. A careful amateurism is still the style (you can still be 'sconced' at some colleges for talking shop at dinner). From outside Oxbridge might appear as a citadel which can only be stormed by the cleverest invaders; but from inside it looks curiously as it always was, with its surface of pageantry, idleness and sport.

Gradually Oxbridge is coming to terms with a more competitive age graduate and angry fathers are finding their sons rejected by the family college. As more grammar schools break into the charmed circle so the pressure to enter the citadel mounts, and the typical undergraduate is changing. But the change from one kind of exclusiveness to another produces new dangers. As the tribal pattern gives way to a meritocracy, so Oxbridge becomes more and more a hot-house of the cleverest men from every class and every area—creaming them off from the other universities, and widening still further the rift between Oxbridge and the rest.

COLLEGES

The main resistance to change comes from the fact that admissions to Oxford and Cambridge are controlled by their forty individual colleges which, like Inns of Court or Eton houses, foster eccentric muddle and fissiparous groups. They retain a jealous autonomy, and they differ as much as Margate differs from Bournemouth. They constitute in themselves a miniature social history of Britain, beginning with University College, Oxford, in 1249 and reaching Churchill College, Cambridge, in 1960. They range from wealthy old colleges with loud, rich undergraduates to poor new colleges, with no endowments and quiet grammar school boys (like St. Catherine's, Oxford or Selwyn, Cambridge).

Probably the richest is Christ Church, Oxford, founded in 1532 by King Henry VIII, with endowments which now bring in more than £100,000 a year. It is the largest Oxford college, with 490 undergraduates in 1960, and a cathedral—the smallest in England —in its garden. It has produced twelve out of forty-four prime ministers, and the road from Eton to Christ Church to politics has been well travelled for two hundred years. In 1960, it had both one of the largest proportion of public school boys (70 per cent) and the largest proportion of failures in the final examinations (8.2 per cent). 'The House', as it's called, has changed little in thirty years: it now takes one hundred and twenty schoolboys a year, compared to ninety before the war. It is obviously impossible for any Christ Church man to write objectively about his own college, and it generates a love-hate relationship in many of its alumni. It contains all kinds of divisions—between canons and anti-clerical dons, between classicists and scientists, or between the four quadrangles with their social labels. Behind the stone walls lurk all kinds of surprising rebels and non-conformists, and I have found (for instance) some of my Christ Church contemporaries some of the most outspoken sources for this book. But the dominant group is still made up of beaglers, sports-car drivers, champagne-party-givers and future Conservative MPs. From the annual newsletter, which records the KCMGs, the ambassadorships and cabinet changes of alumni, one might suspect that the whole of government provided a kind of after-care treatment for Christ Church men; and the influence of the college has managed to promote the question of whether a road should pass through a neighbouring meadow into an unending national debate.

Christ Church is leading the rearguard action against the pressure of democracy. Steven Watson, a Socialist Christ Church don, explained in 1960 the college's system of selection by interview:

'Whatever one's views on the need for social change, it must be admitted that a social revolution cannot be originated in a system of university selection. The need to civilise those who are born to great responsibility, the desire to be tender to claims of loyal old members will, for a long time to come, continue to work to the benefit of the public schools rather than of the obscurer grammar schools.'[1]

[1] *Oxford*, December, 1960.

King's College, Cambridge produces a less conventional group. It began as an annexe to Eton, and until 1856 only Etonians went there: but since then, King's has broken loose from their sister-foundation, and although they still include a wodge from Eton, they like to picture themselves as blending Etonian urbanity with a rebellious independence and intellectualism. 'King's doesn't exist', said the Provost, Noël Annan, an urbane and gregarious humanist, 'to discover reasons for agreeing with the pronouncements of the Archbishop of Canterbury and the Lord Chamberlain'. King's has surprisingly transformed itself from a religious foundation—still with the finest chapel and choir in Britain, and its Dean, Alex Vidler, with one of the few prophetic minds in the church—into a group of agnostic fellows, headed by E. M. Forster. They have a far higher proportion of fellows to undergraduates—seventy-five to three hundred—than any other college, and thus allow more contact between teachers and taught. Kingsmen specialise in the civil service, teaching, and the 'cultural bureaucracy'; up till 1961, the college insisted on handpicking their boys *before* examination, and chose a very noticeable type—precocious, fastidious, very arts-conscious. Many Kingsmen like to appear as prominent critics of 'The Establishment', mocking its pomp and undermining its authority: but one sometimes has the impression that in their anti-Establishment zeal, and the seriousness with which they take the idea, they are—like 'The Establishment's night-club, where King's is well represented—helping to bolster up, rather than to sabotage the idea.

In terms of sheer worldly success, the most formidable college is Balliol, Oxford. Ever since Benjamin Jowett was Master, from 1870 to 1893, Balliol has been preoccupied not so much with scholarship as with success, producing with considerable effort 'a sense of effortless superiority'. In 1960 they had the highest proportion of first-class degrees (18.6 per cent) of any Oxford college (except the minuscule Campion Hall): they also, in 1961, startled Oxford by appointing a lecturer in management studies. 'Life is one Balliol man after another,' Lord Samuel said, and it still is. They include

Harold Macmillan (plus son and grandson)	King Olaf of Norway
	Professor A. J. Toynbee
Lord Kilmuir	Professor D. W. Brogan
Ted Heath	Professor G. D. H. Cole

Henry Brooke	Ivor Brown
Lord Monckton	Cyril Connolly
Lord Beveridge	Graham Greene
Julian Amery	Julian Huxley
Dingle Foot	Aldous Huxley
Prince Wan of Thailand	Raymond Mortimer
Hugh Fraser	Harold Nicolson
Robert Birley	Beverley Nichols

Balliol men are marked not only by their achievements but by their awareness of Balliol, which (like Winchester) gives the impression of being more a cult than a college: they love talking about each other, and in 1957 Balliol men held a special dinner in the City to celebrate the fact that, for the first time since Asquith's government in 1908, the Prime Minister and Lord Chancellor were both Balliol men.[1]

With the growing pressure on Oxbridge from schools on the one side and from industry on the other, the process of 'Balliolization' is spreading, and colleges are judging themselves increasingly by intellectual and worldly standards, less by the social standards of pre-war Oxbridge. The most obvious criterion is the first-class degree: about 8.5 per cent of Oxford's undergraduates take a first, and 10 per cent of Cambridge's. This 10 per cent does not necessarily correspond to outside success. Only six of the fifteen cabinet graduates took firsts, and five of the nine Law Lords. The Foreign Secretary, Lord Home, took a third-class degree, and so did the Lord Chancellor, Lord Kilmuir. The Labour shadow cabinet has a higher intellectual record: in 1960, of the eight that went to university, only two (Patrick Gordon Walker and Anthony Greenwood) had failed to take firsts.[2]

DONS

> Don different from those regal Dons!
> With hearts of gold and lungs of bronze,
> Who shout and bang and roar and bawl
> The absolute across the hall . . .
> > *Hilaire Belloc.*

The exclusiveness of Oxbridge is further enhanced by its teachers

[1] *See The Observer*, July 7, 1957.
[2] *See Time and Tide*, August 13, 1960.

(or 'dons')—about one to every nine undergraduates. 1,500 of them are professors: London alone has *four hundred* professors— nearly three times as many as Oxford and Cambridge. But Oxbridge still sets the pattern—an elaborate one—for dons' behaviour, and clockwise port and high tables have even been exported to Ghana. It was only in 1871 that dons in Oxford and Cambridge were allowed to marry, and Oxbridge still provides a semi-celibate way of life, centring on the senior common room, with special tables for rotating the port and madeira. (Two colleges, Trinity Hall, Cambridge and New College, Oxford, have a special device—a kind of port railway—to solve the appalling problem of how to get the port round without moving it anti-clockwise.) Women cannot dine at the men's high tables except (in some colleges) once a year. Since 1871 matrimony has gradually crept in, but domesticated dons still lead split lives, spanning two centuries, with white-coated men servants and port in the colleges, and nappies and washing up in North Oxford. But this does not apparently lead to broken homes or mental breakdowns, and the two ways of life, like those of diplomats at home and abroad, exist uneasily together.

Most Oxbridge dons maintain a determined detachment from contemporary problems. Some indication can be seen in the post-graduate theses, which show a preference for tiny segments of the distant past, encouraged by their professors to 'crawl along the frontiers of knowledge with a hand-lens'—in Sir Eric Ashby's phrase.[1] These, for instance, were the first four entries in the list of candidates for the degree of Bachelor of Letters in Modern History at Oxford in 1961:

A study of the 'Narratio de Fundatione' of Fountains Abbey.
The rise and influence of the House of Luxemburg-Ligny from
    1371 to 1475.
A bibliography of Henry St. John, Viscount Bolingbroke.
The Archiepiscopate of William de Corbeil 1123-36.

Since the war the outside world of industry and mass media has made inroads on the dons' seclusion, and the trains from Oxford and Cambridge to London have been full of dons travelling up to advise on investment or research, or to appear on television. Some scientific dons make more money as industrial consultants than

[1] 'Universities Today and Tomorrow', *The Listener*, June 1, 1961.

from their university work. The worldly involvement of dons is periodically attacked as a selling-out of their values—'*La Trahison des Clercs*'. But industrialists who subsidise the universities complain on their side that dons do not contribute enough thought and study to Britain's industrial and economic problems.

Dons, like everyone else, have become much more professional; eccentric, drunken or absent-minded dons are all rarer. There is a new race of dons with both feet in the outside world, like Alan Bullock, of St. Catherine's, Oxford, or Sir John Cockcroft of Churchill, Cambridge, who both preside over brand-new colleges with new ideas. But many Oxbridge dons—particularly at Oxford—maintain a profoundly unserious façade: they cultivate frivolous interests and a subtle mortar-board humour, centring on the minutiæ of university rivalries: their outward passions are most deeply aroused on questions such as elections for sinecures or *Lady Chatterley's Lover*, and social romantics encourage them to behave like stage characters. They appear to be delighted, not appalled, by the picture of them painted by C. P. Snow.

But outside this small and not very relevant circle, the large new profession of university teaching is facing a crisis. Already not enough young men are prepared to endure the 'rat-race to publish' which is intrinsic in the present academic ethos,[1] while with the present expansion plans, another eight thousand dons will be needed by the 1970's. At the same time there is growing discontent with the narrow syllabuses of the old universities: there are many reforming parties, but the structure of tutors and professors is so entrenched, like the ramifications of any *ancien régime*, that it is hard to reform one part without upsetting the whole.

Former dons will be scattered all over this book—don-diplomats, don-politicians, don-bishops, even don-bankers and don-chairmen. Scores of dons—people like Sir Oliver Franks, Lord Radcliffe, Sir Ivor Jennings, Hugh Gaitskell, Barbara Wootton—have had an outstanding influence, moving from the world of books and ideas to politics and committees with astonishing ease: and many towards the end of their career go back to Oxbridge as heads of colleges. New disciplines—particularly economics—have forged new links between universities and Whitehall; but Oxford and Cambridge themselves remain as detached as if no one had ever come back from the world outside.

[1] *See* Sir Eric Ashby, above.

REDBRICK

> It's absurd that four-fifths of our undergraduates should be made
> to feel that they're inferior for life.
>
> *Sir Alexander Carr-Saunders.*

The division between Oxbridge and Redbrick—as the other four-fifths is rudely and inaccurately called—is much sharper than the separation, for instance, of the American 'Ivy League'. A Gallup Poll for the BBC in 1960 showed that 80 per cent had heard of Oxford and Cambridge, 50 per cent of London University, 8 per cent of Southampton and Reading. The more the other universities expand the greater, it seems, the centripetal pull of Oxford and Cambridge. In the civil service, politics and law there has been no visible breach in the supremacy of Oxbridge graduates. The division is essentially a class one. While 50 per cent of Oxbridge undergraduates come from public schools, less than 10 per cent of Redbrick do: many public school boys would rather go straight into business, into the services or to a foreign university like McGill, Grenoble or Harvard, than go to a Redbrick university: they prefer no degree to a Redbrick degree.

In England Redbrick has been separate from the beginning. When Oxford and Cambridge were exclusively Anglican, the new Victorian universities were built to provide a liberal education for the poorer boys and dissenters of the provinces—and to give technological training. They grew up outside the old aristocratic pattern, and thus had the austere associations of self-improvement and nonconformism. Oxford and Cambridge graduates scorned them, and London University, which was founded in 1836, was referred to as 'that joint stock company in Gower Street'.

The Scottish universities, like their schools, have avoided the rift of class which divides the English. Even in the fifteenth century there were three Scots universities and the Scots, being poorer and more ambitious, have been more convinced of the necessity of education than the English. But in England, the whole way of life in Redbrick is different. Few of these universities have residential halls and most undergraduates live in lodgings. Few of them have individual tutors. Only a few of the universities have separate colleges, and they lack the strong corporate sense of Oxbridge. No Redbrick university or college has established the continuous relationship with politics or public service which marks Oxbridge colleges. The London School of Economics (which has produced the chairman of ICI and the chairman of the Electricity Council) has often been accused by Tories of breeding left-wing cabinet ministers: in fact the only LSE graduate to reach the cabinet—Aubrey Jones—was a Tory, and he didn't last long.

'Redbrick' ranges from the granite fastness of Aberdeen to the eccentric new buildings of Southampton: an idea of their range of activities and character can be glimpsed from the chart overleaf. Several are in origin 'civic' universities, founded by the mayors and corporations as the product of local pride, many of whom still maintain a town-hall attitude, regarding students' frolics as an affront to civic dignity. In terms of surroundings and architecture, there are different layers of Redbrick. There are the big blackened city universities like Manchester, Liverpool or Birmingham, where most students live in digs on the outskirts and commute like office workers. There are the superior provincials, like Edinburgh or Bristol, which have cleaner air and a tradition of undergraduate spirit. And there is London, in an extraordinary shapeless class of its own, with three times as many undergraduates as any other university, four hundred professors, and departments ranging from the Courtauld Institute of Art to the Imperial College of Science and Technology. The most unusual university is Wales, which has four small scattered components, at Cardiff, Swansea, Aberystwyth and Bangor (which has the distinction of owning a university boat, for the purposes of oceanography—a subject of some interest to the University Grants Committee). But the outward appearance of the universities is no clue to their scholarship: Manchester, one of the bleakest, has produced three Nobel Prize winners in a row, and for twenty years contained the most distinguished British historian, Sir Lewis Namier, while several pleasant places are classed as 'Academic Siberia'.

Many Redbrick universities have established vigorous independent traditions of their own, without too much thought of Oxbridge. Some, like Aberdeen or Liverpool, which are not distinguished by their undergraduates, have strong post-graduate schools. But the breakdown of local cultures and the spread of communications has tended to make the attractions of Oxbridge stronger for teachers as well as for students: and rebellious dons, after a spell in Redbrick, are tempted to return to the womb.

NEW UNIVERSITIES

Between 1960 and 1965 seven new universities will have

University	Founded	Undergraduates[1]	Postgraduates[1]	Professors[1]	Lecturers[1] etc.
Oxford	1249 (1st college)	7,562	1,331	88	71[2]
Cambridge	1284 (1st college)	7,651	1,346	88	65[2]
St. Andrew's	1411	2,314	188	47	262
Glasgow	1451	5,210	529	70	558
Aberdeen	1494	1,775	162	39	248
Edinburgh	1582	4,896	740	65	552
Durham*	1832	4,488	607	79	492
London	1836	16,297	5,400	412	2,860
Manchester	1851	4,127	654	76	593
Wales	1893	5,254	905	111	688
Birmingham	1900	3,316	844	69	538
Liverpool	1903	3,288	558	59	433
Leeds	1904	4,103	613	62	636
Sheffield	1905	2,409	443	56	350
Belfast[3]	1908	3,296	274	51	388
Bristol	1909	2,802	434	47	374
Reading	1926	1,207	273	25	302
Nottingham	1938	2,072	377	38	255
Keele	1949	700	32	15	93
Southampton	1952	1,307	261	25	153
Hull	1954	1,394	192	15	145
Exeter	1955	1,122	160	20	123
Leicester	1957	1,015	180	16	118
Sussex	1961				
Norwich Open	1964?				
York Open	1963?				

* Including Durham Colleges and King's College, Newcastle.
[1] Figures from U.G.C. 'Returns from Universities and University Colleges, 1959–60'.
[2] University Lecturers only.
[3] Figures from *Commonwealth Universities Yearbook, 1961*.

Eccentric Subjects (for 1st degree)[1]	*Notable features*
tary History (art of course)	73 per cent read Arts. 44 per cent from public schools (1957)
te Management	54 per cent read Arts. 56 per cent from public schools (1957)
onomy	Large English contingent. Multi-coloured gowns.
onomy; Marine Architecture	One of the most 'civic'. Large classes, angry students.
idinavian Studies	Very local: most students from near by. Strong medicine.
hnical Chemistry, Linguistics	Powerful medical school. Church of Scotland and Africans. Once a great European university.
physics; British-Roman rchaeology	Part residential. Prestigious but sleepy.
can and Oriental Studies, etc.	Professors of practically everything, including Portuguese History.
nicipal Engineering; itic Studies	Mathematics, Jodrell Bank Telescope. Less distinguished in arts than it was.
ding, Celtic Studies, Cornish	4 per cent from public schools; 40 per cent sons of manual workers(1957).
; Brewing	Technology, Medicine, Sociology. Big-red-brick 'Chamberlain tower'. (recent import) Richard Hoggart.
tronics; Oceanography	Famous School of Architecture. Gipsy Lore.
ther; Synthetic Fibres	Research fellow in TV. Vast expansion.
ss Technology	Excellent in metallurgy.
tiles	
ma	Most sought-after. Medicine and engineering. 35 per cent public school.
ticulture; ltry (part of course)	One-third of students study agriculture.
rying; Horticulture	Very Americanised. Big 'Portland Building' full of cafeterias, etc. Founded by Boots the chemists.
r-year general course	97 per cent residential—but still partly in Nissen Huts. No high table. Smallest University.
	Law school. Basil Spence common-room like a hangar.
idinavian Studies	Only 48 public schoolboys. Many Africans. Poet-librarian Philip Larkin.
tistics	Very remote. Produced Chairman of Esso (UK).
	Intimate, compact society. Only 58 public school boys. Spence buildings. School of European Studies and (later) African and Asian studies.
	Plans to be collegiate à la Oxbridge. Medical studies. Dynamic Vice-Chancellor, Lord James.

The underlined ones are unique.

appeared at York, Norwich, Brighton, Canterbury, Coventry, Lancaster and Colchester—an unprecedented increase. Unlike the Victorian universities the new ones will each aim from the start to draw students from all over Britain. They have none of the old nonconformist or industrial associations: they are not in the middle of blackened towns, but on the edge of (mostly) cathedral cities. Several aim to attract undergraduates, not by local loyalties but by special degrees. The first to be launched is the University of Sussex, which plans halls of residence in a country park outside Brighton, under a vice-chancellor from Balliol and Wales, John Fulton. The university course aims—in the words of the pro-vice-chancellor, Professor Asa Briggs—to redraw the map of learning, and to provide the benefits of specialised and general studies. Brighton hopes to provide a quite new kind of university, but it is characteristic of Oxbridge attitudes that when an article explaining this was printed in *The Times*, containing no mention of Balliol, it was given the heading 'Balliol By the Sea'.[1]

The new universities seem to offer a real chance of breaking the social monopoly of Oxbridge; and it is likely that, lacking the dingy Victorian associations of the big civic ones, they may jump towards the head of the queue. Already three kinds of university are emerging—Oxbridge, Redbrick and New. The new vice-chancellors have a missionary zeal: Lord James has moved from Manchester Grammar School to be Vice-Chancellor of York (where he faces the problem of attracting, rather than shaping, the meritocracy). Frank Thistlethwaite, the Vice-Chancellor at Norwich, has spent much of his life teaching in America. But the capacity of these universities will, until the 1970's, be relatively small— at most nine per cent.

TECHNOLOGY

The cost of new universities is modest compared to the spending on the new subjects of science and technology. The ratio of arts to science students will remain roughly the same, but spending on science is changing the whole financial balance of existing universities. As one minister put it: 'You can buy a professor of Greek for three thousand a year and a Liddell and Scott: but a professor of science may need a million pounds worth of equipment.'

The Industrial Revolution had very little to do with the universities. In the early nineteenth century Oxford and Cam-

[1] *The Times*, August 16, 1961.

bridge took little interest in the new sciences. The technologists, like Watt, Boulton or Newcomen, came from the factories and workshops, while the great pioneer scientists—Priestley, Dalton or Joule—taught in dissenters' academies, mainly Quaker, in the North: so that the rift between science and the humanities was widened by the rift between Anglicans and Nonconformists. It was only after France and Germany had founded their *polytechniques* and *hochschule* for techno-managers that Britain gradually felt the need to adapt their universities to technical education. Hence the new scientifically-minded universities of the 1870's, planted in the middle of the industrial cities of the North and Midlands. They were designed not, like the continental schools, to produce a separate scientific culture, but to bring the new world of technology into the old world of liberal education.[1]

Laboratories and workshops have crept up on the libraries and lecture halls—not only in the new universities but in the old ones. In North Oxford and East Cambridge new scientific cities have grown up beyond the colleges, with government endowments far larger than those of the ancient foundations. The most spectacular expansion has been in the three great 'Techs' of London, Manchester and Glasgow. The biggest of them is the Imperial College in London, officially part of the University of London, but really a proud and complex world of its own. In 1953 plans were announced to spend £12 million enlarging the college. By 1961 the number of students had risen from 1,665 to 2,725, and the teaching staff from 257 to 419, including 45 professors.

On top of these enlargements of old institutions, there has been the creation of new ones, with the unfortunate title of CATS. In 1956, in an effort to raise the standard and output of technological education, three late Victorian technical colleges—Battersea, Birmingham and Salford—were renamed Colleges of Advanced Technology, and between 1957 and 1960 six more 'techs' metamorphosed into 'cats', Bradford, Bristol, Chelsea, Northampton, Cardiff and Loughborough (the biggest and best). The Cats now have 7,786 students (as many as Oxford) and by 1965 there will be 14,000—almost a quarter of England's undergraduate technologists.

The Cats are not too concerned about buildings and facilities —they live in a mixture of original Victorian buildings and gleaming new blocks like the ten-storey new hall of residence at

[1] *See* Sir Eric Ashby: 'Technology and the Academics', 1958.

Battersea. What they want is an ethos of their own, and a status comparable to universities. Their principals are particularly sensitive about their name 'with its deplorable and seemingly inescapable reduction in common parlance to Cats', which they want (characteristically) to be renamed 'Royal Colleges of Technology'. And they insist that 'the educational philosophy underlying the colleges should be clarified'.[1] Cats have been launched in the typically half-hearted style which Britain accords to new institutions. They cannot award their own degrees—some students read for external London ones—and their 'diplomas in technology' can easily be confused with those of ordinary technological colleges. Their courses are mainly limited to engineering and the applied sciences, but most have odd lines of their own—like catering and dietetics at Battersea, environmental hygiene at Birmingham, or architecture at Bristol. The principals want the studies to be widened to include social sciences (for instance, economics and industrial psychology) and they want 20 per cent of their work to be post-graduate research to raise their standing and attract good students. Above all the Cats want to be independent of other universities and the Ministry of Education—to have their own degrees and even their own Technological Grants Committees.

The most vocal spokesman for the world of the 'techs' is Dr. Vivian Bowden, the tough administrator of the Manchester College of Technology, a gloomy red brick building near one of the railway stations. Bowden (an ex-computer salesman) relentlessly attacks what he calls 'the Menace of the Impractical'. 'We mock at Chinese mandarins who let their finger nails grow, to prove that they never had to work', he said to me, 'but we still insist that many of our ablest schoolboys shall devote themselves to intellectual exercises which have little or no connection with the world in which they will have to live.'

UNIVERSITY GRANTS

Who runs the universities? In Oxbridge, the heads of colleges (who take it in turns to be vice-chancellor) each have considerable sway: but all the other universities have professional vice-chancellors who have very wide powers, for instance in deciding syllabuses, allocating funds or patronising architects. They make

[1] Evidence from the principals of Cats to the Robbins Committee on Higher Education.

up a tiny profession of academic administrators, with one foot in scholarship and one in government. Out of twenty-one vice-chancellors, ten were educated at Oxbridge and seven went there later (only eight were at public schools). Two of the most prominent are the Morris brothers, Sir Philip and Sir Charles—vice-chancellors of Bristol and Leeds—and they, with other vice-chancellors, meet regularly for breakfast at the Athenæum, their favourite haunt. The vice-chancellors—though much more worldly than headmasters—are isolated men: they suffer from Oxbridge nostalgia, and a good deal of their time goes into defending university privileges: for instance they refused to allow the new colleges of advanced technology or teachers training colleges to award degrees—only diplomas—thus ensuring that they have junior status.

The real power behind the universities is much less heard of—the nineteen members of the University Grants Committee, who dole out the money. The first grant of government money was £15,000, distributed to universities in 1889: since then the sum has multiplied by 4,000 and in 1960, the UGC gave out £62 million. The committee is a very mixed bag of dons, industrialists, and public servants; among the more vocal are Lord Heyworth, the former chairman of Unilever; Professor Edwards of the Electricity Council; and Edward Russell, the dedicated educationalist from Birmingham. The committee is chosen on the favourite British principle of allowing government money to be allocated, not by the government, but by the profession concerned—a kind of 'indirect rule'. The committee thus act as a buffer between government and universities, ensuring academic freedom, and their largesse is not even inspected by the auditor-general; though the Public Accounts Committee frequently criticize their spending. At the head of UGC is the chairman—the only permanent member—Sir Keith Murray, previously an agricultural economist at Oxford. The powers of Sir Keith are enormous. His committee can, and do, bring whole new universities into being, persuasive letters beginning 'Dear Sir Keith' pour into Belgrave Square from ambitious heads of departments, and the Athenæum is loud with lobbying. Sir Keith is an unobtrusive, cautious committee man, more of a civil servant than a don. This is another case of the divorce between the dignified and the efficient sides of Britain: while Oxbridge dons dress up in flat caps and rich robes to give honorary degrees and mumble Latin compliments to each other—all duly reported and photographed in *The Times*—their future is being settled by nineteen men in mufti, from a shabby office in Belgrave Square. The relations between the UGC and the universities are often fraught with friction and resentment. Sometimes the committee appears like a rich nephew subsidising distressed uncles, provided they pull themselves together, but sometimes more like a rich uncle, on whom young nephews can lean.

Once every five years members of the committee make a three-day visitation to each university in turn, and for a small university the arrival of this mild-looking posse of patrons produces high tension. They are met by the gowned vice-chancellor and his registrar, and shown round the premises. Some vice-chancellors like to reveal only the dingiest professors in the bleakest laboratories, to show that they urgently need money. Others display their sprucest and best, to show that they know how to use money: Leeds University even provides a film-show for the committee. Then at the end Sir Keith, in front of the whole university council, sums up sharply and firmly his impression of the place: faces fall, dreams fade, and the committee departs.

But the committee, though powerful, cannot normally initiate new schemes: they can only approve or disapprove of applications for money, and they leave the universities to spend it as they wish. Nor have they been able to concentrate large grants on one or two places. The committee has to try to treat all universities as equals and this may tend to perpetuate the dominance of Oxford and Cambridge, with their benefit of old endowments.

OXBRIDGE AND POLITICS

The relations between Oxbridge and London politics are full of romantic cross-purposes. In the past the most worldly college has been All Souls, founded in 1437 by Archbishop Chichele with a constitution which other dons dream of—providing a huge endowment for fifty fellows: and the fellows and ex-fellows (called Quondams) are supposed to be the cream of Oxford intellectuals. Among their more arduous duties, at the beginning of every century, they have to parade round the college quadrangles and roofs carrying a dead duck on a pole, and singing their 'Mallard Song'. (In 1900 Cosmo Gordon Lang, the future Archbishop of Canterbury was carried by 'four stalwart fellows'—as is described in his biography—and a cable was sent to Lord Curzon, the Viceroy of India, 'an enthusiastic quondam'.) Before the war

Fellows included the Archbishop of Canterbury, the Foreign Secretary, the Editor of *The Times* and a partner of Lazards; and All Souls could lay some claim to be running Britain—with disastrous results.

Now All Souls still has prestige, but not much influence: their present fellows and quondams include the chairman of the Atomic Energy Authority, the Arundel Herald Extraordinary, Isaiah Berlin, Lord Hailsham and Lord Bridges: but the All Souls dinner table is much less central than it was. The Warden, John Sparrow, who edited Donne's Devotions while a boy at Winchester, is a fastidious bachelor, remaining remote from London and even from Oxford: he even refused the vice-chancellorship. And a younger generation of fellows has emerged including several left-wing rebels, a psychoanalyst, and—to the dismay of some older fellows—an African. All Souls weekends have lost their close links with Downing Street and Lambeth, and two newer post-graduate colleges, St. Anthony's and Nuffield, who include psephologists and Africanists, have established closer and more realistic contact with contemporary affairs.

HARALDUS V. OLIVERUS

The most bizarre collision between Oxford and politics took place early in 1960: and the story of the election of Harold Macmillan as Chancellor of the University throws some light on the London-Oxford axis. The affair began calmly enough, when Sir Oliver Franks, the former Ambassador to Washington, was nominated for the chancellorship—an agreeable sinecure. He was supported by nearly all the heads of Oxford colleges, led by the Master of Pembroke, R. B. McCallum, and the acting vice-chancellor, the witty and worldly Sir Maurice Bowra. His election seemed certain. Then suddenly Professor Hugh Trevor-Roper, an acrid and subtle historian and rival to Bowra, announced that he and others had invited the Prime Minister to stand for the job. Harold Macmillan, at that time spending a grim week with Dr. Hendrik Verwoerd in Cape Town, knew nothing about it, and Trevor-Roper's invitation was assumed to be a harmless frolic. But on the boat back to England a long letter from the Professor (who knew something of Macmillan's repressed rebelliousness) was given to the Prime Minister, explaining in detail why, in spite of the impressive support for Sir Oliver, it should be possible to outvote him. Macmillan replied that he could not commit himself till he returned, that there was nothing in the world he wanted more than the chancellorship, and that he would not shrink from a fight. His advisers and his cabinet, led by the then Chancellor of the Exchequer, Heathcoat Amory, tried to dissuade him—horrified at the suggestion of a premier in office laying himself open to defeat. But Macmillan's curious mixture of theatricality and Oxford nostalgia was aroused. To Oxford's astonishment, the Prime Minister accepted the nomination.

The following few weeks were thick with intrigue and speculation, while the two camps mobilised their supporters: and paltry Oxford politics suddenly overspilled into national politics. It was the kind of totally unimportant issue which can easily engage Oxford's interest, and *The Times* (which attacked Macmillan's candidature), the BBC and the cabinet were all mobilised. All Souls and Balliol were almost solidly for the Prime Minister, but other colleges were caught unhappily between two rival claimants to be 'The Establishment'. The Franks party insisted that they were the voice of Oxford and hinted darkly that the Prime Minister would interfere with Oxford's autonomy. Trevor-Roper, on the other hand, ingeniously insisted that a vote for Macmillan represented a vote *against* the Establishment: the real enemy, he explained, were the faceless men of London and Oxford, aptly represented by the Heads of Houses: while the Prime Minister was a natural rebel. On the day of the election, Masters of Arts filled trains to Oxford to vote for Haraldus Macmillan or Oliverus Franks, under the anxious and threatening gaze of Sir Maurice Bowra who bowed to the voters and doffed his mortar-board. The Minister of Education, Sir David Eccles, took his MA degree only a few days before in order to vote, and was followed to Oxford by the President of the Board of Trade. In the beautiful Gothic divinity school, under TV arc-lights, the votes were counted and the results were declared in Latin which few of the graduates present could understand—Haraldus Macmillan 1,976, Oliverus Franks 1,697.

The discussion as to which side was the Establishment went on. A few days later, in the House of Commons, Anthony Wedgwood Benn, after questioning the Prime Minister, said: 'May I also congratulate him on having proved by his own tremendous victory in a ballot held in Latin, open for all to see, that the Establishment has nothing to learn from the Electrical Trades Union'. 'Except', replied the Prime Minister, 'that on this occasion, I think, the Establishment was beaten.'

The incident was a curious illustration of how, at a time when the country desperately needed to increase the prestige of Redbrick universities, the whole energies of Oxford men, from the cabinet downwards, were devoted to perpetuating the overblown Oxford myth. Oxford and Cambridge still devote a great deal of their energies to boosting their prestige, instead of trying to earn it or export it.

THE RIFT

The rift between Oxbridge and Redbrick, deepened by the rift between schools, cuts right through this book. For Oxford and Cambridge, in so far as they are geared to anything, are geared to the nineteenth century gentlemen's professions—the Law, the civil service or diplomacy, which have adopted their old collegiate traditions. The powerful new professions which between them control the business corporations—accountancy, insurance, actuaries, engineering—have grown up largely outside this charmed circle, in a bleaker and more philistine air. Oxbridge has refused to adapt its curricula to take note of them while Redbrick has found itself trammelled with specialist courses—which helps to explain (for instance) the drabness of modern architecture, and underlies the whole stultifying division between two sides of British life. Here is the most exciting challenge to the New Universities, which may have huge repercussions on the pattern of Britain. For they are not trapped in any curricula, and they can construct courses which are both broad-minded and relevant.

14

CIVIL SERVICE

The Continental nuisance called 'bureaucracy'.
Thomas Carlyle.

Nothing should ever be done for the first time.
Geoffrey Pyke (of civil servants).

WE have already encountered politicians in three different spheres—in parliament, in their party organisations and in cabinet: now we see them in their most important, but least visible rôle—running their departments in the midst of Whitehall: and here, for the next four chapters, we enter the opaque and impenetrable regions of the bureaucracies. A journalist, accustomed to the vivid clash of policies and people in parliament, finds Whitehall a single, grey, anonymous mass, with one policy merging into another, and personalities dissolved in committees and minutes. Nothing in Whitehall is quite what it seems: policy becomes muddled with execution, politicians with officials. When a government changes in Britain, only seventy people change their desks in Whitehall, while in America hundreds of officials migrate. The political masters in Britain can only attend to the broadest principles of policy. The rest of the administration falls on the shoulders of the permanent civil service—and in particular on three thousand men in the administrative grade. The civil service likes to depict itself from the outside as de-personalised, without opinions or policies; but behind the public face, the bureaucracies are still run by individuals, each with their own views and ideas, and as parliament and cabinet find their provinces getting increasingly out of hand, so the power slips ineluctably towards the permanent officials.

Today Whitehall has powers undreamt-of by either party before the war. Public authorities (including local authorities) account for 42 per cent of the nation's investment, and a quarter of its workers. The Ministry of Transport spends £100 million a year on roads alone. The Government can not only control the giant nationalised industries—each bigger than any private company—but by its subsidies, pressures and contracts it can exert huge influence on such industries as cotton, aircraft, agriculture, shipping or engineering. And, as everyone knows, since the war Whitehall has become the universal guardian of the individual, the provider of everything from orange-juice upwards. Sooner or later, all roads lead to Whitehall.

'It's a wonderful place, this Whitehall', said one cabinet minister: 'it has antennae all over the place. If you're thinking of doing something you can put out feelers and in a few hours you know what the reaction's likely to be.'

WHITEHALL

The outward appearance of Whitehall buildings, as a glance at the map following will show, bears no relation to their relative importance: here, once again, is a cleavage between outward show and inner reality. The two biggest—the War Office and the Admiralty—contain two of the oldest but now least important departments: they are both effectively controlled from the Ministry of Defence, with its back door in the 'New Public Offices'. The finest private house in Whitehall—which the prime minister is said to prefer to 10 Downing Street—belongs to one of the least prominent, though most engaging, ministers, the First Lord of the Admiralty. The Ministry of Science, on the other hand, occupies a small eighteenth-century house with a shaky lift, while the omnipotent Treasury is entered through a side door in the 'New Public Offices'. Architecturally the most superb building in Whitehall, if not in London—the Inigo Jones Banqueting House— is occupied by the absurd and unfrequented Imperial Services Museum, full of howitzers, faded flags and dusty models. Many of the most important government departments are now in fact right away from Whitehall: the Ministry of Transport, together with still *more* of the War Office, is in a big block in Southwark, known like so many other buildings as the 'biggest office building in Europe'. Health is in Mayfair, Aviation at the Elephant and Castle.

But the tingling centre of the civil service, where the major decisions are taken, remains the half-mile of stone buildings from Trafalgar Square to Westminster Abbey, with high classical façades, tall cupolas, and heavy marble staircases. The propinquity is important: ideas, misgivings, suggestions can brush from one to another in Whitehall as casually and smoothly as dust on to a coat. In a walk through the park you can have a few casual encounters

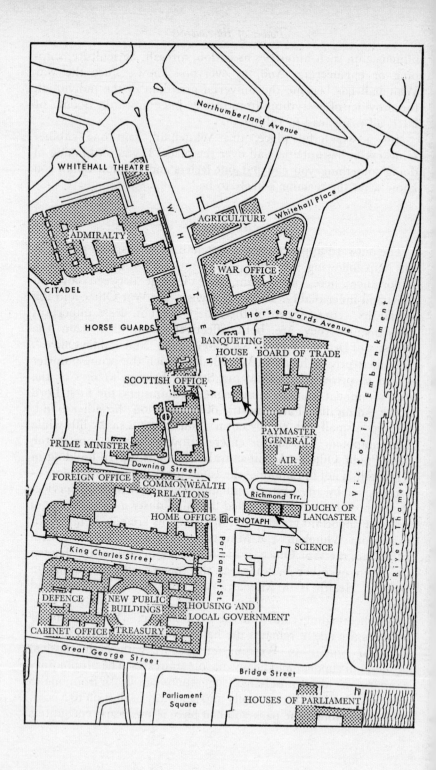

and at once sense the political attitude. And there is the telephone. When it was first invented, it was dreaded in Whitehall: 'Why, anybody could ring me up at any time, and I'd have to answer their questions,' complained one official. But since then, the civil service has taken telephones to its heart—black, green and red ones—and between them comes the dialogue of 'mmms' and 'wells' and 'up-to-a-points' and feelings and agitations, which formulate policies and decisions. (One sign of the closeness of the Whitehall machine and the like-mindedness of its operatives is the speed with which vogue-words are suddenly ubiquitous—pause, *malaise*, shopping-list, marginal, making wrong noises, stop-and-go. The patois of the civil service emphasises the courtly protocol—going native, house-trained, knowing his way around, bowling a fast ball, agreed recommendation, imitate the action of a clam, bull in a china-shop . . .)

It is inside the Whitehall palaces and not in parliament that the sombre day-to-day decisions are taken which shape the future —the awards of subsidies, the placing of factories, the appointment of boards. C. P. Snow has described these 'corridors of power':[1]

> The most characteristic picture of modern power is nothing at all sinister. It is no more or less remarkable than an office— I mean, an office building. Office buildings are much the same all over the world. Down the corridor of one of these offices, of any of them, a man is walking briskly. He is carrying a folder of papers. He is middle-aged and well-preserved, muscular and active. He is not a great tycoon but he is well above the middle of his particular ladder. He meets someone in the corridor not unlike himself. They are talking business. They are not intriguing. One of them says: 'This is going to be a difficult one'— meaning a question on which, in a few minutes, they are going to take different sides. They are off to a meeting of a dozen similar bosses. They will be at it for hours. This is the face of power in a society like ours.

Of all the world's bureaucracies, the British civil servants are perhaps the most compact and self-contained. Their values and opinions are little affected by the values of the press and the public. They have become hardened to ridicule and resentment, and like the Old Contemptibles, turn ridicule to pride. 'Red Tape' is the name of the civil service trade union magazine. 'I

[1] *The Listener*, April 18, 1957.

confidently expect', Lord Bridges (the former head of the civil service) has said, 'that we shall continue to be grouped with mothers-in-law and Wigan pier as one of the recognised objects of ridicule'. 'I think our public image is past praying for', one permanent secretary said to me: 'we're the people who stop you doing things, who interfere, who get in the way. We can never make people *like* us.'

They still conform lovingly to the familiar caricature. They work in gloomy offices in Victorian morgues, guarded by ancient, shuffling doormen, in an atmosphere of—so it seems—contrived squalor. As a visitor, you are passed from one white-haired messenger to the next, down long linoleum corridors, with brown-painted walls, leading into tall ante-rooms, full of knitting, chipped cups, plastic macs and homely typists. There are long telephone conversations about 'HMG' and 'SOS' being exercised, seized, having it in mind, being agitated or embarrassed. The recurring word is 'embarrassment'—a word which signalises the dreaded intrusion of the outside world.

THE MANDARINS

The professional civil service is a Victorian invention—dating back to that dynamic third quarter of the nineteenth century when so many of Britain's institutions took shape. Its origins are so central to the character of bureaucracies, and to contemporary British education and society, that they must be recapitulated here. The civil service is the archetypal bureaucracy (though the word 'Civil Servant' dates from the East India Company, the original 'John Company'), and big businesses are coming increasingly to resemble the Whitehall which they so often mock.

The Victorian idea was that administrators should be chosen, not with special experience of government, but as intelligent, well-educated amateurs—a crystallisation of the amateur ideal which runs through English life. This crucial principle was stated by Lord Macaulay, who recommended the reform of the Indian Civil Service in 1854, in a famous and influential passage:

We believe that men who have been engaged, up to twenty-one or twenty-two, in studies which have no immediate con-nection with the business of any profession, and of which the effect is merely to open, to invigorate, and to enrich the mind, will generally be found in the business of every profession superior to men who have, at eighteen or nineteen, devoted themselves to the special studies of their calling. The most illustrious English jurists have been men who never opened a law book till after the close of a distinguished academical career; nor is there any reason to believe that they would have been greater lawyers if they had passed in drawing plans and conveyances the time which they gave to Thucydides, to Cicero, and to Newton.[1]

In the late eighteenth century the civil service was incompetent, tiny and appointed by patronage: accounting was done in Latin, and the customs department alone had 150 sinecure offices. As the service grew and abuses became more obvious, various reforms were made. Then, in 1853, Charles Trevelyan (Macaulay's brother-in-law, who had spent fourteen years in India) and Sir Stafford Northcote (who had been at Balliol with Jowett) were asked to report on reorganisation. They produced a sensational document. They reported that the public service was 'attracting the unambitious, and the indolent or incapable'. They criticised the system of training men by making them copy out documents (still practised in the City of London). They insisted that the public service must become a profession rather than a job to which 'the dregs of all other professions are attracted'. And they proposed recruiting from the universities by open competitive written examination—turning Greek and Latin scholars into a new race of administrators. It was a compound of Benthamite logic and Chinese experience.

This ruthless report provoked uproar. The secretary of the Board of Trade complained that it would provide 'picked clever young men from the lower ranks of society', and that 'a lower tone of feeling would prevail'. But the incompetence of the Crimean War brought Whitehall into further disgrace. Eventually, in 1870, Gladstone issued an Order in Council which embraced most of the Northcote-Trevelyan proposals. The reform was decisive. It produced, as it was meant to, a profession as dedicated as doctors or barristers, with a powerful collegiate sense, uncorrupt, clever and versatile. The new civil service became part of the core of the middle class, and it grew traditions of its own, with the sons and grandsons of civil servants becoming civil servants. The 'picked clever young men' became—within the limits of Oxbridge—the first great meritocracy, a profession to which any intelligent boy could aspire, a *carrière ouverte aux talents*. It not only reformed the

[1] Committee on Selecting and Training Candidates for ICS, 1854.

civil service, but (as its framers realised) quickened the universities as well—providing a goal behind the examinations.[1]

For the past ninety years, the élite of the civil service, the 'Administrative Grade', have been chosen—with a few modifications—in this way. After the first world war interviews were introduced, and since the last war there have been many more promotions from junior grades: 40 per cent of the 3,000 people in the Administrative Grade now consist of promoted men. But the core of the civil service are still the recruits from the universities, chosen by careful examination and interview by the Civil Service Commissioners (the process of recruitment alone costs half-a-million a year). The recruits remain, as Macaulay meant them to be, highly-educated amateurs: though Macaulay also planned a special college (as there is in France) to teach recruits the basis of their job—such as Indian languages or law—which was not implemented. It is a central tenet of the modern civil service that administration is an art, which can be applied to anything, and the senior mandarins are switched overnight from running prisons to encouraging exports.

OLD BOY NET?

The senior civil servants still form a compact collegiate community. It is often said that they consist of people who have been at school together—probably at Winchester—running the country on the old boy net. Because of the large political implications, the subject has recently been much studied, more than the social background of industrialists or lawyers. In fact it is the old university tie, rather than the old school tie, which dominates the civil service. For the past thirty-five years, the civil service has been a large avenue for the grammar school boy: in 1950, out of 1,045 higher civil servants, only 23 per cent came from boarding schools, only 2 per cent from Winchester, and 1 per cent from Eton. (Even in 1929, Eton and Winchester only provided 3 or 4 per cent.)[2]

In 1950, among 331 senior civil servants,

10 per cent were sons of civil servants
10 ,,   ,,   ,,   ,,   ,, clergymen or ministers
11 ,,   ,,   ,,   ,,   ,, teachers (or dons)
13 ,,   ,,   ,,   ,,   ,, manual workers.

[1] Lord Bridges: *Portrait of a Profession*, p. 9.
[2] R. K. Kelsall: *Higher Civil Servants in Britain*. p. 124.

The Civil Service Commissioners lean over backwards to avoid favouring public school boys: they write a letter of congratulation to every grammar school headmaster who produces a successful candidate, and they were very excited when their first successful candidate from a comprehensive school appeared in 1960. Between 1948 and 1956, only 30 per cent of the young men selected for the administrative civil service came from boarding schools; 40 per cent from local authority schools.[1] (But the proportion of boarding school men in the higher reaches in twenty years' time will be much less—because half of the Administrative class are now promoted from junior ranks.)

The Civil Service is not a public school preserve; but it is very much an Oxbridge—and particularly Oxford—affair. In 1950 out of 332 civil servants above Assistant Secretary, 60 per cent were from Oxford or Cambridge, compared to 69 per cent in 1929 (Oxford's proportion had gone down, and Cambridge's had gone up). Between 1948 and 1956, no less than 50 per cent of the young recruits were from Oxford, and 30 per cent from Cambridge —leaving only 20 per cent from other universities. Fifty-three per cent of the recruits had studied classics or history: only 1 per cent had studied science.[2] These proportions will later be diluted by promotees from junior ranks, and a few scientists changing over: but the Oxford humanist tradition in Whitehall is virtually as strong as ever it was. 'It's partly that the best people are creamed off to Oxbridge at sixth-form level', explained one commissioner, 'but also that the life at Oxford and Cambridge gives people wider interests and more developed ideas—at the other universities so many students have never even left home.'

The old boy net of Whitehall is not the net of Eton and Winchester, but of New College or King's. (The net has wide ramifications: I was surprised in my tour of Whitehall to discover how often Labour politicians had informal contacts with civil servants through their old college friends.) Some colleges—such as Selwyn, Cambridge, or Pembroke, Oxford—hardly ever produce a candidate, but others have a very consistent record among successful candidates. Between 1956 and 1961:

27 were from New College, Oxford
26 „   „   King's, Cambridge
25 „   „   Balliol, Oxford

[1] Recruitment to the Administrative Class: Cmd 232 of July, 1957. p. 25.
[2] Cmd 232. pp. 26 and 27.

19 „ „ Magdalen, Oxford
19 „ „ Trinity, Cambridge
16 „ „ Christ Church, Oxford

Is the civil service maintaining its standard of recruits? Since the war the big industrial corporations have been competing heavily for the best men, and offering larger eventual prizes. 'But it's not industry which is jeopardising our recruitment so much as the universities', one of the commissioners said: 'it's the academic types who tend to try for the civil service, and these are now finding the idea of an academic career more attractive, especially as the new universities make more jobs.' Where industry does compete heavily is in the special departmental classes, where there is now less enthusiasm to become postmasters or inspectors of taxes.

Oxbridge moulds the character of Whitehall, and senior civil servants look back to colleges with nostalgia. 'We are unfortunately lacking', Lord Bridges has said, 'in those expressions of corporate life found in a college. We have neither hall nor chapel, neither combination room nor common room.'[1] But the favourite civil service clubs—such as the Oxford and Cambridge or the Cabinet Office Canteen—take the place of college dining-halls. In contrast to industry, it is not difficult for civil servants to spend most of their life in the company of Oxbridge men. The civil service, in the words of one American observer, is one of the 'forms of corporate social existence which flourish widely in England and the origins of which often ante-date the era of individualism'.[2]

SPECIALISTS

But while the amateur collegiate tradition remains, the whole character of the civil service has changed. It has not only increased in size twentyfold since 1870: it has found itself involved in technical and commercial problems which Macaulay never dreamt of. The old civil service was mainly concerned with regulating people—collecting taxes, running a police force and prisons. The new civil service is occupied in directing industries, allocating vast research programmes, building airports, supervising railways, constructing roads—in fact running half Britain: and the administrators are now entangled in an undergrowth of

[1] *Portrait of a Profession.* p. 32.
[2] S. Beer: *Treasury Control*, 1957. p. 114.

specialists—engineers, scientists, economists, accountants, agronomists. The Ministry of Aviation is much more like ICI than the Home Office, and it employs 3,000 scientists. ICI's board of 22 includes 18 former research scientists: but the Ministry of Aviation is run by Latin and History scholars, headed by an unscientific minister.

The experts not surprisingly resent this *apartheid* and in the last fifteen years a cold war has existed between the two sides. The specialists don't believe that administration is an art in itself: while the administrators insist that their trained minds can deal with any problem. This conflict between amateurs and professionals, between gentlemen and players, runs through many British institutions—more than on the continent or in America—but has its most troubled frontier in the civil service.

Many senior civil servants are worried about their relationships with specialists. Some departments, like the Ministry of Works, are notoriously hostile to experts, while others, like Aviation, are trying to come to terms. 'I don't think we've got the right answer yet', one permanent secretary said to me: 'we don't take enough account of the ambitions of professional people.' 'We don't give our engineers enough scope, or enough money', said another: 'you can't expect first-class men to be happy as simply *advisers*.' 'What we must avoid', said another, 'is having a dual structure all the way up—with administrators on one side and advisers on another, coming up on their own narrow pinnacle. That's terribly wasteful.' Since the war the specialists in the civil service have increased sixfold, as this table shows:

	1939 (thousands)	1959 (thousands)
Administrative	2·1	3·2
Executive	19·3	67·9
Clerical and sub-clerical	112·9	182·1
Typists	15·3	25·6
Professional scientists and technicians	11·0	70·5
Ancillary technologists	25·9	41·9

SILKY MINDS

'They have very silky minds', R. A. Butler said to me, about higher civil servants: 'they've Rolls Royce minds. In fact, the civil service is a bit like a Rolls Royce—you know it's the best machine in the world, but you're not quite sure what to do with it. I think it's a bit too smooth: it needs *rubbing up* a bit.' This image has stuck in my mind throughout this book.

The existence of a strong, professional civil service has immense advantages—often envied by Americans and others. But like most professions it is jealous of its position and self-absorbed. Bagehot predicted that men selected as bureaucrats would 'imagine the elaborate machinery of which they form a part, and from which they derive their dignity, to be a grand and achieved result, not a working and changeable instrument': and his fears were well-grounded. Since the war, it has had to face a vast area of administration which needs new kinds of talent. The old caution and scepticism of civil servants can be disastrous when dealing with dynamic industries of the future: witness the running of British airports, which has been determined not by the excitement of vast expansion, but by the horror of new expenditure and a new shock every year when passengers mount up: or telephones, regarded as a distressing extravagance rather than as an essential tool (the increase in British telephones has been among the lowest in Europe). Both telephones and airports have recently been loosened from the civil service control: but in other fields— transport, aviation, works or stationery—old attitudes remain. It is not only dynamism, and a sense of the future, that these departments need: it is the whole process of opening up and rubbing up—coming to terms with salesmanship, exhortations, public relations, and above all with the public. The conditioned reflex of the civil service is still to imitate the action of a clam, and retire into its shell.

In the war there was much opening-up. Economists, scientists, journalists, businessmen, future politicians, were all imported into Whitehall, to plan the economy, organise rationing, run research, exhort the public. Whitehall was rubbed up by the stimulus of outside connections—particularly industry. But after the war the dons returned to their universities, the scientists to their labs, the businessmen to money-making, and the senior civil servants heaved a sigh of relief, and adjusted their fine machine.

Can this mandarin profession continue unchanged? In the last ten years it has made some concessions—absorbing an occasional economist, promoting scientists, commissioning accountants. But rather than incorporate specialist administrators on a permanent basis, it has built up a second ladder of advisers—scientific, economic or engineering—and a whole web of advisory committees. There are some who say that if you try to interfere with the professional structure of the administrators, their loyalty and confidence will disappear, and the corporate dedication will be lost: but it implies a low valuation on that dedication if, like the dottier Oxbridge colleges, loyalty can only be maintained at the expense of contact with the real world. Of course, it would be disastrous if the sense of public service were to be lost. But the war showed that the civil service was quite able to adapt itself: and today the need for more dynamic attitudes is producing a crisis almost comparable to the war. In 1953 the civil service celebrated the centenary of the Northcote-Trevelyan report with books and speeches about the success of those reforms. They might perhaps more profitably have considered what Northcote and Trevelyan would say now.

THE DEPARTMENTS

These are the largest Civil Service departments, with their permanent and political heads, and their number of employees in 1939 and 1961: the list gives some idea of the expansion of Whitehall, and of the operation of Parkinson's Law—which we shall see more of later. But the numbers in a department do not necessarily bear any relationship to its importance. The two most crucial—the Cabinet Office and the Ministry of Defence—each have only a handful of men.

Department	Number of Staff employed on		Permanent Secretary
	1.4.1939	1.1.1961	
Post Office	196,206	257,979	Sir Ronald German
Inland Revenue	24,974	56,970	Sir Alexander Johnston
War Office[1]	19,827	50,248	Sir Richard Way
Pensions and National Insurance[2]	—	37,347	Sir Eric Bowyer
Admiralty	12,926	30,709	Sir Clifford Jarrett
Air Ministry	19,677	27,787	Sir Maurice Dean
Aviation	—	22,405	Sir Henry Hardman
Labour	28,338	20,333	Sir Laurence Helsby
Customs and Excise	15,017	15,472	Sir James Crombie
Agriculture and Fisheries	2,653	14,921	Sir John Winnifrith
Works	6,274	10,611	Sir Edward Muir
Transport	2,968	7,082	Sir James Dunnett
Board of Trade	4,845	6,974	Sir Richard Powell

[1] On October 21, 1959, the War Office took over part of the functions of the former Ministry of Supply.

[2] The Ministry of Pensions was merged partly with the Ministry of Health and partly with National Insurance on September 1, 1953.

Department	Number of Staff employed on		Permanent Secretary
	1.4.1939	1.1.1961	
Foreign Office	1,729	5,993	Sir Harold Caccia
Dept. of Agriculture for Scotland	658	2,423 ⎫	
Dept. of Health for Scotland	991	1,158 ⎬	Sir William Murrie
Scottish Home Dept.	846	1,858 ⎭	
Health	6,676	5,131	Sir Bruce Fraser
Dept. of Scientific and Industrial Research	1,502	4,449	Sir Harry Melville
Home Office	2,493	3,565	Sir Charles Cunningham
Housing and Local Govt.	—	2,771	Dame Evelyn Sharp
Education (incl. Museums)	2,079	2,760	Dame Mary Smieton
Colonial Office	450	1,726	Sir Hilton Poynton
Power	461	1,586	Sir Dennis Proctor
Treasury	356	1,313	⎰ Sir Norman Brook ⎱ Sir Frank Lee
Commonwealth Relations Office[1]	625	1,183	Sir Savile Garner
Defence[2]	—	394	Sir Robert Scott

DEPARTMENTALISM

'They spend so much time fighting each other', said one civil servant, 'that it's difficult to remember that they're all supposed to be serving the same government.' Each department has what it likes to call its own 'departmental philosophy'; once inside the building, the rest of Whitehall can seem as remote as Scotland. Most civil servants spend their whole lives in the same department, and only the most senior are switched round. A man at the Board of Trade will talk about 'those Min of Ag people' as if they were serving a foreign power. All bureaucracies have this problem: Nikita Khrushchev has complained about the evils of 'departmentalism'—a 'decay of the consciousness of an overriding common purpose . . .'[3]

The departments are much less separate than they were. Before the 1870 reforms they were private empires with no common recruitment policy or salaries. Gradually, as their circles widened and touched, their overlapping segments have become apparent, and the business of 'interdepartmental consultation' is now interminable. It is a surprise to find Whitehall decisions resulting not from anyone taking a broad look at the country, but from a difficult compromise between four rival departments. These rivalries may be essential expressions of democracy, but depart-

[1] Previously Dominions Office and India and Burma Offices.
[2] Constituted in 1947.
[3] Quoted in 'The Ruling Servants' by E. Strauss, 1961. p. 56.

ments often acquire a self-centred momentum of their own. When Commonwealth Relations begins fussing about the rights of Rhodesian settlers, you can never be sure how much of the fuss is self-generated: and when the Ministry of Agriculture makes noises about tomato-and-cucumber growers, they sometimes seem to be anticipating rather than representing market gardeners. The most notoriously self-centred department is the Home Office, who regulate and badger aliens and visitors with little consideration of Commonwealth or foreign interests, or even of human decency: the intense conservatism of the Home Office has trapped nearly every would-be-reforming Home Secretary. The overriding aim of the Home Office, like Bournemouth landladies, is to avoid trouble, however much trouble that may cause elsewhere. And it reached its shabby triumph in the Immigration Bill of 1961.

The departments have very different metabolisms. The GPO, with a quarter of a million employees—more than twice the numbers of ICI—is a kind of industry. The Ministry of Defence is a kind of super-department, like the Cabinet Office, with great power but a small staff. Like colleges or schools, the civil service has its time-honoured hierarchy: and, as usual, there is no real substitute for age. The three most-favoured departments are the oldest—the Treasury, the Home Office and the Board of Trade: while new, important places, like Transport or Aviation, come at the end of the queue.

Departmental characters remain curiously unchanged. The passion for un-reform of the Home Office, or the laissez-faire philosophy of the Board of Trade remain intact through political swings to left and right. Most departments are much more afraid of interfering than not interfering. Some departments—notably Education, Transport and Housing—work at one remove from the public through local councils, maintaining a delicate advisory rôle which inhibits any suggestion of national planning. 'If we started collecting statistics', said one person at Education, 'they'd be afraid that we might want to *use* them.' But the sheer lack of *information* in the great departments of state—about labour, health, schools or traffic—seems, to an outsider, to indicate a serious 'decay in the consciousness of an overriding purpose'.

Even the smaller civil service departments have an astonishing scale of activity. The Stationery Office, for instance, is the biggest publisher in Britain: it publishes 20 million copies of 5,000 books and pamphlets, and 60 periodicals, every year, with annual sales of over a million pounds. Their books range from *The Density of Residential Areas* to museum publications which include such oddities as Fossil Birds, Raphael's cartoons or even Edward Lear's Nonsense Alphabet.

The most despised and unsought-after of the departments (with the possible exception of the Post Office) is the Ministry of Works —which reveals a discrepancy between Whitehall values and others. The Minister is a proverbial parliamentary joke: few people have heard of the present one, Lord John Hope, or can say how he got there; and no recruits (according to a Civil Service Commissioner) choose to go into Works. But it is one of the most potentially exciting departments. The Ministry is best known for its most traditional activities—the upkeep of royal palaces (£605,000 a year), royal parks (£900,000) and ancient monuments (£1,080,000) —including Stonehenge, the Tower of London and Roman earthworks. The kind of thing which makes a minister's reputation is putting crocuses in St. James' Park, or commissioning heraldic lamp-posts for the Coronation. But far their biggest responsibility is in buying new things: they spend *seven million* pounds a year— six times as much as the entire Arts Council grant—on buying furniture, and another *two million* on carpets and curtains. They are responsible for every embassy abroad and everything inside it. They look after the housing of 600,000 civil servants, in 19,000 different buildings: they even look after London statues—the Earl of Balfour recently cost £10,250 and Lord Trenchard £9,350.

The reputation of the Ministry of Works is, quite rightly, appalling. As patrons, they are far richer than any duke has been, and they have dreadfully abused their power. They have built pompous embassies and gloomy post offices. In architecture they have liked to employ underpaid hacks, or discredited fogeys: their safe, old-fashioned taste is well expressed in the new Board of Trade building in Whitehall—'this monument of tiredness and distrust of the world' as Nikolaus Pevsner has called it.[1] When after the war Sir Stafford Cripps tried to improve national design, he did not attempt to reform the Ministry of Works, but, in the Whitehall way, set up a separate Council of Industrial Design to set an example. Recently there has been an improvement, and the Ministry has begun to make some use of enterprising outside designers—most notably in the new High Commission in Lagos. Some of their most depressing products, to be fair, are not their fault: the endless gradations of desks and coat-stands, according to rank, are required by the civil servants, and the fake antique

[1] *Buildings of England; London*, Vol. I, 1957. p. 472.

furniture in Embassies is sometimes demanded by diplomats'
wives (who wage a running war with the Ministry). But the
Ministry still tend to have an amateur, White-Knight attitude of
'it's all my own invention'. In modest schemes, like planning plain
furniture and soldiers' quarters, they are sensible and thoughtful:
but in projects which require imagination and daring—such as
embassies and Whitehall buildings—they reveal the civil service
faults at their worst. Quality and expensiveness are their criteria
rather than design, so that—as in the new Washington Chancery
—the best leather is made to look like synthetic station waiting-
room benches.

MINISTERS

Political heads of departments are necessary to tell the civil service
what the public will not stand.
Sir William Harcourt.

The two heads of each department—the Minister and the
Permanent Secretary—are from two different worlds, and their
relationship is the vital joint in Whitehall—the elbow of government, between decision and execution. On the one hand is the
Minister—famous, extrovert, politically committed. In the waiting-room there is no photograph of the permanent secretary, but
a row of photographs of past ministers, from proud bearded
Victorians in faded daguerrotypes, gradually changing—with the
pressure of universal suffrage—to the beaming and plausible men
of the present. The Minister embodies the whole public personality of his ministry, and he alone is blamed for its public faults.

He must defend and explain his department to parliament: and
this public accountability remains in theory the overriding
difference between a civil service department and private industry.
It takes its most obvious form in parliamentary debates and the
parliamentary question—the 'PQ'. The PQ is the eye of the
public, and it affects the whole character of the ministry: rooms-
ful of filing cabinets, overflowing with trivial correspondence, are
preserved for fear of some future awkward question. Many a civil
servant will dream of the peaceful opaqueness of Unilever and
ICI, where millions can be lost and no questions asked. The
traditional caution of civil servants, their dread of publicity, their
obscurantism, all derive from the dread of the public. The PQ
produces a flurry of activity before parliament. 'We've got
sixty-two questions coming up on Monday', says a private

secretary, rushing through with an armful of files: 'How did the questions go?' asked a permanent secretary, as if awaiting news of a distant battle. But the PQ is a much less seeing eye than it used to be: with the complexity and secrecy of many departments, enormous incompetence can be perpetrated and never come to light.

Listening to cabinet ministers talking with their refreshing indiscretion—behind their big leather-topped desks, leaning back on their chairs or resting their legs on the desk—my main impression was how much, in spite of all the pressure, overwork and underpay, they love their power. I began to understand why they are always reluctant to resign. Compared to the other two parts of his job—parliament and cabinet—here a minister is his own boss, able to do what he likes, with the whole structure of the department built round him, and a private office next door with a handpicked staff at his beck and call. It is here that the manager-ministers, like Marples, Lloyd, Brooke or Watkinson come into their own, away from the bothers of speech-making: and in their ministries they have a quite different *persona*. In parliament every blunder and anxiety is exposed. In the ministry—where he may spend nine-tenths of his time—they have the whole staff to support and defend them. This is what some ministers (and one ex-minister) said about their civil servants:

> Running a civil service department is like playing an organ—you can do almost anything with it. No industrialist gets the same kind of service. A minister can ring a bell, ask for a report on anything, and get it.

> You've got to have a nose for what's important and what isn't—and you've got to know which civil servant can do what. I always like to *persuade* civil servants. Mind you, the power of persuasion is always easier when you've got the power of decision!

> The trouble with the civil service is that it is overstaffed at the bottom and understaffed at the top.

> You know, they've got a wonderful political sense, without themselves being political. They can get the feel of your ideas very quickly.

> They often give you advice based on assumptions of government policy which turn out to be quite wrong.

> Of course I know their tricks: they fill up your in-tray so that you're too busy to make any changes. But I keep a check on things

I've asked to be done and make sure they've done them. They're wonderful people really.

You can't run a ministry like this the way you'd run a business, you know. I never have any time for actual *administration*. Just look at this list of engagements—there's not a free moment.

They can ruin a minister if they want to, you know.

There's no real rule about policy being left to ministers and execution to civil servants. Often civil servants' decisions can have an important effect on policy.

They're extraordinarily adaptable. I remember when we took office in 1951, the same civil servant who had been looking after nationalisation had already got out a plan for de-nationalisation. He went about it with just the same enthusiasm.

Civil servants aren't passive by nature. They're do-gooders, they're Benthamites at heart. They want to reform the world.

Part of the point of the civil service is that people don't take decisions. There are only two or three people who are really meant to take decisions.

Any fool can find the answers to the questions. The difficult thing is to find the questions to the answers.

If the civil service departments are too strong, that's the politicians' fault as much as the civil servants'.

Ministers have very different approaches. Duncan Sandys likes to take what he thinks the most pressing problem, analyse it, argue it, tease it, dissect it if necessary late into the night, infuriating his civil servants with attention to detail. (At the time of the Rent Act, he wrote the letter to householders himself.) Lord Home on the other hand likes to take only the most general problems, and think them out by himself in his leisure—on the grouse moors or in the House of Lords. 'There's only one important distinction in Whitehall', said one of them: 'and that's between ministers who run their departments and ministers who are run by them. Everyone knows which are which: you could make two lists.' Among those in the first list, certainly, would be Duncan Sandys, Iain Macleod, Peter Thorneycroft, Selwyn Lloyd, Enoch Powell. But others are firmly run by their civil servants. There is a story of one Labour minister, who was suddenly asked his opinion in cabinet; he fumbled with his papers and read out slowly: 'The minister is advised to say . . .'

Civil service departments often give the impression of being like
Rolls Royces without drivers. The French civil service, after endless changes of government, seemed to realise that no one was really
driving the car, and quietly moved into the driving seat. But in
Britain the border between politics and administration is more
jealously guarded.

Whoever the minister, a great deal of the power rests with the
bureaucracy. In business, as well as in Whitehall, a chairman may
imagine he is running a company—like a pianola-player, sitting
on the music-stool, varying the speed and volume, while the tune
is being played by the motor. In theory the minister is responsible
for things he knows nothing about: Austen Chamberlain resigned
over the medical supplies to Mesopotamia, and Sir Thomas
Dugdale resigned over the Crichel Down affair. 'The one thing a
minister must never be able to say', said Sir Richard Hopkins, 'is
"why wasn't I told?".' But in the more technical and managerial
ministries, it is impossible for the head to know everything: once
he started asking 'why wasn't I told?' there would be no end to it.
Every minister nowadays finds himself signing minutes he knows
nothing about: R. A. Butler, when he was at the Treasury, used
to sign some minutes with 'R.A.B. at Katmandu'—after the figure-
head King of Nepal. Inevitably, like a good chairman, a minister
must delegate to his juniors—and the frontier between politicians
and civil servants (in some ministries at least) is lost. With the
recent departmental scandals—the Admiralty giving away secrets,
the Ministry of Power breaking the 'pay pause'—there has been no
question of Lord Carrington or Richard Wood resigning. The
doctrine of ministerial responsibility is becoming increasingly
muzzy.

PERMANENT SECRETARIES

> Wise men have always perceived that the execution of political
> measures is in reality the essence of them.
>
> *Sir Henry Taylor, 1832.*

Next door to the ministers, in less spectacular rooms, are the
permanent secretaries. The contrast with their 'masters' is
immediately obvious. The secretaries are, above all, anonymous.
Their comings and goings may revolutionise departments, but they
are unproclaimed: it is not until their obituaries that their
contributions are fully appraised. With many senior civil servants
anonymity is a passion as gripping as fame is for their masters: as

they hear a politician proudly produce a phrase that they invented, they feel a thrill of non-recognition. The names of the permanent secretaries—Cunningham, Powell, Winnifrith, Hardman, Way or Sharp—are rarely heard outside Whitehall.

An encounter between a veteran permanent secretary—inhibited and cautious—and a new young minister—unorthodox and idealistic—provides a sharp antithesis. Ministers—particularly Labour ministers—are full of stories of how they have been told 'it's impossible', 'it's never been done before', 'but it's always been done like this'. Very rarely the permanent secretary is discreetly removed to another ministry: but 'it's very difficult to get rid of 'em, you know', said one present minister, 'things have to get pretty desperate'. More often the conflict is resolved in compromise. For the permanent secretary is the repository not only of caution, but of the armoury of facts, which have a habit of winning: ('facts that seem to live in the office', said Bagehot, 'so teasing and unceasing they are').

The frontier between the civil servants and politicians induces the occupational disease of the civil service—cynicism. Much of their time is spent working out perfect-looking schemes, about roads, welfare, housing, which then disappear into the minister's room, and from there to the cabinet—and then come back mangled and muddled, full of nasty political compromises or stipulations about 'what the public will not stand'. After thirty years watching closely the inner workings of politics, devising schemes for nationalisation and de-nationalisation, most civil servants end up with a profound scepticism about any scheme for improvement: and a few develop a hankering to be rid of the whole business of democracy.

Permanent secretaries are at the top of the gently-sloping pyramid of the civil service hierarchy. This is how the 'Administrative Class' is graded:

Permanent Secretary	£7,000
Deputy Secretary	£5,000
Under-Secretary	£4,100
Assistant Secretary	£2,700—£3,400
Principal	£1,766—£2,468
Assistant Principal	£759—£1,258

Most administrative civil servants stop at the Assistant Secretary level: the next jump, as to Commander in the Navy, is the difficult one. But the bottleneck is not, perhaps, as agonising as it might appear from outside. Many men's ambition has worn out by the age of forty, and the senior jobs are much more burdensome and less financially rewarding than the industrial peaks.

There are thirty permanent secretaries (not all heads of departments: the Treasury, for instance, has five of them). They earn £2,000 a year more than their masters, but less than their equivalents in private industry. They are less well-off in real money terms than they were in 1871, when the head of the Home Office earned £2,000 a year. Their backgrounds are varied: of the thirty in January, 1961, eleven went to public school, twenty-six to Oxbridge, seven to Scottish universities (five went to Oxbridge afterwards), but none to an English Redbrick university. Thirteen have been in the Treasury. All but two began their careers in government service: (Sir Henry Hardman and Sir Lawrence Helsby began as economics dons). Sir Dennis Proctor left for three years to go into Danish business. Nearly all of them have moved between several departments—an average of 2·5 each.

Their status relative to ministers—or at least to Conservative ministers—has risen in the past thirty years. 'There's much less caste difference', R. A. Butler told me: 'in the old days it used to be thought that the minister was chosen by God, and the permanent secretary was just an official. Now they're much more equal.' Some ministers are on easy terms with their permanent secretaries, and dine with them regularly: others remain impersonal and avoid Christian names.

'Establishment is the right word to use about senior civil servants', said one cabinet minister. They form a close-knit homogeneous group. Most of them live either in London, S.W., or in Surrey: their favourite club is the Oxford and Cambridge. 'They mostly go straight home to dinner, and don't meet many people outside Whitehall', one minister said: and this social seclusion brings the permanent secretaries closer to each other. For most of their time they are immersed in their departments, but they keep in touch through the quick antennae of Whitehall. When the permanent secretaries are opposed to something—for instance, aid to under-developed countries—an invisible wall takes shape in Whitehall: somehow or other things mysteriously fail to get done, difficulties prove insuperable. Then perhaps a lever at the top is pulled, and the wall equally mysteriously dissolves: and the gap between policy and execution, between cup and lip, which is the source of the permanent secretaries' power, becomes bridgeable after all. In theory the permanent secretaries do not have attitudes about anything. In practice it would be absurd to expect thirty highly intelligent men to be all politically castrated, and the attitudes they do have can be decisive.

Permanent secretaries are more articulate, more literary, more questioning than most company chairmen. Industrialists are often reluctant to talk about their job, lacking in professional introspection and curiosity: I often had the feeling that they were, after all, simply making nuts or bolts or soap. If you ask them about generalities, trends, or even how they reach decisions, they seem genuinely puzzled. But permanent secretaries enjoy talking about their rôle: in their approach and background they are half-way to dons. They like to see their job less as a trade than an art. 'The work provides', wrote Lord Bridges, '. . . an intense satisfaction and delight in the accomplishment of difficult tasks, a delight which has much in common with that felt by artists on completion of some outstandingly difficult task.'[1] They do not have the same edginess as businessmen: they will often agree that things are far from perfect. On the other hand, they lack the same capacity to *change* things that the industrialist has. They are more intricated in a machine, with committees, balances and gradual modifications.

Yet they remain individuals. Their arrival can transform a ministry more drastically than a minister's—though the minister will always take the credit—and their influence on the minister is often paramount, though they will never say so. This is what some of them *did* say:

> Some people seem to think that we've got a lot of power through the advice we give: but I can't say that I've ever noticed it.

> It's our job to provide the brake rather than the spur. A lot of our time is spent pointing out the snags.

> You have to spend so much time understanding what other men think that you sometimes forget what you think yourself. But I don't think that matters too much.

> There's still plenty of scope for a minister to impose his personality.

> You can't delegate things here as company chairmen do: you have to know all the important things that go on.

> I think we may have to change the whole system before long. It wasn't designed to run big business.

[1] *Portrait of a Profession.* p. 32.

Several permanent secretaries have had unorthodox careers: with many, the war provided new challenges and a shake-up from the sheltered discipline. The men at the top often have more diverse careers than the middle ranks. The most surprising is Sir Robert Scott, the head of one of the most powerful departments, Defence. The son of a Scots engineer, he won a scholarship to Oxford at 15, and joined the consular service in China. He spent the war in a Japanese prison camp, and according to the official report of the Singapore War Crimes trial, 'withstood the most painful tortures, the vilest conditions of incarceration and the strongest moral and physical pressures with a gallantry and good humour the Japanese were quite unable to understand'.[1] After the war he transferred to the Foreign Office, became Commissioner-General in Asia, and was eventually picked—by the inscrutable process of Treasury talent-watching—into the home civil service. Sir Robert's is an example of the heroic career, away from the limiting atmosphere of the bureaucracies.

Another central figure—sometimes tipped as the next head of the civil service—is Sir Richard Powell, the permanent secretary at the Board of Trade, a quiet, articulate bachelor. He went to Cambridge from a Lancashire grammar school, became a shipping expert in the civil service, and then rose to be head of the Ministry of Defence. He moved from there to Trade—from the most secret to the most public department—where he finds himself addressing luncheons and exhorting businessmen, and works on the touchy frontier between government and industry.

Two of the permanent secretaries are women—an astonishing feature after the male preserves of the Church, the Bench and Oxbridge colleges: the civil service is one of the rare fields where women enjoy equal power and pay. They first made their way in the first world war: and by 1925 the civil service—always aiming to be 'model employers'—admitted them to the Administrative Grade (though they still cannot be employed in the service departments: working with generals and admirals would be *too* awkward). Miss Mary Smieton and Miss Evelyn Sharp, both from Oxford, came into the civil service that year, and both rose to be Dames and permanent secretaries, in Education and Housing. Dame Evelyn Sharp, at the Ministry of Housing, is one of the most formidable characters in Whitehall, the daughter of a political clergyman, a keen walker and hiker. She is an expert on town and country planning, a fierce opponent of litter and defender of

[1] *See Daily Telegraph*, June 18, 1955.

green belts, and she has a reputation—very rare in Whitehall—
for calling a spade a spade. She insists that being a high-ranking
civil servant is not really unlike being secretary to any important
man, and that women are just as good at that as men, if not
better. 'You serve your minister whoever he is. I always feel a
man would secretly rather be the minister.'[1]

A permanent secretary can behave like anything from a don to
a tycoon. At the tycoon end of the scale is the Ministry of Transport, whose permanent secretary is a brisk young Scotsman (like
so many), Sir James Dunnett. He appears more like a businessman
than a civil servant; he is outspoken, informal, and draws firm
lines with his pencil on blotting paper. He became head of the
department at only 45. He is one of those many prominent sons of
the Indian Empire (including Professor Tawney, Lord Beveridge,
Robert Birley, R. A. Butler, Hugh Gaitskell). His father was an
administrator in India and his elder brother is also a civil service
knight.

Dunnett is one of the few permanent secretaries who feel
strongly about the need for reform—particularly for engineers,
scientists and economists to be brought closer into administration.
He said in a sensational but largely unnoticed lecture in 1961:

> I think we have got to face the fact that increasingly Govern-
> ment departments are doing much more than merely advising
> ministers. Many of them are, in effect, running his business . . .
> We are in the civil service perhaps inclined to be a little con-
> servative; once an organisation has been set up in a certain way
> we are perhaps inclined to let it run on in that way without too
> much self-examination . . . the Administrative class has not been
> without a certain intellectual arrogance of its own . . . We are
> just a little bit inclined in this country to think we know more
> about administration than anybody else and that we have little
> or nothing to learn from other countries. I do not believe this
> to be true.[2]

All permanent secretaries are overworked: it is almost a point
of pride in the profession that they should stagger home laden
with papers after what is termed 'a hard day's toil'. They must not
only advise the minister, but manage their department and
supervise promotions. Like their masters, they feel they have to

---

[1] *The Guardian*, October 12, 1959.
[2] Reprinted in *Public Administration*, Autumn, 1961.

know what's going on everywhere, in case it might suddenly explode in parliament. They cannot, like Paul Chambers of ICI, go home for tea and thought. They are tied to their departmental machine. 'So the brain of a great administrator', wrote Bagehot in 1856, 'is naturally occupied with the details of the day, the passing dust, the granules of that day's life; and his unforeseeing temperament turns away uninterested from reaching speculations, vague thought, and from extensive and far-off plans.'

The same kind of view has come from Sir Charles Snow, in his book *Science and Government*, though Snow here seem to be (strangely) equating foresight with scientific knowledge:

> I have the greatest respect for the English professional administrators. They are extremely intelligent, honourable, tough, tolerant and generous. But they have a deficiency.
>
> By temperament active men, the nature of their job tends to make them live in the short term, to become masters of the short-term solution. Often, as I have seen them conducting their business with an absence of fuss, a concealed force, a refreshing dash of intellectual sophistication, a phrase from one of the old Icelandic sagas kept nagging in my mind. It was; 'Snorri was the wisest man in Iceland who had not the gift of foresight.'

The three thousand administrators of the civil service include many of the best brains in the country—a unique intellectual corps: but few in Whitehall have disengaged brains, with time to think about long-term problems. Compare, for instance, the human architecture of Whitehall with the structure of Shell—which has seven men at the top, deliberately detached from day-to-day decisions, spending their time travelling, thinking, planning and considering sums over a million pounds.[1] It might be argued that 'long-think' is the job of the politicians: but there are many departments, like Transport, Aviation or Power where planning is often a technical, not a political, business. And politicians are, if anything, closer to the grindstone than their secretaries.

INSTITUTES

Some of the long-think is being undertaken by the new institutes, which provide a kind of shadow civil service, and which deserve a brief digression. There are no fewer than 126 institutes in

[1] See page 433.

the London telephone directory, including the Institute of Breathing, the Institute of Certified Grocers and the Institute of Sewage Purification: no sub-profession is complete without one. But the institutes that concern us here provide a kind of academic, non-party *doppelgänger* to the state departments. Many have been set up with the help of American money— institutes are a favourite American idea—and supplemented by funds from British big business. The first was the Royal Institute of International Affairs, usually known as Chatham House after Lord Chatham's old house which it inhabits in St. James's Square: it was founded in 1920 by a group of rich benefactors including Lord Astor and Sir Abe Bailey, and is now heavily augmented with American money. After the war it accumulated a lot of dead wood, and was even slower than the Foreign Office in realising the importance of Black Africa and the Common Market: but recently it has shown some signs of revival. Since the war, new institutes have followed. These are some of them, with their directors (three of whom were formerly on *The Observer*) and their governmental counterparts:

Royal Institute of International Affairs (Kenneth Younger, Andrew Shonfield)	Foreign Office
National Institute for Economic and Social Research (C. T. Saunders)	Treasury
Institute for Strategic Studies (Alastair Buchan)	Ministry of Defence
Institute of Education (H. L. Elvin)	Ministry of Education
Institute for Overseas Development (William Clark)	Department of Technical Co-operation

Relations between the Institutes and Whitehall are often tricky: in some respects they encourage criticism, by providing ammunition and expertise that political opposition cannot afford. The NIESR, for instance, is a collection of 25 research graduates within a few hundred yards from Whitehall, including several ex-Treasury men, who enjoy firing off salvoes in the direction of Great George Street; and radical admirals like flying provocative kites at the ISS up the road. Whitehall, inherently suspicious of research, does not always enjoy the feeling of being overlooked by ghost-bodies, but the more adventurous civil servants appreciate this new competition. While Oxford and Cambridge have remained proudly aloof from most contemporary studies, the institutes are beginning to provide an academic circumference to Whitehall.

HEAD OF THE CIVIL SERVICE

At the head of the network of permanent secretaries is Sir Norman Craven Brook. 'There are three civil servants who have to know everything that's going on', one former permanent secretary told me: 'one is the Prime Minister's principal private secretary; another is the secretary to the Cabinet: the other is the senior permanent secretary to the Treasury.' Sir Norman Brook is two of them. His official title is 'Secretary of the Cabinet, Joint Secretary of the Treasury and Head of the Home Civil Service'. This troika, together with his personal prestige, gives him unrivalled influence. No one in Whitehall, politician or civil servant, knows as much as Brook. Since 1947, under Attlee, Churchill, Eden and Macmillan, he has attended all cabinet meetings and he has been the confidant of all four prime ministers. As early as 1942 he was deputy secretary to the War Cabinet. For twenty years he has been in the heart of the government.

Brook looks, and is, the quintessential civil servant. He is a tall, grave figure, immaculately dressed, with a rather lugubrious expression and sagging eyes—the look of a thoroughbred bloodhound. He is infinitely unobtrusive. On the Prime Minister's Commonwealth tours, where I first encountered him, he would walk some way behind, through exhibitions, model villages or universities, looking like a casual tourist who just happened to be following. The local officials took little notice of him, and few of them realised that he was the central cog in the British Government machine.

He lives a secluded life with his wife in Chelsea, occasionally playing a game of golf, listening to music or enjoying his favourite (and appropriate) hobby of cabinet-making. He works hard, but not in the obsessive way of some civil servants, and he quite often goes home at seven. He lunches most days, very late, in the Cabinet Office canteen inside the Treasury building, at a special table. He is impenetrably, but not rudely, discreet, and is worried by the indiscretion of others. He generates an atmosphere of unhurried, almost languid calm, talking quite slowly, and making large questions seem small. He has an air of fatherly detachment, as if he had long ago been caught up in an intricate, secret world—which he has. But behind his apparent languor he has immense stamina and a real 'Rolls Royce mind': he can spend a whole day travelling and sit up half the night with cabinet papers—taking five hours' sleep for weeks on end—and with the same fresh imperturbable look in the morning.

Brook's career was rapid and smooth. One of the number of grammar school men who came in just after the first world war, he was at Wolverhampton Grammar School and Wadham College, Oxford. He began his career in the Home Office, where his active mind attracted the permanent secretary, Sir John Anderson. Then Anderson stood for parliament—a rare thing for a senior civil servant—and became a Coalition cabinet minister and Lord Privy Seal. He appointed Brook his private secretary in a succession of ministries, and Brook was thus drawn into the centre of war-time government: by the age of forty he had become deputy secretary to the war cabinet. He was a master of minutes, with one of those well-tempered minds which can digest a succession of confused arguments, and present them—in his small, neat hand-writing—in perfect order: and in 1947 he took over as secretary from his boss, Sir Edward Bridges. In cabinet, he passed smoothly from Churchill to Attlee, from Attlee back to Churchill, from Churchill to Eden to Macmillan: alone of the men round the long green table he had a continuous knowledge of government.

When Bridges finally retired from the Treasury in 1956, Brook took over half of that job too (the other half belongs to Sir Frank Lee), and thus became 'Head of the Home Civil Service'. When Macmillan—who likes to have a close small group near him—became prime minister, he worked very closely with Brook, who virtually became his personal adviser. Macmillan took Brook with him on his overseas tours, relying heavily on his well-stocked, businesslike mind.

When, in fifty years' time, the official secrets are revealed, the name of Brook will certainly feature a good deal in the making of decisions. It will feature, for instance, in the 'Wind of Change' speech of 1960; in the changing relationships with South Africa in 1961; or in the founding of the new 'Department of Technical Co-operation'. There is no sign that Brook has overstepped the civil servant's frontier, but as the central lever of the Whitehall machine, he can understand what needs to be done, and provide ways of doing it, and here his influence has frequently been decisive.

As head of the civil service, he supervises the moving round of the permanent, deputy and assistant secretaries who make up the machine. His scope is far from unlimited. Moves must be approved by the ministers and the senior ones by the prime minister: it is like moving pieces on an overcrowded chess board. Diplomats like to mock the civil servants' obsessions with 'Buggins' Turn Next', and their long queue of second-rate men. But I had the impression that there were more Bugginses in the Foreign Office—a more in-bred department—and that Home appointments are relatively more enterprising. Probably more influential than Brook's headship is his secretaryship of the cabinet. He has the ear of cabinet ministers at any time he wants; he knows Whitehall as none of them can, and with a few discreet words he can achieve what might take others months of negotiation.

Is the headship of the civil service too crucial to be held by any one man? Some ministers—particularly those outside the Macmillan circle—are jealous of the access of the top civil servant. Sir Warren Fisher was head before the war for twenty years, and Bridges for nine—a longer time than most prime ministers: and there is a case for limiting the tenure of office. It has been suggested that the job should be taken over by a committee of permanent secretaries.[1]

But the civil service is already so committee-bound that the prospect of a committee at the *top*, alongside the political committee of the cabinet, is surely appalling. Already it seems likely that when he retires Brook's two main jobs will be split, as they were before, for lack of a man who can combine them. The more complex and departmental government becomes, the more important it is for one or two men to know about everything. *Someone* must cut through the webs of muddle and misunderstandings which accumulate from rival departments and factions. As Dag Hammarskjöld had in the United Nations, Brook has a job which can give direction, decision and execution where otherwise could be chaos.

[1] *See* Thomas Balogh's essay in 'The Establishment', 1959.

15

COMMITTEES

The English way is a committee—we are born with a belief in a
green cloth, clean pens and twelve men with grey hair.

Walter Bagehot.

The ideal committee is one with me as chairman, and two other
members in bed with flu.

Lord Milverton.

A camel is a horse designed by a committee.

Anon.

In Whitehall, sooner or later, individuals always become blurred
into committees. It is in committees that personalities appear to
evaporate: the essence of committeemanship is de-personalisation
—gradually getting your own way by avoiding any kind of
emotional conflict. 'A Government department', it has been said,
'is a collection of people, but if they are to do their work effectively
they must try so far as possible collectively to resemble a *thing*.'[1]
The committee is the embodiment of that thing.

As departments grow in size, and as their problems become more
interlocked, so interdepartmental 'committees' grow up between
them—trying to reach agreement between different points of view,
and to avoid 'departmentalism'. Men from the Board of Trade,
the Treasury, the Home Office and the Min of Ag will come
together with an agenda and a chairman to produce a decision in
no-man's-land. 'Interdepartmental consultation'—that deadening
phrase—is the bugbear of Whitehall: liaison breeds liaison and
committees breed committees. 'It's terrifying, the man-power it
uses up', said one minister: 'some of our best men spend most of
their time in liaison.' Committees are the inescapable penalty of
democracy. This is a characteristic problem of modern organisations: the senior men in the mammoth corporations seem to be—
and are sometimes called—co-ordinators. Bishops, judges, admirals
or scientists are all entangled in committees, all needing the same
qualities of patience and compromise—'all Gerald du Maurier in
the end'.[2]

[1] C. H. Sisson: *The Spirit of British Administration,* 1959.
[2] *See* page 156.

Beyond the civil servants there is a wide untidy fringe of committees connecting with the outside world. There are no fewer than *five hundred* standing advisory committees attached to Whitehall departments, usually containing a mixture of civil servants and outside people: the Ministry of Agriculture alone has fifty of them. The more cut-off Whitehall becomes, the more advisory committees spring up, to provide the eyes and ears of the world: and this penumbra has produced its own race of committee men, nipping in and out of Whitehall from business, farming or trades unions. Once a man is established as a 'good committee man'—'house-trained' as they say—he will move from one committee to another: in 1960 it was found that 34 people occupied 85 places in Home Office committees, while 30 individuals filled a total of 154 places—over five each—on Government bodies.[1] 'Round how many ministerial tables are to be found the same convex waistcoats and bloodshot eyes?' asked the *New Statesman* in 1957.

What are committee men like? This is one romantic description, by William Cooper, who—like C. P. Snow—is a novelist-civil-servant-scientist:

A dozen men are standing about in a nondescript room that contains a carpet, a desk, a glass-fronted book-case, possibly a picture, and a big table: a dozen men of *not* all shapes and sizes. Of all sizes possibly, but of a family resemblance in shape, heavily muscled, substantial, pretty masculine men, men who probably played games well in their youth and have certainly enjoyed sustained robust health ever since. The committee man is characterized by energy and stamina; he can go on for hours—he will never get his way if he cannot. His facial expression is sharp and intelligent but not given to sudden changes, least of all changes indicating passing emotion. His voice is loud—the committee man does not have to be asked to speak up. He stands around chatting genially, possibly jocularly, about one of that morning's letters to *The Times*, until the chairman's voice sounds unhurriedly above the rest: "Well, gentlemen, shall we get round the table?'

The committee man loves his job. It would not be unusual to hear two members of our type of committee reminiscing nostalgically about the days during the war when life was really being lived to the full—when they went home at half-past nine instead of six! . . .

[1] Advisory Committees in British Government. *PEP.* 1960. pp. 53–54.

Is the committee man who governs us a ruthless seeker and wielder of power? asks the beady-eyed, non-committee, governed man. The answer is that he may or may not be, but in any case, *that is not how it seems to him*.[1]

The 'good committee man' is one who patiently lets others speak, guides the discussion, gradually infiltrates his viewpoint, accepts a few compromises, but eventually produces a solution that is nearer his than other people's. An important chairman's technique, when faced with a disagreement on principle, is to discuss not *whether* something should be done, but *how*—to blur the ends in the means—until the question of principle imperceptibly disappears—as happened in the cabinet, one suspects, over Suez and over the Common Market.

To swing a committee effectively involves a good deal of hard work: 'The man who reads his agenda properly', said Dr Charles Hill, 'has a tremendous advantage. You can't really impress a committee unless you've done your homework'. To be a bad committee man is not necessarily an overwhelming drawback in Whitehall. At least one influential man in the Treasury quite often loses his temper, and Sir Solly Zuckerman, the chief scientist in Whitehall, is well-known for his offhand committee behaviour and his habit of suddenly going off to the zoo. But many brilliant, first-class men have been ousted by second-raters because they were 'bad at committees': and for most men, the path to power is through the quiet and patient handling of a group of colleagues.

De-personalisation is emphasised by the minutes—the links which convert committees into actions. A careful memorandum circulates through Whitehall, describing the art of minute-taking, explaining how to play down personal conflicts, to avoid ascribing particular views to particular men, and to compose a corporate committee-view.

The horrors of committees are notorious. They not only waste time and energy: they are apt to produce camel-like decisions which may look sensible inside the committee room, but are absurd in a larger context. The camel image is quite exact, for when given the problem of an awkward hump, like a dromedary's, a favourite committee device is to resolve it by adding *another* hump. In this way the BBC resolved the problem of the dwindling Third Programme by adding a half-hearted extra one, Network Three;

---

[1] William Cooper: The Committee Man and the Technician. *Twentieth Century*, October, 1957.

and the Home Office, faced with the absurdities of an expensive passport, invented a second kind of passport. Similarly, when faced with a conflict between two or three people, a committee will always tend to resolve it by bringing in a fourth. Committees dread 'having a row', however legitimate the row may be. They can often acquire a life and vested interest of their own, continuing with chairman, secretary and agendas long after their original purpose is finished.

Committees are masters of muddle, in their closed world of cross-purposes. Muddle is the extra unknown personality in any committee. This is how one commentator has described it:

> It comes from people not doing what they were expected to do, or doing what they are not expected to do, or simply not bothering to say they have not done what they were expected to do. It springs from the exchanges of memoranda in which everybody puts his position too strongly, from the conference at which complete agreement is reached and which everyone leaves with a different idea of what has been decided, from the order half understood but instantly executed, from the stand on dignity . . .
>
> The most engaging feature of muddle at its best is that it proliferates like yeast in a warm room, and every attempt to explain it gives rise to a new and more complete muddle.[1]

'If our society comes to an end', wrote William Whyte, writing about America, 'it will not be with a bang or a whimper. The sound track will be the soft tinkle of rimless glasses on a conference table.'[2] But in spite of all the apparent deadness and de-personalisation of the committee world, decisions are still pushed and swung by strong individuals: a man with 'fire in his belly' (a good Treasury phrase) can still activate and enthuse other people: and the vital decisions of our time—the move into Europe, the break with South Africa, the making and unmaking of Central African Federation—are the result not of green cloth and clean pens, but of one or two men making up their own minds, tempering and trimming them to the needs of committees, but never fooled into thinking that satisfying a committee is an end in itself.

[1] Patrick White: Not-so-plain Muddle, *The Guardian*, October 6, 1961.
[2] W. H. Whyte: *Is Anybody Listening*, p. 223. New York, 1952.

16

ARMED FORCES

The British Army should be a projectile to be fired by the British Navy.

Lord Grey of Fallodon.

'Two things you must realise about the services', said an air chief marshal. 'Firstly they're all together now: you mustn't treat 'em separately. Secondly they've all had the glamour taken out of 'em.'

No limb of Britain has had such sharp and sudden jolts. The civil service has come up against almost equally pressing new problems, but less spectacular and visible ones. But all three fighting services have come up against inventions which have challenged their core, and faced with these revolutionary situations, they have not been able to say to themselves 'it may seem odd, but it works'. After the afternoon in Hiroshima of August 6, 1945, it seemed as if they might virtually cease to exist. Since then, with the re-emphasis on conventional warfare, they have continued in uncertainty, hovering between H-bombs and rifles, missiles and fighters, aircraft carriers and nuclear submarines. The navy is being forced further under water, for longer times; the air force must envisage planes without pilots; the army is becoming a mobile police force. The old idea of defending the British Isles has become virtually meaningless, and the three services have all become involved in elaborate and tricky alliances.

'The boffin', too, has come into their midst. The services, like civil servants, have always liked to keep experts at arm's length. 'Never let the engineer on to the bridge', has been a naval maxim, and the most technical branches of the army, like REME or RAOC, have been the most junior. Military technology— more than in most other countries—has been regarded as something separate. Naval engineers used to have purple between the gold rings on their sleeves, to mark them off from executive officers. Reluctantly the services are accepting the importance of specialists; engineers are still not allowed on the bridge, and the Board of Admiralty still consists entirely of executive officers. But the orange band has disappeared, and there is now no badge except a Scots accent to distinguish the engineer.

In spite of their contraction and changes, the cost of the services remains by far the biggest item in the national Budget. The estimated cost of Defence in 1961–62 was £1,655 million, which accounts for a quarter of the Budget, and 8 per cent of the National Income—second only to America among Western countries. These were Defence expenditures in NATO countries in 1958.[1]

Country	£ m.	% Nat. Income	Per Head (£)
Belgium	131	3·8	14
Canada	642	6·2	38
Denmark	50	3·2	11
France	1,180	7·0	26
Germany	529	3·2	10
Greece	54	6·4	7
Holland	151	4·8	13
Italy	359	4·3	7
Luxemburg	3	2·1	10
Norway	49	3·8	14
Portugal	31	4·7	3.10s.
Turkey	188	6·5	7
U.K.	1,554	7·8	30
U.S.	16,251	11·2	93

Britain spends nearly three times as much on defence as she does on education: the cost of a single new aircraft carrier—about £50 million—could build five universities the size of Brighton's. The air force costs as much in a year as the entire gross national product of Ghana. This is how the money and men were divided in 1961–2:

Admiralty	£413 million	92,000
War Office	507 „	166,000
Air Ministry	527 „	138,000
Aviation Ministry	190 „	—
Defence Ministry	19 „	—

THE ROYAL NAVY

Pray state this day, on one side of a sheet of paper, how the Royal Navy is being adapted to meet the conditions of modern warfare.
Winston Churchill to First Lord, 1941.

The most dramatic post-war change has been the diminution of the Royal Navy—the arm which, most of all, had been associated with Britain's imperial grandeur. To a schoolboy before the

[1] From Alastair Buchan: *NATO in the 1960's*, p. 39.

war, the navy on cigarette cards, in news films or in the Spithead review, was a visible symbol of 'red on the map'. In 1914, when the navy was at its peak, it had 389 ships, including 71 battleships and battle cruisers, and 148,000 men. In 1939, it was still the largest navy in the world, with 300 ships but 161,000 men. By 1961, it was the third largest navy, with 188 ships, no battleships, but still with 96,330 men. This was the state of the biggest navies in 1960 (the smallest is Thailand's, with five frigates).

	USA	USSR	UK	France
Total strength	635,787	500,000	96,330	67,191
Heavy Aircraft Carriers	9	—	—	—
Large A-Cs	24	—	3	—
Light A-Cs	5	—	6	4
Escort Carriers	20	—	—	—
Battleships	8	—	—	1
Cruisers	60	58	8	5
Destroyers	362	150	39	18
Frigates and Escorts	340	250	85	37
Submarines	157	450	47	20
Nuclear Submarines	17	3	1	—

The old symbol of naval glory was the battleship, the grey floating fortress which was Britain's ultimate weapon. The battleship had the infinite protocol of a floating court, and it provided its own grand mythology of rum, beards and quarterdecks. There are some who say that the battleship was obsolete by the time of the Battle of Jutland, in 1916: but its doom was sealed on May 24, 1941, when the biggest of them all, HMS *Hood*—pitifully unprotected—was sunk by the *Bismarck*. Battleships lingered like dinosaurs until 1960, when HMS *Vanguard*, the pride of the post-war fleet, was towed to the scrap-yard. With it went a way of life. The new kind of navy is as different as porpoises from whales: aircraft carriers and submarines, with eccentric designs, have penetrated under and over the water. In a modern submarine, jammed with pipes, wires and electronic equipment, there is no room for protocol or even for admirals.

The precipitate change has brought agonising adjustments. Young naval officers trained before the war for a life of seamanship have found themselves in the sixties with not a ship in sight. Only one in six senior naval officers is now attached to a ship. At the age of thirty or so, naval officers are divided into a wet list and a dry list. A sea-captain ashore remains a fish out of water.

The enormous numbers in the navy (particularly the eighty admirals) compared to the ships, have aroused a good deal of comment: it was the navy which caused Professor Parkinson to formulate his famous 'Law' (which we will encounter several times in this book) that 'work expands so as to fill the time available for its completion'. Parkinson observed that the fewer the ships the larger the numbers in the Admiralty: and his theory was fully supported, as it happened, by the Select Committee on the Estimates, who published a report in September 1960. They observed with anxiety that although the number of ships between 1952 and 1960 had fallen from 376 to 235, the number of head-quarters staff in the previous year had actually *risen* by twenty-eight. They suggested that naval officers wasted too much time and money travelling by train between London and Bath and that the traditional habit of moving naval officers away from the Admiralty every two years was inefficient and wasteful. They even dared to criticise the navy's conservatism—'Noble traditions of loyalty and service must be jealously preserved', they wrote, 'but they must not be permitted to form a barrier against experiment and reform.'

The admirals, in an official counter-salvo, angrily retorted that designs, stores, research, welfare and treaty arrangements had become far more complicated. A modern cruiser, they explained, needed 2,647 specification pages, compared to 978 twenty years ago: the items in naval stores had gone up from 319,000 to 529,000 in eight years. But the Lords of the Admiralty remain a monument to Parkinson's Law, and their staff and their eighty admirals show no signs of diminishing: in 1961, when many people were expecting a contraction, they moved into a vast glass skyscraper which sticks out, like the bridge of a great ship aground, next to Earl's Court stadium. 'You don't seem to be able to get *hold* of that Octopus at Bath', one Admiralty man told me: 'you can't quite discover what they're all *doing*.' The overseas bases at Gibraltar, Malta and Singapore have accumulated a vast legacy of out-of-date obligations, and Singapore alone employs 10,000 people. The Commanders-in-Chief at Portsmouth and Devonport, whose rôle is now very obscure, have accumulated huge private empires. 'We've got the weevils into 'em', one Admiralty man assured me: 'the places are *riddled* with dry rot'. But the admirals have so far shown themselves very resistant to weevils.

The navy often appears trapped in tradition. At the Royal Tournament in 1961, the navy's two exhibitions showed cutlass fighting and hornpipe dancing at the time of Nelson, and field-guns at the time of the Boer War. Ships, cut off from the mainland, acquire a strange way of life of their own. The navy has always been conscious of being the special and Senior Service (it has the least difficulty in finding recruits) and the unique flavour of the naval officer ashore can be sampled at the Goat Club in Bond Street; or at the R.N.V.R. Club in Mayfair, where the bedrooms are cabins, and taxis are called alongside.

But the navy has always had a tradition of radicalism, tinged with eccentricity alongside its conservatism. It can suddenly be extraordinarily unconventional—as when in 1915 Lord Fisher had two battleships stripped of their guns to carry aeroplanes, thus inventing the aircraft carrier. The navy has a contact with foreign countries which induces a sense of diplomacy, and a certain vulnerability to other ideas: navies are closer to each other than armies or air forces, and they develop a salt-water comradeship. Outside the services, British naval officers are regarded as the smoothest and most adaptable of the three arms—which reflects itself in the ease with which they find jobs in industry.

FIRST SEA LORD

The most striking example of the radical naval tradition is the First Sea Lord himself—the professional head of the navy— Admiral Sir Caspar John. Sir Caspar is very different from the public notion of an admiral. He is, in the first place, the son of Augustus John, and he has the powerful eye of his father, and dark eyebrows which jut out sideways. He is married to a sculptress, and together they are often seen in a Bohemian Chelsea pub. He dislikes pomp and convention. He is tall, rather taciturn, with a dry wit and a clipped way of talking. I found him one of the most impressive and engaging people in Whitehall.

He went to school at Dartmouth, and joined the navy in the year of the Battle of Jutland. From the beginning he was an unconventional kind of sailor. He disliked battleships, volunteered for the Fleet Air Arm at a time when 'bird men' were regarded as very inferior, and was a close friend of another unusual sailor, Lord Louis Mountbatten. John was excited by the problems of the navy in the air age. He spent most of the second world war not at sea, but at desks, first at the Ministry of Aircraft Production, and then in Washington, planning the navy's air strength. He is the first aviator to become First Sea Lord: in his office, looking over the Horse

Guards, there are two jet fighters on the marble mantelpiece.

'We really need a new word for admiral', John said: 'the public thinks of admirals as men with big black beards pacing the quarterdeck. Most of us don't pretend to be admirals in that sense: we're more like general managers of companies.

'We're doing what we can to cut down the numbers, and we're having some success in cutting the top hamper. But the navy's far more complicated than it used to be: the business of design, technical development and production absorbs a lot of our admiral talent. And there are far more senior shore jobs than there were: we have to ante up our quota of officers to NATO and SEATO and CENTO and unified commands as well as to various other allied and inter-service organisations. At these international gatherings you have to have people with brass up the elbow, and all the trimmings: but they're all *ashore*, Sampson—that's the snag.

'Of course we need drastic changes: the navy has to keep on changing. Occasionally I get messages from people who say: "we've got reorganisational indigestion—please let up a bit". I reply: "If you can't keep up with the times, please leave the navy".'

After the war, with domination of the air force, the invention of the H-bomb, and the disappearance, one by one, of British bases abroad, it looked as if the navy's day was done. (I remember cleaning an Oerlikon gun on a cruiser, the day after Hiroshima, and wondering how it could possibly be needed again.) But with the nuclear deadlock, and the development of nuclear submarines, navies reasserted themselves. After a long depression, the British Navy began about five years ago to feel itself important again. And as the Empire dwindled, leaving fewer safe bases for armies and navies, so the idea grew up that the navy itself might constitute a floating base in the Far East, like the American Sixth Fleet, complete with its own air force, commandos, missiles, tankers and depot-ships—capable of remaining at sea if necessary for months on end. This has become the navy's great dream, and if it comes true it will mark a full circle. For the navy was first built up to protect British shipping and interests abroad; then helped to establish Britain's military strength in the great bases of the Empire; now it is retreating from the shore bases, back to the safety of the sea.

THE ARMY

'Britain's a very tribal nation', said one major-general at the War Office: 'that gives the army tremendous moral strength, but it has snags.' The tribal basis of the infantry is the regiment, which is (far more than a ship or a squadron) the repository of loyalty. Regiments in their modern form were invented—like the civil service—in the dynamic 1870's. They were devised by Colonel Cardwell, the secretary of state for war, as a way of ruling the Empire: there were seventy-five regiments, each with two battalions—one at home, the other guarding a distant outpost—and in their static isolation they developed powerful and splendid characters of their own. 'Regiments are not like houses', said Winston Churchill in 1904, 'they cannot be pulled down and altered structurally to suit the convenience of the occupier or the caprice of the owner. They are more like plants: they grow slowly if they are to grow strong . . . and if they are blighted or transplanted they are apt to wither.'

Like most other British institutions, the regiments acquired their strict 'peck-order'. The richer ones insisted on private incomes, and through bequests and private enterprise they acquired large funds (the Grenadiers supplement their funds by sending their band round the world). The younger, poorer regiments fell behind. At the top of the peck-order are the five regiments known as the Household Brigade, or simply 'The Guards'. They are entrusted with guarding the Queen, including marching outside Buckingham Palace in black bearskins, and once a year 'trooping the colour' in front of their Colonel-in-Chief, the Queen.

The Guards are the epitome of the tribal strength of the army. The three oldest regiments—the Grenadiers, the Coldstream and the Scots Guards—all date back to the Civil War, when they helped to restore King Charles II to the throne (though the Coldstreamers, the oldest of the three, had originally been raised as part of Cromwell's New Model Army). The Irish Guards were founded in 1900, to commemorate the Irish bravery in the Boer War, and the Welsh Guards (whose Colonel is Prince Philip) in 1915.

Since the war, the Guards have modified their requirements: officers need no longer buy their own headgear, and men need only be five-foot-eight. Like ordinary regiments, the Guards have had to drum up their recruits as best they can: the Irish Guards have little difficulty, but the others have had to roam the country to recruit their seven thousand. The tribal pattern is beginning to dissolve, and some of their best recruiting areas—Nottingham, Lincolnshire or Bristol are in very unguardsmanlike areas.

But the 550 regular Guards officers form a tightly-knit group which—more even than merchant bankers or the Inns of Court—

have resisted the democracy around them. Half the officers (I was told) are sons of Guards officers: all went to public schools, a large proportion to Eton, and nearly all have a private income. ('Officers commanding regiments', says the recruiting pamphlet, 'discourage parents from giving their boys more than £200 a year at the most when they first join.') They have their own club in Mayfair, their own polo club, cricket club, saddle club, flying club, shooting club. They have a network of ex-officers all over the country, who help in recruiting and providing employment. Guards officers can even, through the Guards Employment Society, arrange to have their houses built, or their suits made, by ex-Guardsmen. Guards officers like to cultivate careful snobberies and, like courtiers, a rigid code of what is and is not said, of a Nancy Mitford kind—like not saying 'cheers' before drinking. You must say servant, not batman; bearskin, not busby; telephone, not phone; go to London, not up to town (the distinctions are proudly explained in the film *The Queen's Guards*). They thrive on the nice distinctions of mess behaviour, and the embarrassment of outsiders. They can be rude, idle, self-satisfied and unintelligent. But they remain what they are supposed to be, a superb fighting force: and it is in the army that tribalism and lack of social mobility—so damaging in other fields—have their greatest justification.

OFFICERS AND TECHNICIANS

But in the post-war years the regiments, magnificent though they are, have become an awkward problem, for they hamper the army in the most crucial modern quality—mobility. Units invented for long campaigns in distant colonies are much less useful for quick flights to unpredictable crises. While the air force and navy can cross-post their men to any ship or base, the army must deal with units of 800. And there have been too many regiments. Between 1958 and 1961 twenty-three pairs of regiments were merged, painfully and with bitter resentments which are still smouldering. Regiments, like the Inns of Court or Oxbridge colleges, produce endless complications of rivalries and non-collaboration. 'A military system so old, so involved and so set about with traditions is cram full of complications and special circumstances; particularly where the various land reserve forces are concerned, the heirs of the Elizabethan trained bands, the Georgian militia and the Victorian volunteers.'[1]

[1] M. R. D. Foot: *Men in Uniform*, 1961. p. 129.

The caste tradition of army officers is followed by most fighting countries. In Russia the officers are much more segregated: the sons of private soldiers cannot become officers, and the highest ranks earn 115 times as much as the lowest (in Britain they earn twenty times, in America fifteen times as much). But tradition and segregation often comes into conflict with innovation, and in the British Army, where technologists have always been regarded as an inferior race apart, the synthesis is difficult. The old separation between the teeth and the tail—the fighting men at the front, and the technicians at the back—is dangerous at a time when the tail must often be swallowed by the teeth. Regimental traditions are apt to encourage officers to believe that they have some ancient moral right to lead men into battle: while the modern army demands technical and professional, as much as moral, qualifications.

The army college at Sandhurst has tried since the war to produce more technical officers, but between its traditions of conformity and discipline and the need for enterprise and innovation there remains a difficult gulf ('A troublesome and erratic figure', said the Sandhurst report on Cadet Montgomery, with a mixture of prescience and narrowness, 'far too self-opinionated and grievously lacking in the polished manner one would like to see in a Sandhurst cadet').[1] And Sandhurst cadets are still recruited from a tiny sector of society: according to the Grigg report of 1958, out of 6,171 cadets, between 1947 and 1958, two-thirds came from public schools, including

399	from	Wellington
302	„	Eton
114	„	Marlborough
114	„	Sherborne
105	„	Cheltenham
97	„	Winchester
93	„	Haileybury

Wellington and Eton have produced nearly 12 per cent of the cadets: and the position has changed remarkably little in seventy years. These were the schools which supplied more than ten cadets in the years 1891 and 1961:

[1] Hugh Thomas: *The Story of Sandhurst*, 1961. p. 173.

1891		1961	
Wellington	37	Wellington	54
Eton	29	Haileybury	21
Clifton	19	Eton	20
Marlborough	16	Ampleforth	17
Harrow	16	Marlborough	16
Haileybury	14	Downside	15
Charterhouse	14	Rugby	12
Cheltenham	12	Cheltenham	11
Westward Ho	11	Sherborne	11
Bedford	11	Bedford	10

The most powerful spokesman for the intensive education of officers is Major-General Hackett, the commandant of the army's scientific college at Shrivenham. Hackett himself, although a great advocate of equitation, is a striking example of a new, rare, egg-head officer. The son of a diplomat, he was a scholar at New College, Oxford. He joined the army—one of very few graduates at that time—and rose quickly, with persistent courage, in the war: he is now widely tipped as a future head of the army. 'Fully to justify a position of superiority for the officer', Hackett said in 1960, 'we must make him in fact a truly superior person . . . Is the service of the Crown in this country's land forces to be left in the hands of those whom industry would reject, young men too dull to get into Shell, or ICI, or Glaxo?' He foresees a future army in which all senior officers will have taken degrees or their equivalents: 'The army', he said, 'cannot be allowed to become a cloistered enclave of privileged idleness.'[1]

RECRUITMENT

Since the decision to end conscription in 1962, the recruitment of infantry has been a mounting problem. The more warlike parts of the kingdom—Northern Ireland, Scotland and Wales—still provide a steady supply of soldiers; but full employment, affluence, television and motor-cars and mobility have made soldier-families harder to find, while affluence has widened the gap between home life and army life: 'The new kind of council-house life, with washing machines and TV, isn't the obvious background for a soldier,' said one general.

The army has tried to attract men with more comfort, higher wages and less harsh discipline, and they have launched a massive

[1] Paper to the Royal United Services Institute, November 23, 1960.

TV advertising campaign, showing contradictory images of jungle warfare and girls on the beach. In 1961 they spent £400,000 —more than half as much as Persil—on advertising with Colman, Prentis and Varley. 'We're competing with industry now', said one man at the War Office, 'and we have to take a different attitude: it's no longer a question of "you're behind the barricades now—go and get your 'air cut".' This 'TV Army' has been mocked by the navy, who have no difficulty in finding recruits. 'They're going about it the wrong way', said a senior naval man: 'telling them that they can have a bedside lamp and a free pass, and see mother every Thursday. Men like to think of themselves as being tough— that's what impresses the girl-friend.' But so far the television tactics have met with apparent success.

WAR OFFICE

The War Office is the biggest building in Whitehall—an extraordinary quadrangular structure, with four cupolas, a giant staircase and cavernous passages leading to subterranean dungeons. It has an extraordinary convoluted life of its own, and ever since the Crimea it has had a reputation for impenetrable muddle; it is still sometimes known in Whitehall as 'the Duke of Cambridge' after the commander-in-chief at the time of Crimea. The division between military and civil servants (usually distinguishable by the stiff backs of the military and the meditative stoop of the civilians) with both sides frequently changing jobs, gives scope for infinite permutations of muddle. 'The civil servants sit embattled behind their own defences', as one civil servant put it, 'busily controlling the ledgers: occasionally the generals get together with a plan and lob it over the wall to the civil servants, who consider it, turn it down, and throw it back again.' In my dealings with the War Office I found myself met with apparently invincible muddle.

The Chief of the Imperial General Staff, who took over in the autumn of 1961, is a new kind of soldier. General Sir Richard Hull, like his predecessors Festing and Templer, is the son of a soldier. He comes from a very military family: his father was a Major-General, and his sister is married to one. But Hull is also a graduate of Trinity, Cambridge—the first graduate CIGS for decades—and a tank-man; for thirty years the CIGS has always been an infantryman. Like his colleagues Pike and John, he combines a fighting career with strong administrative experience.

Since 1948 Hull has been in and out of the War Office, and an important influence in shaping army policy.

It is clear that the soldier of the future will have to be a much more mobile, adaptable person—if only because of the shortage of soldiers and the reluctance to reintroduce conscription. In its White Paper of 1962, the Government hoped to make up for the loss of men by regrouping and cutting down overseas bases.

THE AIR FORCE

Within the lifetime of many airmen, the Royal Air Force has been born, has struggled for survival, has saved Britain from conquest, and then once again has had to struggle for survival. In 1945 it seemed that the air force was the most secure of all the services. Sixteen years later, with missiles, H-bombs and nuclear submarines, it seems possible that the manned fighter and bomber —the very soul of the air force—may become extinct. The main business of future airmen may be to carry the army, and the navy is steadily encroaching on the air.

The RAF, unlike the other two services, has never had a settled existence. Born in the first world war, it was jealously resented by the army and still more by the navy. The RAF fought bitterly for its independence: 'The air mentality', wrote Lord Templewood (political head of the air force in the 'twenties) 'required a special atmosphere of its own if it was to infuse its full power into a new and revolutionary service . . . The very weight and glory of the naval tradition would have prevented the full recognition of the sovereign power of the new service.'[1]

Airmen were looked down on by the others as upstarts, non-gentlemen, raffish and undisciplined. They reacted by being aggressively air-minded: the new 'university of the air' at Cranwell instilled the spirit of independence, and distrust of the Navy. The separateness of the RAF is reflected in its clubs: while generals, admirals and even other professions mix at the United Service Club or the Army and Navy, the RAF club—to which most air marshals belong—is reserved for airmen.[2] The air force, on the other hand, has a broader intake of officers than the army or navy, with fewer from public schools and a much larger recruitment from the Commonwealth; in 1961 three out of seven members of the Air Council, and five out of twelve

[1] Lord Templewood: *Empire of the Air*, 1957. pp. 272–4.
[2] De Witt C. Armstrong: *The Changing Strategy of British Bases*, 1959. p. 115.

of the Commanders-in-Chief were from other Commonwealth countries.

In forty years, the temper of the air force has been transformed. In its 'string-and-glue' period it was a service of daring individuals. Courage and skill were essential, and air squadrons were capable of extraordinary carelessness. The air force hero of the last war was still the brilliant individualist, called to his fighter at a moment's notice. But after the war, jet planes became faster, more expensive and complex, and discipline and technical certainty became much more crucial. The Meteor jet-fighter, a much more difficult plane than its predecessor, brought reappraisal. Several Meteors crashed through carelessness, and the RAF stiffened its discipline and precautions at airfields. The picture of flying as a way of triumphant self-expression soon faded.

The new kind of pilot is a different animal from the old Flying Officer Prune, and the training of one bomber-pilot costs £100,000. More than the others, the air force has found the glamour taken out of it. A pilot is likely to find himself, not alone in the clouds, but flying with a crew of twenty, in a bomber like a power station, watching a row of black boxes in front of him: he may not even— as in the latest American bombers—have a glimpse of the air. A pilot is a technologist—the kind of person so insistently wooed by industry and commercial airlines. But he must still have courage and devotion, and in peacetime and full employment, the mixture is doubly difficult: at the training station at Hornchurch (the Chief of Air Staff told me) 700 people applied to become pilots in a six-month period in 1961, and only 126 were accepted—half what the RAF needed.

The air force today needs equally daring and expertise. (The RAF has proportionately more graduates than the other services, and more officers to men.) The combination of qualifications is apparent at Cranwell, where cadets fly at 40,000 feet in the morning, and come down for Plato and mathematics in the afternoon.

After forty years the RAF already has strong traditions. A large proportion of Cranwell cadets are the sons of air force men. The backbone of the air force is still the group of men, now in their forties, who flew in the Battle of Britain. But unlike the other two, it is far bigger than it was before the war. In the twenties it had 20,000 men: in 1961 it had 138,000.

The modern airman may find himself nowhere near an aeroplane, and he may spend much of his career sitting next to a rocket. The RAF now look after seventy Thors, sticking out like sore thumbs from the English countryside, each with a team of airmen round it: this is the most painful transition of all—for airmen to become grounded. Rocket bases require a new and difficult kind of watchfulness—to wait for years and years in an atmosphere of monastic seclusion and secrecy, at ten minutes' readiness for war. It is a long way from the dogfight. In the past the air force has been led by aviators, as the navy has been led by saltlicked admirals, but in the future air force administrators may grow up in a separate world from the airmen.

The air force remains more easily adaptable than the other services, and it has never had time to become stiff in the joints. Many aviators, like Sir Thomas Pike, learned to fly in string-and-glue biplanes, commanded fighter squadrons in the war, survived to fly jet-planes at twice the speed of sound, and now administer squadrons of rockets and V-bombers. Sir Thomas Pike, the Chief of the Air Staff, belongs to the pioneer generation. Like Hull, he comes from a formidable military family—father an artillery captain, brother a major-general, who married a major-general's daughter. But Tom Pike broke into the new world of the air, went to the new college at Cranwell, and became wholly engrossed in the problems of flying. He belongs to the austere and unobtrusive school: he doesn't smoke or drink, has no large moustache, and is fascinated by flying as an exact science. Like Sir Caspar, he spent part of the war concerned with organisation in London. But 'Killer Pike' was also a formidable pilot. Even at the age of fifty-three he flew a Lightning fighter at 1,021 miles an hour.

Sir Thomas remains a champion of the manned aircraft: in spite of the advent of missiles, he believes, the air force will still need fighters and bombers with men inside them. 'I think', he told me, 'that rockets and planes will gradually come together towards a single design which will give you the best of both worlds. I think we'll be able to have space planes—fast enough to get out into space and to operate there if necessary. As things get more expensive, however, so decisions get very much harder: in the old days, when faced with a choice of planes, we could say "let's build both", now we've got to take a chance, and decide one or the other.

'I don't think missiles have so far made much difference to the character of the air force: we are still predominantly a flying service. And the change to missiles doesn't seem to have affected morale: although airmen have to stay on the ground, they take missiles very seriously. The technical men and the flying men are coming much closer together.'

DEFENCE

'I suppose we'll all end up in a mud-coloured uniform' is a recurring service phrase. The three services are finding themselves, with amphibious modern warfare, more and more entangled. The air force carries the army, the navy carries the air force, and a joint operation of all three—such as the smooth and rapid landings in Kuwait—can find itself commanded by an air marshal. Sea and air still demand, and mould, different characters: but using missiles, commando-carriers or landing craft, the arms can no longer be separated limbs: they stand or fall together.

If Britain had no fighting traditions, and her forces were invented from scratch, she would probably choose one big service for land, sea and air. For the services now spend a great deal of energy fighting each other for money and jobs: (though the position is not as serious as in America where—so one of the service chiefs assured me—'the navy is much more concerned with keeping secrets from the army than from the Russians'). Gradually the British services are coming closer together—trying to compound their individual loyalties and rivalries with the 'tri-service outlook'.

The unifying organisation, the Ministry of Defence, was only invented in 1946, and it has the tactful obscurity (like the University Grants Committee) which marks new but powerful organisations. The Minister of Defence has none of the traditional splendour of the First Lord of the Admiralty or the Secretary of State for War. The Ministry has no separate building. only a corner in Storey's Gate of the 'New Public Offices'; and its staff consists of civil servants and eighteen officers seconded from the three services, including one major-general, one air-marshal and one vice-admiral. But the Minister is all-powerful. Unlike the service ministers, he has a seat in the cabinet. And he controls the money, like a lion-tamer rationing the meat. The services send their ablest officers to Storey's Gate, to make sure that they present the best case in the battle for money.

Once a week the three service chiefs come together at the

Ministry of Defence to form the Chiefs of Staff Committee. The service chiefs are awkwardly caught between the interests of their service and of the nation; but it is a cardinal British principle that (unlike the German war-time high command) the man who has to carry out a decision should have had a say in framing it. 'It's very difficult not to take a single-service view if you think that your own service is about to be sunk without a trace,' said one of the service chiefs, 'You may find yourself arguing against the national interest. But we all try to take a tri-service outlook.'

The top job in the services is the Chairman of the Chiefs of Staff Committee—a post which was only invented in 1956. It is held in rotation by a soldier, a sailor and an airman. The present holder is the most famous and controversial of all serving officers, Admiral of the Fleet Earl Mountbatten of Burma, whose career is a rare example of royalty making a mark on the bureaucracies of Whitehall. He is the great-grandson of Queen Victoria, and his nephew, Prince Philip, married the Queen. Mountbatten's own life has had a quasi-royal aura: he lives in splendour, with liveried servants, at his Hampshire seat—to which he periodically invites the Chiefs of Staff and his Minister—and as the last Viceroy of India he evokes a vanished age.

But he has been determined to drive his own ambitious path. His father, Prince Louis of Battenberg, was First Sea Lord until, in 1916, he was forced to resign because of anti-German feeling, and this helped to give a lasting ambition to his son. As a young naval officer, he became a wireless expert; by the age of 34 he was commanding a destroyer, by 42 he was Vice-Admiral. After his interval in India he came back to the navy and achieved the position he had always longed for—First Sea Lord—followed by the Chairmanship of the Chiefs of Staff. What job he can turn to *next* is a matter of some speculation in Whitehall.

Mountbatten's career has shown a mixture of ambition, courage and showmanship which has made some enemies: at the Admiralty his grandeur is regarded with a mixture of pride and envy—he is known as 'El Supremo', 'Burma', or 'the Earl'. His tall, handsome person, with abrupt speech and authoritative gestures, has never been afraid of obtruding. He has unorthodox views, including a dash of socialism, and he has influenced his nephew's unorthodoxy: as the last of the Viceroys, in charge of the retreat from India, he invoked the hatred of many Conservatives, particularly of Lord Beaverbrook. But his preoccupation has been with the navy. One of his greatest prides is to have invented the new cruiser HMS

Devonshire. His small office at the Ministry is full of his war-time trophies—a model of HMS *Kelly*, Japanese swords, surrender pens. His ambition has been to preside over a new, revivified navy; and he has nursed the idea of a floating base, and seen it come closer to fruition.

At the Ministry, four different strands converge. Lord Mountbatten represents the fighting services. Sir Robert Scott is the Permanent Secretary, from the Civil Service. Sir Solly Zuckerman is the scientific adviser (of whom we see more in Chapter 33). And above them sits the Minister, trying to mould the three elements into a politically acceptable policy.

Between 1951 and 1961 there were eight Ministers of Defence: Winston Churchill, Lord Alexander, Harold Macmillan, Selwyn Lloyd, Lord Monckton, Lord Head, Duncan Sandys, and Harold Watkinson have all held this transient job. Duncan Sandys, from 1957 to 1959, was the most notorious of them. As the hatchet-man of the present government, he has left his mark on aviation and the Commonwealth, but most sharply of all on Defence; he amalgamated regiments, cut down conventional weapons, wielded the 'Sandys' axe to force premature retirement, and concentrated defence policy on nuclear weapons—a policy of 'big bangs and small forces'. He kept the Chiefs of Staff—who had become uppish—severely in their place: he insisted that they met in his room, not he in theirs; he re-drafted their memoranda and questioned their advice. His departure in 1959 was met with relief.

The present minister, Harold Watkinson, is much less in evidence: he is the least known man in the Cabinet—with the possible exception of Frederick Erroll—and the nearest to a technocrat. His approach makes a contrast with that of his showy contemporary, Ernest Marples: it was Watkinson, at the Ministry of Transport, who decided to introduce parking meters and a Pink Zone to London, but Marples, who succeeded him, got all the publicity and credit.

Watkinson is a sombre, unlaughing man with a brusque way of talking: he went to grammar school, then to London University, then into the family engineering business, and later became a technical journalist and broadcaster. He rose to be naval lieutenant-commander in the war. He lives quietly in Woking, and has few Conservative connections. But his rise has been quick: he went into parliament in 1950, made his mark as Parliamentary Secretary to the Minister of Labour during the newspaper strike, and was Minister of Transport by 1955. Watkinson has just the right qualities for a junior cabinet minister: he is managerially tough, politically weak, hard-working and ungrumbling. Defence is always a central political question, since it accounts for a quarter of the Budget, and involves the crucial political issue of conscription. For the Prime Minister it is important to have a Defence Minister who will do what he is told. Watkinson has patiently and toughly set about his task: he has gradually built up the conventional forces which Sandys had cut down; he has cancelled the programme for the rocket Blue Streak; and has resisted the demands of the Chiefs of Staff for the return to conscription.

In the White Paper of February 1962, it became clear that the Ministry of Defence would acquire much wider powers, and that Mountbatten would be able to deal directly with unified commands overseas. The move towards mud-coloured warriors has been accelerated by the shortage of men. What seems clear is that, without conscription, Britain cannot afford the wastage involved in inter-service rivalries: and that, in the resulting rationalisation the navy will come off best—partly perhaps because the Chairman of the Chiefs of Staff and the Defence Minister are both naval men; partly because the navy has the least difficulty in finding recruits: but mainly because aircraft carriers and nuclear submarines have made the sea, once again, the crucial element for Britain's defence.

WAR LORDS?

Politicians remain firmly in control of the services. Britain has never had a very separate fighting caste. The younger-son tradition, it is true, has now virtually died out and has given way to a tradition of fighting families: in 1961, out of seventeen full generals, admirals and air chief marshals who listed their fathers in *Who's Who*, two-thirds were the sons of fighting men. But most service chiefs have (in contrast to Americans) remained part of a broader society: they belong to Boodle's and White's as well as the United Service. They have never had the chance to develop *folies de grandeur*, and they have become used to being cut down and bullied by politicians in peacetime. They have realised that the only way to get money, in the hectic scramble of Whitehall, is to please the politicians.

The men at the top are not at all typical fighting men: they are chosen with an eye to their skill in negotiation, and the services are beginning to develop a special race of Whitehall soldiers. The

Chiefs of Staff are unobtrusive, unpublicised men. In war-time a dozen generals are known: but now few people could recite the names of Hull, Pike and John. Half their careers have been behind desks, and their battles are intricate arguments with the politicians, and with each other, in the corridors of the New Public Offices. The making of defence policy is one of the most secret and guarded activities of Whitehall, and of the clashes between services and personalities it is hard for any observer to get a glimpse. Parliament has to debate £1,600 million a year with very little knowledge of the arguments behind it.

They are far from the 'war lords' of Marxist imagination. Ever since Cromwell's major-generals, Britain has fought shy of giving soldiers too much power. There has been no General MacArthur or General Challe, who can defy political leaders, and there is no powerful military lobby at Westminster like Washington's. Since Haig effectively withstood Lloyd George in the First World War, no warrior has had much political strength. Nor has Britain chosen a general to run the country—like de Gaulle, Eisenhower, Nasser, Khan or Kassim. The last and only military prime minister was the Duke of Wellington.

17

TREASURY

Like inverted Micawbers, waiting for something to turn down.
Winston Churchill.

It is a grave administrative mistake to concentrate this massive
power of negation in the hands of, relatively, a small number of
officials who have no other function but the forthright utterance of
the Everlasting Nay.

Harold Laski.[1]

AT the end of Whitehall, where it turns into Great George Street,
is a huge and ugly building, with cupolas at the corners and a
circular courtyard in the middle, whose special prestige in
Whitehall can be guessed by the presence of window-boxes with
flowers. It contains—so one messenger assured me—a thousand
rooms and nine miles of corridors. It is officially known as 'The
New Public Offices'—the name it was given when it was planned
in 1908. More commonly it is known as 'the Great George Street
Front'. The labyrinthine corridors inside, which curve and
converge like an underground railway, are high and dark, painted
with the hospital colours—greens and creams—favoured by the
civil service; and above the corridors hangs a mass of piping and
wiring, like the lower decks of a battleship.

This is the central citadel of Whitehall. The building contains
the three most important departments—the Cabinet Office, the
Ministry of Defence and the Treasury—and many of the best
minds in the civil service. Here assemble the budget committees,
the cabinet committees, the defence committees, on which the
country's future depends. If anyone were to wish to bring the
British administration to a halt, it is on this building, rather than
on parliament opposite, that he should drop his bomb.

But the Treasury is the most important. Of all government
departments, it is the most abused, mocked and disliked: for it is
their job to say No. They are responsible not only for taxing the
public, but for cutting down government expenditure, and for
questioning every new project. They are abused, not only by the

[1] *Reflections on the Constitution.* 1951. p. 184.

taxpayers, but by every Whitehall department—and most of all by the scientists, who regard the Treasury with venomous incomprehension. Faced with this odium, the Treasury adopt, like judges, an attitude of resigned immunity. In the waiting-room of the Chancellor of the Exchequer is a framed quotation, intended, no doubt, to placate angry deputations demanding money:

> Friends and neighbours, the Taxes are indeed very heavy, and if those laid on us by the Government were the only ones we had to pay, we might more easily discharge them; but we have many others, and much more grievous to some of us—we are taxed twice as much by Idleness, three times as much by our Pride, and four times as much by our Folly; and from these Taxes the Commissioners cannot ease or deliver us.
>
> *Benjamin Franklin, 1758.*

TREASURY MEN

No species in Whitehall is more distinct than the Treasury Men, for they are the mandarins among mandarins. There are only about 1,400 people at the Treasury (compared to 7,000 at the Board of Trade and 630,000 in the whole civil service), but of those less than two hundred are members of the Administrative Grade, and it is they who run the country's finances.[1] They are the pick of the civil service; the Treasury can take the cream of recruits, and later can steal men from other departments, or send its own men to run departments. Treasury men are known to be members of a chosen race, and apart from their actual power, this gives them an edge over the un-chosen.

The compactness of the Treasury astonishes American enquirers, compared to the complexity of Washington. The two hundred all know each other, and information and reputations run through Great George Street as through a school. In the Treasury the literary, Oxbridge character of Whitehall has had its quintessence, exemplified by its previous head Lord Bridges, son of a poet-laureate, Old Etonian, Fellow of All Souls. In the past ten years this atmosphere has been diluted by economists, grammar school men and war-time accretions: but much of the literary mystique remains. The Treasury is half-way between a university and a business, and caught awkwardly between the two—without the academic standards of the first, or the practical engagement of the second.

[1] Even this is a huge increase over previous numbers: in 1914 there were only 35 Administrative Treasury men.

The Treasury are an intellectual, not a social, élite; none of them belong to the world of interlocking relationships in the first chapter, and they are not likely to be seen in the drawing-rooms of 'society'. Most of them live in suburbs, and retire in the evening, with a bulging brief-case on a late train, to a simple meal and perhaps washing up. At lunch time they will either go to the Treasury canteen or walk across the park, down the Clive steps and up the Duke of York steps, to, probably the Reform Club. In one fortnight I had lunch with three Treasury men. Each of them said: 'Where shall we lunch—what about the . . . er . . . Reform?' I found Treasury men accessible, straightforward and with few pretensions; no group could be further from the power-hungry men of popular nightmares.

The corporate spirit of the Treasury is still expressed by its legendary passion for music, which seems to fit with its withdrawn world. Treasury men find it hard to forgive the Prime Minister for not being interested in music, and un-musical men in the Treasury have an uneasy feeling that music is important to promotion. There is no longer, as there once was, a quartet of Treasury knights singing madrigals: but there is still a flourishing Treasury choir, which rehearses in a conference hall inside the building; in 1961 they performed *Dido and Aeneas,* conducted by one of the ablest young Treasury men, Robert Armstrong, son of the head of the Royal Academy of Music. The chairman of the choir is Sir Norman Brook (who had a fine bass voice in his youth), and the three other Treasury knights are all musically inclined: Sir Thomas Padmore plays the fiddle, Sir Denis Rickett frequents the opera, Sir Frank Lee listens to his wife playing the piano. 'The Treasury isn't as *establishmenty* as it was', said one of its political masters, 'but it's still rather cut-off: I think music has something to do with it.'

Sitting in offices round the central courtyard are the four Treasury knights. Sir Norman Brook and Sir Frank Lee are the joint heads of the Treasury. Sir Denis Rickett is in charge of Overseas Finance—which includes the crucial problem of balance of payments. Sir Thomas Padmore is concerned with Home Finance. Three of them went to day schools; the only one who fits a picture of the grand-style civil servant is Sir Denis Rickett, who went from Rugby to Balliol, is a quondam Fellow of All Souls, lives in Hanover Terrace, Regents Park, and is often to be seen at Covent Garden.

Since 1956, when Bridges retired, there have been two joint

permanent secretaries of the Treasury. The first and most far-reaching is Sir Norman Brook, who has already appeared as Head of the Civil Service and Secretary of the Cabinet. Most of his time is spent in the Cabinet Office; but within the Treasury he runs the 'Establishment Division', which controls the civil service, salaries, people and organisation.

The other joint head, Sir Frank Godbould Lee, is at the head of the whole financial and economic side of the Treasury—including the budget, monetary control, and government expenditure. Sir Frank doesn't conform to the Treasury image: neither of the two heads of the Treasury was originally a Treasury man, and Lee is an interesting example of a man at the top being different in background from men in the middle. He is a stocky, untidy-looking man with a down-to-earth manner, a love of gardening and music, Trollope and Gibbon, and a reputation for—of all extraordinary things in Whitehall—unpunctuality. He starts work at *nine* in the morning and in the course of my whole enquiry he was the only man who made an appointment before ten o'clock. His career has been unusual: he went to Cambridge from Brentwood school in Essex, took a double first in English and History, joined the Colonial Office, and served as a District Officer in Nyasaland, where he vigorously organised football as an alternative to tribal feuds: and this individual experience, away from the bureaucratic machine, seems to have given him a very different approach to most civil servants. He was picked up by the Treasury during the war, and his energy and clarity soon made their mark: he was moved to Washington, where he worked with Keynes, and rose to be head of the Board of Trade in 1951. There he made close contact with industrialists and European diplomats, and when he moved to the Treasury in 1960, his impact was emphatic; when he was ill early in 1961 many Treasury people remarked on the running-down and his retirement (back to Cambridge) in 1962 will leave a gaping hole.

THE TREASURY'S POWER

The traditional task of the Treasury has been to save the government money: the Chancellor must reflect the ancient parsimony of parliament, and this still makes up the largest part of the Treasury's job. They finance not only every Whitehall department, but also Covent Garden Opera, the National Theatre, the Royal Society, the Science Museum, the Tate Gallery, the Arts

Council, the University Grants Committee: in all these places the Treasury, as their pinchpenny patron, is mentioned with special dread. Among the more picturesque items which appeared in the 1961–2 estimates were:

> Salary of the Pursuivants, at £16 13s. 4d.—£50.
> Engrossing and copying patents of Arms—£350.
> Grouse Ecology Unit—£1,000.
> £89 9s for the bishop of Sodor and Man to distribute among the incumbents and schoolmasters of the Isle of Man.
> Creation money to Trinity College, Cambridge, for the counties of Cambridge and Huntingdon—£5 6s. 8d.
> £1,000 compensation to Oxford and Cambridge for the loss of the privilege of printing and vending almanacs.

The time-honoured Treasury attitude to spending is summed up by 'candle-ends'—the phrase used by Gladstone to describe minute saving of detail. (In the eighteenth century, the stumps of Foreign Office candles were a perquisite of the housekeeper, who sold them to the gentlemen clerks to light their homes.) Much of the candle-ends attitude survives: Treasury men still enjoy 'teasing' other ministries, particularly the Foreign Office—forbidding an Embassy refrigerator or a new coat of paint. 'The Treasury can argue for months on end with all the subtlety of Duns Scotus about what a day's subsistence allowance ought to be for Bogota', said a former Economic Secretary, Nigel Birch, 'but when really large sums are at stake there tends to be a certain withdrawal of interest.'[1] This is always an ominous sign (as with Sir Anthony Eden at the time of Suez)—the swallowing of ends in a multitude of means.

While the Treasury have continued counting the pennies, the whole nature of their task has changed. In the nineteenth century the Treasury had to control the two fighting services and a handful of Whitehall departments. In 1886 Lord Randolph Churchill resigned because the cabinet would not approve a Budget of £100 million (equivalent to about £500 million today). In 1961, the cabinet approved a Budget of £6,500 million. The Treasury found itself in a position to influence the whole character of the country, to discourage some industries and encourage others. 'Instead of worrying about candle-ends', said one ex-Treasury minister, 'they should have asked themselves the question "in what sense should Britain still be a great power?" ' But with their old aloofness from trade, the Treasury have been astonishingly slow to

[1] *Time and Tide*, August 3, 1961.

realise that they are, in fact, the holding company for the biggest group of businesses in Britain. The drastic techniques of investigation used by the big business corporations—for instance in the re-organisation of Shell[1] have filtered very slowly into Whitehall; the whole new science of 'organisation and management' was for a long time regarded—as one Treasury man put it—as 'third-rate witchdoctory'. Gradually since the war the Treasury have been adjusting their methods. Since 1949 they have given more self-government to departments; they have paid less attention to candle-ends and more to investigation, and 'asking questions' about projects; and they have begun to make use of management consultants, computers and accountants to analyse their departments. Parliament, at the same time, has become less querulous, and has come to regard government expenditure less as a necessary evil, and more as an essential investment. 'Before the war both sides of the House were really against public spending', said one Treasury man: 'since the war they've both been *for* it.'

But the Treasury has not, it seems, fully faced up to its vast new responsibilities. The common complaint about the Treasury's stranglehold is misleading: the Treasury has always been afraid of its own power. They have preferred, like Lord Lugard with African tribes, to practise 'indirect rule'—avoiding putting one of their own men in charge, controlling large spending through the local chieftain—while still keeping petty restraints—the relics of candle-ends. The reluctance to rule directly can be seen in their curious relationships with the Court of the Bank of England—regarded essentially as a foreign tribe—in their tolerant attitude to Parkinsonian tendencies, and in their astonishing cat-and-mouse games with the nationalised industries.

A QUESTION OF MAPS

The problem of control is obviously tricky, and behind some tiresome habits of the Treasury is the desire to behave in a fair and democratic way; democracy has always meant inefficiency, and most of us are happy to pay the price. But there are signs that the Treasury has not really thought out its attitudes to control: as Professor Ely Devons has pointed out,[2] two principles tug in opposite directions—the desire to make departments responsible for their own economies, and the desire to be the public's watchdog

[1] *See* page 434.
[2] *Essays in Economics*, 1961. p. 90.

for every item—and the result often leads to pettiness. A vivid example, quoted by Professor Devons, emerged in the Select Committee on Estimates for 1957–8, when an acrimonious little discussion, on whether it was sensible to limit the expenditure on maps by the Ministry of Defence to £2,000 a year, illuminated some Treasury attitudes:

Mr Robinson (a member of the Committee): But somebody in the Department must keep a close eye on expenditure of maps in the course of a year, because he will get into serious trouble if he spends £2,100 and does not inform the Treasury?

Sir Norman Brook: Is that necessarily a bad thing?

Robinson: I would think that it was.

Brook: I can imagine a Ministry of Defence—I do not say the present Ministry—going quite mad over maps and plunging in with great quantities of expensive types of maps. I do not think it unreasonable that there should be some limit.

Sir Godfrey Nicholson (chairman of the committee): Surely this brings up the fundamental principle, do you or do you not expect your Departments and Heads of Departments to be men of a sense of responsibility and ability? Surely the principle should be to give them freedom and to chase them like hell if they abuse it, rather than this sort of governess attitude of letting them out on a lead?

Brook: I am sorry, but I think that the primary object of these delegations is to avoid a lot of unnecessary correspondence about small things, and that the figures were fixed in relation to each subject at a level which would obviate that kind of correspondence.

Nicholson: And against the Head of a Department showing any sense of responsibility?

Sir Thomas Padmore: Only very partially, because in this case, the maps for instance, Sir Richard Powell[1] said that some of these delegations and some of these requirements for references to the Treasury were helpful to him as accounting officer . . . the extent to which an accounting officer in a Department like the Ministry of Defence can occupy himself with expenditure on maps is very limited.

Nicholson: You are getting yourself into a most dangerous position. You are saying that the function of the Treasury is not only to be the long-stop, but to do the function of the accounting officer?

Padmore: With respect, I am not saying that. I am saying that there is a good deal to be said for having a check on the man buying maps for the Ministry of Defence.

[1] Then Permanent Secretary at the Ministry of Defence.

Nicholson: That is the function of the accounting officer of the Ministry of Defence, is it not?

Padmore: So it is, but there is certainly an advantage in some of the delegation limits in that the check is automatically and easily provided by the necessity, if the expenditure goes beyond what has previously been agreed to be a reasonable level, for a report to be made to the Treasury.

Nicholson: I am very sorry, but I think you are advancing a very dangerous doctrine. You are saying that a Department of that kind cannot be trusted to do its own work, and the Treasury must be in the background to stop the balls which go by the wicket-keeper in order to stop the byes.

Padmore: That is not what I intended to say.[1]

ANTIQUITIES AND SCIENTISTS

Another depressing feature of the Treasury's approach is the reluctance to cut down anything which has become long-established. Anything once started acquires its own momentum, and (as Lord Plowden pointed out in his report on Government expenditure) subsidies which were begun as a temporary 'pump primer' to revive a languishing industry have continued long after the purpose had faded. Few people can seriously doubt that the preposterous ramifications of the Admiralty or the War Office —that slippery octopus in Bath, that Earl's Court skyscraper and those Southwark corridors—could not be cut down in size, or that the weevils now reported to be eating into Portsmouth and Devonport could not work faster. Parkinson's Law seems to have become accepted as having a comic inevitability (it might even be said that the Professor himself, by showing how widespread it was, has encouraged acceptance of the Law). This acceptance would matter much less if ours was an age of unemployment and surplus funds: but the grim corollary of the Treasury's love of antiquities is their reluctance to launch anything new: and it is here that the Treasury's lack of imagination is most alarming—as can be observed in its niggardly approach to any new department or establishment.

The Treasury's suspicions of novelties are most acrimonious in their relationships with science. They have still not quite recovered from the early days of the Atomic Energy Authority when the scientists—as is their way—asked for *carte blanche*, and to their

[1] *Seventh Special Report from the Select Committee on Estimates 1958–9*, Appendix 7, pp. 393–4.

astonishment got it: since then the Treasury have reacted with a special scepticism towards scientific ventures, and scientists and mandarins have been at odds.[1] The Treasury's contact with any scientific project, from jet fighters to Blue Streaks, is embarrassed by the fact that they have no scientists on their staff. Scientists angrily complain that their projects are turned down by Treasury committees containing not a single scientist, and they counter-attack by making outrageous demands for money, knowing that they will be cut by half—but finding them sometimes suddenly accepted. It is in scientific fields—the most foreign tribes of all—that the Treasury's indirect rule can be most dangerous.

Treasury men insist that in choosing between rival projects intelligent laymen, like cross-examining barristers, are just as competent as experts—who anyway never agree. But the acrimony and frequent cross-purposes suggest that the traditional lay criticism has become seriously inadequate.

THE BUDGET

The core of the Treasury's traditional rôle is the annual ritual of the budget. The Treasury's year revolves round the budget, as shops revolve round Christmas: the process begins months beforehand—preparing estimates for the departments, calculating the effect of taxes, working out priorities for future spending. At the end of November departments send their estimates to the Treasury and the Chancellor adds up the claims, and decides on the cuts he wants to make. 'I do not know whether you can visualise what the Treasury is like in December and January', one witness told the Select Committee of 1959, 'but it is absolutely chaotic.' Early in January the estimates come before the cabinet. Sometimes the cabinet succeeds in overruling the Chancellor, but usually the Chancellor has his way. The Chancellor summons a secret 'budget committee' (so secret that no one is supposed to know about it) of his closest advisers—the only committee in Whitehall which has no one taking minutes: the rest of the cabinet are only told about its conclusions on the day before. Finally the tattered black box appears, held up in the air by a smiling Chancellor in front of the photographers, and there is the marathon speech itself.

This is how the sum of £6,440 million, which was allocated in 1961, was raised and spent:[2]

[1] *See* Chapter 33.
[2] From the *Financial Statement, 1961-2.*

REVENUE	£m.	EXPENDITURE	£m.
Income tax and surtax	2,951	Sinking Fund, National Debt, etc.	815
Death duties	240	Defence	1,656
Profits Tax, stamps, etc.	419	Health, Pensions and National Insurance	1,296
Tobacco	835	Housing and Local Government	754
Petrol, Oil and Motor Taxes	568	Agriculture	344
Alcohol	418	Transport, Power and Industrial Research	342
Purchase Tax	525	Education and Broadcasting	243
Other taxes and duties	484	Commonwealth and Foreign	134
		Home Office and Justice	121
		Trade, Labour, Aviation	114
		Miscellaneous	183
			6,002
		Surplus	438
TOTAL REVENUE	6,440		6,440

PLANNING

Planning has become an emotional word. For myself, I have always rather liked it.

Harold Macmillan, December, 1961.

But while the Treasury has been engaged in these traditional controls, it has uncomfortably become aware of a new situation. It is as if a rich man in a small country, running his estate in a thrifty and meticulous way, gradually realises that he is the only rich man left, that he accounts for half the country's wealth, and that he is printing money with one hand and spending it with the other. This is how direct government spending ('supply expenditure') has swelled, compared to Gross National Product:

1870	..	4 per cent
1910	..	6 per cent
1930	..	12 per cent
1961	..	22 per cent[1]

Including spending by local authorities, by the nationalised industries and by national insurance funds, the spending in the whole 'public sector' amounts to 42 per cent of the Gross National Product. And while their spending has grown, the government has accepted a much greater responsibility for the well-being of

[1] *See Plowden Report* (Cmnd 1432), p. 6.

the country. In the words of the historic White Paper of 1944: 'The Government accept as one of their primary aims and responsibilities the maintenance of a high and stable level of employment after the war.' These new responsibilities have altered the whole significance of the budget. As the Plowden Report puts it: 'The budget is seen, not as a simple balancing of tax receipts against expenditure, but as a sophisticated process in which the instruments of taxation and expenditure are used to influence the course of the economy.'

This sophisticated process has brought the Treasury knee-deep into the mysteries of economic policy—the pressures, examples, incantations, exhortations and warnings which generate the economic climate. And with their massive new involvement in spending, they have found the initiative for monetary policy passing inevitably from the City of London to Great George Street. Like a large ship in a narrow channel, they have discovered to their alarm that the waves and currents are being created as much by themselves as by the tide. Inflation has repeatedly undermined their plans for control: 'While they're arguing about messengers with one hand', said one critical former Chancellor, 'they're printing millions of bank notes with the other . . . In one year wages have gone up by as much as the cost of three navies . . . In the last resort, the Treasury don't borrow money, they *print* it.'

The awareness of this new situation has brought with it the most controversial word in Whitehall—planning. The idea has ebbed and flowed since the war. Its heyday was in 1947, under a socialist government, when Sir Edwin Plowden (later Lord Plowden of the Report) was Chief Planning Officer. Even before the end of Socialist rule, planning fell into disrepute, discredited by miscalculations and economic crises. Then, after a long lapse, thoughts of planning seeped back in 1961.

Several factors changed the tide. The nationalised industries had obviously come to stay and, since they involved vast government spending, the Treasury had to forecast the needs of transport and power in ten years' time. The government was deeply involved in research projects, most in defence, which might take a decade to fructify and which affect the future of whole industries. ('Can I see your plans for the next five years', one Minister of Defence asked, on moving into the department. 'I'm afraid we haven't got any', replied the civil servant). And all kinds of government investment demanded longer periods of gestation. The building of teacher-training colleges now will affect the cost of education in *eight* years' time. 'It's like one of those balloons on Hampstead Heath, with bits sticking out', as one Treasury man explained it: 'it takes a very long time to blow up, and it comes out a very odd shape.' This big balloon has compelled the Treasury to think more in terms of five-year plans, and less in one-year budgets. Gradually the Treasury—and the cabinet—have been coming round to considering all government expenditure together, as a single plan.

But the government has become aware that it must not only co-ordinate its own finances and production, but those of private industry too. In the course of 1960 and 1961 the French idea of a *Commisariat au Plan*—of industrialists and civil servants together setting targets for economic growth—slowly filtered into Great George Street, by way of the National Institute of Economic and Social Research. The Treasury, in one of its slow corporate changes from one dogma to another, began to abandon old notions of non-interference, and new words like 'guide', 'pause' and 'regulator' began to be murmured. Late in 1961 a National Economic Development Council—generally known as Neddy—was set up with the help of the trade unionists and industrialists, to act as a mild British equivalent to the French *Commisariat*—to help to map out the industrial future of Britain. Its director-general is Sir Robert Shone, an enthusiastic planner from the Iron and Steel Board. Other members include six trade unionists, the chairmen of the Coal Board and the British Transport Commission, and several of the more analytical tycoons—including Reay Geddes of Dunlops, Francis Cockfield of Boots, and J. N. Toothill of Ferranti. The economic director is Sir Donald McDougall, a widely-travelled Oxford economist.

It is still too early to assess the effects of Neddy: it is not intended to be such a close and powerful council as in France—where the technocrats of industry and the civil service work in harmony, without much trouble from the politicians or the chairmen. But the idea of planning appears to have come back to stay, and the consequences of this are enormous. Firstly, it will mean increasingly that the Treasury will be committing itself to five or eight years ahead—so that the schemes will often outlive the government which approved them. Secondly, the traditional machinery of parliamentary estimates to approve annual expenditure will become still less relevant. Already the estimates are virtually a formality, for the real bargaining and horse-trading has been worked out beforehand between the Treasury and the departments: but long-term planning will make parliament's control still less relevant. Thirdly, if planning is to be successful, the experts of industry and Whitehall must come much closer together, and this new core of planners (helped no doubt by the numbers of ex-Treasury men in industry) will inevitably produce a new and powerful 'Establishment' tending towards the French pattern.

But fourthly and most importantly, planning requires an opposite frame of mind to the old Treasury control. Planning means urging expansion and optimism, staking claims for the future, producing a climate of growth and confidence, which is the antithesis of candle-ends.

ECONOMISTS

> Practical men, who believe themselves to be quite exempt from any
> intellectual influence, are usually the slaves of some defunct economist.
> *Lord Keynes.*

As the government has become more involved in planning, so a new species has begun to settle in Great George Street—the economists. Between the 'administrators' and these experts there has been the usual uneasy rivalry. The economists have resented the amateur, ivory-tower aura (Lord Keynes once described the Treasury as being 'suspended between Heaven and the Scottish Education department'), and many economists have insisted that the whole machinery of the civil service must be changed to embrace economic thinking.

During the war, numbers of economists, such as Hugh Dalton, Hugh Gaitskell, Sir Donald McDougall, Harold Wilson, Roy Harrod, or Lord Robbins, penetrated the heart of Whitehall: and after the war a new post of Economic Adviser to the Government was created, to provide special expertise within the Treasury. The present incumbent (who took over from Sir Robert Hall in 1961) is Professor Alexander Cairncross—a realistic, sceptical Scot from Glasgow University. He, too, came into Whitehall during the war, and has been in and out of it ever since; he was one of the most pungent questioners in the Radcliffe Committee.[1] In the Treasury, he is head of a small colony of fifteen in the 'Economic Division'— several of them borrowed temporarily from universities. He is discreet and discounting about his rôle: 'The principal task of an economic adviser', he said when he was appointed, 'is to prevent

[1] e.g., see page 365.

the government from making crashing mistakes.' How far his influence extends beyond that is obscure: but he has the reputation of being a tough, practical man with a feel for world economic developments.

There are other influences beyond the Treasury itself; the disputes of economists are hardly less bitter than theological feuds. A bevy of unofficial economic advisers proffer their advice, warnings or encouragements from university strongholds. The Treasury is always liable to embrace the theories of one prophet at one moment, another the next; and between the Treasury policy-makers and the academic economists lies one of the most peculiar frontiers of government.

This egghead lobby can be noted at the meetings of the 'Tuesday Club'—a mixed gathering of Treasury men and outside economists, which meets on occasional Tuesdays in a private room at the Reform Club (to which nearly all prominent economists belong: a lot of them, too, live in the Hampstead Garden Suburb). The club was founded by Lord Keynes as a meeting place for Treasury men and outside economists: and it is here that men such as Sir Frank Lee, Sir Denis Rickett, Lord Robbins, Sir Robert Hall, Harold Wincott, Otto Clark, Sir Roy Harrod, will exchange panaceas and nostrums. Every year on budget night they assemble for a special dinner at the Reform, to discuss the economic implications.

It is always important to know in Great George Street which prophets are in, and which out. A small group exert a special influence on the Conservative government, but their influence waxes and wanes. There is Professor Paish, the hearty but gloomy Professor at the London School of Economics (whose father was Economic Adviser to the Government in the first world war), who maintains that a small increase in unemployment would have a dynamic effect on the economy. There is Lord Robbins, chairman of the *Financial Times*, and war-time Economic Adviser to the cabinet, who has had a strong influence on past Conservative Chancellors—now said to be waning. There is Sir Roy Harrod of Christ Church, the biographer of Keynes—a convivial don who sends warnings against the Common Market to the Prime Minister.

But it is inside the Treasury that the economists have their main battleground, and it is here that the conflict between candle-ends and planning is most bitter. While one half of the Treasury insists on cutting down expenditure in overseas consulates, the other half protests that consulates are crucial to encouraging exports and growth. Whitehall has still preferred to keep economists at arm's length: there are only twenty senior ones in all government departments. 'When a specific question of economic policy is referred to a committee, the influence of professional economists is unlikely to be significant', complained one of them.[1] Americans continue to be astonished at this lack of expertise in Whitehall: 'Although I do not mean to criticise', said Professor Paul Samuelson in his Stamp Memorial Lecture in November 1961, 'we are often shocked to find that there are scarcely a dozen fully-fledged economists in the Treasury.'[2]

WHITE PAPERING

A persistent feature of the Treasury is secrecy: and this can be well observed in the character of White Papers—which are meant to explain changes, but are in fact carefully devised to conceal them. Pronouncements about fundamental policy changes are made to appear as vigorous endorsement of previous policies. 'The Treasury is like the Vatican'—as one ex-Treasury economist explained to me—'whenever it says something new, it has to pretend that it's really just the same as before. Like the Pope, it must appear infallible.' When a White Paper appeared in April 1961, about the financing of nationalised industries, few laymen could guess that this marked a revolution in government policy. The Plowden Report of July, 1961 was a revolutionary and critical document: but it appeared as a piece of amiable congratulation—'treading with such extreme delicacy'—in the words of *The Times*—'that its footsteps are scarcely audible'. This is a *locus classicus* of Treasury style: here are some of its phrases, with what I have understood to be their actual meaning:

We hope that it is fully appreciated that . . .
    You completely fail to realise that . . .

Greater emphasis should be laid on . . .
    You haven't bothered to notice . . .

We have the impression that insufficient study has been given to . . .
    No one has considered . . .

[1] *See* P. D. Henderson: "The Use of Economists in British Administration." *Oxford Economic Paper*, February, 1961.
[2] *The Times*, November 10, 1961.

Our enquiry seemed to provide a welcome opportunity for discussions
of problems of this kind . . .

No one had thought of that before . . .

We do not think there is sufficient awareness . . .

There is ignorance . . .

There has been a tendency in the past to overestimate the possibilities
of useful short-term action in public investment . . .

You should look ahead . . .

There should be an improvement in the arrangements to enable
ministers to discharge their collective responsibility . . .

The cabinet should work together . . .

This obscurantism is deep-rooted. It comes partly from the
traditional 'kid glove language' of Whitehall, which always
disguises instructions as suggestions, and instinctively prefers 'not
inappropriate' to 'appropriate'. Departments are never *ordered* to
do anything: they are 'invited to submit proposals . . .' Learning
this language is part of the process of becoming 'house-trained' in
Whitehall; and anyone who says straightforwardly what he thinks
is likely to be labelled as a bull in china-shop. Obscurity is
encouraged, to avoid offending previous ministers and officials. I
asked one Treasury man why, since the White Paper on nationalised industries was so important, it did not say so: he said 'But
what would all the previous ministers think, if it appeared that
they'd been doing it all wrong?'

Much of the fog conceals disagreement. When a report is
unanimous, like the Devlin Report on Nyasaland, it is translucent:
when it is a compromise, like the Radcliffe Report on the Bank of
England, it is opaque. Important Whitehall documents all go
through the process of toning down, passing from department to
department, 'papering over the cracks' (in the Treasury phrase),
until much of the original force—or even sense—has vanished.
'By the time the civil service has finished drafting a document to
give effect to a principle' said Lord Reith, 'there may be little of
the principle left.'[1] A striking example is the Treasury's annual
Economic Survey, which begins its annual progress through Whitehall as a bold and forthright statement, gradually accumulating
qualifications, reservations, inhibitions and misgivings, until it
appears every April in such an innocuous form that few people
bother to read it.

[1] J. C. Reith: *Into the Wind*, 1949. quoted in S. Beer: Treasury Control, p. 120.

Treasury men insist that this process is part of the machinery of democracy, and that the ambiguities stem from the chief committee of all—the Cabinet. The muzziness of White Papers expresses the muzziness of twenty men each trying to get his own way. But in the Treasury, fogginess has long ceased to be a temporary smoke-screen, and has become a permanent camouflage. To compare the Northcote-Trevelyan report, with its hard-hitting language about 'the unambitious, and the indolent or incapable', with modern White Papers, is to see how far the civil service has become turned in on itself. At a time when the Treasury, much more than ever before, needs to exhort and enlighten the public, the idea that White Papers are meant to inform the public and parliament has been virtually forgotten: they are written from one department to another, full of mandarin language. And in the process of fooling the public, one suspects that civil servants begin to fool themselves.

EXODUS

With the progress of planning, the relationships between the Treasury and industry are becoming increasingly important, and those relationships have been somewhat changed by the spectacular exodus of senior civil servants, nearly all Treasury men, into industry since the end of the war. It began in 1951, when Sir Henry Wilson-Smith left to become Deputy-Chairman of Powell Duffryn, and Sir John Woods left the Board of Trade for English Electric; Sir James Helmore left the Ministry of Supply in 1956 for Warburg's Bank; his successor, Sir Cyril Musgrave, left to become Chairman of the Iron and Steel Board. In 1960 there was a greater shock when Sir Leslie Rowan, one of the Treasury knights, left for Vickers; and the next year Sir Edward Playfair, the head of Defence, became chairman of International Computers. One firm, Tube Investments, contains two high-powered ex-Treasury men—Lord Plowden, the chairman-elect and former chief planner in the Treasury; and Sir William Strath. Then there has been the steady migration from the Inland Revenue—a Treasury annexe—including Sir William Coates and Paul Chambers to ICI, and Francis Cockfield to Boots.

The main cause is probably money. Permanent secretaries can earn more than twice £7,000 in industry: and since the war they have been allowed to keep their pensions if they leave after the age of fifty. Also, the life of a tycoon is easier—there is less pressure of work, no parliament watching you, no minister in the way.

There are fewer committees and less frustration, and some civil servants, like Sir Leslie Rowan, had become visibly impatient with the Whitehall machine.

The powers in Whitehall insist that they are not worried by the exodus, and they regard it as a compliment to the excellence of top civil servants. 'There are a lot of first-class men at the top', one permanent secretary explained, 'partly because a lot came in at the same time, just after 1925.' But I found it odd that, with the rapid growth of Whitehall, and the pressure of work at the top, the exodus should be taken so lightly. While civil servants leave, there is no counterflow from industry to Whitehall, for few industrialists, in the present situation, would take such a drop in salary and freedom.

The exodus has helped to encourage a new closeness between the separate worlds of Whitehall and industry. Industrialists like to choose civil servants partly because 'they know their way around Whitehall'—which has growing powers over industry: but also because the industrial giants, as they develop from pioneering and brigandage into vast, settled corporations, feel the need for the patient, analytical intellects of Whitehall.

Is there something alarming about this spreading of the Treasury net? Will eventually ICI, Vickers, British Aluminium, Tube Investments (all of which have, or are likely to have, ex-Treasury chairmen) become part of the charmed Treasury circle? One imagines a clutch of chairmen meeting at the Reform Club, after a brisk round of madrigals, to settle the country's future: for anyone inclined to the 'conspiratorial view' of history, this spread of the mandarins must seem disquieting.

But Treasury men are not as unanimous as they might appear: and as businessmen, they very soon become absorbed—often much too absorbed—in the fissiparous pressures of their own domain. And in so far that they do have a community of thought with the Treasury, it is probably an advantage to the country. For industry has always suffered from too narrow and blinkered a view: and if planning is to shape the pattern of Britain, then closer contact between government and industry—as in France—is essential.

THE CHANCELLOR

In the midst of all these mandarins, planners, anti-planners, knights and economists are the political masters of the Treasury. The frontier between politicians and officials in the Treasury is the most difficult of all: 'Whichever party's in office', Harold Wilson said, 'the liberals are in power'—meaning that the *laissez-faire* policies of the Treasury officials always win in the end. The encounter between a new Chancellor and his senior officials is a crucial test, for here, more than anywhere in Whitehall, the facts live in the office, and the reasons for not doing anything are almost incontrovertible. 'I've had three knights to see me this morning', one Chancellor is said to have complained: 'and each one's given me different advice.' When the Chancellor is certain what he wants to do, and how to do it, then the Treasury will carry it out: when he is unsure and muddled—as Chancellors can easily be—he will be borne along by that mysterious tide called 'The Treasury View'.

Since 1961 there have been two cabinet ministers in the Treasury, Selwyn Lloyd and Henry Brooke. Both of them are manager-politicians, not inspiring to parliament, but quite formidable in Whitehall. The junior of them, known as the 'Chief Secretary of the Treasury' is Henry Brooke, a dedicated administrator who came into politics through local government: his job is to run the watchdog side of the Treasury, cutting down and saying no—to which he seems well-suited. He has a passion for detail, and he personifies the old Treasury attitude of austere and dogged resolve.

But the important figure in the Treasury remains the Chancellor of the Exchequer—the indefatigable Selwyn Lloyd, whose career is one of the oddest in contemporary politics. Among Conservatives Lloyd is in a lonely class by himself: his background has an odd similarity with Macleod's—provincial doctor's son, Fettes and Cambridge. But he is older than Macleod's generation and unlike them he had a successful career (as a lawyer and QC) before he went into politics. Lloyd has none of the *panache* of the successful House of Commons man: he makes prolix and nervous speeches, and is shy in country-house company. He lives simply in London, and has a red-brick semi-detached house in Hoylake, his Cheshire constituency. In parliament and on television he has been the subject of mockery. As a politician he is not confident, and his following is small; in the Suez affair he was easily vamped by Sir Anthony Eden. But in spite of the mockery he remained at the Foreign Office for four years, and remains indispensible to the Conservative government. In Whitehall he shows none of his parliamentary gaucheness. At the Foreign Office his mastery of briefs and shrewd cross-examinations were held in some awe, and in the Treasury he has shown himself a more decisive Chancellor than some.

In theory the appointment of a second minister was supposed to leave the Chancellor free for a general oversight of economic policy, away from preoccupations with candle-ends. Many economists looked forward to a new régime at the Treasury, with the economists and planners rescued from the gloomy atmosphere of the everlasting nay. But in the Treasury this kind of abrupt change never happens: and the double banking has so far, apparently, made little difference to the structure. From information filtering out of Great George Street, it seems that the Chancellor is still kept close to the grindstone. Part of this may be due to the personal attitudes of the Chancellor; though he has accepted the need for overall planning, he has still seen his job in separate compartments—like a barrister dealing with a number of separate briefs, each one disconnected; and he does not quite seem to have got the *idea* of planning. He will turn from cutting down overseas expenditure to discussing Bank Rate, without pausing to survey the country's problems as a whole: and this compartmentalisation showed itself in the emergency Budget of July, 1961, in the pay pause fiasco in November, and in the reluctance (common to other Conservative Chancellors) to recognise that you cannot expect trade unionists to accept a pay pause unless the surtax payers accept one too. Though Selwyn Lloyd might appear to be the modern-minded manager-planner of the cabinet, it is surprisingly the Edwardian figure of Harold Macmillan who is the most interested in planning.

But much of the grindstone attitude remains implicit in the structure of the Treasury. The Treasury appears to be a classic example of bureaucratic machinery, as visualised by Bagehot, being regarded as 'a grand and achieved result, not a working and changeable instrument'. Whatever the Chancellor may intend, he has to deal with a machine which was designed long ago for a different purpose; economists, statisticians and dons have been stuck on to it, to patch it up, but the central apparatus has not been changed. The minute-passing, the budget-preparing and the teasing continue, without time or occasion to take a long look at the needs of the country.

INTO EUROPE

It may be partly as a result of this engrossing machine that the

Treasury has been slow to come to terms with Europe. From the beginning, like most people in Britain, the Treasury was sceptical of the Treaty of Rome: they thought that the European countries would never reach agreement—particularly on agriculture—and they saw the economic ties of the Commonwealth as providing insuperable difficulties to Britain's joining; while at the same time the Foreign Office were inclined to regard the Common Market as a purely economic problem, and to leave it to the Treasury. During 1959, when EFTA, Britain's alternative to the Common Market, was becoming a manifest failure, the cabinet was largely preoccupied with other problems—the retreat from Africa, and the hope of an East-West *détente*: and the question of Europe seems to have been left largely to an unenthusiastic Treasury committee.

Then, in the middle of 1960, several things happened—the most important of which was the arrival of Sir Frank Lee from the Board of Trade. Sir Frank, like most other permanent secretaries, had been doubtful of the feasibility of a European connection, and his background in Africa and his admiration for America both pulled him in other directions. At the Board of Trade he had helped to draft the constitution of EFTA: and though he was more concerned with Europe than most, he saw Britain as having an independent economic rôle with the Commonwealth. Then, in the course of 1959, he changed his mind, and became less hopeful of Britain's Commonwealth rôle, so that by the time he joined the Treasury he was a convinced European. Moreover, he was a tough-minded civil servant, who believed in breaking dead-locks and overcoming difficulties, and he stirred up the general inertia of the Treasury.

In the course of 1960-1961 signs of a new mood became notice-able in the Treasury. Firstly, there was a growing disillusion with the economic future of the Commonwealth, as a result of the break with South Africa, and the obvious reluctance of young countries, like Ghana or Nigeria, to remain dependent on Britain. Secondly, the European Common Market seemed to be a spectacular success. Thirdly, the performance of British industry was increasingly disappointing. The exhortations, the subsidies and the forced marriages had failed to take effect: the word *malaise* began to seep through Whitehall, as words do, and the idea began to take shape that the cure for the *malaise* might be to open the windows and give the patient a shock. While Macmillan was becoming aware of the global importance of a united Europe, the Treasury, reluctantly and with internal resistance, came round to thinking that perhaps, however insuperable the difficulties, a closer union with Europe might be the only solution to Britain's difficulties. But the question that future historians will ask themselves, one suspects, will be not how the Treasury became aware of the importance of Europe when they did, but how they avoided becoming aware of it two years earlier.

18

HONOURS

When everyone is somebodee
Then no one's anybody—
> W. S. Gilbert (later Sir William Gilbert).

Even now, the number of those who are not knighted exceeds the number of those who are. Time doubtless will reverse these figures.
> Max Beerbohm, 1899 (later Sir Max Beerbohm).

TWICE a year, a few weeks before January 1 and June 6, about 4,000 letters, marked Urgent, Personal and Confidential, arrive at British homes from a private secretary at 10 Downing Street. A typical letter reads:

> Sir,
> I am asked by the Prime Minister to inform you that he has it in mind on the occasion of the forthcoming list of Birthday Honours to submit your name to the Queen with a recommendation that she may be graciously pleased to approve that you be appointed a Companion of the British Empire (CBE).
> Before doing so, the Prime Minister would be glad to be assured that this mark of Her Majesty's favour would be agreeable to you.
> I should be obliged if you could let me know at your earliest convenience.
> > I am, sir,
> > > Your obedient servant.

The expression 'has it in mind' (one honorand pointed out to me) is an invaluable piece of civil service phraseology. It infers that the prime minister can quite easily put it *out* of his mind, if the offer is rejected: but that in the meantime all those potential earldoms or Orders of the British Empire are revolving slowly and quietly in the back of his head, waiting to be crystallised. But nearly always the offers are accepted. In official lists at international gatherings foreign dignitaries appear simply with their names: but British delegates will be cluttered with GCBs, GCMGs, KBEs, CHs. However odd they may seem to foreigners, they still have magical importance to the British, with faint emanations from the monarchy and the Round Table, and they have become part of the very fibre of the civil service.

The multiplicity of the 'orders of chivalry' is enough to baffle the most loyal Englishman: Queen Victoria, King Edward VII, King George V all founded new orders—each with slightly different nuances of glory. The grandest order is the oldest, the Garter, founded in 1348, as a reward for skilful jousting: it has not more than twenty-six members who at their investitures wear dark blue velvet garters bearing the inscription 'Honi soit qui mal y pense'. Lord Melbourne (who never accepted the Garter) said 'there's no damned merit in it', but nowadays the Garters are an odd mixture of merit and birth, on the one hand are Royal favourites, such as the Duke of Beaufort or Lord Cranworth (a partridge-shooting friend of George VI), with a tiny band of six fellow-monarchs, including the Emperor of Ethiopia (the Emperor of Japan was sacked for unchivalry during the war, but allowed to wear the insignia in time to meet Princess Alexandra in 1961). On the other hand are genuinely illustrious leaders, such as Churchill and Earl Alexander. Other very cosy orders are the Royal Victorian Chain, mainly for royalty, but including President De Gaulle and the royal physician; and the Imperial Order of the Crown of India, largely restricted to ex-Vicereines of India. There is also the Royal Victorian Order, awarded personally by the Queen, in varying degrees from GCVO to MVO, for faithful service, to such people as the Keeper of the Privy Purse, the Extra Groom in Waiting, and the Keeper of the Swans.

In contrast to the Garter are the twenty-four members of the Order of Merit: the name itself suggests a side-swipe at other orders. OMs have no association with royalty or jousting, and are merely distinguished: they never even meet together, and if they did it is doubtful whether, for instance, John Masefield and T. S. Eliot would have much to talk about. The OM is an impressive little band, from poets and painters to dons and boffins: divorce, promiscuity and atheism are no bar to the OM, though in 1961 the fondness of the octogenarian OMs Lord Russell and the late Augustus John for demonstrating in Trafalgar Square caused some pain to the others. Another side-swipe is the Companionage of Honour—founded in 1917—which likewise suggests that other companions are not wholly honourable. Their sixty-five members include an equally mixed band, from Lord Attlee, Lord Woolton and Lord Malvern to Somerset Maugham, Benjamin Britten and Sir Osbert Sitwell. The distinction between honour and merit in the two orders is sometimes rather obscure.

But most orders are much more mundane, mainly concerned

with rewarding civil servants, and it is here that inflation is rife. The most senior of the civil service orders are the Bath (CB, KCB, GCB), mainly for military men and Treasury officials; and the St. Michael and St. George, whose motto is 'token of a better age', which is distributed to diplomats, colonial servants and Whitehall officials; members rise from CMG (known sometimes in Whitehall as 'Call Me God') to the KCMG ('Kindly Call Me God') to—for a select few governors and super-ambassadors—the GCMG ('God Calls Me God'). The number of CMGs awarded has nearly doubled since the war.

To these older orders was added in 1917 the Order of the British Empire, invented by King George V with the motto 'For God and the Empire'. As the British Empire has dwindled, so its orders have multiplied, until now there are over 75,000 people who belong to its various grades, from the MBE to the OBE to the CBE to the KBE to the GBE. A comparison of New Year honours in 1935 and 1961 shows how the order has grown since the war:

	1935	1961
CBE	50	170
OBE	110	400
MBE	140	700

(The inflation is not as acute as in France, where Napoleon's 2,000 members of the Legion d'Honneur have grown to hundreds of thousands, each with their ribbon in their coat lapel.)

CBEs, CMGs and CBs have become part of the equipment of the bureaucratic machine: to the public their meaning is vague, but in Whitehall they are pregnant with status, and together with carpets, hat-stands and desks they define a man's place on the ladders. Civil servants in the executive or clerical grades will probably end up with the MBE—the equivalent of a gold watch in industry. Assistant secretaries should receive a CB, a CMG or a CBE; in the army, a brigadier should get a CBE, a major-general a CB. Permanent secretaries, generals, and most ambassadors emerge with a knighthood or 'K'. Honours are always said to be a cheap substitute for higher salaries: the CMG, for instance, might be worth £1,000 a year in terms of status. But there is a price to be paid, for the prospect of honours enhances conformity. A civil servant hoping for his CMG is as careful not to put a foot wrong, or to chance disfavour, as a Tudor courtier to escape beheading. 'Poor George, still hasn't got his C', they will say, and George will make his memoranda still more cautious and inoffensive. The minor honours also provide an invaluable method of rewarding political services without resorting to more expensive methods: in the last sixteen honours lists, a quota of about a tenth of the MBEs, OBEs and CBEs have gone to Conservative party workers,[1] and the aura of the palace and peers which they convey are an essential incentive to constituency parties.

The most visible recipient of honour—apart from a peer—is a knight: overnight Mr. J. M. Smith will be transformed into Sir John and—more important—his wife will become Lady Smith. Through all Britain's social revolutions, the charms of knighthood have remained undiminished: echoes of Sir Lancelot and Sir Galahad mingle with more practical advantages: 'EXPECT CLIENTS TO PAY SIR CHARGE' cabled one witty architect after his knighthood had been announced. Nor has the knightage swelled quite as Max Beerbohm forecast: there are about 4,500 knights today—about the same number as in 1935—though there are now fewer Empire knights, and more inside Britain. This chart (from Debrett) shows how new creations of peers (excluding life peers) baronets and knights have varied over the last fifty years:

	1911–15	1916–20	1921–25	1926–30	1931–35	1936–40	1941–45	1946–50	1951–55	1956–60
Peers	41	79	51	54	57	51	71	67	67	69
Baronets	96	192	132	74	52	44	40	6	33	41
Knights	955	1770	1026	856	952	902	1098	1099	1040	924

The bulk of the knighthoods still go to civil servants and to party hacks 'for political and public services'. But the field of knight-worthy activities has been enlarged, albeit in an erratic fashion: there are several acting knights, but no TV knights: three cricketing knights, no football knights. But honours nowadays are awarded for services to motoring, horse-racing, or advertising, and it is doubtless only a matter of time before there will be bingo knights.

Theoretically anyone can recommend anyone for an honour, and thousands of people write to the prime minister suggesting their friends or themselves. But the weighty recommendations

[1] *New Statesman*, December 29, 1961. p. 984.

come from Whitehall departments, from the Conservative Central Office and from the parts of the Commonwealth which still think about honours. They are all sifted by the patronage secretary, and the more important passed on to the prime minister. Occasionally unfortunate mistakes are made, as when before the war they meant to knight a distinguished theatrical figure and knighted an obscure man with the same name. Recent prime ministers have not taken a fervent interest in honours. Sir Anthony Eden, with some advice from his wife, took a lively interest in the honouring of the arts, and was prepared to weigh in the balance the rival claims of a ballet dancer and a managing director for the CBE. But Harold Macmillan does not take much interest in honours below a peerage, and the phrase 'has it in mind' when applied to an OBE is something of an exaggeration.

How many people reply that Her Majesty's favour would *not* be acceptable? There is no reliable information, of course, about the refusal rate (publicly to refuse an honour is at least as vain as to accept it) but are there some signs that honours are becoming more, rather than less, acceptable? 'Fourteen out of fifteen of the people who write back to refuse are obviously annoyed because they weren't offered something better', said one man who had been concerned with honours: 'it's a relief when you come to the fifteenth who really honestly doesn't want it.' Before the war many leading intellectuals, including Professor Tawney, Bernard Shaw, H. G. Wells, refused honours and Rudyard Kipling never accepted one. Today most prominent artists and intellectuals have accepted honours of some kind: even Oscar Kokoschka, the eccentric Czech painter, who made a lifesize wax model of an ex-girl-friend, has accepted a CBE, and nearly all the former Labour leaders have accepted peerages. Most politicians, and some palace officials, would agree that honours have got out of hand: but the Conservative party—confronted with queues of civil servants and party workers waiting for their Cs and Ks—dare not suggest abolition.

The more uprooted and complex our society becomes, the more, it seems, these handles of status are grasped. And at a time when Britain is having to adapt herself quickly to a more commercial and technological age, the honours system helps to perpetuate Victorian values for which most of them were invented. Inevitably, honours have social repercussions. The extension of CBEs to include industrialists—particularly exporters—has done something to widen the field, but the bulk of the honours still reflect a Victorian world. Could the system be reasonably brought up to date? The *Daily Mirror* has suggested a new 'Order of Elizabeth'[1] for 'achievement particularly in keeping with the spirit of the age'. But who can possibly decide what *is* the spirit of the age? Should knights of Elizabeth be football-pool knights, take-over knights, or power-station knights? At a time when Britain is becoming part of Europe, why should we only honour Britons serving Britain? No possible new system could be devised which did justice to all the spirits of the age, and the multiplication of honours involved would soon become still more difficult. In the end, surely, the only real judges of a man's achievement can be his immediate friends, who will honour him with a K or without.

[1] *Daily Mirror Spotlight:* Honours and Awards. p. 16.

19

DIPLOMATS

If you are to stand up for your Government you must be able to stand up to your Government.

Sir Harold Caccia, September 1961.

Dining is the Soul of Diplomacy.
Lord Palmerston.

A STONE's throw from the Treasury, between Whitehall and St. James's Park, is the oddest of all the Whitehall palaces, the Foreign Office. You come at it through an arch in Downing Street, opposite the prime minister's house, and into a great square Italian-ate courtyard surmounted by statues. At the north-west corner of the palace is a tall square tower, looking over the lake in St. James's Park. Inside, the building is still odder: it has the atmosphere of a provincial Italian museum. You walk through a hall of purple wallpapcr, along long arched corridors and mosaic floors, past a room filled with ancient pneumatic tubes, till you come face to face with a marble grand staircase, with two tall alabaster statues at the bottom (one of George Villiers, Earl of Clarendon: one of the first Marquess of Salisbury). At the top of the staircase are huge faded frescoes: one of them, 'Britannia Sponsa', apparently depicts a rape, though called 'The Sea-farers claim Britain as their bride': another called 'Britannia Nutrix' shows a young mother suckling a disagreeable baby: a third shows a buxom girl pointing with a flourish to the word 'Silence'.

In the middle of the frescoes a high heavy door leads into a room, twenty feet high and thirty feet square: the walls are of pale green dotted with gold stars, and above the marble mantel-piece is a life-size romantic portrait of King George III. Round the room are distributed bits of Victorian furniture, deep leather armchairs, lamps, tables, and an old clock. In the middle is a big desk, covered with boxes, telephones, a reading-lamp, and writing paper. Inside this well-preserved museum a live Foreign Secretary works. From this desk, for the past hundred years, British Foreign Secretaries have watched the rise and fall of the

British Empire, two world wars, and the eclipse of Britain's international power.

How potent, one wonders, is the influence of architecture? The Foreign Office was designed by Sir Gilbert Scott to be a tall Gothic castle: the plans were turned down by Lord Palmerston and—with typical Victorian abandon—used for St. Pancras Station. How different would British policy have been in Gothic surroundings, rather than Palladian? Would it be more up to date if it were housed in a steel-and-glass block? Certainly architecture has influenced the *organisation* of the Office. It is because of the high indivisible rooms that junior diplomats have to share their 'Third Room'[1], producing an ethos like a boarding-school dormitory. Surroundings, I suspect, *do* influence attitudes, and it is the social habits and rituals of the Foreign Office that have helped to hold back the realisation of change.

FOREIGN OFFICE MEN

Between the Treasury and the Foreign Office, the twin peaks of Whitehall, there is an old, unfriendly rivalry: they live in worlds as separate and unequal as the army and the navy. You can see both kinds walking across St. James's Park at lunch-time, both with bowler hats and umbrellas, but the Treasury men make for the Reform, while the diplomats go into the Travellers' next door—known in the Foreign Office as the 'works canteen', but with a more pretentious atmosphere than the Reform. The grandest diplomats go farther on to the St. James', with its backgammon and port.

Diplomats, alone of the civil servants, are independent of the Treasury in matters of promotion and policy, and they talk with special scorn of the *Home* Civil Service. Diplomats call themselves the 'F.O.', 'The Office' or simply 'The Service'. They used to be less separate: from 1919 to 1956, Sir Warren Fisher, Sir Horace Wilson and Sir Edward Bridges were Heads of the whole Civil Service, including diplomats, and used to interfere. But when Brook took over in 1956 he was announced as head of the *Home* Civil Service, and the Foreign Office were left to themselves, with their own private pyramid. The Treasury still have their revenge in 'teasing' the Foreign Office over their embassy expenses: in 1961 they scored a temporary victory by cancelling all the Queen's embassy birthday parties.

The diplomats, though usually less important than Treasury

[1] *See* Lord Strang: *Inside the Foreign Office.*

men, are more self-important. Diplomats are aware of being, if not aristocrats themselves, the heirs to an aristocratic tradition: not clerks, but knights. Only since 1919 has it been possible to enter the Foreign Office without a private income, and there is still a family-circle feeling. They know each other by Christian names, exchange chatty telegrams, or cosy letters beginning 'Dear Chancery' and ending 'Yours ever, Far East Department'. Unlike permanent secretaries, who remain anonymous to the end, diplomats write discreet nostalgic memoirs, or little monographs concluding, after mature reflection, that British diplomacy is the best. Two of the last books of diplomats' memoirs were called *The Inner Circle* and *The Ruling Few*. (Sir David Kelly wrote *The Ruling Few* and *The Hungry Sheep*—sometimes unkindly confused as *The Ruling Sheep*.) Diplomats abroad are inclined to regard themselves as representing not the United Kingdom but the Foreign Office; and in London (one civil servant complained) they regard every other department—including 10 Downing Street—as a Foreign Power, to be bullied or cajoled according to their strength.

Many diplomats marry foreign wives, often well-to-do, as a result of spending their lives in expensive society abroad. They have to inform the Office about their wives, who must be approved. Iron Curtain wives, or Jewish wives in Arab countries, cause difficulties, but American wives are a diplomatic asset.

Seven hundred people (including women) serve in the senior branch of the Foreign Service, 'the size of a large public school'—as one of them put it. They are bound together by their Oxbridge background; by the intimacy of Third Rooms; by the perpetual round of embassy parties; and by the flow of telegrams which provide a school magazine, welcoming contributions. Everyone's ambition is to get 'into print'—which means that despatches are circulated to all posts abroad. This corporate spirit—like the Treasury's—has advantages. Members speak the same (Oxbridge) language and understand each other quickly and subtly. The Foreign Office can transact business more quickly and with many fewer cross-purposes than the Americans, for instance. British diplomats are intelligent, hard-working and dedicated: at seven p.m. most lights are still on in the palazzo. They give some evidence of being—as they so often claim—the best foreign service in the world.

But this closed, collegiate society, like the Treasury's, has serious snags. 'A young man who goes into the Foreign Office at twenty-one', one ex-ambassador has said, 'has a change of life at twenty-seven.' Several factors induce this social menopause. The intensity and isolation of embassy life and entertainment—the nightly round of cocktail parties, the formalities and protocol—all contribute to the diplomat's lassitude: 'Diplomacy is hard on the brain', one American remarked, 'but harder on the feet.' Young British diplomats soon lose their curiosity, and achieve a lacklustre expression, an immunity to new experience and new people, and above all an absence of zeal: young recruits are still reprimanded with a reminder of Talleyrand's famous instruction—'*pas trop de zèle*'.

This list of National days in the second half of June gives some idea of the growing burden of international celebrations:

June 17—Anniversary of the establishment of the Republic of Iceland.
　　　　German day of Unity.
　　18—Day of the Republic of Egypt.
　　　　Battle of Waterloo.
　　19—*Dias de Artigas* (Uruguay).
　　20—Independence day of the Republic of Senegal.
　　22—National Tree Day (El Salvador).
　　24—Soviet aviation day.
　　25—Proclamation of the Independence of the Malagasy Republic.
　　27—Buddhist festival of POSON.
　　28—Canadian Army day.
　　　　Treaty of Versailles anniversary.
　　29—Name day of the King of the Hellenes.
　　　　Polish Navy day.
　　30—Anniversary of the Revolution of Guatemala.
　　　　Independence Day of the Republic of Congo (Leopoldville).

Behind its façade of an aristocratic club, the Foreign Office has changed more than it likes to be known.

Firstly, in one man's lifetime it has expanded fifteen-fold. In 1914 there were only 176 people in the Office in London, including forty doorkeepers and cleaners, and only 450 in the diplomatic and consular missions abroad. By 1960 there were over 10,000 people, and the annual cost of running the service was about twenty million pounds—nearly half what the government spends on universities. This colossal expansion, at a time when Britain's power has steadily diminished, exercises the Treasury. Diplomats explain the complexity of modern embassies—the tiresome need for financial, military, technical experts, the growing involvement of the state with economic affairs, the sheer increase in numbers of countries. They decide at length on the necessity for 'keeping up with the Joneses'.

Secondly, diplomacy is no longer a question of negotiating secret agreements only between the chancelleries of the 'Inner Circle': it has become sullied with much more vulgar and technical matters—helping exports, negotiating loans, propaganda and salesmanship—where *zèle* is all-important. And diplomats have had to come to terms with *publicity*. Journalists and diplomats are traditional enemies—the Montagus and Capulets of foreign affairs—and if asperity is detectable in this chapter, this may explain it. Diplomats regard journalists as backstairs intruders, liable at any moment to wreck negotiations. Journalists divide diplomats into two classes—those who tell but don't know, and those who know but don't tell: and the matter is complicated by the repressed desire of many journalists to be diplomats, and of diplomats to end up as journalists.

NEW DIPLOMATS?

How far has a new kind of diplomat appeared to meet the new situation? Diplomacy has always been the most aristocratic of all government professions: in the nineteenth century foreign policy was described by John Bright, in a famous phrase, as 'neither more nor less than a gigantic system of out-door relief for the British aristocracy'. Until 1919 wealth was vital, intellect suspect: Sir David Kelly described how when he went before a selection board in 1914, he overheard the examiners saying: 'Good Lord, he got a first!'

Then in 1941, in the worst part of the war, Sir Anthony Eden, with support from diplomats, set up a committee to advocate reform. One wonders how Britain found time then—and so little time now—to think about so many future problems? It was the time of the Beveridge Report, the Colonial Development Corporation, the Fleming Report on public schools, and other radical thinking: 'When a man is about to be hanged', Dr. Johnson said, 'it concentrates his mind marvellously.' A revolutionary White Paper eighteen months later said (in language which itself has a war-time, Churchillian flavour):

Among the criticisms which have been brought against the Diplomatic Service, the view has been expressed that it is recruited from too small a circle, that it tends to represent the interests of certain sections of the nation rather than those of the country as a whole, that its members lead too sheltered a life, that they have insufficient understanding of economic and social questions, that the extent of their experience is too small to enable them properly to understand many of the problems with which they ought to deal, and that the range of their contacts is too limited to allow them to acquire more than a relatively narrow acquaintance with the foreign peoples amongst whom they live.

These criticisms are often overstated, the White Paper went on: it is, however, true, that the conditions which the Diplomatic Service originally grew up to meet no longer exist unchanged in modern international affairs.

As a result, the 'Eden-Bevin' reforms emerged after the war. Four separate branches—diplomatic, consular, commercial, information—all became interchangeable. Men could be promoted from consulates, or from junior grades, to become ambassadors. Recruits were to be chosen not simply by written examination and interview, but by thorough psychological tests—based on the war-time WOSB tests. A second language was no longer required. Older diplomats who had not come up to scratch could be discreetly retired with a pension before the age of sixty. And *women* were to be admitted to the senior grade. (The arrival of senior women has been smooth, but has produced regional problems. 'If a girl diplomat asks you to dinner in South America', said one diplomat, 'you naturally bring your toothbrush and pyjamas.' No woman has yet become an ambassador, but one, Barbara Salt, is strongly tipped to become Her Excellency.)

The reforms seemed impressive enough: and yet the complaints in the 1943 White Paper—about the narrow circle, the lack of specialists, the seclusion—are still to be heard, even in Whitehall. The Foreign Office is still lacking in economists, and diplomats are still reluctant to talk to non-diplomats. They are still inclined to be too busy mixing with the ruling circles, like Nuri es Said or Batista, to notice potential new rulers, like Kassem or Castro. Their social narrowness, one suspects, helps to explain the insensitivity to new frontiers. The Office is full of experts on the Austro-Hungarian Empire, but when the Congo became independent in 1960 hardly a single man in London knew the difference between the two factions, or could make sense of the stream of crisis cables.

Some seem to imagine that they are in the midst of a tremendous social upheaval: 'Today it is as difficult for an aristocrat to enter the Foreign Service', said Sir Harold Nicolson in 1961, 'as it would be for a camel, loaded with the bales of Eton and Balliol, to pass through the eye of a needle.'[1] But in fact, Eton provides more diplomats than ever. Between 1935 and 1938, six successful candidates came from Eton, six from Rugby and five from Winchester: between 1958 and 1961, seven came from Eton, five from Rugby and seven from Winchester.[2] True, twice as many men go in to the Foreign Office as before the war, and the extra numbers are partly made up by grammar school men. Nevertheless, between 1948 and 1956, 58 per cent of the recruits still came from boarding schools (compared to 44 per cent in the senior Home Civil Service); 62 per cent were the sons of professional and administrative men (compared to 38 per cent in the senior Home Civil Service); and no fewer than 93 per cent came from Oxbridge (compared to 80 per cent in the HCS), while 60 per cent were from Oxford.[3] 'We're trying hard to get more people from Redbrick', one diplomat explained: 'but they don't seem to know what it's about.' Others were more doubtful whether the Commissioners had really tried enough to escape from Oxbridge ideas. A few senior men in South America, including the ambassadors to Paraguay (H. F. A. Gates) and Nicaragua (W. E. D. Masscy), have been promoted from the junior branch ('Branch B'), but the core of the service remains the men picked from Oxbridge at twenty-one.

Out of 78 ambassadors and senior Foreign Office officials in 1961, 63 had been to public school, and with the exception of a deputy secretary, Ralph Murray, the others were in smaller embassies—namely, Nicaragua, Luxemburg, Panama, Ethiopia, Haiti, Costa Rica, Iceland, Korea, Mexico, Sudan, Venezuela, Norway, Liberia, Cambodia. Very few ambassadors had had outside jobs: D. A. H. Wright in Ethiopia was once an advertising man for Senior Service; Con O'Neill in Finland has resigned from the Foreign Office twice—once to become leader-writer on *The Times*; A. J. Ronalds in Malagasy was educated at the Russian Imperial corps of pages, and served in the Imperial Guard. Fifty-nine of the ambassadors went to Oxbridge, seven to London, and none to any other English university.

[1] 'The Old Diplomacy and the New.' David Davies Memorial Institute, March 1961.
[2] *Daily Telegraph*, July 12, 1961.
[3] Cmnd 232 of 1957.

The new flow of grammar school men (or 'Bevin Boys' as they have been called) has been disguised by the influences of the Office—the pressure of the 'Third Room', the cocktail parties, the social menopause; and the powerful influence of the old-style ambassadors, suppressing zeal, recommending the Travellers' Club, has confused new men with the old. Nor has the merging of the diplomatic and the consular services been as complete as appears. The old diplomats soon detected an unease among ex-consuls, did little to alleviate it, and called it *consulitis*.

Gradually those double-barrelled names which move through the pages of diplomats' memoirs—Sir Hughe Knatchbull-Hugessen, Sir Eugen Millington-Drake, Sir D'Arcy Godolphin Osborne, have diminished. A few names would still look well in a romantic comedy—Sir Berkeley Gage, Sir Roderick Barclay, Harold Freese-Pennefather. Ambassadors still have a remarkable faculty for emerging with bizarre Christian names when they are knighted, but there are now many more Sir Johns, Sir Ronalds, or Sir Franks.

Old diplomats also complain that the new men are bringing with them a new conformity; and that, in their unease, they are *plus royaliste que le roi*. They like to reminisce about the grand eccentrics, like Sir John Balfour, the witty former ambassador to Madrid with a bushy moustache, who had a large repertory of risqué songs about Franco and Peron: or Andrew Gilchrist, until recently ambassador to Iceland, who placated an angry crowd by dancing a highland reel in his kilt on the embassy balcony, and sent back witty cables about cod. Diplomats look back nostalgically to the happy hours spent playing shipwrecks round the Third Room.

There is still a good deal of variety in the Foreign Service. I found diplomats much more willing to talk freely about their service than home civil servants: events like Suez or Katanga arouse widespread discontent, and stimulate the Office rebels. But inevitably the growth of bureaucracy, committees and tele-phones has given foreign ambassadors—like judges or tycoons—less scope for eccentric individuality. The greatest blow to eccen-tricity came when Burgess and Maclean disappeared. In the next four years, nine hundred senior diplomats were examined and checked; four were asked to leave the service and six others moved to less important jobs.[1] Nowadays the Foreign Office is much more

[1] *See* Statement by Harold Macmillan (as Foreign Secretary) November 7, 1955.

security-minded: from time to time a notice appears in the arched corridors, saying

SECURITY NOTICE

WINDOW CLEANING TODAY

AMATEURS AND PROFESSIONALS

In spite of the reforms,[1] there is still a suggestion of amateurism among British diplomats, which surprises foreigners: it is reinforced by the curious habit—which pre-dates the jet age—of moving people round every two years, so that they never become expert in any one country: diplomats abroad are apt to give the impression of always having just arrived, or being just about to leave—though recently Lord Home has made the general post less hectic. As we have seen, the Foreign Office, like the civil service or the army, still likes to keep experts at arm's length. While Belgian diplomats have to pass three commercial examinations before they become ambassadors, ours still like to keep trade in a separate compartment. They have recently begun lending diplomats to big industrial firms—to find out about the most unknown country of all, Britain. But like the rest of Whitehall, the Foreign Service is determined not to damage its mandarin structure by embracing (for instance) businessmen, economists or journalists. And they prefer to take on commercial attachés, labour attachés, press attachés, rather than give their ambassadors specialist training.

AMBASSADORS

An ambassador is an honest man sent abroad to lie for the good of his country.

Sir Henry Wotton (Ambassador to James I).

The Foreign Office itself is a 'department' of state: but it is divided into 38 sub-divisions, ingeniously called 'departments'. There are ten political departments, each dealing with different parts of the globe. The 'Northern' department includes Russia; the 'Eastern' department includes Persia and the Yemen. Most people, from the Foreign Secretary downward, are called secretaries (there is a Principal Private Secretary to Her Majesty's

---

[1] Partly indeed, *because* of them: the merging of the special consular services has given less opportunity of specialisation, and it was in the consular line that grammar school boys often made their mark.

Principal Secretary of State for Foreign Affairs). A young man works his way up from being third secretary to second secretary to first secretary (no relationship to a first secretary in the Treasury), to 'counsellor' and then—if he is lucky—to 'minister' and thence, perhaps, to ambassador.

Ambassadors, whatever their nationality, live in surroundings which since the eighteenth century have become deep-frozen so that, like Oxford colleges, they retain grandeur in an age of uniformity. Ambassadors and their families have become a temporary subsidised aristocracy, leading more ducal lives than most dukes, and popping in and out of the gossip-columns, as part of the fantasy-life of Britain. They are called 'Your Excellency' and are usually knighted, with a KCMG. Abroad, they represent the Queen and thus have precedence over cabinet ministers. As a status-symbol, they remain unbeatable—witness the names of night-clubs, cosmetics, hotels, cigarettes, all over the world.

But they are not what they were. Firstly, there has been a spectacular inflation: before 1914 there were 9 British Ambassadors: in 1939 there were 17: now there are 72. Some smaller countries (such as Roumania and the Vatican) are still allowed only 'ministers plenipotentiary', but they feel increasingly insulted if they do not have an ambassador. Iceland for instance actually has an ambassador with a staff of four, and a consul and two vice-consuls, for a population of 170,000—rather less than Croydon's. Secondly, the grandest ambassadors are no longer necessarily the most important. The august ambassadors of the 'inner circle', in Paris, Bonn, Rome or Madrid are no longer very crucial. Their diminution began with the electric telegraph (the telegraph to Constantinople was built as early as 1870), but it has only recently become more apparent, accelerated by jet planes and telephones. 'The Paris embassy isn't really so important now', said one former Foreign Secretary, 'if anything serious happens, you can get over there in an hour. It's some of the smaller places, in the Middle East or South America, where the ambassador can play a really important rôle.' This situation has produced a discrepancy between the dignified and the efficient parts of the Foreign Office. On the one hand are the ancient embassies, with pomp (codified by the Congress of Vienna), chandeliers and colossal *'frais de representation'*, but not much political importance: on the other hand are the small new embassies in remote capitals, without protocol but with perpetual crises. Gorgeous but unimportant posts are useful to the Foreign Office, for they provide a dignified upstairs, a kind of House of Lords. On the other, dumping deadbeat diplomats in remote capitals is now very dangerous: for the most unlikely countries, like Cuba or Laos, can suddenly prove troublesome. 'No more Nicaraguas now', as one diplomat said.

A new kind of ambassador has emerged with the boom in new countries—mostly in Africa in the past three years. No fewer than 17 nations became independent in 1960; the membership of the UN shot up from 82 to 99, and a whole new circle had to be added to the great hall of the General Assembly. Odd-sounding capitals suddenly appeared on the map—Conakry, Tananarive, Yaounde, Abidjan, Mogadishu. This explosion of independence sent a breeze through the Foreign Office: they found themselves called upon at a few weeks' notice to provide complete new emabassies, and a new kind of diplomacy. Young diplomats, instead of arranging *placements* for dinner parties, or writing witty marginalia, were faced with finding an office to work in, paper to write on and discovering who was running the country—without even a *chef de protocol* to help them.

In the young countries ambassadors have to be reporters as much as negotiators, watching for signs of trouble and change, and often salesmen and PROs as well. In Iron Curtain capitals the scope for negotiation is tiny: and the embassy is largely a listening post, to register the tremors of summit opinion. The old habit of sending out ambassadors who can't speak the language, and banishing Russian experts to South America, is gradually being changed: the present ambassador to Moscow, Sir Frank Roberts (an unusual, plain-spoken diplomat from Lancashire) is an old Russian expert.

PARIS AND WASHINGTON

Theoretically the twin peaks of the profession are Paris and Washington. The Paris embassy is the grandest of all: the ambassador occupies a superb mansion, bought from Napoleon's sister and inhabited by the Duke of Wellington, and now jealously watched by the Treasury. It has a courtyard in the Faubourg St. Honoré, a hundred yards from de Gaulle's Elysée Palace, and a long garden leading down to the Champs Elysées. There is a large ballroom, a row of reception rooms full of *boiserie*, flunkeys and bits of the English set in Paris: it is a far more lavish establishment than 10 Downing Street. The ambassador's *frais de representation* are £24,000 a year (apart from heating and lighting)—twice the allowance of the embassy in Bonn.

The present ambassador, Sir Pierson Dixon, is one of several senior don-type diplomats (including Dean, Reilly, Makins, Franks and Hayter). Dixon remains more a scholar than a salesman: he has even written a romantic novel called *Farewell Catullus*. He began as an archaeologist in Athens, then moved to diplomacy, and married a diplomat's daughter. He was principal private secretary (an important stepping-stone) first to Eden then to Bevin, and in 1954 went to the United Nations, where he had the appalling job of defending, without proper instructions, the Suez invasion—which he achieved with dignity. In Paris his position is less exposed: but in 1961 he was given the all-important job of leading the British officials in Brussels, to argue the British case for the Common Market—in which he greatly impressed European negotiators.

In a class by itself is Washington: for since the war the one central plank of British foreign policy—albeit a wobbly one—has been the maintenance of the Anglo-American alliance.The Washington embassy has a staff of no fewer than 500, including five diplomats with the rank of minister, and not including the web of information offices spread over the States. The Washington embassy itself, a huge pillared palace designed by Sir Edwin Lutyens, is (as one ex-Foreign Secretary put it) a kind of microcosm of Whitehall. The total cost of the American embassy and consulates is £1,692,000 a year—as much as the total grant to the Arts Council.

The ambassadorship to Washington is nearly always a controversial appointment, and the choice of David Ormsby-Gore in 1961 was no exception. He is the only current ambassador from outside the foreign service, and such intrusions (much rarer than before the war) are always resented by the professionals. The importance of Ormsby-Gore was obvious: he was not only, as a political minister in the Foreign Office, *au courant* with current predicaments. He was also an old friend and contemporary of President Kennedy. The appointment had an eighteenth-century flavour, for Ormsby-Gore belongs to that large interlocking network of families (following p. 34), and thus closely related by marriage to (among others) Harold Macmillan, Lord Salisbury and the Duke of Devonshire—and very indirectly to President Kennedy himself. He is the heir of Lord Harlech, a former Colonial Secretary and author of *Florentine Sculptors of the Fifteenth Century*: and he farms four hundred acres in Shropshire, for which he became an MP in 1950, when he was thirty-two. But he is not a dilettante: he is hard-working, serious and shy. He looks and walks like a civil servant, with neat, swept-back hair and a habit of putting his hand inside his coat, and he impressed diplomats in London with his avid attention to detail and his adherence—sometimes excessive —to civil service procedure.

His appointment to Washington, the plum of the profession, caused mutterings, and career diplomats insist that their job is too important to be left to amateurs. But outside the Foreign Office the diplomatic machine often appears preoccupied with Buggins' turn next. Career diplomats are apt, towards the end of their career, to 'either go native, or go sour' in the words of one adage; and they are subject (partly perhaps because of their diminished influence) to attacks of *folies de grandeur*, and to writing personal letters to the prime minister.

Modern democracies—Eastern as well as Western—have developed a kind of private court at their centre. The chief executives—Kennedy, Macmillan, de Gaulle or Adenauer—all have their entourage of personal friends, and it is essential that ambassadors should be close to this inner circle of both the home and foreign governments. This seems to be a case where—if there is an able man related to both the President and the Prime Minister—nepotism is invaluable.

As the senior ambassadors have become less influential so London has become more so, and diplomacy has found itself mixed up with bureaucracy. Only since the first world war, in fact, has the permanent under-secretary and his London staff emerged 'from clerkly bondage'[1] into important advisers: Lord Salisbury, for instance, in the 1890's, never consulted his PUS on any matter of importance. But it is arguable that the most influential diplomats today are not the ambassadors but the group of senior men in London—Sir Patrick Reilly, Sir Evelyn Shuckburgh, Sir Francis Rundall, Sir Roger Stevens, Sir Hugh Stephenson, Sir Roderick Barclay, Ralph Murray. And there is also the most unknown influence of all, the Foreign Secretary's principal private secretary (at present Ian Samuel) who can by his sheer closeness to decisions often out-influence everyone else.

But probably the most important is the permanent undersecretary, who is the chief official adviser to the Foreign Secretary, Sir Harold Caccia, who was appointed at the end of 1961, has an orthodox background: Eton, at the same time as his master Lord Home; the son of a forester-diplomat; married (less orthodox, this)

[1] *See* Lord Strang: *The Foreign Office.* p. 147.

the daughter of a Treasury man. He has the reputation of being unpompous, quick, hard-working and not strikingly original. He is an expert on Chinese, and is still a vigorous tennis-player, determined to keep fit. As ambassador to Washington—his previous post—he was genial, popular and suitably American (he horrified London by sending Americanised cables with expressions like *We mustn't pussyfoot the press*).

The PUS, like his opposite numbers in Whitehall, is proverbially overworked; he is, as Lord Strang (a former incumbent) has put it, at the top of a gently-sloping pyramid: 'the apex of a pyramidal structure of the administrative kind becomes the more uncomfortable to occupy, the more gently the sides of the structure slope.'[1] In the Foreign Office there is the same grindstone attitude, the same dislike of unattached thinking, as in the Home Civil Service, but intensified by the extra pressure of telegrams—which give to the Foreign Office, as to a TV studio or the Stock Exchange, a perpetual atmosphere of haste: 'If there is one sense that rules in the Foreign Office', wrote Lord Strang, 'it is a sense of urgency.' (It is symbolic of the urgency that the library is tucked away in a dingy block south of the river.) World events provide the constant stimulus of diplomacy. 'The most important decisions', wrote one diplomat, Sir J. Headlam-Morley, 'are often made, not as a part of a concerted and far-sighted policy, but under the urgent pressure of some immediate crisis.' Decisions which might from the outside look bold, from the inside look merely inevitable. In Lord Strang's words: 'Events are very strong.'

The Foreign Office have always had an aversion to long-term plans: Bevin, when he was Foreign Secretary, started up a planning department, but this lapsed, and has only recently been revived, and long-term ideas still find great difficulty in making themselves heard above the daily din. In the long chain-reactions of the past ten years—the collapse of Middle East régimes, the retreat from one base to the next (from Suez to Cyprus to Aden to Kenya) the emergence of independent Africa, the wave of unrest in South America, the officials have always thought it mildly improper to put up bold, five-year plans to their political masters. 'I distrust anyone who foresees consequences and advocates remedies to avert them', said Lord Halifax before the war; and this old English pragmatism is still glorified.

Here again we find Rolls-Royce difficulty. 'The Foreign Office is like a very sensitive octopus', said one of its members: 'It's

[1] *The Foreign Office*, p. 198.

superbly equipped to receive impressions from all over the world, and to react to them with speed and efficiency. But it's not designed to make positive moves. In Russia, there's a council of ministers who meet regularly and say to themselves, "where do we cause trouble next?"'

In these surroundings, the permanent under-secretary has little opportunity for thinking about the future of the world. One has the impression that much of the time he is more like a nannie, trying to keep his difficult children happy, and keeping the office running smoothly. In this respect he is not unique: many company chairmen, as we will see later, spend most of their time as nurse-maids. To think of top people sitting, like Law Lords, on abstract problems, is misleading. But in the touchy world of diplomacy, nannie-qualities seem particularly valued: men with strong, far-seeing ideas are apt to find themselves *not* becoming permanent under-secretary: in this fine-ground, well-oiled machine, smooth-ness is all.

The permanent under-secretary moves in the chandelier world of official dinner parties and embassy receptions, and it is from this small world that most of his social contacts are drawn, and where much of the casual lobbying occurs. The embassy network is an important source of gossip, pressure and influence. It is also a great psychological force for the *status quo*: so long as the Portuguese ambassador is in friendly evidence, and no Angolan African in sight, the importance of not attacking Portugal tends to remain in the foreground.

The old-fashioned structure of the Foreign Office, and the social unadventurousness of diplomats, reinforces old circles against new. Many diplomats with an entertainment allowance for a fixed number of guests have difficulty in filling their table, and invite old college friends again and again. You have only to look at the list of diplomatic engagements in *The Times*, with a stage army of recurring guests, to see how small the top circles are.

FOREIGN SECRETARY

The frontier between politicians and officials, as in the Treasury, is a shifting and fine-drawn one. But diplomacy is a more tho-roughly political business than Treasury control, and amateurs have more scope and more confidence. A Chancellor need not have a view, or understand the finer points of the sterling area or the Bank Rate, but every Foreign Secretary must have a view about the cold war; and each bend in his policy will affect the cabinet. The assessments of his officials will influence his decisions, but a Foreign Secretary is less likely to be trapped by his diplomats than a Chancellor by his financial advisers.

The ability of a cabinet to defy official advice was established with dreadful clarity on the afternoon of October 30, 1956, after Israel had invaded Egypt. While a Foreign Office spokesman was explaining to journalists in London that Britain's policy was to invoke the Tripartite Agreement opposing the use of force in the Middle East, Sir Anthony Eden was announcing in the House of Commons that Britain had issued an ultimatum to Egypt, and insisting that the Tripartite Agreement was irrelevant.[1] The Suez invasion broke like a bomb on the Foreign Office. Only one diplomat (so far as is known) was privy to the government's plans —Sir Ivone Kirkpatrick, then Permanent Under-Secretary. The Foreign Secretary, Selwyn Lloyd, had flown in and out of Paris without even visiting the embassy. Nearly all the ambassadors were against intervention, and had to defend a policy which none of them had been told about. Suez was an uncomfortable reminder that in spite of the mechanism of consultation, crucial decisions could still be made by a tiny cabal.

Of all cabinet jobs the Foreign Secretary's is the most arduous. 'You're a duty officer seven days of the week', said Selwyn Lloyd —'you can never get away from the telegrams.' The Foreign Secretary fights his battles on three fronts—in the Office, in the cabinet and in parliament: the combination has been described as 'An Impossible Job'[2]: but since 1960, the impossibility has been mitigated by having a Foreign Secretary from the House of Lords, away from the heaviest gunshot, and a second cabinet minister— at present Ted Heath—to relieve the burden: there are also no fewer than four other ministers, including such surprising figures as the Marquess of Lansdowne and the Earl of Dundee.

Between 1940 and 1960 (apart from two very short interregna by Herbert Morrison and Harold Macmillan) there were only three Foreign Secretaries—Eden, Bevin and Selwyn Lloyd. It was not Eden but Bevin—the complete opposite of the traditional diplomat—who was the most popular in the Office, and he alone has a bust in the hall. The legend of Bevin still haunts the Foreign Office: 'of course, I got my education in the hedgerows of experience', he liked to tell his officials. His directness and courage made

[1] *See* Brian Crozier: The Role of the Foreign Office. *Twentieth Century*, October 1957.
[2] Sir William Hayter in *The Observer*, July 24, 1960.

him the perfect boss and, most important to the diplomats, he could win his wars in cabinet.

The arrival of a new Foreign Secretary is such a far-reaching event that it is watched tensely. Alexander Frederick Douglas-Home, fourteenth Earl of Home, took up his office in July 1960. His career up to then had conformed to pattern. His family, from the feudal borders of Scotland, is wealthy, eccentric, ancient: their first title dates from the Wars of the Roses, and Lord Home's brother was author of *The Reluctant Debutante*, and writes poems for Sunday papers. ('Let no one be deceived by his mildness, his good-natured absent-mindedness, his deprecating grin', William said of his brother, '. . . faceless yes-men are not normal products of the Scottish border and the Foreign Secretary is no exception . . .'). At Eton, Home was described by his headmaster —whose daughter he later married—as one of the most un-ambitious boys he had known, and by his contemporary Cyril Connolly, in a passage much quoted by diplomats:

> He was a votary of the esoteric Eton religion, the kind of graceful, tolerant, sleepy boy who is showered with favours and crowned with all the laurels, who is liked by the masters and admired by the boys without any apparent exertion on his part, without experiencing the ill-effects of success himself or arousing the pangs of envy in others. In the eighteenth century he would have become prime minister before he was thirty: as it was he appeared honourably ineligible for the struggle for life.

But the eighteenth-century tradition is still strong. He went to Christ Church, played cricket well, took a third-class degree in history, went into parliament. He became Chamberlain's private secretary, followed him to Downing Street and thus (unlike Churchill, Eden and Salisbury, all aristocrats who stood against appeasement) became implicated in Munich. After the war, when he moved to the Lords, he was a junior minister under Churchill and then in 1955 was promoted by Eden (to many people's surprise) to the Commonwealth Relations Office. He stayed there for five years. He was charming, popular, conscientious and undistinguished: he was very right-wing, closer to Salisbury than to Macleod, and sometimes oddly ignorant of his subject. He was apt to come out with embarrassing clichés about Africans never having discovered the wheel, etc. In the 'wind of change' era, he back-pedalled. People close to him noted a tendency towards hypochondria: he had had TB of the spine during the war and had never fully recovered his strength. At the CRO he seemed—not to put too fine a point on it—rather bored. But in private, and in the Lords, he was a more formidable figure than his public reputation suggested.

In 1960 came the bombshell: Macmillan insisted on appointing him Foreign Secretary. The *Daily Mirror* described it as 'the most reckless political appointment since the Roman Emperor Caligula made his favourite horse a Consul'. His opinions and even his name were hardly known, and the papers had to explain that it rhymed with fume and not with foam.[1] Most newspapers assumed that he would be conveniently subservient. 'He will certainly make a conscientious, loyal and honest lieutenant', said *The Observer*. The social romantics in the Foreign Office (a large cadre), who like a Tory foreign secretary to come from a landed and ample background, welcomed the arrival of a fourteenth earl; his lithe figure, with the neat triangular head, which rolls from side to side as he talks, fitted in much more easily. His grouse-shooting, his butterfly-hunting, his fruity voice and his pleasant sideways smile all generated confidence. In his social ease, his integrity, his lack of middle-class inhibitions, he seemed like Ernest Bevin. But all thought that he would be pliable both with the Prime Minister and the officials.

Nearly everyone (including perhaps the Prime Minister) had guessed wrong. For Home quickly revealed strong and simple ideas of his own: the sleepy peers in the House of Lords, accustomed to hearing second-hand opinions on foreign policy from junior ministers, were astonished by a series of uncompromising speeches. There was not much mention of 'Her Majesty's Government': it was more commonly 'I'. He was determined, in the first place, to expose Communist hypocrisy: 'I want to go over to the offensive', he said in April 1961, 'in exposing the Communists on this charge of imperialism.'

'I must warn people', he said in July, 'that there is a challenge from Communism on an unparalleled scale, which will be pursued quite relentlessly and will demand endurance from our own people over a very long time.' Secondly, he was determined, like the older landed Tories, to maintain 'law and order' in African territories including Rhodesia and Katanga, without bothering too much about Afro-Asian opinion. Thirdly he was convinced of the need of solidarity of the West's American-European axis. With America, while maintaining a reassuring anti-Communist attitude, he was prepared to talk toughly about the need for

---

[1] *See Time and Tide*, October 12, 1961.

L*

negotiation in Laos or Berlin: but Americans seemed almost as sensitive to the charms of the fourteenth earl as the Tory party. Home's ill-health slipped away. His firmness with Russia and sceptical approach to Black Africa fitted well with the disillusionment of British Conservatives, but perhaps less well with the ideas of the Prime Minister. Home's attitude to Russia, to Colonel Nasser or to the United Nations was bolder and more uncompromising than Macmillan's devious interventions, and there were strong indications that the Foreign Office, for the first time for six years, was run by the Foreign Secretary. While Selwyn Lloyd would discuss his speeches with the cabinet or the Prime Minister beforehand, Home's statements often surprised his own colleagues as much as the Russians: and while Dean Rusk, Couve de Murville and Dr Schroeder were all clearly the lieutenants of their Presidents, Home made it clear at NATO that he was 'a model of jaunty independence'.[1]

CRO AND CO

The dealings of the Foreign Office with Africa and Asia are muddled by the existence of two other rival diplomatic bodies, both relics of empire, the Commonwealth Relations Office and the Colonial Office—which between them produce internal rivalries almost as complicated as international ones. 'We must kill the crow!' Ernest Bevin used to say at the Foreign Office—referring to the Commonwealth Relations Office, or CRO, which inhabits an adjoining corner of the courtyard. Set up in 1947 to provide a special relationship between Commonwealth countries, it has its own network of 'High Commissioners' (the equivalents of ambassadors), and its own permanent secretary.

CRO, being new, has suffered lower status than the Foreign Office, who openly despise it, and regard it as a post office or letterbox; and many high commissioners in the past have been inferior to ambassadors, a fact much resented by Commonwealth countries. Recently, after persistent complaints, they have been recruited from wider sources, including Lord Head in Nigeria, a former Minister of Defence and supporter of Suez; Lord Alport in Rhodesia, a former junior minister and author of *Hope in Africa*; Sir Geoffrey de Freitas in Ghana, a former Labour minister; and Sir John Maud in South Africa—a witty and urbane former civil servant and don, of whom one Cape Town wit

Robert Stephens in *The Observer*, December 17, 1961.

remarked: 'You must take the smooth with the smooth.' He has the most tricky and controversial jobs, for he combines being Ambassador to South Africa and High Commissioner to the British Protectorates—two conflicting responsibilities, sometimes called 'Maudledum and Maudledee'. But since 1961 his job has been outside the Commonwealth, split between the Foreign Office and the Colonial Office.

The existence of two organisations side by side has duplicated experts and bureaucracies, and given great scope for inter-departmental muddle: at the United Nations they each have their separate groups, thus ensuring that the Foreign Office doesn't know enough about the Commonwealth, and vice versa. Their separate organisation seems to make the influence of Commonwealth countries less rather than more potent, and it has helped to shield the Foreign Office from African influences, rather than expose it to them. The Foreign Office feels the impact of Portugal or France more forcibly than that of Ghana or Australia, with whom they have no direct contact. Moreover, the CRO is apt to be too preoccupied with defending the interests of Sir Roy Welensky (who comes under CRO) against Kaunda and Banda (who come under the Colonial Office) to have much energy left for pressing the interests of their African clients.

From time to time efforts are made to merge the CRO either with the Foreign Office or the Colonial Office: but the Commonwealth Secretary in the cabinet always resists, and the two bodies continue to glare at each other across the courtyard.

No institution in Britain has seen such rapid change as that extraordinary residue of Empire, the Colonial Office. In 1946 the Colonial Secretary was responsible for 65 million people and 37 separate colonial territories. Today (1962) he has 31 million people under him, and by 1970 the number will be nearer 4 million. One by one the countries are struck off the colonial list and pass over to the Commonwealth Office. But until the trouble-spots of Africa are resolved—as dangerous in Westminster as in Africa—the Colonial Secretaryship will remain the hottest seat in Whitehall.

With the colonies are departing a remarkable breed—the governors. Fifteen years ago there were thirty-four of them—they were monarchs, prime ministers, judges rolled into one. They lived in vast, draughty palaces and castles, called 'Government House', and teams of flunkeys and gardeners trimmed their tropical lawns.

Their bold, tall, cocked hats were covered with swan-plumes—bought for £20 from Moss Bros.—and they toured their colonies to the sound of brass bands. Their lives were punctuated by old-fashioned hazards: they were liable to be shot at, or to have their palaces stormed by settlers.

After 1947, with considerable sang-froid, the governors set about liquidating their powers—imprisoning the revolutionaries one moment, making them prime minister the next, and then retiring to the English countryside. Only a few remain. In Kenya there is still the colossal Government House outside Nairobi, surrounded by parkland, with the life of a miniature court—inhabited by Sir Patrick Renison, who has worked his way up through the diminishing outposts of Empire—Ceylon, Trinidad, Honduras, Guiana—and is now holding the shaky balance between the rival factions in Kenya. The present-day governors are a much less rugged breed than their predecessors, more like civil servants. At the most tricky of all gubernatorial posts, in Northern Rhodesia, is Sir Evelyn Hone, the epitome of the businesslike governor of the last phase of Empire—quiet, efficient, former Rhodes Scholar, tough, but looks awkward in his cocked hat.

Governors will soon be almost extinct. A few outposts will remain, mostly Pacific or Caribbean islands, too small or un-developed for self-government. They include the Seychelles (population 41,452), Ascension Island (418) and the Falkland Islands (2,800) of which one ex-governor said 'the only memorable thing about the Falkland Islands is the wind'. Also, according to the *Colonial Office List*, 'various islands and rocks throughout the world are British territory but are not included in any country ... Many of them have no permanent inhabitants'. Some of the surviving governorships, like the Bahamas, Bermuda, Gibraltar or Malta, are virtually 'grace-and-favour' appointments, ideal for retired generals, admirals or monarchs (the Duke of Windsor governed the Bahamas during the war).

Out of the ashes of the Colonial Office itself is gradually rising a new and important institution, drily named the 'Department for Technical Co-operation'—a discreet phrase for aid. It was launched—with the typical secrecy and with the tiny funds accorded to anything new—in July 1961, and now inhabits part of Carlton House Terrace. As the last colonies become independent, the Department will probably absorb the Colonial Office. At the head of the Department is one of the most unusual of Britain's proconsuls—Sir Andrew Benjamin Cohen, an enormous, shy man, given to long, disconcerting silences, with a large appetite and untidy hair. He belongs to a distinguished Anglo-Jewish family; his sister is Principal of Newnham College, Cambridge; he had a brilliant Cambridge career and married the daughter of a don. In the Colonial Office in London he had a strong and radical influence on post-war policies: then in 1952 he was sent out to the stormy post of governor of Uganda—where he first exiled the Kabaka, then welcomed him back. After a spell at the United Nations in New York, he came back to London to build up the new department. A characteristic story is told of Cohen in Malta—where he served for a time during the war. The dockyard workers had made angry complaints about the bad food: their leader insisted on an interview with Cohen, and sent in as an exhibit beforehand a piece of mouldy bread, which had been served at the dockyard canteen. But by the time the angry worker arrived, the exhibit had disappeared. Cohen had absent-mindedly eaten it.

Cohen is an appropriate symbol of the transition from gubernatorial pomp to practical technical aid. He is an intellectual idealist, with strong views on Britain's continued rôle in poor countries. Though he has spent his life as a civil servant, he maintains an open-ness to new ideas and new people. The department itself is a test of whether Britain can give disinterested help to new countries with the same enthusiasm with which she governed them.

COMMON MARKET

The gradual impact of European unity and the Common Market can be traced through many British institutions: but one of its central battles has been round the Foreign Office. Here, as elsewhere, diplomats have been reluctant to take a long view. Since the war the Foreign Office, like the rest of Britain, has been sceptical of European unity: Lord Boothby has recalled how the diplomats poured 'repeated and invariable douches of cold water'[1] on the Council of Europe at Strasbourg: and international organisations were looked on as rivals to their own profession—threatening to by-pass the whole splendid mechanism. About the first moves towards economic unity, beginning with the Coal and Steel Community in 1951, the Foreign Office were sceptical: they regarded it as a purely economic matter, and passed the problem to the Treasury. The fact that the Foreign Office had few econo-

[1] House of Lords, August 3, 1961.

mists, and the Treasury knew little about Europe, helped to muddle the issue. When the Six Powers met at Messina in 1955 (while Macmillan was having a brief spell at the Foreign Office), the British sent an observer to the talks, but later withdrew him: it was thought that the talks were in danger of duplicating existing organisations. Even when the Treaty of Rome was signed in 1957 —at a time when Whitehall was preoccupied with troubles in Cyprus and Nyasaland—it made little impact on the Foreign Office, and hence on the rest of Whitehall (one sign was the official translation, reprinted over the following five years, which was indifferent and inaccurate). In the following year various voices began to be heard. Sir Gladwyn Jebb, then British Ambassador to Paris, sent dramatic despatches about the rebirth of Europe, and within the Foreign Office Sir Evelyn Shuckburgh (a former PPS to the Foreign Secretary and expert on Western organisations) and Sir Paul Gore-Booth (now High Commissioner in Delhi) were among the prominent pro-Europeans. But the Office remained torn between the Commonwealth and the Common Market, and continued to put faith in the ineffective Free Trade Area. Selwyn Lloyd had other things on his mind.

By the middle of 1960, the Prime Minister had been converted, and Ted Heath had joined the Foreign Office with the special bailiwick of Europe. The Treasury were dropping their financial objections, the malaise of industry was becoming more evident, and the press—headed by *The Economist*, which diplomats read— was becoming louder.

When the political decision had been taken, in July 1961, the Whitehall machine moved quickly and adaptably: it is characteristic of our bureaucracy that, once told what it has to do—like the Rolls Royce when given a driver with a map—it can react with spectacular vigour. It is then that 'the absence of fuss, the concealed force, the refreshing dash of intellectual sophistication' come into their own, and the machine dashes forward. The team that was mustered to negotiate in Brussels was the pick of Whitehall, headed by Sir Pierson Dixon, the British Ambassador in Paris: his second-in-command was one of those unconventional men who sometimes lurk in senior Whitehall offices—Sir Eric Roll, from the Ministry of Agriculture: educated in Vienna, speaks French and German perfectly, ex-professor at Hull (the reddest brick of all) and an expert in international economic negotiation. He is a wholly international man; he has worked in OEEC and

NATO, has close friends in the Washington administration. The rest of the team were:

Sir Roderick Barclay	(Foreign Office)
G. R. Bell	(Treasury)
Sir Henry Lintott	(Commonwealth Relations Office)
Sir William Gorell Barnes	(Colonial Office)
G. H. Andrew	(Board of Trade).

The team, with Sir Frank Lee and the Treasury knights in the background, moved swiftly: the long opening statement by Ted Heath—later leaked to the Canadians and then published under pressure—was a model of analytical clarity, and in Brussels the German and Italian bureaucrats were reported to be delighted to find a team which could at last give the French bureaucrats a run for their money.

20

PRIME MINISTER

I rather enjoy patronage. I take a lot of trouble over it. At least it makes all those years of reading Trollope seem worth while.
Harold Macmillan at Oxford, June 1959.

FROM time to time, in one of six of the more conservative London clubs (Pratt's, Buck's, the Carlton, the Beefsteak, the Turf or the Athenæum), a tall, grey-haired man with a drooping moustache can be observed walking slowly—almost shuffling—up the stairs, alone. He walks in, orders perhaps a dry martini, and then may turn to talk to one of the members. He talks well, in a casual, relaxed way, with a sardonic wit. He has a habit of picking his teeth with concentration, and of brushing down the side of his moustache tiredly. Everything about him seems to droop—his moustache, his eyes, his mouth, his floppy cardigan. Even his black bow tie, which he wears in the evening, is tucked beneath his collar, in the Edwardian fashion. He is one of the few men left in England who literally puts his tongue in his cheek when making a joke.

His repertoire of languid gestures includes the pulling in of his mouth, tongue in cheek, as he prepares a quip; the pulling down of the corner of his eyes, while he pauses for a point; the fastidious wobbling of his hand, as he searches for a nuance; the opening of his mouth—squarely, like a trap—as he feigns amazement. He might be any aged clubman, imagining himself to be important. But in fact he is, of course, the Prime Minister: and it is in clubland —in this old-fashioned, faintly histrionic setting—that he seems at home.

'There are four different Harold Macmillans', one observer of him has remarked: 'and you never know which one you're talking to. There's the crofter's grandson. There's the Balliol scholar. There's the man of business. And there's the Duke's son-in-law'. To these might be added a fifth Macmillan, the Guards officer. In the person of the Prime Minister several different strands come together. Dukes, Eton, Balliol, the Guards, clubs, the Church and Whitehall all jostle together behind that moustache: his career provides a kind of epitome of the Conservative party.

Macmillan, like many a Scotsman, likes to refer to his simple ancestry: he has carried from ministry to ministry, and finally to 10 Downing Street, a faded photograph of the stone-and-thatch cottage on the Isle of Arran, where his grandfather was brought up. But his crofting connection is distant: his grandfather, Daniel, left home as a young man to find work in London, where he founded the publishing house of Macmillan. Daniel's son, who began life as a music student and then joined the family firm, was already wealthy and well-established. He married an American girl, also a music student, a doctor's daughter from Kentucky. It was this American infusion, rather than Scottish blood, which forged Harold Macmillan's ambitions. He adored his mother, and still talks often about her: she was strong, upright, and very ambitious for her three scholarly sons. It was Mrs. Macmillan who had built the big neo-Georgian villa at Chelwood Gate in Sussex, with wide passages and small rooms, where the Prime Minister now lives.

Harold, like his elder brother, went as a scholar or 'tug' to Eton —a life very different from being an ordinary Etonian, or 'oppidan'. (Nineteen out of Britain's 44 prime ministers have been Etonians, but only Macmillan and Walpole were scholars: 34 went to Oxford or Cambridge, 12 were at Christ Church, 8 were at Harrow.) The Eton scholars live a highly competitive life of their own, looked down on as unsporting and gauche. It was as a Balliol scholar—or strictly speaking as an exhibitioner—that the intellectual Macmillan came into his own. At Balliol he acquired a donnishness, a fascination with ideas, a sense of intellectual power which marks him from most other politicians. He loved Oxford, its ceremonial and high tables and Latin speeches, its rigorous intellectual standards. He likes to talk about the secluded Oxford of his day—without factories or motor-cars. 'The only industry when I was up', he has said, 'was marmalade—which seemed somehow appropriate.' At Balliol he was regarded by his contemporaries as a worthy, ineffectual idealist.

War broke out when Macmillan was twenty. He belongs to that dwindling generation of 'survivors' (including Lord Monckton, Lord Salisbury, Lord Chandos, Lord Avon, Lord Attlee and Sir Winston Churchill), whose boyhood was spent in the legendary days before 1914, when the future seemed so secure. He joined the Grenadier Guards, and was wounded three times; out of the six exhibitioners and scholars in his year at Balliol, he was the only survivor. He is proud of his military career: he wears a Guards tie on the few occasions when he is not wearing an Old Etonian tie. He loves inspecting guards-of-honour, chatting with old VCs, reminiscing about regiments. He looks down on people (like Hugh Gaitskell) who have never led a platoon of men into battle, even if they were doing vital war-work. This is one example of an important trait in Macmillan, typical of many Conservatives, a cleavage between his rational side—realistic, analytical and slightly left-wing, which was consummated at Balliol—and his emotional side—old-fashioned, high Tory, prejudiced, which had its apotheosis in the Guards. The two strains, though often at odds, proved politically valuable; but the second emerged more strongly as he grew older.

After the war he became ADC to the Governor-General of Canada, the ninth Duke of Devonshire. A year later he became engaged to one of the Duke's daughters, Lady Dorothy Cavendish. He came back to London for a very fashionable wedding at St. Margaret's, Westminster. A wedding photograph shows Major Macmillan sitting solemnly beside his bride and bridesmaids, in a wing collar and black cravat, with a big black Groucho Marx moustache. The wedding was to change the whole pattern of the major's life. His relationship with the Devonshires was crucial but complicated. For a young Tory politician at that time there could have been no connection more advantageous. The Devonshires, of all the ducal families, had the widest connections: they were richer than the King, and to marry a Cavendish was like marrying a princess. The tenth Duke, together with his brother-in-law the fifth Marquess of Salisbury, was at the very centre of the cousin-hoods who had been interwoven with politics for the past centuries. Macmillan found himself overnight related to sixteen members of parliament.

But the Devonshires were proud and exclusive, and Macmillan's relationship was far from easy. They lived a sumptuous, quasi-royal life, travelling between three large houses—in London, Derbyshire and Ireland. They were inclined to patronise the young, shy commoner who had married into them. One daughter, Lady Blanche, had already married a brewer: and when the old duke heard his other daughter wanted to marry a publisher, he is reported to have commented wryly: 'Well, books is better than beer'. The young Macmillan had an equally ambiguous relationship with the aristocracy. He enjoyed their company, was a good shot, stayed in the great houses, but he was bored by racing, horses and philistinism, and they were bored by his bookish

324

talk. It has been said that Macmillan did not feel entirely on top of the aristocracy until he had not only become Prime Minister, but had sacked his cousin Lord Salisbury, and given his nephew, the young duke, a government job.

'I was a bit of a rebel once myself', Macmillan likes to tell young Conservatives. Four years after he married he became Conservative Member of Parliament for Stockton-on-Tees, a bleak industrial town in the North of England. It was there—where most of the workers voted Tory—that he saw the effects of unemployment and poverty, and this experience moulded his political attitudes.

It is important not to underestimate the influence of Stockton-on-Tees on Macmillan's later policies: in the Treasury since 1957 it has become something of a joke—but it is a serious joke. The memory of unemployment has left Macmillan with a horror of slump and deflation which affects British economic policy today.

In parliament between the wars he became one of the group of earnest young Conservatives—including Bob Boothby—who were dubbed the 'YMCA': he wrote several dull books, including *The Middle Way*, and referred to the Conservative leaders as 'disused slag heaps' (one of the many signs of the strong early influence of Disraeli, his favourite prime minister). He attacked his own party both for its unemployment and appeasement, and joined Churchill in his attacks on Hitler: as a result he was in the political wilderness. He was shy, nervous in public speaking, and unnoticed. 'Quite able, but I think, rather pedestrian', is how Tom Jones described him in 1931.[1] He worked hard and efficiently as a director of Macmillans, enjoying his contact with historians and authors, but with a strong business sense, not misled by the romantic aura of publishing; in his house there is an empty niche which, according to a family joke, is reserved for Hall and Knight —whose mathematical school books helped to found the family fortunes.

In 1942 Churchill—remembering old allies—asked him suddenly to go to Algiers as resident minister: there Macmillan flourished, establishing a good connection both with the American general, Eisenhower, and with the French chief, de Gaulle. 'Remember that we are Greeks in their Roman Empire', he told a group of British officers one day: 'it is our job to change their minds without their realising it.' He was a good Anglo-American, and watched, without apparent resentment, Britain's rôle pass

[1] Thomas Jones: *A Diary with Letters,* 1954. p. 2.

from senior to equal to junior partner. After the war he was talking without bitterness about Britain's diminished rôle long before most Conservatives could face the fact.

In the post-war parliament he was still not a prominent figure: with his gravity, his histrionic manner and his slight pomposity, some backbench Tories regarded him as the Walter Mitty of the party, day-dreaming about statesmanship, and in the years out of office he appeared deeply disillusioned by the Labour victory. But with Churchill back in power in 1951, his second great opportunity came: he became Minister of Housing, publicly committed to build 300,000 houses a year. Macmillan welcomed the challenge: he brought in a businessman he had met during the war—Percy Mills—and a thrusting, ambitious young MP, Ernest Marples. From Housing Macmillan rose under Churchill to be Minister of Defence; when Eden took over as Prime Minister, he became Foreign Secretary and then, at the time of Suez, Chancellor of the Exchequer. In neither office did he make a very strong mark. In the Treasury he launched the Premium Bonds, annoyed some of the mandarins, and introduced a new, spot-check device for estimating the financial situation ('it's like looking up trains in last year's Bradshaw', he complained about the Treasury's system). But he was far from dynamic as Chancellor, and during 1956 he seemed to many of his colleagues to be tired, old, and ready for retirement.

Between Macmillan and Eden there was a marked antipathy. Macmillan, who was apparently relaxed and phlegmatic, was irritated by the nervous tenseness of his prime minister: and right-wing Tories—restive with the humiliating retreat from Empire—regarded Macmillan as a more robust leader. When Eden began envisaging a Suez invasion, Macmillan (in spite of his Anglo-American loyalties) encouraged him and was a member of the inner cabinet: but when, half-way through the operation, he withdrew his support—on the grounds that it threatened the gold reserves—he was not (as Butler was) regarded as betraying the right. Macmillan's full rôle in the Suez affair will remain obscure for many more years; what is clear is that he was deeply implicated, and that without his support it would probably never have happened.

When Eden resigned, a hundred Tory MPs wrote to the Chief Whip, saying they could not support Butler—who was regarded as too liberal and unreliable. The Queen consulted three Conservative leaders, Churchill, Salisbury and Eden, about the successor, while behind the scenes Lord Kilmuir was sounding out the cabinet, Ted Heath (then Chief Whip) was questioning Conservative MPs, and Salisbury was reporting on the Lords. All three reported that only one man would be acceptable—Harold Macmillan.

Macmillan brought to Downing Street a sense of unflappability. The klaxon of the official Humber, which blared through the traffic in Eden's day, was thenceforth silent, and the change was symbolic. Macmillan wrote a notice to hang on his secretaries' office, with the words from Gilbert and Sullivan: 'Quiet Calm Deliberation Untangles Every Knot.' He was able to work hard without fuss: he normally wakes at six, does two hours work on his papers before breakfast, spends the day on official business, and works on his 'boxes' at night, often till two in the morning. There were long chats with his secretaries about books and people; there were long weekends in the country; there were no more anxious telephone calls to ministers. The tiredness which seemed to have overtaken him suddenly dropped off. Like Home when he became Foreign Secretary, Macmillan emerged at the top of the tree not only with a new energy, but with a blossoming personality which few would have previously suspected. It is apparently one of the dangers of the tremendous concentration of power at the top, that ambitious subordinates have to be so cautious and so trimming that their real personality is largely concealed: 'the path to political preferment passes through the field of party orthodoxy.'[1] Not till they reach the top is it fully expressed—as Britain learnt with Sir Anthony Eden.

The several aspects of Macmillan all proved useful in the difficult course he had to steer after Suez: he shuffled off to the left, while appearing to head right. He came to terms with Nasser, patched up relations with America, released Archbishop Makarios from exile—which induced Lord Salisbury, his cousin-by-marriage, to resign in protest: and his gradual retreat from the right reached a climax in January 1960, with the 'Wind of Change' speech in Cape Town. All these moves could have outraged the die-hards. But the Balliol scholar was concealed by the ducal exterior, his Edwardian appearance was infinitely reassuring. In Cape Town, the day after he had unmistakably dissociated himself from the White men's aspirations in Africa, I remember watching the White South Africans cheering him as he drove through the streets, looking unchangeably imperial, to his ship.

Sir Ivor Jennings: *The British Constitution*, 1958. p. 160.

In his first three years as prime minister, Macmillan rode high: he had rescued his own party from the humiliating shipwreck of Suez: he had personally mediated between Moscow and Washington in a way which, though unsuccessful, captured the electors' imagination: he had exploited the boom of the late nineteen-fifties, and led his party to an easy victory in the general election of October 1959. He was referred to by left and right as Supermac and Macwonder—first satirically, then seriously.

But as Britain escaped from past crises into the more humdrum future—productivity, education, Europe—so Macmillan's leadership seemed less adequate. The calm now appeared complacent. 'Whoever bothered to say that Churchill was unflappable?' said Hugh Gaitskell. At the same time the Trollopean side of Macmillan's character seemed to be winning. The House of Lords, which had been withering away, experienced an astonishing comeback: little-known peers with ancient titles, like the Earls of Perth and Dundee and Earl Waldegrave, emerged to take posts in his ministry. The Earl of Home became Foreign Secretary. And a regiment of cousins-by-marriage marched in: his nephew the Duke of Devonshire became parliamentary secretary at the Commonwealth Relations Office; his son's brother-in-law, David Ormsby-Gore, became ambassador to Washington; his wife's cousin, the Marquess of Lansdowne, became a minister at the Foreign Office; a distant cousin, Lord Cromer, became Governor of the Bank of England; his son-in-law, Julian Amery, became Secretary of State for Air. 'I don't think Harold appoints aristocrats to show off; he's used to their company. But I don't think it does his popularity any good', said one minister. 'There has been nothing like it in England since the days of the eighteenth-century Duke of Newcastle', wrote a former Conservative MP, Christopher Hollis: 'and the record is today unparalleled by any country in the world save only Laos, Saudi Arabia, and perhaps the Yemen.'[1]

At first his party showed little discontent: the idea of having a duke, a marquess and four earls in the government was, after all, in the best Tory tradition. But backbenchers, waiting for promotion, became restive. Macmillan, they noticed, was happy enough with aristocrats or self-made men. But he seemed increasingly reluctant to come to terms with the middle classes.

When he discusses the future of Britain, Macmillan can sound realistic enough: he likes to *talk* about the precarious, challenging

[1] *Political Quarterly.* July, 1961. p. 220.

times of the New Elizabethans, and the excitement of living on the verge of bankruptcy. He can speak with enthusiasm about television or nuclear energy; about the 'new men' of science and technology; about exporters and industrialists as the new merchant adventurers; and about the race between two kinds of British business, the old-fashioned Victorian firms and the new corporations.

But as he talks about scientists and technocrats—'those H. G. Wells people'—a certain unreality seems to set in. In 1960 he told a hallful of businessmen that 'Exporting is fun'. The businessmen were not amused. He combines the traditional interests of the cultivated squire—Greek, foreign policy, shooting, literature, regiments—with an apparent faint dislike for factories, laboratories, the City and trade.

In this he is in many respects typical of his party, and even his country, and in the first years of his ministry, when Britain took refuge in nostalgia, the identification seemed close. But as Britain moves further towards Europe, trade, competition and the future, so Macmillan's entourage of peers, dons and clubmen seems more obviously anachronistic. His allies maintain that he retains scholarly, aristocratic values in a brash, commercial age, his enemies that he is an old-fashioned snob. But by either reckoning, Macmillan's ministry seems likely to go down in history as a curious diversion in the social evolution of Britain.

Macmillan talks wittily about the popular misconception of 'The Establishment'; how the press and the public are still obsessed by 'they', as something separate from themselves; how people still regard the Foreign Office or the banks as if they were run by a few noble families; and how gossip columns disclose a world of dukes and butlers, like drawing-room comedies. Yet he himself often seems to enjoy this ancient illusion, and to prefer, as Disraeli often did, a romantic setting of gorse and clubs to the real managerial world.

In his early years Macmillan seemed to enjoy discussing the hard technical problems of industry; he liked meeting the ICI scientists in his constituency of Stockton. But now he seems uninterested—perhaps slightly distressed—by technology and the social change which it is bringing about. Compare *The Middle Way*, published in 1938, full of statistics about pig-food, butter prices and unemployment, with his pamphlet in 1958, *The Middle Way: Twenty Years After*, full of Tory clichés. There had of course been an important change of occupation in that twenty years, but at the same time an earnest, pedestrian politician had become an aloof country gentleman.

Another change has occurred. Before the war Macmillan was regarded as a somewhat puritan 'YMCA man'. He has remained religious and upright; he reads the lesson every Sunday at church, treats his employees considerately, and enjoys dining off cold mutton. He talks with feeling about the moral dangers of rootlessness, and the moral weaknesses of some politicians. But in his premiership this is not quite what he has conveyed, and to the public he has become a 'never had it so good' prime minister. Part of this has been bad luck; the phrase 'you've never had it so good' was meant to reflect not the boom of easy money, but the end of the pre-war misery which he remembered from Stockton. It was an unlucky coincidence that, in the middle of the Suez crisis, he should find himself in Trafalgar Square launching the premium bonds, or that the cabinet should be arranging to exclude West Indian workers just at a time when batches of French croupiers were being imported. Partly, too, the Prime Minister seems to have enjoyed the cartoon-image of the faintly rakish Edwardian. But behind this outward picture there does seem to have been a basic change—whether because of the war, Suez, a growing historical pessimism, or merely the gaining of power—in Macmillan's approach over those twenty years.

THE PRIME MINISTER'S POWERS

One suspects, indeed, that ever since the emergence of Lloyd George as the national leader in the first world war the prevailing tendency has been towards the exaltation of the Prime Minister at the expense both of his colleagues and of the House of Commons.

Professor Max Beloff (August 1960).

Is the prime minister's power increasing? Is he becoming less the chairman of a cabinet committee, *primus inter pares*, and more of a president, with powers quite distinct from his colleagues?

Provided a premier can keep his party, his colleagues and parliament reasonably happy, there are no rules for the job. Churchill established a private court of overlords and personal advisers: he had little cause to worry about his party or parliament, since he was virtually irremovable, but he left great areas of government to departmental ministers. Whatever Churchill was, Attlee wasn't: 'he was much more like a chairman', as one of his successors put it: 'mediating between his directors—Bevin and Cripps.' Or as

Attlee described it: 'The job of a prime minister is to lead and co-ordinate a team, not to seek to be an omnipotent minister.'[1] Eden bombarded nearly every department with minutes, phone calls and questions. He did not in the long run carry his party with him, though in the short run he revealed dramatically the powers of a prime minister. Yet in spite of the personal interpretations, developments in the last century have altered the prime minister's rôle. Among the factors are:

Universal suffrage. Since the vote was extended to everyone, the prime minister has become more a personification of his party, and general elections have become, in the public's eyes, a contest between two men—with all others subordinate. There are apparent exceptions to this: for instance in 1945 Bevin with his trade union and war-time career was in many respects a more popular and familiar figure than Attlee. But the pressure of publicity tends to concentrate increasingly on one man: Macmillan is 'Mr. Tory' and Gaitskell is 'Mr. Labour', and this has helped to produce a more Presidential situation.[2] Once in office, the press are apt to ascribe all government policies to the boss. The prime minister's special relationship with the electors can short-circuit the powers of the cabinet, and television has given him a powerful new medium for direct access: it is one of which he has to be careful—for it infuriates parliament to be by-passed—but which can be invaluable in a cabinet issue such as Suez, or the Common Market.

Secondly, the expansion of the government machine. The growth of the Cabinet Office, the spread of cabinet committees, and the wider scope of the civil service, have all brought a larger concentration of information to 10 Downing Street. The more complicated government becomes, the greater the need for co-ordination, and in the nervous system of Whitehall, the prime minister's office must be the ganglion. Much of the influence of a premier depends on sheer information, and the messages that go to and from the limbs of government. A cabinet minister may know less about the current of Whitehall than the civil servants at 10 Downing Street.

The prime minister is not perhaps as central as he might appear from outside: one might suppose that it would be like being in the middle of the piazza of St Peter's in Rome, where the pillars, which from the edges seem confused and patternless, suddenly come into line, all pointing to the centre. But that is not, it seems, an accurate analogy: for the area of muddle and fog, so noticeable

---

[1] *See Daily Telegraph*, August 9, 1960.
[2] Sir Ivor Jennings: *The British Constitution*. p. 162.

in government departments, is equally apparent here, and the prime minister, like the cabinet, is constantly having things done *to* him—by America, Russia, the TUC, the Opposition, and even his colleagues, which spoil any pattern he may be devising, and provide further muddle. The more puzzling of the prime minister's actions, like those of the Chancellor or the Foreign Secretary, become less astonishing if one takes into account the vital signicance of muddle. But nevertheless, 10 Downing Street is much better informed than other departments, which sets the prime minister apart from his colleagues.

Thirdly, summits. Jet planes and international telephones have made foreign affairs much more a matter of exchange between chief executives, rather than foreign ministers or ambassadors. The position still fluctuates with the personality of the foreign secretary, and has changed, as we have seen, with the arrival of Lord Home. But if Khrushchev, Kennedy and de Gaulle look after their foreign affairs, they expect to deal with the British prime minister, and no one else. And the heads of smaller countries are at least as sensitive about dealing with the chief executive: to the world at large, Macmillan *is* Britain. In theory the Monarch is supposed to take over much of the ceremonial representative rôle: in practice, every visitor knows where the power lies, and wants to be there.

How has the job of prime minister changed from before the war? I asked Macmillan:

To some extent, of course, the prime minister's job is what he makes of it. But the number of inescapable things has increased—and they always were considerable. The tempo has quickened too.

At home the Government carries many more direct responsibilities than it did. In foreign affairs things have become more complex because of the proliferation of new nations, new groupings, new organisations.

With the use of modern communications you get the difficulties that arise from differences in time. At the Foreign Office you can be woken up in the middle of the night from the United Nations, where it is only 7 o'clock, and be asked which way we should vote about something, and you have got to decide. The Foreign Office is the most exacting post: it is like editing a daily paper: the Treasury is more like a weekly paper.

Also this flying business. That has certainly made a difference.

Nowadays there is no particular difficulty about having a meeting almost anywhere in the world at the drop of a hat. So you get pressures to have them. And, of course, quite a number of countries—it isn't only Russia—choose to do the really important business at the summit. So the prime minister tends to get more and more caught up in meetings, in travelling, in receiving visitors. Don't think I am saying it's all a waste of time. Much of it is really useful. And travel does give you opportunities earlier prime ministers didn't have—for example in getting round the Commonwealth.

Then again, the business of parliament has changed enormously. When I was a young man it used to adjourn from August to February. People really had time to think. Nowadays parliament takes up much more of a prime minister's time. Parliamentary Questions, for example. Fifty years ago it was not "done" to raise broad policy issues at Question Time. Nowadays it is: questions leading up to a debate, really, and they take up a good deal of work.

Keeping yourself straight with the press is something else that seems to have become more complicated. Partly because the pace is so much quicker. But also far more people demand to be seen. On top of that, there's television. Learning to cope with television isn't easy. Either you get involved in a kind of circus act with interviewers or you try solos—if they let you—and solos are just about the most difficult television technique. How *can* you give a fireside talk to a television camera?

The fact is that you can't be prime minister nowadays unless you are prepared to stay up late. A great deal of the hard work doesn't begin until the evening, when the boxes start coming in. Much of the time you can't get out at night except for official occasions. I don't mind myself, but some people wouldn't like it. If you go off to Scotland, everyone seems to assume you are on holiday. They don't realise that you have to take secretaries with you: that you have to keep in touch with London all the time.

What it all adds up to is that these days a prime minister must have the constitution of an ox. It's no longer just a question of intellectual and mental capacity.

MEN AROUND MACMILLAN

Round the Prime Minister are the small group of personal

advisers at 10 Downing Street. American observers have been astonished by the compactness and casualness of the staff—only a handful of private secretaries—compared to the massive White House secretariat. The building itself has the easy, informal atmosphere of a well-run country house, with secretaries strolling about like permanent guests and friendly butlers hovering by the door. But it is an undeniably efficient organisation—one of the few which have not succumbed to Parkinson's Law. It is quick, adaptable, capable suddenly of working through the night: everyone from the typists to the switchboard operators are handpicked. The telephone is always answered immediately—it never rings twice (at the Foreign Office, on the other hand, even the telephones seem afflicted with absence of zeal: they often ring for two minutes). The Number Ten switchboard can get Tokyo in ten minutes, and keeps track of anyone who might be needed, so that the prime minister has only to mutter a name into the telephone for the man to be found. No one who has worked at Number Ten ever seems quite satisfied with the organisation anywhere else.

Certainly the most important of Macmillan's advisers is Sir Norman Brook, head of the civil service: he has become increasingly close to the Prime Minister, as his personal adviser, accompanying him on all his major tours, and he represents the main link between the premier and the Whitehall machine. But apart from this official link, there is a subsidiary system, known in Whitehall (sometimes resentfully) as the 'Number Ten Network'—the web of ministers' private secretaries, each exceptionally well-informed, each keeping in close touch with the prime minister's private secretaries. They work the bush-telegraph of Whitehall, and it is they who actually transact much of the day-to-day business, lubricating the wheels between ministers, and adding their own advice on the way. 'Master's in a bit of a worry over that second bit of the Bill', one of them might say: 'do you think your master might get it changed?' And the other private secretary will consult *his* master, carefully taking the political temperature, and reporting back the result.

At the heart of this network are the four private secretaries to the Prime Minister, who sit in offices round the cabinet room, and observe all the comings and goings, the ups and downs, and the ins and outs. One of them, Philip de Zulueta, seconded from the Foreign Office, represents the important link between Number Ten and the F.O. The private secretaries are the pick of the younger civil servants. Usually in their late thirties, and destined for high promotion, their task is an odd combination of the menial and the crucial; on the prime minister's tours they can be seen trooping out of the aeroplane at the tail end of the party, carrying the red or black boxes which contain state papers, and standing in a huddle together with the typists. But they also draft telegrams, keep contact with ministers, collect and assess the news and reactions, and frequently give advice. Close to the private secretaries is the prime minister's public relations adviser, Harold Evans, known as 'Evans the Leak', but much more unobtrusive and discreet than his American equivalents.

Among the secretaries' jobs is the drafting of speeches. A secretary will collect the material, insert the suitable compliments, gratitudes, jokes and local references—usually if possible with a joke about the Scots: the speech will very often begin with the words 'My wife and I are delighted'. Then the draft will be passed to the prime minister, who will look through it and dictate his own version, after a certain amount of 'wombling' (as Gladstone's private secretary described his master's preparation: 'He lies down on the sofa and *wombles* it in his inside'). Finally the speech will be typed out with big letters on small sheets of paper, held together with a bit of red string; the words will be divided into short lines like a poem, to indicate the separate cadences—a device introduced by Churchill in the war, and followed by prime ministers since:

> I confess that
>   as the Vice-Chancellor read out my record
> it sounded rather like
>   an obituary notice.

Even then, the speech is often changed at the last minute, and Macmillan is at his best when ad libbing. With major speeches, many advisers may have a hand. With the 'wind of change' speech, for instance, a first draft was written six weeks beforehand by the High Commissioner in South Africa, Sir John Maud, who had flown to London to discuss it. The speech was then worked over by the Prime Minister, Sir Norman Brook and others, and at various stages through Africa, as the political atmosphere changed, it was taken out, amended, and slightly toned down. Finally it burst, as if from nowhere, on an unsuspecting Cape Town parliament.

One civil servant apart from Sir Norman Brook must know everything of importance that happens in Whitehall—the prime minister's principal private secretary, who occupies the centre of the Number Ten network: his office adjoins the PM's, and the private secretary is nearly always a special *confidant*[1]. The present incumbent, Tim Bligh, is a Winchester-and-Balliol man with the kind of sceptical, agile mind on which the Treasury prides itself: he leads a quiet Kent life, between the glamour of conferences and tours. His independence and lack of pomposity is unusual in Whitehall (as a war-time naval officer, he had a legendary career, commanding an MTB with ferocious daring), and Macmillan evidently respects his strong integrity.

Often the Prime Minister will be followed on his tours by a tall, lean secretary, peering through thick-lensed spectacles with a grave clerical expression. He appears in official lists as 'John Wyndham, MBE'. Once, when Macmillan was being shown round a model village outside New Delhi, an old man in a tattered uniform was introduced: 'This is one of the largest land-owners in this district'. The Prime Minister shook hands and then called out, 'Wyndham!' John Wyndham said 'Yes, Prime Minister', and came hurrying up. 'And this', said Macmillan to the old Indian, 'is one of the largest landowners in *my* district.'

This was an understatement, for John Wyndham is one of the richest (and most surprising) men in Britain. The friendship between him and Macmillan—a kind of Johnson-and-Boswell relationship—is an important clue to the Prime Minister's character. For Wyndham, in spite of his clerical look, generates an exotic seventeenth-century atmosphere, full of wild jokes and outspoken comments, like a young lord in a Restoration comedy. He is a very uncontemporary character: he lives with his wife, a famous society beauty, in Petworth House, a magnificent Tudor mansion in Sussex—which he inherited with a fortune from his uncle Lord Leconfield, author of *The Early History of the Thoroughbred Horse in South Africa*. But for the past six years Wyndham has chosen to be unpaid private secretary to Macmillan, whom he has admired intensely ever since he worked for him in Algiers in the war. Wyndham followed his master from ministry to ministry (though while Macmillan was Chancellor, Wyndham had to leave temporarily because he was himself negotiating with the Treasury over his uncle's death duties). Macmillan finds great solace in Wyndham's irreverent talk—there is a whole catalogue of Wyndhamisms—and his disinterested loyalty; often he will go over to Petworth, not too far from his own Sussex home, and stay till late at night. The extent of John Wyndham's influence over

[1] *See* Sir Charles Petrie: *The Powers behind the Prime Ministers*, 1958.

government policy is a subject of constant speculation among his friends.

Apart from these official advisers, there is Macmillan's small circle of friends. They are fairly predictable—mostly Etonians, aristocrats and relations, including the Duke of Devonshire, Lord Lansdowne, Lord Swinton, Gavin Astor, and Lord Stuart of Findhorn. There are a few more intellectual friends from his old Balliol or publishing days: the late Sir Lewis Namier and the late Monsignor Ronald Knox were both important influences, and Macmillan still enjoys his frequent visits to Oxford (where his grandson is at Balliol). But the grouse-moors seem to have won over the high tables, and Macmillan is evidently at his happiest in the country-house world.

MACMILLAN AND EUROPE

It is in keeping with the tradition of Victorian prime ministers that Macmillan should have found his main satisfaction in international, rather than in home affairs—even though Britain's scope for world diplomacy is dwindling. He has flown further than any previous premier—round Asia, Australia, to Washington, the West Indies and Canada, and to Moscow, Kiev and Leningrad. He has blossomed out abroad with a fulness that he never quite achieved in England: 'At home you're just a politician', he remarked in Australia, 'abroad you become a statesman.' The Berlin negotiations, the Wind of Change in Africa, the application to join the Common Market, the conciliation of South Africa, have all hung on Macmillan's decisions. In many home fields, such as industry, science and education, Macmillan has shown very little interest, and he hardly sees the heads of home departments, like Eccles or Marples. 'As he gets older', said one of his colleagues, 'he thinks mainly about three things—the cold war, the Common Market and the Atlantic alliance.' His absorbing interest has been in international affairs, and he is at his most eloquent talking about Britain's historic rôle in the world. Almost alone among the cabinet ministers, he has the faculty—and the time—to take a broad, detached view of Britain, to state its problems in his mind; and as a result it was Macmillan—the cartoonist's joke Briton—rather than the more ardent and involved Europeans, who provided the initiative for Britain's move into Europe.

In 1960 two events came as a serious blow to Macmillan's international operations. The first was the disastrous summit meeting of May in Paris, when Khrushchev, in one savage out-burst, wrecked all hopes of an East-West *détente*—thus reducing to ruins Macmillan's hopes of the previous two years. The second was the election of President Kennedy in November, a man twenty-five years younger than Macmillan, who made it plain that he had no need of an international go-between; the press emphasised the discrepancy between this vigorous young administrator and Macmillan's quaint régime, and forecast the end of the 'special relationship' between America and Britain. It was the first blow which most wounded Macmillan, and he made no secret of his depression; he saw the world threatened with a new dark age—with the Russians and Chinese as the new barbarians, America as a Byzantium, and Europe as Europe, once again the threatened bastion of civilisation.

In early 1961 Macmillan, with some difficulty, adjusted himself to this new situation. He set about (with the same tact he had shown with Eisenhower during the war) establishing a close avuncular relationship with the young President. It was not easy, and Kennedy's speed was often disconcerting: their first meeting was in March 1961, when they shared a canteen lunch at the naval base at Key West, at Kennedy's suggestion, on the way back from the West Indies. When Kennedy arranged a meeting with Khrush-chev in Vienna in June, it came as a slight blow to Macmillan's pride (though Kennedy had consulted him beforehand). Kennedy was not obviously of the same temper as Macmillan and seemed in many ways closer, in his donnish curiosity and detachment, to the Labour intellectuals. But Macmillan *had* succeeded in establishing a relationship closer than that with Eisenhower.

After Khrushchev's Paris outburst, and the further explosions in New York in October 1960, Macmillan's main pre-occupation had become the survival of Europe: he did not take the view, as others did, that Khrushchev's fury was directly due to the U2 incident, but rather that the U2 gave an excuse for a new intransi-gence, dictated by more serious internal reasons. He saw the world involved in a new kind of holy war, and the spectre of the Russian and Chinese hordes, already a billion people and still multiplying, was foremost in his mind. Already by the end of 1960 he had decided that a united Europe was the only hope of Western survival: and that, compared to this central problem, the problems of individual countries in the Commonwealth must inevitably be secondary. Up till that time his interest in Europe had not been outstanding: he had been a keen member of Churchill's United

Europe movement after the war, but his enthusiasm had waned; in 1956 he talked privately about the need for European competition to stimulate British industry but in 1957 he had been very doubtful about the Treaty of Rome. Although in his Commonwealth tours he had been well aware of the economic limitations of Britain's rôle, he retained a strong romantic attachment to this club—which showed itself forcibly in March 1961, when he tried with every kind of argument to prevent the Commonwealth prime ministers forcing South Africa out. And Macmillan, like others in the cabinet, was slow to realise the extent of Europe's industrial success compared to Britain's. The cold war and the developing dark age pattern drew Macmillan towards the Common Market, coupled perhaps with the feeling that if Britain joined Europe quickly—particularly while de Gaulle could still provide a counterweight to Germany—she still had a prospect of playing a dominant part in Europe's future. By the spring of 1961 Macmillan's historicist view had begun to meet with the view of the Treasury and industrialists—who had worked round to the conviction that joining Europe was the only chance of revivifying British industry.

Much of Macmillan's place in history (it seems, writing in March 1962) depends on the success of the entry into Europe. If it fails, then Macmillan's obsession with statesmanship, his trips to Moscow, the Commonwealth and Washington, together with his lack of interest in home affairs, will look merely absurd. If it succeeds he will have made his mark on the shape of the world.

Once he had made up his own mind, Macmillan had to press his cabinet gradually to the same conclusion. It was not easy. On his side Macmillan had not only the veteran 'Europeans', such as Sandys and Thorneycroft, but more recent converts, notably Iain Macleod and Ted Heath. Other ministers, such as Marples and Watkinson, were becoming more aware of the malaise of British industry, and the need for new stimulus. But there were several members, notably Butler, Maudling and Hailsham, who were antipathetic.

It was here that Macmillan's practised committeemanship was invaluable: he knew his own mind, but let other people speak theirs, allowing his ideas to infiltrate: he was able to take meetings slowly, and to stop before they reached outright disagreement. In the course of 1961, urged on by an almost unanimous press, the cabinet slowly came round to accepting the Common Market, without ever reaching a crisis, and (as happens with committees)

M   339

found itself gradually discussing not *whether* to do it, but *how* to do it.

On July 31st, 1961, Macmillan made his statement in parliament announcing the Government's intention to apply to join the Common Market. Two days later, in the Commons debate, he outlined his view of Britain's situation:

> It may, of course, be that there are some people in Europe who believe that this small but richly endowed continent can lead a rich, fruitful and prosperous life, almost cut off from contact with the rest of the world. But I do not believe that such people, if they exist, are to be found among the leading men or the governments of Europe. Certainly, this island could never join an association which believed in such medieval dreams, but if there are little Europeans, and perhaps there are, is it not the duty of this country, with its world-wide ties, to lend its weight to the majority of Europeans who see the true perspective of events? I believe that our right place is in the vanguard of the movement towards the greater unity of the free world, and that we can lead better from within than outside. At any rate, I am persuaded that we ought to try . . .
>
> I think that most of us recognise that in a changing world, if we are not to be left behind and to drop out of the main stream of the world's life, we must be prepared to change and adapt our methods. All through history this has been one of the main sources of our strength.

How does Macmillan see Britain's rôle in Europe? Would Britain, I asked him, still have an individual rôle within the Common Market?

> Why not? This isn't a society for giving up national identities. Is anyone less conscious of France as a nation since she joined the Six? Has General de Gaulle become a 'stylised' character? It's not really that at all. It's more a matter of working together imaginatively—or, if you like, putting together various national gifts, talents, experience, to achieve common ends by agreed means. How can the British stop being what geography and history have made them? We are the point at which three circles intersect—Europe, America, the Commonwealth. Making our ties with Europe closer and stronger doesn't mean weakening the others. On the contrary. I believe we are all the

more valuable to Europe because of these other ties. And in strengthening Europe and strengthening ourselves by going into the Six we would be likely to make ourselves all the more valuable to our Commonwealth and American friends.

People don't often realise that the Victorian Age was only an interruption in British history. The hundred years of British naval and to some extent political supremacy which ended in 1914 was a very rare thing in history. The age of the 'Concert of Powers' was a sort of Antonine Age: we can't expect it to happen again. The trouble is that a lot of people look back to that time of stability and don't think enough of the circumstances as they are in the world today. They talk a lot about the glories of the Old Elizabethan Age, but they forget it was a time when Britain was politically very insecure, facing much greater countries. We only kept this country going then by brains, courage and adventure. Now we've got to do it again.

The Anatomy of Britain

PART TWO

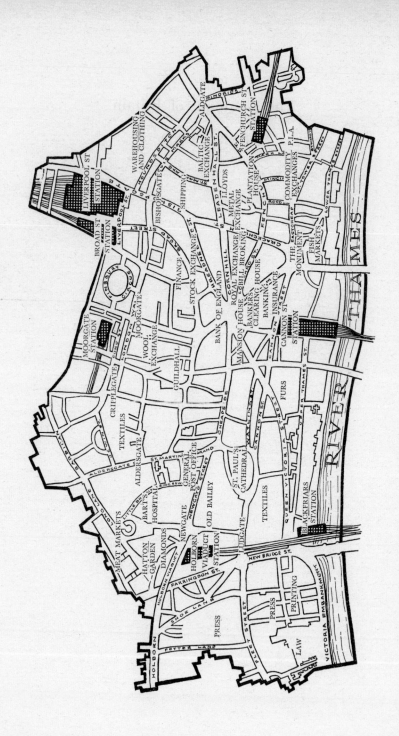

21

THE CITY

I believe that our system, though curious and peculiar, may be
worked safely; but if we wish so to work it, we must study it.
                                    Walter Bagehot (Lombard Street).

There was an Old Person of Bow,
Whom nobody happened to know;
    So they gave him some Soap,
    And said coldly, 'We hope
You will go back directly to Bow!'
                                    Edward Lear.

LONDON is two cities—the city of Westminster, and the city of
London, each with its own cathedral. Although the green fields
and river banks between them have long ago been built over, the
difference in character remains: Whitehall and Bishopsgate are at
the opposite ends of Britain's affairs—government in Westminster,
and finance in the city. Here we enter a territory much less
mapped than Whitehall, and harder to report accurately. Only
two documents since the war—the astonishing Bank Rate
Tribunal of 1957, and the Radcliffe Report of 1959—have helped
to open up the interior: there are no royal commissions, select
committees or parliamentary debates to throw light on its activities,
and city men are very unreflective about what they are doing. But
as Britain begins competing more hotly with Europe and America
so the character of the city becomes more central.

The city is still almost as concentrated as a hundred years ago:
it breathes a far more restricted air than Westminster. It is still
bounded by the 'square mile' of EC2, which can be crossed in
twenty minutes, and which contains most of the important
financial institutions in Britain. In the middle of this square is a
still smaller area, a quarter-mile across, centring on the Bank of
England and the Lord Mayor's Mansion House, which forms the
heart of the city: it includes the stock exchange, several insurance
companies, the commodity markets and nearly all the banks.
Concentration is the most important characteristic of the city:
within the square mile, though only 5,000 live there by night,
400,000 people work by day. Apart from the newspaper industry

on the Western edge, none of them makes anything except money. The propinquity of the financial offices, their steady rubbing, shaping and polishing, has provided the 'sensitive mechanism' (to use the favourite city phrase) on which their reputation rests.

The inner square has an intense atmosphere which no visitor can fail to notice. Nearly everyone wears a dark suit, a bowler hat and an umbrella, and discount brokers or gilt-edged stockbrokers still wear top hats. The restaurants are crowded with rows of pale-faced, black-coated men. Since the war tens of thousands of girls have strayed into the city, to work on the adding machines, type-writers and files, and their stiletto heels and jaunty walk contrasts with the solid lope of city men: but they are kept well apart, and have giggling lunches at the tea-shops while the men have beer and steaks. 'The city is a village' is a favourite saying: the streets and bars are full of people meeting, recognising, discussing each other. They are pressed closely together by their work, and isolated from the rest of London or the country. But even the different sectors of the city are very introverted: few stockbrokers have even been inside Lloyd's. The city is really a group of villages, with a moat round them all.

The moat, like that round other professions, has grown wider in the past thirty years. In spite of the inter-marriages, and politico-financial dynasties in the chart following page 34, the city no longer enjoys very close connections with the Conservative party. There are still strong bonds between right-wing Conservatives and the more imperialistic city companies, such as the British South Africa Company and Tanganyika Concessions, and city companies still subsidise the Conservative party. But the new generation of professional politicians, such as Macleod or Powell, have no love for the world of EC2, and Harold Macmillan treats the city with some disdain.

The rift no doubt has mixed causes. The landed interest have always liked to be aloof—or at least seem aloof—from trade, as at White's club: but the professionalisation of politics has increased the distance, and the Conservative Central Office look more anxiously to the electors and their subscriptions than to the city.

TRADITION AND PROGRESS

It is the pride of the city that it can combine formality with adaptability, tradition with enterprise—the first giving security to the second. Much of the paraphernalia is still Dickensian; the shiny Victorian drinking saloons, down small alley-ways; the ancient mahogany offices with worn brass-plates beside the front door; the liveried uniforms of waiters and butlers. But city men point out the electronic apparatus alongside their aged butlers, and ancient offices furnished with teleprinters. 'Tradition and Progress' is a stock heading to articles about the city, in annual surveys about steady advance.

In training its people, too, the city is traditional; much of it is still run on the 'fagging system'—the habit rejected by the civil service in 1870, of employing young men, often intelligent and expensively educated, at menial tasks for several years, copying transfers, writing in ledgers, or checking figures. The docile 'public school proletariat' (most from the 65 per cent who do not go on to universities—see chart, page 184) are employed on jobs which for some years may need no part of their expensive education except simple arithmetic. The analytical Oxbridge mind of Whitehall is noticeably absent in the city. There is a City University club, founded in 1885 (Oxbridge only, of course), but it is eclipsed by the more philistine halls of the city companies—the Fishmongers, Stationers or Haberdashers, and by the grand premises of Armoury House. It is the loyal unquestioning spirit of the regiment rather than the enquiring approach of universities which pervades the city, which contains whole light brigades of men at their desks, not reasoning why. The repression, like that of fags at school, achieves an awful continuity, with the older men remembering their own young drudgery. Although since the war the city has seen a large influx of graduates, much of the old discipline survives.

'It doesn't matter *what* you know, but *who* you know', they say in the city: personal contacts, and the personal background which provides them, are still decisive. This helps to account, perhaps, for the fact that the city remains the unchallenged bastion of the minor public schools, and within the square mile you hear more talk about men's schools, background, and above all their families, than anywhere else except perhaps in the Guards. The waves of the meritocracy, of examination wallahs and managerial revolutions which have swept through the civil service and industrial corporations, have hardly rippled the city. The 'Old Boy Net' which has become a sheepish or satirical phrase in other areas, remains a venerable concept.

The justification is that the city is based on *trust*. 'My word is my bond' is the motto of the Stock Exchange: 'Fidentia' is the motto of Lloyd's. The speed of the city's operations depends on acceptance of verbal promises, and this has been increased by the invention of the telephone—which allows hundreds of thousands of promises to be made every day. This quick trust, it is argued, depends on knowing to whom, or to what kind of person, you are talking—knowing he is 'one of us'. Unlike New York or Paris, which have a less homogeneous tradition, the city of London has a tribal past, and this eliminates—as in the Foreign Office—fuss and lawyers. The public school proletariat help to provide the lubricants to the sensitive mechanism.

But it is often thought that trust is the *only* requirement. What-you-know is gradually gaining over who-you-know. Since the war many clever young men with no connections have made fortunes and reputations. Stockbroking, insurance and banking are becoming increasingly specialised, and with specialisation the expert enters his kingdom. But it is still surprisingly possible to build a city career by knowing everyone, and knowing very little: the city, like the Conservative party, still loves the ignorant but reliable amateur, but even the most calculating professionals often like to appear as amateurs in the end.

Most English institutions are weighed down with Victorian furniture, but none so heavily as the city. For every part of the city is conscious of its glorious past: from 1815 to 1914—the 'English Era'—London was the undisputed financial capital of the world. Since 1914 the city has suffered a series of shocks—the shift of power to Wall Street, the dwindling of foreign loans, the growth of nationalism, the Labour government, the loss of Empire, the disappearance of China. The city has survived these buffets with a resilience which has surprised many critics: the Dickensian-looking men in their mahogany parlours have turned from financing foreign governments to devising hire-purchase schemes; the Lloyd's underwriters have continued sitting in front of dog-eared ledgers, but now insuring atomic power stations and jet planes. The city (which is full of self-praise) congratulates itself on remaining the leading international market for commodities, chartered shipping, foreign exchange or insurance, and providing the 'invisible earnings' which help to redress Britain's balance of payments, and this fact alone has been enough to dissuade Labour governments from trying to tamper with that sensitive mechanism. City people justify their curious archaisms—the ceremonial of discount brokers, the fagging, the ritual of Lloyd's—with the phrase so often used of the House of Lords, the election of bishops, or the gobbledigook of barristers: 'It may seem odd to you', they say, 'but there is one thing to be said for it—it *works*.' But the phrase 'it works' is of course inadequate: Liberia works, avoirdupois works. The city is never likely to collapse suddenly, with a broken mainspring; its danger is that it might, like the Hapsburg court, gradually become irrelevant to modern Europe.

STOCK EXCHANGE

In the city
They sell and buy
And nobody ever
Asks them why.

But since it contents them
To buy and sell
God forgive them!
They might as well.
Anon.

The city of London is full of exchanges, buying and selling *things*—wool, meat, gold, metals, rubber—but since the joint stock system was invented in the seventeenth century, allowing the public to buy shares of companies, the most important market has become the market for shares. There are no fewer than twenty-two stock exchanges in Britain, from Aberdeen to Exeter, but by far the biggest is in London. The London stock exchange is the main market for 40 billion poundsworth of investments, in 10,000 different kinds of shares. £16 billion are in government stock, representing part of the National Debt. The rest are shares in anything from banks and shops to steel-mills and shipping companies. The centre of the market is the big block of offices, shaped like the bow of a ship, just next to the Bank of England. Round the block and in neighbouring buildings are stockbrokers' offices, each with their ticker-tapes and blackboards showing the latest prices. In the middle of them is the dingy Victorian hall of brown marble, filled with two thousand men in dark suits, which is the stock exchange itself.

The hall is essentially a market-place, with men—no girls— busily buying and selling, and it is the nervous centre of the city of London. The stock exchange is dingier and rowdier than the insurance 'Room' of Lloyd's—which may reflect its seedier origins: the 'rascally' stock-jobbers of the eighteenth century who clustered round 'Change Alley' were much less solid citizens than the insurers at Lloyd's coffee-house. The stock exchange has the atmosphere of a superannuated schoolroom. On an afternoon when I was there, one lugubrious-looking broker was walking round the room with a feather duster, tickling the other side of men's bald heads, so that they looked round to discover nobody; another broker was kicking a newspaper, crunched into a football, round the hall; another was throwing paper-pellets, with careful marksmanship, at his colleagues.

Looking down on the 'House', you can see the different parts of the market at work. Government stock ('gilt-edged') on the left is usually sedate, with a few men in silk hats—the gilt-edged uniform. On the right are Mines; in the middle are Oils, Breweries, Steel. Round each section are the 'jobbers', the middle-men (who provide the market and quote the prices)—a unique English profession, whose necessity is often questioned. Weaving round the jobbers are the stockbrokers, the agents of the public, trying to buy or sell their shares. From time to time a bell rings in the House, a notice is put up on a board, and yellow words begin to move across a big screen on the wall. They may announce an important dividend or a new industrial issue, and now the activity on the floor becomes more comprehensible: brokers rush to the jobbers, trying to buy or sell stock after the news, while the jobbers try to decide how the news will affect their prices.

Several changes have impinged on the conservatism of the stock exchange since the war. In the first place, the 'small investor' has loomed larger: a poll conducted for the stock exchange in 1960 reckoned that about three million people—or 6 per cent of the population—in Britain now invest in stocks and shares; 18 per cent were manual workers, 45 per cent were women, 16 per cent were under 34.[1] The proportion is not as high as in America (10 per cent) or in Japan (18 per cent), but the British total has almost doubled in 15 years, and is still rising by about 2,000 a month. In the past few years, in order both to attract investors, and to counter political attacks, the stock exchange has tried to endear itself to the public. Since 1953 a public gallery has been opened behind a glass screen, from which visitors can look down on the astonishing spectacle beneath. Solemn-looking girls in scarlet uniforms answer questions; a pamphlet explains 'Why the Stock Exchange is Indispensable'; and a film called 'My Word is My Bond' is shown every three-quarters of an hour. Stockbrokers are touchy about their reputation. 'Just how well are they—the

[1] *See* 'The Private Investor'. Gallup Polls, February, 1960.

public—getting to know you?' asks a writer in the *Stock Exchange Journal*: 'more important: when they know you, do they *like* you?'

The present Chairman of the Council, Lord Ritchie of Dundee, is an eloquent spokesman. He is a handsome, rather theatrical-looking stockbroker with a monocle and pearl tie-pin, and three two-tone green telephones in his panelled office above the main hall. 'We're trying to dispel the Victorian idea that the stock exchange is something mysterious, doing fiddles on the side', he said: 'we're showing that it's a straightforward job, and part of the nation's business. But we've avoided approaching stock exchange with advertising like "you want the best shares, we've got them".'

Stockbrokers, like joint stock bankers, are still not *very* keen on widening their custom: they want to be liked, but they do not welcome a rush of new small customers. They look aghast at the activities of American stockbrokers, who advertise in newspapers and sell shares over the counter at Grand Central Station. British stockbrokers sometimes explain that it is wrong to sell shares like soap, but one suspects that the real objection is that it is not worth the *bother*; they are much less mechanised than the Americans, and the cost of arranging a small share transfer often exceeds the profit.

The major new influence on stockbrokers has been not the small investors but the new giants of the city—the 'institutions'.[1] The one-and-a-half millions a day that come from the insurance companies, demanding to be invested, has influenced the market much as the arrival of the SS *Caronia* in an African port. When the insurance companies buy, they buy in tens of thousands, and they hardly ever sell: by favouring some kinds of shares, they can push the price up steeply, so that the whole market turns round. But the insurance companies, like rich men, are fussy, and demand much more information and service than individual investors. Stockbrokers, like solicitors, have watched since the 1880's the eclipse of rich private clients by the new corporate wealth. Like lawyers' firms they have had to become bigger, more concerned with statistics and research, and have begun to acquire independent information about industry. The big firms have become regarded as intelligence service for the city, at the centre of the telephone network of mmms and wells and meaningful grunts. 'Better ask Cazenove's', a banker will mumble, and the answer will come back with the authority of the market-place.

Stockbroking has become a more specialised, organised business: the big firms no longer rely entirely on relations and friends

[1] *See* Chapter 25, page 398.

351

to provide their young men, but recruit university graduates of proven intelligence—a new idea for the city. Here, at last, we see the upthrust of the professional meritocrats against the ingrained English respect for the amateur. What-you-know is steadily gaining on who-you-know, and the institutions have had the effect of institutionalising their brokers, too. Many stockbroking firms have their own department of 'investment analysts' who watch trends in share prices, and even visit factories and offices—however unwelcome that may be. Many brokers never go near the rowdy hall, or throw darts or play with feather dusters, and the 3,500 stockbrokers have become a rather more respected clan. In Victorian times they were looked down on as a get-rich-quick trade, with vulgar Gothic mansions in South London for pretentious dinner parties. Today, coming closer to industry and insurance, brokers, like admen,[1] feel themselves to be indispensable and expert agents, not private profiteers.

But one suspects they are apt to exaggerate the extent of their professionalism. According to the *Financial Times*, a graduate in a stockbroking firm might earn £2,500 in his middle thirties: this may be true of many, but the attraction of the stock exchange remains, as it always was, its closeness to the roots of money, and the information and scope it provides for augmenting personal capital. The opportunities which built those stockbrokers' mansions in Victorian times are still at work, and a clever young stockbroker can still make a fortune before forty. However much it may have the appearance of a profession, dedicated to service, stockbroking remains close to money-making. Most stockbrokers have their 'peck-order' of clients to whom they will pass on quick tips. Near the top will be close friends, important contacts, large clients, perhaps a duke or an earl; for a client interested in making money, it is always important, through friendship of favours, to be near the top of his broker's list. But usually at the top of the list is '*self*': and it is this first peck at the corn which gives the stockbroker the chance of his fortune.

GREED AND TRUST

The greedy basis of the stock exchange may seem sordid and deplorable, compared to the ideals of public service or the dedication of teachers: after spending two months talking to people in the city, I felt oppressed and dispirited by its narrowness

[1] *See* page 583.

and bleakness, the quasi-sexual fascination with money concealed behind large layers of humbug, and the sheer boredom of it. And yet (it seems to me) it would be disastrous if the city were to become *genuinely* professional—with aims overriding the making of money. There is no doubt a strong case for limiting the colossal scope for capital gains since the war which, alongside high income tax, has made a mockery of high salaries. But if one accepts the necessity for stock exchanges then money-making must surely be the inspiration: Western capitalism has not yet discovered a dynamic substitute for the self-advancing entrepreneur. Only the prospect of personal gain can provide the lively eye on the future, the gambler's skill, the restless awareness of what industries are finished and what still to come, on which the city's reputation must eventually stand or fall. This might seem trite: and yet, I found myself surprised how often the city seemed to have turned its back on its money-making origins, and to have become, not too greedy, but not greedy enough.

'The rough and vulgar structure of English commerce is the secret of its life', wrote Bagehot, 'for it contains "the propensity of variation" which, in the social as in the animal kingdom, is the principle of progress': and Bagehot went on to emphasise how much of the enterprise and progress of the city came from the self-made men, who did not have the protective instincts of the already rich. Does the city still have this 'rough and vulgar structure'? The protective instinct has certainly grown stronger since Victorian times, providing a vast haven of non-competition. There has grown up a thick web of 'gentlemen's agreements' arranging for banks, insurance companies or lawyers not to steal each other's business, and the phrase 'it's not done' is always lurking to frighten the newcomer and console the mediocre. The city, it is true, has an old trick of being first appalled by a new-comer—as we will see—and then accepting him as soon as he's obviously unsquashable (perhaps the same instinct which allows Britain to jail prime ministers one moment, and invite them to Buckingham Palace the next). Several rough and vulgar men have come up since the war, and behind some stately boardrooms of doddering peers you will often find a few clever upstarts from the suburbs running the business on long-distance telephones: the city, like so many other places, instinctively maintains the gap between dignity and efficiency.

But with protective tariffs, the collapse of foreign governments, and the strictures of exchange control, the roughness and vulgarity have had less scope, and much of the city has become entangled in the 'Old Boy Net'. To a surprising extent, the big new developments of the last fifty years—hire-purchase, building societies, industrial life assurance, property development—all of them keyed to the future—have been exploited by men outside the square mile, and outside the Net.

In the next five years the city may face its crucial test—to show whether or not it can become the financial capital of Europe. The scope, for the present at least, is limited by high interest rates and exchange control (more stringent than in Italy or Germany, and about as severe as France's): and much of the city has the disadvantage of being geared to the English-speaking world of the White Commonwealth—more interested in Rand gold and Canadian oil than German chemicals. What the city can do will depend eventually on its balance between those two contradictory strains in the British character—trust and cunning. All the odd totems and mumbo-jumbo which we will find in the next chapters —the scarlet robes, the brokers' top hats, the Governor's ritual— can be justified as the trappings of trust, the badges of a stable and confident machine. Businessmen like a certain fustiness in their bankers, and impatient young men in the city are sometimes appalled to find Wall Street even more pompous. But the city must operate, behind that misleading ritual, with cunning and speed: it must adventure into Europe with the same ruthlessness that it showed before its Antonine Age. Many British businesses, like Courtaulds, can change their character abruptly when faced with real disaster, and the new closeness to Europe may reveal some interesting transformations. For the survival of the city as an international financial centre depends in the end not on top hats, but on the ability to see into the future and supply its needs more quickly than anyone else. 'All *sudden* trades come to England,' Bagehot wrote: that was in 1873.

22

BANK OF ENGLAND

Lord Radcliffe: It is very deep in history that bankers have been regarded with suspicion?

Lord Brand: And always will be by people who cannot get credit.

Memoranda of the Radcliffe Report. Question 10739.

IN the centre of the city, next door to the Royal Exchange and facing the Lord Mayor's Mansion House, is the massive quadrilateral of the Bank of England. Its appearance aptly symbolises its famous secrecy and obscurantism. Round the whole building at street level is a blank, windowless façade broken by corinthian pillars, above which rise five storeys of offices. Inside the Bank has the look of an eccentric court; tall men stand in the hall wearing long brown overcoats and top hats with gold bands; other men, in black trousers, pink morning coats and red waistcoats, escort visitors into high-ceilinged rooms perfectly air-conditioned at 67 degrees. Few people would think that this was the home of a nationalised industry.

The Bank is proud of its nickname of the 'Old Lady of Threadneedle Street': in the exhibition room there is the original cartoon by Gillray called 'Political Ravishment or The Old Lady of Threadneedle Street in Danger', in 1797, showing Pitt as prime minister assaulting an aged hag sitting on a trunk labelled 'Bank of England', shouting 'Murder! Murder!' (the fear of financial rape has haunted the Bank since). 'The Old Lady' is the title of the Bank's own house magazine, with the crinkly cover favoured by nineteenth-century quarterlies, and the Bank is fascinated by its own past. In the 'Court Room' there is a weather-vane so that the directors can see if their sailing ships are in difficulty. Every night a troop of guardsmen in bearskins and scarlet tunics arrive in the height of the rush-hour, to guard the building against rioters. It is much easier to find out about the seventeenth-century origins of the Bank than about its present activities.

The secrecy is obsessive—particularly compared to other central banks. 'We are after all a bank', said Lord Cobbold, the previous Governor, 'doing business for customers, and nobody wants their

bankers to talk too much': the idea that they should try to
enlighten the public is quite foreign to them, and their secretive-
ness rivals that of the Treasury. Nationalisation in 1946 made
little difference; the Bank has never accepted the notion of
public accountability, and over the past hundred years its
activities have become more, not less, clandestine. For this book
they would not commit themselves as to the names of the Committee of Treasury who are (in theory anyway) the nation's
advisers on monetary policy. When the committee headed by
Lord Radcliffe published their Report in 1959 on the monetary
system, it let some light into the darkness, but the members were
politely exasperated by the lack of information: they mentioned
the Annual Report, 'the meagreness of which has become a by-
word', and even made the wild suggestion that there should be
'a revival of the 1844 idea that the Bank should publish certain key
figures exposing its operation in the monetary system'. Since then
the Bank *has* begun issuing quarterly reports, but they remain
ingeniously obscure. 'It isn't so much that they don't *want* to tell
you what's going on', one banker explained it: 'it's more that they
don't know how to explain it: they're like a Northumbrian
farmer.'

THE COURT

On the first floor is an interlocking set of rooms reserved for the
Governor and Directors, decorated in the twenties' Adam style,
with the splendour and peace of a rich man's country house. A
wide carpet leads past the green dining-room, past a pillared hall
full of bankers' portraits, into the heart of the Bank—the long
white room, known as the 'Court Room', flanked with columns
and filled with an ornate, hundred-and-fifty coloured carpet. A
blue-cloth table stands in the middle, with nineteen chairs round
it: here, every Thursday morning, sit the nineteen members of the
'court'.

These nineteen are chosen to advise the Treasury on financial
policy and 'feeling in the city'. Before the war they consisted
almost entirely of city men—a phenomenon which helped to explain
the appalling insensitivity of the government to unemployment.
Today (partly because of that criticism), they are more diversified:
four are full-time members of the Bank of England; six from
banks, seven from industry and commerce; and one from a
trade union. These, in January 1962, were the nineteen directors,
with their most important other position:

† Lord Cromer	Governor of the Bank
† Humphrey Mynors	Deputy Governor
Maurice Parsons	Bank of England full time
John Stevens	,, ,,
Sir Cyril Hawker	,, ,,
† Lord Bicester	Chairman, Morgan Grenfell
Sir George Bolton	Chairman, Bank of London and South America
Sir Charles Hambro	Vice-Chairman, Hambros
Lord Kindersley	Chairman, Lazards
Michael Babington Smith	Deputy Chairman, Glyn Mills Bank
† Sir Alfred Roberts	Gen. Secretary, Amalgamated Card, Blowing and Ring Room Operatives
Sir George Abell	Bank of England full time
† Geoffrey Eley	Chairman, Richard Thomas & Baldwin
† Sir John Hanbury-Williams	Chairman, Courtaulds
Sir Harry Pilkington	Chairman, Pilkingtons
Lord Sanderson	Director, Shaw Savill
William Keswick	Managing Director, Jardine Matheson
Lord Cobbold	Ex-Governor of the Bank
George Nelson	Managing Director, English Electric

† Member of Committee of Treasury.

Many of these names will recur in the next hundred pages. The Directors of the Bank are conservative, traditional men, most of them sons of bankers or industrialists. Of the nineteen, nine are over sixty, seventeen went to public school and seven went to Eton. At least seven of their surnames have been well known in the city for the past hundred years.

At the head of the Court is the Governor of the Bank of England, the headmaster of the city. In the square mile he is known as 'Grandma', 'the little white father', or mysteriously as 'the Authorities': and it is his job, among many others, to enforce the unwritten laws and codes of city behaviour—with the same kind of unstated rule as the Lord Chancellor has over barristers, but with larger powers. His weapons seem mild enough: he will 'drop a hint', 'make observations' or 'frown'; but in the closed society of the city, his disapproval can—and very occasionally does—mean ruin.

BARINGS

To the authority of the job the present Governor, Lord Cromer, brings an extra command, for he is not only an earl, but the head of the Baring family—the oldest of all the British banking dynasties. The family are all the descendants of a deaf clothing manufacturer, Sir Francis Baring, who was known as the 'first merchant

357

in Europe' when he died in 1810, leaving seven million pounds. The Barings established themselves as one of the most powerful and richest of the great Whig families: in 1818 it was said that there were six great powers in Europe—England, France, Russia, Austria, Prussia and Baring Brothers. Since the slump in South America in 1890, when Baring Brothers collapsed and had to be rescued by the Bank of England, their power has been much less. But the influence and wealth of the family has remained, and they have footholds not only in the city, but in the Palace and in Whitehall—a rare combination. There are now no fewer than five separate Baring peerages—Cromer, Northbrook, Revelstoke, Ashburton and Howick. They have provided two Chancellors of the Exchequer, a Governor-General of India (first Lord Northbrook), a poet (Maurice), a Lord Chamberlain (second Lord Cromer) and a Governor of Kenya (Lord Howick). 'Nothing is more like itself, nothing less like anything else, than a Baring', wrote Lord d'Abernon: 'Strong, sensible, self-reliant men, with a profound belief in themselves, their family and in their country . . . not subtle or mentally agile, but endowed with that curious combination of character which lends authority even to a doubtful decision.' Part of the Baring family tree is shown on the following page.

THE GOVERNOR

The present Lord Cromer has followed a Baring pattern of moving between private banking and public service. After Eton, Cambridge and the Guards in war-time, he spent ten years as a managing director of the family bank, and then two years as Economic Minister in Washington, where his combination of ability, charm and title made a large mark, and he was even talked of as a possible president of the World Bank. (He had married a daughter of the present Lord Rothermere, chairman of the *Daily Mail*—of which he was for a time a director.) The appointment of an earl to the Bank of England, after a long period of speculation (during which time Sir Oliver Franks was offered the job and said no), produced the same kind of mixed reactions as greeted those other earls at the Foreign Office and the Ministry of Defence. There were many who thought that a charming and clever Baring, of 'Kennedy's age', with American connections, was the right man to induce confidence in the city. Others insisted that Cromer's lack of experience in industry, economics and general banking were serious drawbacks: the three previous Governors

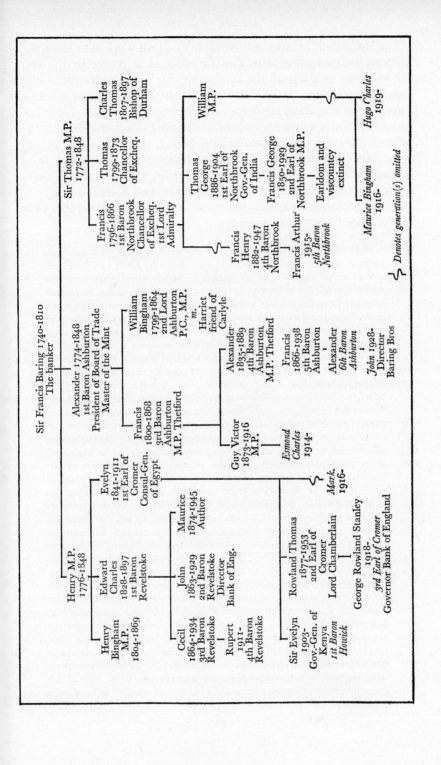

Sir Francis Baring 1740-1810
The banker

Henry M.P.
1776-1848

Alexander 1774-1848
1st Baron Ashburton
President of Board of Trade
Master of the Mint

Sir Thomas M.P.
1772-1848

Henry Bingham M.P.
1804-1869

Edward Charles
1828-1897
1st Baron Revelstoke

Evelyn
1841-1911
1st Earl of Cromer
Consul-Gen. of Egypt

Francis
1800-1863
3rd Baron Ashburton
M.P. Thetford

William Bingham
1799-1864
2nd Lord Ashburton
P.C., M.P.
m.
Harriet
friend of Carlyle

Francis
1796-1866
1st Baron Northbrook
Chancellor of Excheq.
1st Lord Admiralty

Thomas
1799-1873
Chancellor of Excheq.

Charles Thomas
1807-1897
Bishop of Durham

Cecil
1864-1934
3rd Baron Revelstoke

John
1863-1929
2nd Baron Revelstoke
Director Bank of Eng.

Maurice
1874-1945
Author

Alexander
1835-1889
4th Baron Ashburton
M.P. Thetford

Guy Victor
1873-1916
M.P.

Francis Henry
1882-1947
4th Baron Northbrook

Thomas George
1886-1904
1st Earl of Northbrook
Gov.-Gen. of India

William M.P.

Rupert
1911-
4th Baron Revelstoke

Francis
1866-1938
5th Baron Ashburton

Esmond Charles
1914-

Francis Arthur
1915-
5th Baron Northbrook

Francis George
1850-1929
2nd Earl of Northbrook M.P.

Sir Evelyn
1903-
Gov.-Gen. of Kenya
1st Baron Howick

Rowland Thomas
1877-1953
2nd Earl of Cromer
Lord Chamberlain

Alexander
6th Baron Ashburton

Earldom and viscounty
extinct

Mark.
1916-

John 1928-
Director Baring Bros

Maurice Bingham
1916-

George Rowland Stanley
1918-
3rd Earl of Cromer
Governor Bank of England

Hugo Charles
1919-

⌇ *Denotes generation(s) omitted*

(Lords Cobbold, Catto and Norman) had all worked at the Bank before their appointment, and to bring in a young Baring was interpreted as a slap in the face to the city's very tentative managerial revolution. It is still too early to assess Cromer's actual impact on the Bank: but there is some evidence that his international outlook and his realism are helping to remove some of the complacency from Threadneedle Street, and that he is not altogether at one with his more protective co-directors from Lazards, Hambros and Morgan Grenfell[1]. He delivered a quite menacing speech at the annual Lord Mayor's dinner—traditionally an occasion for congratulation—in the autumn of 1961, only three months after he took office:

> If we are to maintain our present standard of living, let alone improve it, we have to work for it and not against it. There are, I believe, a number of factors working against it, stemming in part from our national tendency to revere the past to an excessive extent, to hanker after the good old days or to use our energies to fight evils and abuses, many happily long disappeared, of the bad old days. Are there not still many outdated customs and practices in industry which owe their origin to mitigating the dire hardships of the years of depression between the wars, but which today only result in limiting the advance in the standard of living? Is it perhaps not possible that the overall level of government expenditure today has grown to levels that the population as a whole is not willing to support by forgoing personal consumption to the extent necessary? Is our system of taxation matched by the present needs of the nation? Are the money rates we have seen in this country in recent years the most appropriate to achieving the rate of progress we would like to see? Are we saving enough? Is the high level of government expenditure overseas not perhaps based more on our Imperial past than tailored to our changing position in the world or the need to confine financially unremunerative expenditure overseas to what, as a nation, we are prepared to earn overseas? Do the remnants of the 'siege' economy which remain with us from the last war make any positive contribution to our good or merely restrict our earning capacity? These are some of the questions that are crossing my mind in my first few months of office. These are only some of the questions that we have to find an answer to in the breathing space we have obtained.
>
> We are faced with a great challenge and I welcome the Chancellor's reference to a new sense of purpose, for it is absolutely essential that we make full use of the opportunities provided by the support of the International Monetary Fund, to accomplish what we have not yet achieved; that is to adapt our economic way of life to our present position in the world and to the present age. I read recently that we are in fact nearer the year 2000 than the year 1920, so let us look more to what we wish to achieve between now and the year 2000. One of the great heritages of the merchants and bankers of the city of London is

[1] *See* page 384.

their ability to adapt themselves to changing circumstances. Were this not so we would not be gathered here tonight and I certainly would not be replying to this Toast, but I know that I can speak with complete assurance when I say that, given the opportunities, the merchants and bankers of the city of London will continue to make an increasingly significant contribution to our economic strength.

NATIONAL DEBT

The Bank's basic rôle is not very different from that of other central banks. Firstly it is the government's banker, borrowing money for the state when required. Secondly, it is banker to the other banks—arranging free exchange between them and banks abroad, printing their bank-notes (except in Scotland) and providing their reserve of money. But the Bank of England has other duties. It has to regulate Britain's overseas investments—the highest per head of any country. It has to enforce exchange control. And it has to act as custodian of the Sterling Area, holding balances on behalf of the other sterling countries.

The Bank's largest service to the Government is to manage the National Debt, which occupies about two thousand people in a crescent-shaped building facing St. Paul's called 'New Change', built since the war in ugly Neo-Georgian style. It was the National Debt which brought the Bank into being: William III needed a million pounds quickly, to raise money for his war against Louis XIV, and was advised, very ingeniously, to borrow it from the public. In 1694 the Bank of England was established with a staff of seventeen clerks, to fix the loan. Since then, the Debt (it is usually given a capital D) has never looked back: governments have gone on using it to raise money quickly without waiting for taxes—particularly in war-time. The Debt multiplied seven times in the first world war, and doubled in the second—by raising such loans as 'Victory Bonds' or 'War Bonds'. By March 31, 1961 the Debt stood at

$$£28,251,676,714.^{[1]}$$

Some people, including Ted Hill of the TUC, find the idea of a Government in debt rather shocking, and a few have even helped to pay it off: in 1929 Lord Inchcape gave half a million pounds towards reducing it. But it has gone on growing, and no Western country has managed to do without this handy device.

The Debt is made up of about three million separate accounts,

[1] But this figure does not bear much relationship to the real indebtedness of the government to the public—which was estimated by Professor Victor Morgan at £17,000 million in 1955 (see *The Structure of Property Ownership in Great Britain, 1961*).

and six million payments a year are made to stockholders from New Change. New government loans—known as 'gilt-edged stock' because of their thorough reliability—are raised from the stock exchange, through one of the most mysterious men in the city, William de Wette Mullens, who occupies the almost hereditary post of Senior Government Broker. He provides the main link between the Bank and the stock exchange. He is surrounded with feudal dignity, so that it is difficult to remember that he is actually making money. He is a large courteous man who, like all gilt-edged people, wears a top hat in the city. Officially (and rather hopefully) he is known as 'Broker to the Commissioners for the Reduction of the National Debt': he inhabits the mock Florentine offices of 'Mullens and Co' in Moorgate, only a few yards from the Bank of England, where portraits of Mullenses look down from tall panels: the first Mullens became government broker in 1829. The other seven partners include Peter Daniell, whose grandfather was government broker, Robin Peppiatt, son of a former chief cashier of the Bank of England, and David Bewicke-Copley, heir to Lord Cromwell. (Gentlemen prefer bonds, they say in the city.) Being privy to the government's plans, Mr. Mullens is the object of immense interest in the city, and his selling of bonds can generate panic in the stock exchange.

The Debt is no longer regarded by the Bank as a regrettable consequence of wars, to be reduced as quickly as possible. It has become so vast, and so involved with the country's economy, that its management affects the whole circulation of money. By adjusting the interest and the quantity of new government stock—and by the curious operation of 'funding'—changing the debt from short to long term loans—the Bank through Mr. Mullens regulates the money situation. Controlling the money supply is the most important rôle of the Bank, and it is here that the Bank's goings-on are most intricate and obscure. For in the city, money becomes (in Sir Oscar Hobson's phrase) 'two dimensional'—varying in character according to interest rates and time of repayment. The Bank deals in all kinds of money—cheap money, dear money, liquid money, frozen money, long-term money, short-term money, safe money, risk money, dollar money, sterling money, and even with 'moneyness'.

MONEY MARKET

Among these odd kinds of money are the short-term loans raised for the Treasury, through 'Treasury Bills'. These Bills—invented by Bagehot in 1877—are government IOUs for sums ranging from £5,000 to £100,000, to be repaid (usually) within 91 days. They allow the government to raise money quickly, later to be repaid from taxes and long-term loans: every Friday morning the Treasury announces how much money it will raise by these Bills the following week—usually between £200 and £300 million.

These huge sums of money are in effect borrowed from the only people who can possibly afford them—the joint stock banks, with their enormous deposits. But as intermediaries between the joint stock banks and the Bank of England there has grown up one of the most astonishing professions in Britain—the Discount Brokers, or 'Bill Brokers'. They are not numerous or important, but they are so much part of the extraordinary 'sensitive mechanism' of the city that they deserve a special mention. Their job is to borrow large sums from the joint stock banks and then lend it, through Treasury Bills, to the government. Every Friday the discount brokers arrive in their top hats at the Bank of England to buy the Treasury Bills, at a price agreed beforehand between them, and 'deliberately manipulated' (in the words of the Radcliffe Report) to exclude outside tenders.

The Treasury Bills are the largest quantity of floating money in the city, and round them revolves the 'money market'. The ease with which one can borrow a few million pounds for a few days is one reason why sudden trades come to London. With such large sums involved, the difference between one-sixteenth and two-sixteenths becomes crucial. The discount brokers nibble their tiny percentage from the Treasury Bills, and grow prosperous on it. On days when 'money is scarce', the top hats can be seen rushing from bank to bank—just before 3.30 when the Bank of England stops dealing—trying to find a cheap million pounds or so, at one sixty-fourth per cent less, with which to balance their books. Here we might pause to note the indifference of the city to the decimal system: the first strong official recommendation for decimalisation was made in 1841, but only in 1961 was a full enquiry instituted. ('These things take time', said a Treasury man.) In the meantime the city is still burdened with calculations of one-sixty-fourth per cent.

The discount brokers—only about eighty in all—are unique, not surprisingly, to the city of London. They lead lives of antique formality: every morning they call *in person* at the joint stock banks, to discuss the weather, cricket, and perhaps the money market. No other country makes use of them: *their* Treasuries go direct to the banks. Since the discount brokers fix prices between themselves, they cannot be said to make the money market any more competitive. The city's justification for them is that they provide a kind of cushion—a pet city word—to the money market, making it less volatile and neurotic than Wall Street, and also (of course) that 'it works'. The discount brokers awaited the verdict of the Radcliffe Report with some trepidation, but they need not have worried. 'It would not be beyond human ingenuity', Lord Radcliffe concluded, 'to replace the work of the discount houses; but they are there, they are doing the work effectively, and they are doing it at a trifling cost in terms of labour and other real resources.'

BANK RATE

The Bank can influence the supply of money in three principal ways. First, it can adjust the operations and requirements of the National Debt. Secondly, it can bring pressure on the joint stock banks to restrict loans to their customers. Thirdly, it can wield its most controversial weapon, the Bank Rate—the rate of interest at which it lends money, and hence (by tradition) the interest rate of the joint stock banks to their customers—which affects the cost of borrowing all through the country. Every Thursday morning the Court considers Bank Rate, and at 11.45 Mr. Mullens, accompanied by a stock exchange waiter, walks in his top hat from the Bank of England to the stock exchange—a journey which takes exactly two and a half minutes—enters the hall, gets up on a chair, and announces Bank Rate. From 1932 till 1951, which marked the era of 'cheap money', it was always two per cent. Since then it has been used by successive Conservative governments to control the rate of spending, oscillating between seven and three per cent.

The efficacy of the Bank Rate is fiercely debated. Several factors have weakened its power. Firstly, the great industrial corporations now largely finance themselves out of profits: a succession of industrialists—including Lords Godber of Shell, Fleck of ICI, Heyworth of Unilever—explained to Lord Radcliffe that their investment plans were virtually unaffected by Bank Rate.[1] Secondly, government spending has enormously increased: 'nearly half the total volume of investment is now financed by public authorities', wrote the Report (para 49), which 'does not respond in the same way as private investment.' Thirdly, the hire-purchase

[1] *See* page 448.

business has multiplied, thus allowing the government to stop public spending much more quickly by changing hire-purchase conditions, and decreasing the sales of cars or refrigerators.

The techniques for influencing spending are still shrouded in mystery, as much psychological as economic. It is reassuring to the layman to find in the Radcliffe Report the economy frequently described in homely terms—'stoking up the boom', 'spitting into the wind', 'going off the boil'. The uncertainty about Bank Rate was vividly expressed by Professor Cairncross,[1] questioning Lord Cobbold, then Governor of the Bank, in the Radcliffe Committee:

> PROFESSOR CAIRNCROSS: There is an old saying that prayers and incantation, with a little arsenic, will poison a flock of sheep. I wonder whether the Bank Rate plays the rôle of the incantations here. If I may put the question in a slightly different form, just how do you visualise a change in the Bank Rate as affecting the demand in the economy?
>
> MR. COBBOLD: This is a very arguable subject and anybody can have his own opinion. My own view is that it has still quite a considerable effect both in its general psychological influence, and on reality. On reality it has a far higher effect when you get towards the higher rates. I regard the seven per cent Bank Rate, particularly in conjunction with the trend of emphasis of policy in general, as being in its own right a very effective weapon in reducing demand.

The Radcliffe Committee concluded that, without control of public spending or hire-purchase terms (which rest with the Treasury, not with the Bank), an increase of Bank Rate would be —in the Governor's phrase—like 'spitting into the wind'.

TREASURY AND BANK

Who is really responsible for Britain's monetary policy? The answer is characteristically obscure. In the first place the Court of the Bank of England is not quite what it seems: 'There's a lie in the heart of the Bank', as one banker put it. For while the Bank retains the trappings of a joint stock company, as it once was, its reality is quite different—not primarily because of nationalisation, but also because of the huge rôle of the Treasury, and the personal authority of the Governor (who is appointed not by the Court, but by the prime minister). The Court, for all its splendour and dignity, is not a very decisive body. 'It would be unrealistic', said the Radcliffe Report in its kid-glove language, 'to regard the meetings of the Court as the source of effective decisions on policy

---

[1] *See* page 282.

made by the Bank.' The Court delegates many decisions to the 'Committee of Treasury' consisting of the Governor, the Deputy-Governor, and five other nominated directors (marked with a †ot on page 357). 'It is in the Committee of Treasury', wrote the Report, 'that the Bank's views are formulated on matters of central banking.' But even the Committee of Treasury 'is and must be in essence advisory to the Governor'. The most crucial decisions are taken by the Governor in consultation with the Chancellor of the Exchequer (who, by the Act of 1946, has power to give directions to the Governor). The Radcliffe Report urged that Bank Rate, the most important decision of the Bank, should be announced in the name of the Chancellor, not of the Governor—thus making it clear where the responsibility lay. But the suggestion was not followed up, and Mr. Mullens still stands on his chair.

Is the Bank of England the city arm of the Treasury, designed to impose the government's policy on the banks? Or is it still, as it was, a part of the city—a bank which happens to have one huge client, the government? In its internal character, with its secrecy and splendour, the Bank is much more like an old-fashioned business enterprise than the civil service. The relationship between the Bank and the Treasury is one of the most peculiar of all, complicated by the personal contrast between bankers and Treasury men, two miles away. As one commentator put it, 'men who have never been to boarding-school often feel that they are dealing with men who never left it'.[1] The Bank embodies the unquestioning regimental spirit of the public school proletariat, and graduates are rare. Clean-limbed young men show visitors round the building with the reverence for trophies and pillars shown by schools or regiments. Their spirit is at odds both with the introspective musicians of the Treasury, and the blasé graduates of the Foreign Office. The men in Threadneedle Street are on top of the day-to-day abrasive mechanism of the city, in the midst of sixty-fourths, fine rates, moneyness, etc. They are inarticulate but confident, tilling the financial fields with an almost agricultural rhythm, and their senior men are held in some awe by Great George Street when the mandarins work in their ivory tower surrounded by abstractions. Although Treasury men nowadays visit the city more often, the Bank are not very welcoming, and the idea of exchanging bankers and mandarins—which seems a sensible remedy for cross-purposes—is not encouraged.

The Treasury, too, regards the Bank, more than any other parts

[1] *Time and Tide*, April 6, 1961.

of its empire, as a foreign tribe who must not be interfered with, and here the doctrine of indirect rule is very evident. The Court of the Bank, odd and unrepresentative though it is, is regarded as voicing 'city opinion', and the Governor is expected to carry the Court with him. Even the Labour party, thought it nationalised the Bank and Sir Stafford Cripps said jokingly 'the Bank is my creature', dreaded any kind of outright clash with Threadneedle Street, and the mystique of the city remains a powerful influence on Westminster. The British government is not alone in not wanting to interfere with the central Bank. The American Federal Reserve and the German Bundesbank can both openly contradict their government, but Britain prefers to keep the relationship obscure and concealed. The balance of power between the Governor and the Chancellor varies with the personalities: during the governorship of Lord Cobbold (who was quite prepared for a showdown) Treasury men used to recite:

> Two voices are there; both are of the C
> Cobbold and Chancellor; each a mighty Voice.

There are signs that Lord Cromer is prepared to be outspoken and independent, and that he is not allied either with the Treasury or the Court. But the obscure division of responsibility seems to have helped to increase the scope for financial muddles such as spitting into the wind, or stoking up the fire with one hand and damping it down with the other.

Britain—whether in the form of the Chancellor or the Governor —has long ceased to have full control over her monetary policy, as over foreign policy, and much of the future rests with those shadowy speculators in Zurich, and with the central bankers of Europe. Britain's dependence came home sharply in the economic crisis of July 1961, when after a very heavy run on sterling, the Treasury had to apply to borrow up to £892 million from the International Monetary Fund—more than half the Fund's lendings for the year. Dr. Per Jacobsson, the Swedish managing director of the Fund (although an Anglophile, father-in-law of Dr. Roger Bannister and author of detective stories in English) took a stern view of the British economy. He and his fellow-bankers made it clear that they expected strong disciplinary measures if the loan were to be granted, including a steep rise in Bank Rate and large cuts in government spending—a view with which the

Treasury concurred. In Vienna, two months later, Dr. Jacobsson made no bones about his attitude:

'Britain has been given help', he told the *Guardian* correspondent, Richard Fry, 'not in order to carry on as she was doing but to gain time in which to put her house in order. The Fund stands for monetary discipline. A change of policy is essential for Britain's future rôle in the world. What would be the good if people were to say the British are nice people but they no longer have money?'[1]

See The Guardian, September 16, 1961.

23

BANKERS

Most bankers dwell in marble halls,
  Which they get to dwell in because they encourage
    deposits and discourage withdralls,
And particularly because they all observe
  one rule which woe betide the banker who fails to heed it,
Which is you must never lend any money to anybody
  unless they don't need it.

Ogden Nash
('Bankers are just like anybody else except richer').

WHEN ordinary people talk about a bank, they mean one of the 'joint stock banks' or 'clearing banks' whose names are to be seen, above stone façades and frosted glass, in every high street in the country. They have become, like town halls or public libraries, part of the unchanging face of town life; and their character is almost equally institutional, for they exist in a strange limbo between nationalisation and free enterprise. They long ago reached a truce between each other, about the limits of gentlemanly competition. Being among the richest financial institutions in the country, they are carefully watched and controlled by the Governor of the Bank of England, who prints their banknotes, acts as their master-bankers, and keeps an eye on their reserves. The joint stock banks are in the midst of that curious city world, so difficult for the outsider to comprehend, where competition only exists between small but unwritten limits, where 'it's not done' lurks behind every counter, with a headmaster in the background.

THE BIG FIVE

There are only eleven joint stock banks in England, and those are dominated by the 'Big Five', which are, in order of size:

Bank	Deposits (Dec. 1961)	Chairman
Barclays	£1,728 million	John Thompson
Midland	£1,673 ,,	Lord Monckton
Lloyds	£1,336 ,,	Harald Peake
Westminster	£1,050 ,,	Lord Aldenham
National Provincial	£933 ,,	David Robarts

The remaining six banks—Martins, District, Williams Deacons, National, Glyn Mills and Coutts—are much smaller; their total deposits are less than Barclays. But many of them—and the Scottish banks—have their specialities, and the Royal Bank of Scotland even has a drive-in branch in Trafalgar Square.

The Big Five are among the biggest banks in the Western world: before the devaluation of the pound, in 1949, the Midland was *the* biggest. American banks are restricted by law to a single state, while the British ones have national coverage: Barclays and the Midland each has more than 2,000 branches. These giants took their present shape, after a succession of swallowings of smaller banks, at the end of the first world war, after which the Treasury became worried, and 'made it known' that they would disapprove of any more amalgamations—one of the first cases in Britain of monopolies being prevented.

The Big Five had their roots not in the city, but in the provincial banking families, most of them Quakers, who grew up in the seventeenth and eighteenth centuries: many old banking names still survive on the boards. The Quakers were a close-knit, persecuted community, who were used to helping each other with money, and they soon became trusted by others as money-keepers. After some early disasters the banks settled down into cautious, conservative businesses with a strong public conscience and an emphasis on trust over enterprise: the last bank to get into difficulties was the military bank of Cox and King's in the Haymarket, now absorbed by Lloyds and still with a military tradition. The banks regard themselves, first and foremost, as the guardians of the public's money. They insist that they cannot lock up money in long-term ventures, and five years is (in theory but not in practice) their longest loan. They do not invest in industrial companies, and by tradition they keep around thirty per cent of a bank's deposits 'liquid'—available for immediate recall. The vast deposits of the banks are invested in government stock, Treasury Bills, hire-purchase companies, or loans to industrial or private customers. This is how the eleven London joint stock banks held their total deposits of £7,929 million, on December 31, 1961:

Capital paid up and reserve funds:	4·2 per cent
Liquid Assets:	
Cash in hand and balances with Bank of England	8·4 per cent
Treasury and other Bills	17·0 per cent
Money at call or short notice	10·6 per cent

Special Deposits with Bank of England:	2·8 per cent
Other Assets:	
Government stock and other investments	14·1 per cent
Advances to customers with other accounts	42·0 per cent
Balances with other banks and 'items in transit'	7·7 per cent
Bank premises, etc.	1·6 per cent

It is the 42 per cent which is lent to customers, amounting to over three billion pounds, which affects the social life of the country: this web of credit, largely controlled by the branch managers, can provide a new dress, a new house, or a new factory. This credit clearly concerns the government, for by ordering the banks to restrict their lending, the Treasury can reduce the amount of money in circulation. For nearly twenty years, from 1939 to 1958, this is what they did, to the vexation of the bankers and the borrowing public. Overdrafts were restricted and banks imposed their 'self-denying ordinance', promising not to compete for customers by offering better loans. The main business of banks—lending money for profit—became uncompetitive and the Big Five were united in their unwillingness to lend. 'The banks were anaesthetised', as one banker said, 'it was like driving a very powerful car at twenty miles an hour.'

In July 1958 the 'credit squeeze' was quite suddenly relaxed: the banks, to their astonishment, found themselves able to lend more money and they began competing. Anthony Tuke of Barclays had already astonished his fellow-bankers by taking a share in a hire-purchase business: but soon after the end of the squeeze Lord Monckton of the Midland announced a new kind of 'Personal Loan' for customers, and other banks followed with mild counter-attractions. The freedom was very limited, and in 1960 the banks were forced to make 'special deposits' (one or two per cent of their total) with the Bank of England—as a new kind of governmental control. But since 1958 a slight competitiveness has remained between banks: 'They have been able to stand up,' to quote the same banker, 'to breathe—and even to walk.'

BARCLAYS AND MIDLAND

The walking-pace is set by the two biggest, Barclays and Midland: the others—even Lloyds—are apt to follow behind. Whenever Midland opens a branch in a new suburb, Barclays are likely to follow. Their competition is a little more vigorous, and their characters more different, than one might suspect from their uniform architecture, scratchy pens, or rates of interest. Their chairmen, though they meet once a month to discuss banking problems and blossom out into long, philosophical reports every January, are quite keen to steal a march.

The biggest, Barclays, still retains something of its old Quaker family character. Twenty-five Quaker banks, mostly in East Anglia, came together in 1896 to avoid being swallowed by other combines, and they determined to keep their character by a system of 'local directors'. They still have old family names—a Barclay, a Bland, a Bevan, a Seebohm—on their board. Anthony Tuke, who was chairman for eleven years until 1962, was from a component Quaker bank. He is an amiable and witty Wykehamist, with a bushy grey moustache and a habit of quoting Greek or nursery rhymes in his annual reports. A liberal, *laissez-faire* banker, he is sometimes known as 'the Iron Tuke': he has led the complaints against Government interference, and the Government's own extravagance: 'we keep on having to mop up the water', he said, 'which is being spilt by Government spending.' The new chairman, John Thompson, is also from a Quaker banking family.

The Midland, sometimes known as the 'small man's bank', has a less gentlemanly past than Barclays, with Midlands roots and a reputation for thrusting methods and 'gimmicks'—including a bank on the *Queen Mary*. The Midland, like other big banks except Barclays, is largely run by its managers, but with a less heavily titled board: as chairman since 1957 they have had the versatile elder statesman Lord Monckton, Minister of Labour under Churchill and Eden, and creator of the Monckton Report on Central Africa. Monckton leaves most of the day-to-day running of the bank to the managers, and his most important decisions are largely to do with handling people, making sure that the succession is right, and seeing that staff relations are good.

NEW CUSTOM

In spite of the occasional competitive gestures of the joint stock banks, their most surprising trait to outsiders is their lack of competition for new kinds of custom. 'There have been two important changes in the field of banking', one chairman told me, 'one is the development of medium-term credits for British export —which has the effect of locking up more of the banks' capital.

The other is the growth of banking for the weekly wage-earner. We're still feeling the effects of the post-war social revolution. What's happened to money in Britain since 1948 means that now there's often very little difference between the wage of a secondary school headmaster and a man on the line at the Nuffield works: this has meant that huge sections of the population have become bankable. We're slowly moving towards the weekly wage-earner, and this will probably mean a new kind of bank—looking less frightening and less like a magistrates' court—and a new kind of bank manager.'

But so far there is little sign of such transformation, and American tendencies which have appeared in journalism, business or shopping have not penetrated to banks. Few Anglo-American contrasts are more striking than this: in the newest banks in New York the customer goes up to a long open counter without glass in a vast open hall, containing an expanse of young crew-cut men behind desks, with hardly a single private room. Banks may have floral displays, dog-shows, ice-skating exhibitions, or chamber music to attract their customers, and tempting booklets describe the easy arrangements to borrow money. In Britain, the customer stands in front of a cage, with a pen on a chain, a few bleak booklets about foreign exchange, and a view of severe girls in front of big ledgers. The puritan, nonconformist conscience of the early days still hangs over them.

Traditionally the banks—even the 'small man's bank'—were the custodians of the rising middle class; and they are as sceptical about small savings as stockbrokers about small investors. Their hours of opening (from ten to three) do not exactly encourage working men, and their advertising and the placing of their new banks is designed for the middle class. 'The clearing banks', in the words of the Radcliffe Report, 'have broadly, as a matter of deliberate and concerted policy, stood aside while small savings have fed the development of building societies, savings banks and other specialised financial intermediaries.' Working men and their wives have preferred the Post Office Savings Bank, where money can be paid in or out at any Post Office counter, with a fixed interest of $2\frac{1}{2}$ per cent. On March 31st, 1961, the Post Office deposits stood at

$$£6,045,000,000$$

—only just less than the total deposits of all joint stock banks. Much of this huge sum was built up during the last war, with

strong savings campaigns and little scope for spending. Nowadays
—as the Treasury told the Radcliffe Committee—'we have to
work very hard to stand still'. The six billion pounds is looked
after by the Commissioners for the National Debt—i.e., the Bank
of England—who invest it in government stock; it accounts for
nearly a quarter of the National Debt.

BANK CLERKS

The social revolution is most apparant among the staff of the
banks themselves: for the 126,000 bank employees—most of whom
work in joint stock banks—are white-collar workers whose wages
are being overtaken by the working-class. An average bank clerk
starts work at sixteen with £295 a year, rising to £915 at the age
of thirty-one—by which time he may still be earning less than a
docker or factory-worker. Some bank managers earn as little as
£1,500 a year. Bank clerks work long hours, including Saturday
mornings, under strict conditions—their own bank balance is
regularly inspected. But they are reluctant to join a trade union
and press for better wages: the National Union of Bank Employees
(NUBE—pronounced Newby) can only claim 40 per cent of the
bank workers, and only Barclays and the National Bank, of the
eleven, recognise it. Most clerks prefer the 'Staff Association' of their
own bank, which enjoys the patronage and subsidy of the management. The rift between the Staff Associations and NUBE is
symptomatic of the predicament of the modern clerk—suspended
between his middle-class aspirations and proletarian wages.

In the unthrusting atmosphere of the banks, opportunities for
quick advancement are small. At the Midland some years ago a
local manager wanted to upgrade a brilliant young man; but this
would have meant breaking the normal promotion arrangements,
and his request was refused. He resigned, decided to read for the bar,
and now finds himself, fifteen years later, a leading expert on Trust
Law, earning £10,000 a year and advising the joint stock banks.

Meanwhile, new intruders are affecting the bank clerk—machines and computers. The banks find that women work better
with machines than men; at the Midland (with a total staff of
20,000) the proportion of women, I was told, has risen by 5 per
cent in ten years, to 40 per cent. These regiments of women are
liable at any moment to marry. 'After the first war, there was a
rush of young men into the banks', said one chairman, 'which
tends now to produce some frustrated men in their fifties, with not

enough managerial jobs to go round. But I'm afraid we may be leaving our successors with the opposite problem—of not enough young men to provide managers for the future.'

The scope for initiative among joint stock bankers is not large. With their customers they try to neutralise themselves as far as possible: bank managers are taught never to use the words 'I think', and in their approach to loans (as Ogden Nash suggests of American banks) they favour the big battalions and the status quo. Industrial giants, like Hawker Siddeley, have colossal overdrafts; but the British banks do not, like the Americans, have their own big investigation department to discover which smaller firms are deserving of credit. Only occasionally do the banks appear in controversial fields (Lloyds lent money to Charles Clore to help him try to take over another of their customers, Watneys, and the National Commercial Bank of Scotland has helped Hugh Fraser to take over Harrods). In their dedication, their lack of greed, and their sense of quiet service, the joint stock bankers provide a placid, safe centre to financial Britain: one can no more imagine a bank going bust than the monarchy falling. But for large opportunities and an eye on the future, we must look elsewhere in the city—to merchant banks and financiers.

HIRE-PURCHASE

Two new kinds of bank have grown up during this century—building societies and hire-purchase. Both have had enormous social consequences: the 'incentive goods revolution' has brought men back into the home, strengthened the position of women and 'deproletarianised' working-class homes.[1] Both of them are essentially extensions of banking, geared to the future, and building societies are really a kind of hire-purchase. But both fields have been ignored and often scorned by the old joint stock banks, and have grown up from quite different roots, with peculiar histories.

Building societies began as poor men's clubs during the early nineteenth century: the first recorded was in Birmingham in 1781, when subscribers arranged to meet once a month at the Fountain tavern, paying half a guinea a share towards a building scheme.[2] Houses were chosen by ballot, and 'ballot-and-sale societies', often based on pubs, grew up all over the Midlands. At the same time the Nonconformist churches in the Midlands and Yorkshire began

[1] *See* Norman Macrae: The Incentive Goods Revolution: *Credit*, March, 1961.
[2] *See* Sir Harold Bellman: *Bricks and Mortals*, 1949. p. 14.

thrift clubs and sick benefit clubs, which expanded into house-building: and the movement had great support from social reformers, like Bright and Cobden, who saw property as a key to the franchise. The Abbey National Building Society with its big white tower, sometimes thought to be the site of Sherlock Holmes' rooms in Baker Street, represents a merger of chapel and pub—the Abbey Road Baptist Chapel, and the National Society, which met in the London Tavern. Forty years ago the combined assets of the two societies were two million pounds: in 1960 they were £390 million. The biggest of all is the Halifax, still based on Halifax, and patronised since 1853—when it was founded—by the Halifax family. It keeps its North Country independence—nearly every member of its board comes from the West Riding[1]—and remains absolutely separate from the Building Societies Association.

In spite of their vast expansion, the building societies have kept much of the character of Nonconformity and self-help. The building society knights are earnest, moral men, who have seen a movement become an institution in their lifetime; Sir William Cash is related to John Bright: Sir Bruce Wycherley, managing director of the Abbey National, comes from a methodist family.

The co-existence of the building societies with banks is odd. 'Borrowing short and lending long is anathema to the banker', said Sir Harold Bellman, chairman of the Abbey National and author of *Bricks and Mortals*: 'but we know that default by our members is very rare. There's no hostile competition between banks and building societies—we regard our work as complementary.' Like all building societies, the Abbey National is conservative about architecture. 'It's all right for the house-buyer to indulge in architectural whims with his own capital, but a freakish house might be unsaleable if we had to use our mortgage powers, and we prefer not to risk our members' funds. There's still enormous scope for progress in the field of home ownership. Less than a third of people in Britain own their homes: in the U.S. it's more like two-thirds.'

Hire-purchase has a more commercial and less moral origin, and for a long time was regarded as disreputable. It began, rather oddly, with the invention of the sewing-machine in the mid-nineteenth century: being expensive, long-lasting and productive, the Singer company found it useful to sell it by hire-purchase, and their idea was followed by piano-makers and furniture-makers.

[1] *See* Oscar Hobson: *A Hundred Years of the Halifax*, 1953.

The Civil Service Mutual Furnishing Association was founded in 1877, by a group of senior civil servants—a surprising activity for deputy secretaries—to assist their juniors to furnish their homes.[1] Meanwhile during the 1860's 'wagon companies' had been formed in the North of England, to provide hire-purchase for railway trucks (which the railways did not provide) to take coal from the mines to the merchants. From filling this gap, the companies expanded to cars and equipment: the 'North Central Wagon and Finance Company' and the 'British Wagon Company' became two of the biggest hire-purchase concerns.

The idea of hire-purchase, unlike that of building societies, often outraged the Nonconformist conscience: and the companies, like the insurance collectors, could be ruthless in enforcing 'snatch-backs' if payments had lapsed. Not until 1938 was a Hire-Purchase Act passed which partly protected the hirer. Further legislation, long overdue, was passed in 1962. The prejudice against hire-purchase has largely dissolved since the post-war boom: TV, washing machines, refrigerators and cars have all multiplied under the never-never. The total hire-purchase debt has risen steeply: in 1959 it was £700 million, compared to £2,500 million owing to building societies, and about the same figure owing to banks. By the end of 1961 the debt was £953 million, or about £18 per head.

Like the building societies, hire-purchase firms have grown up outside the city nexus, looked at askance by most bankers—until in 1958 Barclays took a share in United Dominions Trust, and other banks followed. The companies vary widely in stature: the great boom of 1958, when hire-purchase shares rocketed, was followed by heavy losses. The biggest and most belligerent is the omnipresent United Dominions Trust, with a huge white building in Eastcheap.

It began as an American idea, established in 1919 by a young Scots barrister, J. Gibson Jarvie, as a branch of a New York banking house. By 1923 it had become a British company, with Jarvie as chairman. Mass-production of cars made hire-purchase much more respectable and, after a long period of disapproval, by 1930 UDT was sufficiently regarded for the Bank of England themselves to buy half-a-million pounds worth of shares.[2] Now Gibson Jarvie, at 79, is accepted as a master-banker, and one of the city's grand old characters. He is a stocky, cigar-smoking, bullet-headed man, working in a dark-panelled room with a deep-

[1] *See* Hire-Purchase in a Free Society, Institute of Economic Affairs ,July, 1959.
[2] The UDT Group of Companies'. 1960.

throated grandfather clock and bound law volumes, and photographs of himself, in a kilt and in a wig. He breeds cattle in Suffolk, shoots on his Scottish estate, has a son who is a joint deputy chairman and racing-car enthusiast, and enjoys himself making speeches telling the Government to 'set the people free'.

Jarvie has seen his business grow from an upstart lender into a major city institution, and his letterhead says firmly at the top 'United Dominions Trust Ltd. Bankers'. His group now has huge ramifications in industry, for they provide not only the capital for hire-purchase, but expert advice for farmers, engineers and small businessmen, and like other bankers have found themselves increasingly involved in industrial problems (they have lent money for the steel balls used in making the Kariba dam, or for engines for trawlers). Jarvie himself often expounds, with unrelenting energy, the importance of credit, and has set himself up as one of the prophets of the new credit society. The UDT, in spite of the setbacks of bad debts, continues to be the most aggressive of the hire-purchase companies, and in 1962 they caused a new flurry by outbidding others with a new bonus system for their agents—a step which caused a furore in the city, but which forced other companies to follow.

MERCHANT BANKERS

Who hold the balance of the world? Who reign
O'er congress, whether royalist or liberal?
Who rouse the shirtless patriots of Spain?
(That makes old Europe's journals squeak and gibber all)
Who keep the world, both old and new in pain
Or pleasure? Who make politics run glibber all?
The shade of Buonaparte's noble daring?—
Jew Rothschild and his fellow-Christian, Baring.
Byron: Don Juan. Canto V. 1823.

The merchant banks stand with relationship to Barclays or the Midland rather as a barrister to a firm of solicitors, or a bookie to the tote. They are much smaller (they employ between them less than 4,000 people) and most are privately controlled. They do not have cheque books or counters for small customers: they deal with big firms and rich individuals. 'You live on your deposits', Lord Brand used to tell his joint stock banking friends: 'we have to live on our wits.' The merchant bankers are wealthy, usually hereditary, and are still widely regarded as the princes of the city.

They are the descendants of seventeenth-century merchants, most of them from Germany, who developed into bankers—selling their signatures instead of their goods. They found it more profitable to deal in credit than materials, and they made money both by guaranteeing other people's credit (accepting houses) and by raising loans (issuing houses). In these delicate operations, their integrity and judgment became their chief asset—their justification for hereditary bias. Ever since the Medicis of Florence, the merchant banks have been dynastic, passing down know-how, wealth, and sometimes brains.

In the early nineteenth century the London merchant bankers were richer than governments; Rothschilds financed whole armies, and Barings developed South America. The first heavy setback came with the South American slump of 1890, when Barings had to be rescued from ruin by the Governor of the Bank of England (who ordered the other bankers to come to their assistance). But a new decline in foreign business came after the first world war, when nationalism and the rise of Nazi Germany made foreign loans far more risky. Since then the London bankers have turned more to advising industry at home—a connection once considered undesirable.

In the meantime the wealth of the merchant banks was being eclipsed by the Treasury, the industrial corporations, and the provincial institutions which were pushing their way up—insurance companies, building societies and joint stock banks. New financiers, working through investment trusts, had become more powerful, if less respectable, than the bankers. The city, which can be dazzled by romance, often credits merchant bankers with more influence than they have. Many have lived on their names, and clung to old business instead of looking for new. But their connections and knowledge still give big opportunities; and a few banks have had a visible effect on the pattern of trade.

A 'merchant bank' corresponds roughly to an American 'investment bank' and a French *banque d'affaires*. The élite of the merchant banks are the seventeen 'acceptance houses', who have the backing of the Bank of England to accept other people's bills—to guarantee payment by one firm to another. The 'acceptance business' is less important today, when many firms are richer than their banks, and can finance themselves; and most banks are more active as 'issuing houses'—floating new issues of stock. But the partners (about 140) of the acceptance houses, backed by the Bank of England, are regarded as part of the city 'Establishment'. These were the seventeen banks of the Accepting Houses Committee, in January 1962, with their date of foundation and committee members:

1763	Baring Brothers	Sir Edward Reid (Chairman)
1804	N. M. Rothschild	Edmund de Rothschild
1804	J. Henry Schroder, Wagg	H. W. B. Schroder
1805	Wm. Brandt's Sons	W. A. Brandt
1808	Antony Gibbs	Lord Aldenham
1810	Brown Shipley	Angus McKinnon (Deputy Chairman)
1830	Kleinwort, Benson	Ernest Kleinwort
1831	M. Samuel	Lord Bearsted
1833	Arbuthnot Latham	S. R. Allsopp
1836	Guinness, Mahon	H. S. H. Guinness
1838	Morgan Grenfell	Viscount Harcourt
1839	Hambros	J. H. Hambro
1853	Samuel Montagu	Louis Franck
1877	Lazards, de Stein	J. Macartney-Filgate
1896	S. Japhet	R. A. Harari
1907	Philip Hill, Higginson, Erlanger	R. A. F. de Trafford
1946	S. G. Warburg	Geoffrey Seligman

BANKING FAMILIES

The merchant bankers work in a formal atmosphere, conditioned by trust and steeped in tradition. In many banks the partners still work together in one large room: in one of them all partners' letters are opened every morning, and put on a table for the others to see. Mahogany, black-coated waiters and grandfather clocks set the tone of privacy. Nearly all are hereditary firms, and only two were founded since 1900. All but two of the senior partners are sons of bankers, and families dominate the boards. This, for instance, is the list of partners in Wm. Brandt's Sons:

H. B. Brandt
R. E. Brandt
W. R. Brandt
H. A. Brandt
W. A. Brandt
J. M. Brandt

In merchant banking hereditary privilege remains unassailed. But several family banks, while maintaining control, have introduced able outsiders to enliven or run their businesses, like Sir George Erskine of Morgans, Gordon Richardson of Schroders, or Louis Franck of Samuel Montagus. This is part of the recurring pattern of the city—helping to provide the balance between trust and enterprise—solid, long-established families in control, with clever outsiders, often from the Continent or Scotland, providing the dynamic.

The banking families have an influence beyond their own banks. Many of the partners of the accepting houses are directors of insurance companies, and a growing number have become directors or chairmen of industrial firms, or powers behind them: 'I've sacked a dozen chairmen in my time', one banker told me. And since the eighteenth century, bankers have repeatedly inter-married with the aristocracy, and with the other bankers. Brands, Hampdens, Hambros, Barings and Financial Smiths interlock in the chart following page 34. Their connections with the political and ducal families are perhaps not as close as they look, but they help to give merchant bankers wider horizons and contacts than other men in the city.

The family with probably the most remarkable financial ramifi-cations is the 'Financial Smiths' (not to be confused with the bookselling Smiths, headed by Lord Hambleden, or with the descendants of F. E. Smith, later Lord Birkenhead). Every summer a lunch is given by the Smith Family Club, presided over by Sir Alexander Smith, which is confined to the descendants of Thomas Smith, born in 1631, who founded a bank in Nottingham. In 1959 17 descendants were reported to hold city appointments: between them they held 87 directorships in 75 companies, including 6 chairmanships and 3 managing directorships. They include the heads of two merchant banks—Lord Bicester of Morgan Grenfell and Reginald Abel Smith of Arbuthnot Latham—partners of two others, Hambros and Schroders, and directors of two joint stock banks, Coutts and the National Provincial (which absorbed the original Smith family bank at the end of the last century). The Smiths have traditionally favoured Eton, Cambridge and the city, but recently young Smiths have gone into industry, and one, Brian Abel Smith, is a radical economist at the London School of Economics.

Some of the more prominent Financial Smiths[1] are shown on the following page.

ROTHSCHILDS

Apart from Barings who maintain enterprise as well as autho-rity, specialising in South America and beer) the oldest, and

[1] *See The Economist*, March 28, 1959.

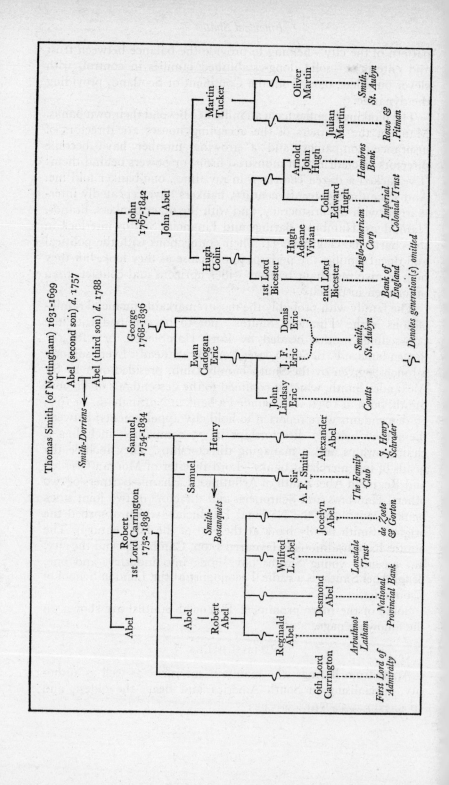

Thomas Smith (of Nottingham) 1631-1699

Abel (second son) *d*. 1757

Abel (third son) *d*. 1788

Smith-Dorriens

Abel

Robert, 1st Lord Carrington 1752-1838

Samuel, 1754-1834

George 1768-1836

John 1767-1842

Abel

Robert Abel

Henry

Samuel

John Abel

Hugh Colin

Smith-Bosanquets

Reginald Abel — *Arbuthnot Latham*

Desmond Abel — *National Provincial Bank*

Wilfred L. Abel — *Lonsdale Trust*

Jocelyn Abel — *de Zoete & Gorton*

Sir A. F. Smith — *The Family Club*

Alexander Abel — *J. Henry Schröder*

John Lindsay Eric — *Coutts*

Evan Cadogan Eric — *Smith, St. Aubyn*

J. F. Eric — *Smith, St. Aubyn*

Denis Eric

1st Lord Bicester

Hugh Adeane Vivian — *Anglo-American Corp*

2nd Lord Bicester — *Bank of England*

Colin Edward Hugh — *Imperial Colonial Trust*

Arnold John Hugh — *Hambros Bank*

Martin Tucker

Julian Martin — *Rowe & Pitman*

Oliver Martin — *Smith, St. Aubyn*

6th Lord Carrington — *First Lord of Admiralty*

ξ. *Denotes generation(s) omitted*

certainly the most famous is Rothschilds. At New Court, behind the Mansion House, hangs the sign of the five arrows, to commemorate the five Rothschild brothers who first scattered to London, Paris, Vienna, Naples and Frankfurt. The English house was founded by Nathan, a cotton merchant in Manchester, and his great-great-grandsons are the present partners. Rothschilds is now less romantic: no longer does the Rothschild pigeon bring in the news, the Rothschild boat lie waiting off Folkestone, or Rothschild couriers leave daily for the capitals of Europe. Armies (such as Wellington's in Spain) no longer need wait for Rothschilds' support. But they continue to be enterprising in less romantic fields, such as founding hire-purchase firms and unit trusts, developing Labrador, and (to the city's astonishment) having Labour leaders to lunch.

Rothschilds are very *haute banque*, and at New Court you feel the full weight of family tradition—particularly in the unique ritual of the bankers' lunch. Bankers' lunches, in quiet panelled rooms with silver platters and crested china, help to bring their country-house life into the middle of the city. They entertain clients or guests in a hushed Victorian setting, well away from ticker-tapes or telephones; and they can use prestige as a weapon. One or two banks have up-to-date lunch rooms (the Ionian bank, an unorthodox place, has a row of three modern dining-rooms, a fish-shaped table and specially designed cutlery). But most banks prefer to evoke safe nineteenth-century glory.

The visitor to Rothschilds arrives at a Victorian Palazzo, like a private house, with a panelled entrance hall hung with bearded Rothschilds, where the guests are assembled. A butler greets them, and at the stroke of one the door is thrown open into 'The Room' —a long and perfectly preserved Victorian drawing-room, filled with bric-a-brac, relics, framed letters, portraits and partners. A blind is pulled down, to separate The Room from the adjoining office. Rothschilds rise to greet the guests with sherry, and ten minutes later move into the dining-room, with a carefully planned *placement*, for conversation about industry, gardens or music. At a quarter-past two the hosts rise, the guests depart, and the partners go back to work among the bric-a-brac.

GENTLEMEN V. PLAYERS

At first glance the merchant banks, each with their lunches, insurance companies, butlers and discretion, might seem to be a united club. But since the war—and probably since their beginnings—they have been divided into two rough groups, sometimes described as Gentlemen v. Players, where the two spirits of the city, the protective and the aggressive, have come into conflict. The two sides have often skirmished, and often made truces: but the sharpness of the conflict was revealed in the most extraordinary affair in the recent history of the city—the 'Aluminium War' of 1958-9. 'It was a watershed', said one banker, 'the city has never been quite the same since.'

On the one side are the gentlemen, or as the American magazine *Fortune* describes them, the 'Old Freddies', who 'quietly partition the city's vast business among themselves—which is why the city can put over a huge money deal in half the time it takes Wall Street'.[1] The most prominent of them is Lazards—descended from the French-Jewish *Lazard frères*, but now wholly and emphatically British. Lazards lies at the heart of the hereditary banking nexus. They have five important peers on their board— Lord Poole, a former Chairman of the Conservative Party; Lord Brand, a director of *The Times* and former member of Lord Milner's kindergarten, sometimes called Mr. Establishment; his nephew, Lord Hampden, thought to be the ablest of the partners, related to the Dukes of Beaufort and Devonshire; Lord Kindersley, the senior partner; and the man who owns two-thirds of Lazards' shares, Lord Cowdray. Lazards is an interesting example of the blending of old wealth with new—of ducal and mercantile. They are capable of being both stuffy and ruthless, and they represent the British aristocracy at its toughest—though not necessarily at its shrewdest.

Behind the bank is the legendary personality of Lord Cowdray, a cousin of Churchill and one of the richest and most formidable men in Britain. He is the heir to the oil fortune of his grandfather, Weetman Pearson, who founded the Mexican Eagle oil company, later merged into 'Shell-Mex'. The present Cowdray interests include three important trusts (Whitehall Securities, S. Pearson and the Cowdray Trust, which work at the top of the Vickers skyscraper), the Westminster Press chain of provincial newspapers and the Financial News Ltd., which owns the leading financial papers in Britain, headed by the omnipresent *Financial Times*. Cowdray is a man of relentless energy, with the reputation of making money out of everything he touches—even polo, which he organises on Sundays, with a good profit from spectators. He lives

[1] *Fortune*, June 1959—to which I am indebted to some of the facts in this section.

in two big Victorian houses in Sussex and Wales, and (although he has only one arm) goes shooting with an energy which wears out his guests. Once a year he tours through Texas, where he has large interests, exhausting Texans with questions. He is one of those aristocrats who have never lost their ancestor's urge to make money. Although he touches political circles, he is hardly interested in politics. His actual intervention in Lazards or Whitehall Securities is believed to be slight: he appears for lunch with the managing directors, but leaves most decisions to his representative, Lord Poole, and was not much concerned with the Aluminium War.

The senior partner of Lazards, 'primus inter pares' as he describes himself, is Lord Kindersley—a tall, confident banker with a military moustache, and the quiet, superior manner of hereditary bankers. It was his father (then Sir Robert) who gave Lazards their high reputation for shrewdness, and in those days it was Lazards who were regarded as upstarts. ('I remember when Baron Schroder crossed over the street to avoid meeting Sir Robert', one banker told me, 'because Sir Robert had pinched the Brazilian coffee business from him.') But his son is the personification of the city insider (as vividly emerged in the Bank Rate Tribunal of 1957)—director of the Bank of England, Governor of the Royal Exchange Assurance, Chairman of Rolls Royce, and senior partner of Lazards.

Working closely with Lazards is the stately establishment of Morgan Grenfell, still associated with the New York firm of Pierpont Morgan, and founded by the American philanthropist, George Peabody (builder of model Victorian dwellings). The partners of Morgans include Lord Harcourt (related to the Morgan family and brother-in-law of Lord Ashburton, of Barings), who is also chairman of the huge Legal and General Insurance Company; Lord Catto, a son of a former Governor of the Bank of England; Lord Rennell, a former diplomat; and his brother-in-law Lord Bicester (one of the Financial Smiths), senior partner and director of the Bank of England. 'Morgans and ourselves', Lord Kindersley explained to the Bank Rate Tribunal in a famous and revealing passage, 'are probably closer than any other two issuing houses in the City of London; we discuss intimate details of every kind and description. I do not think Lord Bicester would find it in the least surprising that I should come to him and say to him: "Look here, Rufie, is it too late to stop this business or not?" '

Other 'gentlemen' banks are Hambros, entirely controlled by

the Hambro family, who came from Copenhagen in 1814 and still have a large Scandinavian connection; and M. Samuel, founded by Marcus Samuel, the East End trader who later founded[1] the colossus of Shell. Samuel's is still run by Samuels, headed by Lord Bearsted, who have a family director on the board of Shell, but compared to the Royal Dutch-Shell annual turnover—more than £3,000 million—the bank which helped to create it is now tiny—symbolic of the change in financial power over the last century.

The traditional bankers move in similar circles: they meet at the favourite bankers' clubs—Brooks's, Boodle's, White's—stay at each others' country houses at weekends, and shoot each others' grouse in Scotland in August. Some have more cultural habits: Barings and Rothschilds share a permanent box at Covent Garden, and Lazards and Morgan Grenfells share another. Most of their business has been inherited, and has not much expanded in the past ten years: 'The position of the traditional banks', one of them said to me, 'is rather like the British Empire after the war. There's nothing much more to gain, and a lot to lose. But it's a bit less of a closed club than it used to be; newcomers are always coming along, and seem like strangers until they're not new any longer. It's rather like a village.'

Confronting this club is a small band of strangers, with very little to lose and a lot to gain. The most unusual intruder is Lionel Fraser, the tall white-haired chairman of Helbert Wagg, which merged with Schroders in 1962, for he is that rare phenomenon—the self-made banker. At the age of sixteen he answered an advertisement for a job with a small banking firm, now part of Helbert Wagg's. 'The city meant precious little to me, for I was completely without background or connection. It was just somewhere to scrape a living.' Now, at the age of sixty-six, he is a major figure in banking and industry: he controls an industrial holding company, Thomas Tillings, which includes such varied businesses as Pyrex Glass, Cornhill Insurance, Newey & Eyre Electrical Appliances and Heinemanns, the publishers. His tall white-haired head, with a bow tie beneath it, is often to be seen at private views and art galleries: his Knightsbridge flat is overflowing with modern paintings and sculpture, including an Epstein bust of himself. In spite of his success, he has not become a country-house banker, and he enjoys writing provocative articles and cocking a snook.

Another stranger is Kenneth Keith, the managing director of Philip Hill, Higginson, Erlanger—who occupy a modern air-

[1] Or helped to form it: see p. 430.

conditioned building in Moorgate, equipped with the usual bankers' butlers. Keith, though he served in the Guards, comes from an unbankerlike profession—chartered accountancy: after the war he was brought into Philip Hill's by Sir Brian Mountain of Eagle Star Insurance (who have a large interest in the bank); he became managing director in 1951, at the age of 35. He is a tough, casual, feet-on-the-desk banker, with swept-back grey hair and a brisk way of talking. He has found new fields in the Commonwealth and set up a branch in Nigeria: and he is determined that London should become the financial centre of Europe. 'We're all rather jealous of him', said one prominent banker. Philip Hill's includes a prosperous investment trust, which gives them strong contacts with industry, and one of their directors is the omnipresent Harley Drayton.[1]

But the most spectacular newcomer is Siegmund Warburg, from an old Hamburg banking family, who came to England as a refugee, and established his bank in 1946. Cultured and sensitive, with dark, deep-set eyes and a quick intuitive mind, Warburg has fluttered the city since the war. He perceived very early the new trends in British banking—particularly the importance of industrial mergers. He advised Associated Television, Roy Thomson in his buying of the *Sunday Times*,[2] and the *Daily Mirror* in buying Amalgamated Press and Odhams. Warburg's 'Mercury Securities' owns among many successful properties an advertising agency, Masius and Fergusson. Warburg has recruited his staff and partners, from a wider range: they include two ex-civil servants (Sir Andrew McFadyean and Sir James Helmore), a former journalist (Ronald Grierson) and the former ambassador to Paris (Lord Gladwyn). In the city Warburgs are notorious for hard work and perpetual travel. They work in a new building in Gresham Street, furnished in bankers' contemporary, with a grandfather clock and old prints, but full of electronic devices.

THE ALUMINIUM WAR

These were the main city forces assembled on each side of the extraordinary 'Aluminium War' of Christmas 1958 which, in one dazzling fortnight illuminated the workings of the city and industry. It was a conflict between old and new banks, between American and British approaches to industry, and between shareholders and directors. The new won.

[1] *See* chapter 24.
[2] *See* page 119.

The seeds of the war were sown in 1957, when the American Reynolds Metals, run by four aggressive brothers, had decided to try to buy British Aluminium (the *only* British aluminium company) in order to acquire their new plant in Quebec. Reynolds were advised by their bankers, Kuhn Loeb and their London correspondent, Siegmund Warburg, not to antagonise British nationalism by an outright American bid, but to operate with a British company. After much exploration, they went into partnership with Sir Ivan Stedeford of Tube Investments, a self-made engineer from the Midlands[1]—whose adviser was the other maverick banker in the city, Lionel Fraser. Stedeford was at first anxious about an Anglo-American take-over of a sedate British company: but eventually he was persuaded. Through Warburgs, Tube Investments and Reynolds secretly began buying British Aluminium shares.

By October 1958 TI had bought about 10 per cent of the shares, and BA were anxiously trying to find out who was buying them. To avoid antagonising the city, Stedeford decided to come out into the open, and he arranged a meeting with British Aluminium in St. James's Square on November 3, 1958. On the BA side was their chairman, Lord Portal of Hungerford, the war-time Chief of Air Staff, and his bearded managing director, Geoffrey Cunliffe, son of a former Governor of the Bank of England—advised by *two* bankers, Hambros and Lazards: together they symbolised the Old Guard of the city. Sir Ivan, together with Reynolds' agent Joe McConnell, told Portal that they would like to have an association with British Aluminium: Portal and Cunliffe replied stiffly that they could not consider any proposition, since they were negotiating with another group. Stedeford and McConnell made a definite offer for BA shares two days later. Portal, in a second encounter on November 28th, replied that he had already reached an agreement with Alcoa, Reynolds' American rivals, and could not pass on Sir Ivan's offer to shareholders. Sir Ivan, furious, summoned a press conference revealing the whole story, and the terms of his offer to BA shareholders (which was far more attractive than Lord Portal's arrangement). The press sided quickly with Sir Ivan: ('it is hard to believe that the British Aluminium Board would sign the Alcoa agreement . . . without exploring the Tubes proposition', wrote the *Financial Times*), and the big insurance companies who held shares in BA were annoyed at not being consulted. Portal insisted

[1] *See* page 484.

that 'your company has never done a better piece of business
than completing this agreement with Alcoa', and (replying to
suggestions that he might have consulted shareholders) said in
a classic phrase—'those familiar with negotiations between
great companies will realise that such a course would have been
impracticable'. On December 14 TI sent a formal bid to shareholders of 78/– for each BA share. Five days later BA's board announced that they would increase the 1958 dividend from 12 per
cent to 17½ per cent—an opportunist move which provoked
further scorn from the press. But it still seemed likely that the BA
shareholders would hang on to their shares.

Then, on New Year's Eve, the bombshell came: fourteen august
financial institutions wrote to BA shareholders, in a letter signed
by Lord Kindersley and Olaf Hambro, to announce that between
them they were holding two million shares in BA, that they were
prepared to buy shares at 82/– each, and that the TI take-over bid
must be resisted in the 'national interest'. The consortium included
Lazards, Hambros, Morgan Grenfell, M. Samuel, Samuel
Montagu, the Whitehall Trust, and the British South Africa
Company. Between them they made up the heart of the interlocking city establishment. Lionel Fraser, to the fury of Lazards,
replied with an interview in the *Evening Standard*:

'It all seems like Alice in Wonderland when really calm judgment is called for. How my friends on the other side can say their
proposals are in the national interest astounds me.

'I cannot understand selling millions of shares, to an American
company at 60/– a share, when the other side now recommends
BA shareholders not to sell at the present price of 82/–. The whole
thing smacks of fear. It is unprogressive.'

Looking back on the incident, it seems astonishing that such a
group, with so many able men, should have behaved so unwisely:
the consortium's appeal to 'the national interest' ('saving British
Aluminium for civilisation' as one banker put it) had little
support, since both schemes involved equal American participa-
tion. Reynolds retorted easily to the consortium by buying
1,300,000 BA shares in the first two days of the New Year, and
made an improved bid on January 5th. In the meantime the
Governor of the Bank of England tried to patch up the row by
inviting the parties to talks on January 1 and 2, but without
success. Many big insurance companies which had agreed not to
accept the Reynolds offer quietly sold their shares on the open
market where the price stayed above 82/–, and the Church

Commissioners, refusing to take sides, did the same. By January 9, Reynolds and TI held 80 per cent of British Aluminium shares. The war was over.

Soon afterwards Lord Portal and Geoffrey Cunliffe resigned from the board, with compensation of £88,000 between them, and Lord Portal was appointed as chairman of the British Match Corporation—an 'Establishment' job previously held by Lord Kindersley: while Lord Plowden, the nominee of Sir Ivan, moved into St. James' Square and began to inject new life into the company.

Recriminations soon followed. Olaf Hambro wrote to *The Times* on January 12, to complain that 'it is very unclear why the majority of city editors of the press seemed to be against city opinion and openly wrote in favour of the take-over bid'. *The Times* in a leader two days later pointed out that, in terms of Americanism, there was nothing to choose between the two bids. Anthony Crosland, the Labour MP, writing to *The Times* about the consortium, said 'their outlook appears about as contemporary as the architectural style in which the city is now being rebuilt—both make one shudder'.

AFTER ALUMINIUM

Behind the allegations about the national interest lay a deeper resentment—that the new bankers, by their secret buying and by-passing of boards, were undermining the network of trust and authority on which the city rested, and (a subsidiary charge) were coming too close to industry, in a continental, un-British way. For some months the two sides in the city would not speak to each other: but then, as happens in the city, out of the sharp antithesis a synthesis emerged. Warburgs, after other successful deals, began to be accepted as part of the 1960's, and soon to acquire a *haute banque* flavour, while Lazards rapidly increased their home industrial business. Only two years after their patriotic appeals in the Aluminium war, Lazards were engaged in buying British Fords shares for the American company. Meanwhile in the quieter old banks amateurism since the war has been slowly giving way to professionalism: bankers have been arriving at 9.30 instead of 10.15, moving from Hampshire into London flats, and talking shop at lunch.

'The Aluminium affair was the beginning of a new spirit', said Lionel Fraser, 'there's much more cut-and-thrust these days, much less of the "you scratch my back, I scratch yours", and the "dear old boy" business: the old Etonians aren't as powerful as they used to be, and people no longer feel that they have to stick to their own preserve. I suppose it's still tremendously useful in the city to be a son of a lord—it starts you off with other people's trust. But banking is a very professional business nowadays— technique is what matters, knowing where to find the right kind of money: there's a *touch* to the city—a sense of service: you have to know how to *play* the investment market, just as people play the piano.'

'The city is becoming more competitive than you'd think', Kenneth Keith told me: 'some sides of the business—particularly dealing in securities—will probably change out of recognition in the next ten years. There'll be a lot more rationalisation, and probably more mergers. Nowadays a bank has to be able to provide specialist services right along the waterfront.'

Siegmund Warburg believes that the important thing is whether firms are allowing the wind of change to blow from generation to generation through their offices: he doesn't think most of them have. People have always been saying that the city's in a state of transition, but the rebels of one generation become the conformists of the next. 'In the sense that bankers provide money for industry', Warburg has said, 'they're becoming less important: but in the sense of being consultants—what I call "financial engineers"—they're becoming much more important.'

There is still a suspicion—partly a residue of the 'Bankers' Ramp' of 1931—that bankers are plotting the economic future of the country. But I have the impression that most of them, while invoking the national interest, are too absorbed in the day-to-day worries of the city to call on the Chancellor or nobble the Treasury. In spite of their family networks, the old bankers appear to spend much more time weekending between themselves than with politicians or industrialists: and Harold Macmillan has shown no great fondness for 'banksters' as he has called them. Ever since the Labour government—when more than one merchant bank made preparations for moving their headquarters out of England—there has been a lingering distrust between bankers and the Treasury, and on the issue of the Common Market, where one might expect bankers to lobby strongly, their influence was small. The Aluminium War and other encounters suggest that, far from having a bold picture of their future opportunities, many bankers are being dragged into the mid-twentieth century. On the other hand there are signs of some very enterprising, internationally-minded young bankers, some with famous names, who are longing to get to grips with the future: and the events of the next few years may well provide the challenge to bring out the city's strength and speed.

24

FINANCIERS

Avarice, the spur of Industry.
David Hume.

ALL over the city, men in small offices are buying and selling little bits of industry. They range from 'bucket-shops' which make a living out of speculating in shares, to imposing investment trusts, which raise money from the public and invest it, at a profit, in hand-picked companies. Among the newest are 'Unit Trusts', designed to enable quite small investors to buy shares in a whole group of industries.

Historically the city, though closer to industry than the Wall Street bankers, has been separate from industrialists. The bosses in the North and Midlands have nursed a bitter (and sometimes well-founded) suspicion of bankers and financiers. There are many city stories about the encounters between bluff Yorkshire men and smooth Bishopsgate bankers. Many big firms like ICI, Courtaulds or Unilever have prided themselves on their independence from EC2. 'We are suspicious of banking', said Samuel Courtauld in 1942, 'because we think it is often overpaid for its services, and also because we doubt its efficiency. Historical development has given it a privileged position on which it is apt to trade. We are suspicious of company promoters and gamblers in stocks and shares, because they want something for nothing, and do far more harm than good.'[1] In a time of crisis, as when ICI threatened Courtaulds, they become very aware of the city and shareholders; but in their normal operations the industrial Leviathans have become virtually independent of the city.

But Britain remains a country of small businesses: and for thousands of them, particularly the fast-growing ones, finding money is still crucial and very difficult. The city, like the joint stock banks, operates on the principle of lending large sums only to those who have large sums. It is easy enough for big companies to go to the stock exchange and insurance companies, but for smaller firms there is a gap in the city machine—known since the Macmillan committee of 1931 as the 'Macmillan Gap'. Various

Quoted in *The Boss* by Roy Lewis and Rosemary Stewart, 1958.

industrial holding companies have grown up to help smaller firms with finance. Among them are the Charterhouse Group, controlled by Sir Nutcombe Hume, which owns ten companies, including a merchant bank (S. Japhet) and a publishing house (Methuens), and has shares in seventy-five others; and 'Credit for Industries Ltd', a subsidiary of the hire-purchase firm United Dominions Trust. Others are Tillings, the 'family of companies' controlled by Lionel Fraser; Firth Cleveland, the engineering group run by Charles Hayward; and Norcros, the 'club' of firms controlled by John Sheffield.

Two more philanthropic groups have been set up since the war. One is the 'Finance Corporation for Industry' (FCI), subsidised by the Government. The other is the 'Industrial and Commercial Finance Corporation' (ICFC), set up by the joint stock banks and run by Lord Piercy—that rare phenomenon, a Labour peer in the city.

The word financier is one which city men nowadays avoid: it brings back memories of thirties scandals, and names like Clarence Hatry, the financier who financed United Steel but then crashed and went to jail. With their talk about 'families of companies', 'nurseries', 'clubs', 'filling a gap' and 'providing services', financiers provide an impression of paternal—almost maternal—care of industry. They, too, have been influenced by the vogue for professionalisation, and the fact that they make private fortunes out of industry is sometimes forgotten. The independence of the industrial Leviathans, run by their own managers, sometimes suggests that the city entrepreneur is a dodo-person, killed off by the war and the managerial revolution. But among the hundred biggest companies in Britain, as we shall see, there are still more than a score which are controlled by such entrepreneurs. There is no chance in this book of dealing with all their various characters: here I picked only one—perhaps the most spectacular—Harold Charles Drayton, usually known as Harley Drayton.

117 OLD BROAD STREET

At number 117 Old Broad Street is a door with a list of 48 companies printed on metal strips, beginning with 'Alcoy and Gandia Railway and Harbour Ltd', and ending with 'Vector Securities Ltd'. Upstairs, the offices have the usual musty city smell, and sense of historical standstill. These are the headquarters of Harley Drayton, chairman of twenty-three companies, led by

British Electric Traction, which owns 14,000 buses in Britain and 60 per cent of the shares in the biggest TV company, Associated-Rediffusion. He controls, among others, Mitchell Cotts, the African traders; Advance Laundries; the Antofagasta and Bolivia Railways; Provincial Newspapers Ltd, with four newspapers; and a group of twenty investment trusts. The 'Drayton Group', as this is usually known in the city, is probably the most striking example of a group of industries financially controlled from the city.

Into these offices comes every morning a big, bucolic man with a red face, white hair brushed back, a monocle dangling over his pin-stripe suit, and tall, laced boots. He looks, as he is, a strong man from country stock who has somehow strayed into the city and applied laws of tough common sense. Drayton likes to gaze out of the window in his old leather chair, puffing at a cigar, philosophising about the world and the city, and quoting the Bible: 'The twenty-fifth chapter of Ecclesiaticus is the only economic system which ever worked. It tells you how to run a sinking fund, how to manage a business, how to make an issue.' At weekends he retires to his 700-acre farm in Suffolk, and reads the lesson at Plumton parish church. In the country he loves his country-squire life, walking and shooting, and his greatest pride is to have been High Sheriff. He collects illuminated manuscripts, and lives in 'Millionaires' Row' in London (one of the last three private residents to do so). His interests outside his companies are not large, and his political attitudes are antique. He stood as a Liberal candidate after the war, but largely because he thought the Conservatives were becoming too Socialist; and the Liberals have since disillusioned him. He belongs to the Council of the Institute of Directors, and put a lot of money into South Africa after the war —one of his few financial mistakes. He operates almost entirely from the city, only occasionally going out to inspect his interests in Africa, Canada or South America, or Television House in Kingsway (he goes there when his nephews want to look round). 'You have to pick your man and give him final responsibility for the day-to-day management. My job is the final financing, picking of high executives. You have to make yourself available when they're in a hole. Otherwise I don't interfere. Sometimes I just give them a bit of advice like "Boys, be careful, copper's going up".'

Drayton is a self-made man. His grandfather was a Lincolnshire farmer, and his father was a gardener who settled in Streatham. At fifteen he answered an advertisement for an office boy, and joined 'Government Stock and Other Securities Ltd'—a group of very successful investment trusts then run by Lord St. Davids, who had built up a large business in South America. Young Drayton's ambition and quickness with figures soon made a mark on Lord St. Davids' associate Jack Austen—a pioneer in transport who had built up British Electric Traction. When Austen died in 1942, he left Drayton the running of the business, and his house, Plumton Hall in Suffolk: and Austen's portrait now hangs above Drayton's fireplace, between two paintings of the Bank of England. 'All that I am', Drayton said to me in an expansive conversation, 'I owe to him. When I was young, you had to catch the eye of someone who would help you—and there were only eight or ten people who would do that. Nowadays it's much easier—there are far more people who can help you—about thirty or forty: and you can make profits much quicker. But in the old days they helped you out of kindness: nowadays they all want their cut from you.'

Drayton never thought, 'it just isn't done', and the name Drayton, even though it now appears on the board of the Midland Bank, can still cause grunts in the city. But like other ex-rebels in the city, he has become respectable; he is proud of having the Earl of Airlie's son as one of his protégés. I asked Drayton what had distinguished his own career from others':

Most of the city has the idea that you must conform. What stops most people in the city is snobbery. You don't have to worry about being popular. You have to take risks and stick your neck out. If you're an artist, nobody worries if you're a failure: but in the city it's regarded as a crime almost against the Holy Ghost to make a mistake.

Some people are born with a bug inside them: if they are, they can do anything: if they're not, they might as well settle down to be a clerk—it's like the parable of the talents. You have to have a burning belief in what you're doing, and sell it to people who will back you. I'm still prepared to see people in my bath at eight in the morning, and I'm ready to do a deal at midnight. Before the war, when business was difficult, you really had to *sell* things. We used to say: any damn fool can make electricity; it takes a genius to sell it.

The city by and large lost its position after the first world war and still more after the last war—but most people didn't tumble to it. Between the wars, big money was still in the hands of merchant banks—Lazards, Rothschilds, Barings, Morgans—

each with one, two or three million. But with inflation, and the rise of the new financial institutions, one or two millions became chicken feed. The big people were either the ones who had a great deal of money of their own, or the industrialists. I think it was the new industrialists who proved themselves to be the descendants of the great old adventurers, like Drake or Raleigh.

Drayton showed his independence from city opinion in 1955, with the arrival of commercial television. While nearly the whole of the city was sceptical, Drayton had a hunch that it would make large profits; British Electric Traction bought a large share in Associated-Rediffusion, in partnership with Lord Rothermere's Associated Newspapers (*Daily Mail, Daily Sketch*, etc.). Drayton reckoned to lose one-and-a-half million: in the first nineteen months BET lost £3,719,000. But he stuck to his hunch. When Lord Rothermere decided that the losses were too high, Drayton's representative casually suggested that he might be able to find a buyer, and Rothermere thankfully sold out. The buyer turned out to be none other than BET. Very soon afterwards the television tide began to turn and the advertising rolled in. 'I thought it would make two-and-a-half million a year', said Drayton: 'in fact, it's making seven million . . . I think I've always been more enterprising than most. But there was quite a lot of wear and tear on the tummy.'

25

INSURANCE

By means of which Policies of Assurance it cometh to pass upon the loss or perishing of any ship there followeth not the undoing of any Man, but the loss lighteth rather easily upon many than heavily upon few.

Act of Elizabeth, 1601.

When you want *really* big money, you usually find yourself talking to people who *didn't* go to Eton.

A banker.

DEMOCRACY, in finance as well as in government, has put power into bureaucracy. It is a parallel to the shift of power from parliament to the civil service. The financial giants of the city today are not the bankers or financiers, but the great anonymous bureaucracies of the insurance companies and their cousins, the pension funds. In investment the insurance companies, trustees for millions of individuals, have taken the place of the magnates, dukes and Rothschilds who dominated the city a century ago. 'The Institutions'—as the insurance companies and pensions funds are enigmatically called—pour about eight hundred million pounds of new money ever year, enough to finance a new ICI; in five years the new investments of insurance companies have gone up from a million a day to one-and-a-half million.[1]

The power of the institutions is one of the most important developments of the mid-century. But it has grown up outside the traditional mythology of Britain: there are no good novels about insurance, no fashionable memoirs of forty years with the Pru. Decisions are taken by clerkdoms much more remote than the civil service, away from parliamentary questions, and the institutions emerge into the headlines even less than bankers.

Insurance is split into two species. Firstly, insurance against accidents—ships sinking, buildings burning, cars running over people. Secondly, insurance (or technically 'assurance')—of a man's life against a *certainty*—death. The first kind is hazardous, based ultimately on a calculated gamble. The second is largely

[1] *The Economist,* July 22, 1961. p. 381.

predictable, for the average span of men's lives—when hundreds of thousands are involved—can be quite accurately calculated.

The first kind, gruesomely called 'Non-Life Insurance', has the oldest origins. Insurance of ships followed Vasco da Gama's voyage: the first recorded British policy was for the vessel *Sancta Crux*, in 1555. The 'Fire Office' was founded by Nicolas Barbon, son of Praise-God Barebones, in 1680, fourteen years after the Great Fire of London. Insurance followed the path of new inventions—against railway, car, or aeroplane accidents, or the indisposition of prima donnas. International insurance was a British development; in the eighteenth century the symbols of British insurance companies— suns, phoenixes or globes—spread over Europe as the marks of trust in British money. In nineteenth-century Germany, villagers saw the Sun symbol—the face of a man inside a radiant sun—and knelt down to worship it.[1] London no longer dominates insurance in Europe, but it remains its biggest insurance market.

The traditional heart of 'non-life' insurance has been the collection of rich individuals and their friends known as 'Lloyd's'— the city insurance market, containing 'The Room', which claims to be the biggest room in the world. It is a curved hall of green-and-white marble 340 feet long, like a covered-in swimming pool, surrounded by a gallery: a sedate and sedentary version of the stock exchange. It contains sometimes as many as four thousand people, all selling or buying insurance. Unlike most city activities, what is happening is quite clear; Lloyd's still keeps its simple seventeenth-century routine, when men gathered in Edward Lloyd's coffee-house to offer insurance for ships. Sitting on medieval-type benches, four-in-a-row, in front of shelves and leather-bound ledgers are the 'underwriters' of insurance, looking like overgrown schoolboys. Wandering between the 'boxes' (as the desks are called) are the 'Lloyd's brokers', holding long folded cards, or 'slips', representing a ship, fleet, cargo or pair of legs to be insured. The brokers queue up in front of the underwriters, to ask them to add their name on the slip: if the underwriter agrees, he puts his signature, with the premium and the proportion of the risk he is prepared to take, under the name of the proposition (hence 'underwriter'). The broker then goes round The Room until the signatures and proportions add up to 100 per cent.

The Room contains a typical city mixture of new and old devices. In the middle is a raised rostrum containing a man in a

[1] *See* P. G. M. Dickson: *The Sun Insurance Office*, 1710–1960.

big red robe with a wide black collar, looking like a town-crier, reciting the names of brokers through a microphone. Above him is the old 'Lutine Bell', which is rung once for bad news about ships, twice for good news, and beside it an electronic notice board, showing names of brokers. When a broker is wanted, one of the 'waiters' (who stand round the room in scarlet uniform) writes his name on a special instrument, and the name is reproduced by an electronic hand in front of the town-crier, who then calls for the broker. There are no typewriters, computers, dictaphones, teleprinters or girls in The Room. Clerks inscribe the details of premiums and clients in their crowded, dog-eared ledgers. The system looks medieval, but in its simplicity and lack of paper-work, is not unlike some of the newest Marks and Spencer ideas of office efficiency. Round The Room are ante-rooms, diningrooms and committee rooms all built since the war in a heavy style which emphasises the country-gentleman image of Lloyd's: the Adam committee room has a ceiling and chimneypiece brought intact from Bowood, the Marquess of Lansdowne's house in Wiltshire.

The financial backbone of Lloyd's is made up by the five thousand 'names', grouped in 140 'syndicates', who provide the capital and must pay in for disasters—with unlimited liability. Each of the outside names has to be worth at least £75,000 (though many nowadays are guaranteed by their syndicates), but two-thirds are sleeping partners or 'back-woodsmen' who never go near The Room. The Names form a proud club: to be elected you must be sponsored by six members, and cross-examined by the Council, and the list includes large numbers of old city families. Old school ties dominate The Room: people working at Lloyd's who are not members—known as 'substitutes'—are kept severely separate; they even have their own 'substitutes' lavatory'.

Lloyd's, like merchant banking, depends on a mixture of trust and daring. Syndicates vary enormously in their profits: several, helped by the inflation of the fifties, have made spectacular postwar profits, but the majority make not much more than 10 per cent on their investment. The pride of Lloyd's is its foreign business (estimated in 1955 to earn about £17 million a year in foreign currency[1]): American film-directors, Italian ship-owners, Chilean wool-growers, have all come to Lloyd's. Their reputation depends not only on their reliability, but on their readiness to insure almost *anything*, all in one big room, very quickly and without fuss: the

[1] *See* William M. Clark: *The City's Invisible Earnings*, 1958.

speed is part of the justification of the club. But with the growing insurance centres in New York, Paris or Frankfurt, many underwriters doubt if they can maintain their proportion of international business, particularly marine insurance.

Two-thirds of non-life insurance now comes not from Lloyd's but from 'The Companies'—the big joint stock insurance companies, which stand to the 'Lloyd's Boys' as a bus to a taxi: they are bureaucracies, run not by free-lancers but by salaried managers. Most of them (the biggest exceptions are Eagle Star and General Accident) belong to 'The Tariff'—fixing the minimum premium for common objects like cars. The competition between Lloyd's and the Companies is an interesting contest: Lloyd's (like barristers) have low overheads, quick decisions and personal connections, while the Companies have the advantage of mass-production. But Lloyd's are gradually developing fewer and bigger syndicates, more specialists, and mechanised statistics in separate offices. Competitors, here as elsewhere, grow like each other.

Most big companies handle both Life and non-Life, and are thus called 'composite', although the two businesses are kept separate. These are the biggest non-life companies, with their total 'premium income' in 1960, and their chairmen.

Royal Group	£144,163,080	T. H. Naylor
Commercial Union Group	£112,739,745	R. C. Brooks
Northern & Employers	£78,874,323	Lord Knollys
General Accident	£74,910,018	Sir Stanley Norie-Miller
Royal Exchange	£50,705,712	Lord Kindersley
Sun Alliance Group	£45,482,321	T. D. Barclay
Phoenix	£40,862,080	Sir Edward Ferguson
Guardian	£35,130,682	Lord Blackford
Norwich Union	£34,113,951	Sir Robert Bignold
London (& Sea/Beacon)	£34,772,166	Harald Peake
Eagle Star	£27,272,754	Sir Brian Mountain

A frivolous city story describes a mythical merger between four of the biggest insurance companies. A young artist (the story goes) was commissioned to design a large crest for the new building of the combine, which was kept veiled until the opening ceremony. The chairman's wife pulled the veil away, and a gasp of horror went through the crowd as a set of four designs, each showing a lascivious scene, was revealed. 'What the hell's the meaning of this?' said the chairman. 'It's quite simple,' said the artist: 'up on the left is a man with his wife—that's the Legal and General:

below it is a man with a prostitute: that's the Commercial Union. On the right a man's discovered with another man's wife: that's the General Accident. Below is a man with his secretary: that's the Employers Liability.'

Most insurance companies are old-established city institutions, with head offices within the Square Mile. Their boards are part of the network of interlocking city directorships, usually with close connections with one or two merchant banks. Like the joint stock banks, they are made up almost entirely of outside directors, including peers, generals and admirals and old city surnames, who meet once a month for discussion and lunch. In 1959 it was calculated that out of 182 Insurance Directors, 59 had titles, 33 were bankers and only 29 had worked in insurance companies. A recent cartoon in the *Insurance Guild Journal* showed a decrepit old man staggering through the office: 'No, that's not an accident claim, Clogg', said one clerk to another, 'that's a Director.' Many managers, on the other hand, insist that they welcome a board of outside directors. 'The managers have more influence than anyone on the board', one of them told me: 'but management is a lonely occupation, and we appreciate the moral support of the board: they're a comforting and valuable part of the machine.'

The Companies, of course, have their peck-order. The most aristocratic—'the Eton of insurance'—is The Alliance (now merged with an even older company, the Sun) founded by Nathan Rothschild in 1824, and still with a Rothschild on the board. Their chairman is T. D. Barclay, a Suffolk landowner from the banking family. It specialises in high-class clients and ducal estates, but also enjoys taking exotic new risks: they were the first company to insure radioactive isotopes. One of the oldest surviving companies is the Royal Exchange, granted a royal charter in 1720, with its head office beside the tall portico of the Royal Exchange itself. Lord Kindersley is their 'governor' and their twenty-two directors include a duke, and an earl, two viscounts, and a baronet. They meet once a month: 'it's just a jolly good club', one banker chairman explained, 'hardly any of the directors know anything about insurance. All the real decisions are taken by their sub-committees.'

Some companies prefer chairmen who have actually worked in insurance, like Sir Stanley Norie-Miller and Sir Edward Ferguson. Lord Knollys (who was chairman of the Vickers industrial giant combine until 1962) was an insurance managing director for fifteen years. Sir Brian Mountain of Eagle Star (which has two marquesses, three baronets, two mountains and Kenneth Keith among its directors) is a former general manager, son of the founder of the company, and a member of an old Lloyd's family. Other large companies keep provincial roots: the Yorkshire in York has a local landowner, Lord Middleton, as its chairman. And the Norwich Union, still firmly rooted in East Anglia, has a former Lord Mayor of Norwich, Sir Robert Bignold; it is exceptional in having an old interest in property, and a large share in Anglia TV.

The biggest company for non-life business is the Royal, with strong Liverpool roots: it originated in 1845, when Mersey businessmen decided that London rates were too high, and it still has several Liverpudlians on its board, with an Etonian Liverpool merchant, T. H. Naylor, as its chairman. It was only in 1960 that it moved its boardroom to London. Like most other companies, the Royal is effectively run by its chief general manager, Sir Charles Trustam—an enterprising actuary from Cambridge, who worked his way through insurance; he has helped to improve the public relations of insurance and to introduce graduates.

In the last three years insurance companies, like other businesses, have been merging, and familiar old names like the Sun, the Atlas and the Sea have been absorbed with others. The numbers of competing offices, behind their frosted glass in the high streets, are diminishing. The mergers are partly the result of the particular hazards of insurance in America, where, since the end of the Civil War, the big British companies have been well established. The companies draw 70 per cent of their income from overseas, and the Royal group receives a bigger premium income from America than from Britain. But American claims are heavy: the San Francisco earthquake and fire in 1906 (when fifteen American companies could not pay up) cost eighteen British companies £11 million: and fires in America in the last few years have been heavy. When General Motors lost £12 million in the great fire of Detroit in 1953, half was paid by London companies. One company, the Yorkshire, has now decided to give up its American business, but most are waiting for better days, and strengthening themselves by mergers and 'rationalisation'. Larger volumes and smaller profits have made the insurance companies, like joint stock banks, settle down into big and staid institutions.

THE LIFE COMPANIES

But the most spectacular new insurance power lies with the big

Life companies, whose backgrounds are more humble and provincial. The Life companies (with relatively small initial capital) receive their money week after week, month after month, and pay back their lump sums only after a lifetime: and so they have funds ten times bigger than the non-Lifes'. The largest Life companies, like so many of the new powers of the last century, originated not from the city but from nonconformist movements of lower middle-class men in the provinces. That these poor men's clubs should have become the giants of the city is one of the ironies of twentieth-century finance. These are the ten biggest Life companies (most of which also do non-Life business) with funds, premium incomes and chairmen:[1]

	Life Funds	Premium Income	Chairman
Prudential	£947,987,973	£122,205,493	Sir Frank Morgan
Legal & General	£369,041,155	£46,510,676	Viscount Harcourt
Standard[2]	£260,225,063	£32,838,810	Sir James Campbell
Pearl	£257,167,279	£35,140,967	Geoffrey Kitchen
Co-operative	£211,362,852	£36,983,394	S. L. Kassell
Norwich Union Life	£181,163,085	£24,870,089	Sir Robert Bignold
Liverpool Victoria Friendly	£167,601,825	£21,944,780	F. J. Howe
Refuge	£151,489,456	£20,029,773	Sir W. Proctor-Smith
Sun Life	£139,561,093	£16,387,746	C. G. Randolph
Royal London	£138,363,356	£15,569,591	E. H. Haynes

THE PRU

By far the biggest is the legendary Prudential, with the motto 'Fortis Qui Prudens'. To the public, 'the Pru' is best known for its 16,000 'men from the Pru', the army of local travellers, many with small cars, dark suits and little books, who call at five hundred doors a week collecting the weekly insurance contributions. But to the city of London, the Pru presents a different face, for it is the largest single investor in the country: its *total* assets (a sixth of the assets of all Life companies) are more than a billion pounds. Though this is less than Barclays Bank, the Pru does not need to keep its money ready, like a bank's, for quick withdrawal: it can invest the whole sum, for a whole generation, without the need to call it back. Every week, the Pru has another two million pounds to invest—pouring from a bottomless well into government stock,

[1] Year ending December 31, 1959.
[2] Year ending November 15, 1959.

industry, or property. Pru and her colleagues, with their massive wealth, have stolen the thunder from the bankers. One city story tells how an industrialist called on his merchant banker to discuss raising some money. 'Can I discuss it with my colleagues?' said the banker. 'All right', said the industrialist, 'but don't pinch my taxi to go round to the Pru.'

The Pru is the biggest and oldest of the 'Industrial Life Companies'—those Life companies which grew up from the weekly savings of industrial workers. It originated as a company in 1848, but in June, 1852 a deputation of working men called on the secretary of the new company, and two years later a director appointed agents, to collect weekly savings from the Potteries and the weaving districts of Cheshire and Lancashire. Eager for thrift and self-help, and determined to avoid state aid, the artisans and workers embraced the new security of life insurance; by 1886 the Pru had more than *seven million* policies, with three-quarters of all the industrial life business.[1]

The proud Victorian character of the Pru is expressed in its towering Gothic castle in Holborn, just West of the city. The topography is significant, for like its rival the Pearl up the road, the Pru stands at arm's length from city influences.

The castle is an astonishing fantasy: outside there is a jumble of pointed windows, pinnacles, gables and steep roofs (in contrast to the plain red glass slab of the *Daily Mirror* opposite, which Pru men deplore). In the hall are walls of polished yellow tiles, Gothic pillars spring up between stained glass windows, and black-letter notices, like hymn-boards, announce the managers' offices.

Through the hall every morning 3,000 clerks and typists stream in to file, check and transcribe thirty million policies. In long, vault-like offices, rows of teenage girls write on cards behind wooden desks, or feed facts into punching machines. On the top floor is the Pru theatre, for amateur theatricals, in the basement are the diesel engines, on the second floor is the ecclesiastical board-room, with a square throne in the middle. In one corner a big glass goblet engraved with aeroplanes, trains and pylons, by Laurence Whistler, commemorates an unusually big sale of government stock from Messrs Mullens and Co. But in spite of the Gothic surroundings, the Pru people are very down-to-earth: lunch there is a much less pretentious and formal than lunch at a merchant bank—more like a liner than a country mansion. Drinks are served on the sideboard, there is lager instead of wine, wait-

[1] Dermot Morrah: *A History of Industrial Life Assurance.* p. 53.

resses instead of butlers, and plain English food. The conversation is matter-of-fact and professional.

The Pru tries to compose its board equally from three elements —management, old 'Prudential families' (Deweys, Harbens, Hornes, Lancasters, etc.) and outside directors. But nowadays fewer come from the families, and more from the managers. The chairman, Sir Frank Morgan, is a self-made man who has spent his whole life in the company, and so have the triumvirate who run the company (who are not on the board, but sit in on board meetings)—K. A. Usherwood, the General Manager, Leslie Brown, the Secretary and Chief Investment Manager, and F. M. Reddington, the Chief Actuary.

ACTUARIES AND CLERKS

Nearly all the senior managers of the Pru—and of other Life companies—carry after their names the initials FIA—Fellow of the Institute of Actuaries.[1] There are only eight hundred actuaries, more than half employed in Life insurance offices: ever since the Institute of Actuaries was founded in 1848—the same year as the Pru—the stability of Life insurance has depended on them. Actuaries are specialised mathematicians who, after a course which may take six years or more, are versed in the intricate statistics of men's lives on which life insurance depends, and prepare the expectation-of-life tables. Their training is narrow and bleak: most of it is done by correspondence, with a few lectures and classes, and there is a large proportion of failures. Only one in four of actuaries are graduates. Life insurance draws its meritocracy from a self-made, specialised world from outside the universities; a different world from the boardrooms of merchant bankers or Lloyd's. The actuaries are one of the highest-paid professions: the graph opposite shows the findings of the Pilkington Report on Doctors' Salaries in 1960.

The other 80,000 insurance workers (Life and non-Life) are less well placed: like bank clerks, they are caught between trade unionism and professionalism, and there is similar friction between the trade union, the 'Guild of Insurance Officials' (with 18,000 members), and the larger Staff Association, which they call 'the yellow union'. Since the war the wage of many insurance workers has slipped below manual workers', and at twenty-one their wage is much less: 'a marrying wage at a marrying age' is a union slogan.

[1] or FFA (Fellow of the Faculty of Actuaries, in Scotland).

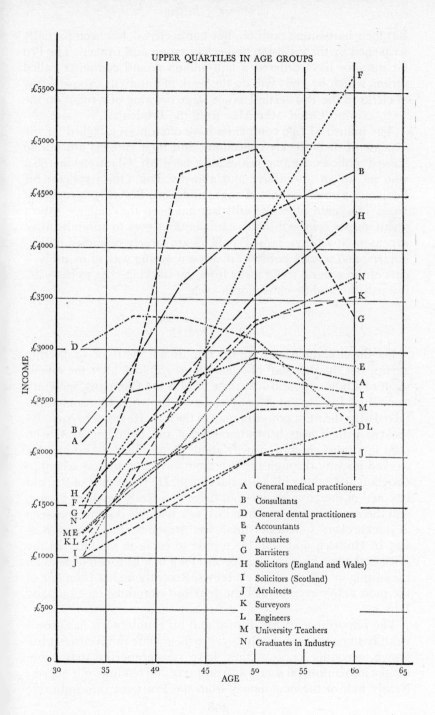

UPPER QUARTILES IN AGE GROUPS

A General medical practitioners
B Consultants
D General dental practitioners
E Accountants
F Actuaries
G Barristers
H Solicitors (England and Wales)
I Solicitors (Scotland)
J Architects
K Surveyors
L Engineers
M University Teachers
N Graduates in Industry

But their bargaining position, like banks clerks', has been partially weakened by the intrusion of mechanisation and women. The Pru for instance have ordered a half-million pound computer called Orion, which by 1963 will do the work of hundreds. Above a row of clerks in the Pru castle I saw a large drawing of a robot on the wall, saying: 'Orion—the Man from the Prudential.'

The industrial Life companies have often been attacked for the expense of their weekly collections, and their ruthless attitude to 'lapsed' policies. Among critics have been Mr. Gladstone in 1864, who set up an alternative and abortive Post Office system; Sir Benjamin Cohen's report of 1931; and Lord Beveridge's report of 1942. The main object of criticism has been the 'expense ratio'; about 30 per cent of a man's contributions goes to administrative expenses. Nowadays 'lapsed' policies are largely repaid to policy-holders, and weekly policies are anyway giving way to monthly— part of the general trend away from the working-class week-cycle, towards the middle-class month-cycle.

LESLIE BROWN

For the city, the Men from the Pru are not the 16,000 collecting agents, but the tiny staff of twenty-four who look after the investment of a billion pounds. At their head is the Company Secretary and Chief Investment Manager, Leslie Brown, FIA—sometimes talked of as the most powerful man in the city. He is stocky, quietly-spoken, with a neat bristly moustache and twinkling eyes, who talks in a frank, humorous way about the problems of his job. He worked his way through the Pru after leaving grammar school in Croydon and taking his actuarial course. He is not part of the 'old boy net' of the city: he does not drive in a Rolls, or shoot grouse, and there is no mention of him in *Who's Who*. He is sometimes seen at stockbrokers' lunches or financiers' banquets, but he prefers to stay in Holborn and wait for people to come to see him. In the stock exchange, his name is a legend: for a new issue can depend on the raising or falling of his eyebrows. Recently he has been one of the most active members of the Jenkins Committee on Company Law.

The importance of Mr. Brown and his counterparts has grown steadily since the war, firstly because their share in investment has grown, secondly because they have put proportionately more money into industrial shares and property and less into 'gilt-edged'. Nearly half of the new money from the Pru went into industry;

and between them the insurance companies have about £2,000 million invested in industrial companies. In some major industries, notably steel, the insurance companies together now hold nearly half the shares: they own about 37 per cent of the ordinary shares of the Steel Company of Wales, and there are few big industrial companies where the Pru is not a sizeable shareholder. When in 1953 the Conservatives began denationalising steel, the operation largely depended on the insurance companies' willingness to take up the shares.

The insurance companies are the elephants of the city, but chained elephants. In theory, they could combine to direct the Steel Company of Wales, and appoint its chairman; in practice, they carefully avoid entanglements with management. This shyness has several causes. Firstly, their money is not their own, but held in trust for their millions of policy-holders: their job is to obtain the maximum interest, not to run Britain's industry; insurance men murmur the word 'fiduciary', and (like civil servants) talk about 'those whom we serve'. Secondly, they know that if they tried to exercise their financial power, it could soon be circumscribed or nationalised. Thirdly, they don't *know* anything about management of industry.

Brown tries not to buy more than 7 per cent of the shares of any one industrial company: but even so, the Pru often finds itself the biggest single shareholder, and occasionally has to exercise its power. 'There was one small company where two groups of directors—one young, one old—were equally divided', Brown told me, 'and they came to me to ask what view the Prudential would take.' The idea of the Prudential taking a view was essentially repugnant, but eventually Brown did express his opinion—in favour of the older directors, who found a compromise.

Something of the potential influence of the Pru emerged in the dispute in the BSA company in 1956. A group of directors, led by John Sangster, opposed the sitting chairman, Sir Bernard Docker. For two months there were accusations and counter-accusations. Sir Bernard bought time on television to appeal to the shareholders. Lady Docker told the *Daily Telegraph*: 'We just had not got a Daimler any more. This has been the hardest day of my life.' But behind the battle between the Dockers and the directors, the Pru suddenly stood out as the most important factor. They were by far the largest shareholder, with 260,000 ordinary shares compared with the Dockers' 100,000, and they had recently approached Sir Bernard with a demand for an independent investigation into the company's affairs.

The climax came at the wild and noisy shareholders' meeting of August 1, 1956. Docker made an emotional appeal, and accused the directors of revealing the company's private affairs to the Pru behind his back: it transpired that Sangster had gone to the Pru as early as January with his worries. An anonymous 'Man from the Pru' explained their rôle, and told of the meeting with Sangster: 'I then learned about his own particular anxiety about the company. The action which the company took was in no way sponsored by the Prudential . . . It is our clear policy in the Pru not to interfere in the management of industrial companies in which we invest. In this case, when there were no other large shareholders whom we might consult, we came to the conclusion that we had a duty to all the shareholders as well as ourselves to take some action.' But it became clear that wherever the initiative lay, the revolt could not have happened without the Pru's support. By the end of the meeting Sir Bernard had been defeated, and John Sangster confirmed in his place.

The insurance companies (they insist) never compare notes about making investments: they normally only come together on the 'investment protection committee' (IPC), which meets once a month. Occasionally, when a company proposes a change of articles affecting shareholders' rights, the committee recommends companies to withhold their approval: without their support, a new share issue has small chance of success. Their most evident objection has been to the extension of 'non-voting' or 'A' shares, enabling families to retain their control through ordinary shares.

Can the insurance companies, with their growing investment, maintain this aloofness from industry? Should the biggest shareholders in the country be sleeping ones, only wishing to be woken in moments of outrage? It seems likely that the Pru will play a less passive rôle as it becomes more accustomed to its power, and already they are beginning to take rather more than a purely accountants' view: their staff of eight economists—as many as the Treasury's—provides an independent view of the industrial future. At the same time, insurance companies are becoming more aware of the responsibilities of their wealth and investment. One interesting innovation came from Sir John Benn, Chairman of the United Kingdom Provident Institution, the most original of the insurance chairmen, with many philanthropic interests. In 1961 he persuaded various insurance companies and other city institu-

tions to provide capital for a new company to exploit inventions—
a favourite interest of his—and to help fill the 'development gap'
to which the Radcliffe Report had drawn attention.

PENSION FUNDS

Since the war, an even more sudden wealth has emerged in the
city—pension funds. Nearly all big firms now have their own
pension schemes and, though many are administered by insurance
companies, the biggest are independent. The accumulation of
savings has risen so fast in ten years that the biggest pension funds
invest more than all but the top insurance companies. In 1958 the
total investment of pension funds in all shares amounted to
£1,625 million (for 'internally administered schemes and nationalised industries'). Since then (the Radcliffe Committee were told)
the increase has been about £150 million a year.

The pension fund controllers are not a spectacular cabal: they
have their own association, with an office above an ironmonger's
shop in Kensington, and a twice-yearly journal called *Superannua-
tion*. But they do not see much of each other. To the stock exchange,
the names of the investment managers—Brimblecombe of the
Airways fund, Andrews of Unilevers, Neil of Combined Petroleum,
Mulligan of Courtaulds—are more important than the chairmen
of the companies: each of them control millions of new money a
year. Probably their most prominent spokesman is Ross Goobey,
an actuary who runs the Imperial Tobacco pension fund in
Bristol; like other investment experts, he does not like to be too
close to the city.

Many pension funds are heavily restricted by their constitution:
some can only invest in gilt-edged, others have 50 per cent of their
money in industry. In a few, such as Marks and Spencer's, the
provident fund comes near—in theory—to controlling its own
company (in America the Sears Roebuck mail-order firm is
virtually controlled by the Sears Roebuck pension fund).

The biggest pension fund belongs, as one might expect, to
Britain's biggest employer, the National Coal Board. Its investments are run by an unobtrusive former stockbroker, P. D.
Johnstone, from a small office next door to *Coal* magazine, in
Chancery Lane. Johnstone administers two funds, one for staff,
one for mineworkers, which between them produce about £17
million of new money a year, and will amount to about £450
million of investment by 1970. He is responsible to 'investment

o*   411

committees', consisting of members of management and the mine-workers' union. But apart from occasional objections (such as an unwillingness to invest in oil shares) they do not interfere with investment policy. Johnstone doesn't see much of the other pension funds except at such functions as stockbrokers' lunch parties. The Coal Board prefer to paddle their own large canoe.

THE PARAPROPRIETORS

The British insurance companies are more powerful, and more free, than their counterparts in most Western countries. In America insurance firms, after scandals early in the century, were restricted in many states to investing only 5 per cent of their money in industrial shares: and they received a sharp shock in the slump, when Manhattan was full of half-empty buildings owned by insurance companies. In Britain there have been no such disasters.

The most persistent critic of insurance is Richard Titmuss, Professor of Social Administration at the London School of Economics, who helped to frame the Labour Party's pension plan: he has the distinction of having *worked* in an insurance company—the County Fire Office—before becoming a don. In his pamphlet *The Irresponsible Society* in 1960 Titmuss attacked the secrecy of the insurance companies (they refused to disclose the value of their assets to the Radcliffe Committee), their untrammelled freedom, and the narrow social attitudes of the 'Pressure Group State'. He maintains that this concentration of investment leads to centralisation and social irresponsibility. 'It is power concentrated in relatively few hands, working at the apex of a handful of giant bureaucracies, technically supported by a group of professional experts, and accountable, in practice, to no one.' The insurance companies reply that they are acting simply as the honest trustees of their policy-holders. 'We are not at all *eminences grises*', said Geoffrey Kitchen, chairman of the Pearl: 'it is not our policy to approach the government. We never try to use our influence—except when we are attacked, as with nationalisation. We're always trying to get the best possible return for our policy-holders. We have a very active and lively investment policy. We made almost 7 per cent on our investments last year—that's not bad.' But the insurance companies, after attacks on their methods of collection and their irresponsibility, and threats of nationalisation, are aware that their image is not too good: and they have spent some money on advertising their service to the public, with coy fables about animals and bees and a TV hero called Fred.

The economic power of insurance and pension funds is a phenomenon not only in Britain, but in the whole of the West, and its consequences are still unresolved. Father Harbrecht[1], a Jesuit economist, has compared the new financial institutions to the 'Great Domains' of eighth-century Europe—when feudal landlords, without actually owning property, had property vested in them by their occupation, and by the services and armies they provided. Similarly, Father Harbrecht suggests, 'control over property has gravitated to the managers of the financial institutions because they perform a function which is valuable to society. This function is to distribute among the generality of people the wealth which the corporations (that is, the big industrial companies) are creating.' To this new system he gives the name 'the paraproprietal society', 'because in it the connection between men and things, which is another way of saying property, is so attenuated that the fundamental function of property is not dominant . . .' He concludes that 'a man's relationship to things—material wealth —no longer determines his place in society (as it did in a strong proprietary system) but his place in society now determines his relationship to things. This is the consequence of the separation of control over property from individual ownership.'

The growth of insurance companies marks the latest stage in the divorce between property and power, which we will note in the ownership of the industrial Leviathans: the men whose money is used by the Pru and the Pearl to invest in ICI or Unilevers have no say in the running of those companies. 'Divorce between men and industrial things is becoming complete', wrote Adolf Berle: 'a Communist revolution could not accomplish that more completely.'[2]

In Britain this new power of the paraproprietors has grown up suddenly and obscurely, away from traditional institutions. However much they may see themselves as mere intermediaries, the investment managers, in their narrow funnel between the wealth of millions of policy-holders and the corporate wealth of industry, have a scope for patronage, for enterprise and social improvement scarcely equalled by any other group. But it is one of the tragedies of contemporary Britain that this powerful group has grown up in a bleaker, narrower atmosphere than

[1] Pension Funds and Economic Power. New York, 1959.
[2] Adolf A. Berle, Jnr: *Power without Property*, 1960. p. 76.

the old estates—with few of the cultural and social influences that play round the old professions and the universities. The failure of the old humanist world to come to terms with the new corporate institutions has had melancholy consequences.

26

PROPERTY

IN five years several of Britain's biggest cities have been face-lifted: they have changed from horizontal to vertical skylines. Steel and glass cliffs have pushed up between old churches; rows of Victorian shops have given way to big white office buildings; skyscrapers have grown up round St. Paul's. Two causes are discernible. Firstly, the relaxing of controls and the credit squeeze in 1958 after twenty years of restrictions. Secondly, the booming value of metropolitan land, which has turned the centres of London, Birmingham or Manchester into miniature Manhattans. Office space in the middle of London is now more expensive than New York's: the best sites in Manhattan (Jack Cotton told me in 1961) command 45/- per square foot, including rates and services: the Cheapside equivalent costs £3 per square foot.

The land itself in most cases is owned by the only people who could possibly afford it—the insurance companies. In property they have found an apparently safe resting place for part of their money-gusher. But the buying-up of the land, the planning, designing and leasing of the buildings is in the hands of a handful of speculator *entrepreneurs*—the property developers. There are few more astonishing collaborations than those between the cautious insurance bureaucracies, preoccupied with trusteeship and security, and the flamboyant self-made millionaires who, by borrowing huge sums from the insurance companies, have changed the face of the cities, and made their fortunes.

Property is a difficult commodity: it involves assessing and visualising the potential of sites, patiently bargaining and buying up clusters of old buildings, negotiating with local councils, planning new blocks to cram in the maximum office space. In New York, which was laid out from the beginning in large criss-cross blocks and where laws are more cut-and-dried, the operation is easier. But the very jumble and messiness of London, its zigzags, curves and old buildings, yield great prizes for those who can disentangle it.

In London and other cities surprising amounts of land are still owned by the old aristocratic families who first developed it—the

Dukes of Bedford and Westminster in Bloomsbury and Pimlico, or Lords Cadogan and Howard de Walden in Chelsea and Harley Street. Other large tracts are owned by the Crown and the Church Commissioners and other bits are still owned by individuals, department stores or British Railways. But it is the property developers—subject to the wayward controls of local councils—who are taking over the rôle of master town-planners, which was once the prerogative of dukes, earls or the monarch himself.

These tycoons are nearly all self-made millionaires, from modest middle-class families; most are Jewish, a few Scottish or Canadian. Among them are Harold Samuel, the unobtrusive chairman of Land Securities Investment Trust, in partnership with his cousin Basil, Bernard Sunley of Sunley Investments, Walter Flack of Murrayfield Real Estate Company, Maurice Wohl of the Wohl group, and the two biggest, Jack Cotton and Charles Clore of City Centre Properties.

The exploitation of property has helped to produce quick profits in other businesses; shops, breweries, or department stores which own sites in city centres have found their value multiplied. The property boom has helped to enrich the financier Charles Clore—who, for example, after buying the shoe-shop chain of Freeman, Hardy and Willis, sold the freeholds to insurance companies with a large capital profit: and tried to do the same by bidding for Watney's breweries, which has pubs on precious corner sites. Sir Hugh Fraser, the Glasgow draper who owns Harrods and Eskimo Foods, has made large profits by selling his freeholds—such as John Barkers and D. H. Evans. It might seem odd that so many English businesses sit on precious sites without exploiting them, and so fall an easy prey for take-overs. The loyalty to freeholds runs deep in the English character.

But the most successful property developer has concentrated on property alone. 'You can't diversify the human brain', says Jack Cotton: 'I only know about one thing—property. I've been in the property business only, all my life.'

THE WORLD OF JACK COTTON

To move from the gloomy castle of the Pru to Jack Cotton's suite at the Dorchester makes a sudden contrast. Cotton works always from suite 120, surrounded by Renoirs, vivacious secretaries, brisk surveyors, maps of London, press cuttings, and a stream of visitors. He sits talking, drinking and laughing at the long table in his drawing-room, sometimes till two in the morning, occasionally striding jauntily to the telephone to talk to Charles Clore, Erwin Wolfson, or somebody. 'Allo', he says. He is short, red-faced, fifty-nine, with smooth black hair, shrewd eyes, a pointed handkerchief in his pocket with a bow tie to match, a red carnation. His cars are called JC1 and JC2. He exudes the atmosphere, not of a businessman but of an impresario: he reminded me of the late Mike Todd. He likes to throw back his head with a chuckle, saying 'terrific thing!' In an age of conformity, Cotton's exuberant Dorchester life has become a legend. He loves publicity and has none of the suspicion of the press of Clore, Fraser or, Harold Samuel.

He can see large opportunities, backed up by attention to tiny details (when I first went to see him, a copy of my last book was lying on a table by the door). He is said to be able to walk down any of London's main streets, and reel off the value of each site; 'JC is like a computer', his bearded personal assistant explains, 'he can remember *everything*.' But he is also a master-salesman, enthusing others, and adept at dealing with local authorities (the former Chief Valuer of the LCC is one of his directors). In acquiring large sites, he works through a large private intelligence system of surveyors, patiently assembling the pieces of land until the jigsaw has been completed. Cotton sees himself as a creative person, boldly re-shaping the city skylines. 'Let's look at my Canalettos', he says, producing panoramas of projected sky-scrapers behind the Thames. 'It's a terrific thing, you know, to watch a building being demolished, creating plans for something to take its place and watching it rise and grow from the ground for the coming generations to look upon. Providing you think things out in the first place, you can't go wrong—always remembering that you can't please all the people all the time.'

His work is his life: he spends weekends at his house by the river at Marlow, loves the Crazy Gang, collects miniature bottles, and is very ambitious for his three sons—all in the business (one a surveyor, one a company secretary, one a solicitor). But like Roy Thomson he is single-minded, and buildings and 'big deals' (he has a paper clip called that) are his obsession. Apart from the vast capital gains involved, he is as excited by change as others are appalled; he visualises buildings with the same zest, if not the same taste, as dukes did before they lost interest in contemporary architecture and became professional preservationists.

Cotton is the son of a Birmingham Jewish export agent, who had South African connections. After school, first at King Edward's, Birmingham, then at Cheltenham College, he set up an estate agency business at the age of twenty-one. He soon began developing valuable sites and by the end of the war (which he spent partly in America, organising Jewish immigration to Palestine) he had several important Birmingham properties. He acquired a public company in 1946, to develop London and Birmingham properties with insurance companies—which grew enormously in the following ten years. In 1956 Geoffrey Kitchen, of the Pearl, noticing that Cotton was making large profits from property, suggested that the Pearl and Cotton should go into partnership. Since then Cotton has formed a host of subsidiaries with insurance companies (notably with the Pearl and the Legal and General) and also with industrial giants, including ICI, Shell-Mex, BP and Barclays Bank DCO—who all felt the need of Cotton's expertise in developing their properties. In 1960, when Cotton's company merged with his friend Clore's City Investments, they created the biggest property development group in the world, with assets of £67 million, and with Cotton at the helm. 'It's really quite simple', Cotton told me, sitting at the long table in his drawing-room. 'At one end of this table is an insurance company, which wants to invest its money, or a big concern looking for safe investments for its pension fund. At the other end is a company we are associated with—like City Centre Properties (Stores Developments), which wants money for development. And there, in the middle, sits Jack Cotton, who brings them together and works it all out.' It seems odd that these giant corporations, with all their resources, were not able to acquire the expertise and foresight to develop their own properties, but they were apparently too preoccupied with their own grindstones to have the time or staff to think about property. So more and more business has fallen into Cotton's lap.

The scale of property development has steadily grown. In the fifties, fortunes were made by Cotton and others, by buying up small sites and selling them together. When small sites began to be scarce, whole areas were developed—as in Hammersmith or Birmingham, costing as much as ten million each. Finally, Cotton and Clore have taken to buying up whole companies (like the Royal Exchange in Manchester), and developing the developers. These are some of the ramifications of Cotton and Clore's companies:

London:
  Bow Bells House
  Berkeley House
  Empress State, Earl's Court
  Royal Palace Hotel, Kensington
  London Casino
  Prince of Wales Theatre
  Hilton Hotel, Park Lane
  St. Christopher House
  Villiers House
  Constitutional Club
  Moor House
  70–88 Oxford Street
  Athenæum Court
  Verulam House
  Park Lane House
  Monico Site, Piccadilly
  Royalty Theatre

Birmingham:
  Tube Investment House
  Piccadilly Arcade
  Big Top
  Woolworth Building
  Mappin and Webb Building
  New Street Sites

Others:
  Manchester Royal Exchange
  Sheerness Harbour Company
  Alan House, Nottingham
  Avenue Foch/Rue Picot, Paris
  40 Wall Street, New York
  Grand Central City, New York

His joint companies have brought Cotton into contact with many leading British institutions—ranging from the Church Commissioners to the Zoo—and he is proud of his personal connections with the city and industrial establishments. ('They couldn't afford to let him fail,' one banker said.) Once a year at the Dorchester, Cotton holds a huge company luncheon. The small tables are presided over by his directors, his chief executives and his sons: while the high table is made up of Cotton's closest allies and friends. The list of names gives some idea of the scope of Cotton's operations. For instance, Mr. Cotton's high table for October 1960 is on pages 420 and 421.

PROPERTY AND PATRONAGE

In Britain Cotton's most celebrated project was his scheme to rebuild half Piccadilly Circus, in conjunction with Lord Harcourt's Legal and General Assurance. The Piccadilly plan came to light only by accident, because Cotton showed his plans on TV. A rumpus followed, culminating in a public hearing in December 1959. It not only exposed the haphazard approach to London's town-planning, and the uncertain hand of the LCC: it showed, too, how far the ownership of new buildings had become divorced from responsibility. The freehold owners of the Piccadilly site were the Legal and General, but they had little say in the design of the building, which was fixed by Cotton, his architects, and his surveyors (Jack Cotton and Partners). The eventual tenants have

1	2	3	4	5	6	7	8	9	10	11	12	13	14	15	16	17	18	19	20	21
CHARLES FORTE, ESQ.	SIR JOHN ELLIOT	BASIL MAVROLEON, ESQ.	ALDERMAN C. JAMES HARMAN	SIR IFOR EVANS	EVELYN B. BARING, ESQ.	SIR ANDREW MacTAGGART	C. M. VIGNOLES, ESQ.	LORD COTTENHAM	SIR LEONARD SINCLAIR	E. A. BINGEN, ESQ.	F. M. SIR CLAUDE AUCHINLECK	DR. VAN EYLE	SIR ROBERT RENWICK, BT.	E. A. KEKICH, ESQ.	CHARLES CLORE, ESQ.	SIR MORTIMER WARREN	THE HON. WALWORTH BARBOUR	SIR SOLLY ZUCKERMAN	SIR CHARLES HAMBRO	ERWIN S. WOLFSON, ESQ.

(1) Chairman, Forte's Ltd; (2) Chairman, Thos Cook & Son Ltd; (3) Chairman, London & Overseas Freighters Ltd; (4) Alderman & Lieutenant of the City of London; (5) Provost, University of London; (6) Director, Baring Bros & Co Ltd; (7) Chairman, Power Securities Ltd; (8) Managing Director, Shell-Mex & BP Ltd; (9) Director, Lockhart, Smith & Co Ltd; (10) ex-Chairman, Esso Petroleum Co Ltd; (11) Deputy Chairman, ICI; (12) Chairman, Murrayfield Real Estate Co Ltd; (13) Director, Philips Electrical Industries Ltd; (14) Director, ATV; (15) Commercial Attaché, U.S. Embassy; (16) City & Central Investments Ltd; (17) Secretary, Church Commissioners; (18) H.E. American Ambassador to Israel; (19) Scientific Adviser, Ministry of Defence; (20) Deputy Chairman, Hambros Bank Ltd; (21) President, Grand Central Building

no control over the architecture. The owner and the occupiers were equally irrelevant. The decisive planner—the 'paraproprietor'—was the go-between, Jack Cotton.

In nearly all new building, Cotton works through his own firms of architects, Cotton, Ballard and Blow—who employ over seventy architects. But his most spectacular coup has been in Manhattan, where he put up nine million pounds to collaborate with the American Erwin Wolfson in building Grand Central City in Park Avenue 'the largest office building in the world', with 59 storeys, 63 lifts, eight moving staircases and 25,000 office workers. In America the insurance companies have fought shy of large property investments since the slump: but Cotton, with his massive support from British insurance giants, was able to barge in, and having found Pan-American and other tenants, quickly recouped his

	GEOFFREY KITCHEN, ESQ.	W. LIONEL FRASER, ESQ.	S. C. JOSEPH, ESQ.	B. HUBERT CHAPPELL. ESQ.	SIR SIMON MARKS	HUGH FRASER, ESQ.	SIR MILES THOMAS	HAROLD SAMUEL, ESQ.	SIR NUTCOMBE HUME	L. FRANCK, ESQ.	F. A. COCKFIELD, ESQ.	ERNEST TAYLOR, ESQ.	J. H. BUSCOMBE, ESQ.	LORD LUCAS OF CHILWORTH	SIR HOWARD ROBERTSON	H. N. SPORBORG, ESQ.	SIR CHARLES TAYLOR, M.P.	A. DICKSON WRIGHT, ESQ.	SIR RONALD M. HOWE	SIR GERVAIS TENNYSON-D'EYNCOURT
ESQ.	22	23	24	25	26	27	28	29	30	31	32	33	34	35	36	37	38	39	40	41

Inc.; (22) Chairman, Pearl Assurance Co Ltd; (23) Chairman, Helbert Wagg & Co Ltd; (24) Chairman, Clifford Motor Components Ltd; (25) President, American Chamber of Commerce; (26) Chairman, Marks & Spencer Ltd; (27) Chairman, House of Fraser Ltd ; (28) Chairman, Monsanto Chemicals Ltd; (29) Chairman, Land Securities Investment Trust Ltd; (30) Chairman, Charterhouse Investment Trust Ltd; (31) Managing Director, Samuel Montagu & Co Ltd; (32) Managing Director, Boots Pure Drug Co Ltd ; (33) Chairman, Unigate Ltd; (34) Director, Shell-Mex & BP Ltd; (35) — (36) Architect; (37) Director, Hambros Bank Ltd; (38) Chairman, Grosvenor House Ltd; (39) Surgeon; (40) Chairman, Vine Products Ltd; (41) Director, Buxton Estates Ltd.

capital sum. He loves talking about Grand Central City, and a special song has been recorded to commemorate it:

Hoi, but it's big.
It's gotta be big.
Why does it have to *be* so big?
Because it's gonna be the heart of business and industry—
and man, that's gotta be big.
Big—because it's
Grand Central City,
Grand Central City.

From its skeleton of steel
to the structure very real
for the largest office building in the world . . .
Oh men who have courage, of Anglo-American fame:
Erwin Wolfson, Jack Cotton!

Jack Cotton's connection with the Legal and General is fairly typical of the British property pattern: the insurance companies are usually content to leave the building to the developer. This delegation of responsibility has a depressing effect on patronage, for the speculator, using the money of an anonymous insurance company to build for anonymous tenants, tends towards anonymous architecture—squeezing in the maximum possible floor space. The building will not express the personality of the owner, or the tenants; it need only be a safe investment. Some developers are relatively daring: Maurice Wohl for instance (who collects modern paintings) built a handsome ribbed edifice called State House in Holborn—off the beaten track for expensive buildings— with a Barbara Hepworth sculpture in the courtyard. It lay empty for two years, and was eventually taken by a civil service department, the Department for Scientific and Industrial Research.

Some big firms—such as Shell, AEI, or English Electric—still commission their own buildings. But most office blocks are designed for no one in particular. Whether this is worse for the architect than designing for a wilful and tasteless client, like Shell or AEI, is debatable: the Vickers skyscraper, owned by the Legal and General, is a much more up-to-date and exciting affair than Shell's. But at least the company's buildings express some kind of personality, with someone to take the blame.

Will the insurance companies continue to leave property development to outsiders? Some insurance men, including Lord Harcourt (who is not only chairman of the Legal and General, but chairman of the Oxford Preservation Trust) are beginning to take a larger interest in development, and the Legal and General already has its own development schemes. But most companies are content to take their profits from their joint companies, and avoid interfering in management, as with their other investments. 'We couldn't hope to have the kind of staff and expertise that someone like Cotton has', said one insurance man, and Cotton agrees: 'you can't pay a man £10,000 a year in an insurance company and expect him to be in the same street as a man who's making money for himself.'

Anatomy of Britain

PART THREE

27

CORPORATIONS

As the banker, as a symbol of economic power, passed into the shadows, his place was taken by the great industrial corporation.
J. K. Galbraith: American Capitalism.

As the twentieth century moves into afternoon, two systems—and (thus far) two only—have emerged as vehicles for modern industrial economics. One is the socialist commissariat; its highest organization at present is the Soviet Union. The other is the modern corporation, most highly developed in the United States.
Professor Adolf Berle.

WE come to a new and crucial sector of British life which is ostensibly unconnected with earlier institutions—the industrial corporations and their professions and managers. The world of country-house amateurs, though it has influenced their way of life, has little relevance to the provincial factories and offices of corporation scientists, salesmen, technicians, accountants. Since the last war, the corporations have bothered little with parliament (few now employ a Member as their spokesman), and lobby direct with Whitehall bureaucrats. The old professions of the universities, the Law and the Church have few points of contact with them, and the press, busy with the romantic regions of politics, parliament or diplomacy, hardly ever penetrate inside the walls and pyramids, except on missions of congratulation. The boards and managers of Shell or Unilever are less known than the obscurest backbencher.

The bankers and financiers, who helped to give birth to some of the industrial giants, have seen their offspring becoming far richer than themselves. Even politicians now accept their inevitability. The biggest corporations have become supra-national bodies, with interests far wider than those of the British economy, involved in an elaborate balancing trick with rivals and governments all over the world. And as European countries come closer to each other and to the Americas, so the corporations (it seems) will grow to American dimensions.

THE NEW LEVIATHANS

The names of ICI, Shell, Unilever or Imperial Tobacco

dominate hundreds of thousands of Britons. To visit the head-quarters of a big industrial corporation is like visiting a foreign country and, talking to their managers, one is aware of a complex, self-enclosed microcosm, held together with oil, soap or steel. These industrial organisms, inside and outside the organism of a nation, are one of the most mysterious phenomena of the Western world. Shell-land or Unilever-land are kingdoms without kings. When in 1651 Hobbes wanted to depict the nature of the modern State, he showed on the frontispiece of his book *Leviathan* a sceptred king whose body was entirely made up of small men. In the twentieth century the industrial corporations—both publicly and privately owned—have taken over much of the rôle of Leviathan. But they have no kings. No one man controls or owns them; and at their head are committees of men who are themselves an organic part of the body of the whale.

Their nebulous characters are aptly expressed by the French word for limited company—*anonyme*. Their palaces staring at each other across the Thames (like those of 17th-century dukes) are different universes, and to the conformity of work is added the conformity of their home life—with Shell suburbs and ICI suburbs crystallising over the country. They have bureaucracies in many ways similar to Whitehall's or the Pru's, but much more self-contained and all-embracing, with their own factories and territories and international ramifications.

There are many features of these new Leviathans which are disturbing—their conformism, their introversion, their secretive-ness, the narrow limits of their competition, and, above all, their endemic elephantiasis. But few critics can suggest any alternative system for running an industrial economy. The difference between private corporations and nationalised ones is diminishing, as also in Russia and America. It is difficult to visualise the great corporations being replaced in the next fifty years; they have begun to achieve the staying power of nations themselves. Big whales can still gobble up smaller ones, and the giants at the beginning of the century—Bradford Dyers, Fine Cotton Spinners, J. & P. Coats—are no longer the biggest. But it is hard to imagine the big diversified companies, like ICI or Unilever, losing their supremacy.

Before considering British giants, we must take a glance at America, for there the corporation is most developed and most thoroughly studied, and British companies are rapidly approxi-mating to the American pattern. For the past thirty years American

professors of economics and law have been observing, with unconcealed bewilderment, the inexplicable growth of big business. Since
the thirties, about 130 corporations have been responsible for half
the manufacturing industry of America;[1] the *number* of giants has
hardly changed during that time, but their power has steadily
increased. Though they certainly compete in salesmanship, advertising and research, their competition in prices is narrow; and the
classical economists' free-for-all competition, with firms subjected
to the 'judgment of the market-place', is not evident when a few
vast firms make up an oligopoly.

What is uncanny is the manner of their development. For as
Professor Berle and Dr. Means first explained thirty years ago,
their nominal owners, the shareholders, have no effective control
over their policy; and more recently ownership has separated still
further from control, through the emergence of the insurance
companies (the paraproprietors) as the principal shareholders
(see pp. 412–413). The days of autocratic heads, such as Henry
Ford, John D. Rockefeller, or Lord Nuffield, are largely past, and
most of the Leviathans have broken away from the families and
financiers who first founded them. It is the absence of controlling
owners which makes the corporations such an odd development in
Western economic history. 'The capital is there', Professor Berle
has written, 'so is the capitalism. The waning factor is the
capitalist.'

The board of directors, except in cases of spectacular mis-
management or feud, when shareholders unite to rise in revolt
against them, are responsible to no one but themselves. They are
managers without bosses, and they elect one another: they are
'tiny self-perpetuating oligarchies'. The extent to which the
corporation can be controlled from outside the firm is severely
limited. Economists are led to the confusing conclusion that the
corporations, like perpetual clocks, run themselves—a conclusion
which many of them reach with obvious distress and alarm.
'The young lad mastering the technique of his bicycle may legiti-
mately shout with pride, "Look, Ma, no hands", but is that the
appropriate motto for a corporate society?' (Berle).

In the terms in which left-wing critics were accustomed to
regard capitalist organisations in the thirties, the existence of this
small group of giants would be hardly short of a nightmare. But
even quite radical economists have been surprised to discover that
the corporations behave better, and more in the public interest,

[1] Edward S. Mason: *Corporation in Modern Society*, 1959. p. 5.

than they had ever expected. Several explanations have been offered: the development of a managerial class, concerned with prestige as much as profits; the competing pressures of specialist departments; the growth of a 'countervailing power' from trade unions or retailers; or the emergence of a 'corporate conscience'. But most American economists agree that this elephantiasis is inevitable and not necessarily overpowering.

The rôle of the corporation in modern America is the subject of heated and anxious debate: should they stick firmly to making profits (as the British are inclined to prefer) leaving the individual, the State and local communities to look after the rest? Or should they face up to new responsibilities of patronage, of building up new communities, of culture and education? Some critics have found the last alternative more alarming than the first: 'Our ancestors feared that corporations had no conscience' (to quote Berle again); 'We are treated to the colder, more modern fear that, perhaps, they do.'

In Europe since the war industries have tended to the American pattern: instead of a mass of local or family firms competing, there are now often only three or four huge rivals. In Britain the concentration has increased rapidly in the last few years. In 1953 (according to Sigmund Prais) the hundred largest companies in Britain, measured by net assets, accounted for 31 per cent of the total industrial profits:[1] since then, with take-overs, mergers and growth, concentration has spread.[2] Like the Americans, the British giants have become independent of financiers and the city. They, too, are often without single dominating heads, and are ruled by tiny self-perpetuating oligarchies: they, too, have continued much the same under different governments. European firms have found themselves competing increasingly with Americans, and competition, whether between firms, nations or newspapers, often makes competitors resemble each other.

There are big differences. In Britain the amalgamation is still continuing. The British managerial revolution is less developed than in America. The nationalised area of British industry is much larger, and all industry has been influenced by the threat of nationalisation. British corporations are apt to be less ruthless, more tolerant than the Americans, and perhaps more prone to administrative corpulence and gout. The very biggest firms in

[1] *See* S. J. Prais: The Financial Experience of Great Companies. *Economic Journal*, June, 1957.
[2] *See* pages 494-5.

Britain—notably Shell and Unilever—are bigger in proportion to the country than their American counterparts and belong more to an international, than a national economy. And in the Common Market they are likely to become much more supra-national.

And the British corporations are much less known than the Americans. Many firms since the war have spent large sums on prestige advertising, but that has been designed to divert, rather than to inform, the reader, with eccentric dialogues, joke drawings, or photographs of children: in fact to show the corporations not as important, but as unfrightening. When Shell celebrated their golden jubilee in 1957, they sent a superbly illustrated book to all their shareholders—not about oil, but about sea-shells.

To generalise about corporations is dangerous; their histories, products and managers have moulded very different personalities. I have therefore tried to describe the three biggest firms in Britain, which are not only important in themselves, but also show patterns into which other industries are shaping.

In terms both of sales and assets the three largest are Shell, Unilever and ICI (excluding British Petroleum, which comes just above ICI, but has 56 per cent of its shares owned by the British government). These three are enormous even by world standards: Shell is the third biggest, by sales, in the world, and Unilever sixth. These were the world's largest companies in 1961, as calculated by *Fortune* magazine:

Company	Headquarters	Sales ($ 000)	Assets ($ 000)	Net Profits ($ 000)	Employees
1. General Motors	Detroit	12,736,000	8,553,085	959,042	595,151
2. Standard Oil	New York	8,034,736	10,090,437	688,573	140,000
3. Royal Dutch/Shell	London/The Hague	5,481,316	8,900,080	496,958	250,000
4. Ford	Dearborn, Mich.	5,237,889	4,031,506	427,886	160,181
5. General Electric	New York	4,197,535	2,551,258	200,072	250,621
6. Unilever	London/Rotterdam	3,883,510	2,259,454	149,470	293,351
7. U.S. Steel	New York	3,698,495	4,780,849	304,171	225,081
8. Socony Mobil Oil	New York	3,178,064	3,455,382	182,610	69,000
9. Chrysler	Detroit	3,007,049	1,368,534	32,154	105,410
10. Texaco	New York	2,980,309	3,646,773	391,751	56,658

SHELL

By far the biggest in Britain is Shell, third in world sales after General Motors and Standard Oil. Its size is difficult to comprehend. It produces 14 per cent of the free world's oil. Its annual income, of £2,603 million in 1959, is bigger than the entire national income of Switzerland or South Africa. Its annual expenditure is more than the whole annual investment of Britain overseas. Its tankers alone, amounting to ten million tons of shipping, form by far the biggest fleet in the world—four times the tonnage of the biggest passenger group (P and O). The towering importance of Shell in the British economy—and its conservatism—is aptly symbolised by its stone skyscraper block on the Thames, containing 6,000 people and dwarfing the Houses of Parliament opposite.

Shell is the most inscrutable of the corporations in Britian: oil has its own complex, convoluted problems, and oilmen have been sufficiently harassed and attacked in the past to be defensive and touchy about their affairs and their size. 'Groupthink' is a noticeable characteristic. The outsider might see Shell as a single, solid force with firm opinions. But inside, the picture is much more fragmented—like the inside of Whitehall—with hundreds of smaller Shells interacting, engrossed in technical problems.

Shell is not strictly a British firm. More properly known as 'Royal Dutch/Shell', it was the result of the spectacular merger of 1906 between Henri Deterding, the brilliant little Dutch financier, and Marcus Samuel, the trader from Whitechapel who began by importing sea-shells from the Far East—which gave their name to his vast oil empire. The resulting combine of Royal Dutch/Shell—generally referred to as 'The Group'—is controlled by two parent companies, and the British parent—confusingly called 'Shell Transport and Trading'—controls only 38 per cent. But the financial headquarters of the Group are in London, and it is there that, three times a week, the managing directors meet. The British have 38 per cent of the shares, Americans 24 per cent, and Dutch only 16 per cent. Correspondence is in English, finance in sterling, and the whole Group is English-speaking. The collaboration between English and Dutch, with their complementary characteristics, is difficult but workable.

But to speak entirely in terms of English and Dutch is misleading, for Shell in its staffing is probably the most international firm in the world, and its internationalisation over the last fifteen years has been an operation without commercial parallel. Shell, more than any other giant, has found itself on the angry frontiers of nationalism and race; and unlike its American rivals it had no safe home oilfields to which it could retreat. The word nationalism sent a shiver down its spine, and as early as 1938 it experienced its first great trauma, when the Mexican Government expropriated the rich oil wells of the Shell subsidiary, El Aguila. Its overseas branches were then run largely by British and Dutch graduates, with benevolent paternalism of the District Commissioner kind. There is an old Shell story about a cable received from Shanghai before the war: 'Lubricant sales dropped 5 per cent. Send urgently two more cricket blues.'

The fate of El Aguila showed that paternalism was not enough. And so, after the war, the seven managing directors instituted a vast scheme for 'regionalisation'. They realised that their only chance of retaining their vast and valuable empire was to make every possible concession to local nationalism. They pushed through—*ahead* of politics—the quick recruitment and promotion of Asians, Africans or South Americans, giving them as much independence as they dared. They tried to avoid choosing local managers by Western or 'old boy' standards, and to accept the values of local communities. For many of the old-style adminis-trators the change was appalling (I remember seeing their bewilderment in East Africa in the early fifties when apparently incompetent Africans were promoted). But it was carried through, helped by Shell's hard international experience, and the geo-graphical detachment of the seven men. In tricky countries such as Ceylon or Sudan, they tried to recruit key political figures—to 'buy in the bell-wether', in their own phrase. They became deeply involved in local problems—subsidising education, creating a 'commercial class', bringing Africans to London. It was a painful operation, full of disappointments and mistakes, but it achieved quickly and relentlessly—and in striking contrast to BP—the obliteration of the imperial idea alongside which Shell had been built. As regionalisation progressed, so Shell was able to send a Ceylonese to Thailand, an Egyptian to Trinidad, a Thai to the Philippines, or a South African to Brazil.

The regionalisation made it not only international but looser. 'The Group' now has about 500 separate Shells all over the world, each with its apparently autonomous general manager. In many countries the Group holds only a proportion of the shares (65 per cent in America, 70 per cent in France). When one looks at the headquarters or house magazines of West African Shell, South

American Shell or Shell Française, one could well be unaware that any other Shell existed: for the employees it is this local entity, rather than the shapeless mass of the Group, which commands their loyalty. Likewise the British subsidiary, jointly owned with BP and awkwardly called 'Shell Mex and BP', has quite separate existence, in its own big squat building on the north side of the river. Like Shell Française or Shell Italiana, it is purely a marketing organisation.

Regionalisation has made the Group's job more subtle, more specialised, and needing relatively fewer metropolitan people. In ten years, though Shell's output has nearly doubled, the numbers of British and Dutch recruited to the Group has remained the same, and the need for the old-style administrators, as for district commissioners, has virtually disappeared. But the hard core remains the 5,500 'expatriates', of whom 2,100 are British—of whom in turn about 1,000 are administrative, as opposed to technical. These thousand can be compared roughly in their numbers and in their jobs with the Foreign Office, and in most Asian or African capitals Shell men have a status second only to the diplomats.

They are the earliest corps of industrial graduates. Shell was the first firm to recruit systematically from the universities: in 1910 it gave £10,000 to set up an Appointments Board. Four-fifths of the young Shell administrators are now graduates—and they are recruited widely from Redbrick.

Shell is less formal than the Foreign Office and less bound by hierarchies and titles, but for that reason Shell men are apt to be very *protocolaire*. They have been immersed in oil abroad, living in Shell houses, or in Shell compounds, going to Shell parties at Shell country clubs, travelling in Shell planes to visit Shell towns in Shell oilfields. They talk about oil and the Group in the same tone diplomats use for HMG. 'I wish the administrators wouldn't talk about oil as if it was a *faith*', said one senior Shell rebel: 'anyone would think it was a church. At least the technologists aren't fooled by that.' Shell deals in a single commodity, but many executives have never actually dirtied their hands with oil. One told me how he was once attending a conference about marketing naphtha. 'By the way', he asked half-way through, 'has anyone actually *seen* any naphtha?' Nobody had.

SEVEN MEN

At the head of the Group, meeting three times a week in the

skyscraper boardroom are the managing directors, 'The Seven Men'. They are a legend within Shell and in the city. Their salaries (secret) are each around £50,000 a year—five times the prime minister's. Much of their lives is spent flying in private Shell planes between London, The Hague, and foreign Shells; luxury planes, with beds, dressing-rooms and arm-chairs are waiting at two hours' notice.[1] At their London meeting they do not bother themselves with sums of less than half a million pounds.

The seven are very much a product of the managerial revolution. All of them have worked their way through the firm, without any considerable shareholding. They have a smoothness in sharp contrast to the founders, and are distinctively committee-men—though they dislike the word: ('Only a committee', one Shell man remarked, 'could have commissioned that South Bank building.')

Four of the seven, as stipulated by Deterding's agreement, are Dutch, and the first two live in Holland. They are Lykle Schepers, aged fifty-six, the expert on research and chemicals; Jan Brouwer, an ex-geologist in charge of exploration and production; Arnold Hofland, a tall, tough multi-lingual ex-Brigadier in the British army, in charge of marketing; and the chairman, John Loudon. The three British directors are Harold Wilkinson, a former head of Canadian Shell, in charge of North America and the Far East; John Berkin, a quiet engineer in charge of co-ordinating oil, considered by many to be the most brilliant; and David Barran, a Winchester and Cambridge man, who came from marketing oil in America—the youngest and perhaps most interesting. But the differences of nationality are not very evident; all the Dutchmen speak fluent mid-atlantic English, and all the seven have spent long periods abroad, becoming international men.

The most obviously international is the chairman, John Hugo Loudon, who has a house in Holland, a flat in Grosvenor Square, speaks five languages and spends 150 hours in the air every year. Although born and brought up in Holland, he speaks polished, slightly nasal English, which sounds more American that Dutch. He is tall, elegant, with wavy grey hair and restless eyes. He has the manner of a diplomat, not a tycoon, and he comes from a Dutch diplomatic family. His grandfather was a Governor-General of the Dutch East Indies, his uncle was Foreign Minister, and he himself is a Jonkheer—a kind of Dutch baronet—and a KBE. He has a fine collection of paintings in Holland, including a

[1] *See The Aeroplane*, April 27, 1961.

Rembrandt self-portrait. His father was chairman of Royal Dutch, and one of his sons is a successful young Shell engineer, married to an English baronet's daughter. The Loudons have become a Shell royal family.

John Loudon thus grew up in a statesmanlike home, at a time when much of the oil business was still rough and tough, but international tact was beginning to be valued. He showed his diplomatic gifts in Venezuela, when he went as general manager in 1944 and pushed through rapid Venezualisation. Three years later, at forty-one, he became one of the Seven Men—taking over as chairman ten years later.

'Most of my job', Loudon told me, 'is strictly commercial . . . I'm concerned far more with inside problems than with outside ones.' The diplomacy, he insisted, is in the hands of the local general managers. He is, like most chairmen, concerned with public relations—'I don't know why, but oil always seems to me to have a smell to it'—and he spends much time trying to dispel damaging ideas. 'The dogs may bark, but the caravan moves on.'

SHELL RE-SHAPED

Shell's managerial revolution after Deterding's departure produced massive problems, and large areas of bureaucratic muddle. The Dutch-British sides, entrenched in London and The Hague, gave wonderful opportunities for cross-purposes and duplication. Private princedoms still lingered.

Loudon took a sensational step. In 1959 he and his board engaged an American firm of efficiency experts—called McKinsey Inc.—to recommend changes of organisation. It was by far the biggest investigation ever commissioned in Britain. A team of crew-cut graduates flew over to London and The Hague, sat on a committee with Shell experts, interviewed managing directors, tramped round the offices. After nine months—the usual gestation period—they gave birth to a drastic and largely secret report, which was almost totally accepted. Many of the ideas indeed were thought to be Loudon's own, and McKinsey provided timely corroboration.[1]

London and The Hague were to have quite separate functions —London's including finance and marketing—and the two centres were to be run as one. Several senior men were discreetly declared redundant. A big and growing subsidiary of the Group, Shell

[1] *See* Professor Parkinson, p. 457.

Chemicals—which deals with an expanding line of business—was to be hived off as a separate company. The Seven Men were to have more time for thought and were told to detach themselves (as the Cabinet signally fails to do) from day-to-day problems (one of them had to be ticked off for taking too much interest in detail), and to relieve them a new race of 'Co-ordinators' or 'Solomons' was devised. The new scheme was an attempt to produce the 'perfect pyramid' which is every efficiency expert's dream; in Shell, as in most companies, there were bound to be bumps in the pattern where personalities obtruded; the Group still has a lot of top hamper, and Parkinsonian tendencies successfully defeated a good deal of the reorganisation of the chemical side. But the McKinsey plan is an example of self-analysis more drastic (though no more necessary) than any in Whitehall.

There is something inherently baffling about finding at the top of a huge department a boss with the evasive title of co-ordinator: but this is, of course, part of the discreet rôle of Shell headquarters which, like the Treasury, prefer to issue advice instead of instructions. Its activities are incomprehensible to the outsider, for it is turned tightly in on itself, with its own commercial ambassadors negotiating between one Shell and another. (See chart on page 437.)

Between the distant outposts of Shell and the London headquarters lies the same contrast of improvisation and formality as exists between African embassies and the Foreign Office. But the bureaucracy of Shell headquarters—as of other Leviathans—is more opaque than anything in Whitehall. No parliamentary questions or select committees disturb *its* workings, whose deadening fatuity is terrifyingly conveyed in Thomas Hinde's novel about Shell, *For the Good of the Company*. The cream of Oxbridge graduates find themselves confronted with the rules of a third-rate clerkdom, and a jargon of 'Shellese' more fatuous than Treasury language: 'the price is going down' is transformed to 'we would think the price is going down' and finally to (since 'feeling' is regarded as more democratic than 'thinking') to 'we would feel that in view of the depression in the general market level'. One Shell graduate recorded for me a selection of the actual changes that superiors had made on various people's letters:

urgent	a matter of some urgency
we hope you will let us know	we would ask you to let us know

please let us know if you need further help	we would be pleased to assist on receipt of your detailed advice
uneconomical	anti-economical
also	a further complication is the fact that . . .
without a precedent	. . . lacks an established historical background
will lower the prices	will have a depressing effect on the general market level
we would prefer to defer alteration of these prices until the necessity occurs	we suggest that the question of possible alterations to the present transfer prices should be considered in the event of competition arising when they may be reviewed in the light of the situation at that time

The vital question for Shell is the price of oil, and on this point most oil men are sensitive. For although the cartel arrangements of the thirties are now broken up, the oil giants, or 'seven sisters'— Standard Oil of New Jersey, Socony Mobil Oil, Shell, BP, Caltex, Gulf and Compagnie Française des Pétroles ('Total') —still dominate the western world, all selling petrol *at the same price*. Shell is insistent that the uniformity of prices at the retail pumps (which is only 17 per cent of its business in Britain) does not represent any lack of competition. In other respects their competition is genuine, though often depressing and defensive—buying up service stations, clubbing together to keep a new man out. The fight of the seven sisters can be seen all through Europe—in the clamour of advertising from the shells of Shell, the flying horses of Mobilgas (Socony Mobil Oil) or the blue-and-red ovals of Esso (Standard Oil of New Jersey). At the pump, they compete with wash-basins, maps, motels, radio commercials or special ingredients—with almost everything except price.

The fight is dominated by Standard Oil and Shell, and their world-wide duel—involving sheikhs, geologists, garages, prime ministers, universities, café-owners—has transformed deserts, created cities and modernised countries. In the last ten years, mainly because of its large share of the markets of Asia and Europe, Shell has been catching up on Standard Oil, and in the next ten may well overtake it. Both companies have cut themselves loose from outside finance. Shell poured £1,900 million of capital into building and exploration in the five years from 1954 to 1959; but less than 10 per cent of that came from outside the Group. 'The capital requirements of the international oil business', said Lord Godber to the Radcliffe Committee, 'have outgrown the money markets of the world.' More than half Britain's income from

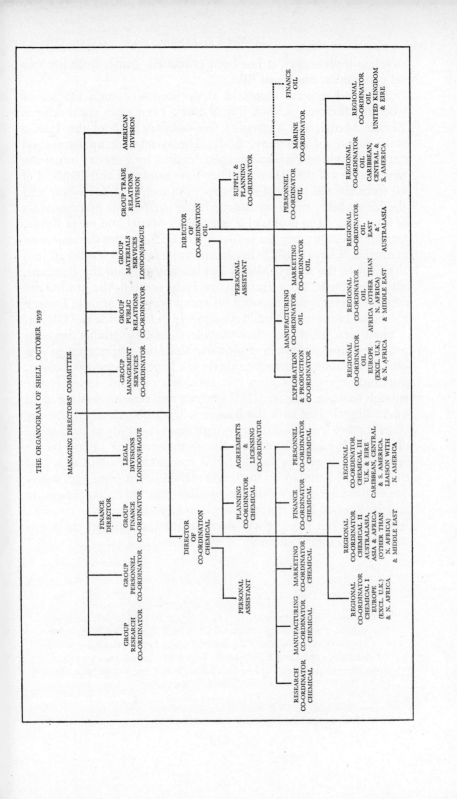

THE ORGANOGRAM OF SHELL   OCTOBER 1959

MANAGING DIRECTORS' COMMITTEE

GROUP RESEARCH CO-ORDINATOR

GROUP PERSONNEL CO-ORDINATOR

FINANCE DIRECTOR

GROUP FINANCE CO-ORDINATOR

LEGAL DIVISIONS LONDON/HAGUE

GROUP MANAGEMENT SERVICES CO-ORDINATOR

GROUP PUBLIC RELATIONS CO-ORDINATOR

GROUP MATERIALS SERVICES LONDON/HAGUE

GROUP TRADE RELATIONS DIVISION

AMERICAN DIVISION

DIRECTOR OF CO-ORDINATION CHEMICAL

PERSONAL ASSISTANT

PLANNING CO-ORDINATOR CHEMICAL

AGREEMENTS & LICENSING CO-ORDINATOR

MANUFACTURING CO-ORDINATOR CHEMICAL

MARKETING CO-ORDINATOR CHEMICAL

FINANCE CO-ORDINATOR CHEMICAL

PERSONNEL CO-ORDINATOR CHEMICAL

RESEARCH CO-ORDINATOR CHEMICAL

REGIONAL CO-ORDINATOR CHEMICAL I EUROPE (EXCL. U.K.) & N. AFRICA

REGIONAL CO-ORDINATOR CHEMICAL II AUSTRALASIA, ASIA & AFRICA (OTHER THAN N. AFRICA) & MIDDLE EAST

REGIONAL CO-ORDINATOR CHEMICAL III U.K. & EIRE CARIBBEAN, CENTRAL & S. AMERICA. LIAISON WITH N. AMERICA

DIRECTOR OF CO-ORDINATION OIL

PERSONAL ASSISTANT

SUPPLY & PLANNING CO-ORDINATOR

FINANCE OIL

EXPLORATION & PRODUCTION CO-ORDINATOR

MANUFACTURING CO-ORDINATOR OIL

MARKETING CO-ORDINATOR OIL

PERSONNEL CO-ORDINATOR OIL

MARINE CO-ORDINATOR

REGIONAL CO-ORDINATOR OIL EUROPE (EXCL. U.K.) & N. AFRICA

REGIONAL CO-ORDINATOR OIL AFRICA (OTHER THAN N. AFRICA) & MIDDLE EAST

REGIONAL CO-ORDINATOR OIL. EAST & AUSTRALASIA

REGIONAL CO-ORDINATOR OIL. CARIBBEAN, CENTRAL & S. AMERICA

REGIONAL CO-ORDINATOR OIL. UNITED KINGDOM & EIRE

overseas investments, it has been estimated, comes from her two oil companies, Shell and BP.[1]

Some oil experts maintain that, however much the giants liberalise themselves, their day is done. Their most vocal critic is Enrico Mattei, the aggressive free-booting head of the Italian state-owned oil company, ENI. 'The system set up by the oil cartel', he said at Piacenza in 1960, 'cannot long survive under the new realities of the situation. They have outdated and deprived of all force the old ideas of a monopoly of technical know-how and the inevitability of oil operations being carried out by companies of huge size.' 'The profits of *le sette sorelle*', Mattei told me in Rome, 'are far too high: they get between the producer and the consumer countries. They're still living in the colonial age.' To break into the field of the sisters, Mattei has bought oil from the Russians, undercut them by a fraction in Italy, outbid the traditional fifty-fifty agreements between oil companies and Middle Eastern rulers, and arranged to build refineries in North Africa and Ghana.

Shell men insist that they provide a necessary buffer between producer and consumer countries, that the alternative to the orderly squabble of the seven sisters is a hopeless free-for-all of two hundred sisters, scratching one another's eyes out, never secure enough to make long-term investments, and possibly leading to an international crisis with the Russians. Undoubtedly Shell and the other six face a difficult future—with an over-supply of oil, a surge of economic nationalism, and Russia undercutting prices. In the last decade, Shell has shown that it can change its attitudes, and they are still haunted by the words: 'If only, ten years ago, someone had foreseen . . .'[2] But it is possible that Shell, like dinosaurs and Hollywood film studios, may disintegrate from sheer out-size. In the next ten years it will need all the ingenuity of the seven men to keep their five hundred Shells intact.

UNILEVER

Avis Unileverensis (managerialis).
Plumage: highly variegated; habits: too numerous to list; habitat: the world; distinctive characteristics: a high flyer. The birds who run Unilever come in many shapes and sizes. For a marketing man, for example, a spell in a sales team in Yorkshire may lead to experience in an advertising agency in London. Later, from London, our man may go to Brazil—or Pakistan, or Australia, or to one of many overseas

[1] Andrew Shonfield: *British Economic Policy since the War*, 1958. p. 113.
[2] *See The Evolution of an International Service*, Shell, 1959.

stations. The Parent Board of Unilever itself and the Management of
our 400 companies are peopled by men like this. So if you are bird
that likes a varied habitat, above all, if you're feather for flight into
the higher realms, Unilever's atmosphere may be congenial to you.

Unilever advertisement for recruits.

Business History has as yet been but little studied in Britain and the
inquiring reader still has to choose between what are virtually two
sorts of propaganda: an heroic mythology on the one hand and a kind
of economic Crime Club on the other.

Charles Wilson: History of Unilever, 1954.

Unilever has many likenesses to Shell. It is Anglo-Dutch,
international, decentralised (with four hundred separate companies). It, too, has come to terms with nationalism: as the
expropriation of the Mexican company shook Shell, so was
Unilever shaken in 1948 by the looting of the Kingsway Stores in
Ghana. But one need only step inside the Unilever building, half
a mile down the river, to notice the contrast. In Shell you sense an
unchanging hierarchy of men in pin-stripes discussing pipelines or
South-East Asia. In Unilever House a salesman might stroll down
the corridors discussing frozen doughnuts. While Shell is concerned with its one holy commodity, Unilever sells a fantastic
range of stuff, including Lux Soap, Stork Margarine, Gibbs
Toothpaste, Walls Sausages and Ice Cream, Birds Eye Frozen
Foods, MacFisheries, Atkinsons Perfumes, Omo, Vim and Persil.
Shell men talk reverentially about 'The Group', but Unilever
people have been heard to refer to 'Dear Octopus'. They keep
their central identity in the background, and do not shout too
much about the connection between Stork and Omo. One of their
mandarins told me that when he was first approached at Cambridge, he assumed that Unilevers had to do with cantilevers.

While Shell is one big pyramid, Unilever is a collection of small
pyramids, constantly changing their size and position and forming
zigzag routes to the peak. A man in Unilever can (and has)
become managing director of Walls Sausages at the age of twenty-
eight, and from there might move through soap, timber or toothpaste up to the central board.

Unilever is probably the most sophisticated corporation in
Britain, and also one of the least pretentious. It still has something
of the character of the institution from which it grew—a cosy,
efficient grocer's shop. But it has also developed psychological
selection, computers, ergonomics, elaborate costing, and scrupu-
lous care for its 23,000 managers (when senior managers go on long

439

air journeys abroad, they are encouraged to come home by ship). It has even had its history objectively written—a kind of corporate psychoanalysis.

It is rash to generalise about the Dear Octopus. Its biggest limb of all, the United Africa Company, is engaged in quite separate activities, including making cement, beer and plastics. But Unilever is concerned above all with salesmanship. There is no sense, as in Shell, of purveying a noble and indispensible product. 'The kind of problem we're facing at the moment', one senior Unilever executive explained to me, 'is whether you can sell collar studs in fish-shops.' Unilever is mixed up in the social change of Britain and forty-nine other countries and while Shell's ultimate strategy might be said to depend on handling a sheikh, Unilever's depends on handling a housewife.

LORD LEVERHULME

All this is implicit in Unilever's tempestuous past, and in the character of the founder of the British side of the business, the brilliant and impulsive first Lord Leverhulme. It was William Lever (as he then was) who first introduced mass-advertising to Britain, in the soap business in 1885. He repeatedly quoted the old American jingle:

> If you whisper down a well
> About the goods you have to sell
> You will not make as many dollars
> As the man who climbs a tree and hollers.

By 1920 Lever controlled more than three-quarters of the British soap trade. But he had also embarked on other rash and eccentric enterprises. He fell in love with the Western Isles; to help the fishermen there he set up companies to process their fish. To sell the fish he bought a chain of high-street shops, called Mac-Fisheries; to sell alongside the fish he bought Walls Sausages; and Walls, to keep themselves busy in the summer, had started making ice-cream. The original fishery business in the Western Isles was a total flop, but MacFisheries, Walls and the food business which grew around them are now the third largest section of Unilever's business.

Still more rashly, Lever decided in 1920 to buy a company which traded in oil-seeds for his soap and margarine—the Niger Company in West Africa. It nearly ruined him. But it survived as the United

Africa Company to become by far the biggest of all Unilever's subsidiaries, with a large chunk of the trade in Ghana and Nigeria.

When Leverhulme died in 1925, Francis D'Arcy Cooper, who had been his accountant, became chairman. He was one of the first of many cases of accountants rescuing crumbling companies, and without him Lever's would probably have collapsed. The firm was then in hot competition with Continental rivals—notably the margarine-and-soap firms of Jurgens, Van Den Berghs, and Schichts, who had merged in 1928 into the 'Margarine Unie'. The two rivals, the *Unie* and Lever's, opened talks, and in September, 1929, they merged as the Anglo-Dutch firm of Unilever, with two holding companies and twin boards, called 'Unilever Limited' and 'Unilever NV'. It is an arrangement similar to Shell's, but more centrally based on London. This huge and awkward conglomeration, through the slump, went through a time of agonising 'rationalisation'; for a time, in the D'Arcy Cooper era, there was an attempt to centralise the whole outfit until, as one Canadian executive complained, 'you had to cable London before you went to the bathroom'. But later Unilever took on an opposite tendency, leaving its local managers largely—and sometimes too much—in control.

HEYWORTH'S MANAGERS

In 1942 Cooper was succeeded by Geoffrey Heyworth, later Lord Heyworth, who ruled the British end of Unilever for the next eighteen years. Heyworth is a quiet, thoughtful man, a self-made intellectual given to long pauses and meaningful but ambiguous grunts. He has now retired from the chairmanship, spending his time on government committees, as probably the most distinguished elder statesman of British business. 'The Lord', as he is known by the staff, left a decisive mark on the character of Unilever and much else. He embraced the new problems of marketing and growth with an un-English enthusiasm: the idea of change, of one product pushing out another, of detergents pushing out soap, stimulated him. He told me how he had urged the young Unilever men to 'make change your ally'. He generated a sense of un-complacency in Unilever, welcoming anything which was new.

He pushed ahead schemes for training graduates, and took a close interest in universities, sitting on the University Grants Committee, becoming a fellow of Nuffield. He gave annual reports which have since become a model—choosing each year one main theme, on advertising, managers, or investment. Above all, Heyworth pressed on with the managerial revolution which D'Arcy Cooper had initiated, building up a new 'meritocracy' of managers from inside the firm, watching their training, and encouraging 'cross-fertilisation' between the different Unilever companies, 'keeping the fences low'. As Unilever decentralised and diversified, so the managers became more important. 'The firm isn't really run by the board, it's run by five hundred managers', Heyworth said to me. Unilever came to see itself more as a central management service. 'You can raise ten million pounds in two days', one Unilever man said to me, 'but it takes ten years to produce ten managers.' They built up an 'industrial civil service', almost as apolitical as Whitehall; they are 85 per cent Conservative, according to one estimate, but two of the Unilever board are Socialists and several are Liberals.

Unilever managers come from two strains—the graduates, and the promoted clerks or salesmen, from the 'University of Hard Knocks', as Lever called his own education. Since the war Unilever has tried to introduce a more dignified, civil service atmosphere—graded carpets, canteens and morning tea (tea-and-cake for senior managers, tea-and-biscuit for middle managers)—and to dispel the undergraduates' prejudice about super-grocers. Today about half the senior managers are graduates, and the proportion is still rising.

The 'royal families' of the founders gave way to self-made and self-perpetuating managers. Old Leverhulme luckily had no truck with nepotism: 'The surest way to annoy the old man', said Lord Heyworth, 'was to promote one of his relations beyond his merits.' Today, of the twenty-four members of the Unilever board, all have been in the business all their lives, and only four belong to 'royal families'. Lord Leverhulme, the son of the founder, comes up from his Cheshire farm once a month, as an 'advisory director', but his share in the company, like that of the Dutch descendants, is tiny in proportion to the total shareholding. The final stage in Unilever's managerial revolution was reached a few years ago, when it was announced that directors no longer had to have any financial stake. None of the present directors are from the city, insurance companies, or other firms. Unilever has, in fact, become entirely self-perpetuating, virtually independent of the city. Like those of Shell, the financial operations of Unilever are dictated, not by the stock exchange or by the financiers, but by the necessities of international competition. 'If we feel that we must keep up with the Joneses', Lord Heyworth explained to the

Radcliffe Committee, 'whether we have to pay 8 per cent or 6 per cent doesn't make much difference. It is a horrible business, keeping up.'[1]

THE CHAIRMAN

The present chairman of Unilever Limited, George Cole, took over from Heyworth in 1960, at the age of fifty-four: he thus belongs to the new generation of bosses, too young to fight in the first world war, less isolated and perhaps more competitive. In a gathering of businessmen, Cole seems unobtrusive, and not part of the intimate confident circle of the city's Old Boy Net. But within Unilever he is regarded as something of a superman. He went to the 'University of Hard Knocks'; he comes from North Country stock and went to school in Singapore. He joined the Niger Company as a junior clerk, at the age of sixteen, and worked his way up through the West African business. In his boldness and down-to-earthness he remains basically an African trader; he enjoys criticism more obviously than Heyworth, and has the same zest for change.

He is a large, broad-shouldered man—high bald head, humorous deep-set eyes, unpompous manner, soft voice. I was tempted to divide British businessmen into those who sat behind their huge bare desks, and those who come forward to relax on a chair or a sofa: Cole belongs to the second, Chambers of ICI to the first.

Cole rules Unilever jointly with his Dutch co-chairman, F. J. Tempel, whose office has a communicating door, and most of the day-to-day decisions are taken by a triumvirate of the two chairmen and a vice-chairman, Dr. E. G. Woodroofe, a scientist and ex-head of the research division. To help them they have 'mandarins'—not unlike the co-ordinators of Shell—each in charge of a division: technical, personnel, marketing, finance and tax, company secretary.

Cole's main preoccupation is with managers: when I asked him what was his most important job, he said immediately, 'finding successors'. The special committee only considers sums above £25,000: but they try to ensure that their subsidiaries are not becoming involved in businesses they don't understand. That is a central tenet of Unilever's: 'We are not an investment trust', wrote Heyworth,[2] 'concerned to find capital and leave management to others. We normally go into businesses we can run ourselves.'

---

[1] Proceedings of the Radcliffe Committee, 1960. Q 11479.
[2] Lord Heyworth: *Capital Investment*, 1960.

Both Heyworth and Cole have tried to leave their companies to themselves: like Shell, they believe this gives Unilever an advantage over American competitors. But the balance between centre and perimeter is difficult to keep, for there is always a danger (as Heyworth put it) that 'the business might fly apart by centrifugal force'.

How will the Octopus grow in the future? The pattern of 'diversification', first set by the eccentricity of Leverhulme, has proved an immense advantage in the sixties: while other 'one-track firms' have been shopping around for new and different businesses, Unilever already has its eggs in several different baskets. 'I think that the decision to buy Birds Eye Frozen Foods in 1943', Cole told me, 'was just as bold as Lever buying MacFisheries.' Birds Eye now produces 66 per cent of the frozen foods in Britain.

There is one significant reason why this giant firm must grow larger. 'Unilever must diversify', Lord Heyworth told me, 'if only because the cost of getting inside the mind of the consumer is now so high that once we've got inside the housewife's kitchen to find why she buys kippers, you might as well find out why she buys everything else.'

Marketing, motivational research, depth interviewing and mass advertising lie at the heart of Unilever's operations. The process which began with William Lever's hoardings for Sunlight Soap has culminated in the huge apparatus of modern advertising. Last year Unilever spent about £100 million on advertising, of which probably about £20 million was spent in Britain—5 per cent of the total British expenditure, and the biggest single advertiser. The annual cost of Unilever advertising is roughly the same as its annual profits. Unilever products—1,200 different brand names throughout the world—advertise not only against their rivals but against each other—Gibbs against Pepsodent, Summer County against Stork. Unilever men discuss the toothpaste war as intently as if it were an international crisis: in the belly of the Octopus groupthink and conformism are rife, and men easily become absorbed in the tiny limits of their competition.

The pace has been enormously quickened by commercial television, of which Lord Heyworth has been a firm defender. TV advertising can bring Birds Eye or Lux on to the screen in the housewife's home on the same day all over the country. Three weeks after Walls had produced a new steak-and-kidney pie, Cole told me, it was selling 100,000 a week. And TV breaks down the British loyalty to established products—'brand loyalty'. In the past, while Americans have enjoyed changing their soaps, tooth-pastes and cars, the British have stuck to Sunlight, Persil and other established brands, and have mocked the Americans' fickleness. But now we too are becoming more changeable. Unilever is urging us on, pushing out one product with another, analysing the housewife's subconscious desires, and stimulating them into spending. TV and supermarkets (Cole told me) have made the old-fashioned huckster-salesman out of date, and the television screen has taken over the function of the foot-in-the-door. Instead of the brash salesman in a van, talking an old grocer into buying more soap than he wants, Unilever now has subtle executives planning a nation-wide advertising campaign, plotting when to move in Omo, or pull out Vim. The marketing men have always been the top dogs of Unilever. Scientists, who resent the grocer-image, are becoming more important, and research now looms much larger. But marketers remain the mainspring: they have been paid more and sacked more. With the complexity and centralisation of advertising, their value grows; they are on the profitable frontier between industry and salesmanship.

'Keeping up with the Joneses' is the centre of Unilever's business. To some starry-eyed youths who join it, the operation may seem narrow: 'It's difficult to feel very serious', said one Oxford recruit, 'about making a housewife buy two sausages when she needs only one.' But Unilever is proud of what it is doing. 'Some people, who have spent years castigating the evils of poverty', to quote Lord Heyworth again, 'now seem disconcerted by prosperity, and they make very sour noises about it. We cannot follow their logic. We like to see people well off, and although we realise that mass prosperity brings new and unfamiliar problems we would much rather face those than poverty's ancient curse.'

'The most important thing for Britain', Heyworth said to me, 'is growth. There are two things which produce growth—inventions and advertising. You may not like advertising, but without it you can't produce growth. Without it, you're just in a stagnant pool.'

ICI

On board the RMS *Aquitania* in October, 1926, Sir Alfred Mond, Sir Harry McGowan and other chemical industrialists sketched out an agreement on Cunard notepaper. Thus Imperial Chemical Industries was born. In the following thirty-five years ICI has come to be regarded as Britain's superman. It has tripled in size since its birth and ridden high on the post-war chemical boom, proliferating new factories, new products and new ways of life. Today it employs about 112,000 people, but this number (which is diminishing) belittles it, for the proportion of capital to men in ICI is enormous (four times, for instance, the ratio of AEI). If one wanted a symbol of ICI, it might be a huge clean chemical plant with a mass of pipes and towers, and one technologist standing by a gauge.

In the World Series, ICI is (by sales) twenty-fourth from the top. Though it has big overseas subsidiaries, it is much less international than Shell or Unilever. But in Britain it is the biggest of them all, and wholly British. 'People talk about *us* as a sinister Anglo-Dutch concern', said one of the Unilever mandarins, 'but they regard ICI as part of their patriotism, as if it were the army or the navy.' In many important products—caustic soda, soda ash, nitrogenous fertilisers—it has a monopoly, which leads to some unreal and uncommercial attitudes; ICI salesmen go through the motions of persuading customers who have no option but to buy from them. But monopolies have also made it unusually aware of public opinion; it has been a sensitive giant, and taken its responsibilities seriously, looking after its people, giving scholarships to universities, and anxious to do the right thing by the country. It is afflicted with the usual problems of giants. There is a macabre story about a director of British Railways arguing with a director of ICI as to whose organisation was biggest. 'Of course we're bigger—look at our turnover!' said the Railways man. 'Aha', said the ICI man, 'but we've got more *passengers*.'

ICI does not have the same closeness to the customer as over-the-counter companies like Unilever. Most of its products are sold to other firms: only an odd mixture of things, like paint, zip-fasteners, drugs, Terylene or cartridges are sold direct to the public. Scientists, not salesmen, are the key men of ICI: out of the sixteen executive directors—though all have long ceased to be specialists—only three (Chambers, Bingen and Todhunter) are non-scientists. The preoccupation of ICI with scientific research has been helped by its monopolies, and partly because of this ICI men have often been uncommercial. But in the past few years, as we shall see, the personality of ICI has begun to change. The old heavy industries—such as explosives or alkalis—have remained relatively static, while new, more domestic ones have brought ICI closer to the customer, generating competition. And a new chairman, Paul Chambers, has arrived.

The roots of ICI are in the sprawling chemical factories of the provinces, and it is still essentially a group of big provincial companies, bound together by common finance. The merger was a federation rather than a union; although McGowan built a great imperial palace on the Thames, with tall nickel doors, much of the power of ICI remained in the manufacturing divisions in Glasgow, Billingham or Manchester. The early slump years of ICI saw bitter resentments from the divisions, rivalries, feuds, axings and suspicion of London. But gradually, with enlightened directors and paternalism from Alfred Mond, later Lord Melchett, the components got together as a single company, and the letters ICI became a source of pride. The character of the company was formed by two men— McGowan the shrewd Scot, and Mond the benign German Jew.

But the separate divisions—now eleven—remained strong. 'You'll never understand ICI', one veteran scientist told me, 'until you realise how *different* the divisions are—as different as parts of the United States.' From the country-squire aura of Winnington Hall, the port-drinking club in the Alkali Division of Cheshire, to the self-made, no-nonsense atmosphere of Dye-stuffs in Manchester, they are all worlds of their own: few of the chemists or managers move outside their division. They are immersed in the family atmosphere of their chemical towns—the alkali town of Winnington, the Terylene town of Harrogate, the ammonia town of Billingham (where I was born). Some divisions, like Harrogate or Wilton, are young and expanding; others, like Winnington, have settled down to a comfortable middle age. There is not much contact, either between the divisions or with the outside world. They have their own clubs, sports, theatricals and charabanc tours, and they quite often marry company wives.

These provincial roots have given the combine its strength and weaknesses. The strength has lain in its vigour, its capacity for advancing self-made men, its lack of pomp, its closeness to the workers. Since the days when Mond and Brunner encouraged the trade unions, ICI has been a model of labour relations and works councils, and later of profit-sharing. ICI has had, too, a provincial dislike of the city; many ICI men in the divisions like to talk disrespectfully about the world of high finance and stocks and shares. ICI does not normally deal through a merchant bank, but direct through stockbrokers; and some directors have taken a pride in *not* knowing the morning's stock market quotation of their shares. They think of themselves as enlightened industrialists, rather than businessmen. Directors are expected to spend a good deal of their time in the provinces, and British Railways are proverbially full of ICI men. ICI has been able to feel independent of the city and such matters as Bank Rate: it has spent the staggering sum of £535 million on new plant and projects since the war—of which £410 million has come out of its own profits. 'It would be wrong to say that Budgets are of no interest', Fleck told the Radcliffe Committee in 1959, 'but I cannot recall any of them that made any significant change in our approach to what we were thinking of doing.'

From the provinces, and from its monopoly, come some of its weaknesses—its insularity, its complacency, its old-fashioned approach to organisation, its resentment of metropolitan and non-scientific intruders. It has a conservative respect for hierarchies and an almost medieval attitude to women, who rarely get promoted above secretaries. And there is its snugness: anything less than un-qualified praise—such as this chapter—ICI is liable to regard as a stab in the back, and their public relations still has an old-fashioned blustering, threatening quality. A great deal of money and energy goes into the business of self-congratulation. When they celebrated their thirty-fifth birthday, ICI arranged for a twenty-two page supplement in *The Times* devoted to untarnished admiration, in-cluding an article on 'South Africa: Need for Faith', and accom-panied by a congratulatory editorial. A few months later their image looked very different, and *The Times* led the attackers.

Invention is the life-blood of ICI. Its long-term future depends less on capital and managers than on research. It spends roughly £14 million a year on 'research and development'—more than is spent by all the universities put together. The 6,000 research workers are ICI's spearhead to the future, producing such inven-tions as Polythene, 'Perspex', 'Paludrine', 'Procion' dyes or Terylene (bought from Calico Printers), which have changed our pattern of living. But research brings the insoluble problem of running a commercial civil service side-by-side with difficult eccentrics. Every organisation scientist is aware that individual-ists such as Rutherford, Whittle or Fleming, who do not take easily to organisation, are supremely important.

Holding a balance between discipline and eccentricity is one of ICI's hardest tasks. In its early years its scientific achievement was impressive: before the war it built a whole school of research chemists, with a sense of freedom and challenge and close contact with universities; they had a fair record of inventions, and still have an FRS as senior deputy-chairman. But some of their scientists are doubtful whether they will have such a free rein in the future, and whether the organisation men may not be winning over the individualists.

As its factories become more mechanised and automated, ICI is becoming increasingly a firm of technologists. Already in 1959 15 per cent of its staff had university degrees. The total number of ICI employees (in spite of its vast expansion) has fallen, while the number of 'staff'—or monthly-paid people—has risen: the ratio of weekly-paid to monthly-paid has fallen in ten years from 2·7 to 1, to 2 to 1. This huge heavy industry, in fact, is quite rapidly becoming an industry of white-collar workers.

Into their technological jungle ICI has recruited since the war hundreds of an unfamiliar species—the arts graduate. The meeting of test-tubes with the humanities has been painful; the two sides have found themselves staring across the deep divide between the 'two cultures', almost equally illiterate in each other's subjects. Several young graduates have described to me the frustration of leaving university to do drudgery work in an alien atmosphere, and ICI has been accused of recruiting first-class brains, and then wasting them on workaday jobs. In some fields, particularly selling, arts graduates have reached top positions rapidly; the chairman of the metal division and a managing director of dye-stuffs are both arts men, and in the next few years, as the first post-war generation comes to the top, the company will probably acquire a more humanist character. But it remains predominantly a technological firm. ICI has the particular problems of a company thirty-five years old—an awkward age, when the first young men have grown old, and pioneering opportunities are fewer. It is a pyramid with a square base—an awkward bulge of men in the middle, and not enough jobs at the top.

The provincial (and particularly Scottish) roots are apparent in the succession of chairmen. After Mond (the first chairman), McGowan, Bain (his deputy), Rogers and Fleck were all self-made Scots boys, two of them from the same street in Glasgow. Fleck— who retired in 1960—embodied the most attractive ICI qualities: he rose from being a Glasgow lab.-boy at fourteen to being not only chairman but also a Fellow of the Royal Society. He is a rugged man with huge bear-like shoulders and a rich Glaswegian accent, who still fells trees at Billingham at week-ends.

PAUL CHAMBERS

But in 1960 ICI made a clean and dramatic break with this

scientific tradition, appointing Paul Chambers, who joined the board straight from the civil service in 1947. Chambers is a Londoner, an intellectual, a graduate of the London School of Economics, the son of a city wine-merchant. He went to the City of London School, which educated amongst others Asquith and Kingsley Amis. He has spent half his life in the Inland Revenue—where he invented the PAYE system and reorganised Indian taxation. He is short, articulate, quick-thinking, with a photographic memory. In Whitehall he had the reputation of a wonderman, and had even been tipped by some as an eventual head of the Treasury. He has kept in touch with cabinet ministers, who tend to regard him as 'Mr. Big Business'—rather as Lord Chandos once was. Since he became chairman, Chambers has emerged (unlike Cole of Unilever, or Loudon of Shell) quickly into the political foreground: he has criticised budgets, urged lower surtax, attacked Britain's 'sentimental softness towards inefficiency' and insisted that the profit motive must prevail in nationalised industries. He has been in the van of the movement into Europe: 'for too long sections of British industry have been becoming increasingly insular, introspective, restrictive, reactionary and inflexible'. Unlike Chandos, Chambers has nothing of the amateur about him: he is a single-minded and uncompromisingly professional man, not afraid to talk about taxation and rationalisation all through a cocktail party. Chambers belongs to the new unflamboyant school of chairmen; he can travel up in one of the grand nickel lifts of ICI house without being recognised (McGowan would have had the lift cleared for him). He lives unpretentiously in a big house in Bishop's Avenue, Hampstead, with his second wife—who worked in ICI—and three daughters; he has a brother who earns £10-£15 a week as a stores clerk in an Acton electrical firm. He likes going home early, enjoys gardening and mending greenhouses, and plays bridge or scrabble in the evenings. He earns £50,000 a year.

His arrival in the ICI boardroom caused a flutter. Chambers did not try to conceal his cleverness, loved talking and was quick to point out the mistakes of his colleagues; with some of the un-money-minded senior scientists there were some difficult scenes. But Chambers had the mastery of the intricate financial affairs of the giant, which the scientists lacked, and by the time Fleck had become due to retire in 1960 it was clear to most—though not to all —directors that Chambers must be chairman.

The transition showed how dangerous it is to personalise a company by 'Mr. ICI', for whatever Fleck is, Chambers isn't.

But the change of chairman *did* represent a shift of emphasis in the company's character—away from the provinces and scientists, towards the city and finance. Not only Chambers but the finance director and treasurer also came from the Inland Revenue (all introduced by the former treasurer, Sir William Coates). ICI veterans soon noticed—sometimes with sadness—a new concentration on financial expertise. Helped by its monopoly position, ICI had managed, like other manufacturing companies, to reach a position of colossal financial strength with a surprising indifference to finance. But all that was now changing. Special courses in finance and taxation were introduced, an investment committee was set up, and more 'outside' directors were introduced—including the head of the National Provincial Bank, David Robarts. The pure scientists became less confident that science was supreme.

Chambers' position as a non-scientific head of a chemical giant was not easy, but he had a gift for quickly absorbing new situations, following the threads of his complex organisation and talking about chemical compounds accurately and enthusiastically. He brought to ICI a broader view of economic trends and world trade—which was shown in his successful negotiations with Russia, which reached a climax in the ICI exhibit in the British Trade Fair in Moscow in the summer of 1961.

Chambers presides over the twenty-two directors of the main board—sixteen of them full-time, each earning £24,000 a year. The day-to-day control of finance is in the hands of a quadrumvirate of the chairman and three deputy-chairmen (Holroyd, Bingen, Williams). But the main board has delegated most of its control to the divisions. Like Shell's seven men, the directors of ICI normally consider only seven-figure sums, and in 1960 there were further moves towards decentralisation, giving more power to the provinces, and cutting board meetings from fortnightly to monthly. A scheme (which took the usual nine months to devise) was instituted to leave the directors, like Shell's, more free for long-think, and to remove proliferations: 'we have, you know, read *Parkinson's Law*', explained E. A. Bingen, the deputy chairman. At the same time, by more careful financial control, the main board actually increased its oversight of divisions. Most of the effective decisions rest with the divisional boards and their chairmen (£12,000 a year): to the people at Wilton or Winnington, the local chairman is the boss.

In such a disparate empire, it might seem that no single head could dominate. And yet, in two astonishing months of 1962 it became clear that one man, Paul Chambers, lay behind the move which transformed the public personality of ICI—the attempt to take-over a rival Leviathan, Courtaulds.

This is not the place to tell the complicated story of that frustrated effort, which has been dramatically chronicled elsewhere.[1] But the take-over illuminated the changed character of the company with a clarity which appalled many of its employees (in one long statement Chambers succeeded in never once mentioning the word employees). Looking back on my encounters with ICI when preparing this chapter a year earlier, I recall how different it then appeared; a company known primarily for its care for workers and research, associated with profit-sharing and university scholarships, suddenly emerged as one of the most relentless of all big businesses, prepared to enlarge its monopoly to the point of embarrassing even a Conservative government, and disturbing thousands of its managers. Some humbug accompanied the tut-tutting about 'ICI's image': if ICI's character had changed (as it had) into a profit-minded, competitive concern, it was just as well that this should be known to everyone. What seemed most distressing was that ICI, after its years of self-congratulation and bland publicity, should conduct its bid with an insensitivity to its own scientists and workers, which threatened the climate of scientific achievement and self-respect on which the company's greatness had been built.

The bid for Courtaulds affected not only the two companies, but all British business: for it revealed that in an extreme crisis (like men in love or war) the conventional trappings, the opaque annual reports, the secrecy, the smugness, become suddenly ridiculous, and are thrown overboard in the desperate need for help. To read ICI's articles in *The Times* in 1961, or Courtaulds' 1961 annual report in the light of the subsequent events, is to see how far large companies are prepared to ignore their shareholders, and the public—until they need them.

[1] See Roy Jenkins in *The Observer*, March 18-April 1, 1962.

452

28

MANAGERS

The last word on how we may live or die
Rests today with such quiet
Men, working too hard in rooms that are too big,
Reducing to figures
What is the matter, what is to be done.
W. H. Auden: The Managers.

Management, like war, is made up of long periods of routine
divided by short bursts of intense activity and peril.
John Tyzack.

EVER since James Burnham's book was published in 1941 the
phrase 'the managerial revolution' has become something of a
bogey-word, conjuring up those anonymous men in huge rooms,
running vast industries by means of some unspeakable expertise.
The word manager, like general or permanent secretary, has
acquired its own mystique. In clubs or in the old professions—
where there is not much contact with managerial men—the phrase
is full of dread: managers represent the antithesis of the old
knightly ideals. It is sometimes difficult to remember that the
managers are ordinary men doing very ordinary things—selling
soap, finding oil, making chemicals—and that the senior managers
are simply junior managers promoted. This shock confronts many
young graduates going into large companies. They expect to be
led into a *métier* as intricate and challenging as Greek iambics,
and they find themselves selling kippers in the high street, slowly
moving up to selling more kippers in more high streets, until they
find themselves regarded as 'managers'.

In 1956 Unilever, out of 270,000 employees had, 23,000 managers
in all—6,000 senior and middle, 16,400 junior.[1] When the Acton
Society Trust conducted a survey of managers in thirty-seven large
firms,[2] they found that the median ratio of managers to employees
was about two per cent. The status of this two per cent has risen
spectacularly since the war. The post-war export crisis, the
collapse of imperial jobs in the Indian Civil or Colonial Services,

[1] Lord Heyworth: *The Managers*, 1956.
[2] *See Management Succession:* Acton Society Trust, 1956.

the reaction against the civil service with its associations of coupons, and the new attitude to big corporations as being themselves a kind of public service—all generated a new respectability, and an inrush of able young graduates into industry. These figures show the numbers of Oxford graduates going into industry, as recorded in the files of the appointments board:

1906	6
1926	39
1936	77
1946	49
1956	277
1957	291
1958	275
1959	292

'For ambitious young undergraduates', C. E. Escritt of the Oxford Appointments Board told me, 'industry and the foreign service are now the twin tops.' The universities now send more men into industry than into any other occupation: about 30 per cent of the graduates in arts, science and technology in 1949–50 went into industry.[1]

Many are reluctant recruits. Dr. Mark Abrams has analysed the results of a Cambridge survey of 927 undergraduates in 1959, which showed that though 17 per cent were choosing a career in business management or advertising, only 8 per cent would have chosen it if other professions—notably teaching, writing or social work—were equally remunerative. Analysing the replies of the reluctant majority, Dr. Abrams concludes: 'Their leisure activities suggest that they have comparatively little taste for individualistic competition, and less than average liking for the responsibilities of leadership and organisation. When they take part in group activities they show a preference for anonymous and passive rôles. They find information more satisfying than ideas, and entertainment more attractive than controversy . . . Business might regret ever having recruited them.'[2]

The Leviathans began to tumble over each other to recruit the cleverest young graduates. ICI, Shell and Unilever sent spies to Oxford and Cambridge, to woo potential managers with lunches, tours and pamphlets. Old Oxford men are sent as bait to lure

---

[1] *Opportunnities in Industry*. PEP, 1957. p. xv.
[2] Mark Abrams: Business Aspirants from Universities. *The Manager*, September, 1961.

other Oxford men into their trades. 'Each year the courtship grows a little more feverish', wrote J. G. W. Davies, of the Cambridge Appointments Board in 1956, 'every device being exploited to acquire prestige in the university.' Several pressures induced this new interest in graduates. One was the 1944 Education Act, which businessmen believed would scoop up nearly all the able young men into the universities, leaving less talent on the shop-floor. Another was pure fashion; bosses like to have graduates in the firm, even if (as so often) they don't quite know what to do with them. But the main pressure was the obvious shortage of 'manager material', and the urgent need to buy the best brains quickly. Only three hundred companies are registered with the Oxford and Cambridge Appointments Boards; small and middle-sized family firms are still resistant to Oxbridge recruits. But the three hundred include all the big corporations.

The new scramble for managers can be seen in the pages of appointments advertisements in the quality newspapers—particularly on Sundays—where the variety, salaries and habitat of managers and technocrats can be observed. The growth of this 'market-place' in the past five years has caused a minor business revolution, for here are large and dignified firms publicly bidding against each other for senior men, stating quite plainly the kind of salaries—even five-figure salaries—which they would pay. For many of the old school, the clamour from this market-place is horrifying; it cuts across two old industrial traditions—secrecy and lifelong loyalty.

The market began quite suddenly with the foundation of selection specialists in London, offering to serve as 'job brokers' for managers and technicians. The first and biggest—responsible for more than half the appointments—is Management Selection Limited (MSL). Others are:

Personnel Administration (PA),
Associated Industrial Consultants (AIC),
Executive Appointments (EA).

In discreet West End offices they interview managers, to marry them with new employers. These selection firms have set a new pace by providing shop-windows, generating curiosity, ambition and envy. This, for instance, was the 1960 Christmas Message of MSL:

On Christmas Day . . . we send our greetings to all who read these columns regularly. We would not exclude, of course, those who are merely curious to see how their lot compares with others, those who

455

feel compelled to keep a watchful eye on their competitors, or even those who find it a diverting weekly exercise to speculate on the identities of our clients . . .

In 1959, 900 jobs were advertised through consultants: in 1960, 1,300.[1] There are now about 18 separate consultant firms in London, and the big corporations have stepped up their own advertising for staff, with large spaces, more romantic headings, and more challenging requirements. In 1961 I collected a small anthology, of which these are two:

PROMETHEUS UNBOUND

As Shelley interpreted the Greek myth, Prometheus was released by Hercules. His crimes, in the eyes of Zeus, were making man from clay and teaching him the use of fire. We need neither to be made nor exactly taught.

Morgans—104 years old—make more foundry crucibles from clay and graphite than anyone in the world and know a good deal about their uses.

We now seek a man—AN EXPERIENCED CERAMIST—who can join us as a Technical Manager, take charge of technical control and development for both our large crucible factories and, by planning an ambitious programme of new uses for our traditional materials, qualify for the post of Technical Director within two years.

This Prometheus (yes, a demi-god) must have creative urge restless curiosity, leadership, the talent for choosing good men, initiative, strength of personality and youth—say 35 years.

THE UNITED STEEL COMPANIES LIMITED
DEPARTMENT OF
OPERATIONAL RESEARCH
AND CYBERNETICS

CYBERNETICIAN to join in our long-standing research into self-organising systems. It is not enough to have read Wiener: candidates should be familiar with international progress in cybernetics over the last fifteen years, and will preferably have experience of inter-disciplinary research.

The 'headhunters', as the consultants are called, have had a large influence on industry: many of them, apart from supplying staff, provide a management consultant service, moving into organisations, as McKinsey's did with Shell, to reconstruct pyramids and re-arrange staff. Inevitably a good deal of mumbo-jumbo surrounds this new profession, and things are not always what they

---

[1] 'The Headhunters': *The Director*, January, 1961.

seem: 'A careful survey has now established the fact that the clients who approach a business consulting firm do so with one of two motives', wrote Professor Parkinson: 'On the one hand they may want scapegoats for the reorganisation upon which they have already decided. On the other they may want to prevent such a reorganisation taking place.'[1]

But the consultants are the shock-troops of industry, and they have succeeded in storming the walls of companies, increasing the flow of ideas between them. On the careers of managers they have had a noticeable effect. They have helped to push up salary scales, and have increased the mobility of managers between firms. The consultants have exhaustive punch-card systems to match the right man to the right job, and some executives, even after having been placed in one firm, keep their names on the books.

Till recently, British managers were more obviously loyal to their companies than Americans, more likely to stay in one firm all their lives. The zigzag career of an American executive, hopping from one firm to another up to the top, was frowned on, and 'poaching' for staff on other companies' land was not done. 'We like to grow our own timber', said a Shell personnel manager, and most of the timber is still home-grown. Many senior pension schemes are still non-transferable; a married man in his forties knocks away a large prop if he leaves his firm. He is bound to it (in Lord Heyworth's phrase) by 'chains of gold'.

But the pattern is changing. I spoke to John Tyzack, a former Group-Captain who runs his own selection firm, specialising in senior managers. 'Two opposite things are happening', Tyzack said: 'on the one hand big companies are encouraging more of the corporate spirit. On the other hand, it's becoming easier for managers to change their firms, on the American pattern. There are several reasons: one, I think, is a general restlessness—partly perhaps because there's no longer an Empire to provide an escape route, so that people want to move about more inside Britain. Also, American firms in Britain, like Hedley's, have had a tremendous influence on their British rivals. The Americans are still much more ruthless about jobs: while an American executive is with a firm, he regards himself as belonging wholeheartedly to that firm, but if he gets a better offer from elsewhere he feels no guilt about changing. But it looks as if, while we are moving towards the American idea, the Americans are becoming loyal to their firms. I think we need some really new thinking about this: I'm

[1] *The Director*, June, 1960.

afraid we may do tomorrow what America discarded yesterday.'

Why do managers change jobs? 'It's like divorce', said one personnel consultant: 'money only comes into it when the marriage has already collapsed.' Advertisements often lay more emphasis on 'The Challenge of Tomorrow', 'Rapid Expansion' or 'a pleasant part of Southern England' than on the actual salary. A recurring motive for change is frustration—because of a bottleneck, a hidebound board, a lack of appreciation of technical skills, or simply overpowering boredom and absence of challenge. The situation of Home or Macmillan, who apparently needed a new challenge to bring out new energy, is often echoed in industry. 'Sometimes a man of fifty can become transformed in a different job', said Tyzack, 'because he's given a new challenge, which brings out the best in him. But sometimes he's just past his peak—and then there's not much to be done.'

Big firms compete hotly for first-class managers, but do they make full use of them? The impact of unqualified, analytically-minded graduates on the provincial, home-grown world of industry has often been painful: in some firms after the war as many as 75 per cent of the graduate recruits had left after a few years. The Leviathans are full of able young men doing crosswords and watching the clock; if they were coming to grips with factories and shop-stewards the wastage might be more forgivable, but all too often they are learning nothing except patience, and how to live with frustration. The older men resent the young 'management trainees' without technical knowledge, while the trainees feel the lack of a definite job or stimulus. The Acton Survey in 1956 found that:

> The creation of an élite corps tended to spoil the trainees and to antagonise other employees. Trainees became bored because they had so little opportunity for exercising responsibility, and because so much of their time was spent watching other people and being given useless information, such as that 'the pink slips go in this tray and the yellow in that'. And finally, at the end of the training period, companies were apt to find themselves landed with too many 'nice' people not suited for any particular job.[1]

But recently the big corporations have tended to adopt a more informal and less irksome approach to recruits. The idea of a 'management trainee' has—at least on the surface—become disguised: graduates are given definite workaday jobs and 'unobtrusively earmarked' for quick promotion.

[1] *Acton*, page 45.

A MANAGERIAL PROFESSION

Are managers a profession? 'The difference between industry as it exists today and a profession is, then, simple and unmistakable', wrote the late R. H. Tawney, forty years ago, in *The Acquisitive Society*: 'the latter is organised, imperfectly indeed, but none the less genuinely, for the performance of *duties*.' Tawney saw the new managerial class and the 'gradual disengagement of managerial technique from financial interests' providing the beginnings of professionalism. 'It marks the emergence within the very heart of the capitalist industry of a force which, both in status and in economic interest, is allied to the wage-earners rather than to the property-owners.'

Tawney also believed that the new managers could only be rescued from preoccupation with money-making by nationalisation. But in the forty years since, without wholesale nationalisation, managers have become much more professional-minded, in Britain as in America. 'In a short thirty years we have passed from a corporate order whose managerial style was derived from the so-called 'robber-barons', the divine-right Bayers, and the public-be-damned Vanderbilts, to the business-school-trained, public-relations-conscious professional of the highly complex corporate bureaucracy of today.'[1]

In Britain, professionalisation has been the catchword since the war. The British Institute of Management produces papers and awards diplomas in management. The Administrative Staff College—a big country house on the Thames near Henley—provides three-month courses for middle-managers. But these courses do not compare in their rigour and intensity with the 'Case Method' instruction of (for instance) the Harvard Business School. On the other hand, in America recently, after such attacks as William Whyte's and Vance Packard's, there have been signs of a reaction against the mystique of management, with its 'elaborate witchcraft replete with high priests (public-relations experts and public-opinion testers) with rituals (brainstorming, market research), with incantations (business serves the public) and with a vast literature of holy writ'.[2] 'Management is a means to an end, not an end in itself', William Whyte pleaded: 'The role of the manager is quite tough enough without being saddled with theology.'[3]

[1] Norton E. Long: Chapter in *Corporation in Modern Society*, 1959.
[2] Bernard D. Nossiter: *Management's Cracked Voice*. Harvard Business Review, 1959.
[3] Eric Moonman: *The Manager and the Organisation*. (Introduction), 1961.

The extent to which management can become a profession is obviously limited. Industry is no less concerned with profit and money-making. Profit remains the criterion of success—the means of controlling, judging or organising: it cannot be said of a manager, as it could be of a doctor: 'he's first class, but he doesn't make much profit'. The manager's prestige is identified with profits as a civil servant's is with the CMG. 'Not only his corporate loyalty to the firm', Anthony Crosland has written, 'but all his personal motives—professional pride, ambition, self-realisation, desire for power and prestige—find their fulfilment in high output and rapid growth, and hence high profits.'[1] Even in Russia profitability is the yardstick of industry. What has changed is the way of achieving profit. 'To make long-term profits nowadays', said Tyzack, 'you have to consider the community, the trade unions, the international situation and what the government is going to do next.' The corporate manager must be more circumspect, more aware of others: 'they'—a critical, left-wing they—are always looming in the background.

THE MIND OF THE MANAGER

Industrial managers are a very mixed bunch. Among the 3,300 analysed by the Acton Society Trust, average age 46, over half began as manual and clerical workers, one or two went to elementary or secondary school, one in five to a public school, one in five had a degree. But graduates and qualified men were much commoner among the younger ones, and by the mid-sixties the first post-war inrush of graduates will be reaching senior jobs— which is likely to bring industrial corporations closer in character to the other graduate professions of Whitehall, the law and the universities themselves.

Old businesses which have stopped growing, like railways or shipbuilding, can easily defeat scientific managers with what John Tyzack calls the 'law of maximum mediocrity': conformity and loyalty press managers to the toleration of the same second-rate uniformity. But in expanding firms—chemicals, electronics, television—there is more scope. Special managerial diseases (according to the Acton survey) afflict firms between twenty and thirty years old, where young men have grown old together—leaving a gap in the middle age-group. The go-ahead company of one generation—like Distillers' or Dunlop—can often become the

[1] *Corporation in Modern Society.* p. 266.

laggard of the next: and to a remarkable extent corporations behave like individuals, becoming middle-aged, corpulent, and sometimes just dying from old age. But some old-established firms, faced with threats or opportunities, have succeeded in reorganising themselves efficiently—Wallpaper Manufacturers, Ind Coope beer, South West Gas Board—and even the threat of take-over can transform a complacent firm—as Charles Clore, without buying it, transformed Watney's.

But the main opportunity for a modern manager comes with size. However conservative or ancient, big companies find themselves having to establish a proper management structure, or else disintegrate. A pyramid is built, with 'lines of responsibility' and layers, and once a firm grows beyond the ken of the board, managers enter their kingdom. In the industrial giants, the managers evolve their own values, and the social problems of the American manager are becoming visible here. The career of a corporation manager cuts across traditional societies and local communities; he is a 'spiralist'—moving towards the top in narrowing circles, from one community or country to another, gathering local experience before he settles in the head office as a senior executive.[1] He has no local obligations, and is preoccupied with his company. 'The young business executive in Wigan', wrote William Watson, 'is likely to have more interests and friends in Manchester and London, or even in New York, than he has in Wigan.' The British manager, like the American organisation man, becomes a 'free loader on the body politic'.[2] Taxation increases the enveloping influence of the corporation: the lunches, cocktails, chauffeur-driven cars and cigars inside the corporate womb contrast with the shepherd's pie in the suburban home. High income tax makes it hard for an individual family to compete against the neopaternalism of the company.

The impact of corporate communities on the traditional communities, centred round the squire, the church and the small town, has so far been very little studied in Britain: as the corporations become more international, revolving their 'spiralists' in wider circles, so they will presumably cut across local societies more sharply, substituting for the old landed aristocracy and its values the new aristocracy of the company managers (as in America). But so far this conflict, like others, has been blurred by the amateur tradition, and the reluctance of managers to appear to be managers.

[1] *See* William Watson: The Managerial Spiralist. *Twentieth Century*, May, 1960.
[2] *See* Norton E. Long: *above.*

Bigness creates vast new problems. The more layers there are, the longer a man takes to reach the top, and the less he can see all sides of the business. A young graduate, taken on for his 'broad horizons' (a favourite management cliché), will find himself in a thicket of specialist problems, with no glimpse of horizon in sight; and specialisation is worse for the young technologist, moving from a university lab to a works lab, with little scope for handling people. ('The arts graduate needn't worry about competition from the scientists', said one personnel expert: 'they're like pygmies. They treat people as if they were chemicals: they want to wait until all the variables have been eliminated.') Thousands of scientists escape from laboratories to become managers—helped by the frequent weakening of scientific curiosity at the age of thirty. 'It was as easy as getting up in the morning', said Lord Fleck, of his change from research to management. But the Acton survey suggested that arts graduates were more likely to reach top management than scientists.[1] A PEP survey showed that though arts men began with salaries on an average £70 lower, four years later they were more successful than scientists.[2] According to two American writers, Harbison and Myers, in an international survey, in Britain 'recruitment in top management is still biased in favour of the former public school boy and the Oxford and Cambridge graduate, and against persons with other educational qualifications such as engineers'.[3]

The Leviathans have developed an intricate mechanism of management, like the hierarchies of the civil service, geared not to parliament but to profit. 'Management by exception' has spread, defining the day-to-day responsibilities of junior managers, beyond which exceptional cases are passed to middle managers, with *their* defined responsibilities, who pass *their* exceptions to senior managers, and so to the board. Each manager can authorise expenditure up to a standard figure: he will evolve from a hundred-pound man, to a thousand-pound man, and eventually (like the directors of Shell) to being a half-million-pound man. The amount he can authorise, like his carpet or his desk, can define his status.

COMPUTERS

Into this intricate pyramid an alarming new master-manager

---

[1] *Acton*, p. 24.

[2] PEP: *Salaries of Graduates in Industry*, March, 1961.

[3] Frederick Harbison and Charles A. Myers: *Management in the Industrial World*, 1959. p. 314.

has entered: a brain which can remember everything about everyone, which can check figures, write cheques, calculate turnovers and notice exceptions in every factory and shop. No manager can ignore the influence of the neat grey machines, with their menacing names—Leo, Pegasus, Orion—silently working in their air-conditioned rooms, disgorging their ticker-tapes of figures. The computer is still only in its infancy in Britain, which has only about two hundred of them (compared to four thousand in America), of which sixty are in industry; but clearly computers will eventually have a drastic effect on managers. A big one—like the £2 million machine installed by the Atomic Energy Authority —can discover quite new kinds of information, and every computer provides a brain-box of centralised knowledge which must strengthen the central management—and the accountants, who can unravel it. A computer can report on monthly sales from hundreds of shops a few days after the end of the month and can analyse changes and qualifications of staff. It can organise 'management by exception', by letting out a mechanical scream when the figures go wrong. As one consultant put it: 'A big computer can put a giant corporation back into being a one-man firm.'

Computers' usefulness varies, and is often exaggerated. Some giants, like BMC, have refused to install them: others use them more for keeping up with the Joneses than for radical re-organisation. But if the computer is properly exploited, a company must be 'bent round' it, and the pyramid changed in quite painful ways.

Computers will certainly encourage centralisation, allowing managers to control branches at a distance: in iron curtain countries the computer is already held in some dread. In Boots or Marks and Spencers, computers will enable headquarters to keep count of every article sold, to have it automatically replaced, and to note the daily trend of sales. 'It will put the shop manager into the position of being not much more than a housekeeper', said one management consultant. This centralisation may make it harder for junior men to gain the experience—particularly the scope for mistakes—which can train them for senior management. The emergencies which have given so many office-boys their first lucky break, revealing them to the boss, are in danger of being eliminated. The computer cannot usurp the rôle of the *senior* managers: a man must still assess the problem in the light of the facts, through his own instinct. But, rather as television can by-pass the small salesman, so computers may by-pass the small manager.

A MANAGERIAL ÉLITE?

Not only computers, but bigness, specialisation and the tools of scientific management have all tended towards the formation of a much more defined race of managers separated, discreetly but firmly, from the rest. 'The experience of those who have paid most attention to management development', wrote the Acton survey, 'suggests that such early selection and training is essential if managers are to have the necessary variety of experience, and if they are to be given opportunities to develop while they are still flexible enough to do so. To those who object that this creates an élite, the answer is that this is inevitable.'[1] Although much of industry is still concerned with ordinary people doing ordinary things, the Leviathans are beginning to evolve their own breed of mandarins, like the Whitehall ones, and with the same dangers of separation and unconscious arrogance. Much of the argument about the professionalisation of management boils down, in the end, to how far such an élite is desirable: and the argument flared up again when in June, 1961, Balliol College announced that they were establishing a research fellowship in Management Studies, endowed by the Institute of Directors. 'The same services that Balliol has rendered to the civil service, to politics, diplomacy, the Law and the Church', said the Master of Balliol, with the usual Balliol smugness: 'it is capable of rendering to business. In the last century the Northcote-Trevelyan Report transformed the civil service into a model of integrity and efficiency. A similar reform has long been overdue for recruitment into business administration. The universities have been slow to respond, and where they have responded the result has not always been what is needed. But we believe that we should make a start here and now.'[2]

But Balliol's blessing was not welcomed with unmixed enthusiasm: a long *Times* correspondence ensued. 'One can see it clearly', said Dr. V. L. Allen on the BBC: 'not a new struggling discipline but one sumptuously provided for, dominating and dominant, with the rest of the social sciences serving it from odd corners, basements and attics . . . Universities which run management training schemes are helping to rationalise the present power structure in industry. They are, therefore, providing a service for the controlling élite . . . Perhaps the possibility of serving the country's centres of economic power is irresistibly attractive when

[1] *Acton.* p. 49.
[2] *See The Times,* June 2, 1961.

compared with the task of investigating the underdog, the unemployed, the pathological case, a task which has so often been their lot.'

'The universities must come to terms with management,' replied J. H. Smith in a broadcast the following week: 'I think Dr. Allen finds it difficult to accept this because he has little enthusiasm for managers, or for élites. I can sympathise, but feel bound to draw his attention to an authority whom I am sure he respects: more than forty years ago, Sidney Webb wrote: "Under any social order from now to Utopia a management is indispensable and all-enduring . . . The question is not: 'Will there be a management élite,' but 'What sort of élite will it be?' " '

29

ACCOUNTANTS

Cold, passive, noncommittal, with eyes like codfish ... minus
bowels, passion or a sense of humour.
            Elbert Hubbard (describing the typical auditor in America).

They are almost business doctors, are they not?—That is an expression I have seen used.
            Examination of Sir W. Plender (Departmental Committee of 1930).

THE accountants, the fastest-growing profession in Britain, stand
to the world of corporate business much as the lawyer stood to the
nineteenth-century world of rich men's property. They are the
priesthood of industry: the more fragmented and diversified a
company becomes, the more important becomes the man who can
disentangle the threads of profitability that hold it together. Few
people in a vast company are in a position to see over the tops of
the trees. An able accountant can, and from his knowledge comes
his power.

The growth of the profession has been spectacular. In 1940 there
were about 34,000 accountants: by 1958 the number was estimated
at 58,000—three times the number of lawyers and 29 times the
number of barristers. Their power has been enormously enhanced
by taxation, which can mould the shape of a corporation, of which
few people except accountants can make sense. The 'innumeracy'
(as Crowther called it)—the ignorance and fear of figures—of the
average British businessman has added to the accountants' mystique. 'It's pathetic', said one management consultant, 'to see
how accountants pull wool over the eyes of the engineers.'

Accountants or former accountants play a decisive rôle in British
Industry. In the slumpish times of the twenties and thirties,
several large firms were rescued by accountants, as Lever Brothers
was rescued by Francis D'Arcy Cooper, and since the war
there has been a massive flow of accountants into industry.
According to one estimate, they quadrupled in 25 years, reaching
10,000 in 1958.[1] Among the most powerful present-day accountants are Sir Ellis Hunter, chairman of Dorman, Long: John Davis,

[1] *See The Future Rôle of the Accountant in Industry* by W. W. Fea, Institute of Chartered
Accountants in England and Wales, 1958.

the managing director of the Rank Organisation; John Spencer Wills, chairman of Associated-Rediffusion and other companies in the Drayton Group; Halford Reddish, chairman of Rugby cement; and Henry Lazell, chairman of the Beecham Group. Paul Chambers of ICI comes from that sanctuary of the priesthood, the Inland Revenue.

But the accountants, however powerful, remain a pariah profession. They are a striking example of the British reluctance to accept new occupations; like actuaries or scientists, they have come in through the back door. Their beginnings were squalid. The first accountants, who began practising in the city about 1840, were invariably associated with bankruptcy and liquidations; like undertakers, they had an aura of gloom. With the passing of the Companies Act of 1862 and the Bankruptcy Act of 1869—which provided for the appointment of an accountant for creditors—the occupation became much more important, but still associated with calamity. Ernest Cooper, a founder of Cooper Brothers, has described their position when he first went to the city in 1864: 'We could hardly, south of the Tweed, claim to be a profession. There was absolutely no organisation or co-operation, no Institute or Society, no examinations, very few articled clerks, no newspaper, no library, no benevolent fund, and not even a dining club or golf club. Our social position was not enviable . . . I well remember that to be seen talking to, or having your office entered by, an accountant, was to be avoided, particularly in the stressful times of 1866.'

In 1880 'The Institute of Chartered Accountants in England and Wales' was founded, and the job became a profession with its own rules of conduct. With the expansion of the joint stock companies, which required independent auditors by law, and the advance of taxation, accountants multiplied, and soon became associated with normality, rather than disaster. But they never acquired the dignity of lawyers or doctors. Their education remains stark: there are few university courses, no Inns of Courts, little sense of brotherhood. Most accountants are taught at evening classes or at 'crammers', run by commercial firms for profit—a bleak initiation. Clever graduates often prefer to wait for unprofitable briefs in barristers' chambers to jostling with self-made clerks at accountants' crammers.

In Scotland the status of accountants, as of teachers and engineers, is higher—partly because the courts made earlier use of accountants: Sir Walter Scott, as early as 1820, recommended that his nephew 'cannot follow a better line than that of an accountant'. Edinburgh had its society of accountants in 1854, thirty years before England. The Scots training for accountants is broader, and insists on higher preliminary qualifications.

More than half the 60,000 accountants practise in accountants' firms, run by partnerships, like lawyers or doctors—varying from single men advising on tax-dodging, to international institutions. Four firms dominate the profession: one or other of their names can usually be seen above the annual reports of any industrial giant. This is their likely order of size (they are much too secretive to divulge the size of their staff):

> Peat Marwick Mitchell
> Price Waterhouse
> Deloitte Plender Griffiths
> Cooper Brothers

In the city, their incantatory names have acquired a respectability equal to Baring's or Freshfields. The arrival of their senior partners, in bowlers and black coats, far from suggesting calamity, brings calm and confidence.

Their main job is still auditing, and once a year their emissaries arrive at their client's offices to check through last year's ledgers. It is a job of massive tedium, checking the past rather than visualising the future; though nowadays with the mechanisation and standardisation of accounting, auditors can concentrate on checking systems, rather than go through all the figures. The auditor is the key to the company system—the representative of the public's interest, the licensed spy for the shareholders. His essential quality is independence: if figures are wrong or misleading, he must say so. For Deloitte's or Cooper's to 'qualify their report'—to suggest that sums have not been accounted for—is worse than an 'observation' from the Governor of the Bank.

Auditing occupies about 80 per cent of the accountants' time, but as the large partnerships have grown in resources, so they have provided other services. After going through a company's books, they can know more about its workings than most directors; they can advise on taxation problems, systems of costing, pension schemes, economic trends—and more recently on office organisation, for which the big firms have special departments, rivalling the management consultants. The 'Big Four' have broader international connections than most bankers and consultants, with networks of branches, and their services and advice are much cheaper than the banks'.

As corporate business has become more complex, so the advice of the auditors has grown weightier: they can analyse not only honesty and competence, but general health and prospects. Travelling from one corporation to another, they can compare their problems—acting as business doctors, specialists on industrial anatomy, putting their stethoscopes near the heart, checking the blood stream, diagnosing the curious diseases and intestinal troubles of Leviathans. In a crisis their advice can be at least as valuable as bankers'—for instance Binder Hamlyn's advice to Courtaulds in 1962.

A heavy new weapon is the 'special investigation'. A large company planning a project, a bridge, or a take-over, will often commission accountants to report on its feasibility, and (in accountants' words) 'generally to introduce a sense of realism'. After engineers have drawn up plans for a dam, a group of accountants will fly out, peruse the figures, compare them with other projects, cross-examine the engineers, and produce their own—often more pessimistic—report. Broad investigations are now beginning to be used by the government and even the Treasury: in 1961 Ernest Marples, the Minister of Transport, commissioned Peat Marwick's—often regarded as the Establishment accountants—to prepare a report on shipbuilding contracts, as part of his campaign to stimulate the industry. But the Treasury is only beginning to make use of accountants as an instrument of control: it is now clear that if a full investigation had been made into the British Railways modernisation plan before it was approved, scores of millions could have been saved.

This kind of accountancy is concerned not with the past but with the future, and it requires from the accountant what he (like a solicitor or a bank manager) most shrinks from—an opinion. 'Clients are not impressed by a report', wrote Henry Benson, senior partner of Cooper Brothers and son-in-law of D'Arcy Cooper,[1] 'however detailed or painstaking, unless it is concluded by a firm opinion. I do not suggest that the accountant's traditional attitude of caution should change or that he should cease to be impartial. The point I am seeking to make is that if we are to be of real use to our clients, we must be prepared to give a common-sense judgment on the facts that we have discovered.'

This new scope depresses some other businesses—particularly

[1] Paper to the Institute of Chartered Accountants in 1958.

engineers. For, in so far as accountants are known to make decisions, they are likely to say No. To a team of engineers, no nightmare is worse than a group of men arriving to introduce realism (=pessimism), to envisage bad weather, floods and 'contingent liabilities' —that menacing accountants' phrase—to shake their heads and ask awkward questions. Accountants indignantly deny that they are habitual no-men: 'a full and fair picture' is their object, and some accountants, certainly, can become quite romantic about vast and risky expenditures. But their whole history, beginning with bankruptcies and flourishing in the age of slump, has filled them with a vivid sense of disaster. Imagination and sense of change are not their first requirements; and the business doctors are sometimes unable to diagnose the most deadly of diseases—the creeping caution and hypochondria induced by some of the doctors themselves.

TAX

The strongest source of power for the accountant is tax. Since income tax was introduced by Pitt in 1799, taxation has influenced the pattern of society: it helps to account for the spate of weddings in March, the generosity of fathers to children, the number of authors living abroad, the boom of life assurance, the largeness of businessmen's lunches and the smallness of their dinners. While in America taxation has become the province of lawyers, in Britain it has been largely taken over by accountants. (Some suggest that the lack of lawyers specialising in tax, coupled with accountants' ignorance of law, gives the Inland Revenue too strong a position.)

Company tax brought the accountant into the industry, income tax and surtax brought him into the home. Tax avoidance, juggling with schedules, covenants, domiciles and beneficiaries, have made the accountant as important to the middle-class family as a dentist or solicitor; avoidance is regarded no longer as a nasty trickery, but as a private duty—a perpetual and inevitable war.

'No man in this country', said Lord Clyde, President of the Scottish Court of Session, 'is under the smallest obligation, moral or other, so to arrange his legal relations as to enable the Inland Revenue to put the largest shovel into his stores. The Inland Revenue is not slow . . . to take every advantage which is open to it under the taxing statutes for the purpose of depleting the tax-payers' pocket. And the tax-payer is, in like manner, entitled to be astute enough to prevent, so far as he honestly can, the depletion of his means by the Revenue.'[1]

The techniques of tax avoidance have produced angry comments from judges. In June, 1961, the manager of the Midland Bank's branch in Pall Mall, Mr. Gordon James Brown, appealed against a refusal to have his membership of two clubs, the Devonshire and the Royal Automobile, allowed as tax-free expenses—in front of Lord Evershed, Lord Justice Harman and Lord Justice Donovan (who seemed curiously unaware of the common practice of firms' paying for club subscriptions). 'But he is not employed to sit in the coffee room and eat roast mutton', said Lord Justice Harman. 'I think there is something in the social aspect, some element of "social snobbery",' said Lord Evershed, 'if Mr. Brown were seen about the Devonshire Club it gave him a certain status...' 'It seems to me', said Lord Justice Harman, 'to poison the wells of hospitality altogether if you ask a man to lunch, not because you like him, but because of some ulterior motive...' 'It shocks me, it really does', said Lord Evershed, after discussion with Brown's Counsel: 'that is why income tax is a sort of game, a battle of ingenuity, unrelated to any principle of commonsense or ethical considerations, and it is extremely bad for respect for the law. I can only plead that some time some day those who instruct you will pay regard to the prestige of the law and possibly the welfare of society.' The appeal was dismissed.[2]

At the centre of this great tax web is the much-abused Board of Inland Revenue. 'The Revenue' itself spends £46 million a year maintaining a corps of about 3,000 inspectors, and a staff of 20,000.

Tax-collecting is not very popular, and since the war the Revenue have had difficulty in recruiting—and keeping—enough people: by 1961 they were 300 inspectors short. Tax experts have become more and more in demand by industry, moving from one side of the fence to the other—from gamekeepers to poachers. As the rules have become more intricate, so both sides have come to talk a private language—like burglars and safe-makers, progressing from new evasion devices ('scissors', 'share-stripping') to new attempts at safeguard.

'There are two million people who assess their own income tax,' said one (anonymous) tax inspector complaining about the

---

[1] Quoted in *The Tax Gatherers* by James Coffield .1960. p. 98.
[2] *The Times*, June 27, 1961.

'crying abuses': 'if one is suspected of fraud it will take several weeks of work to run him to ground, and there are not enough income tax inspectors to investigate the millions of probable offenders. All we can do is to investigate the most blatantly fraudulent: a fruit-seller, for instance, who takes his wife and children for a two weeks' holiday in Majorca and charges the holiday to business expenses. £30 million is collected every year from dishonest tax evaders, but hundreds of million more are lost annually by legal tax evasion. In big business companies, the companies themselves have little opportunity for evading tax, but directors and executives can lighten the burden by arranging their business so that the maximum personal expenditure is made directly out of business—which isn't of course illegal. The ordinary wage man can do little more to evade taxation than claim on a luncheon voucher. The worst tax offenders are butchers and doctors—but the explanation rests on opportunity rather than type. The Edwardians paid hardly any tax and showed remarkable honesty. Tax evasion goes up in geometrical progression. The tax laws are added to every year, but the accountants and legal experts are as clever as our men.'

The Revenue successfully preserves an impassive façade. But it is not entirely rigid in its methods of extortion. If it cannot obtain money from someone who is visibly broke, it is quite capable of making a bargain, and settling for a monthly payment—keeping the cow alive in order to milk it. With show business—where large sums of money are made, spent, and then demanded—the relationships with the Revenue are most bitter. Actors and musicians, unable to pay taxes, find themselves bonded for life to the Revenue, like Elizabethan spendthrifts to usurers.

But the Revenue are not wholly inhuman. Sir Alan Herbert once wrote a cheque, duly stamped and crossed, in this form:

Dear Bankers, PAY the undermentioned hounds
The shameful sum of FIVE-AND-EIGHTY-POUNDS £85.0.0
By 'hound', of course, by custom, one refers
To SPECIAL (INCOME TAX) COMMISSIONERS
And these progenitors of woe and worry
You'll find at LYNWOOD ROAD, THAMES DITTON, SURREY.
This is the *second* lot of tax, you know,
On money that I earned two years ago
(The shark, they say, by no means Nature's Knight,
Will rest contented with a single bite:
The barracuda, who's a fish more fell,
Comes back and takes the other leg as well).

Two years ago. But things have changed since then.
I've reached the age of three-score years and ten.
My earnings dwindle: and the kindly State
Gives me a tiny pension—with my mate.
You'd think the State would generously roar
'At least, he shan't pay SURTAX any more'.
Instead, by this unChristian attack
They get two-thirds of my poor pension back.
Oh, very well. No doubt it's for the best;
At all events, pray do as I request:
And let the good old customs be enforced—
Don't cash this cheque, unless it is endorsed.

The cheque was cashed and an official reply came back from the Office of the Special Commissioners of Income Tax:

S.T.H.31097/40
Dear Sir,
It is with pleasure that I thank
You for your letter, and the order to your bank
To pay the sum of five and eighty pounds
To those here whom you designate as hounds.
Their appetite is satisfied. In fact
You paid too much and I am forced to act,
Not to repay you, as perchance you dream,
Though such a course is easy, it would seem.
Your liability for later years
Is giving your accountants many tears:
And till such time as they and we can come
To amicable settlement on the sum
That represents your tax-bill to the State
I'll leave the overpayment to its fate.
I do not think this step will make you frown:
The sum involved is only half-a-crown.
Yours faithfully,
A. L. Grove.

Sir Alan replied:

Your Ref. S.T.H.31097/40
I thank you, Sir, but am afraid
Of such a rival in my trade:
One never should encourage those—
In future I shall pay in prose.

30

CHAIRMEN

I wish I knew if I was chairman of this company,
It would make a lot of difference at conferences:
Gorgeous conferences we have, simply gorgeous,
Finest in the City, I imagine.
I am always in the top chair, but the boys will never
let on if I'm chairman or not.
D. B. Wyndham Lewis, Lament.

WITH all the talk in the past twenty years about the 'managerial
revolution' it is often assumed that the revolution is virtually
complete—that most of industry is run by committees of managerial men, divorced from ownership or inheritance. This is far
from the truth. Only in a few giant companies which have outgrown their families—Shell, Unilever, ICI—has the revolution
been complete; at the top of most companies an individual or a
family still wields large influence. The old race of managers, who
worked their way up through the factory without special training
or outside experience, like insurance or bank managers, have not
often been strong enough to break into the board and achieve a
dominant position. Only since the war have the new race of
graduate professional managers—like Shell or ICI men before the
war—had the confidence and all-round experience to challenge
the old boardroom traditions, and most will not be reaching the
boardroom age for ten or fifteen years. The conflict between the
old family tradition, still with shades of the amateur squire, and
the new professional managers (though often confused) is fundamental. It is the few hundred top industrial managers, rather than,
for instance, a few hundred MPs, who will determine the future
economic strength of Britain.

The typical British business is not the anonymous corporation,
but the family firm. In 1959 a third of the profits in the manufacturing, building and distribution industries were earned by private
companies, not quoted on the Stock Exchange.[1] Even after private
companies have 'gone public', as we shall see, family interests
remain dominant. When Dr. Copeman in 1955 conducted a
survey of 1,243 directors in public companies with assets over £1

[1] *See* Radcliffe Report, p. 82.

474

million, he found that 28 per cent of the directors had succeeded their fathers in the same firm and no less than 8 per cent had succeeded as the fourth or fifth generation.[1] In the older industries, such as shipbuilding, cotton or printing, many firms are still run by the great-great-grandsons of the founders, descending from the industrial revolution.

FAMILY FIRMS

The old family firm has a character as different from the managerial corporation as a tree from a house. Over the decades it has taken on some of the characteristics of an estate. Portraits of the bearded founder and his progeny hang in the front office, retainers reminisce about the chairman as a schoolboy, the chairman's secretary looks after tomatoes from the kitchen garden or the children's return to school after the holidays, between invoices for machinery. The sense of family spreads out from the boardroom to the whole factory, and in a small town the company can dominate the social life; at Richard Clay's printing works in Suffolk (where I once worked) a sixth of the population of Bungay worked for the firm, and nearly everyone had a son, a brother or a husband in the company.

To the workers in the smaller companies, the family *is* the firm. They may resent young Mr. Charles, straight down from Cambridge, being introduced round the factory, to become a director over their heads in a few years' time; or doing odd shopping jobs for the chairman's wife; or the patronising airs of Mrs. Peter, Mrs. Tom and Mrs. Alan at the annual staff outing. But the family represents a simple embodiment of something which is impersonal and complicated, and young Mr. Charles is its continuity. Compared to a managerial corporation, a family firm is like a monarchy to a republic:[2] it is more interesting and more comprehensible. The mystique and inertia which can gather round a family chairman after a few generations may eventually bring the whole company to disaster; but in the meantime it is very reassuring, for trade is insecure and restless, while a family is secure and continuous, loyal and visible.

Some family firms have achieved equilibrium over generations, settling to a convenient size, gathering subsidiary families round them—of book-keepers, factory hands, craftsmen, handing down jobs from father to son. In the smallest firms—shops or builders—

---

[1] *See* G. H. Copeman: *Leaders of British Industry*, 1955. p. 97.
[2] *See* Bagehot, page 48.

there may be no incentive to grow beyond a single boss.

A few family firms have grown to international dimensions, while still remaining private companies. Probably the most celebrated is Wedgwood's, founded in 1759 by Josiah Wedgwood —who himself came from a long line of potters. He personally invented most of the designs and processes which made Wedgwood famous: he was an extraordinary mixture of eighteenth-century dabbler, technician, businessman and Fellow of the Royal Society. Since then Wedgwood's have maintained a continuous family tradition; not only the board, but many of the workmen are descended from the original eighteenth-century people. The present chairman, Josiah (author of *The Economics of Inheritance*) belongs to the sixth generation, and by 1920 the tenth generation of Wedgwoods was already in the company. The *Wedgwood Review* has such headings as 'Mr. Josiah reviews 1959', 'Mr. Josiah on the US recession', or 'Brush up your Wedgwood', a quiz about the firm's history. But the Wedgwood family have branched out into barons, historians and artists, intermarried with the Cambridge intellectual dynasties: recently there has been a shortage of young Wedgwoods interested in business, and the family tradition seems likely to dwindle.

Pilkington's, the glass makers at St. Helens, are the other most prominent private family firm. Their founder, William Pilkington, made a success of the family wine business, and invested some money in the St. Helens Crown Glass company in 1826. Two years later the firm ran into trouble; William bought out all the partners except his brother-in-law, and set up as Greenall and Pilkington. His four sons were equally dynamic and fascinated with new processes: they experimented with electric light and installed a telephone as early as 1880. In the next decade the experimental instinct waned, and they were slow to develop safety glass, but later they did a deal with Triplex, and now control safety-glass factories in Australia and South Africa and South America, with large shares in Canada's biggest firm, Duplate. By the 1950's, with the help of an enterprising young Pilkington, they had caught up again technically, and spent £4 million on the new 'float glass' process.[1] Their chairman, Sir Harry, is not only a very successful businessman, but has been a director of the Bank of England (to which he bicycles) and chairman of the royal commissions on doctors' salaries and television.

[1] *See* J. C. Barker, *Pilkington Brothers and the Glass Industry*, 1960.

476

Another remarkable family firm is Ferranti's, the electronics firm with 18,000 employees, mostly in Manchester. The present chairman, Sir Vincent de Ferranti (an ex-president of the Electrical Engineers) was the son of the founder, and Sir Vincent's son, Mr. Sebastian, aged 34, is managing director. The Ferrantis succeed in presiding with a mixture of paternalism and aggressive enterprise—they commissioned a sculpture by Paolozzi, but also built the first commercial computer in Europe ten years ago, and have been building a £2½ million computer for the Atlas rocket.

Family firms can break up in several ways. The family may lose interest, or die out. They may encounter such powerful competition that—like the components of Barclays Bank, Imperial Tobacco or ICI—they have to merge with other families. They may find death duties insuperable. They may need extra capital for development and be forced to 'go public' on the stock exchange. The change-over from a family firm to a managerial corporation is a recurring drama of our time. Instead of the loved and hated old name, like Morris or Austin, there are initials— BMC, AEI, BAC. Instead of an impossible old boss there are committees and 'they'. The workers who cursed the old man now have only a committee to blame, and reminisce gloomily about the rough old days of the bicycle shop.

The British readily feel sentimental about family firms. Where the firm revolves round one dynamic personality, the transition to a committee can mean a loss of vigour, but many second or third generations are more likely to be complacent than dynamic. Not many families—even of bankers—are ruthless enough to exclude nitwits from the succession, or fecund enough to produce enough first-class managers. The drawing-room privilege which hangs about the boardroom can easily act as a disincentive to ambitious outsiders. The chairman himself, who must be moderately efficient to survive, is not the main obstacle: it is the periphery of nephews, cousins and particularly sons-in-law who so often clog the wheels of management, and by the assumption of privilege damage the dignity of professional managers.

In the more backward industries, family complacency must take much of the blame. The incompetence of shipbuilding, the obstinacy of machine-tool companies, the medieval habits of many printers, often emanate from grandsons and great-grandsons of founders: the company is handed down, with the furniture, the heirlooms and the country house, and the ships and machines become part of the family estate. The undeniable charms of the family firm, like those of the palace or the squire, are dangerous for a country that must come quickly to terms with change.

TWENTY-THREE CHAIRMEN

Among the largest firms in the country, there is still often a family or an individual with a dominating influence on the board: even among American giants, Fords and du Ponts are still controlled by Fords and du Ponts. The managers may be in control of the day-to-day running, but in major investment decisions—which can make or break the company—the family can still be decisive. Opposite are the twenty-three companies which in 1961 qualified for the 'hundred million club'—having (British) assets of over £100 million. (Assets are not a satisfactory guide to size, but the other two yardsticks, profits and turnover, can be equally misleading, and turnover is still frequently secret.) Below are brief notes on the twenty-three firms and their chairmen.

1. *Shell Transport and Trading*[1] *(Assets £853·2 million)*
   (see pp. 430–438).

2. *Imperial Chemical Industries (Assets £695 million)*
   (see pp. 445–452).

3. *British Petroleum (Assets £563·4 million)*
   Half-owned by the British government—though their influence is small: the two government directors are regarded as having 'gone native'. BP, like Shell, is a vast oil concern, owning 50 per cent of Kuwait oil, 40 per cent of the consortium in Iran, and 24 per cent of the Iraq Petroleum Company. BP (formerly Anglo-Iranian) have been less crafty and sensitive to post-war changes than Shell, as they learnt to their cost in 1951 at Abadan—since when they have quickly put on a more international face. Like Shell, they long ago grew beyond the control of one man. Their present chairman, Maurice Bridgeman, belongs to the civil-service school of oilmen; he has spent his career in BP or in government service, but he has an Eton-and-Whites background and banking connections. His father was Lloyd George's Home Secretary; his brother, Lord Bridgeman, is a director of Warburg's Mercury Securities, his daughter married a Baring.

---

[1] This does not include the Dutch part (see p. 430).

Company	Headquarters	Assets (millions) £	Employees
Shell	London	853·2	250–300,000
ICI	London	695	113,699
British Petroleum	London	563·4	100,000
Unilever (UK only)	London	355·1	74,000
British-American Tobacco	London	325·9	100,000
Imperial Tobacco	Bristol	292·8	46,000
P and O	London	197·4	35–45,000
Courtaulds	London	192·3	48,000[1]
Bowater Paper Co	London	187·8	14,500
Steel Company of Wales	Port Talbot	183·3	24,500
Esso	London and New York	180·5	14,000
Guest, Keen and Nettlefold	London and Smethwick	179·9	80,000
AEI	London	170·6	103,000
Tube Investments	London and Birmingham	168·5	60,000
Distillers	London and Edinburgh	150·7	21,000
Vickers	London	142·9	70,000
Stewarts & Lloyds	Corby, Lincs.	137·7	40,000
United Steel	Sheffield	130·8	39,000
Dunlop Rubber	London	124·4	under 100,000
Ford Motor	Dagenham	114·8	47,863
Great Universal Stores	London and Manchester	112	65,000
Ind Coope, Tetley, Ansell	Burton-on-Trent	108.4	31,000
J. P. Coats, Paton & Baldwins	Glasgow	106·7	45–50,000

[1] UK only, plus 12,000 overseas.

4. *Unilever (UK only) (Assets £355·6 million)*
(see pp. 438–445).

5. *British-American Tobacco (Assets £325·9 million)*

A brother-company to Imperial Tobacco (see below) formed in 1902 to grow and sell tobacco abroad (it still sells no cigarettes in Britain). It employs 100,000 people with 100 factories in 50 countries, but has only 4,000 employees in Britain. Its American subsidiary is estimated as the fourth largest tobacco company there. It has some of the characteristics of Imperial, and tobacco families on its board. But their chairman, Duncan Oppenheim, is a very civilised solicitor who came from the city firm of Linklater and Paines—a comparatively rare example of a lawyer-chairman. He has exhibited an action painting, and is chairman of the Council of Industrial Design.

6. *Imperial Tobacco (Assets £292·8 million)*

An extraordinary example of continuing, rather sleepy family influence in a giant firm. It was formed in 1901, as a protection against American invasion, out of three big family firms—Wills, Players and Churchmans—and several smaller ones. Together with Gallahers—of which they own 42 per cent—they produce 90 per cent of British cigarettes. Their headquarters is a great red-brick palace in Bristol, from which they direct their various subsidiaries—which are left to compete with each other on a narrow but hectic territory.[1] The parent company, known as 'IT Co' maintains an aloof, mahogany attitude to the sales race, but they benefit from their monopoly position by their influence with shops. Wills have always been the dominating influence, and Lord Dulverton, head of the family, is on the board. The chairman, Roger Clarke, comes from one of the family firms (William Clarke) which made up Imperial—his father was 'Leaf Manager' of Imperial. He and his board have reacted to the 1962 report on Lung Cancer, and to revelations about their monopoly, with the old-fashioned sang-froid of unreconstructed businessmen.

7. *P and O Steam Navigation (Assets £197·4 million)*

The biggest shipping line in the world, with 366 ships and a large interest in the biggest private airline. It has the conservative characteristics of shipping lines—very long city lunches, a great divide between the crews and 'the Company', and largely ship-owning families on the boards. Shipping, like the navy, faces

[1] *See* Players v. Senior Service, pp. 590–592.

extreme changes, but has been slower to face up to them. Cunard is run by Brocklebanks and Bates's, Union Castle and Clan lines are run by the Cayzer cousins. P and O, though a huge public company, has strong family traditions: there are three Geddes on the board, plus an Earl and two Viscounts. But the company is largely run by two Etonian brothers, Sir Donald Anderson, the chairman, and Sir Colin, an art-collector who lives in a big old house in Hampstead. The sons of the previous chairman, they came up through Anderson, Green, part of the P and O empire. They have helped to change the face of P and O, with comparatively daring ship-designs and civilised décors by Sir Hugh Casson.

Sir Donald has made tough statements about the shipping industry: 'so far as shipping is concerned this country suffers under the delusion that Britannia rules the waves not by human effort but by divine right' (1954), and has rejected the idea of government subsidies as 'a form of artificial respiration for the half-drowned' (1960). But by March, 1962 the shipping position had become still bleaker and P and O even had to cancel their shareholders' ancient privilege to visit new ships.

8. *Courtaulds* (*Assets £192·2 million*)

Up till January, 1962 Courtaulds seemed, and in many respects was, a stately company of the less aggressive kind. Its board included two Courtaulds, an ex-cabinet minister (Aubrey Jones) and the chairman, Sir John Hanbury Williams who belonged to the courtier tradition—son of a general, born in Windsor Castle, married a princess, Director of the Bank of England. Courtaulds were secretive, public-spirited, afflicted with troubles in textiles, and not much interested in their shareholders. The chairman-elect, Sir Alan Wilson, F.R.S., had the reputation of being an outstanding scientist, but not primarily a businessman.

Two months later ICI had tried and failed to take them over, and Courtaulds emerged with a very different face: they spent £250,000 on ruthless advertising, effectively accused ICI of a poor research record compared to their own, and convincingly revealed their own programme of expansion and future profits; with this and other attractions pushing up their shares from 30/- to 50/-. They also displayed an impressive director, Frank Kearton, an F.R.S. who began with ICI, who did much to save the company from absorption. He and his colleagues swept away reticence and protocol, and gave an impression of both scientific and commercial enterprise. By March 12 it was clear that ICI had only got

37 per cent of their shares—which Courtaulds celebrated with a thanksgiving service. The outward transformation of Courtaulds was an astonishing example of how, when fighting for its life, a company can reveal a totally different character.

9. *Bowaters* (*Assets £187·8 million*)

Spectacular example of a huge expanding corporation still controlled by one individual, Sir Eric Vansittart Bowater, known as 'the Emperor', who has a large pent-house flat on top of the Bowater building in Knightsbridge. The firm was founded by Sir Eric's grandfather in 1881, and was still comparatively small when Sir Eric became chairman in 1927: he bought out his uncles who wouldn't agree to his expansionist policy, and went into partnership with Lords Beaverbrook and Rothermere—later advantageously buying both out. He bought plants and timber in Newfoundland and Scandinavia, and after the war forged into Tennessee, New Zealand and more recently into Europe. Sir Eric supplies much of the dynamic: when there was a forest fire in Newfoundland, Sir Eric personally flew out to look at it. He broadcasts to his company's Canadian employees on Christmas Day, and is adept at public relations: Bowaters have a sumptuous illustrated annual report, surmounted by the symbol of—guess what?—the bow and the water. Recently Bowaters have been reorganised, and the managerial structure bent round a large computer, but Sir Eric cannot be bent round anything, and the company still has a private court in the middle of it. Bowaters is like a pyramid, with a big private plateau on the top, but in the next generation it will be run by a committee of managers.

10. *Steel Company of Wales* (*Assets £183·3 million*)

An unusual company invented from scratch in 1947, with no family traditions: it was started by, among others, Richard Thomas and Baldwin and GKN[1] to produce sheet-steel and tin-plate in South Wales, and now has the largest integrated steelworks in Europe, producing 3 million ingot tons a year—the 'City of Steel which never sleeps'. It was nationalised and denationalised, and now has wide share-distribution but with big blocks belonging to GKN and with the chairman of Metal Box on the board. But the company is run by a triumvirate who were largely responsible for building up the steel-works (the first two both came from Guest Keen's), Sir Julian Pode, the chairman, an ex-accountant who

[1] *See* page 483.

breeds horses; Frederick Cartwright, the managing director; and David Young, a Scots financial expert. Like most steel companies, SCOW is close to the factory, proud of its provincialism and not showy.

11. *Esso Petroleum (Assets £180·5 million)*

A subsidiary of Standard Oil of New Jersey, and Shell's main competitor, both outside and inside Britain. Their London office— a skyscraper near Buckingham Palace—is allowed fair independence, but the parent company keeps them on their toes; their most striking Americanisation was the building of the Fawley refinery near Southampton—the biggest in the Commonwealth— in record time. Managers arrive at the same time as the workers. Their chairman, Hugh S. Tett, often assumed to be American, is in fact a Redbrick technocrat, in contrast to nearly all the other twenty: he took a science degree at Exeter university, did research at London on tetro-ethyl lead, and worked his way up through Esso technical sales. He became a petroleum expert, looked after Esso's research in Europe, and became London chairman in 1959.

12. *Guest, Keen and Nettlefolds (Assets £179·9 million)*

Made up of eighty steel and engineering firms, making things from safety-pins to welding equipment. They are run from Smethwick in Staffordshire, with a modern office in Kingsway, London. Parts of GKN go back to the industrial revolution, but they are not atrophied by old age, and have been expanding suddenly. There are still family influences, but GKN has become largely a managerial company. Their chairman, Kenneth Peacock (also a director of the Steel Company of Wales) is the son of a former managing director, and went into GKN from Oundle. He is an adept committee man, skilful in dealing with his eighty companies, and keeping quite a strict hold on investment.

13. *Associated Electrical Industries (Assets £170·6 million)*

The biggest electrical company, making everything from electric light bulbs to power stations and railway engines ('We have both elephants and rabbits in our zoo,' said Lord Chandos). The result of several mergers, absorbing such famous names as British-Thomson-Houston, Ediswan, Siemens and Metropolitan Vickers —names that they have ruthlessly suppressed, imposing a new corporate personality with the help of glamorous advertisements. The divisions remain separate, dominated by engineers—except for Hotpoint (refrigerators, etc.), run by a celebrated Scots super-salesman, Craig Wood. But the main board is very un-managerial, including the omnipresent Lord Bicester. The chairman on-and-off since 1945 has been Lord Chandos.[1] The heir-apparent, Mike Wheeler, went into steel from St. Paul's School, and worked with Chandos during the war. After the war he rose to be chairman of a division of GKN, until he was invited by Chandos to AEI. He is expected to display the familiar apparent contrast between new chairmen and old—a civil servant more than a politician, quiet, professional, son of a GWR manager, Master of the Beagles in Bucks. But he is a tough, incisive man, capable of making shrewd decisions quickly on the telephone and not bothering too much with subordinates.

14. *Tube Investments* (*Assets £168·5 million*)

Another mixed engineering group, with products from scaffolding to hypodermic needles. Based on Birmingham, where they have an ugly, Cotton-and-Clore building and a Midlands accent, but with a growing back-base in London. 'Tubes' have been built up by its chairman, Sir Ivan Stedeford, a dynamic Methodist engineer from Birmingham who married the boss's daughter (he has a son and a son-in-law in the business). He preserves an aggressive Midlands independence, as emerged in the Aluminium War against the 'Old Freddies' of the city.[2] He is now an elder tycoon-statesman for government committees. He has been able to choose good men and leave them alone—notably his successor, Lord Plowden.

Plowden is an interesting new-style chairman—formerly chief planner at the Treasury, and head of Atomic Energy. He is a quiet Treasury man, precise and very influential: an intellectual,with an analytical approach. Behind his mild exterior he can be bold and critical, particularly of Old Freddies and family firms: a late but effectual convert to the Common Market.

15. *Distillers* (*Assets £150·7 million*)

A near monopoly of Scotch whisky, including most of the well-known names: it was formed from a group of family distillers in 1877, based on Edinburgh. Since then, its whisky profits have been

[1] *See* page 506.
[2] *See* pp. 387-390.

so huge that it has expanded first into industrial alcohol then into petro-chemicals, antibiotics, plastics, etc. But Distillers, like Imperial Tobacco, shows signs of monopolitis, and are less enterprising than before the war. Between the whisky and the industrial sides is a strange contrast: the whisky people are mellow and family-bound, entrenched in Edinburgh society, each brand with its own board, competing with other brands. The industrial people are much more technical and self-made. The two converge on the main board, which includes Major Macdonald-Buchanan of Black and White, and Lord Forteviot of Dewars. The chairman, Sir Graham Hayman, is a tough manager from the chemical business who ran a rival company and was bought out: he is now fairly aloof and does not (as he likes to put it) go much 'into the kitchen'. He maintains a secretive attitude to the different sides of the business: 'Some of my horses are lagging, others well out in front.'

16. *Vickers (Assets £142·9 million)*

Engineering giant, originated in Sheffield 150 years ago, now with four big divisions—aviation, shipbuilding, engineering and steel. All are headed by engineers and are kept separate: the enterprise of the aircraft division (which produced the Viscount) does not cross-fertilise the more somnolent shipbuilders: though a Vickers research company does span all divisions. The head office, in its glass skyscraper, is becoming more of a holding company, and in some of its satellites, like the British Aircraft Corporation or Vickers overseas, it shares ownership with others. Vickers, the biggest armament company, has become very close to the government after two world wars. In the passages are notices saying 'The official secrets act affects *you*', and faded pictures of battleships. People sometimes talk of 'the army, navy, air force and Vickers'.

Vickers has difficulty in finding enough engineers with enough breadth of experience for top jobs: their board includes Sir Sam Brown, the city lawyer, Lord Bicester (of course) and a vigorous Treasury knight, Sir Leslie Rowan, as managing director. As chairmen they have preferred generals or peers: the two previous chairmen, Lord Weeks (a general from Pilkington's) and Lord Knollys (an insurance peer, page of honour to two kings) were both brought from outside the company, and the new chairman, Major-General Dunphie—son of a courtier and banker, married a general's daughter—was brought into Vickers by his friend Lord Weeks.

17. *Stewarts and Lloyds (Assets £137·7 million)*

A steel giant, merged in 1903, with a Lloyd on the board until 1961, and Graham Stewart as their chairman. He is a vigorous Wykehamist who was in the forefront of the campaign against nationalisation—'a long step towards the setting up of communism . . .' (January 28, 1958). Much of the company is run by managing directors, but Stewart flies 35,000 miles round England a year, and takes a large hand in investment decisions. United Steel, Stewarts and Lloyds, and John Summers have all been interlocked with directors—making up the 'Holy Trinity' of steel.

18. *United Steel (Assets £130·8 million)*

A merger of family steel companies in 1918: like other steel companies, it has a superstructure of old families, with self-made managers and numbers of Oxbridge graduates. It is technically very advanced, but maintains a wide divide between managers and the board of seven, which is largely hereditary. Until 1962 the chairman was Sir Walter Benton Jones, an octogenarian Welsh baronet from a coal-owning family, whose son is a director. James Peech, the new chairman is (as usual) less flamboyant and political than his predecessor, with no bow ties or literary references, but he also comes from a steel family. He went from Wellington and Oxford to the city, and joined the company in his thirties.

19. *Dunlop (Assets £124·4 million)*

Founded by John Boyd Dunlop, a vet, who invented an inflatable tyre for his son's tricycle: but since then have become less dynamic, and have tended to rest on their rubber, without much diversification. Their territory stretches from Malayan plantations to Midlands factories—making tyres, rackets, tennis balls, cushions, etc. (Their London office is very rubbery, rubber tiles, rubber floors.) Their chairman, Sir Edward Beharrel, is the son of a former chairman (who worked his way up from being Assistant Goods Manager to the LNER). Most of the day-to-day running is done by Reay Geddes, the managing director, whose father, too, was chairman of Dunlops. He read economics at Cambridge, went into the Bank of England, and then joined his father's company. He is a transport enthusiast, one of the early agitators for the Channel tunnel, and organised a road conference in Rhodesia, to 'revive Rhodes' dream of the all-red line'. He is also a member of the Treasury's 'Neddy'.

20. *Ford Motor (Assets £114·8 million)*

The biggest car company by assets, although BMC produce more cars. Since 1961 wholly owned by Fords in Detroit: their vast Dagenham works are Britain's most spectacular example of American 'vertical integration'. In many ways very American in their approach—ruthless, quick-changing, cosmopolitan—using American and German inventions freely. A visit from Henry Ford is preceded by weeks of panic. There is a whole corridor of segregated dining-rooms for different layers of bosses—amusing for a visitor, less so for a junior manager. Their chairman, Sir Patrick Hennessy, is a tough Irishman who began his career making Model T Fords in their Cork factory. He worked under Beaverbrook—with continual rows but mutual admiration—in Aircraft Production in the war. At Fords he likes to move from one department to another, finding out about them in detail: when something went wrong in the Ford Stand in the 1960 Motor Show, he put it right himself. In major investment matters he is controlled from Detroit, but in most decisions is independent.

21. *Great Universal Stores (Assets £112·0 million)*

The largest giant created by a single entrepreneur, who still controls it. Sir Isaac Wolfson, by a series of take-overs (when they were still unfashionable) built up the shop empire, including a merchant bank and a travel agency, called 'Gussies': it includes the biggest mail-order business in Europe, with lush catalogues which rival Sears Roebucks'—which provided his original inspiration. Gussies still revolves round their dynamic founder—a tireless, teetotal tycoon—and his son will probably succeed him. By issuing non-voting shares[1] the Wolfson family retain complete control, as Marks and Spencers remains with Markses and Sieffs.

22. *Ind Coope, Tetley, Ansells (Assets £108·4)*

The biggest of the breweries, as a result of a merger arranged at two Derbyshire picnics in February, 1961 ('that infamous patch of grass'—*Daily Worker*). 'This is not a take-over', said the chairman, Edward Thompson: 'it is a commonwealth concept—and a new one to the British brewing industry.' The group controls an eighth of the pubs in England, and is the most spectacular of several recent

See page 410.

mergers which, by May, 1961, had concentrated half the British pubs in the hands of ten companies:[1]

	No. of Pubs
Ind Coope, Tetley, Ansell	9,250
Watney, Mann	5,100
Bass, Mitchells & Butlers	4,200
Courage, Barclay & Simonds ..	3,500
Whitbread	2,500
Charrington	2,400
United Breweries	2,000
Scottish & Newcastle	1,700
John Smith (Tadcaster) & Assoc. ..	1,650
Greenall Whitley & Assoc.	1,650
Total for 'Top Ten'	33,950
Total number of pubs in UK ..	69,184

Much of the recent drive in brewing has come from men outside the brewing families or 'beerage', including Alan Walker of Bass, Mitchells, and the Canadian E. P. Taylor. Ind Coope's has no Inds or Coopes on the board; Thompson is a former solicitor who became managing director of Ind Coope in his thirties, a follower of American methods and a believer in high-pressure marketing and branding (Double Diamond, Skol, etc.). He has been described as 'a man who could as easily be running a chain store or a steel combine'.

23. *J. P. Coats, Paton & Baldwins (Assets £106·7 million)*

Founded by James Coats in Paisley in 1824, producing a large dynasty: between 1910 and 1930 nine Coatses and two Clarks died millionaires. In 1910 they had the biggest profits of any company in Britain, as the chart opposite indicates:[2] it also shows how transient some of the Leviathans have been.

Since the war Coats have lost ground, and have been slow to diversify into more expanding fields: but in 1960 they merged with Paton and Baldwins, which gave them a big holding in wool. Their board is full of family: they have three Coats, a Clark, a Clark son-in-law (Lord McCorquodale). But their chairman, Sir Malcolm McDougall, is a self-made Scot who walked into Coats' at the age of 14, and got a job in the accounts department as an office boy.

[1] *Sunday Times*, May 21, 1961.
[2] *See* P. E. Hart: Business Concentration in the United Kingdom. *Journal of the Royal Statistical Society*, Vol. 123. Part I. 1960. p. 57.

Largest 10 business units by profits, 1908–50

1908–10	1924	1938	1950	
1. Coats	Imp. Tobacco	Imp. Tobacco	Unilever	1.
2. Imp. Tobacco	Lever	ICI	ICI	2.
3. Guinness	Courtaulds	Lever	Imp. Tobacco	3.
4. Brunner, Mond	Coats	Woolworth	Distillers	4.
5. Fine Cotton	Guinness	Distillers	Coats	5.
6. Vickers	Brunner, Mond	Stewarts & Lloyds	Woolworth	6.
7. Dunlop	Dunlop	Courtaulds	Courtaulds	7.
8. Lever	Fine Cotton	Coats	Vickers	8.
9. Armstrong Whitworth	Distillers	Watney	Dunlop	9.
10. Bradford Dyers	Guest, Keen & N.	Dunlop	Stewarts & Lloyds	10.

FAMILIES AND FIRMS

Among these twenty-three—all with thousands of shareholders, usually headed by the Pru—the 'managerial revolution' is far from uniform or complete. Although committees of managers and technicians make up their middle ranks, at the top of many there continue to be individuals whose bold decisions—as with ICI or Courtaulds—can change the character of the company: some, like Chambers, have succeeded in imposing their character on vast concerns; others, like Bowater, have virtually created their concerns; others, like the heads of breweries or shipping companies, have inherited a special authority.

In some companies, such as Great Universal Stores, Marks and Spencers, or the House of Fraser, families can keep control by issuing non-voting shares: young Fraser, young Wolfson, young Cotton, young Sieff are all likely to succeed as chairmen. But even without a majority of voting shares, families can often dominate Leviathans. Among thousands of small shareholdings they may own the biggest block, or enjoy the tacit support of the biggest shareholders, usually the Pru and the Legal and General; or the other directors may have such a strong hereditary loyalty—particularly when the firm carries a family name—that they elect a family chairman with all the regularity of Hatfield Conservative association electing a Cecil. Sons-in-law, too, remain an enduring phenomenon, as in the Conservative party, the court and banking: Sir Ivan Stedeford of Tube Investments, Willoughby Norman of Boots, Sir Philip Warter of Associated British Pictures, all married the daughter or grand-daughter of the boss.

The position of families varies widely. Some chairmen have virtually private sheikhdoms with their own miniature court which cuts right across the managerial pyramid. Others are more like a constitutional monarch, chosen by a board of executives as a personification of the company, and a wise adjudicator in times of crisis: as the Queen's most critical function is to choose a prime minister, so the chairman's may be to choose a managing director. Often big businesses experience the ambiguous condition of the eighteenth-century government, with power somewhere between the king and the cabinet. The firm gets more complicated, the managers more indispensable, the family's holding proportionally smaller: the balance gradually—sometimes suddenly—shifts from the family to the managers, from a court to a committee. Often an autocrat retires, like a Caesar, leaving a disorganised empire to be run by a triumvirate: the end of the pioneer generation, like Leverhulme's, is nearly always difficult. Lord Nuffield and Lord Austin, two heirless pioneers, left the jumbled inheritance which became the British Motor Corporation—only now achieving a tidier pattern: the aircraft companies, built up by brilliant pioneers like de Havilland or Sopwith, are passing painfully into an era of accountants and organograms.

THE CHAIRMAN'S JOB

The most distinctive characteristic of the businessman—the thing that most sharply distinguishes him from the lawyer, college professor or, generally speaking, the civil servant—is his capacity for decision.
J. K. Galbraith: American Capitalism.

What does a chairman's power amount to? 'Ninety per cent of the time I'm just a superior nursemaid', said one of the chairmen: 'I spend my time deciding to move Mr. Smith to replace Mr. Brown, trying to find another place for Mr. Brown by persuading Mr. Robinson that it's time for him to retire. The other 10 per cent of the time is spent deciding about capital investment: and a lot of these decisions are forced on you by the competition. That's what I was told when I took over—but I didn't believe it then. Most of your time is spent in the engine room. Only occasionally do you go up on to the bridge: then you lash the helm and go down again.'

'The most important change that has come with the managerial revolution is the need for good communications', said another: 'More and more the man in the centre is left with nothing to do except sit and write: that's one of the ways in which British business is falling behind—they're not used to the idea of presenting business to the community, and the gift of the gab is still suspect in the boardroom. Not that American businessmen are much more articulate than we are: the main difference is that they hire ghost writers and we don't.'

'The difference between politics and business', Lord Chandos has said, 'is that in business you finish something. If you spend £10 million and employ, say, 3,000 or 4,000 people, and the project produces a profit of 25 per cent you can safely go home and leave criticism to Michael Foot or anybody else who likes to have a go at it. The work has been finished and is in being. That's the attraction of business.'[1]

Businessmen remain, in spite of the encroachment of bureaucracy, much freer to decide things than Whitehall committees. 'In the civil service', said one ex-Whitehall tycoon, 'most decisions came up from below: you might not always take the advice of junior men, but you always expect them to give an opinion. But in business, I was surprised how often decisions come straight from the top.'

But the decisions are not perhaps quite so far-sighted and wide-ranging as they sometimes appear in chairmen's philosophic reports. 'How did you find the tycoons?' asked one cabinet minister, 'I find they've got minds like searchlights: they light up a narrow strip very brightly, but that doesn't mean that they can see all round. I'm often surprised how little they understand about other things.' After talking to chairmen, I found myself abandoning images of ships and tillers, and visualising instead roundabouts and swings in a foggy fairground. As Bagehot described it in 1872:

> Most men of business love a sort of twilight. They have lived all their lives in an atmosphere of probabilities and of doubt, where nothing is very clear, where there are some chances for many events, where nevertheless one course must be determinedly chosen and fixedly adhered to. They like to hear arguments suited to this intellectual haze.

Or, in the description by Lord Heyworth, to the select committee on nationalised industries in 1953:

> No one can tell at the point of having made a decision whether it is going to prove right or wrong ... The point is that decisions have got to be taken. That is the thing which matters. It is

[1] Interview with Malcolm Muggeridge. Granada TV, July 25th, 1960.

dynamic. You have got to do something. As I always put it, I look upon myself as someone who is perpetually in a fog; you get used to being in a fog. Occasionally you think the fog has lifted while you have made a decision; and then it obscures again.

CHAIRMEN AND EUROPE

Yet in spite of all the apparent limitations of a chairman's scope —the fog, the muddle, the committees, the sheer effort required to counteract centrifugal force and Parkinsonian tendencies— there is no doubt that even in the most intractable managerial corporations, a dynamic chairman can have a crucial effect. Many of the companies with the most spectacular growth since the war have a single dominating man at their head. Any chairman must spend much of his time in nursemaid duties, but his moments of decision remain crucial. Many companies may find it agreeable and reassuring to have a constitutional head, leaving most decisions to managing directors. But when a vigorous chairman does appear—a Chambers, a Bowater, a Cole—the change can affect every limb of the company. Whether such changes are desirable or gentlemanly may be debated: what seems clear is that if Britain is to survive industrially alongside Europe and America, she has to play the business game with competitive rules. It is, as one chairman put it, 'no longer a question of *whether*, but *how*'.

31

COMPANIES

One of the curses of the political atmosphere of Britain is the sentimental softness towards inefficiency.

Paul Chambers, October, 1961.

The world is fast becoming a supermarket and Britain is being crowded off the shelves.

E. P. Godden (Managing Director, Beecham Services Ltd).

BRITAIN has traditionally been a country of small businesses, but the past ten years have shown a rapid concentration. The trend is not new: at the turn of the century many giants arose, such as the Bradford Dyers' Association, Imperial Tobacco, or Calico Printers, and another crop came with the depression of the twenties, when ICI, Unilever, AEI were all formed. During and after the war there was a lull:[1] but then came a new wave which has changed the whole pattern of business.

In some fields, such as chemicals (largely due to ICI) and entertainment (due to Ranks and the TV companies) giants already prevail. In building, small firms are well entrenched (in Britain as in America). But in other trades—cars, cotton, printing, shops or beer—small firms have been quickly swallowed by big ones. All of them except cars are old industries and have faced cold winds—foreign invaders, decreasing demand, or rising costs. Beer has been traditionally very secure, protected by the system of 'tied houses'. But the drift from pubs to TV, the rising costs, and the arrival of an invader (E. P. Taylor from Canada) and a would-be invader (Charles Clore) have produced a flurry of mergers. In the words of Colonel Whitbread: 'We must integrate, or disintegrate.'

These figures from the *Financial Times*[2] suggest the increase in concentration between 1954 and 1960. The first column shows the proportion of assets in each group held by the top 10 per cent companies (out of the leading 2,100). The second shows what those assets *would* have been, had the mergers in the following six years already taken place.

[1] *See* P. E. Hart: Business Concentration in the UK, *Journal of the Royal Statistical Society*, Vol. 123, Part I, 1960.

[2] March 30, 1961.

	1954	1960
Food..	61 per cent	64 per cent
Drink	54 ,, ,,	64 ,, ,,
Chemicals	81 ,, ,,	82 ,, ,,
Metal manufacture ..	62 ,, ,,	69 ,, ,,
Engineering..	56 ,, ,,	59 ,, ,,
Other metal ..	62 ,, ,,	66 ,, ,,
Vehicles	58 ,, ,,	65 ,, ,,
Textiles	62 ,, ,,	71 ,, ,,
Clothing	45 ,, ,,	64 ,, ,,[1]
Bricks, etc.	54 ,, ,,	55 ,, ,,
Paper, printing ..	60 ,, ,,	67 ,, ,,
Leather, timber ..	63 ,, ,,	65 ,, ,,
Construction ..	33 ,, ,,	33 ,, ,,
Wholesalers ..	40 ,, ,,	43 ,, ,,
Retailers	69 ,, ,,	78 ,, ,,
Entertainment	74 ,, ,,	74 ,, ,,
Transport, other services ..	57 ,, ,,	58 ,, ,,

TAKE-OVERS

Jungle red in tooth and claw, and particularly Clore.
Lord Attlee (House of Lords, 1961).

Many mergers have been voluntary, but several have been the result of take-overs, which have often transformed the characters of firms, by-passing the old directors. Several factors have encouraged the raiders, and the situation has been not unlike America at the time of Coolidge. The boom in city property has increased the potential value of many companies; the ploughing-back of profits has given companies tempting hoards; the combination of high income tax without a capital gains tax has made quick capital appreciation very attractive; and the issue of non-voting shares has enabled single entrepreneurs to keep control of huge public companies. A small group of raiders—most notably Isaac Wolfson, Charles Clore, Sir Hugh Fraser, Cecil King, Roy Thomson—have become the heads of colossal empires within ten years. The most celebrated and successful of the raiders is Charles Clore, the son of a Russian-Jewish refugee who had built up a small textile business. Clore began his property career by buying the Cricklewood Ice Rink at the age of twenty-two: now, at the age of fifty-seven, he owns among other things half the shoe-shops in Britain, Furness shipbuilding yards, the Hampstead Garden Suburb,

[1] This figure, as the *Financial Times* points out, is misleading, since the biggest company in this field, Sears Holdings (controlled by Charles Clore) includes many other industries.

Loch Ness, and 16,000 acres of Herefordshire; and together with Jack Cotton he controls the biggest property company in Britain. He is restless, single-minded and secretive (he refuses to see any journalists). His business philosophy was tersely expressed when he told the Jenkins Committee that it did not matter if a director could read or write, provided he maximised the returns.

In the early fifties, when Wolfson and Clore were most active, take-overs were rare and frowned on. Even in late 1959, when the Aluminium War[1] burst on the city, they were still thought disgraceful by half the city: but by 1962 ICI itself was trying a take-over. The raiders transformed whole areas of business: sleepy and comfortable firms have been rationalised, combed and costed, their properties sold up, their products standardised, their managers re-valued[2] with unsuspected thrusting men emerging from the undergrowth. Some take-overs aimed only at quick plunder, but many have brought greater efficiency as well as exploitation. The attitude of the city remains ambivalent, as it was in the Aluminium War. 'Generally speaking, bidders have created new employment rather than the reverse', wrote the authors of one study of take-overs.[3] 'There may be occasions', said Anthony Tuke in 1960, 'where something more drastic than a gentle kiss on the brow from a Prince Charming is needed to awaken the sleeping beauties. It may even be necessary sometimes to tip them right out of bed. But it can seldom be wise to pull down the whole house or even to sell it as it stands to a stranger.'

'THEY'

Giant firms have similar problems. Their mergers bring together proud separate units, with the same kind of agonies as those of federated countries or amalgamated regiments. Some component companies appear independent and competing—Players against Wills cigarettes, White Horse against Johnny Walker whisky. Some federated firms like Unilever or Imperial Tobacco keep their central organisation in the background. Others, like AEI or ICI proclaim their unity. The amalgamation is often painful: new giants have to make great efforts—by advertising, tours or house magazines—to persuade their workers that AEI, ICI or English Electric really *exist*. 'When a previously independent business

[1] *See* page 387.
[2] *See* the Thomson Empire, p. 119.
[3] *See* George Bull and Anthony Vice: *Bid for Power*, 1958. p. 24.

becomes incorporated into a group', wrote H. P. Barker, chairman of Parkinson and Cowan, 'a change of atmosphere often occurs . . . The executives feel that some measure of responsibility has been lifted from their shoulders, the carrot seems further away, the stick less frightening, and an entirely new factor has appeared on the scene. This factor is the arrival of "they".'[1]

Many giants are still working out the relationship between centre and circumference. But most are tending towards greater decentralisation of units, while maintaining shrewd financial checks—preferring to regard themselves more as a holding company or a family bank. British business is still unaccustomed to bigness: most giants have not been giants for long, and the nationalised industries have produced quite new dimensions.[2] The relationship between the parent and its subsidiaries is still an unresolved problem—how to control without stultifying, how to advise without interfering—and even the words 'parent' and 'subsidiaries' are begging the question. The rôle of a modern industrial headquarters is subtle and complicated: 'Headquarters', said Lord Heyworth, 'always seems a half-crazy place anyway.'[3] But how this problem is solved—how 'they' appear to the men in the factories and local branches—is a question more important to millions of workers and managers, whose life is bound up with their company, than the workings of Whitehall or Westminster.

DIVERSIFIERS

Business has become both bigger and more mixed: 'diversification' has become a craze. Some companies, such as Unilever or Beechams (pills, Brylcreem, Lucozade, etc.) have gathered a gallimaufry half by mistake: but others have deliberately 'gone shopping'. Courtaulds were worried about cotton, and bought their way into chemicals, engineering, paint and packaging. The Ross trawler-fishing business, headed by Carl Ross of Grimsby, were faced with a shortage of fish, and went into printing, lorries, hire-purchase, chickens, crop-spraying and frozen foods. De La Rue expanded from bank-notes and playing cards to formica, oil heaters and computers. Charles Clore's empire, Sears Holdings, not only owns half Britain's shoe-shops, but also makes socks, ships, pumps, laundries, pipes and jewellery.

Even stubbornly one-track firms have branched out. Ever since

---

[1] Quoted in *Business Enterprise* by R. S. Edwards and Harry Townsend, 1958. p. 199.
[2] *See* page 533.
[3] *See* Select Committee on Nationalised Industries, 1953. Q. 705.

1799, Guinness have concentrated with fantastic success on one product, but they have now turned to selling butterscotch and Irish salmon. Some companies have extended into an adjacent territory: Booker Brothers have moved from shipping to shopping; Marks and Spencers have developed from selling shirts to making them. Many mixed groups have a common denominator: all Beechams' stuff is very dependent on advertising, all ICI's revolves round research, all Vickers is concerned with 'making big things out of metal' (as Lord Knollys put it). But several groups, like Sears, Tillings or De La Rue, have no perceptible common thread—except profit.

This hectic mix-up has changed the outlook of the top business-man. He need no longer be a brewer, a shoe-maker, a shipowner or a printer, with the smell of a dock or a print-shop: but he must be a master-manager. Paradoxically, in an age of specialisa-tion, big firms—like country trading stores—must specialise in everything. Many find the implications disturbing, widening the gap between the factory, with its technicians printing or brewing, and the headquarters, dominated by finance, controlling their shoes and ships and sealing wax purely through their profit and loss account. This it seems leads both to a more mandarin head-quarters élite and also, at the same time, to an exaggerated depend-ence on the men-on-the-job.

Bigness has strengthened the lure of London. In the nineteenth century the centres of industrial power were Manchester, Birm-ingham or Glasgow and the directors lived and worked near them. But as companies merge and grow, their headquarters need to be close to Whitehall, the city, their rivals, lawyers, advertising agents, London airport. Now most of the giant companies have their board meetings in London. The big steel companies are still run from the North, and the car firms from the Midlands: but as with insurance companies, building societies or banks, the drift is still towards London. Britain is less centralised than France, where Paris is the dominating centre. But compared to Chicago or Los Angeles, Hamburg or Dusseldorf, British provincial centres are depleted, and the trend is threatening to turn London into a nightmare megalopolis.[1]

Provincial companies suffer a transmogrification when they reach the metropolis. Who would guess that the new English Electric building in Aldwych, with its portland stone, second empire boardroom and ornate executive suites, was the centre of a

[1] *See* London Diaspora? *The Economist*, January 13, 1962.

rugged provincial empire? The décor and architecture of London headquarters seems to represent a conscious desire to be part of an imaginary immemorial London with emanations from Buckingham Palace and the Bank of England. But to the men at the factory, the London palace is the physical embodiment of 'they' or —as headquarters are sometimes called—'the Kremlin'.

INTERNATIONAL BUSINESS

The main pressure to bigness has come from foreign invaders, who can afford to take large risks, draw on international experience, and regard Britain as a suburb; while in the reverse direction, international British companies need huge resources for their battles in America and Europe. The invasion of American tobacco, as early as 1901, produced Imperial Tobacco; German chemicals helped to give birth to ICI; continental margarines produced Unilever. Since the war the international battle has intensified— for instance the detergent war between Unilever and Hedley's (Proctor and Gamble); the oil war between Shell and Esso; the car war between American Vauxhalls and Ford, and British BMC and Rootes; the chain-store war between Woolworths (American) and Marks and Spencers (British). In many fields like typewriters, cameras, sewing machines, vacuum-cleaners, razor-blades, tinned soups, cornflakes, foreigners dominate the field.

Canadians have a special aptitude for invasion, for they combine aggressive North American attitudes with an evident fondness for Britain. Garfield Weston (Allied Bakeries, ABC teashops, Fortnum and Mason, etc.); Roy Thomson following Lord Beaverbrook; E. P. Taylor (United Breweries) have all helped to disturb the placid stream of British business. For some, like Weston or Taylor, their British business is only an extension: 'Remember, a bad year for United Breweries is just a bad *day* for Mr. Taylor', one brewer was told. But often, as with Thomson or Beaverbrook, the British business becomes the major interest, with much greater scope for exploitation and glory than on the Canadian side. 'There must be *something* wrong with this country', Roy Thomson is reported to have said, 'if I can make money so easily out of it.'

PIGMIES

Where, in this Brobdingnag, is the place for Gullivers? There is still no lack of small firms: in 1957 there were about 291,000 companies; one man in a hundred was his own boss. But only 11,500 were public companies, of which 3,000 are quoted on the stock exchange, and those three thousand account for 46 per cent of the employment, and 60 per cent of the profits, in un-nationalised industry.

Some kinds of firms refuse to grow in size—notably builders and civil engineers: apart from a few big contractors whose names stare out from the tops of new buildings—Laings, Taylor Woodrow, Cubitts, etc.—the building trade remains defiantly fissiparous, in Britain and also in America. Between the Leviathans, small fish can still swim and grow without being gobbled.

The self-made businessman is now less likely to make his fortune in manufacturing than in 'service' industries—a shop, a launderette, a window-cleaning business. As Britain becomes more prosperous, so these services increase, and *by 1960 more people were employed in services and distribution than in manufacturing*—as in America and Sweden, but in no other Western industrial country. Britain's centre of gravity is moving away from mines and factories, towards shops, hairdressers (100,000 in 1959), lorry-drivers, or TV technicians: and like an Arab bazaar, we are busying ourselves with persuading and entertaining each other.

Britain, following America, is slowly moving away from a steel-based economy, with motor cars and washing machines among the most precious possessions, towards an economy where services predominate. Spending on travel, food, security, hygiene, medicine is rising: 'the past year or two has seen the end of consumer durable society', wrote the *Financial Times* in its after-Christmas editorial in 1961: 'in the past year there was first a boom in clothing sales, then in better class foods and delicatessen, and finally in drink of almost every sort'.[1] It is in providing services—particularly for comfortable leisure—that the large opportunities for the self-made businessman will occur. The one-man success stories will be not so much about engineers, aircraft designers or inventors—those fields are developed by laboratory teams or committees of managers—but interior decorators, grocers, property dealers, supermarket owners. The era of Nuffield and de Havilland is being succeeded by the age of Charles Forte and Jack Cotton.

---

[1] *See* New Patterns of Affluence: *Financial Times*, December 27, 1961.

32

DIRECTORS

England is the last home of the aristocracy, and the art of protecting
the aristocracy from the encroachment of commerce has been raised
to quite an art,
Because in America a rich butter-and-eggs man is only a rich
butter-and-egg man or at most an honorary LL.D. of some hungry
university, but in England he is Sir Benjamin Buttery, Bart.

Ogden Nash.

'FOR the first time in English History, the businessman has
reached the Top', wrote a left-wing critic, Ralph Samuel, in 1959.
'It has not always been so. It is scarcely two decades since business
was in disgrace, business leaders suspect, and the capitalist system,
to all appearance, disintegrating . . . How are the fallen mighty!
Today the Businessman is everywhere. Whoever you are, where-
ever you are, it is hard to miss him. If you're a writer, he's probably
bought out your publishers, or holds important interests in them.
If you're an artist, his commission will certainly be the best that
comes your way: perhaps you already work for him, designing his
products or his "packaging", laying out his advertising, his
brochures, his "House" magazine . . .'[1]

The new acceptability of the businessman can be detected
everywhere: in the cosy gossip-paragraphs in newspapers; in
photographs in *The Times* of boards of directors staring at their
blotting paper; in the university 'Magnates Club' at Oxford; in
advertisements showing lovable chairmen on winter cruises. The
old aristocratic prejudice against trade—always hypocritical—has
weakened: 'When I was a boy', said Sir Miles Thomas, chairman
of Monsanto, 'I was always told that the gentry didn't want to soil
their hands with trade: nowadays it's very different. I'm a member
of White's for instance, and people like Lord Dudley and his
brother are very proud of their place in business.'

The British attitude is a long way from the American enthusiasm. A detergent salesman or a cornflakes tycoon is still something
of a joke in St. James's Street, and businesses are socially classified
not by their profits or size—as in America—but by their respect-

[1] The Boss as Hero: *Universities and Left Review*, Autumn, 1959.

500

ability, with books and beer[1] near the top and scrap metal near the bottom. Nor have tycoons come nearly as far out into the open as in America. The British approach of 'please address all communications to the secretary' remains well entrenched.[2] 'There's still a hole-and-corner tradition in British business'—to quote Sir Miles again: 'the British businessmen still hate being criticised: they like to present a front of constant achievement and progress.' Secrecy is still deep-seated; the annual reports, with phrases like 'taxation equalisation account', remain incomprehensible to the lay shareholder compared to American or even Japanese reports. Only when a company desperately needs the support of its shareholders, as Courtaulds did in 1962, does it begin to give serious facts.

But in the sunnier post-war climate, directors have been coming out of their holes, stretching their limbs and basking. One sign of their new confidence can be seen in the company reports in newspapers: ten years ago most of them were grey rivers of text, usually beginning with an obituary ('his ability and wise counsel will be greatly missed'), following with bare trading figures, and ending with a tribute ('long and loyal service of which I think we can all be proud'). Now each year a few more chairmen look out benignly from a photograph, explaining their progress in stirring language. 'Eight Bells from the British and Commonwealth bridge'— announced Sir Nicholas Cayzer, Bart, of the British and Commonwealth Shipping company in 1961. 'Yesterday is interesting, but it's only history. It is tomorrow we want to know about . . .' began Sir Walter Benton Jones, Bart, of United Steel. The caustic comments of Cecil King, of the *Daily Mirror*; the Latin tags of Anthony Tuke, of Barclays Bank; the gnomic utterances of L. Nidditch, of Ely Breweries; the right-wing explosions of Gibson Jarvie, of United Dominions Trust; the annual apologia of Harry Oppenheimer, of the Anglo-American Corporation—all these are expanding into more confident types—more readable, more plausible but not much more revealing.

DIRECTORS' BACKGROUNDS

What kind of men are directors? The *Directory of Directors* lists over 35,000, of companies with assets of more than £25,000. A survey of the more important ones was made by Dr. G. H. Copeman, editor of *Business*, in 1950: he sent questions to 3,215

[1] Books is better than beer. See page 324.
[2] Roy Lewis and Rosemary Stewart: *The Boss*, 1960. p. 221.

directors of companies with assets of over a million pounds, of whom 1,243 replied; they showed that:[1]

58 per cent went to public schools
36 ,, ,, went to university
11 ,, ,, started work at fourteen or before
60 ,, ,, (roughly) started with some business connection in the family
21 ,, ,, became directors before they were thirty, and
54 ,, ,, became directors before they were forty
60 ,, ,, held no other directorship, outside the main group
19 ,, ,, were sons of directors of the same firm
22 ,, ,, began as executives
17 ,, ,, began as engineers
16 ,, ,, began as accountants
41 ,, ,, had never changed their jobs from one firm to another that was independent of it.

Comparing these figures with American studies, Dr. Copeman found that American businessmen were more likely to come from the 'lower occupational classes', to be better-educated, to have changed their jobs, to be sons of farmers or labourers; but that both in America and Britain about 60 per cent of businessmen were the sons of businessmen.

A sidelight was shed by the Institute of Directors which in 1959 sent out 5,000 questionnaires, of which 60 per cent were completed. According to this directors' picture of themselves:

14 per cent have a university degree
64 ,, ,, depend on experience alone
68 ,, ,, drive to work
21 ,, ,, arrive before 9 a.m.
38 ,, ,, work every Saturday
59 ,, ,, take three weeks holiday a year, or more
34 ,, ,, have lunch every day without discussing work
19 ,, ,, have only a snack lunch
40 ,, ,, think they are overweight
$4\frac{1}{2}$,, ,, are teetotal
70 ,, ,, never smoke cigars
20 ,, ,, have over $\frac{3}{4}$-hour of exercise a day
63 ,, ,, have no voluntary commitments at week-ends or evenings.[2]

This is an (anonymous) description of the life of a provincial director:

[1] *See* G. H. Copeman: *Leaders of British Industry,* 1955.
[2] This contrasts strikingly with senior American executives of whom (according to a *Fortune* survey) more than half took part in civic or charitable activities.

He will probably drive a Jaguar to the office every day, in a large industrial town; he will live 15 miles out in a modern house with eight bedrooms and five acres. His wife will be as old as he, but ageing faster and will look rather exhausted with the effort of keeping up with him. He may well conduct a few unserious affairs, probably when he visits the Head Office in London. He will be well-preserved and extremely well-turned out; he will take *The Times*, but read the *Express*; his staff will be devoted to him; his wife will run an Austin; he will have children at boarding school. There will be very few books in the house; holidays will be taken in Spain; he will be drinking rather more whisky than he should and will rely on television for relaxation more than he should; he will be well up in the supertax class, but not saving very much. In the home, talk will be seven-eighths of his colleagues at work and about his friendly but lethal struggles with them; he will know his job backwards, despise outside experts, but be secretly worried about the prowess of his junior colleagues. At 50 he may well have a heart attack, perhaps in the bath, and after that will have to work at half-speed.

Directors' salaries are surrounded by secrecy: by law only the total salaries paid to directors need be published. When the government revealed that Dr. Beeching, the chairman-elect of the British Transport Commission, was earning £24,000 as a director of ICI, the news came as a bombshell to the civil service. Many people assumed that this was a typical industrial salary, but in fact, it is higher than most. These were the *average* emoluments of directors in some large companies in September, 1960 (but since there are normally some part-time directors, the average pay of full-time directors is usually higher):[1]

	Average emolument
Turner and Newall	£29,331
Shell Transport & Trading ..	22,051
ICI	21,517
Bowaters	19,700
F. W. Woolworth	17,762
Unilever	16,708
Tube Investment	12,434
J. Lyons	11,597
Distillers	10,253
AEI	7,757
Sears Holdings	7,456
Rank Organisation	7,449

[1] *Financial Times*, March 17, 1961.

503

The highest paid director is said to be Sir William Lyons, founder-chairman of Jaguar Cars, said to earn £100,000 a year: the four main board directors of Jaguars between them are paid £205,000—apart from pension contributions.[1] Other prosperous bosses are Ronald Soothill, chairman of the asbestos combine, Turner and Newall; and Paul Chambers of ICI. But salaries above £20,000 are quite rare: some clues come from the Inland Revenue, who revealed that among earned incomes in 1960

        2,777 earned over £10,000
of whom 1,681 earned £10,000–£15,000
       534 earned £15,000–£20,000
       562 earned over £20,000 (with an average salary of £33,000).

But these figures are misleading; pension schemes, cars, flats and other 'fringe benefits' are more important than an extra £5,000.

How do British directors compare with others? According to F. X. Olanie, of McKinsey's, managing directors of smaller companies (turnover about £1 million) compare favourably with their continental counterparts: but in firms with turnover around £40 million, they are paid less than in France, Germany, Italy or Belgium.[2] The American corporations, of course, offer salaries which far outstrip Europe: in 1960 Frederick Donner of General Motors was paid £205,000 and Henry Ford £165,000.

INSTITUTE OF DIRECTORS

One pointer to the new self-confidence of bosses is the Institute of Directors, in three mansions in Belgrave Square. After the war it was moribund, and then was revived by a ginger-group led by Lord Chandos and Sir Edward Spears: it aimed to become a 'Bosses Trade Union', and to encourage a 'warm family feeling' among directors—a kind of counter-revolution to the Socialists. Since then it has multiplied a hundredfold, and now has 38,000 members, including (they told me) 109 MPs and 186 members of the House of Lords.

The Institute presents a kind of caricature of directors, as in satirical films. Its club is called 'The Number 10 Club'. A long

[1] *Evening Standard*, November 25, 1960.
[2] Deciding the Executives' Salary: *Financial Times*, December 20, 1960.

bar is filled at lunch-time with large and leisurely men, who progress to the dining-room for big long lunches (some of the best in London), served by Italian waiters on Wedgwood Napoleon Ivy plates (as used on Elba), followed by endless cups of coffee. At three-fifteen directors are still in the coffee-room, while the chauffeurs wait in Jaguars and Zephyrs. A thick, glossy magazine, *The Director*, including a regular feature called 'the View from the Chair', is sent monthly to members. Every November the Institute holds a jamboree of five thousand directors, addressed by Conservative figures. At the Albert Hall in 1961 the chief guests were Harold Macmillan, Paul Chambers and Sir Roy Welensky.

The Institute encourages a mystique of directorship as opposed to managership, and stays aloof from the British Institute of Management, their less effective rival, which they describe as 'madly serious'. The Director-General of the Directors is an Etonian baronet, Major Sir Richard Powell—bluff and amiable, with wavy grey hair, a humorous moustache and enormous charm: he inhabits a big office with a coal fire, murky paintings, a row of gadgets on the desk, and a patio outside. 'There are three different classes in industry—labour, managers and directors', said Sir Richard: 'the board itself doesn't have to be experts: technicians and accountants should be available, to be consulted by the board. Generals are often the best kind of men to run businesses. We believe that directors are a kind of aristocracy: they should be men of parts, and they should have interests outside their business. Directors have become noticeably less selfish in the last seven years: it's easier now to find men to join committees.' 'I know it is dangerous phrase', Sir Richard has said, 'but you could say we were a gigantic Old Boy network.'[1]

LORD CHANDOS

Among the more influential members of the Institute's council are three powerful backers of commercial television: Harley Drayton[2] of British Electric Traction (whose matter-of-fact and authoritative statements are held in some awe); Sir Robert Renwick, the tough baronet stockbroker; and C. O. Stanley, chairman of the Pye group—both co-founders of Associated Television.[2] Also prominent on the council are Sir Frederick Hooper, known

[1] *See Daily Mirror*, November 9, 1961.
[2] *See* page 394.
[3] *See* page 606.

as 'Daddy Schweppes'; and Sir Edward Spears, known as 'Beau-caire'. The high priest of the Institute has been their president, Lord Chandos, who speaks with bravura at their annual rallies. He stands as a director-hero (a long study of him went through three numbers of *The Director*) and an important symbol of bossmanship. He is a bulky man with a huge leonine head, like a Ronald Searle drawing, and a big pearl tie-pin. He speaks bluntly, wittily, full of classical tags, and with authority. He lives at Trafalgar House, the old seat of the Nelson family: and he drives a Bentley called LC 1.

Moreover, he represents a rare phenomenon—the aristocrat as businessman. He comes from an ancient family with coal interests and academic habits, the Lytteltons, who have intermarried with Peels, Gladstones and Asquiths. He was brought up before 1914, and his career began like Macmillan's or Duff Cooper's—Eton, Guards, survivor, married duke's daughter. But he turned not to politics, but to the city, becoming an expert on metals and cartels: from the age of thirty he never earned less than £10,000 a year. He was an intellectual as well as a shrewd businessman, and this rare combination gave him special usefulness: in the war Churchill made him Production Minister, in the War Cabinet, and he was put in charge of clothes rationing, bargaining with American tycoons, and other big-business operations.

After the war he became chairman of the newly-founded electrical giant, AEI, and retreated from politics—apart from occasional forays (he called nationalisation 'the Frankenstein of Universal Suffrage'). In 1951 many expected he would become Chancellor of the Exchequer, but instead Churchill made him Colonial Secretary—which his father and grandfather had been. He pushed through Central African Federation, dealt firmly with Mau Mau, and paved the way for Nigerian independence. But he was not a parliamentary success: he confronted questions with the brusque manner of a chairman interrupted at a meeting. After three years he went back to AEI, while at the same time promoting Northern Ireland, presiding over the Directors, addressing meetings, and remaining an advisory tycoon to the Conservatives. He wrote a secret report advising the building of Cunard's Q3, which was later dropped with a clatter. He has always been an important link between Tory politics and big-business, and he is one of many to have been called 'Mr. Establishment'. Lord Salisbury, congratulating Lord Chandos on his maiden speech (in support of the Common Market) in the House of

Lords in 1961,[1] reminded him of how they had been together at the same private school, at the same house at Eton, had joined the same battalion of the same regiment on the same day; in the second world war they had joined the government together, been made privy councillors on the same day. As a lobbyist, he is, in Harold Macmillan's words, 'pitiless in pressing the claims of friendship'.[2]

INSTITUTE AND POLITICS

The Institute should not be taken too seriously. To become a 'Fellow', as members are called, requires no more than any kind of directorship, plus three guineas a year: 40 per cent of the fellows come from companies with assets of less than £100,000. Fellows can be divided into those who use the letters 'FInstD' after their name and those who don't: 'when somebody writes to me using those initials', said one management consultant, 'I'm inclined to discount him: it suggests that he doesn't realise how meaningless they are.' Most Fellows use the Institute less as a trade union than as a handy hotel, a car-park and a club.

Few Fellows are politically active, or take any part in the Institute's affairs: but the politically minded officials, like trade unionists, are not afraid to invoke their whole membership, and they have their own '10 per cent democracy'. The Institute has assembled large funds from industry, and has a special 'Free Enterprise Fund' for advertising and other campaigns against nationalisation: before the 1959 election they put out a good deal of anti-Labour propaganda, and publicised a list of doomed firms. Many modern Tories, conscious of their new image, see the Institute as either a joke or an embarrassment: its political support, with its aura of expense-accounts and amateur boardrooms, like the support of Lord Beaverbrook, is not an unmixed blessing. 'The idea of a businessmen's lobby isn't altogether attractive', said one former Conservative chairman: 'the Institute aren't a particularly *nice* collection of people.' But the Institute do have some political influence with the Conservative party. Before budget-time they are always very active and vocal, and after the surtax relief in 1961 there were special celebrations.

The Institute has taken over part of the lobbying rôle of the Federation of British Industries. Before the war the FBI successfully intervened with the government over tariffs in 1931 or the

---

[1] August 3, 1961.
[2] Speech to the Institute of Directors, November 8, 1961.

amalgamation of coal mines in 1938: but since then—partly perhaps because of the war—its power has been much less evident. In the decision to negotiate with the Common Market the FBI played no apparent rôle, and some businessmen now complain that it is more on the side of the government than of industry. 'The notion of the FBI as the *eminence grise* of British politics must be abandoned', wrote Professor Sam Finer in 1956: 'even with a Conservative government in power the FBI is but one voice— albeit a very powerful one—among many.'[1]

The Institute of Directors has done something to educate and professionalise their directors. It stresses the importance of labour relations ('without that, nothing goes right: it's like sex in marriage'), provides an advisory service, holds courses on management and mass meetings about exports, and publishes provocative and critical articles. They have a neon sign (above Coca-Cola) in Piccadilly, which rather fitfully says 'either exports go up, or Britain goes down'. But in their country-squire cult (business documents, as at White's, are regarded as *de trop*), they confuse the real priorities of business, the images with realities. 'They are', as one chairman put it, 'a kind of rearguard action against the managerial revolution.'

[1] *Political Studies*, February, 1956.

33

SCIENTISTS

If we could lock up all the scientists for five or six years, we might possibly have a consistent defence policy.

Harold Watkinson: House of Commons, November 4, 1960.

CONSTANTLY undermining, outdating and disorganising the organisation men, accountants, civil servants and politicians, are the scientists who, in the past twenty years, have stepped on to the administrative stage. While diplomats are discussing disarmament, scientists are discovering weapons which make their decisions useless. While accountants are estimating profits, scientists are discovering processes which wreck their assumptions. While mandarins entrench themselves at headquarters technologists can counter-attack with devastating practical discoveries.

Already early in the century the scientists were changing the shape of the future but up to the last war their importance was largely unacknowledged. 'This war was the turning point. Whereas previously scientists were seen, according to the interests of the observer, either as dedicated scholars, or as the source of invention, or as the technical guardians of the social service on which an urban civilisation depends, today they also appear in a number of new guises—as the backbone of national defence; as pioneers of outer space; and even as the counsellors of presidents and prime ministers.'[1]

The suddenness of the change has been as bewildering for the scientists as for the others. Men accustomed before the war to scrounge for equipment as government 'boffins' or university pariahs, have found themselves wooed by government and industry, with new labs, vast equipment, nervous respect and multiplied staff. 'The feeling of being a depressed class has quite gone', said one science knight: 'When I told my father I wanted to read physics at Cambridge he said "surely you want to be well off: if you read science you'll never be able to have a car". I remember in 1940 the young naval officers all had nice girl friends and the

[1] Sir Solly Zuckerman: Liberty in an Age of Science. *Nature*, July 18, 1959.

scientists had plain wives. Now the scientists are the privileged class. I suppose the arts people actually have to live on their *salaries*.' At schools and universities the old 'stinks' departments have become a status symbol, and output of scientists has raced ahead: three-quarters of the scientists and technologists who have ever lived, one of them has calculated, are alive and practising today.[1]

But the scientists remain a separate breed. In 1961 Martin Madden, one of the few scientific members of parliament—which is confused and bored by science, as its sporadic scientific debates suggest—pointed out that:

> Of 36 heads of Oxford colleges 2 are scientists;
> 24 heads of Cambridge colleges 6 are scientists;
> 31 vice-chancellors (or their equivalent) 10 are scientists;
> 20 members of the cabinet 1 is a scientist;
> 22 permanent heads of government departments 2 are scientists;
> 20 editors of national newspapers 0 is a scientist.[2]

In the seventeenth and eighteenth centuries, science was still a gentlemanly pursuit: the first President of the Royal Society was an Irish peer, Lord Brouncker, who was the first man to give a series for quadrature of a portion of the equilateral hyperbola. The Marquess of Rockingham, when not prime minister, whiled away his time trying to turn coal into oil. But the fragmentation of science, its narrow educational syllabus and exclusion from the 'humanities', made it a less fashionable subject. Arts men still take pride in not knowing how motor-cars or jet planes work, and science has come to be regarded as a career for ambitious, single-minded men, not for the worldly all-rounder or talented amateur. A scientist who *does* become part of the politico-literary world—like C. P. Snow, Professor Bronowski or Sir Solly Zuckerman—is regarded as an ambassador and invited to talk endlessly on the problems of being a scientist. Scientists have begun to produce their own dynasties—the Huxleys, Braggs, Thomsons or Darwins—but they have remained surprisingly separate. The current 'swing' towards science may help to bridge this gap in twenty years' time, but the educational rift is a deep one, for the English fondness of the amateur is biased against the specialised scientist. And the scale of scientific experiments has become so large that scientists have lost some of their apparent individuality. 'A century

[1] *See* Dr. Bowden: Too Few Academic Eggs. *Universities Quarterly*, November, 1959.

[2] *See The Times*, August 26, 1961: 'scientists' here includes engineers, mathematicians and doctors.

or more ago the scientist was as much an individual as a poet is: he was a "cultivator of science", a savant. More recently he has been regarded as "one of A's team", or "a product of B's laboratory". There is now a risk that he may become simply a unit of scientific manpower.'[1]

Scientists, on their side, have resented the supremacy of arts graduates in politics and the civil service, and have felt ostracised from decisions and influence. 'They' and 'the Establishment' are often muttered by scientists. 'There's a kind of war between the two sides', one scientific civil servant explained: 'sometimes I begin to feel that they are determined to keep us down, and that they put their narks in everywhere.' 'People like Macmillan or Hailsham are ambivalent about science', said one scientific knight: 'they regard it as a regrettable necessity. They accept it but wish it wasn't there.'

In spite of this rift, the scientific achievement of Britain, particularly in physics and chemistry, has been out of all proportion to her size: in radio astronomy or molecular biology Britain is preeminent. One index (though not significant behind the iron curtain) is the number of Nobel Prizes, awarded by the Swedish Academy of Science. These are the leaders since 1901:

	Physics	Chemistry	Physiology or Medicine	Total
USA	19	13	25	57
Germany	12	20	9	41
Britain	15	11	11	37
France	7	6	3	16
Holland	5	2	2	9
Sweden	2	4	2	8
Austria	3	1	3	7
Switzerland	–	3	4	7
USSR	3	1	2	6

I found my conversations with scientists a relief after the more guarded dialogues with managers and bureaucrats. They talk freely and wittily, maintain a buccaneering attitude to the Treasury. They are used to fighting for recognition and they love describing the subterfuges involved in raising a million pounds. Most of them remain unpompous, do-it-yourself people with boyish enthusiasms and little snobbery; not all the most eminent have knighthoods. Several answer their own telephones, and get straight down to business: there is not much amateur rigmarole. Many

[1] *See* Sir Eric Ashby: *Technology and the Academics*, 1958.

enjoy fast cars, gadgets and music—noisier music, one suspects, than Treasury men, Brahms not Bach. Their new involvement with power and destruction has worried many of them, as it has worried Americans and Germans, but in the face of the blandishments of government, most of them have retained a stubborn independence.

Yet the enormous new involvement of British government with research is inevitably transforming the situation of scientists and their institutions. In 1958 Britain spent 2·35 per cent of her national income on research, about the same that she spent on advertising or schools (in America the proportion was 2·74 per cent—over 11 billion dollars). The British ratio is rising, and the flow of money into scientific research and education is changing the whole balance of power in government, industry and the universities. These were the sources of finance for research and development in 1958–9 (this does not indicate where the research is *done*: much government research is undertaken by industrial firms and universities):

Government	
Defence Departments	£234·3 million
Civil Departments	67·9
Research Councils	17·6
Public Corporations	7·8
Private Industry	136·0
Universities	1·5
Other organisations	12·7
TOTAL	£477·8 million

THE ROYAL SOCIETY

The new *largesse* in the first place has affected the scientists' own most ancient and venerable institution, the Royal Society. 'The Royal' is a society of all Britain's most distinguished scientists. King Charles II founded it, and its tercentenary was celebrated in 1960, culminating in a rally at the Albert Hall. Its headquarters at Burlington House, opposite the Society of Antiquaries, is full of white pillars and red leather chairs, where Fellows can read faded volumes and listen to each other's lectures. The Royal holds regular 'Conversaziones' with a Queen Anne flavour, when Fellows and wives walk up the grand staircase in evening dress to shake hands with the president, and mingle in the reception rooms, watching other Fellows conducting small experiments.

In the seventeenth century the Society was the hub of scientific discovery. Newton, Halley, Dryden and Pepys gathered to chat about inventions and even though Pepys (who was President) couldn't understand Newton's *Principia*, they could all understand telescopes and comets. Since then specialists have learnt more and more about less and less, and the renaissance ideal of the 'universal man' has faded. It was in 1901 that the Fellows decided to exclude altogether the 'human' sciences—economics, for instance, or philosophy—and their proceedings have become steadily less intelligible to the layman. The Society has been split into two sides—the 'A' side (mathematics, physics, chemistry, etc.) and the 'B' side (geology, botany, physiology etc.), and one side has great difficulty in understanding the other.

The Fellows are elected by a series of sub-committees, with extraordinary care; the initials FRS are often more coveted than a knighthood. Some complain that the qualifications are too narrow and exacting so that many Fellows are elected after their active research is over: Sir Alexander Fleming was elected years after his discovery of penicillin.

Past presidents include Wren, Newton, Davy, Huxley, Kelvin, Thomson, Rutherford, Bragg, Dale, Adrian. The present one, elected for a five-year term in 1960, is Sir Howard Florey, the co-discoverer of penicillin, who won the Nobel Prize for medicine in 1945. Florey sits once a month on an old leather throne under a portrait of King Charles II, with beside him a treasurer (Sir William Penney), three secretaries (Sir Lindor Brown, Sir William Hodge and Dr. Thornton) and sixteen councillors.

The Royal Society has all the dignity of a scientific parliament: over three centuries it has grown up alongside monarchy, government and Church. But, like the House of Lords or the Court of the Bank, it is not as decisive as it looks. Many Fellows suspect that, in vast new scientific oceans, the Royal is becoming increasingly irrelevant: of over £450 million a year spent on research, the Society disperses only £235,000. The rebellious Fellows—quite a large segment—regard the Society as pompous and obsequious to government. 'The only important thing the Fellows do is elect other Fellows', said one radical Fellow: 'it's like one of those marine organisms which has lost every faculty except that of reproduction.'[1]

The Royal has many indirect contacts with government. Nearly every important scientific adviser is an FRS and the initials open the door to government and industry. The Society elects members

[1] e.g. the Pacific Palolo Worm (Eunica Viridis)

to committees; provides the cabinet with advice when asked; and acts as a kind of scientific Foreign Office, maintaining a network of international connections: science is the same kind of *lingua franca* as Latin was in the middle ages, and remains determinedly international in spite of the cold war. As a body the Royal has never been closely involved in major government decisions, but its aloofness has become much more apparent with the vast new expenditure since the war; they have fought shy of the government who in turn have sometimes found them too fussy and pure. 'They had a pathological and unnecessary horror of being controlled by government', one eminent Fellow said: 'They had the choice after the war of remaining a mutual admiration society, or really taking part in the control of science. They chose the former. They threw away the handles of power.'

SCIENTISTS AND INDUSTRY

Science is no longer simply an academic pursuit but, primarily, a matter of national survival.

'We are entering now upon the most serious struggle for existence to which this country was ever committed. The latter years of the century promise to see us in an industrial war of far more serious import than the military wars of its opening years.' That was written, not in 1962, but by T. H. Huxley in 1872. Most of British industry has never taken kindly to scientific research. The industrial revolution, as we noted in Chapter 13, owed nothing to the universities or the government: spinning jennies and steam engines were built by practical factory mechanics (though several, like Arkwright—a classical scholar—were well educated). Already in the 1860's and 1870's, when continental technical colleges were establishing close relationships with industry, Britain was lagging behind. The English exhibits at the Great Exhibition in Paris in 1867 were described as 'slovenly intruded heaps of raw materials mingled with pieces of rusty iron'.

In the light of these warnings, repeated over the past ninety years, it seems surprising that British industry has survived at all, and the monotony of these Cassandras encourages some people to think that Britain can always 'muddle through'. But in the 'second industrial revolution' of automation, science-based industries and mass-production, the integration of research with industry has become far more important, and this awareness has increasingly involved the government in industrial science.

It was to counter the research effort of German industry that in 1916 the government established the 'Department of Scientific and Industrial Research'. Today the DSIR spends about 14 million pounds a year, with five thousand employees and fourteen Research stations, the largest being the National Physical Laboratory, and a head office in Holborn. It subsidises fifty 'research associations', where rival firms (reluctantly) collaborate on research projects.

Newer 'science-based' industries—chemicals, electrical, aircraft—are deeply involved in research: they know that without it they could not survive, and in 1958 these three employed 65 per cent of the scientists in industry. ICI or Albright and Wilson work closely with universities: 'We've grown up together', said Sir Alexander Todd at Cambridge, 'with ICI people, Glaxo people, Monsanto people: the only difference between the kind of work that I do and what ICI does is that they necessarily have an economic objective.' Research has become a main weapon in fierce competition: 'It's becoming more and more a battle between the back-room boys,' said H. D. Lazell of Beechams.

But in older industries—shipbuilding, machine tools, coal, laundries, building and even motor-cars—research is still tiny, and a far smaller proportion of turnover in Britain than in America. For forty-five years the DSIR has been trying to persuade these industries to adopt new methods, usually working gingerly behind the scenes, terrified of publicity (I cannot even name the people I spoke to there). 'It's no good criticising industrialists in public; they just button up their coats: we want them to come into the party and join us. We hate fuss and headlines. What we're doing is missionary work, introducing scientific ideas to the factories.' But occasionally they come out into the open, publishing papers—on machine tools or shipbuilding, which both caused a large furore: or an appropriate minister—Lord Hailsham or Ernest Marples— makes an outburst. Soon after he became Minister of Science, Lord Hailsham complained in an explosive interview about the difficulties of the DSIR in encouraging builders to use a better kind of hod. 'That they should have to try and persuade a major industry to accept such a development in this modern age is pathetic.'[1]

Another large industrial weakness is the 'development hump'— the obstacle between discovering things and developing them: all too often they are left to be developed in America, from lack of

[1] Interview with the *Financial Times*, November 4, 1960.

interest or finance. One device to fill this gap is the National Research Development Corporation, founded after the war to allocate money for promising inventions. One NRDC project, the 'Hovercraft', has proved exciting and fruitful, but the inventions coming forward have so far been disappointing. Another scheme has been the idea of 'developing contracts', placed by the DSIR with industrial firms to experiment with new devices—computers, for instance, or new kinds of ship. But it has so far been difficult to place contracts without any particular customer in mind—like not knowing what gun to design when you don't know who the enemy is.

This is part of the nub. For nearly all the major engineering and scientific advances—jet planes, atomic power, ball-point pens, radar, transistors—have been precipitated by war, or the fear of it. The most destructive inventions produce constructive by-products: missiles can launch satellites for radio-communications. To provide a substitute for war, giving the same stimulus and financial incentive to industry, is the heart of the government's problem. Americans achieve it partially by giving a wide interpretation to 'defence', using it as a pretext for subsidising computers, electronic devices, new kinds of aircraft: the USAF even sponsors research into grasshoppers. But in Britain defence is less popular, and the solution less easy.

ENGINEERS

The profession of Civil Engineer, being the art of directing the Great Sources of Power in Nature for the use and convenience of man.
Charter of the Institute of Civil Engineers, 1828.

Some people suspect that the insuperability of the development hump is partly due to the decline in the influence of engineers. Compared to engineers on the continent, or in Russia (where they are one of the most respected professions) British engineers are not much in evidence. In Victorian times names like Brunel, Naesmith or Telford were national heroes: in the railway boom, ambitious engineers set up their offices in Victoria Street, close to parliament where they pushed through their bills. The consultants are still there, several of them earning as much as £20,000 a year: but they are far less noticed by parliament or the public. The Institute of Civil Engineers, a stately palazzo off Parliament Square, still evokes the grandeur of Victorian technocrats, with rooms full of portraits of past presidents, including Bidder, the mathematician who could multiply twelve figures by twelve figures in his head. It has a council room with a horseshoe table, holding the names of present councillors—Manzoni, Baker, Owen Williams, Skempton, Bugsby.

Hundreds of contemporary engineers, including these and men such as Sir George Edwards (who designed the Viscount), Sir Christopher Hinton (who planned the first nuclear power stations) or Lord Nelson of Stafford (chairman of English Electric) have had a large effect on British life. But engineering has become much less associated with individual names. Partly this is because much exciting British engineering takes place abroad, for such projects as the Indus dam in Pakistan or the Kariba dam in Rhodesia. But the men behind new projects in Britain, like the M1 or the Forth Road Bridge, have become much more anonymous. Since Victorian times engineers have no longer dealt with single patrons like the Duke of Bridgewater, but have become involved with teams and committees, and this has helped to weaken their influence: 'Up till 1900', said the secretary of the Institute, Mr. Macdonald, 'the Engineer's word was law: but since then they've had less and less of the last word.' Many engineers feel that they have lost their initiative to the businessmen—particularly accountants.

Engineering has lost a good deal of its panache: it is sad to compare the astonishing speed and boldness of Victorian projects —the Crystal Palace took a few months from drawing board to completion, and the first fly-over, the Holborn Viaduct, was built a century ago—with the delays, committees and qualifications of modern engineering: the extension of the Victoria underground has been at the discussion stage for the past ten years. Much of the slowness is due to the delays of democracy, and the sheer *poverty* of modern Britain: but it is partly, too, due to the lack of powerful engineers at the top.

Compared with the continent, the *average* British engineer is as well trained, but there is no British equivalent for the rigorous two-year course of the French *polytechniciens* who have had such a large influence on their industry and civil service, and the British schools lack their high standing. Continental engineers have a strong schooling in theory, which helps to give them a daring and enterprise, shown in the French monorail, the French pavilion at the Brussels Fair, or Nervi's Olympic stadium at Rome. Initiative for the Channel tunnel has come from the French engineers, with little excitement from London.

The scope of engineers has been further limited by the fissiparity of the profession which, like the Inns of Court, has produced complicated internal rivalries. The oldest of the institutes, the 'Civils' (bridges, roads, dams) took a high-handed line with new-comers, and actually refused to elect George Stephenson a member, which led to the foundation of the 'Mechanicals' (trains, cars, aeroplanes). Others, the Electricals, Chemicals, etc., followed, so that by 1929 there were already more than a hundred societies for engineers. And since 1900 the architects have stolen some of the engineers' thunder: the two professions have been at daggers drawn, and much more separate than in Europe. But the different branches of engineering are now, more than ever, interdependent; a dam can involve Civil, Mechanical and Electrical—and engineers are aware that this fragmentation has weakened their scope: 'a multiplicity of bodies and an attitude of mind which seems to elevate the importance of the part above that of the whole.'[1]

A brave new bid for unity was made by Sir George McNaughton, chief engineer to the Ministry of Housing, in his presidential address to the Civils on November 7, 1961. 'If engineers are to gain their old position of policy makers and financial controllers in the work they undertake,' he said, 'they must be able to express views on wider fields than the purely technical.' He criticised the fragmentation of the profession, and suggested that there should be a high-level co-ordinating body between the Civils, Mechanicals and Electricals, 'so powerful that other chartered bodies could not afford to stand aside' (which produced an angry retort from the Chemicals). Talking about the decline in engineers' influence, he said: 'One can only speculate as to the cause of the present position. Can it be the absence of a higher standard of education in the humanities and the social sciences amongst the entrants to the profession?'

SCIENTISTS AND WAR

Half the scientific research in the country—costing £230 million a year—is undertaken by the Ministry of Defence—engaging 60 per cent of all British research scientists and technologists. This is the murkiest region of all, for what happens to that £230 million is known to only a handful of people. Most of the scientists work in isolated stations scattered over the country, knowing little about each other.

[1] J. G. Orr, General Secretary of the Engineers Guild: *The Times*, November 13, 1961.

Secrecy is anathema to scientists. Discovery depends on communication. Scientists have, since the end of the seventeenth
century, been internationally-minded. Science knows no real
frontiers; and a Russian scientist can soon find himself at home in
Burlington House. The creeping expansion of *secret* research,
largely devoted to means of destruction, has depressed scientists
all over the world.

Defence inevitably is an area of preposterous waste. Extravagant
projects can take seven or eight years to complete, rolling on with
their own massive inertia, only to find themselves hopelessly
unwanted, for either political or technical reasons. 'Research' still
conjures up test-tubes or microscopes, but more often it means
gigantic engineering contraptions, lumps of radio-active hardware,
and intricate electronic devices—enough to build a whole town,
and all liable to be scrapped. Only momentarily does parliament
and the public glimpse the waste—as when the government
abandoned the project for the Blue Streak missile in 1960 after it
had cost £100 million.

The decisions for these vast outlays are taken by the Chiefs of
Staff, the Minister of Defence, and ultimately by the cabinet. But
a key position—probably the most important scientific job—is
held by the Scientific Adviser to the Ministry of Defence. He lies
in the centre of the committee-web: and he is the main link
between science and war.

The occupier since 1960, Sir Solly Zuckerman, is a surprising
person to find in this sombre position: he is a gay ex-South
African with a restless, overflowing mind. He is an expert on
baboons and thirty years ago wrote the standard work on the social
life of monkeys. He is a gregarious, drawing-room man: he
married the daughter of Lord Reading and unlike most scientists
moves in several unscientific circles. He remains, in spite of his
Whitehall commitments, Professor of Anatomy in Birmingham,
and still spends time at the London Zoo, of which he is secretary.

Since the outbreak of war, Sir Solly has been involved with
government science: he studied the effects of bombing and blast,
and belonged to the school opposing the wholesale bombing of
homes. His perceptive mind, charm and persuasiveness brought
him into the midst of committee-country;[1] he made easy friend-
ships, and remains the confidant of ministers on both sides. He
enjoys the corridors of power, but he remains a sensitive intellectual, well aware of his social responsibilities. Some people in

[1] *See* Chapter 15.

Whitehall complain that he is not sufficiently interested in war.

'While essential in matters of defence, the business of secrecy also has great drawbacks', Sir Solly said, 'It makes it most difficult to get cross-fertilisation between the different branches: and the lack of communication is demoralising for scientists. You get too many people retreating to scientific establishments in the provinces, soaking themselves in their specialised subject, without knowing how it relates to some other subject, or how it will be applied. With the growth of science and specialisation, the isolation is getting worse, everywhere in the world. Scientists nowadays don't think much about the social consequences of science—they're only interested in their specialised fields. When I deliver lectures about the social responsibilities of science, the young scientists regard me as an old square.'

ATOMIC ENERGY

The most expensive part of defence research is concerned with nuclear fission: and here the Ministry delegates its task to the mammoth nationalised industry, dealing both with peaceful and warlike applications—the Atomic Energy Authority. It is the most inpenetrable industry: even to enter their London headquarters in Charles II Street, a visitor has to wear a yellow 'V' badge. The annual report of the 'Atomic Iceberg' reveals little about how its £78 million from the Treasury has been spent. It is divided between two clients—the Ministry of Defence, for whom it makes weapons, and the Electricity Generating Boards, for whom it designs power stations. Between them the AEA manages to be accountable to no one.

It was founded in 1954, full of high promise, as an off-shoot of the Ministry of Supply, which had made the first atomic bombs. The American AEC farmed out all its nuclear research to universities and companies, but the British decided to have it all in one rich national organisation, separate from industry or universities. The new Authority was full of enthusiastic scientists, headed by Sir John Cockcroft, and Britain seemed on the verge of leading the world to cheap nuclear power. The AEA was determined to free itself from the civil service, to become a flexible organism, run by scientists for scientists.

But the excitement wore off. Nuclear power turned out to be far more expensive than coal or oil. Building power stations produced unsuspected problems, and large losses for the contractors. 'Zeta', which it was hoped might produce power from the sea, did nothing of the kind. And AEA grew from exciting youth to corpulent middle age. In seven years the staff doubled to 40,000, and assets increased from £155 million to £250 million. Scientists complained that the administration became top-heavy, bureaucratic and cluttered with protocol—that it was becoming just a bureaucracy with a small eccentric fringe—a BBC of science. For a time the scientific knights wouldn't talk to each other. The administration of research has appalling problems; for often there is no obvious output like broadcasts or oil sales, no clear distinction between means and ends, and the spending of millions may depend on one uncertain hunch. The ups and downs of public excitement have their effect on Harwell's morale: 'First they put us up on a pinnacle which was much too high', said Sir William Penney, 'then we went down into a hole which we never deserved: in five years they may regard us as quite a reasonable bunch of men.'

At the head of the Authority is Sir Roger Makins, who spent most of his life as a diplomat, rising to the head of his profession as Ambassador to Washington in 1953. After a spell as joint head of the Treasury he moved to the Authority in 1960. He is a tall man, with a booming voice and half-spectacles on the end of his nose; he made himself felt quickly in the scattered empire of the Authority—from Dounreay in Scotland to Winfrith in Dorset. His problems, he insists, are basically no different from other diplomatic problems. 'My job is half-way between a permanent secretary's and a minister's', he said: 'I have a certain amount of independence, and my own little cabinet. But because we are financed directly from the Exchequer and are therefore subject to full Treasury and parliamentary control, and because of the defence part of our work, we have to be very close to government on several levels. We are part department, part research and development organisation, and part commercial enterprise. This makes for problems of organisation and management. We're facing in at least two directions, and we're not quite as free as we may look.'

Under Sir Roger is a board of five knights, each in charge of a department, with six part-time members, headed by Sir John Cockcroft. The most important is the vice-chairman, Sir William Penney. More than anyone, he was responsible for the British A-bomb and H-bomb. He makes a contrast both with Sir Roger and with the other influential Whitehall adviser, Sir Solly. For he is the epitome of the self-made, dedicated scientist. He has a boyish-looking face with a thatch of hair, large glasses and an ambling walk. He lives a quiet, suburban life. He talks in a sing-song, almost apologetic way, answers his own telephone and has a matter-of-fact attitude to questions. Penney is one of the 'new men'—the race of scientists growing up with a background quite separate from the old class-structure. He was the son of an army warrant officer, and went as a boy to Sheerness Technical College where he discovered his mathematical flair. He became assistant professor at the Imperial College, and during the war (like Sir Solly) he investigated bombing effects. In 1944, as one of the most brilliant of Britain's young scientists, he was invited to America to study the atomic bomb; and on August 9, 1945, he was one of two Englishmen to watch the explosion on Nagasaki. Since then he has been bound up with nuclear research, perfected the A-bomb in 1952, and the H-bomb in 1957.

He is known for his unpretentious approach to problems. A story is told of Americans in the New Mexico desert discussing expensive methods for measuring atomic blast. 'Why don't you try', said Penney diffidently, 'putting a row of tins cans across the desert, to see how they get dented by the blast.' It worked perfectly.

Penney remains ultimately responsible for all Britain's nuclear research. The centre for basic research is at Harwell in Berkshire, the most expensive of the AEA's establishments, which claims to be the biggest atomic research establishment in the free world—employing 6,000, including 1,500 scientists.

Like so many modern research centres, Harwell is remote and isolated. It looks like, and was, a war-time air force base, sitting by itself in the Berkshire countryside, with rows of married quarters, a high fence all round, and inside, a mass of fantastic ironmongery, like a deserted fairground. It is dominated by the reactors, with names like GLEEP, BEPO or LIDO, built inside great concrete cubes in the middle hangars, full of strange noises—beeps, tapockatas, boinks and pssts. The biggest look like two outsize dustbins coming up from the ground, called Dido and Pluto, with some of the characteristics of strange gods: outside one is a notice saying: 'If Dido sounds siren, run to Pluto'. Dido and Pluto together cost nine million pounds to build, and another two million a year to run. Thick double doors lead into a jungle of engineering round the central reactor. It is a world on its own: there are TV screens, dashboards of dials, and a travelling crane. Bits of radioactive metal are taken out of the reactor and carried in lead caskets to laboratories where scientists in rubber gloves study them behind glass screens.

Scattered round Harwell, standing round the reactors or inspecting bits of metal in the labs, are the 1,500 scientists; they include three FRSs, but in their dingy white coats they are difficult to tell from lab assistants or mechanics. At lunch the scientists sit at long tables in sports coats and baggy flannel trousers, with the informality of a camp. Age and sex are irrelevant: there are about fifty women scientists, and the head of one division is twenty-eight.

Harwell is a long way from the conversaziones at the Royal Society and the ideal of the universal man. It is typical of the fragmented state of science, where one man can spend a lifetime experimenting with one vast, possibly quite fruitless, contraption. No one yet knows whether Harwell will become a forgotten white elephant, like Zeppelins, or the forerunner of the dawn of a new age. For at Harwell a layman realises with apprehension what in his own awe of science he can well forget, that scientists are not omniscient or prophetic, but groping in the dark like anyone else.

GOVERNMENT AND SCIENTISTS

The relationship between the freedom of scientific institutions and the controlling power of government finance is a problem in all Western democracies, made more pressing by the immense concentration of Russian scientific effort. How to co-ordinate research without directing it, how to have different kinds of research without jealousies and rivalries, are problems that no democracy can finally solve.

In Britain the problem is complicated by the low science quotient among the administrators—notably in the cabinet and the higher civil service; and here the Whitehall division between specialists and mandarins is most serious of all. 'If you go to a ministry they proudly produce an assistant secretary and say: "here's a man who's got a science degree"', said one scientific knight, 'but it wouldn't do any harm if a third of the assistant secretaries had a scientific training.' The introduction of 'scientific advisers' to provide the link between Whitehall departments and research organisations has not been very effectual, since the advisers do not often become closely involved in policy-making: 'Unless this type of integration is assured', said Sir Solly Zuckerman's report in 1961, 'we do not think that many good scientists would find the job attractive in certain departments; they would have few staff and would have no direct responsibilities for research, and they would be uncomfortably placed between the main body of the department and the research establishments of other organisations.'[1]

Between the Treasury and scientific departments there remains a wide distance: Sir Solly's report pointed out in kid-glove language some defects—the lack of 'forward looks', the arguing in a 'financial vacuum', the way projects 'drift on from one stage to another without strict control at critical points', and the preservation of old projects through inertia: 'Lay officials in the Treasury . . . must inevitably tend to focus their attention on new major projects, on new fields of research, or on unforeseen increased expenditure on old projects, and less on the elimination of existing items because they have declined in importance.'[2]

Differences in background exacerbate the relationship—inevitably bitter—between science and politics. 'You pursue a thing up to a certain point and then the whole thing disappears into a higher political level, and the decision is taken—and nobody quite seems to know why', as one leading scientist put it: 'the people who take the decisions really don't know anything about them. You might just as well toss a penny—in fact that would be better than not deciding at all, like Blue Streak. They tend to put off decisions until *nature* decides.'

The integration of scientists into government is obviously not easy. Many are naturally radical, dis-organisation men, not 'house-trained' and quite enjoying their battles with Whitehall. And very often—as civil servants love explaining—they fail, like economists, to agree among themselves. But the present exclusion of scientists from the centre only makes things worse: it is here that the closed collegiate tradition of Whitehall, and the amateur tradition in politics, is most obviously hopeless. When politicians *do* take science seriously, there is the danger that they adopt a court favourite, like Lord Cherwell, taking his advice as more infallible than any scientist's could possibly be.

COMMITTEES AND COUNCILS

Whitehall, partly because of the lack of scientists in its midst,

---

[1] *Management and Control of Research and Development.* HMSO 1961, p. 80.
[2] *Ibid.* page 44.

partly because of its healthy democratic respect for the independence of other institutions, has approached the control and co-ordination of research with great hesitation. As far as possible, the government has left the scientific dons to themselves, while giving them large grants: 'In our view', wrote the Zuckerman report, 'pure basic research is best carried out in the environment of a university rather than in that of a Government research establishment. It is characteristic of universities that they provide their members with the necessary freedom to pursue any line of enquiry they wish to follow and, broadly speaking, at whatever pace their inclinations dictate.'[1]

The aristocrats of science remain the university dons: of the 616 Fellows of the Royal Society in 1960, 126 were at London University, 107 at Cambridge, 50 at Oxford, 16 at Edinburgh, 13 at Manchester, 13 at Bristol, 11 at Birmingham and 60 at all the other universities.[2] Cambridge remains the phenomenal seed-bed of British science, as it has been, off and on, since Newton's day: and perhaps the most concentrated area of scientific talent in the world.

But applied government research is controlled by a whole cluster of councils—committee-country with a vengeance. A single scientist may sit on a score: 'I *loathe* advisory committees: there are far too many', one of them said. 'If only committees had actual control over spending, they'd be much more responsible.' 'There's a small group of committee-people who the civil servants have got used to', explained another scientist: 'it's not so much that they've got *confidence* in them, but they know they won't make a nuisance of themselves, by telling things to the *Daily Mail*.'

But some of the councils have clear-cut powers, with annual funds to allocate for research projects. These are the four government councils, each with their full-time secretary:

Department of Scientific and Industrial Research	Sir Harry Melville
Medical Research Council	Sir Harold Himsworth
Agricultural Research Council	Sir William Slater
Nature Conservancy	Max Nicholson

The councils exist, like the University Grants Committee, in a no-man's-land between the civil service and the universities, and their position is often delicate. 'Committees only get moving under

[1] Zuckerman, p. 26.
[2] From *Discovery*, July 1960.

the pressure of applied forces', as one scientist put it: 'Blackett turned the DSIR upside down.' The relations between the councils and the universities are often awkward: 'You've no idea what happens when you connect the DSIR and the university in series', said the same source: 'you get disputes over who drank the Nescafé.'

MINISTER FOR SCIENCE

But the most curious feature of British scientific research expenditure is the lack of a central co-ordinating body. The nearest thing to a scientists' cabinet is the Advisory Council on Scientific Policy (ACSP), founded after the war, largely by Professors Blackett and Zuckerman, to keep going the war-time connections between science and government. The sixteen sages of the ACSP include the four secretaries of research councils, the chairman of the University Grants Committee (Sir Keith Murray), two scientific industrialists (Lord Fleck and Sir George Edwards), a man from the Royal Society (Sir William Hodge), four scientific administrators (Sir Solly Zuckerman, Sir William Penney, Sir Frederick Brundrett, Sir John Cockcroft), a Treasury man (A. W. France), two other academics (Professor Bennet-Clark and Dr. J. S. Tait), and the chairman, Professor Sir Alexander Todd.

Todd is a tall, formidable Nobel prize-winner, with a rich Glaswegian accent; he is Professor of Organic Chemistry at Cambridge, where he sits behind a large desk in the new chemistry building, beside a complicated model of a molecule. He is the son of a Glasgow JP, and he married the daughter of one of the princes of science, Sir Henry Dale.

But the phrase a 'scientist's cabinet' is misleading: for the ACSP is a disparate body of very busy men with large other commitments, who only meet one afternoon a month: they begin at 2.30 and by 4 p.m. some members are already looking at their watches, and worrying about their trains back to Oxford, and in the long summer holidays they don't meet at all. That this should be the central advisory body for the government is, on the face of it, absurd. They have no opportunity to discuss many major problems: when, for instance, a much-criticised report was published under their name, suggesting that there would be an excess of scientific man-power by 1970, it turned out to have been written by a sub-committee of a sub-committee: the Committee itself had not had time to discuss the report.

Somewhere in the middle of the committees is the nebulous

bailiwick of the Minister of Science, Lord Hailsham, on whose influence in cabinet they all ultimately depend for support. Hailsham is one of the ablest and probably the most independent of contemporary Tory politicians: his ebullience and his evident personal friction with Macmillan have at least temporarily set back his career. He is boyish, impetuous, with a flow of witty conversation and an alarming cackle of a laugh, which rocks him in his chair. He has a first-class mind, an optimistic sense of the future, and a romantic showmanship which can be attractive or (as at Suez) dangerous. He has an oratory of the moving, old-fashioned kind, backed by Christian convictions, and he is one of the few men in cabinet who give the impression of passionate beliefs. But his appointment as Minister for Science was not widely welcomed by scientists: neither he nor his Minister of State, Denzil Freeth, knows anything about science, and scientists are doubtful about his strength in cabinet.

His office is one of the oddest institutions in Whitehall. To begin with, it is not a ministry, only an 'office of the Minister for Science' —or an un-ministry as *The Economist* calls it. It inhabits a small eighteenth-century house off Whitehall, with a staff of fifty-five (including six doorkeepers and five messengers), a tiny lift which breaks down, and a gas lamp outside the front door. His job is to advise, coax and co-ordinate. But the Office is still weak in authority, with a relatively junior deputy secretary and small funds. 'The Office is in an indeterminate state', one of its staff told me, 'between being a post-box, not often emptied, and having real influence.'

ADMINISTERING SCIENCE

Most scientists seem to agree that with the present and future involvement of the government, the hold at the centre will have to be strengthened. I asked Sir William Penney, at the Atomic Energy Authority, about some of the problems of scientific administration: in the first place, about secrecy, and how far it inhibits scientific freedom:

Penney: I think both industry and the defence scientists of the government are fully on guard against the risk of small groups getting isolated comfortable jobs—with no real knowledge of how other people are getting on. Efforts are made to stop this settling into a rut. But I think secrecy is more subtle in its effect than just first-order things. If a very clever young man

527

or woman in science, who is offered a job in a secret place on secret work, is offered an equally well-paid job with equally good facilities where there's no secrecy, well there's no doubt where the choice is, and this shows up in time. Not that a good man in a secret place is handicapped. What is handicapped is the organisation, because secrecy is regarded, naturally enough, as a bit of a disadvantage.

Sampson: With AEA the public sometimes has the impression that there's simply not enough information given out, so that nobody really knows what to criticise. Is there any way that that is being overcome?

Penney: As regard basic science, I don't think the complaint has any justification. Our scientists are in and out of conferences all over the world, we report our work and so on. But when one gets nearer to military application, then of course we have to be very careful. We're very much aware that the quality of our people depends on how we handle them—that they are better people for mixing and reporting what they're doing. Even at our most secret place at Aldermaston, quite a lot of our staff are attending open conferences. They perhaps don't man for man contribute new papers as much as those who are in unclassified places—because they can only describe certain aspects of their work. But we do everything we can.

Sampson: How far do you think the relationship between scientists and government has sorted itself out?

Penney: It's changed enormously. Our government know how vital science is, and the scientists have no cause for complaint. Now where I think the change is happening—and it's going to accelerate—is using scientists in government, in industry, in commerce, even in foreign affairs, not as scientists but as *people*—chosen for qualities of common sense and judgment, and having the advantage of understanding science. No, I think there haven't been enough of those people. Science is a very exacting profession, and to succeed you have to work very hard and you have to be single-minded. Young people making their reputation in science are devoted to their own expertise, and therefore in a sense are late starters in the broader issues. It isn't that they are out of sympathy with them, but their science takes every ounce of their energy. Now, I think that in this country, and certainly in America too, the governments need people of judgment, management, policy-makers, all those things, and some of these people should have scientific knowledge. And we're very short of these.

Sampson: Do you think there *is* a basic difference between the classical and scientific disciplines—a serious field of cross-purpose?

Penney: In the last analysis the discipline doesn't matter. What matters is the intelligence and brainpower, sensibility, feeling for human relations. But what does also matter is that in an organisation you have some of each—where a man can say 'Yes, I understand that because I learned about it'. So I think it would be very dangerous to have, for example, all the directors of a large industrial company with classical degrees. They'd make a mess of it, however gifted. At present scientists are not sufficiently represented in these things, not because they haven't got men of intelligence and personality, but because until recently science has been so consuming. I think the increase in the number of scientists and the efforts which scientists are making to broaden the training are going to have very beneficial effects.

Sampson: How far do you think there is still a social barrier here, which makes scientists less easily absorbed into government?

Penney: I suppose there is; there have been difficulties here. First because the scientist, as I have explained, is almost *unilateral* when he's young. Secondly, because in these other fields there have not been many scientists there already to bring them in. But the steps that we're taking will correct that position.

Sampson: But still, one has the impression talking to scientists that there is a minor cold war between scientists and civil servants.

Penney: In military fields thirty, forty years ago, this was very true. I think it was probably true even later in some other fields. But at the Whitehall end at any rate, that has disappeared. The government and the top civil servants are desperately keen to get in scientists with two qualities: the ability to take a big position and, secondly, the ability to make good judgments in scientific fields.

Sampson: Is science in danger of getting bogged down in committees, swamping the individual element in research?

Penney: It's commonly said, sometimes jokingly but often seriously. To some extent it's unavoidable, but I think also that a lot of executive work can be done by people who've had a scientific training but are not specialists in science. And we ought to be able to use older people better. As a rule, scientific originality doesn't last to the age of retirement—in some cases it disappears much earlier. The methods of using these people would be worth studying: scientists haven't made any time-and-motion studies. I think they've got to see that the really fertile scientist at his most creative period does research which really does matter: because he's brilliant there's no reason for shoving him on committees. You should wait until he's got a little older.

Sampson: The relationship between this great flood of government money that's going into science and the freedom and independence of the various units—do you think we've got that right?

Penney: No, we haven't. It is one of the most difficult matters in science today, and both the government and the scientists know it. Science now, even fundamental science, requires so much money that it must be considered by politicians, because it's such a substantial slice of the total budget. I think some new steps are required, and they must start from Whitehall, but the decisions must be on the advice of scientists. The problems are beyond the analysis of a body like the ACSP which has such a short time. These are big problems; they want much more careful and detailed consideration. Take a major issue—for example, high energy accelerators: the unit of coinage is a million, perhaps ten million, and future ones may cost a hundred million. The Atlas computer costs three or four million pounds, and lots of subjects will require the services of such a computer. If you project this forward ten or twenty years, we've simply got to have a machinery for sorting this out. You can imagine what ticklish questions come in: one man wants ten million quid, though another can do miracles for ten quid. And the irony of it is that that may be right: one man with a few thousand pounds might have a bigger impact on our civilisation of thirty or forty years' time than a man who gets ten or even a hundred million pounds. Who's clever enough to judge that? One of the most important problems of today is the financing of science—getting a balance—realising that some projects have to have expensive things because they can't get on without it, and yet those sums of money might have revolutionary effects in small areas where a few thousand pounds provides a piece of equipment that permits somebody to do something quite outstanding.

Sampson: But if much more planning is needed, can we avoid having a full-scale ministry of science on the Russian model?

Penney: Well, no one wants the regimentation of science. I think this gives us scope for originality. We are original in our ways of managing government, and both the government and the scientists realise that both have a decisive interest; the government has to have a power of veto if it's too expensive, and the scientists have got to sort it out. We haven't got a method at the moment: we've had some tentative shots at it. It must mean in the end a bit more concentration. The machinery has to be more centralised in a Minister for Science's department. But he's got the problem of carrying the scientists with him, knowing that the scientists are competitive with each other.

34

NATIONALISED INDUSTRIES

> If you keep pulling up the plant to see how the roots are getting on,
> it does not grow very well.
>
> *Lord Heyworth (Select Committee 1953. q. 723)*

> It may be regrettable, but it seems to be a fact that people's enthu-
> siasm about almost any group to which they belong is enhanced by
> competition.
>
> *Hugh Gaitskell: Socialism and Nationalisation, 1956.*

NATIONALISED industries are the major innovation of post-war
Britain; unlike most British institutions they have not grown
slowly out of the past, but have been deliberately imposed, appearing fully armed, like Athena from the head of Zeus. Ever since
they disappeared from the stock exchange, they have become
a battleground of theory—a rare thing in so pragmatic a country—
crossed and recrossed by armies of commissions, select committees, politicians, dons and consultants—all trying to decide
what to do about them.

They are an odd jumble of properties. The state has been landed
with many of the most unprofitable estates in the country, in most
cases because they have apparently become unworkable by anyone
else. The full list includes the Sugar Board, Cable and Wireless Ltd.,
the North of Scotland Hydro-Electric Board, Short Brothers and
Harland Ltd., the Atomic Energy Authority, and, of course, the
Post Office—a nationalised industry in every country, but which
in England has grown to become a banker, telephone company,
tax-collector and pension agent. But the Post Office is a separate
case, run directly by the civil service. The core of the state industries is made up by the great national utilities—coal, gas,
railways, electricity and airways.

They all have exciting histories: they represent, in that order,
the layers of Britain's industrial revolution. It was on coal that the
industrial revolution was based: the invention of gas (in 1798), of
railways (in 1829), and electricity (in 1881) built up the urban
industrial country which we know. Today they have grown from
daring pioneers into ancient, reviled and unwanted retainers. And
as Britain becomes more involved in affluence, cars and private

property, so the fabric of public services becomes increasingly taken for granted, like waterfalls or rivers, and only noticed and cursed at when strikes interrupt their flow.

Their most obvious characteristic is size: they make the private industrial giants look like midgets. British Railways employs six times as many people as ICI, and the Electricity Board devours enough capital to build a new ICI every three years. Each of the Coal Board's nine divisions is bigger, in turnover, than English Electric. These are the six leading public corporations, with their assets, numbers of employees, profit, turnover, and date of nationalisation:

	Employ-ees 1960	Surplus or Defi-cit 1960 £M	Net Assets[1] 1957–58 £M	Turn-over[1] 1957–58 £M	Date of national-isation
British Transport Commission	729,000	−36·3	1,694[2]	726·7	1947
National Coal Board	634,000	−21·3	852	937·3	1946
Electricity Council and Boards	193,174	+16·3	1,514	340	1947
Gas Council and Boards	124,443	+2	502	388·6	1949
BOAC	20,787	−2·5	103	53·5	1939
BEA	13,240	+1·5	33	27·4	1946

Their size, as much as their ownership, has made them problem children, for when they were nationalised in quick succession, no one had had experience of running huge concerns except generals; and industrial corporations are not at all like armies. Their teething troubles were not unlike those of private giants, like ICI or AEI. In retrospect, perhaps the most surprising fact about the nationalisation was how, in spite of all the theorising and discussion that preceded it, hardly any of the nationalisers had any idea of how large corporations could, or should, be run. This was part of the price of the divorce between parliament and the world of managers before 1951, and when the Conservatives took over in 1951, their knowledge was hardly greater. As the problems grew, several of the heads of private firms were called in: Lord Heyworth from Unilever, Lord Fleck and Paul Chambers from ICI, Sir Ivan Stedeford from Tube Investments—they all

[1] As calculated by Ralph Harris and Michael Solly in *A Survey of Large Companies*, Institute of Economic Affairs, 1959.

[2] But see page 541. The deficit for railways alone is very much larger.

533

gave their diagnosis and prognosis, but none had had experience of malaise on such a massive scale. As Lord Heyworth put it to the Select Committee in 1953: 'Anyone can find out what is wrong at any moment of time, but very few people can get it better . . .' The problems of the big corporations are compounded of size, old age, service and neglect, for which there is no quick cure.

While cabinets were slow to understand the organisational problems, the Treasury were slow to realise the economic implication. The industries added enormously to the government's responsibilities, not only in appointing their heads and directing their policies, but in allocating their capital. And nationalisation changed the whole balance of economic power. Between them, in 1959, they invested £760 million—nearly as much as the £820 million spent by the whole of private manufacturing industry. In its responsibility for regulating this sum, Treasury policy can drastically affect and alter the country's economy, but it has come to this realisation slowly and reluctantly.

Though nationalisation is associated with Socialism, these industries had been moving steadily towards state control since the nineteen-twenties. The nationalisation of coal was first proposed by the Sankey Commission of 1919. BOAC was created by a Conservative government in 1939. Nationalising electricity was considered by Lord McGowan in 1936, and nationalising gas was recommended by Lord Heyworth in 1948. The state had been intervening in railways and coal as they declined through the twenties and thirties: and vigorously though their nationalisation was opposed by Conservatives, few openly advocate de-nationalisation. But both parties still argue about what these bodies are supposed to *be*.

The concept of the public corporation was first fully expounded by Herbert Morrison who was responsible for creating the London Passenger Transport Board. 'The public corporation must be no mere capitalist business, the be-all and end-all of which is profits and dividends', wrote Morrison in 1953: 'Its board and officers must regard themselves as the high custodians of the public interest.' But the 'high custodians' are caught between the ideals of service and the demand for profitable running. We have seen how the whole dynamic of private industry is provided by the profit motive—how their structures, hierarchies, prestige and self-respect only make sense in terms of profit. The Socialist founders of nationalisation wished to substitute the service motive as the driving force. Profits and service are bound to be at loggerheads. Telegrams, airways to the Hebrides, country electricity and branch-lines all lose money but are all essential services. No one likes to be associated with loss. 'Our chaps hated our making a loss', said Lord Douglas of Kirtleside of BEA: 'they used to go into the pub and someone would say, "Well, Bill, how much money have you lost today?" When we started making a profit, the whole atmosphere was different.'

NATIONALISED CHAIRMEN

And who should run these corporations? Morrison insisted that the public corporations should be largely independent of government interference: they would not, like civil service departments, have a minister sitting in the building. Their boards would be left to get on with their job, like the boards of private companies, with parliament, as shareholders, occasionally surveying the scene, and the appropriate minister maintaining contact with the board. But the relationship has not worked out that way. At first, ministers left the corporations pretty much alone: 'I think they were too ready to abdicate to the Frankensteins which they'd created', one ex-minister said to me. Then, as things began to go wrong, parliament became restive. Conservative ministers and civil service departments (who have often resented the freedom of the corporations) have intervened more in running the industries. 'Three years ago', said one chairman bitterly, 'it looked as if we were becoming a kind of mammoth ICI: now we're becoming more and more like the Post Office.' Between these two poles, ICI and the GPO, all the nationalised industries are still wavering.

It is perhaps not surprising that these bodies have no strong personalities of their own. Their names are elaborately confusing: the electricity people have changed three times—from BEA to CEA to (now two names) EC and CEGB: who now knows the difference between CEGB—which employs 55,000 people—and EC, which employs 514. The two million people who work for these organisations, from the SWGB to BR (ER), appear as a single government army. The nationalised managers, like insurance managers or accountants, are largely separate from the public school nexus and the old boy net: they have their roots with provincial engineering schools or branch offices. The CEGB has not yet acquired the institutional aura of ICI, and the words Coal Board can still produce a titter.

In this unhappy no-man's-land between government and commerce are placed the chairmen of the nationalised boards. They are not much envied and, compared to the chairmanship of a joint stock company, their task is nightmarish. They are appointed for five years only—not long enough to see the fruits of their capital investment: and though one chairman has survived thirteen years, many have resigned before the end of their term. They have to run their vast and complex properties with an inquisitive parliament and usually a determined minister looking over their shoulder. There must always be disagreement between a chairman trying to run a commercial business and a minister trying to placate the public—whether the chairman wants to raise the price of coal or fares, to make large capital investments, to buy American aircraft, or to give in to wage demands. The argument is not usually settled by open directives from the minister, but by the 'fireside chats' or 'old boy messages'—the traditional British technique. The outcome of the chats is the secret test of the chairman. Many of them are over-ruled or persuaded by the minister, many have been discreetly sacked. But a few have held their own. When Lord Citrine ran the electricity authority, Labour ministers complained that he was harder to control than the chairman of ICI. More recently, both Lord Robens and Dr. Beeching have shown signs of holding their own against their ministers.

Consequently the chairmen have yet to emerge as an identifiable species. Most of them have come from outside their industries—from the armed forces, from private industry or politics. The four major chairmen all come from outside the traditional civil service background:[1] they include a professor, an engineer and a scientist. Here, as in insurance or hire-purchase companies, new institutions are run by new men. They are unflamboyant. Their battles, though heroic, are unsung. Compare the unobtrusive rôle of Sir Henry Jones with Enrico Mattei, the head of the nationalised oil-and-gas combine in Italy—who runs his own newspaper, openly attacks the government, subsidises political parties and works his industry as a private empire.

When the corporations were created, it was hoped that a new kind of person would emerge—someone half-way between a civil servant and a businessman, between the world of budgets and the world of profits—a new 'industrial civil service'. The salaries followed this pattern: most of the chairmen earned £10,000 a year—more than the civil service heads, but much less than the private tycoons. Many chairmen, and some of their boards, had

[1] *See* page 193.

accepted large cuts of salary. The ideal of public service showed itself in the austerity of the dingy corridors, bleak offices and chipped cups of tea on the civil service pattern, with little of the expense-account splendour of private industries.

But into the midst of these assumptions was dropped in March 1961 the 'Beeching Bombshell'—announcing that the new head of British Railways, Dr. Beeching, would earn the same salary as he had as director of ICI—£24,000 a year. It happened that, in the following week, I was interviewing three chairmen of nationalised industries. Their reaction was immediate: 'Absolutely deplorable', 'thoroughly demoralising', 'tremendous repercussions'. It was almost as if it had been announced that the Royal Navy had sold out to Shell.

Behind this furore lay the whole proud history of the public service—which in Britain, unlike in America, has in the past been more highly regarded than private industry. The nationalised industries—particularly coal and electricity—still have many managers who have an idealistic dedication to state service, and a fixed dislike of private industry. But since the war the private industries have become more concerned with prestige, and the public ones with profit, while the public corporations, at a time of full employment, have had to compete strongly for their managers. The Beeching bombshell seemed to imply that public and private service were indivisible, that service was no longer its own reward.

Meanwhile a fundamental force had pushed all the corporations in the direction of private industry—competition. When first nationalised, they were indispensable services at a time of shortage, sure of their market, in danger of producing too little rather than too much, and all basically dependent on coal. But road transport, natural gas, airways and oil have made all of them less secure, setting coal against oil and natural gas; gas against electricity; railways against cars, lorries and airways; airways against foreign airways. The fights have not only made the industries more cost-conscious; they have gradually made them emerge as separate entities to the public eye, as more aggressive, positive bodies. The desirability of competition has, of course, been emphasised by the Conservative government; an important White Paper in April 1961 (suitably disguised in Treasury language) on the 'financial and economic obligations of the nationalised industries' said: 'They are not, and ought not to be regarded as social services absolved from economic and commercial justification.' This is the antithesis of Herbert Morrison's high custodians: but part of the change would certainly have continued under the Labour party, which has come to recognise, as Hugh Gaitskell wrote in 1956, 'that people's enthusiasm about almost any group to which they belong is enhanced by competition.'[1]

One pointer to competition is provided by advertising, to which parliament has often objected. But the public corporations have increasingly advertised not only to attract people from roads to railways, from oil to coal, from electricity to gas, but also to improve their labour relations and present a better image to the public. These figures[2] show how their spending on advertising has grown:

	1950	1955	1960
National Coal Board	£732	£4,128	£700,658
British Railways	239,834	288,960	646,513
Electricity Council and Regional Boards	42,788	180,610	358,256
Gas Council and Regional Boards	65,755	649,646	1,242,828
BEA	33,700	100,516	127,396
BOAC	62,240	120,719	304,357
GPO	2,934	8,543	161,082

COAL

Coal is the oldest, most basic industry of all. Deep mining began in Britain three hundred years ago, and by Dr. Johnson's time all the present coalfields were being worked. Coal production reached its peak—like the navy and the city—in 1913, with 287 million tons a year, when a third of the coal was exported and the mines employed over a million men. Today, with 200 million tons a year, Britain is still the fourth biggest coal-producer, next to America, Russia and China.

Coal mining is part of the life of the country: the black slag heaps and pitheads which jut out of the landscape in South Wales or Durham have grown their own villages and communities. In many ways coal mining, like some family firms, is closer to agriculture than industry, rooted in local communities, cut off from the towns, dependent on manual labour. In spite of mechanisation, 60 per cent of the cost of coal is the cost of labour. It is the mining village, with the lodge, the pub, the club, the union branch-office, which still determines the character of the industry. 'We're

[1] *Socialism and Nationalisation*, 1956, p. 26.
[2] Source: *Legion Statistical Reviews*.

still putting holes in the ground in green fields', said a senior man
at the Coal Board, 'and putting villages round them—following the
coal towards the North Sea. We only recruit miners from miners'
families and miners' villages. The difference is that the villages are
much less isolated than they were thirty years ago—with cars,
television and more money.'

Coal has an unhappy history—exploitation, child labour,
unemployment and strikes, which reached a climax in 1926, when
the miners continued on strike for six months after the rest of
the country had gone back to work. The mines had been built on
cheap labour and the coal-owners faced the twentieth century
with reluctance, little research, poor labour conditions and no
co-ordination.

The nationalisation of this sad run-down industry in 1946 was an
operation without parallel in British history: the new 'National
Coal Board' bought 200 separate companies at the cost of
£338,000,000. The new board established itself in Hobart House, a
big rabbit-warren near Victoria. For the miners, the day of
nationalisation was a day of triumph—the end of a twenty year war.
Hobart House still has an atmosphere of dedication, partisanship,
and bitterness about oil, quite different from other corporations.
The forging together of these scattered collieries was a gigantic
task. Few men had experience in large-scale management, and
many who did left the industry on nationalisation. The separate
collieries were proud of their independence, and the colliery
managers were often a law to themselves. The industry remains
dominated by the mining engineers, whose training is concerned
with machines rather than men. 46 out of 48 of the area general
managers, the 'barons of the industry', are mining engineers. The
impact of a national organisation on these rugged communities
was bound to be difficult: 'It was such an upheaval', one observer
said, 'that there was no humus left: there was nothing on which
managers could grow.' The Coal Board was accused of a stifling
centralisation, and Hobart House became a favourite Tory symbol
of Socialist bureaucracy. But when the Fleck committee reported
in 1955, they said that there had been too *little* centralisation, and
that separate divisions were given too much freedom in staffing,
organisation and capital expenditure, with some area general
managers allowed to authorise projects up to £100,000: 'This
degree of delegation cannot be matched in any well-run industrial
undertaking within our knowledge.'

The Coal Board maintains a vast subterranean empire, including

s*

1,000 railway engines and 14,000 miles of roadway under the surface. They are the second biggest brick-makers in the country (half a million bricks in 1958), and one of the biggest landlords (143,000 houses and 236,000 acres of farmland). They maintain a vast private railway system, with 78,000 wagons and 4,000 miles of track.

The coal industry is not at heart competitive. It is indispensable, and it knows it. For nearly twenty years, since 1938, there was no alternative to coal—for gas, electricity, blast furnaces, central heating or railway engines. In the post-war years the government urged the Coal Board to produce as much coal as possible, without too much regard to cost: salesmanship was not needed, and quantity was preferred to quality. The consumption went steadily up, from 186 million tons in 1946 to 218 million in 1956. And then, in 1957, against all predictions of economists, it went down. It continued to go down for the next three years. Between 1958 and 1960 the Coal Board had to cut production by 28 million tons; they cut their manpower by 120,000—equivalent to the whole of ICI, and in 1961 they were still losing men at the rate of 80 a week. Several unexpected factors created this slump. Industry had a recession, the use of coal became more efficient, railways began to turn to diesels, there had been three mild winters and a brilliant summer. But most menacing had been the increase in the use of oil —for power stations, central heating, road transport. Oil consumption doubled in two years, and the Coal Board found itself with international new enemies—Shell, Esso, BP—armed with the menacing slogan 'anything coal can do, oil can do better'. At Hobart House they talked sourly about the Ministry of Power as the 'Ministry of Oil'.

Grappling with this new situation is the new head of the Coal Board, Lord Robens, a big welcoming man with a comfortable Yorkshire accent and long legs which sprawl over the chair. Alone of the nationalised chairmen, he is a politician: he left school at 15, worked his way up through the Co-op, became a Labour cabinet minister at forty, and took over the Coal Board in 1961, at fifty. He has the toughness, the fluency, the expansive gestures of a politician—wagging a finger, shrugging big shoulders. In Hobart House he is known as 'Our Alf'. He has identified himself with the new situation of coal, and projected a new vigour; he is the first nationalised chairman to have a private aeroplane.

'Competition has changed the whole psychology of the industry', said Robens: 'it means we've really got to *sell* coal, and provide a service all the way through. For twenty years the nation had been a captive market for coal. But the market for coal is changing; in the future it'll be supplied mainly through the pipe or through the wire. What we want is a few large customers, not millions of small ones. Mechanisation is being planned to a degree undreamt of three hundred years ago: this year (1961) we'll install four hundred power-loading machines. The miners, thank God, aren't Luddites: they don't mind machines, provided they get the money.'

Robens is determined to assert his independence if necessary: having been in the Ministry of Power as a politician, he knows both sides of the frontier. 'If the government gives a direction that goes right against our commercial interest, I'm bound to protect myself: if they want us to be commercial they must say so openly in a directive—and publish it in the balance sheet.'

RAILWAYS

Coal problems were bad enough, but the problems of railways were worse. When the 'Big Four' railway companies were nationalised in 1947, the new British Transport Commission became the biggest employers in the country: today they employ more men than the army, the navy and the air force put together. They took over not only railways, but canals, docks, road haulage, Pullman cars, Cook's travel agents. Pickfords' and Carter Paterson's delivery services. They became the biggest hoteliers and caterers in the country, with a chain of Victorian railway palaces. They inherited the most extravagant railway system in the world: no country has such a large amount of railway track (50,000 miles) for its size. You have only to compare a railway map of Britain, with its veins stretching out to remote country areas, with one of Germany or France. And in 1960 it was found that on the average, three out of four seats on British Railways were left unoccupied.[1] Like mines, the railways were built with cheap labour. Armies of navvies covered the country with railway tracks. They built no fewer than 13 main-line stations in London—New York has two. This complex of stations, viaducts, tunnels, bridges, workshops, marshalling yards, engines and rolling stock is by far the most expensive property in Britain. In 1960 the British Transport Commission estimated that the gross replacement value 'could hardly be less than £5,000 million'.[2]

[1] *See Select Commitee on Nationalised Industries*, 1960, para. 326.
[2] *Ibid.* para. 243.

The railways are the most embarrassing of all Britain's Victorian leftovers. In the 150 years since they came into being, they have acquired a picturesque, feudal and delightful way of life of their own, presided over by top-hatted stationmasters in cavernous station halls. Local traditions and loyalties persist; it's said that no Western Region man can talk for more than *eight* minutes without mentioning the name of Brunel.

It is difficult to remember that the railways were once as daring as supersonic jets today. The question of profits gradually receded into the background, as mysteriously happens with old industries: the system of railway accounting, riddled with what the select committee called 'financial archaeology', has been the despair of investigators. Ever since the arrival of the internal combustion engine, all railways have been in difficulties. French railways with much less mileage (Dr. Beeching told me) lose more money than the British. But in Britain, where the railways are the oldest, the problem is thorniest.

MARPLES AND BEECHING

Into the midst of this placid railway empire arrived in October, 1959, the disturbing phenomenon of Ernest Marples, Minister of Transport. It is dangerous in Whitehall to give credit for changes to the men who claim it: a new permanent secretary (Sir James Dunnett) and a new cabinet had an important influence here and so did Marples's predecessor, Harold Watkinson. But the personality of Marples was central. He is an unusual British minister, much more typical of North America or Germany, and almost unique in the upper reaches of Conservatives. He is a self-made tycoon, with no political connections, and a passionate interest in business which distinguishes him from the rest of the cabinet. He sees himself less as a politician than a technician, devoted to efficiency: like Paul Chambers of ICI, he cannot bear incompetence. At a time when the government was finding itself concerned with running hundreds of businesses from airlines to hotels, most ministers were much more interested in the traditional fields of foreign policy, the Commonwealth, parliament or social reform. Marples is first and last a businessman.

He is a spry man in his fifties, with wavy grey hair and a North-country accent. Efficiency dominates him: he likes to draw diagrams or make lists on a sheet of plain paper in front of him while he talks. He lives in an air-conditioned house in Belgravia with a mass of gadgets, walks, skis, cooks, climbs rocks, goes on long bicycle tours and talks about them all. He gets up at five, completes his paper work before eight, plays a game of tennis, and then begins his normal day's work. He doesn't even pretend to be an amateur.

Marples began life as the only child of a Socialist charge-hand in a turbine shop in Manchester: he won a scholarship and left school at fifteen to join a firm of accountants, auditing the books of bankrupt firms—which gave him an important early insight into finance. At twenty-one he moved to London, and soon began making money by converting houses into flats. In the war he rose from a private to regimental sergeant-major to captain: and in 1945 he became a Conservative MP. Soon afterwards he founded the firm of Marples Ridgway, with a brilliant engineer. In a few years he had made his fortune, and begun to turn his interests from money to power.

In 1951 he was made parliamentary secretary to Harold Macmillan, helping him to build all those houses. Six years later— after a period of disfavour with Eden—he became Macmillan's Postmaster-General, reorganising telephone charges and launching glamorous publicity, and after two years he reached his longed-for job, Minister of Transport. The snarled-up situation exactly suited him—London crawling with traffic jams, British Railways losing millions, roads built without planning or research. He bustled into his new office, read every available book on transport, hired Colin Buchanan, the author of the best of them (who happened to be working in the Ministry of Housing), flew round America and Europe inspecting flyovers and traffic systems, and devised new schemes for London parking, one-way streets, and long-term road-plans. 'I'm a great believer in committing myself', he told me: 'that's how you get things done, by committing other people too. You get the experts and then you say, "well, now you must do it".'

His largest problem was the railways. He did not disguise his contempt for their incompetence, and he was visibly out of sympathy with their chairman, Sir Brian Robertson. He inspected the modernisation plans, the costing systems, the potato-peelers and the frying pans, the centralised lump of administration, and compared it all to Marples Ridgway. He appointed the Stedeford Committee with wide terms of reference, and after their secret report appointed one of its members, Dr. Beeching, a director of ICI, to be the new chairman: soon afterwards two other new full-time members of the Transport Commission were appointed—Philip Shirley, an Australian accountant from Unilever at £12,000 a year, and Leslie Williams from Shell at £7,500 a year. The new appointments—one each from the three pillars of private enterprise—underlined the new order in nationalisation.

I found Dr. Beeching one of the most reassuring of all the administrators I talked to. He approaches his vast problem—itself a kind of caricature of all Britain's problems—with the dispassionate expertise of a surgeon. (The fact that he is always known as Doctor, without his Christian name, Richard, reinforces the image.) He is a big, relaxed man with a high dome, a bristle moustache and a slow gravelly voice; he might be mistaken at first for one of those large phlegmatic men who tell long stories over a pint of beer in a country pub. The contrast with Marples, short and tense, is immediate, but the two evidently fit together; there are some people who say that Marples' most important achievement was the hiring of Beeching.

Beeching rose through ICI with apparent effortlessness. The son of a journalist, he took a first in physics at the Imperial College, did research into electrons, and in ICI soon showed a flair for management. He built up a reputation both for efficiency and for fundamental niceness. Like Marples he likes drawing diagrams, but in a more leisurely, expansive way; he takes life easily, arrives at the office at ten, and generates an atmosphere of homely confidence. He gives the impression above all of a striking intellectual honesty, and the political shibboleths about nationalisation seem to dissolve in his presence.

His arrival in British Railways has within a year already produced a new situation. He succeeded, remarkably quickly, in obtaining the trust of the unions, but he had little sympathy with the traditional attitude of assuming that all railways (like coal mines) were permanent and unchangeable, and that it was their duty to provide any service that was required. He was visibly astonished by the sheer lack of *information* about traffic and costs, through all the years of furious controversy. He described the deficit as an 'open-ended sock' and brought a whole new vocabulary of words like 'fine-scale cross-subsidisation', 'conditions of origin' and 'built in flywheel'. He shuffled about general managers, introduced accountants, and wobbled the staircase of promotion. Against the anger this produced was the realisation by able men, stuck in a long and inevitable queue, that their talents might now be noticed.

'You can't have a confused set of motives', he said to me, 'you can't say one day you're giving a service and ignoring the profit, and the next day that you're hoping to make it pay. . . . It's true that it's not so *nerve-racking* to be deep in the red as it is to be hovering between the red and the black; but on the other hand being in the red can be very demoralising.'

GAS AND ELECTRICITY

The other nationalised industries (even gas) became more accustomed to competition. The incandescent flame was invented by William Murdoch in 1798; the Gas Light and Coke Company was formed in 1798 and the next year Westminster bridge was lit by gaslight. It was an astonishing innovation, which revolutionised urban society. For most of the next century gas had the field to itself, until in 1881 the first electric light system was installed, in Godalming in Surrey: (Lord Salisbury, the prime minister, was one of the first people to have his house lit by electricity— showing an aristocratic interest in technical innovations not much followed since). Electricity won in lighting, but gas kept its supremacy in cooking: there are now 9 million gas cookers in Britain, compared to only $1\frac{1}{4}$ million electric ones. Competition made gas more efficient, and it found ways to cheapen production and use its by-products (which include coal tar, benzine and ammonia): it also took to heavy advertising and invented the engaging 'Mr. Therm' before the war. Since 1955 electricity production has overtaken gas, which has remained roughly static. 'Gas is fighting for its life', said a gasman.

A new and unexpected frontier of competition developed when the gasmen, finding coal in short supply, decided to bring liquid natural gas (which has revolutionised cooking on the continent) from the Sahara to Britain by ship. But coal soon became abundant and the Coal Board (who sell an eighth of their coal to the gas board) complained bitterly to the government, but without success.

Gas was built up by a number of local firms—some private, some municipal—which after nationalisation in 1948 kept much of their local character. It is the most decentralised of the nationalised industries: though the Gas Light and Coke Company was renamed North Thames Gas, it remained a proud and separate entity, still setting the pace for others. Gasmen remain a special, loyal breed, not greatly changed by nationalisation. The chairman of the Gas Council (the co-ordinating centre) is Sir Henry Jones,

545

whose father and grandfather were both in gas: he is a neat, white-haired man with a precise speech, who went into gas from Cambridge and maintains a deep interest in the fluid.

ELECTRICITY

Between a coal mine and a power station there is all the difference of two centuries. One new power station produces enough electricity to run Birmingham. Labour accounts for 60 per cent of the cost of coal, but only 15 per cent of electricity. In spite of tremendous capital costs, electricity has consistently made a profit. Although it has been extended to uneconomic country areas, its price fell from £60 a kilowatt in 1948 to £37 in 1961. Productivity has increased, the number of 'men per megawatt' has fallen; while production has doubled, the number of employees has remained static. This is due more to world-wide trends and improvements than to the efforts of the staff: ('Anyone would think', said one member of the board, 'from the way some electricity people talk, that *they* were responsible for doubling consumption'). But the expansion and profitability has given it a special dynamic, and it has the advantage of a very short past.

Electricity has a confusing and much criticised organisation, devised by a new Act in 1957. There is a Central Electricity Generating Board in charge of producing electricity, twelve area boards in charge of distributing it, and an Electricity Council which in theory is the central, decisive body. Its chairman, Professor Ronald Edwards, is an unusual kind of don-tycoon. He went to grammar school, became an accountant for nine years, then joined the London School of Economics as Lecturer in Business Administration, and later as Professor of Economics: he became one of the very few British experts in industrial organisation, and presided over seminars of dons and industrialists. He was a member of the Herbert Committee on Electricity and then (like Beeching) turned from outsider to insider and in 1961 became head of the industry he had criticised.

But although the Council is theoretically the centre of the industry, the Generating Board is the most powerful: they own, commission and place the power stations, and they have at their head the formidable personality of Sir Christopher Hinton, a tall technocrat who works behind a huge desk overlooking the Bankside power station in London. He is very much one of the 'new men', who can alarm non-technologists and political amateurs.

546

The son of a country schoolmaster, he began his career at sixteen, 'nut-scragging' at Swindon railway works: from there he gained a scholarship to Cambridge and then joined the newly-formed ICI. After the war—when he organised factories—he ran the industrial side of atomic energy, and the building of the first nuclear power station. His drive and ruthlessness led, extraordinarily quickly, to the opening of Calder Hall in 1956 (he was never 'house-trained').

In electricity, he has expanded research, strengthened public relations, made a succession of outspoken speeches and statements. He told me: 'The trouble is that the British public haven't decided what they want the nationalised industries to do; in fact quite a slice of them don't want them to succeed at all. Whatever the nationalised industries do the public like to find fault with them and that has a bad effect on morale—it's a viscous drag on the whole operation. No body of men does its best work unless it is prepared to make mistakes. It is easier for men to risk mistakes when shielded by the seclusion of private industry than when, as in a nationalised industry, they will be dragged under the same spotlight of criticism that is turned on politicians. Much of my job consists of seeing that staff are free to do administrative and executive work exactly as in a large privately owned firm.'

The most spectacular development has been the building of nuclear power stations, which Sir Christopher himself had begun. They cost as much to build as a small town: the biggest of them at Sizewell will have cost £58 million to build, employing 2,000 workers for four years: it is rising from a cliff on the Suffolk coast, a silent and solitary factory, sucking in 27 million gallons of seawater an hour, and belching it out again, through tunnels ten feet high, at near boiling point, warming the sea by ten degrees for miles around and attracting interesting new kinds of fish. It will produce 580,000 kilowatts of electricity—enough to supply a city: but after twenty years it will be unusable—a colossal monument to the earlier nuclear age.

Will the nuclear power stations prove white elephants? So far, they have been very extravagant—partly because electricity-from-coal has become cheaper: in 1962 nuclear power stations were costing about £100 a kilowatt to build, compared to £40 a kilowatt for 'conventional' stations. Sir Christopher insists that by about 1970 nuclear power should be cheaper: 'We're now entering an extremely interesting period', he said, 'when we are becoming a three-fuel economy. We have as our available fuels coal or oil or the nuclear fuel. This gives a breadth of interest which is quite unusual.' On whether the power stations are the forerunners of cheap easy power, or a sad dead-end, depends a great deal of Britain's future prosperity.

AIRWAYS

'We're the most competitive industry in the world', said Lord Douglas of Kirtleside, chairman of British European Airways: 'and that makes us different from the other nationalised industries.' The two national airlines are far smaller than the other corporations: they have only 5 per cent of the staff of British Railways. But their business expands by roughly 15 per cent a year, and they are involved, unlike the others, in a world-wide battle. The competition between national airlines becomes each year more hectic, but it is a very circumscribed competition, controlled by the most formidable cartel in the world, the International Air Transport Association (IATA), which settles everything from fares and legroom to the size of luggage and sandwiches—leaving the airlines to compete with planes, hostesses, courtesy and advertising. The more similar the services become, as with detergents, the more intense the advertising.

Airlines have a separate, international atmosphere of their own, and their staff has a classless, placeless character, freed from the past, as different from railways as coffee-bars from pubs. But in their short lives the airways have already accumulated entrenched Parkinsonian bureaucracies and a self-contained 'Kremlin'—as the BOAC headquarters is called: 'There are too many people flying typewriters in this place and not enough flying aircraft', as one pilot put it.

Britain, being compact and crowded, is one of the least airminded countries: London Airport, although it is the world's biggest international airport, with 600 planes a day from 51 airlines, is smaller than a dozen airports in America.

For British European Airways the competition is fairly unhampered by obligations—apart from a few routes like the Scottish 'Highlands and Islands' service, which costs £350,000 a year. Their chairman has had the job for thirteen years—outlasting all other chairmen. Lord Douglas of Kirtleside is a huge square man with a chin like a spade, who presides over the office as an indestructible father-figure. He was a scholar at Oxford, became a life-long Socialist and rose to be Marshal of the RAF. He brought to BEA authority and idealism: he runs the airline with easy informality from a converted school, called 'Bealine House', along-side Northolt Airport. He knows when to keep Whitehall in its place.

BOAC—the second biggest airline in the world—has had a much more troubled history. They have had to show the flag in unprofitable places like Caracas for the sake of national pride, and to subsidise a cluster of associates, including Nigerian, West Indian and Middle Eastern airlines. 'My aim', said Sir Matthew Slattery, the chairman, 'is to try and keep the Commonwealth linked with Commonwealth airlines.' No other major airline has the same kind of commitment as BOAC has to the Common-wealth. BOAC too has been pressed by successive governments into buying British planes. The original Comets, followed by the Britannias, proved costly failures—unlike BEA's Viscounts and Comet 4s. The frontier between airlines and the aircraft industry which depends on them is perpetually subject to government intervention. And BOAC have had much greater trouble with engineers and unions, and have lacked the hard core of managers (mostly from Imperial Airways) of BEA.

Their troubles have been increased by the growth of the com-mercial 'independent' airlines, led by the merger of British United Airways and British Aviation Services, who have 150 aircraft and 80 per cent of the independent business. Their board represents a large slice of city interests, including Sir Donald Anderson of P and O, Sir Brian Mountain of Eagle Star insurance, Lord Poole of the Cowdray group and Sir Nicholas Cayzer of British and Commonwealth Shipping. Both nationalised airlines are bitter about the Conservative government allowing private competitors to use profitable routes, without paying for unprofitable ones. 'My job', said Sir Matthew, 'is to protect the public's investment by not letting other airlines take our profits. I'll fight every alloca-tion to the independent airlines.' Here again the conflict between high custodians and the profit motive is inducing a crisis.

These and other troubles have made the chairmanship of BOAC one of the least enviable jobs in the country. There have been no fewer than eight different chairmen since 1945, including Sir Miles Thomas, Lord Knollys and a part-time banker, Gerard d'Erlanger. The present occupant, Rear Admiral Sir Matthew Slattery, came from the nationalised aircraft company Short Brothers and Harland, and so was already house-trained for Whitehall. He is a tall, withdrawn figure, who spends half his time flying round BOAC's empire. He has no illusions about the difficulty of his job: 'It's not easy being the head of a nationalised industry, you've got to be used to dealing with governments, and knowing how they behave. You can't run BOAC on a hundred per cent commercial basis; the national commitments are bound to cost money.'

The running of the nationalised industries still presents an unsolved problem to both political parties. They have not reached the comfortable confidence of private industry—self-perpetuating, self-financing, self-admiring. The relations between Whitehall and the state industries—the largest of all parental problems—is still unhappy. The nationalised boards are very far from being any kind of team: they are Leviathans with their heads lopped off, and the procession of chairmen and directors in and out of the boardrooms has spread insecurity, while the incursions of private-enterprise experts have disturbed the old public service ideals. As private enterprise bosses move to public industries, civil servants switch to private industry, and industrial managers acquire a stronger professional sense, the old contrast between public service and private ambition will become blurred, and the question of ownership less relevant. 'The Labour party recognises that, under professional managements, large firms are as a whole serving the nation well. Moreover we recognise that no organisation can operate effectively if it is subjected to persistent and detailed intervention from above.'[1] 'The basic fact', wrote Anthony Crosland in 1956, 'is the large corporation, facing fundamentally similar problems, and acting in fundamentally the same way whether publicly or privately owned.'[2]

But how public services can be dynamic, competitive and animated with profit, while still remaining 'high custodians' and servants of democracy, remains a recurring problem for many Western countries. As Britain becomes more exposed to the competitive winds from America and the continent, and to the lure of private property, so the essential services may, as in America, become regarded as the tail-end-charlies, the forgotten drudges under the pavements and pit-heads. This should be a field where Britain, with her old democratic conscience, should make a major contribution: and now that the furious party controversies are over, and the muddles and elephantiasis of the public corporations are being dispassionately analysed, there could still arise new organisms, having vigour without selfishness and service without somnolence.

[1] *See Industry and Society.* Labour Party, 1952.
[2] *See* C. A. R. Crosland: *The Future of Socialism*, 1956, p. 480.

35

TRADE UNIONS

Thirty years ago their job was on the street corner, today it is in the conference room.

Charles Dukes, General Secretary of the NUGMW, in 1941.

SINCE the war in the whole of industry, nationalised and otherwise, there has been one force with which all managers and directors have had to come to terms—the force of organised labour. Trade unions have been hailed, praised and cursed as the 'fifth estate', and no one can ignore them. Their position has enormously changed since the pre-war years. As they have become closer to government, less militant, less sure of their real destination, so their power has become harder to analyse. 'The trade unions', one observer has written, 'have never been more powerful—and seldom used their power less. They have never attracted so many members—and have never had members so apathetic. There is an intense deep-seated loyalty—and there are frequent revolts against the chosen leadership. They hold the future in their hands—and cling to the present.'[1]

But they have remained insistently separate from the other estates, their smoother metropolitan world, their façades, and pomposities. In the trade union world things usually *are* what they seem, and their leaders have kept an inherent suspicion of 'them' and the corridors of power—most notable in their attitude to the nationalised industries for which they had been so long pressing. 'They weren't always willing to cross over, nor were their men always willing for them to go in', said Lord Attlee: 'a curious contradiction, because they talked of labour running the show and yet when you put a trade unionist in they tended to regard him as a bosses' man.'[2]

The separateness of trade unions is evident at the TUC's annual conference—so different from the sort of meetings of peers, commoners, churchmen or directors which mark the other estates. In a cinema or music hall the delegates sit on tip-up seats, in rows according to their trade—garment workers in open-necked shirts, road-menders in cloth caps, civil service clerks in dark suits; it is

[1] Eric Wigham: *Trade Unions*, Home University Library, p. 6.
[2] Francis Williams: *A Prime Minister Remembers*, 1961, p. 92.

like the Labour Party conference, which takes place a month later, but with the intellectuals and the constituency radicals noticeably absent. In the gallery are academic observers, personnel officers from the corporations, foreign labour attachés: every year United Steel throws a lavish party for delegates. The numbers of outsiders in the unions' caravan increase every year.

On the platform, sitting behind green cloth, are the thirty-five members of the General Council. The chairman—appointed annually—sits in the middle behind a large silver-plated bell; to his left is George Woodcock, the general secretary, behind leather-bound volumes in the front row are ex-chairmen, mostly knights—the 'Trade Union Establishment', or 'Old Pals Club'. There is Sir Tom O'Brien, the small, dapper ex-cinema worker, who began as an errand-boy at twelve, and has toured the world as a trade unionist. There is Sir Alfred Roberts, the Lancashire factory worker who is now a Director of the Bank of England. There is Anne Godwin, the leader of 60,000 office workers. And most prominent of all is the great shape of Ted Hill, General Secretary of the Boilermakers—the embodiment of the tough, immovable union spirit of the thirties: an enormous Cockney, shaped like a hippo, with a deep voice growling 'nuffink', 'where is 'e?' or 'get on wiv it'. Since as a boy he mended boilers, for P and O at the London Docks, he has never swerved from his distrust of all bosses, who he still often refers to as 'rascals', and he retains a simple, vivid approach to national problems. 'Our economy's like Tower Bridge', he said in 1960, 'always up and down.'

Proceedings are homely but brisk: in ninety-four years the congress has evolved its own language and ritual, combining emotional appeal to men with strict authority. The atmosphere is mainly North Country and Scottish: only three of the thirty-five councillors are Londoners. A Minister of State will be called 'that laddie', and one ex-president, Sir Will Lawther, told a delegate from the rostrum to 'shut your gob'. Tough bargaining will be interrupted by waves of sentimentality. At the end retiring members are given gold medals and make nostalgic speeches about colleagues and wives, which may end in tears. A vote of thanks is proposed to the Press (who have a close though touchy relationship) and Auld Lang Syne is sung by the whole hall holding hands.

Rows of bald heads shine under the arc-lights, for most delegates are over fifty. They have taken part in the General Strike of 1926, seen the dole queues of the thirties. 'The Movement' has a magnificent history of struggle and 'the giants'—Bevin, Deakin and Lawther—who forged it: every year the local Mayor is presented with the Webbs' *History of Trade Unionism*. Much has changed since the days of the giants, but what still distinguishes the TUC from other power-groups is the sense of being on the receiving-end of all the legislation and management decisions which emanate from Whitehall or the West End boardrooms: here you feel the human outcome of the committees, the management studies, the rationalisations and maximisations. It is not the geopolitical resolutions—so often forgotten or reversed by the following year—that matter most to the rank and file, but the hundreds of tiny resolutions about occupational deafness, home confinement grants or protection against fire. Nevertheless, the passionate views on defence, foreign policy and nationalisation, however little material result they may have, are still a very important part of the movement, distinguishing it from most other trade union movements. For they reveal the residual ideological strains—Catholicism, Methodism, Marxism—which lie behind the ideology of 'trade unionism' and give it dignity and passion.

GENERAL SECRETARIES

Seven years ago you could talk about the TUC as a solid political force: three big leaders—Arthur Deakin, Sir Thomas Williamson and Sir Will Lawther—commanded a majority of votes, and together urged wage restraint, supported Gaitskell against Bevan, defended the H-bomb and the Atlantic Alliance. But since Lawther retired and Deakin died—to be succeeded a year later by Frank Cousins—the balance has been upset. The individual leaders have large and personal powers, fortified by tough constitutions and publicity, and massively increased by TV. Only one man stands out in most unions. 'When Bevin was there, who'd heard of Deakin?' said one general secretary: 'When Deakin was there, who'd heard of Cousins?'

When you see the thirty-five men on the dais you can easily imagine them as a miniature cabinet; but their power in fact is only the total of the powers of the individual unions, frequently at loggerheads: 'baronies in a kingless kingdom', as one general secretary said. The general secretaries of the biggest unions, who are all members of the Council, are the sinews of the movement: they have grown out of the rank and file, and spent their lifetime working—with small salaries and hard lives. They are an isolated group, cut off from others in this book. Several live in the North-west suburbs of London, commuting to their London offices and periodically touring the branches. At home they live quiet domestic lives, nearly all keen on gardening. At work, they are immersed in their own unions, usually seeing their opposite numbers only at TUC meetings (once a month), at deputations in Whitehall, or on trade union delegations abroad, or at social occasions, such as Embassy parties. One moment they will be facing rows of spectacles and pens in the Treasury, the next pleading in a branch office with inarticulate strikers. They cut across all classifications. Their background (as Anthony Crosland has said) is working-class, their way of life middle-class, their power upper-class. They have the influence of eighteenth-century dukes, the background of factories. They do not, like politicians, create dynasties, and their sons often go into white-collar jobs (like Woodcock's son in ICI or Cousins' sons in BOAC and AEA) where the movement is weak.

Most of the leaders have gained power late in life. Some have been caught up in a high-living round of conferences, parties and continental tours, but their wives usually act as a sheet-anchor and they remain solidly unpretentious and very accessible: to talk to them you do not need to make long-term appointments, you need only buttonhole them in the passage at a conference. Few stayed at school after sixteen. They are the only group who show no signs of being invaded by graduates: of the thirty-five members only one, Woodcock, has a degree. They are the only group of leaders who could never be mistaken for any other group—judges, civil servants, accountants or managers. Will the impact of the 'meritocracy', catching all clever boys at the age of eleven, drain the movement of future giants, leaving 'no more Bevins'?

THE BIG SIX

Of about 9,000,000 trade unionists in Britain, 8,056,493 are affiliated to the TUC. Their range is exotic, and the conference mixes ancient and limited crafts with new technicians and mass-producers. The smallest unions include:

51 London Jewish Bakers
56 Wool Shear Workers
90 Spring Trapmakers
127 Coal Trimmers
142 Spindle and Flyer Makers
162 Military and Orchestral Musical Instrument Makers

and delegates come from such surprising trades as

9,676 Actors
5,492 Doctors
28,317 Musicians
2,212 Footballers
2,323 Variety Artistes
15,244 Journalists

But the weight is with the giants, and in 1961 six big unions held half the membership as the list overleaf shows.

Two of the biggest are 'general unions', which straddle scores of industries. Others, like the railwaymen, miners, or seamen, are 'Industrial Unions', within a single industry. Many smaller ones are 'craft unions' linked to the apprentice system, but most have been diluted with unskilled labour.

The cost of the untidiness, 182 unions, is heavy; they argue about 'demarcation' and one union by striking may put members of other unions in the same factory out of work. Britain has paid the price for pioneering trade unions, as for the industrial revolution which begot them. Each union has a proud, jealous history, and only the desperate pressures of the twenties and thirties persuade small ones to combine. Now, with less pressure, there is less chance of effective merging, and their constitutions are as diverse and old as South American governments.

TRANSPORT AND GENERAL

The biggest union in the Western World is the Transport and General Workers', whose leadership has become one of the most influential posts in Britain. Its 1,300,000 members—ranging from London bus-drivers to North Wales quarrymen, with the militant dock workers at the heart—command a sixth of the votes at the TUC. It was formed by Ernest Bevin from fourteen separate unions in 1922, when wage cuts and unemployment had produced a critical need for workers' unity. After *ten years* of discussions, Bevin persuaded them to yield their autonomy: 'nothing in his career more clearly bore the stamp of his own creation'.[1] To impose unity Bevin framed a constitution to give huge powers to one man, the general secretary—the job he himself filled from 1922 till 1940, when he became Churchill's Minister of Labour. The general secretary is the only full-time official who is elected by a ballot of all

[1] Alan Bullock: *Life and Times of Ernest Bevin*, p. 185.

Union

| Transport and General Workers (TGWU) |
| Amalgamated Engineering (AEU) |
| General & Municipal Workers (NUGMW) |
| National Union of Mineworkers (NUM) |
| Union of Shop, Distributive & Allied Workers (USDA\ |
| National Union of Railwaymen (NUR) |

the members and on the union's council he is much the most powerful: for the rest are all part-time members. The general secretary of the 'T and G' enjoys the same kind of power as the president of the United States:[1] he is the only member of his cabinet who has been directly chosen by the majority of his people. But the general secretary is appointed until retiring age.

This one-man rule is often resented—particularly the fact that full-time officers are all appointed. Rebellious groups have paraded the streets with the slogan: 'We were *elected*, not appointed.' A persuasive general secretary can make sure that officials are sympathetic to him, and his election by the very unsophisticated rank and file encourages demagogy. All the general secretaries of the T and G, from Bevin to Cousins, have been powerful speakers. But the organisation gives a lot of freedom to the five thousand branches and the sixteen 'trade groups': and more than any other, the T and G suffers from the threat of breakaways—which compels the leaders to take notice.

The headquarters of the T and G, 'Transport House', is a plain brick building in Smith Square, Westminster, part of which is used by the Labour party. It was the first of the big union buildings, and Bevin saw it opened in May 1928: 'To him it was nothing short of marvellous that a working men's organisation, with a subscription of sixpence a week, could rise from renting a house in a back street, to building, at a cost of well over £50,000, an eight-storey office building of its own within a stone's throw of the House of Lords.'[2]

Since its foundation the T and G has had only four secretaries —Ernest Bevin, Arthur Deakin, Jock Tiffin (who died a few months after taking office) and Frank Cousins, elected in May 1956. We

[1] V. L. Allen: *Power in the Trade Unions*, p. 207.
[2] Alan Bullock, *Life and Times of Ernest Bevin*, p. 406.

Head	Members	MPs (1959)	Contributions to 1959 Election Fund	Funds per member (1957)
ank Cousins	1,302,080	14	£35,000	£8.14
ill Carron	972,587	8	50,000	11.11
ck Cooper	796,121	4	25,000	4.14
ill Paynter	586,361	31	42,000	1.13
—	355,271	9	26,000	5.11
id Greene	333,888	5	14,630	14.19

have already seen[1] the large impact of Frank Cousins on the Labour Party—the most startling example of the individual power of union leaders. In the setting of his union he appears a less isolated figure: he has a good deal of support for his unilateralist policies, and his relentless suspicion of bosses reflects the resentments of dock workers and lorry-drivers. Like Hill he has stuck to his pre-war attitudes: 'Every time that we ease—every time we slacken off a little—then capitalism shows its teeth against us, and shows that it has not removed its thinking very far from where we were twenty years ago'. At one time in 1960 his militancy seemed close to bringing a crisis between the unions and the party, but since then his support—though still formidable—has waned. He is convinced that the trade unions and the Labour party are inseparable, but he dislikes the middle-class leadership: 'I would prefer to see a trade unionist in leadership of the party'.

AMALGAMATED ENGINEERING UNION

The Amalgamated Engineering Union, the second biggest, has a more anarchic character. Its oldest component began in 1851, the year of the Great Exhibition, as a 'craft union' of skilled engineers, but the present union was formed in 1920, out of ten craft unions, which have since become diluted with unskilled workers, and even with women (all craft unions are suspicious of women). An elaborately democratic constitution was drawn up, headed with the words 'United we stand—divided we fall', and modelled on the Soviet trade unions (before their powers were circumscribed by Stalin). In theory, the AEU is ideally democratic. Every official in the union is elected for varying terms: the factory workers elect the district committees, who elect the

[1] *See* pages 94–96.

divisional committees, who elect the National Committee of 52 members, while the Executive Council of seven is elected by the whole membership in each of seven regional divisions. But in practice only one in ten members vote, and the AEU leadership is quite unrepresentative. 'It is', as one of them described it to me, 'even more self-perpetuating than the board of ICI.' In 1960, according to the president, Bill Barron, 12 of the committee of 52 were Communists, and 6 fellow-travellers: the 'ten per cent democracy' of the AEU has become a by-word.

With this awkward constitution the president, who is the most powerful official, is never in a strong position: but the current president, Bill Carron, has nevertheless had a massive impact on the movement. He is a short, bald man with a jutting chin, large shrewd eyes, small turned-up eyebrows and the impassive expression of a mandarin. He is unpompous, fond of photography and television, not attracted by banquets, and completely dedicated. A Roman Catholic—one of four on the General Council—he first stood as a union candidate when he was a young fitter in Lincoln in 1931 to keep Communists out, and ever since he has been unremittingly anti-Communist. As the right-wing head of a left-wing union, he has had awkward situations, but he is tough, persistent, with superb stamina: he can go on arguing till late at night, unswerving and good-humoured.

Like others', Carron's attitudes were forged by the general strike and the depression, but he accepts that the unions' outlook must change. He told me how when he talks to his daughter, who works for the South East Gas Board, he realises the different assessments of the young. 'I can't help remembering the time when my wife was in hospital having a baby, and I asked my foreman if I could take a few hours off to see her: he said, "Why must you people always be bothering about your families: you're here to *work*,".' 'That's one of the moments', said Carron, 'which gave me my outlook on politics: but you can't expect young people, who haven't experienced that kind of thing, to think the same.'

GENERAL AND MUNICIPAL WORKERS

The General and Municipal Workers have a similar wide range of unskilled workers to the T and G, and similar strong powers for the general secretary: until Cousins, the two were traditional allies—the core of organised manual labour. 'Thorne House', the headquarters of the 'NUGMW' in Bloomsbury (the trade union quarter of London), has big metal doors with engravings of all the jobs, from road-menders to gas-workers, which make the union. There have been only four general secretaries of the G and M—Will Thorne, who founded it in 1924; Charles Dukes, later Lord Dukeston; Sir Thomas Williamson, who ruled for sixteen years; and Jack Cooper, who took over from Williamson in 1961. He is the son-in-law of Lord Dukeston—a rare example of the beginnings of a union dynasty. He went to a council school, made soap for Levers, worked his way up through the G and M and Manchester City Council, and for a year was a Labour MP. In politics he is a Gaitskellite, more independent than his predecessor Williamson, but equally at loggerheads with Frank Cousins. It is too early to judge his impact on the movement.

MINERS

The most distinctive and close-knit is the National Union of Mineworkers. No miner can work without a union card. There is no 'ten per cent democracy' about them: their self-contained communities have an intense union tradition, and every pit-head has its local office. They have the most sponsored MPs—thirty-one—of any union, and parliament is full of their Welsh or Yorkshire accents (though like other unions they tend to regard parliament as a secondary service—a resting-place, not a front line). At conferences, the miners sit and cheer together, stay in their own hotels, sing their own songs.

Because of their local loyalties, they are the most decentralised union; only in 1945 did their forty-one organisations combine in a single body. They have a modern black office in the Euston Road, with a sculpture of an underground miner in the entrance: but most of their staff are scattered through branches. Their general secretary, Will Paynter, is perhaps best known as the leading Communist at the TUC—though he was voted off the General Council in September 1961. His influence with miners is partly counterbalanced by a very anti-Communist president, Sid Ford. But Paynter is a forceful leader—short, wiry, and eloquent in a soft Rhondda accent. He went down the South Wales pits at fourteen, and joined the Communist party at twenty-nine. He has never lost touch with his fellow-miners. He sits in a polished office in London with red leather chairs and white telephones, but is constantly away touring the pit-heads, and though he lives at Edgware two of his seven sons are miners.

Paynter is convinced that the TUC have lost contact with *their* rank and file, and he mocks their 'statesmen': 'There's a tremendous ferment at the lower levels: it's got to be harnessed somewhere', he told me. 'And when the recession comes, the young people will be much more rebellious than *we* were. They don't have the restraint and inhibitions that we had. The difference between the workers' share and the employers' is as great as it ever was.' He insists that his Communist and trade union activities are kept quite separate, and laughs at suggestions that he is in secret contact with other Communist leaders.

RAILWAYMEN

The railwaymen—the other big nationalised labour force—are less close-knit. The National Union of Railwaymen (NUR) is far the biggest railway union, but they have two proud rival unions, the Associated Society of Locomotive Engineers and Firemen (ASLEF) and the white-collar Transport Salaried Staffs Association (TSSA)—who both look down on the ordinary railwaymen. More than any other group, the NUR (telegraphic address 'Beware') has changed from militant opposition to co-operation with governments and boards. The general secretary, Sid Greene, began his career as a Paddington porter, and now seems the quintessence of the modern moderate—clerical grey, quiet voice, neat white handkerchief, garden in Middlesex. 'They wouldn't go ahead with the modernisation plans', Greene said to me, 'without consulting the Unions first . . . Whenever I go over to Euston Station to have a chat with the General Manager, and walk up the grand staircase past the statue of Stephenson, I can't help thinking "Old Stephenson must be turning in his grave to see a trade unionist walking up those stairs: it wasn't for people like *us* that he built the railways".'

Greene's railwaymen are among the lowest-paid of all workers, and their bargaining is weakened by the heavy loss made by the railways. But the NUR are more inclined to see the British Transport Commission as their allies, against the meanness of the Treasury, than as the Government's agents. Greene's hardest task is to make his members aware of their rôle: 'You've got to make the rank and file feel that they've got a *niche* in the industry.' The railwaymen, more than anyone, can bring British industry to a halt—'I'm a bit afraid of the extent of our economic strength', Greene said 'I hope we never have to use it: it can so easily turn public opinion against us.'

Sid Greene

USDAW

A more expanding and very different group are the Union of Shop, Distributive and Allied Workers (USDAW); for their members are involved with 'service industries'[1]—shop assistants, clerks, packers—between the open-necks and the white-collars. They are on the wage-earning end of the boom in service industries since the war, and they represent an important part of the union movement of the future. USDAW has difficulty in organising, because 47 per cent are women, who usually move or marry: the manual unions are inclined to regard them as a 'cosseted union'. Much of their original membership was in the Co-operative movement, which encouraged trade unionists. But USDAW has shot ahead since the war, creeping into the big chain stores (Marks and Spencers, Great Universal Stores, Woolworths, etc.) which are the bane of their organisers. Their secretary until 1961, Sir Alan Birch, was an appropriate white-collar leader, though more right-wing than his executive: a grave and statesmanlike leader who had been an accountant, less emotional than most unionists and less personally involved in hardships. He was the most prominent theorist and planner on the TUC, and his death in 1961 left a large gap in the movement.

The youngest of the General Secretaries is Clive Jenkins, aged thirty-six, who belongs to the most rapidly-growing union, a body of 25,000 white-collar workers, prominent in airlines, called ASSET—the Association of Supervisory Staffs, Executives and Technicians. Jenkins is a smooth and left-wing Welshman, who writes books about the conspiracies of power and brings to his union an ingenious energy. ASSET has started its own insurance company, advertises for members on television, and has bought small shares in several large companies—so that Jenkins can complain at shareholders' meetings. Jenkins belongs to a tiny circle of intellectual trade unionists and he even edits a highbrow trade union journal.

UNIONS AND BUSINESS

All the big unions face similar problems—most notably the fact that with full employment factory workers can bargain directly

[1] *See* page 499.

with the bosses, and the union leaders thus have difficulty in keeping and controlling their members. Most unions since the war have been challenged by 'wildcat strikes' and rebellious shop-stewards. It is the shop-stewards who collect union dues at the factories, recruit new members, and enforce the factory agreements: the T and G has 25,000 of them, and altogether there are said to be 200,000[1]—more shop-stewards than soldiers. Ever since a menacing 'Shop-Stewards' Movement' grew up during the first world war, the unions have tried to keep stewards in check. But with full employment, power drifts towards them, for they can often make better bargains than at the national level—producing a 'two-tiered' system—with the union headquarters negotiating one agreement in London and shop-stewards negotiating a better agreement at the factory.[2]

Another problem for unions: how far should they take on the pattern of 'business unionism', as in America and Germany, where the big unions are capitalist businesses in their own right? How far should union leaders have the salaries and surroundings of top businessmen? Do they need trained economists and financiers to assess their wage claims and to look after the unions' investments? There has been a long tradition in the British movement that union leaders should be self-sacrificing men, living close to their people. Cars, chauffeurs and big salaries are suspect, as signs that the leaders may have joined the bosses. Frank Cousins earns £2,260, Sid Greene £2,000. And the members hate to increase their subscriptions; in 1958 the men paid an average of ·75 per cent of their basic wages to the unions, compared to 1·5 per cent in 1939. The dues for the AEU were 4 per cent of wages in 1912, but only 1 per cent in 1959. Subscriptions vary from 8d. a week for the 'T and G', to from 4/6d. to 9/6d. for the London Typographical Society.

Many unions still dislike being mixed up with 'tar'—the goings-on of capitalists. The nominal capital of trade unions in 1958 was £84 million, an average of £10 per member, but very little of this is invested in industry (which would have multiplied its value over twenty years) and three-quarters is in gilt-edged stock. The American mineworkers think nothing of buying up large shares in coalfields, but British unions are only now beginning to make tentative investments, usually in unit trusts, which avoids the embarrassment of having holdings in a particular industry.

---

[1] Henry Wilton: *The Trade Unions, the Employers and the State*, 1959, p. 116.
[2] *See* B. C. Roberts: *Trade Union Government and Administration*. Bell, 1956.

Several unions still have rules forbidding investment in equities.

The background of trade unionism as a class struggle has left a strong prejudice against importing specialists, graduates and middle-class men from outside the movement: but gradually a more professional attitude is emerging. An example is Harry Douglass, a big benign Yorkshireman, Secretary of the Iron and Steel Trades Confederation. He comes from one of the richest unions, the steelworkers, who earn up to £40 a week: they are the aristocrats of trade unionists and in their booming towns—Middlesbrough, Scunthorpe, Corby—acres of cars wait outside the steelworks. In their co-operation with bosses and lack of class feeling they are closer to American unions. Harry Douglass, with his well-cut suit, his salary of £4,000 and his chauffeur-driven car, could easily be mistaken for a steelmaster, and he is the most business-minded of the leaders. 'The trade union movement today is a very powerful machine', he said at the 1960 Congress, 'and it can only be driven by experts. . . . Are we going to be like the sons of rich men, having inherited a wonderful machine, to allow it to be destroyed by our envy, and our selfishness?'

Others agree: 'If I am told that I am proposing that unions should adopt some of the methods of big business', said the President of the 1960 Congress, Claude Bartlett, 'my answer is that we have to deal with big business—and that trade unionism is no small business. We cannot urge initiative and experiment on others and stay defiant of change ourselves.'

Another equally pressing problem is the growth of the white-collared and white-coated workers—the growing middle class of bank and insurance clerks, civil servants, local government officers, teachers. Several hundred thousand 'white-collared workers' *are* represented at the TUC—including for instance the 144,000 members of the Civil Service Clerical Association, or the 40,000 members of the Inland Revenue Staff Federation. The Post Office Workers, under Ron Smith, have emerged as one of the most militant groups, and Smith himself has become a significant member of 'Neddy'. Others, like the National Union of Teachers and the National and Local Government Officers (NALGO)—the fastest growing union of all, which jumped from 146,000 to 274,000 between 1946 and 1961—are outside the TUC. But Men from the Pru, bank clerks, white-coated workers in laboratories fight shy of unions.[1]

[1] *See* page 374.

The proportion of white-collared to manual workers is steadily rising, and the total figure of trade union membership has been slowly falling—accelerated by the big drop in mining, textiles and railways. About 23,000,000 people are engaged in *some* kind of work in Britain, including cabinet ministers, bookmakers, bishops, stockbrokers and others reluctant to join trade unions, and hundreds of thousands of farm labourers, builders' men, dock workers and odd-job men who are too apathetic, temporary or far-flung to be reached by the unions. But they include, too, the lower-middle-class who see themselves as growing socially superior to trade unions.

The unions still dominate the vital industries—mining, railways, power stations, lorries—which could bring the country to a halt. But as they move away from militant strikes towards a closer relationship with the government, so these 'key industries' become a less viable weapon, and white-collared workers—who bring strength in negotiations and a larger stake in the future—become more important. Trade unionists know from their own sons and daughters that the future Britain will be a white-collar country. Recently, with the pay-pause and the resulting militancy, there have been signs of a new solidarity, and both NALGO and the teachers seem likely to join the TUC. But the conjunction is difficult; for while the white-collar people, conditioned to large bureaucracies and committee-work, bring a negotiating skill, they are often less articulate and persuasive than the manual workers, who have been used to fighting from the beginning. The TUC needs both talents equally—to be able to stir up its people at mass-meetings, and then bargain skilfully in committee-rooms— but they fit uncomfortably, and white-collar people remain alarmed by the political connections of the TUC.

TUC

From Easter until August the individual unions hold their seaside conferences, where delegates come together to pass resolutions on anything from peptic ulcers to missile bases. If the resolution is passed, by however small a majority, it then stands as the corporate opinion of the whole union, and the delegates are sent on to the Trades Union Congress meeting armed with the 'block vote' of the total membership. The block vote is often spoken of as a kind of modern pocket borough, as if the union bosses could do what they like with it. But though a persuasive leader may be able to swing his conference behind him, a current feature of many unions is the opposite: general secretaries, including Carron and Greene, have found their unions' block vote adamant against them.

In September the unions come together for their conference, and for one week in the year the TUC suddenly blazes into the headlines, its leaders fill the TV screens, its dramas and conflicts become exposed and analysed. But for the rest of the year the TUC is not much in evidence. The TUC itself is relatively tiny. The actual Council of thirty-five is made up of busy general secretaries (including those of all the six biggest, except Will Paynter), who normally meet only once a month round the horse-shoe desk in the new Congress House in Bloomsbury (with a statue outside of one worker pulling up another). Few central union organisations are as weak as Britain's. The TUC cannot order a union to strike or not strike: it can only advise, cajole or bring careful pressure. In 1961 the unions paid only sixpence per year per member to it, producing a total of about £250,000 a year, which had to pay for staff, scholarships, publicity, international affiliation fees, and organising the conference

The actual staff of the TUC consists of only 87 people, including maintenance staff. The senior people are engaged in researching, reporting and recommending: each subject has a special sub-committee, headed by a member of the General Council. Probably the most influential is the Economic Sub-Committee; Sir Alan Birch, who was its chairman before he died, talked to me about some of the problems of the TUC: 'We must bridge the gap between the workshop and the General Council. The unions advised us long ago of the need for a national body on welfare questions: but there is a kind of taboo on the TUC against wages policy being discussed. Some of the wealthy, well-organised unions don't want to be dragged into other people's troubles, and the Communists argue that it would be "trying to bring in wage restraint through the back door". But we've got to get down to planning. The only real planners in Britain today are people like Clore—they're people who decide what they want to do, and do it. But Britain's become so compact today that it's got to be planned as a *business* in the interests of the community as a whole. Future developments in British industry may present British unions with new problems that they can't solve, as in automation and new industries—so they'll have to get together . . . The biggest influence in the TUC is environment. When the environment changes, the trade unions must change. They may be slow, but it's bound to happen. It's like natural selection.'

GEORGE WOODCOCK

The most important figure at headquarters, and probably in the whole movement, is the General Secretary, George Woodcock. He is the only full-time member of the Council, and he runs the permanent staff, with a salary of about £2,500 a year. He is a kind of secretary to the cabinet, but his cabinet is more fissiparous and fitful than the government's, and he has none of the limitations of a civil servant: he can, and does, speak boldly at meetings and emerges as a tough political figure in his own right. He is unmistakable, with a shock of grey hair above enormous black bushy eyebrows; he has a soft Lancashire voice, precise and measured, which conceals surprising passion and impatience. Like a wise ghost, he is nearly always to be seen at TUC gatherings, looking, listening, watching, nodding, occasionally speaking out. Alone in the movement, he combines a working-class upbringing with a (literally) first-class education. He was the son of a Catholic millworker, and at twelve he was working half-time on the loom near Preston, to help his family's wages: at twenty-five, he had won a scholarship to Ruskin College, Oxford, then to New College where he took a first-class degree. (His Economic Adviser at the TUC, Len Murray, is also a New College man.) Woodcock fought shy of political trade unionism, and dislikes soap-boxes. He worked for a time with the civil service, which bored him, and then for ten years was senior economist at the TUC. Walter Citrine—one of the moulders of the movement—impressed Woodcock with professionalism and careful decisiveness, and he still often seeks Citrine's advice. He was also strongly influenced by Bevin, who taught him how to run committees. For fourteen more years Woodcock was assistant to the next general secretary, Sir Vincent Tewson, when he could watch the Council at work, but had no power: and in 1960, after this long and awkward vigil, he became general secretary himself.

He is one of the most articulate men about his job that I encountered: he is wide awake to the new problems of the TUC. The crucial change, for him, was during the war, when the government accepted responsibility for wages and employment: he remembers Neville Chamberlain telling the TUC delegation in 1938: 'We have only a little more control over labour than we do over the weather.' But since 1944, when the government accepted responsibility for the economic weather, the trade unions' job (Woodcock thinks) is bound to be different. 'We created the Labour party to get what we wanted. Now we've got it, we don't need it in the same way. The Labour party's job is to get votes. Our job is to get wages.'

He sees his own rôle as very limited. 'The TUC doesn't *do* anything: it can't tell the unions what to do. All I can do is to try and see the way things are going, and help them along. I have to try to get the feeling of the council, and then help them to reach a decision.' He admits the shortage of young trade unionists, and the old-fashionedness of many attitudes. 'But it will change as the men at the bottom change. Trade unions are not like family firms, or a religion: the movement is made by the people who come into it at the bottom, and they're pulled into it not by personal ambition but by their own self-respect. We'll have to buy economists and experts in the market-place, and pay well for them: but the men who run the movement will always come up from the rank and file.'

THE CART-HORSE

The TUC has always been tolerant, and slow to criticise: Low depicts it as a cart-horse, clumsy but indestructible. Only occasionally is it compelled to take action against one of its unions, but such a moment came with the Communist-controlled Electrical Trades Union. The ETU is the seventh biggest union, with a quarter of a million members. Its Communism is not entirely due to its leadership: it was noted by Marx, among others, that the most radical workers are not the lowest paid—such as railwaymen or dustmen—but prosperous, semi-skilled men, such as lorry-drivers, engine-drivers or electricians. The electricians—who began as a small group of telephone men in Manchester in 1889—know their power and potential, in everything from television to aircraft. 'We are in everybody's business.'

But after the war, the ETU was captured by the Communists—partly through the apathy of others, partly by simply rigging the ballot. Their offices in a suburb in Kent were shrouded in evasion and secrecy. For years they remained an open scandal, exposed by the press and television, on the initiative of Woodrow Wyatt, but still tolerated by the TUC. Then in 1961, the unsuccessful candidate for secretary, John Byrne, brought a court case against the excutive, including the Communist secretary Frank Haxell. Mr. Justice Winn found Haxell and others guilty of 'fraudulent and unlawful devices': 'not only was the Union managed and controlled by the Communist Party', he said, 'but so run as to suit the ideals of the party.' Haxell was ordered to resign, and John Byrne took his place: the Communist president, Frank Foulkes remained in office.

After long, worried meetings, the TUC decided that it could not tolerate the ETU in its midst. At their meeting at Portsmouth in September 1961, George Woodcock sadly and soberly recounted the sins of the union—not the sins of Communism but the sins of fraud. At last the president, Ted Hill—an old friend of Foulkes—slowly announced: 'It is with profound regret that I have to ask the ETU delegation to withdraw from Congress and surrender their credentials.' Frank Foulkes sadly walked out of the hall, saying 'au revoir, Ted'. 'It was like some very unfortunate family severance'—as one observer put it[1]—'in which all the instincts of flesh and blood give way, in the last analysis, to the good of the greater number.' Four months later the ETU was thankfully readmitted.

THE POWER OF THE UNIONS

The strength of the unions is now much harder to define than in the pre-war head-on clashes. It is not a mailed, but a kid-gloved fist, showing itself little in actual strikes. In 1960, according to the Ministry of Labour, the time lost by strikes amounted to only 0·5 per cent of the total working time, or three million man-hours—compared to 300 million man-hours lost through illness. 60 per cent of the time lost by strikes was in four industries, which account for only 7 per cent of the working population—motor-cars, docks, ship-building and coal mines, all known for their bad labour relations and old-fashioned management. 'Docks have always been bad', said a man at the Ministry of Labour: 'that daily slave queue doesn't give the docker a chance to have a loyalty to his employers. And in shipbuilding they can still sack a man at an hour's notice.' Britain is not, contrary to frequent impressions, a country very prone to strikes: these were the total number of days lost per 1,000 workers in mining, manufacturing, construction and transport in the Western industrial countries in the decade 1950–9:

US	13,830
Finland	10,555
Belgium	7,310

[1] Peter Jenkins: *Time and Tide*, September 7, 1961.

Canada	7,270
Italy	6,330
Australia	5,930
France	5,470
UK	2,460
Norway	2,200
Denmark	1,595
W. Germany	940
Sweden	635
Netherlands	440
Switzerland	110

Among these fourteen, Britain has fluctuated between tenth and fourth place in the past decade; these were the days lost per thousand each year:

1950	100	10th highest
1951	130	11th
1952	140	9th
1953	170	9th
1954	190	9th
1955	280	8th
1956	150	8th
1957	620	4th
1958	260	5th
1959	420	5th

Two big factors restrict strikes. One is the unions' small funds, which amount only to an average week's wages to each man. The other is public opinion, which looms like a genie: the TUC knows well that strikes by public services, as by the London busmen in 1958, can make the genie scowl.

Much of the unions' power treads softly and invisibly, through the corridors of Whitehall, through boardrooms of nationalised industries (where trade unions have their nominees), and through a hundred joint committees—the British Productivity Council, the Monopolies and Restrictive Practices Board, the Ministry of Labour Advisory Committee on Cost of Living Index, and now the most important, the National Economic Development Council. At the factories there is always suspicion that at those pow-wows the leaders are being bought off by the glamour of government. Many militant demagogues have become fascinated by London power and society. *From Workman's Cottage to Windsor Castle* was John Hodge's autobiography, and J. H. Thomas the railway leader was mocked for his love of aristocracy.

569

The dubbing of trade union knights—'the knights and belted earls of the TUC',[1] as the ETU has called them—has added to suspicion.

The unions' power in this kid-glove era hangs on a tricky balance. The TUC must be close enough to government and boards to influence them, yet separate enough to bargain ruthlessly, keeping their members behind them, clenching the fist inside the glove. With their militant street-corner past the unions are still unequipped for this balance: lobbying, persuasion and public relations have become complex arts, and the TUC lacks sophisticated negotiators, with economics and tactics at their fingertips; chairmen and politicians concur: 'We all want a strong trade union movement', said one minister: 'the trouble is, how can we help them to achieve it? If they think we're interfering, they'll do the opposite.' The advent of planning—with the invitation to the TUC to take part in NEDC—will bring trade unions further into Whitehall, with greater conflicts between their two loyalties. To many of the old street-corner school, this secret committee-world is inherently sinister, and many are very sceptical of the Treasury's good intentions. But to some younger unionists, planning is a new and exciting responsibility. It will certainly give trade unionists a new beachhead in Whitehall, and may result in a further by-passing of Parliament's power, a possibility which has already worried some MPs. As F. J. Bellenger wrote:

What will now be the position when the Chancellor comes down to the House to explain some revolutionary change in his fiscal policy and says by way of recommendation that it arises out of ideas unanimously agreed or formulated in his N.E.D.C.?

Could the opposition oppose such Government policy in those circumstances? Would, for example, the T.U. group of nearly 100 MPs sponsored by various trade unions be willing to oppose policy which their union representatives had already approved? Might not those Labour M.P.s who took an independent line be in danger of swift reaction from their own Party which is so closely associated with the trade union movement both nationally and locally?

My own intuition is that parliamentary democratic forms are going to change in the next 10 to 20 years. Big business is

---

[1] In 1961 there were 5 knights on the Council, but no earls: the only union peers are Lord Citrine and Lord Williamson.

getting bigger. Labour is getting better organised. (Witness for example the suggestion that local government personnel should now through their trade union affiliate to the Labour party.) Government has to consult with these two estates of the realm before introducing legislation and parliament will no longer be the main watchdog of the executive—at any rate in economic affairs.'[1]

A great deal of the power of the unions is of a conservative, negative kind, devoted to preventing the spread of technological changes which might threaten full employment. There are signs of a new attitude, both from the Ministry of Labour and from unions, towards reducing restrictive practices in return for greater security. But the determined rearguard action against the new world of the boffins remains one of the most solid and depressing aspects of the unions' power.

The most visible power of the TUC is over the Labour Party which it invented, and it is this which has recently underlined the annual conference, for trade unions finance and supply 92 of the 258 Labour MPs.[2] They contributed £326,000 out of the total of £346,000 of the Labour Party's General Election Fund in 1959. And they determine 18 of the 27 members of the Labour Party's national executive. When a resolution is passed at the TUC, it is likely to be passed at the Labour Party conference, too. The connection is difficult and unhappy—for the Labour parliamentarians, duly elected by their constituents, resent being pushed by the block votes from the TUC: while the TUC, having invented and subsidised Labour, naturally wants its money's worth. The outcome is still to be settled: but it seems likely that the TUC will gradually become less concerned with issues of defence and the cold war, and more, like American unions, with planning and industrial welfare. There is both sense and sadness in the change: for in the passionate workers' speeches on world issues—muddled and maddening though they can be—there is often the authentic voice of the nation's conscience.

[1] *The Times*, Feb. 1 1962.
[2] *See* Martin Harrison: *Trade Unions and the Labour Party Since 1945*, 1960, p. 267.

36

LEISURE

All the time we keep avoiding leisure we keep talking about it.
Sloan Wilson.

WHILE trade unionists fight successfully for shorter hours, scientists perfect new substitutes for labour, and computers, TV and supermarkets take over the drudgery of industry, the problem of leisure looms larger. No institutions can be kept in perspective without reference to this large outside, which is changing everyone's character. The old nonconformist ethos, the sense of work being itself virtuous and self-improving, is being undermined by the new prosperity. The success story of today is less likely to be about a man who got up earlier and worked later, like Ernest Marples: even the 'hard day's toil' of the civil service is not necessarily desirable. The modern tycoon, like Jack Cotton, often gives the impression of work being not an improving drudgery, but a glorious romp: and the dress-designers, restaurateurs or decorators who are today's young heroes would have appalled Samuel Smiles. The notion that a worker or clerk can reach the top by working harder has become less convincing, and further undermined by gambling: the real success stories are the winners of football pools or premium bonds. Who would have imagined, even thirty years ago, that a British government would be putting out advertisements like this:

> There was a clerk with a worried frown
> Who got his fellow workers down
> Until one happy day he found
> He'd won a prize—£1,000

In spite of the slow industrial growth, the adverse balance of payments, the economic crises, Britain continues for most people to be an increasingly pleasant place to live in. Behind the daunting façades of British institutions, the drab architecture, economists, imperialists and the Board of Trade, Britain is in a state of galloping consumption, in the age of Bingo, Babycham or Chemmy. At one extreme leisure is organised and commercialised with juke boxes or glossy magazines, at the other it revolves round philosophical paperbacks and correspondence courses. But either way there's more of it, and more money to spend on it. The average working week has dropped from about 50 hours in 1939 to 44 hours in 1961, the teenagers alone spend £850 million a year on themselves. When Thorstein Veblen wrote his *Theory of the Leisure Class* in 1899, leisure, 'conspicuous consumption' and extravagance were the hallmark of the upper class, the visible proof that they could remain apart from sordid industry. Today the aristocratic prerogative has spread downwards, and all England is putting on the style.

The traditional pursuits of rich Englishmen have taken on a new lease of life: of the three classic sports only shootin' is still largely the preserve of the gentry and the rich. A lot of estates where the owner can't afford to run a shoot by himself are now shot over by syndicates. But syndicates don't make shooting less private, and anyone answering the rare 'gun wanted' advertisement will be carefully screened to make sure that he's 'safe'. Hunting, on the other hand, which doesn't need a big private estate, has been taken up by far more people. The number of packs of foxhounds has stayed at about 185 since 1905, but while before the war the hunts had difficulty in finding enough subscribers, today they are booming, and famous hunts like the Belvoir and the Quorn can usually muster over 200 mounted followers. The Horse as a focal point of country life has made a comeback with prosperity in the same way as the London clubs. But the Pony has had an even more startling success. The countryside is fuller of shaggy little horses than ever—membership of the Pony Club has risen from 17,000 in 1947 to 60,000 in 1961[1]—reaching their climax in the summer gymkhanas:

> Oh wasn't it naughty of Smudges?
> Oh, Mummy, I'm sick with disgust.
> She threw me in front of the judges,
> And my silly old collarbone's bust.[2]

Side by side with these ancient County activities, a jazzier social world has grown up round the 'cocktail belt' outside big towns—a world of stockbrokers' Tudor houses in large gardens where people drink Pimms in the summer. Social life centres round the golf and country clubs, and the club dance is the annual equivalent of the

---

[1] *Britain: An Official Handbook.* COI, 1962.
[2] John Betjeman: *Collected Poems*, John Murray, 1958.

hunt ball. Weekends are in American style, with tennis, picnics, drinks, parties—hectic in comparison with the country walks and quiet dinners of the deep county. Some of the clubs can be as exclusive as their American counterparts, and it may take a long probation to get into one. The world of the cocktail belt (typified by Sunningdale) still follows the English ideal of country life and the great outdoors, but it is based on money, not land, and peopled by successful businessmen and managers.

The pastimes of the old, and even the new, aristocrats are gradually becoming less relevant. The leisure of the British fifty years ago could be analysed in class terms, from caviare to fish and chips, from the Riviera to Blackpool: the tastes of upper and lower only met in a few national obsessions like cricket, gardening or the races. But since the war there has been more money to spend (taking the 1947 average as 100, wages have risen to 230 in 1960 and prices only to 170), and mass media have multiplied (there were 2 million television licences in 1953 and 11.4 million in 1961). There has been a spectacular change. Traditional leisure is losing ground. Cricket and football, though still enormously popular (Charlie Chaplin and Professor Ayer are devoted followers of Fulham and Spurs), have dwindling devotees. (It is impossible to imagine a campaign for 'brighter cricket' before the war.) The cinema has lost its hold—except among unmarried teenagers, two-thirds of whom go at least once a week, perhaps to snog in the doubles—and audiences have dropped from 1,365 million in 1951 to 514 million in 1961, producing a fall in expenditure from £108 million to £65 million. Television is largely to blame, but these are some of the other things people are finding to do instead:

Motor racing is booming, from the big national meetings (16 in 1959) to odd local events like hill climbs organised by the 500 driving clubs. Between the leisurely atmosphere of Ascot, with its careful status distinctions between Royal Enclosure, Silver Ring and Heath, and the noise, fumes and thousands of classless young men in sweaters and girls in tight trousers at Brands Hatch, there is the gulf of a social revolution.

Bowling. Some cinemas have turned themselves into bowling alleys: Ranks have converted seven since March 1960, and reckon there are already 30,000 bowlers in Britain. An American import, it's a brilliant answer to the demand for gregarious, exhausting, 'fun for all the family' evenings—with licensed clubs for drinks and snack bars.

Bingo. Since the Betting Act of 1961 made them possible, Bingo halls have taken over from cinema shows. Four out of five British adults gamble in some way, and Bingo has provided a safe new excitement for housewives, with the tense dedication of a casino and without the disasters. The washing is abandoned at 3 p.m. as wives rush out to get a good place at the Bingo tables. It costs 2/6 or 5/- to get in, and as much again to play—but it's almost impossible to lose more than a pound a session.

Sailing. There has been a 1,000 per cent increase in owners of boats over the past ten years: in 1961 the Royal Yachting Association's small boat class was 14,770, and this is probably only a third of the small boats in the country. In 1958 Prince Philip estimated that there were 'a quarter of a million people messing around with boats'. The only likely future snag is a shortage of parking space: already friends are arranging their weekend's sailing on a 'you can have our mooring and we'll take yours' basis.

Another old playground of the rich, Abroad, has been invaded. In 1961 3½ million Britons went abroad for their holidays—the numbers have *doubled* since 1950 and *trebled* since 1937, and (according to Cook's) go up by about 250,000 a year. Most families still prefer an August week by the sea, but many young people who used to flood holiday camps have discovered that the £15 a week can be better spent in Spain. A new kind of cheap holiday has come with the vogue for renting villas—'A Millionaire's holiday for a few pounds'. No less than 100,000 people are having villa holidays in 1962. The repercussions of travel can be seen in the changing face of Britain's town life: Britain has come out of dowdy isolation and responded to gay foreign influences—Italian shoes, French fashions, Gaggia coffee machines, juke boxes, delicatessens—and people are bringing back new tastes like wine-drinking; wine sales in Britain have doubled since 1939. Coffee bars, with chromium and foreign names, have influenced town life all over Britain.

The British have become increasingly a nation of dancers—five million people go dancing at least once a week in the 5,000 dance halls, and 5,000 dancing schools teach them. Fred Astaire has just opened one. But upper-class Englishmen are still bad at dancing, and the 'guardsman's shuffle' and inhibited jitterbugging of deb dances still contrasts with the swooping ballroom dancers and the intricate jives at Mecca halls. Ballroom dancing is one of the few world championships which Britain holds.

Tastes in food are more adventurous, and foreign restaurants—Chinese, Italian, Indian, even vegetarian—have proliferated over big towns, notably in the North. Spaghetti bolognese has become a staple lunch-time food for thousands of secretaries. Tax dodges have encouraged big lunches, smoked salmon and champagne on expenses. (We are the world's biggest importers of champagne, drinking 26 million glasses a year.) If Britain's past greatness depended on being able to talk politics after dinner,[1] her future may depend more on talking business soberly after a four-course lunch. But even outside the expense-account round, eating-out in the evenings has become much more of a habit as in France, and new restaurants quickly produce new clienteles.

Although there are 30,000 fewer pubs than before the war, they are fuller—largely because, like other male bastions, women have invaded them. On the whole Britain is a sober country—Frenchmen drink three times as much alcohol, New Zealanders drink more beer—and consumption of alcohol has gone up very little in ten years. But real night life depends almost entirely on clubs thanks to the amazing and tortuous laws. To buy a drink after 11, play roulette, hear lampoons about the Establishment, or see an uncensored film, you must join a club, and nearly all clubs are booming: almost anyone can get a licence to start one with twenty signatures and five shillings. There are jazz clubs for teenagers, strip clubs for middle-aged businessmen, night clubs for debs, dining clubs for gourmets, and, since 1961, gambling clubs for millionaires.

Clothes have set a new gayness and style. Marks and Spencers started a revolution with mass-produced copies of foreign designs, and others followed. Here too there is no longer one style for the rich and one for the poor; Britain, once only recognised, rather drearily, for the 'quality' of her tweeds and twinsets, is now famous for the speed and cheapness with which Paris copies are imported. Men are becoming more dandified, lured by the trade into fads like striped shirts and square ended ties, and Teddy Boy extremes have been enviously followed by Etonians. Mockery of Italian men for their vanity and toiletry is now less often heard.

All these changes have given great scope for businessmen who can, like Lord Marks, provide for, or even invent, new tastes. Travel agents, restaurateurs, hairdressers (employing 100,000 people), the owners of boutiques and dress shops, the promoters of new crazes like bowling, are the beneficiaries from the £16

[1] *See* p. 55.

billion which consumers spend every year; leisure is a field where a bright idea can be as valuable as big capital resources.[1] Here is how some of the money was spent in 1960, compared to 1950:

	1950 £ million	1960 £ million
Total personal spending	9,438	16,608
Food	2,689	4,860
Drink	760	1,001
Beer only	497	563
Tobacco	766	1,140
Clothes	1,063	1,632
Books	35	75
Newspapers	71	143
Magazines	109	214
Motoring	181	1,031
Cinema	108	65
Other entertainments	96	106
Travel	362	573
Servants	98	86

In the middle of this Bingo age, are there signs of a more cultured society? The social philosophy of the industrial revolution—the doctrines of self-help, hard work and profit concealing the undergrowth of poverty and drunkenness—still lingers to promote austere notions of leisure: material prosperity and full employment have undermined their basis, but little has come up to replace the old puritanism, shown for instance in the State's attitude to the arts. 'The purchase of instruments of amusement for the rich with money raised by taxes on rich and poor alike is depredation', said Bentham, giving as examples: 'Edifices, although for the use of the public, in so far as rendered costly by ornament . . . Pictures, statues and other products of the imitative arts.' The *total* annual government grant to the arts in 1961 was £8 million—one 200th of the defence budget, and of this the main state patron, the Arts Council get a meagre £1·7 million. The whole collection in the National Gallery (mainly provided by benefactions) cost the nation £2½ million, and the stolen Goya portrait of the Duke of Wellington, bought for £140,000, cost £15,000 more than the National Gallery's ordinary annual purchasing grant. Private patronage, with its huge potential influence, is largely in the hands of commercial middlemen who sponsor the safest mediocrity—the cinema distributors, property developers,[2] building societies, television tycoons. They blame mass

[1] *Cp.* p. 499.
[2] *See* p. 420.

577

tastes, but some of the nicest tastes, like olives, have to be acquired by familiarity.

But the increase in time, money and education has urged on a cultural revolution, with egghead paperbacks and classical LPs in the forefront. The British are buying and borrowing more books: 17,000 separate titles were published in 1930, 21,000 in 1960—twice as many as in America—and between these years books in public libraries jumped from 42 million to 71 million, and their total annual loans from 311 million to 445 million. Booksellers agree that the greatest rise is not in novels, but in religion, travel and philosophy (Hatchards has trebled its philosophy turnover in three years). In London the theatre is booming—'half the theatres would have been dark through August pre-war. Now they're full', said one manager. In the provinces, though big theatres are un-adventurous, small repertory companies (often supported by the Arts Council) are doing well. Audiences at concerts are growing; before the war the Proms ran for 30 nights in a hall holding 2,000, now they run 48 nights in the Albert Hall, which holds 7,000. The total number of concerts has risen from 400 before the war to 2,000 today. But Britain has only 12 national orchestras, five of them in London, and music lovers are very dependent on radios and gramophones (of the 80 million records sold a year, one-fifth are classical). The greatest single musical influence, the BBC, under its new musical director William Glock, has been weaning the public from endless Tchaikowsky and Tannhauser to modern and little known works. Do-it-yourself music still goes strong: in 1949 there were 617 'official' music clubs and societies belonging to the National Federation of Music Societies: now there are 820 with 80,000 members. The growing interest in music and theatre makes the dearth of patronage all the sadder. While in Germany the state supports a symphony orchestra in every town, and the Berlin Philharmonic alone gets £150,000 a year, the Arts Council have to finance orchestras and theatres, amateur societies, exhibitions, opera and ballet on its £1·7 million a year—enough to build 4 miles of M1.

The visual arts too are booming, from the stately homes business to the Tate Gallery's Picasso exhibition of 1960, which drew a record crowd of 460,000. But the art market is one preserve of the rich which has not been invaded. Dealers and auction rooms are prospering, and in 1961 fifteen new London galleries were opened: but the growing attitude to pictures as investments has made them, like diamonds, a rich man's game.

But with all the new activities, tastes and expanding interests, there remains a strong anti-social element in the national character. George Orwell wrote of the 'English characteristic which is so much a part of us that we barely notice it, and that is an addiction to hobbies and spare time occupations, the *privateness* of English life. We are a nation of flower growers . . . of stamp collectors, pigeon fanciers, amateur carpenters, coupon snippers, darts players, crossword puzzle fans'.[1] More gambling is done at home than anywhere else, filling in football pools—in three-quarters of British homes somebody does the pools once a week spending over £90 million a year. Fishing, the most defiantly private sport, is booming (the *Angling Times* has a circulation of 123,000). There are 19 million spare time gardeners, from banking magnates to trade unionists. Pets abound—one in three families has a cat, one in four a bird, and one in five a dog.

Will the privacy and mild eccentricity of English leisure be gradually worn down by the bombardments of motor cars, Wimpy bars, bowling alleys and, above all, mass advertising and TV—producing a gregarious Americanised society, with the same status-races? Many people fear that the Common Market will induce as frenzied a race as America's into the world of steel and glitter—which would make Europe a great public fairground. If 'growth' (the catchword of industry) is taken to mean only steel-production, consumer durables and industrial productivity, then the ultimate achievement will be a country clogged with honking cars and criss-crossed with motorways. But if growth also means social services, education, books, art and gardens, then Britain—whose aristocratic and landed tradition has produced more subtle (and often more sensible) status symbols—may not only find her own solution to the problems of twentieth-century leisure, but even export it.

[1] *The Lion and the Unicorn*, 1941.

37

ADVERTISING

I'm the most superficial man on earth, and yet I am the dean of my profession. So there must be something wrong with my profession.
    Albert Lasker (the 'founder of modern advertising').

The trade of advertising is now so near perfection that it is not easy to propose any improvement.
    Dr. Johnson, 1759.

RECENTLY a big American food firm in Britain held a sales conference, to pep up its salesmen. The sales manager began by blowing up a balloon, and bursting it with a small bang. 'That wasn't very good, was it,' he said to the company: 'Now each of you will find a balloon under his chair: would you mind bringing it out and blowing it up.' The salesmen pulled out their balloons and all blew them up. 'Now we'll all burst them together'—and they did, with a loud bang. 'That was much better, wasn't it? You see that goes to show that one man by himself can't do much, but if you all work as a team you can make a big bang.' This is part of the rumpus of salesmanship which is advancing on Britain: each year the sales conferences become more dedicated and more absorbed, with more gimmicks and pep-talks. The American ballyhoo, which Britain has so much enjoyed mocking, is gradually winning. The most obvious manifestation of this is the advance of advertising.

For most years since the war, spending on advertising has increased by a steady ten per cent, and only in 1961 has the increase begun to slacken off. It has grown faster than the gross national product: advertising has, in effect, been shouting louder and louder about less and less. In 1960 Britain spent £456 million on advertising—roughly the same as she spent on schools, or on scientific research. Four years before she spent only £305 million. Here are the percentages of national incomes spent on advertising:

	1953	1959
USA	2·6	2·9
UK	1·6	2·1
W. Germany	1·6	1·7
France	·6	·6
Italy	·3	·6

The British have always regarded themselves as more resistant to advertising than Americans. But during and since the war (which made great use of it) the admen's prestige has steadily grown. In America, Madison Avenue has recently suffered a setback: bogus television quizzes, payola, faked-up commercials, and the cut-throat competition between agencies have revealed an ugly and pathetic mendacity and have damaged the admen's social position. In Britain, advertising has been steadily on the up, and the agencies have attracted some of the ablest university graduates. As so often Britain is accepting what America is rejecting: here once more the two ships seem to be crossing in mid-Atlantic.

Commercial TV and fatter newspapers have quickened the pace of expansion in the past five years. As Britain becomes saturated with increasingly similar goods, so her advertising comes closer to the American pattern. The more identical the soaps or detergents, the more the adman is in his paradise, using all his skill to devise the 'unique selling proposition', to unearth irrational motives, to dress soap with romance, sex, security or self-advancement.

But in the past year or so, there have been signs of revulsion. Commercial TV has made advertising much more aggressive— breaking into the middle of popular programmes, shouting about detergents in the drawing-room: the growth of political advertising (the Conservatives spent half a million pounds before the last election) has aroused suspicions, and the Consumers' Association and their magazine *Which?*, with a circulation of 295,000—bigger than *The Times*—began to make some readers more sceptical. At the meeting of the Advertising Association at Brighton in May, 1961, there were distinct signs of worry: an anxious debate was held on the themes of 'Advertising has never been menaced so much by public opinion', and 'Why is it that so many people dislike us?' Admen, even more than stockbrokers, are aware of an unfavourable image.

Advertising has no direction, no centre, no obvious tycoons (though those can be found in America). It exists as a hectic go-between, between the two great wheels of industry and the public, taking a series of quick and temporary decisions, existing from hand-to-mouth—constantly half-surprised by its own existence. You will look in vain (despite what some churchmen think) for a room-full of advertising chairmen deciding how best to corrupt the public mind and extend their power: only occasionally do they get together to defend their trade or—very rarely—to chuck out a member. In the one great recent advertising revolution—the creation of commercial television—a few agencies took an important rôle but most were more alarmed than exhilarated by the prospects, as appears in the next chapter.

The influence of advertising on the press is not as bludgeoning and restrictive as many people, including Northcliffe, feared: no one has succeeded in proving that advertising has a secret effect on editorial policy. Advertisers like newspapers to be credible; the more absurd an advertisement is, the more they like it to be alongside convincing news. But advertising has, in less direct ways, immensely influenced the character of the press—more obviously in the 'quality' papers which are more dependent on advertising.[1] Subjects which are supported by advertisers—notably fashion, travel and consumer goods—have all received mounting editorial attention compared to serious news: women's magazines and supplements, linked to advertising, have boomed while general news magazines have slumped. No major paper or commercial television channel will dare put forward strong criticism of advertising or advertisers: the only large medium which is invulnerable is the BBC, and this has taken little advantage of its position, though in 1961 it began a cautious consumers' programme called 'Choice'. The influence on newspapers has not been so much the direct corruption of the editorial puff or boost, as the general muffling of criticism and the magnification of the adman's interests and the tendency for advertisers to press newspapers into the same mass markets as themselves. Advertisers have also encouraged a debased new travesty of journalism, the 'advertising supplement', with vapid articles of praise designed to be printed alongside advertisements.

Modern advertising was an American invention. There were British pioneers, like Lever and Lipton, but the pace was set by New York. High-pressure advertising began with a young Texan-Jewish salesman called Albert Lasker, who in 1904 first invented the principle of 'salesmanship in print'. He transformed advertising from a series of sedate announcements into a cunning art of appealing to secret desires, and in the next forty years he made 45 million dollars out of it.[2] But as the business became more complicated, so advertising became less of an art, more of a science. On to the original wagon of salesmanship was loaded an extra-

[1] *See* page 130.
[2] *See* John Gunther: *Taken at the Flood*, 1960.

ordinary baggage of statistics, pollsters, committees and analysts: the technique of probing and goading the human mind became more specialised. 'Advertising', complained Lasker, who had a gift for epigram, 'has been lost in the advertising business.'

But advertising, in spite of its impedimenta, still has the histrionic atmosphere of a second-hand Hollywood. Advertising agencies are a compound of ballyhoo, calculations and creative energy: in their curious caravan are included accountants, film producers, salesmen, poets, artists, showmen and straightforward businessmen. But it is an industry which still manufactures only one fragile commodity—ideas; nothing is actually *made* in an agency building, except words, and when all the committees are finished, the advertisement still depends on someone to write it. The copywriters who compose the advertisements and the artists who design them make up the frail heart of the advertising business: as the flood of advertising has swelled, so these 'creative men' have moved from agency to agency at ever higher salaries. Advertising and television between them have created a sudden and insatiable market for the more malleable kinds of creative talent: and a copy-writer in his early thirties can earn £5,000 a year. Here is one of the most spectacular changes in thirty years; with the growth of TV, advertising and 'posh' journalism, any creative talent is in furious demand, and anyone prepared to bend his talent to commerce is more likely to collapse from long lunches at the White Tower than from starving in an attic.

The adman's trade depends on harnessing abstract ideas to the machinery of selling—and the resulting conflict shows itself in their characters. They are like lawyers—as they often point out—in their one-sided advocacy, but without the law's object of the whole truth. The earlier, pre-war generation of admen were often reluctant recruits, writing sonnets or painting abstract pictures between slogans. But since the war, advertising has become much more a self-contained career, with its own circles and revolting obscurantist jargon. 'Environmentally and market-wise', an accomplished adman will tell his client, 'I think we've minored this too much: we need to make a *major*: we've got to plus it up a bit.'

The smoothest of the admen are the account executives, who look after clients; they are the salesmen for salesmanship. They are masters of ploy and one-upmanship—knowing just where to live, who to know, what to say, where to take their clients to lunch. They inhabit the Connaught, the Savoy or the Stafford, welcomed by waiters and signing bills with casual bravura. The art directors can be seen at the Arts Club in Dover Street, full of large men gripping each other by the shoulder, exchanging bonhomie. Two different elements can be noted in the British adman—the Madison Avenue type, with lightweight suits and Italian ties, constantly searching for lusher and more expensive restaurants, and the Guards officer type, with an old English double-breasted cut and a sober tie, frequenting mahogany regions: the Guards Club itself is now a favourite advertising haunt.

Most senior admen come from Oxford or Cambridge.[1] Advertising is a favourite destination for the public school boy, and men who thirty years ago might have gone out to rule India or pace the quarterdeck may now be selling detergent campaigns at the Connaught. 'Advertising seems to need face-to-face communicators', said Dr. Mark Abrams, a detached market researcher at the London Press Exchange, 'which is the special skill which Oxbridge provides: people who know when to be flippant and when to be serious, who can say the right things about Wimbledon and Glyndebourne.' Advertising is a very professional affair, with a large front of professional amateurism. 'Never have I met', someone said, 'such a high ratio of ignorance to intelligence.'

There are about five hundred advertising agencies in Britain: but about half do 90 per cent of the business. These were the twelve biggest agencies in 1960, together with their 'billings'—the total cost of the advertising they placed (excluding international billings):[2]

A	J. Walter Thompson	42·6 million dollars
	London Press Exchange	40·8
	S. H. Benson	30·6
	Colman, Prentis and Varley	26·8
	Mather & Crowther	25·2
A	Erwin Wasey, Ruthrauff and Ryan	23·0
	Masius and Fergusson	20·5
A	Young and Rubicam	19·0
	Lonsdale-Hands	16·3
A	Foote, Cone and Belding	16·0
	W. S. Crawford	15·6
A	McCann-Erickson	13·9

Five of them (marked A) are American-owned. In the last few years several big American agencies have bought London firms,

[1] At the LPE, for instance, three-quarters are from Oxbridge.
[2] From *Advertising Age*, 1961.

or set up their own branches—bringing a new surge of ballyhoo, statistics, and higher salaries. Some admen have complained that this American invasion is destroying the authentic British way of life: and that American sledgehammer tactics—like 'Brand X' of Hedley's—are quite un-British. But others are doubtful whether there is any longer such a thing as a British approach, in such a very American business. Or rather the British approach seems to have become American while the American has become less so.

J. WALTER THOMPSON

The biggest agency in America is also the biggest in Britain—and in Australia, Argentina or India—the omnipresent J. Walter Thompson. 'The great days of advertising are over', said Commodore James Walter Thompson, a bearded pioneer, when he sold his agency to Stanley Resor in New York in 1916: since then the turnover has increased by 120,000 per cent, and the firm has spawned over the world. J. Walter Thompson is not a typical agency (there is no such thing) but, both in America and Britain, it has set the pace for others. It was the first agency to develop exhaustive research about markets—ever since 1912 when it produced a small dry book called *Population and its Distribution.* JWT men in New York like to regard themselves as a 'University of Advertising', and to think of themselves as part of a serious profession: they are opposed to nepotism, and there is hardly a son-in-law in the business. Their entrance tests rival those of the Foreign Service. They are anti-romantic and thorough, and have imposed bureaucracy and science on the young wild trade of advertising: the poets and artists, like scientists, bishops or trade unionists, have found themselves sucked into committees.

Thompson's have pioneered 'Reason why' advertising, which unearths motivations for buying products and then projects them to the public. They love testimonials from famous people (Pond's Cream, Lux Soap, etc.) and have a special testimonial department. Gilbert Harding earned £5,000 a year advertising indigestion cures, but most subjects are much cheaper, and film stars are usually free. Thompson's also go in for scientific evidence ('laboratory tests show that . . .'): they have a whole team of highly-paid consultants from universities to help them with special ingredients and secret formulae. Thompson people are taught to ask themselves five questions—known as the 'Thompson T Square':

'What are we selling?
To whom are we selling?
Where are we selling?
When are we selling?
How are we selling?'

The London office of J. Walter Thompson, though ultimately controlled from New York, sees itself as thoroughly British. It has made the point that its staff includes a member of the House of Lords (Lord Tennyson), and three members of the House of Commons (John Rodgers, Richard Hornby and Ian McArthur). The chairman, vice-chairman and directors are all British, and New York (which holds 65 per cent of the shares) only rarely interferes. When you walk through Thompson's offices—nine floors in Berkeley Square—you feel immediately the heightened atmosphere of the 'Agency Game'. Activities which might seem merely fatuous outside the building, like collecting testimonials for face cream, immediately acquire an urgent significance. In advertising, ends are forgotten in the excitement of means and techniques, and the one question which cannot be asked is '*why* are we selling?' Young men in bow ties and suede shoes stride through the corridors, pretty, confident secretaries sit talking in clusters (pretty girls are very important for impressing the clients), senior executives sit with their doors open, occasionally shouting a Christian name into the passage. Words like 'creative', 'emote', 'subconscious' are bandied about like merchandise. Even the notice boards have an extravagant theatrical atmosphere: 'Dear Art Department, just to thank you for my lovely lovely rug.'

Along the corridors are long display boards, covered with sexy photographs, seductive advertisements and slogans such as 'The best creative people are definitely unreasonable'. Inside the offices are framed advertisements and glass cases containing packets of Kelloggs, Persil or Horlicks—like a museum. These names are the gods of Thompson's business, referred to with a mixture of familiarity and reverence. Into their promotion goes all the care that went, in medieval times, into church building. JWT use five hundred artists and 67 writers—writing, unwriting, rewriting their lines of praise. In the Thompson pub, the 'Coach and Horses' behind Berkeley Square, you can hear stories of past campaigns ending with 'and the sales went up like this'—and the speaker tilts his hand to suggest a steep graph.

Some of the Thompson campaigns are legendary. There were those heavenly Black Magic chocolates in the thirties, with a

586

page from a romantic letter, implying that chocolates were the prelude to love. There was the invention of 'night-starvation', with endless strip-cartoons showing haggard and unloved girls being transformed into beauties and successes by Horlicks. There was the procession of film stars washing themselves with Lux, starting in 1928, which began the long association between Unilever and J. Walter Thompson. 'Both Unilever and JWT', said Unilever's glossy magazine, *Progress*, 'are modestly proud of having so successfully analysed the woman/soap/complexion/glamour relation.' (It is surprising, in looking at past campaigns, to see how little techniques of advertising have changed in thirty years.)

'An agency is like an army consisting entirely of officers', said Thompson's managing director, 'and that makes it difficult to run.' Out of Thompson's staff of 1,075, 259 are 'creative', and no fewer than 51 are 'associate directors': it helps to impress the clients. Television has swelled this creative army: it has brought the admen into the heart of show business, and the film-makers are becoming the aristocracy of advertising. Above all, TV has made the big advertising agencies much richer.

Thompson, like all advertising agencies, is a young man's world—and a young woman's. The right enthusiasm, ideas and salesmanship are all more likely to be found in the young than in the old. The managing director, Tom Sutton, who looks after the day-to-day administration, is the boy-wonder of British advertising, aged only thirty-eight. Sutton is the quintessence of the modern adman. He joined Thompson's from Oxford, in 1949—one of the first of the post-war rush of Oxford men into advertising. He is half English, half Viennese-Jewish, and he has a driving energy which goes straight to the point: he is absorbed in the world of selling. As a young man he was sent to start up a new Thompson office in Frankfurt, and built it up to a staff of three hundred; when he left to become managing director, he was presented by his staff with a juke-box, with a supply of records about himself. Sutton is boyish, extrovert, full of enthusiasm for every product and campaign: he enjoys practical jokes. He gives no hint of the guilty pangs sometimes ascribed by social commentators to admen. He works hard, starting at 8.30 in a modest office, facing a huge box of cigarettes and a Roman map of Francofurtum.

Thompson's are a sophisticated agency, aware both of the subtleties of their profession and its perils. Their men are often in touch with other Thompson offices. 'The British attitude to advertising is still different from the American', said one Thompson man, 'the Americans *like* to be sold new things—they haven't got the same loyalties that we have: compare their treatment of plays on Broadway to our loyalty to the Crazy Gang. But I'm sometimes worried about the sudden growth of advertising here: if the decibels of persuasion get too loud, there may be a revulsion from advertising—as there was in America.'

AGENCY WARFARE

The five hundred agencies exist in a state of jungle competition, not only for clients but for staff: successful writers or account executives move from camp to camp, sometimes taking clients with them. But the larger agencies are beginning to settle down to a more placid existence. The oldest agency, the London Press Exchange, was founded in 1893 as a news agency supplying a London Letter to the provinces—hence the odd name (their chairman, R. C. Sykes, is the son of the founder). Soon they discovered—as others have found since—that advertising is more profitable than journalism, and with the help of such lucrative clients as Cadbury's chocolate and Beecham's pills they have grown into one of the biggest agencies in Europe.

The largest British agency—if we include its overseas business— is S. H. Benson, founded in 1893 by Samuel Benson, a naval officer with a crippled leg who turned to advertising: the office has a ship's bell in the entrance-hall room, and a plaque to commemorate Dorothy Sayers' *Murder Must Advertise*, which was written about Benson's. The present chairman, Robert Bevan, is a cultivated man with a taste for painting and good furniture. He is the son of one of the Camden Town school of painters, and he was one of the first men to go straight from Oxford into advertising (in 1929). Among Benson's early clients (still with them) were Bovril, Colman's Mustard, Skipper's sardines and the coveted Guinness—who spend nearly a million a year.

The agencies are perpetually wooing, with lunches, diagrams, drinks and statistics, the large industrial companies—particularly the tiny group of giants like Unilever, Imperial Tobacco or Shell— on which their fortunes depend. They subsist on the fifteen per cent commission from the placing of advertising, and the transfer of one million-pound product brings £150,000 a year to an agency. The meetings with the clients or prospective clients mark the tense climax of an agency's salesmanship. Magnificent lunches are spread out in private rooms. Tape-recorders, films, sheafs of drawings and dossiers of figures are marshalled. Sometimes a whole book is produced to explain the agency's virtues.

ADVERTISING AND INDUSTRY

The collision of the youthful world of advertising with the reticent world of business is bizarre. In Britain, as opposed to America, businessmen have inherited a distrust of advertising and a feeling that, if what they make is good enough, there will be no need to boast about it. They have regarded advertising as a useful luxury, not an essential tool. An elderly director of a family firm and a young advertising executive from Mayfair talk different languages. But gradually the admen and salesmen have come closer to industry: 'Thirty years ago people were shocked at the idea of a marketing man on the board', said Dr. Mark Abrams, 'accountants and engineers were all right, but not people who *sold* things. In those days an advertising man was likely to have a chat with a manager at Lyons Corner House: now he'll be talking to a member of the board in the directors' dining-room.'

But many industries in Britain have been built on advertising and never forget it. Margarine, patent medicine, cigarettes or cosmetics were born into an age of posters, and the firms which make them, the Unilevers or Beechams, are dominated by 'marketing men'. It is the older industries, which existed before posters or newspapers—like food, beer or coal—which resist advertising most strongly. This is how the cost of advertising compares with the value of retail sales, for some products (in 1959):

Margarine	4·3 per cent
Soup	6·7
Breakfast Ccreals	5·4
Health Drinks	11·5
Hair preparations	13·5
Indigestion cures	20·0
Cold cures	20·0
Car oil	12·5
Soap and detergents	10·4
Butter	·5
Fruit	·2
Bread	·4
Coal	·1
Crockery	·3

In advertising circles, a special magic surrounds products

which spend more than a million pounds a year. These were the ten products which spent most on advertising in 1960, with the firms that make them:

Persil	Unilever	£1,160,000
Tide	Hedley's (US)	1,124,000
Omo	Unilever	1,030,000
Daz	Hedley's (US)	945,000
Stork	Unilever	899,000
Guinness	Guinness	891,000
Nescafé	Nestlé's (Swiss)	862,000
Surf	Unilever	855,000
Maxwell House	Alfred Bird (US)	669,000
Ford	Ford (US)	642,000

Four of the big ten are made by Unilever: none of them are made by a strictly British firm. The ding-dong battles between Unilever and Hedley's (owned by Proctor and Gamble of Cincinnati) raise the stakes higher and higher. From time to time there is talk of a truce and Unilever sometimes show signs of embarrassment at the hideous aggressiveness of the detergent war. But the two are implacable enemies, and are locked in a noisy and costly conflict. Some indication of our cockeyed economy is provided by the fact that Tide and Omo between them spend more on advertising than the Arts Council spends altogether in a year.

Where the ratio of advertising to cost is small, the effectiveness of advertisements is hard to judge: no one, for instance, *knows* whether 'Drinka Pinta Milka Day' makes more people drink milk. But with cold cures, detergents or hair oil, the sales ebb and flow with advertising, and the adman enters the heart of business. Often the adman not only provides the posters, television commercials and newspaper displays: he moves in to redesign the packaging, to analyse the market, to recommend on the strategy of selling and even—in some cases—to suggest new kinds of products. Like bankers or management consultants, advertising men can act as a kind of sheepdog to a sleepy flock.

THE WAR AT SEA

Several advertising wars, engaging thousands of troops on both sides, are currently being waged through the newspapers and TV screens—the detergent war, the instant coffee war, the soap war, the cornflakes war. But perhaps the most restless and mysterious is the cigarette war, the great advertising epic of our age.

Why do smokers prefer one cigarette over another? And what is the mysterious connection between cigarettes and the sea? In spite of all the market research and opinion polls, the answers remain obscure. Is it the excitement of wetness, the suggestion of manliness, or the echoes of naval supremacy? Whatever it is, the lure of the sea is everywhere—as in Anchor, advertised by manly men in oilskins (aptly taken off in *Beyond the Fringe*), singing a ditty about how they hanker for an anchor: or Capstan, which requires an unfortunate young man to lug around a bollard with his girl friend.

But two main contenders eclipsed all others—Senior Service and Player's: and their naval engagement has gone on for thirty-five years. Their placards and slogans, both in light blue, stare out from nearly every tobacconist—Player's Please; Senior Service Satisfy. Each of them sell about 20,000 million cigarettes a year. In size, taste and colour they are apparently almost identical (Player's are slightly thinner and longer) and they are thus an ideal subject for the adman's art.

The fight began in a small way in 1925, when Player's were already triumphantly established: they had a bearded sailor on their packet, unquestionably masculine, from HMS *Hero*. Together with Wills' Gold Flake and Woodbines—all belonging to Imperial Tobacco—they ruled the cigarette roost. Then an enterprising Greek called Pattreiouex (the only man I can discover who has five vowels in a row) began selling cigarettes in Liverpool, with the cunning name of Senior Service: they had a very unusual *white* packet with a galleon, two gulls, and the curious inscription 'a product of the master mind'. The master mind prospered, and a few years later Pattreiouex was bought out by a larger firm, Gallahers—though they kept the five vowels on the packet. But at the beginning of the war Player's were still several lengths ahead.

Then, during the war, Senior Service were sent out in quantities to the troops, and they managed to maintain a high quality of tobacco. The tobacco, the name and the plain white packets attracted the army as much as the navy, and the lower deck as well as the wardroom. By the end of the war they were famous and full of heroic associations. When tobacco was finally freed from rationing—as late as 1954—Senior Service leapt ahead, doubled their sales in a year and quadrupled in five years—to the astonishment of the tobacco world. The smaller brands which had subsisted in the days of rationing were all knocked aside by the two big brands—Senior Service and Player's. Both of them stepped up their advertising. Senior Service had an advertising agency called Service, full of ex-naval people, who took the challenge with gusto: cameras went down to aircraft carriers to photograph more and more manly naval smokers—helping to advertise the navy as well as the cigarettes, which crept steadily up.

Player's became seriously worried—more so because it appeared that *young* smokers were avoiding them, associating Player's Please with the square old smokers of the thirties. What was the secret of the master mind? Was it the white packet, the galleon, the slogan, or the naval bombardment? Player's moved to a new agency, Mather and Crowther, the Drinka Pinta people, well known for their prize-winning pictures and their accent on *love*. Mather's gave bold and drastic advice: they decided to move ashore, and to show young lovers dawdling through damp woods and lingering on the beach, lighting each other's cigarettes with that look of sleepy eroticism so beloved by advertisers. They produced a new, more sexy slogan—'People Love Player's'. And to commemorate their diamond jubilee in 1960, Player's took four pages in *The Times*, and produced a new flip-top packet, not blue but *white*.

In the meantime both sides decided to bring out filter-tip cigarettes, to compete in the growing new market. Gallahers called their brand 'Nelson', with the simple slogan 'made by the makers of Senior Service': Player's, after rummaging through every conceivable naval hero, called theirs 'Admiral', with four gold bands round the packet. But while Nelson scored a victory, Admiral was sunk without trace, and Player's brought out another much more successful brand, Gold Leaf, to compete. Senior Service continued their advance (though Player's lovers appeared to be having some success). By 1961 Senior Service and Player's had moved into the one million pound advertising bracket, and were running neck and neck. Fatuous though this vast expenditure might seem, it at least appeared as an example of vigorous free enterprise, so it came as something of a shock when in July 1961 the Monopolies Commission revealed that Imperial Tobacco had a large secret holding in Gallahers—forty-two per cent of their shares. And the sense of the absurdity of the battle was brought home still further by the Physicians' report on cancer in March 1962.

PRESTIGE ADVERTISING

Since the war there has been an uprush of advertisements not obviously concerned with selling: a headline announcing 'This is the age of Shell': eccentric dialogues about ICI: an announcement from ATV beginning 'Quot Homines, Tot Sententiae': huge photographs of Associated Electrical Industries, showing exploits throughout the world. Ironically these big-business advertisements are most prominent in the left-wing *New Statesman*.

This is 'prestige advertising', 'company advertising', 'reputation advertising', 'institutional advertising', 'good-will advertising'— the multiplicity of names, as for lavatories, suggests embarrassment. Sometimes the object is clear: South Africa justifies *apartheid*, steel attacks nationalisation, television is mindful of the Pilkington Committee. But often the advertising has a broader objective—a fostering of goodwill, a 'projecting of a corporate image'—to use a favourite advertising expression. 'Company advertisements', says a significant pamphlet issued by the Institute of Practioners in Advertising, 'can influence the public to regard the company in a certain way: as forward-looking people with a vigorous policy of scientific research; as friendly, helpful people with enough humanity to laugh at themselves; or as craftsmen in the English tradition to whom "automation" and "assembly line" are naughty words.'

The growth of institutional advertising since the war has been spectacular: one advertising chairman estimated that it now constituted ten per cent of the total. It marks an important trend, for it shows advertising trying to act as interpreter for the business corporations, and beginning, in some fields, to usurp the rôle of journalism. There are several ways of describing its rôle. According to Colonel Varley of CPV, it is a question of 'producing a fusion between the consumers' and the producers' attitude. You have to find out where technological developments are taking you, and try to equate those with consumers' attitudes'.

Many Leviathans avoid institutional advertising. Unilever, for instance, prefer to remain a shadowy presence (when, recently, they conducted a poll among the intelligentsia, to discover attitudes to detergent advertising, they found that many were shocked by Omo advertising, but had no idea who was responsible). Few people connect Pepsodent with Unilever, Lucozade with Beechams, Dettol with Reckitt and Colman. But other firms love to proclaim themselves to the public. The eccentricity of Accles and Pollock, the whimsicality of Albright and Wilson, the heroism of English Electric, the enterprise of Bowaters, the sensitivity of the Electricity Generating Board, the broad-mindedness of De La Rue—all these are beginning to enter into our folklore. Frequently, the advertising has very little relation to the real personality of the company: as the IPA pamphlet points out, it may like to suggest that an assembly-line is really a group of craftsmen. The jolly, eccentric directors in the advertisements, singing ditties and exchanging merry quips, can hardly be more different from the actual boards.

PUBLIC RELATIONS

Organised lying
Malcolm Muggeridge.

A most degrading profession
Harold Wilson.

The deliberate, planned and sustained effort to establish and maintain mutual understanding between an organisation and its public.
Definition by the Institute of Public Relations.

December 10th is Public Relations Day. Every year three hundred or so delegates from the Institute of Public Relations come to the Festival Hall to celebrate their trade, and men with double-barrelled names come up to the platform to discuss their problems. 'There is still a vast job of explanation to be done', said the retiring President, R. A. Paget-Cooke, on Public Relations Day in 1960: 'I have been deeply concerned about the public relations of public relations.' 'Since people are looking more closely at the public face of public relations', said the incoming President, Alan Eden-Green, 'we must give it a little of the attention it needs. We must watch our make-up.'

The trade had an appropriately disreputable beginning. The first public relations officer was Ivy Lee, a persuasive American who was employed by the first Rockefeller in 1914 to explain away the massacre of strikers in Colorado: in 1934, when he was had up in court, he turned out to be acting as PR man to the Nazi government. Since Lee's day public relations in America has galloped ahead: there are now reckoned to be 100,000 American PR men, spending two billion dollars a year.

Britain has advanced more cautiously, and about thirty years behind America. The first PRO in Britain was Sir John Elliot, who began on the *Daily Express* (which his father edited), became the first PRO for Southern Railways, later chairman of the London Transport Executive, now chairman of Thomas Cook's. Before the war public relations—except in fashion or show business—was regarded with suspicion. The war made it, like advertising, respectable and Whitehall found PROs very convenient for explaining unpopular actions. Since the war the trade has raced ahead. In 1948 the Institute of Public Relations was founded with 248 members: in 1961 it had 1,447 members. One public relations man—Eric Williams of McCann-Erickson—has estimated that by 1970 there will be 10,000 of them: 'Everyone will want to get into the PR act.' Already the Church of England, Paul Getty, Hambro's bank, debutantes, the Army, the Aga Khan, all have their PROs: even the Queen has her PRO, Commander Colville (though he is as much concerned with keeping his client *out* of the papers).

British public relations have roughly followed the American pattern, but there are important differences. In America PR is a trade very separate from advertising, with its own large firms: in Britain, most advertising agencies have their own PR departments, and this combined front makes the machine more formidable. Another difference is that Britain has stronger traditional social networks and communications—the networks of schools, universities, clubs, families, or parliament—which public relations persuaders come up against. But this does not necessarily make PR less effective: by operating *through* clubs, school ties and old boys nets it can and does take over traditional networks, and public relations is a lucrative field for the old boy net and the public school proletariat.[1]

Hundreds of public relations men are steadily employed by large corporations, keeping newspapers and television informed of their employers' achievements, suffused in a rosy light. Many others are employed by advertising agencies to supplement their other services. But there are also more subtle, independent practitioners, often called 'consultants', who work in a more personal way and are the aristocrats of the profession. They have firms of their own, with plush offices in the West End. They work among chandeliers and marble mantelpieces, telephoning, entertaining, introducing, arranging, conciliating, explaining—lubricating the wheels between corporations and the public. Sometimes they make use of institutional advertising, but their real art consists of *unseen* promotion—inspiring headlines, television programmes,

[1] *See* page 194.

v

questions in parliament, letters to *The Times*. They cultivate an old-fashioned, long-established atmosphere: they wear stiff collars and dark suits and sit in Regency offices.

They are the new diplomats of British society: they have the suavity, the social poise, the adaptability and flexibility of diplomats, and a sprinkling of titles and double-barrelled names. There is the Earl of Kimberley, whose clients include Gilbey's gin and Gina Lollobrigida: Lady Joubert de la Ferté, who looks after the London Fashion Designers: Prince Yurka Galitzine, who handles, among others, P and O, IBM and the Suez Canal Company: Alan Campbell-Johnson, once Lord Mountbatten's press attaché, now explaining Esso, Thomas Hedley and Imperial Tobacco.

One of the most celebrated is Toby O'Brien, a languid, soft-voiced Irishman (he has a brother known as 'Post Office Toby', who is PRO to the GPO). O'Brien has all the proper trappings of public relations: he sits in an office in Old Burlington Street with a soft carpet, a grandfather clock and a huge oil painting of William O'Brien, a seventeenth-century ancestor on horseback.

O'Brien was once part of 'Peterborough', the gossip-column of the *Daily Telegraph*: later he became Public Relations Officer to the Conservative party, and helped to reconstruct their propaganda machine after 1945. He works in a personal and intimate way, giving small parties for selected opinion-moulders, arranging little wine-tastings, press conferences, statements and expeditions, and doggedly promoting his clients' interests, undeterred by criticism. 'I've always been brought up to believe that public relations people should be seen and not heard', he said, 'it's your job to boost your clients, not yourself.' His clients include Cunard, the Channel Tunnel, Gonzalez Byass sherry, Spanish Turismo, and the Katanga Government, for whom he has produced a regular news-sheet and a Congo-Africa fortnight: 'The point is I never take anything on that I can't believe in a hundred per cent', he told the *Daily Mail*: . . . 'They are still cannibals you know, literally.'

Public relations is penetrating further into the world of politics —both national and international. Several of the PR consultants are employed by foreign governments (a relationship forbidden in America), and are taking over part of the rôle of ambassadors: they have an informality and a technique with the press which conventional diplomats lack. Among these quasi-ambassadors are Michael Rice, a young Conservative who has publicised Ghana; Patrick Dolan and Associates, who have handled the publicity for Western Nigeria; and Frank Owen, a former Fleet Street editor who has represented, among other people, the King of Siam.

The most celebrated political advisers are Colman, Prentis and Varley who (with their subsidiary public relations firm, called Voice and Vision) have advised the Conservative party, the army and Sir Roy Welensky's government in Rhodesia. The success of their free plane trips, tours and advertising in influencing members of parliament pointed dramatically to the power of public relations, as the organisers were quick to demonstrate. 'The public relations gimmick of bringing out parties of British MPs on fact-finding tours of the Federation has paid off handsomely', the Federal Director of Press and Public Relations is reported to have said in Lusaka on November 14, 1961: 'Public relations men "went to town" on various media to get Sir Roy Welensky terrific coverage for his recent speech at the Institute of Directors.'[1] The fact that MPs are dependent on 'gimmicks' for their excursions abroad has caused worry among some cabinet ministers,[2] but MPs earning £1,750 a year who want to travel find it hard to resist invitations.

Writing a newspaper column one soon uncovers the mechanism of public relations, bombarding the office with handouts and gimmicks to attract attention. In the course of a year I received an invitation written on a plate, another written on silk, several invitations by telegram, a pile of visiting cards with my name printed in Greek (to advertise *The Guns of Navarone*). There was an invitation to a tea party at the Imperial Turkish Baths (to meet 'Miss Slenderleaf' of Tetley's teas); there was a jumping party in a gymnasium to advertise a book; a champagne party to look at a £250,000 man's suit; an invitation to meet a Haitian Voodoo priestess; and an invitation from Derry and Toms which began:

His Royal Highness the Duke of Edinburgh
having graciously consented to a
Display of the Personal Gifts . . .

The PROs outbid one another to find spectacular and exclusive

[1] Letter to *The Times* from Gerald Percy: December 1, 1961.
[2] *See* page 60.

venues for their parties; lately they have taken to invading clubland and parliament—of which increasing numbers of PR men are members. The *Financial Times* has estimated that there are twenty Conservative MPs working in some capacity for PR or advertising agencies: 'the question "whom do you represent"' they comment, 'may become quite ambiguous'.

The public relations officers have become part of the daily machine for manufacturing news: behind every issue of a newspaper lie their contraptions—the handouts, outings, free trips, press conferences or fashion shows.

Journalists oscillate between the undoubted agreeableness of the PR men's blandishments—the plane trips to Athens, the lunches at the Connaught, the ready-made photographs and printable little stories—and an uneasy sense of dependence and obligation. Early in 1961 a group of journalists—headed by Nicholas Tomalin, former editor of the Londoner's Diary in the *Evening Standard* and now editor of *About Town*—went so far as to found a 'Society for the Discouragement of Public Relations', which holds dinners at Bertorelli's; members pledge themselves to refuse lunch invitations and exchange information about publicity outrages. But not all journalists are so antagonistic, and women journalists are uncomfortably aware that, but for the PR machine, the whole calendar of fashion news would collapse.

As Britain becomes more fragmented, more professionalised, so the persuaders enter their kingdom. The old methods of communication—the club, the coterie, the country house, even the newspapers—are weak in the face of this well-oiled machine. Some people have suggested that the attempt to influence MPs, for instance, by free trips to Rhodesia, is no *more* sinister than the pressure of dinner-parties and country houses before the war. But public relations is much more directed and purposeful than any private hostess, and their 'social engineering'—a favourite PR phrase—is far more resourceful.

The picture that Britons have of themselves is already warmly coloured by public relations and advertising: in so far as people have an impression of AEI or Bowaters it is not through the press or through private information, but through the announcements of AEI and Bowaters themselves. In front of every corporation and institution, like the court praiser dancing and singing in front of a shaky Zulu king, is the PR man—explaining, interpreting, scattering handouts, telling stories of fabulous achievements.

The public relations men are comfortably aware that, after

their years of tribulation, the future is theirs. 'If all these forecasts are realised', Eric Williams has written, after adumbrating the glorious future, 'how splendid it will be for PR wives. At last, without uncertainty, evasion or embarrassment, they will be able to reply quite simply (even without a slight soupçon of status?) to the neighbourly query about their spouses' occupation: he is in public relations.

'And there will be a smile of instant mutual understanding . . .'[1]

It is easy to adopt, as I have done here, an intolerant approach to the whole business of advertising, and much harder to work out what its relationship should be to contemporary Britain. Advertising is an inescapable part of the capitalist system, the visible part of the iceberg, which has to be faced. But the British, because of the traditional reticence and intimate character of the old institutions, have often tried to forget it and to wish that (like science) it wasn't there. Partly as a result, advertising and public relations have been associated with the newer, more ruthless, and often mendacious causes.

In fact, of course, the need for some kind of 'social engineering' is implicit in the complexity of modern society; but the more idealistic and entrenched institutions, including Whitehall departments, the United Nations, the BBC and the Labour party, maintain their suspicion of all kinds of advertising. As advertising trespasses further into journalism, so the resulting imbalance becomes more serious. The public faces a barrage from tobacco makers, industrial corporations, political pressure groups, the fashion industry, but hears scarcely a word from social services, Whitehall and the nationalised industries. The older institutions are apt to suspect all new forms of communication, both external and internal, and continue to behave in a club-like, secretive way long after they have grown themselves into mass organisations. The dangers of this withdrawn tradition were very abruptly discovered by the BBC.

[1] *Advertiser's Weekly*, January 20, 1961.

599

38

TELEVISION

TELEVISION has affected nearly every other estate in the country. Commercial TV was not something, like schools, universities or the press, which 'just growed'. It was an innovation more sudden and dramatic than the nationalised industries, and like them full of doctrinal implications: while *they* stood as a monument to socialist doctrine, commercial TV is a monument to the free-enterprise lobby of the Conservative party. In six years it has grown from an idea in the minds of a few tough enthusiasts into colossal companies, the most powerful patrons in the country, with profits larger than newspaper groups. Commercial TV, with the combined assault of technology and big-business, has undermined many old attitudes, and turned the managerial revolution on its head; while the new medium itself is still having repercussions on parliament, the monarchy, the Church, the press and even the position of the prime minister.

BBC

I believe that the success of a business depends on one man.
Lord Reith[1]

Writing in 1962, it is already difficult to recall the days of an unchallenged British Broadcasting Corporation: for as with other competitors—life peers v. hereditary ones, Shell v. Esso, Lloyd's v. Insurance companies—the rivals are becoming more alike. But basic differences remain and much of the BBC's character is the product of its short but spectacular history. Its thirty-year monopoly, from the royal charter of 1927, seemed for most of that time as inevitable as the air force, and it acquired its own massive corporate character. It has some claim to be the first public corporation: for largely through the personality of J. C. W. Reith it succeeded in wresting itself away from the control of the Post Office, its nominal master, to become a separate organism, responsible to parliament only, who renewed its charter every five years. (The rivalry between the BBC and the GPO continued, and helped to let in the commercial lobby.) But the BBC had none of the anonymity and apparent headlessness of later nationalised

[1] Interview with John Freeman: *The Listener*, November 10, 1960.

industries, for its whole personality revolved round Reith. As one of his staff, Mary Adams, later recalled it, 'He was Queen Victoria, Genghis Khan, Leonardo, rolled into one. He was Headmaster, Field-marshal, Permanent Secretary, Commoner, Captain of the Ship, Father wielding a cane, a baton, a pen, a telephone, a secretary with an effortless ease. . . . Around him we were all dwarfs.' Partly from Reith, partly from its closeness to government, the BBC acquired that reverent attitude to British institutions— particularly the monarchy—which has made it the most visible and disliked symbol of the Establishment. 'It moves sluggishly with all that is worst in British life, all that find prevailing opinion safe and comforting', wrote Henry Fairlie. 'Ever since a generation thrilled to an announcer intoning the lines about its King's life moving peacefully to its close, the BBC has produced a staff of highly trained palace lackeys with graveyard voices, and a ponderous language stuffed with Shakespearean and semi-Biblical echoes', wrote John Osborne. The image of the BBC has changed in the past six years, but some of its reverential tone persists, most aptly expressed in the hushed tones of Richard Dimbleby. Its authority reached its peak in the war, with the nine o'clock news and Churchill's speeches. A competitor to the BBC would in those days have been unimaginable.

With its quick expansion and wartime accretions, the BBC became an unparalleled 'cultural bureaucracy', far larger than newspapers or advertising agencies. Like the AEA or ICI it had to combine disciplined hierarchy with a wild strain of creative energy. It had—and has—a substructure of civil service rules with an eccentric over-layer. Most BBC offices have the same careful squalor—the dusty notice-boards of out-of-date announcements, the peeling linoleum, the chipped cups—as Whitehall departments, and directors are likely to receive the CBE. But in the midst of the workaday bureaucracy are subversive poets, mutinous scriptwriters and unreliable actors. The BBC has never made a virtue of its creativity, as advertising agencies do: there are no 'creative directors' in Broadcasting House, no sexy notice-boards or wild brainstorming sessions to inspire the muses. A pleasant austerity and lack of hokum still surrounds the 'old Corp', as commercial men call it, almost as if the Board of Trade, through some terrible crisis, had been forced to earn its living by light entertainment. It is the strange juxtaposition of this grave bureaucracy with creativity which makes it both loved and hated.

At the top the BBC has a stately organogram, leading down from

Governors to Directors to Controllers to Producers; with this at the head in 1960:

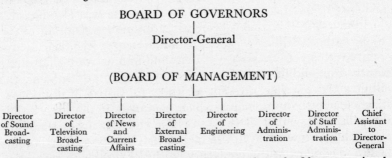

The governors are chosen from the usual pool of house-trained committee-people on the amateur principle: they are not required to have an interest, or knowledge of, broadcasting, and when Sir Arthur fforde was appointed Chairman in 1957 he told reporters that he did not possess a television set. These are the present governors, with their profession:

Sir Arthur fforde (Chairman) ..	Solicitor, Ex-Headmaster of Rugby
Sir James Duff (Vice-Chairman) ..	Ex-Vice-Chancellor of Durham
Sir David Milne (Scotland)	Ex-Permanent Under Secretary, Scottish Office
Mrs. Rachel Jones (Wales)	Sociologist
J. Ritchie Mckee (Northern Ireland)	Northern Ireland Arts Council
G. E. Coke	Chairman, Rio Tinto Company
Dame Florence Hancock	Ex-TUC General Council
The Earl of Halsbury	Ex-Managing Director, National Research Development Corporation
R. F. Lusty	Chairman and Managing Director, Hutchinsons

But the governors are not much more apparent than the governors of a school with a strong headmaster, and their main task is the choosing of a Director-General, who is the executive head. These are the seven Director-Generals since 1927, with their previous occupations:

Lord Reith (1927–1938) Gen. Manager, Wm Beardmore & Co.
Sir Frederick Ogilvie (1938–1942) Vice-Chancellor, Queen's University, Belfast
{ Sir Cecil Graves (1942–1943) BBC
{ R. W. Foot (1942–1944) Gen. Manager, Gas Light & Coke Co.

Hugh Carleton Greene

Sir William Haley (1944–1952) *Manchester Guardian*

Field Marshal Sir Ian Jacob (1952–1960) Chief Staff Officer, Ministry of Defence

Hugh Carleton Greene (1960) BBC

Carleton Greene is the first D-G to have made his career in the corporation, and his appointment suggests that the BBC hierarchy has now become self-perpetuating. In his background Greene has some elements which suggest the typical BBC executive. He is a tall, pale man, with a quiet smile and intimidating reserve, like a cultivated permanent secretary. He is one of the four sons of the headmaster of a public school, Berkhamsted, which educated them all: one, Graham, became a novelist; another, Raymond, is an eminent physician who climbed Everest; a fourth, Herbert, has been an ardent defender of the nine o'clock news and opponent of his brother Hugh's policies. After Oxford Hugh became Berlin correspondent for the *Telegraph*, and joined the BBC in wartime, specialising in propaganda to Germany. He had tact, drive and administrative skill, and he rose quickly through the hierarchy, becoming Director-General in January, 1960.

From his dark-blue office in Broadcasting House—with a bronze bust of Lord Reith outside—Carleton Greene supervises his jumbled empire, from cowboy films to electronic music. He does not have grand ideas about the power of broadcasting. 'Can one point to any single occasion on which in its short life broadcasting has changed the course of history . . . ?', he said in Germany in April, 1959. He believes that the BBC is the best possible system and that the alternatives of purely commercial broadcasting (as in America) or state-controlled broadcasting (as in France) are far more dangerous: 'Radio and television are too powerful in their eventual long-term effects for their control to be entrusted to politicians—or businessmen.' He does not have the grand Hegelian ideas of Lord Reith; but while accepting that the BBC must be impartial between Right and Left, he insists that it cannot be neutral between Right and Wrong. 'I should not for a moment admit that a man who wanted to speak in favour of racial intolerance has the same rights as a man who wanted to condemn it.' He maintains that the BBC is quite independent of government pressure, and he has not disguised his contempt for 'the commercial monster' and the men who control it. 'Commercially controlled television tends in the long run to undermine the intelligence, at any rate of its constant listeners and viewers.'

Television took the BBC farther away from the austere discipline of Lord Reith, and showmanship quickly impinged on the informational, civil-service habits: 'You couldn't just stare into the camera looking anonymous', one of the news announcers said to me: 'you *had* to start smiling and putting across a personality.' Showmen and cantankerous panellists, like Gilbert Harding, became national figures, and the Board of Trade element was in retreat. And the size and resources of the cultural bureaucracy multiplied: by 1948 the BBC was able to put no fewer than a thousand people to cover the Olympic Games at Wembley: and today it employs 17,000 people. The BBC bent its old character, but did not break it: the hierarchy were still 'sound men'. (The corporation is still run, not from the television centre in Shepherd's Bush, but from the sound headquarters in Portland Place.) The governors came from the sheltered worlds of universities and public service. With its size, its lack of international competition and its insulation, the BBC was in 1950 largely unaware of the threat to its future.

THE COMMERCIAL LOBBY

> We have our typically British way of resolving problems of taste, just like any other problem.
> *Sir David Maxwell Fyfe* (later *Lord Kilmuir*), *June 11, 1952*

The launching of Commercial TV was an operation which throws light on several people and institutions in this book, and provides a unique glimpse of the mechanism of power. It was due, not to any strong popular movement, but to the misgivings about monopoly of two leading Conservative politicians, a vague sense of dissatisfaction with the BBC and the old-time attitudes of the cabinet among younger Tory backbenchers, and the active political pressure of a handful of lobbyists with a strong financial interest. The influence and tactics of this lobby have now become apparent from the important study by Professor Wilson of Princeton University, to which I am indebted for part of this material.[1] The lobbying was certainly made easier by the small majority (only 17) of the Conservative party, which enabled a few backbenchers to be a tail wagging a dog: but the success of the lobby, against a united Labour party, an apathetic public and a divided Conservative party, remains an extraordinary and still partly unexplained phenomenon.

[1] Professor H. H. Wilson: *Pressure Group*, 1961. Some important material is also in 'The Men and the Money in ITV': *Sunday Times*, May 14–28, 1961.

The first strong criticism of the BBC came from one dissenting member of the Beveridge Committee in 1951, a little-known Conservative MP, Selwyn Lloyd. The report recommended that broadcasting should remain under a single public corporation, but Lloyd criticised the BBC for its size (it had expanded from 2,500 to 12,000 between 1935 and 1951), for its monopoly and for its excessive power: he quoted critically Lord Reith's statement that 'it was the brute force of monopoly that enabled the BBC to have become what it did; and to do what it did; that made it possible for a policy of moral responsibility to be followed', and he complained that 'it is just as though a British Press Corporation were to be set up with a monopoly of publishing newspapers'.

After the report a committee of ten Conservative back-benchers was set up, including John Rodgers, director of J. Walter Thompson,[1] Charles Orr-Ewing, and John Profumo, who reported that the broadcasting monopoly should be broken. But in debates in the Commons and the Lords there was little apparent discontent with the BBC, with the important exception of Lord Woolton, an ex-salesman and shopkeeper who was excited by the idea of mass-marketing. When the Conservatives took office in October 1951 there was no enthusiasm in the cabinet. But a strong lobby of advertising and other MPs had formed itself, including Lady Tweedsmuir, Ian Harvey of Crawford's advertising, and Anthony Fell of Pye Radio. In March 1952 Lord Woolton became minister in charge of broadcasting, while as chairman of the Conservative party organisation he saw the potential of the new medium and under him the Central Office helped to promote it. In May 1952 a white paper was published, saying that 'in the expanding field of television, provision should be made to promote some element of competition'.

Lord Reith in the House of Lords bitterly attacked the white paper: 'Somebody introduced Christianity into England and somebody introduced smallpox, bubonic plague and the Black Death. Somebody is minded now to introduce sponsored broadcasting. . . . Need we be ashamed of moral values, or of intellectual and ethical objectives? It is these that are here and now at stake'. He was supported by Lords Halifax, Waverley, Hailsham and Brand. In the Commons, there was less Conservative opposition, and John Profumo effectively attacked the 'guardians of the BBC', who were 'almost powerful enough to be able to intimidate the government', and insisted 'we are not a nation of intellectuals'.

[1] *See* p. 585.

But there was not much enthusiasm either, and as John Rodgers later said, most of the credit was due to 'five or six Conservative backbenchers who worked day and night on the project'. 'It is still not clear', wrote Professor Wilson, 'how so small a group was able to make its influence decisive.'

Working behind parliament was the 'unique and powerful triumvirate' (as Wilson calls them)—Norman Collins, Sir Robert Renwick and C. O. Stanley—who between them brought together three quite different strands of influence, and who are all still major influences on the TV scene. Norman Collins, the novelist, journalist and publisher, had been controller of BBC Television from 1947 until, in 1950, he was passed over for the newly made post of TV Director, and promptly resigned: rarely can a passing-over have had such momentous consequences. Collins immediately devoted all his energies to destroying the BBC monopoly, disgusted by 'an organisation which hadn't even got a TV set in the board-room'. He set about the attack with what he later called 'sheer bloody-mindedness'.[1] He brought invaluable energy and respectability to the campaign: he knew the inside workings of the BBC, could convincingly attack its monopolism, and persuaded bishops and dons that a commercial rival would not mean Americanisation or excesses.

With him was Sir Robert Renwick, an adventurous stockbroker in Old Etonian braces, who held fourteen directorships in the electrical industry. He had wide contacts; he was on the council of the Institute of Directors, he had been wartime controller of communications at the Air Ministry, and he had close Tory connections, including a friendship with Orr-Ewing, one of the early supporters. 'Some participants in this controversy', wrote Wilson, 'believed that Renwick's influence in party circles and with Lord Woolton may have been enhanced by what they assumed to have been his substantial assistance to raising the Conservative Fighting Fund.'[2] Renwick had been chairman of one of the biggest electricity companies, and was a believer in untramelled enterprise: 'After the war very few Tories really believed in free enterprise', he told me: 'my industry was nationalised, so I wanted to try and get my own back'. Both Renwick and Collins thus derived their main stimulus from getting their own back.

The third, Charles Orr Stanley, is a chubby Irishman who had built up Pye Radio from a small bankrupt company into an

[1] *Sunday Times*, May 14, 1961.
[2] *Pressure Group*, p. 147.

international company. Stanley is one of those implacable non-Englishmen who never succumb to the charms of monopoly or rings: he saw the commercial prospects of commercial TV at an early stage and set about pressing for it remorselessly through allies in parliament and elsewhere. The triumvirate worked closely together, and met at the Reform Club to work out their tactics and extend their allies.

The oddest feature of the ensuing campaign was the indifference or even hostility of most groups which were to benefit from commercial TV. The cinema industry, including Sidney Bernstein's Granada Theatres and Sir Philip Warter's ABC group, were originally opposed to it, as were the West End Theatre managers, including Prince Littler. The majority of radio manufacturers were apathetic. 'I am amazed that in a young and virile industry such as yours there should be such hesitation and timidity in putting the competitive television knob on the set', complained Sir Robert Renwick. Nor were most of the advertising agencies at all enthusiastic: 'They were making too much money too happily to be interested in TV', Collins told me: 'but in fact they've done better out of it than anyone—15 per cent of £50 million'. Many agencies resented American infiltration, and were afraid of the capital expansion and know-how required ('we'll have to get an American in to run it'); only a few of the biggest— notably Thompson's, Erwin Wasey (American), Masius and Fergusson (controlled by Warburg's) and the London Press Exchange —were enthusiastic. The City of London, which might have been expected to be alive to the commercial prospects, remained bored and sceptical, with the notable exceptions of Harley Drayton, Siegmund Warburg and Renwick. Newspapers were equally sceptical, or afraid: when Renwick organised a lunch of newspaper proprietors, only Cecil King of the *Daily Mirror* (who later became a shareholder in Associated Television) showed any interest. 'In a hundred years there may not be newspapers', he said later, 'but there will certainly be television. We want to learn about it and we are in it for keeps.'

Not only was there this commercial apathy, but by June 1953 an impressive counter-lobby, the National Television Council, organised by Christopher Mayhew, had been set up to dissuade the government, with supporters including Lords Halifax, Brand and Waverley, Lady Violet Bonham Carter, ABC cinemas and the chairman of the TUC, Sir Tom O'Brien. The new council, with its strong Establishment flavour, alarmed the cabinet: and its warnings of vulgarisation were helped by the recent American televising of the Coronation, which had been heralded by commercials featuring J. Fred Muggs, the TV chimpanzee.

But Collins, Renwick and Stanley were undeterred by the counter-attack, and with the support of Lord Woolton they prepared a more impressive front. In July the Earl of Bessborough—a merchant banker and ally of Renwick's—met with the Earl of Derby and Norman Collins at the Turf Club, to invite Derby to become president of a new 'Popular Television Association', with support from Pye and others, and with the collaboration of the Conservative Central Office and unofficial blessing of Woolton. The new association succeeded in presenting a non-party front, attracting Socialists including A. J. P. Taylor, and had as its main object 'to awaken the national conscience to the dangers, social, political and artistic, of monopoly in this rapidly expanding field of television'. It had less impressive names than the anti-commercial council, but it had large funds, masterly techniques, and three tireless men. While the government gave the impression that changes would be distant and vague, the lobbyists pressed for a quick bill, and devised ingenious ways of satisfying Conservative qualms. All the usual public relations devices were employed, and 'Aims of Industry', the anti-socialist PR firm (which had invented Mr. Cube) worked closely with the association. Massive letters-to-the-editor campaigns were organised, public figures, including Lord Derby, Alec Bedser and Gillie Potter, made suitable speeches, and a service of news items were provided for newspapers: an impression was conveyed of a nation demanding TV advertising. The campaign, together with back-bench and cabinet pressures (whose details are still obscure), had its effect, and by the end of 1953 the cabinet had decided to press through with commercial TV. 'This study would seem to establish the fact', concluded Professor Wilson, 'that a small number of MPs, well organised with good connections among both party officials and outside interests, and pushing a definite, limited programme, may exert considerable influence and even overwhelm an organised majority in their own party.'[1]

By March 1954 the Television Bill came up for its second reading: the debate was bitter and split the two wings of Conservative thinking—those who believed in the paternal, aristocratic rôle of government, and those who believed in commercial free enterprise at all costs. It was partly a division between the Salisbury-type

[1] *Pressure Group*, p. 208.

and Macleod-type Tories which we have seen elsewhere, but many liberal Conservatives were torn between the dislike of monopoly and the dislike of unrestricted salesmanship. But in the end no Conservative MPs voted against; the Bill was passed by 296 votes to 269, and fourteen months later the first television advertisement —for toothpaste—appeared.

ITA

'Television, this titan of communication between man and man, this surging, sweeping power, rationed and controlled for us before, is in our hands.'
Sir Robert Fraser, September 24, 1955

To supervise this sudden innovation a new public body, the Independent Television Authority, was constructed, to erect the transmitters and give licences to 'contracting companies'—a system partly copied from Chicago. The ITA was empowered by the Act to provide 'television broadcasting services, additional to those of the BBC and of high quality both as to transmission and as to the matter transmitted' and that 'nothing is included in the programmes which offends against good taste or decency or is likely to encourage or incite to crime . . .' A Chairman and 'Members of the Authority' were appointed by the government, not unlike BBC governors, and not necessarily interested in television: their first chairman was Sir Kenneth Clark, the art historian, and the second Sir Ivone Kirkpatrick, former head of the Foreign Office. As with the BBC, the executive head was the Director-General, a job first advertised in *The Times* in 1953. Sir Robert Fraser, sunbathing in Spain, saw the advertisement and applied for the job, in some of the same spirit of adventurousness as Reith twenty-seven years before. Fraser had worked with Sir Kenneth in the war, he had the right background and experience, and he was chosen.

But Fraser had none of Reith's austerity or Calvinism. For their offices the ITA took one of the finest private houses in London— the former American Ambassador's mansion overlooking Hyde Park, with a huge Second Empire drawing-room for the D-G: later they moved into a brand new building next to Harrods, with hand-picked furniture, pent-house flats and tinkling lifts, outdoing the TV companies themselves in its comfort. Fraser himself is an unusual paradox—Australian, once an intellectual Socialist, close friend of Laski, Dalton and Durbin, wrote leaders for the *Daily Herald* and stood as Labour candidate, worked in information during the war, and later ran the Central Office of Information. He is tall, confident, very articulate, well attuned to modern publicity, and loves talking about his job. His new post surprised many of his old left-wing friends, but he justifies it at length. He regards himself as a 'liberal with a small l', and sees himself as a Benthamite, believing in democratic choice, in contrast to the Platonic ideals of the BBC. He likes to think of Commercial TV as 'people's television': 'If you decide to have a system of people's television', he said in Manchester in 1960, 'then people's television you must expect it to be, and it will reflect their likes and dislikes, their tastes and aversions, what they can comprehend and what is beyond them.' From their offices, Sir Robert and his staff of 118 keep a check on the quality of TV programmes, with a rota of senior men watching the screen all day, recording dubious moments. They forbid advertisements from moneylenders, marriage bureaux, undertakers or the *Daily Worker*, and occasionally insist on programmes being withdrawn. But most interventions are secret; how far television would be more violent and unscrupulous without this watchdog is not known. Certainly the wording of the Act about 'good taste or decency' has an ironic ring in face of the subsequent free-for-all.

The most important job of the ITA was to choose the contracting companies. The selection was made by all members of the authority, but Fraser's influence was often decisive. At first the pessimism about the new medium was such that competition was not very intense. Only when profits were apparent did the value of the ITA's patronage become obvious: 'There's been nothing like it since Charles II doled out patents for making soap', said one TV lawyer. But in the first year the potential losses were so large that only the richest groups were prepared to contemplate investment, and the eventual result was to make big groups bigger, and rich men richer. The allocation of TV stations resulted in many situations which parliament had most hoped to avoid: the extension of the power of a few already powerful showmen, the exclusion of newspapers (largely through their own fault) from all but one of the biggest stations, and an effective tie-up between the 'big four' producing an effective monopoly of commercial TV, making apparent nonsense of the stipulation of the Act that they should be 'independent of each other both as to finance and as to control'. These were the thirteen commercial TV stations in February 1962 (two new stations, Wales TV and Channel TV have not yet started transmitting).

	Net Profits 1961	Area	Chairman	Main Shareholders
Associated Television	£3,172,089	London weekends Midlands weekdays	Sir Robert Renwick	Moss Empires Daily Mirror Pye Norman Collins, Val Parnell, etc.
Associated-Rediffusion	£3,931,591	London weekdays	J. Spencer Wills	British Electric Traction (50%) Rediffusion (37½%) J. S. Wills, H. C. Drayton, etc.
Granada TV[1]		Lancashire and Yorkshire weekdays	Sidney Bernstein	Granada Group (85% Bernstein family)
ABC TV[1]		Lancashire and Yorkshire weekends Midlands weekends	Sir Philip Warter	Associated British Pictures (large holding by Warner Brothers)
Scottish TV[1]		Scotland	Roy Thomson	Thomson interests (80%) Howerd & Wyndham (10%)
Southern TV		Southern England	John Davis	Rank Organisation (37½%) Associated Newspapers (37½%) D. C. Thomson (25%)
Television Wales and the West (TWW)	£662,341	S. Wales and West of England	Earl of Derby	Lord Derby (25%) News of the World (20½%) Liverpool Daily Post (14½%) Jack Hylton
Tyne-Tees	£439,316	Newcastle area	Sir Richard Pease	George and Alfred Black (21%) Daily News (21%) Northern Mercantile and Investment (17%)
Westward TV	(started 1961)	South West England	Peter Cadbury	Keith Prowse Emile Littler
Anglia TV	£329,531	East Anglia	Marquess Townshend	Guardian (20%) Romulus & Remus films (20%) Local interests, industry Norwich Union (55%)
Ulster	£117,100	N. Ireland	Earl of Antrim	Belfast Newsletter, Lord Antrim, etc.
Border	(started 1961)	The Border	John Burgess	Cumberland Newspapers George Outram and Co. Sir Michael Balcon
Grampian	(started 1961)	East coast of Scotland	Sir Alexander King	700 shareholders, mostly local.

[1] Granada, ABC and the Thomson Organisation do not publish their TV profits separately.

The first company to be formed, Associated Television, had as its nucleus the original triumvirate of lobbyists who all still have shares in it: Collins' original investment of £2,250 was worth £501,750 by November 1958.[1] But the triumvirate did not originally have enough money to satisfy the ITA; and in the meantime two prominent showmen, Lew Grade and Val Parnell, on the initiative of a publicity agent, Miss Suzanne Warner, had combined to form their own TV company, financed with the help of Warburg's bank,[2] who were quick to see the potential. But they were refused a station—partly because Parnell's theatre company, Moss Empires, was already thought powerful enough: they therefore eventually merged with Collins' group, which already had a contract. Since the showmen had most of the money, they gained control, and Prince Littler, chairman of Moss Empires, became chairman: later, after ATV suffered heavy losses, Cecil King (again through Warburg's) brought in the *Daily Mirror* with a 19 per cent share.

These different strains formed—and still do—a bizarre partnership. But the showmen's influence made ATV a kind of 'Palladium of the Air', with its climax in Val Parnell's 'Saturday Night Spectacular'. Val Parnell and Lew Grade, known as Val 'n' Lew, share a glossy office, and their breezy, casual style permeates the building. Both are straightforward box-office men with attitudes far removed from the stately early manifestoes of the commercial lobby: 'I'm Woolworth-minded', Parnell has said: 'I cater for the masses.' Parnell is the son of a professional ventriloquist who worked his way up from office boy to running variety, and his greatest love remains the Palladium: he is a big rugged man who combines a casual friendliness—'S'long' and 'Cheerybye'—with organisational toughness. Lew Grade is a legendary figure often depicted as a modern Sam Goldwyn, credited with the same kind of stories. He came, called Louis Gradowsky, to England from Odessa as a child-refugee with his two brothers, and from being a Charleston champion climbed up to running (with his brother Leslie) the biggest variety agency (credited with saying 'the trouble with this business is that the stars keep ninety per cent of my money'). He is a jovial, uninhibited man with loud ties and fat cigars, a long nose jutting from a bald head, and a combination of shrewdness and salesmanship reminiscent of Jack Cotton.

[1] According to the *Sunday Express*, August 23, 1960.
[2] *See* p. 387.

The original prime mover, Norman Collins, now occupies a less central position: he sits in a huge leather club chair, in which he is usually photographed, in a panelled office with Sheraton furniture and a TV set behind a Chinese cabinet—a symbolic contrast to Parnell's. He is vice-chairman, supervises the more cultural programmes, and as the company becomes more dignity-conscious his position has become more important. But the business pace—fast and relentless—is set by Val 'n' Lew. Like other theatrical businesses ATV has developed its own wild Parkinsonian disorder, with small private empires and large rivalries: the atmosphere was not made easier when in 1961 Val Parnell did not oppose Charles Clore's attempt to take over Prince Littler's Moss Empires. Since then Littler has resigned as chairman, and has been succeeded by the omnipresent Sir Robert Renwick, who comes in from the city in the afternoons.

More than any company, ATV has an international, half-American feel: its offices themselves—foliage in the waiting room, Muzak in the hall, open-plan corridors—have the de-nationalised character of airports or UN agencies: and ATV has produced a race of compères with mid-Atlantic accents, in contrast to the public school tones of the BBC. They have close relations with America, both buying and selling programmes, and therefore producing their own programmes with a not-too-British flavour for export. Parnell likes to visualise a future of completely international TV, with British programmes and advertisements appearing direct on American screens.

The other London company, Associated-Rediffusion, had a quite different genesis, and here we are back again into the territory of Harley Drayton, who had such confidence in the new medium that he not only put up a large share but, when the losses were biggest, bought out his co-owner, Lord Rothermere.[1] Now 50 per cent of the shares are owned by Drayton's British Electric Traction, and another $37\frac{1}{2}$ per cent by Rediffusion, the piped-radio company in which BET has a large interest: part of the remaining $12\frac{1}{2}$ per cent, too, is personally owned by Drayton. But Drayton himself is almost as aloof from the company as he is from the Antofagasta Railway; he shows his nephews round, but normally never goes there, and the company is run by people with no previous experience of show business, films or newspapers: the chairman, Spencer Wills, is an accountant who worked his way up through

[1] *See* p. 397.

the bus business of the Drayton Group. The managing director is a former radio engineer, Paul Adorian, who came from Hungary as a young man and helped to build up Rediffusion. The general manager, who has a large influence on the company's character, is a retired naval officer, Captain Brownrigg, who runs the business with the brisk authority of the quarterdeck, and explains how he organised AR, with its elaborate hierarchy, in the same way as he reorganised Singapore dockyard. AR like to suggest that television is a logical extension of their shareholders' earlier businesses—trams, buses, electricity, coal-gas, etc. 'Is it surprising', said Spencer Wills in his annual report of 1961, referring to the Pilkington Committee, 'that we should have been entrusted with the task of furnishing television programmes to the largest city in the Western hemisphere?' Whether the purely business attitude of the heads of AR is better or worse than the showman's attitudes of ATV is often argued among television men: AR lack any strong sense of corporate character, but programmes are less subject to interference from the top.

ABC Television, unlike any others, is wholly owned by one company, the Associated British Picture Corporation, which runs 400 cinemas in Britain, and in which the American Warner Brothers has a large stake. The chairman, Sir Philip Warter, is one of the most respected men in the medium: he is a quiet, civilised businessman, who married the daughter of the man who built up the cinema chain; he is also vice-chairman of the British Transport Commission, and keenly interested in railways. But ABC are as bound by profit-motive as other companies, and rigorous in their pursuit of mass viewing.

Granada, based on Manchester, is the only major company dominated by a single personality—its chairman, Sidney Bernstein, who with his family owns 85 per cent of the shares: Paul Adorian has said, 'only one man has *real* power in this business—Bernstein'.[1] He belongs to the small group of left-wing millionaires (including Jack Hylton, Lord Walston, Alan Sainsbury, Lewis Cohen, etc.) and is the only major tycoon who proclaims strong political views, with strong links with the Left. He talks passionately about the social and cultural rôle of television and describes himself as a 'Reithian'. He is the most autocratic of the chairmen, supervising details of presentation, typography, publicity and taste. His wide range of interests include the

[1] Quoted by Clive Jenkins. *Power Behind the Screen* 1961. p. 93.

publishing firm McGibbon & Kee. He also collects pictures and cattle, holds left-wing dinner parties and loves showmanship: he is a lifelong admirer of Barnum, and a friend of Alfred Hitchcock. Probably alone of the contractors, he would like to have the same kind of power as a newspaper-owner, commanding editorials and crusades, and presenting a consistent political view. He is the nearest that television has to a Northcliffe or a Beaverbrook: but he is deprived of editorials, columnists or comment, and to Bernstein the neutralising requirements of ITA present a constant frustration. But in other respects Bernstein's career has been less frustrating: he has the biggest personal holding of anyone in commercial TV. His programmes are culturally superior to others and his patronage more enterprising, but he is not markedly less interested in ratings and advertising revenue.

The smaller TV stations which followed have a less heavy influence from showmen; as TV became more obviously profitable, respectability was considered more important for candidates. More traditional directors have emerged, and TV has provided a large bonanza for the local aristocracy. Rival contenders for Sir Robert Fraser's favours have tried to outdo each other with lord lieutenants and mayors, and a marquess, three earls, three viscounts and coveys of local gentry have appeared on the boards, alongside entertainers and popular newspapers. The most blue-blooded is the Earl of Derby, now chairman of Television Wales and the West, with a 25 per cent holding, next to the *News of the World* (20½ per cent), followed by the chairman of Ulster Television, the Earl of Antrim. Probably the most mixed group is Anglia Television, whose chairman is the Marquess Townshend, descendant of the turnip pioneer, and whose board includes representatives from Cambridge University, the *Guardian* and Norwich Union Insurance. But the most spectacular of the secondary TV tycoons is Roy Thomson,[1] with the major interest in Scottish Television. The ITA originally expected that newspaper groups would extend their influence into commercial television, but Thomson turned the process on its head. By acquiring Scottish TV—a 'licence to print money'—he made enough to buy the *Sunday Times* and its surrounding provincial newspapers, and thus brought the restless salesman's world of TV into the heart of Fleet Street.

[1] *See* p. 119.

The small stations give the appearance of local autonomy with their boards and programmes, and provide (in theory) 15 per cent of the programmes from their own studios; but they are heavily dependent on the Big Four for their syndicated programmes arranged by the 'Network', which effectively prevents competition between stations, and gives the country the same mass-produced pabulum. From time to time the TV tycoons entertain each other—usually at the Savoy—to organise the Network: they try to outdo each other in the splendour of the meal at those extraordinary gatherings—Lew Grade, the Earl of Derby, Captain Brownrigg, Sidney Bernstein, the Earl of Antrim, etc.

POWER OF THE TYCOONS

What does the power of these new tycoons amount to? Their political scope is severely limited by the ITA: 'They tell us what's sex and what isn't, what's politics and what isn't, what's violence and what isn't', said Val Parnell. Labour views must be balanced by Tories, and contentious programmes are submitted beforehand. But in the social and cultural character of their programmes, the tycoons can still have enormous scope. Their sudden emergence has defied the managerial revolution: they are a throwback to the days of early press barons. 'You must remember that the ethos of a company doesn't flow from the structure of its Board', Sir Ivone Kirkpatrick told Clive Jenkins, when cross-examined about TV ownership[1]: but although the companies are hedged round with managers, technicians, producers in their solid bureaucracies, the personal influence of the owners stands out in all companies: they control the key business of 'programming'—arranging for the worst programmes to go on at the peak viewing times, and the best late at night; and they can, if they wish, allow experiment. But few of the TV contractors are much interested in television, art, plays, or news; they are interested in quick, safe profits, and have in varying degrees allowed the programmes to be dictated by the relentless commercial pressures of the Tam ratings and the advertisers. Like insurance companies, popular newspapers or advertising agencies, they have preferred to abdicate their power of patronage in favour of profitability.

The influence of advertisers, as with newspapers, has been more general than specific: the TV Act was framed to prevent any kind of link-up between advertisers and programmes, but the

Power behind the Screen, p. 250.

pressure of big advertisers—Daz alone spends £700,000 a year on TV—is such that it forces programmes into the same mass-mindedness as soap and detergents, squeezing minorities into the late evening.

Looking back on the original TV debates, it seems odd how much the two sides were considered in black and white—a rigid monopoly on one side, a huckster's free-for-all on the other, a choice between the governess state and the Omo state. Many supported commercial TV mainly out of exasperation with BBC complacency, and the sluggishness of the BBC provoked the vulgarity of commercial TV. Here again we find the deep British gulf between the old collegiate tradition on the one side and the brash outsiders on the other, between Gentlemen and Players. The lack of awareness in the BBC—like the unawareness of Lazard's or Courtaulds—of the forces that were assembling against it remains one of its most astonishing characteristics. The BBC is an outstanding example of an institution which could not apparently move except under applied forces.

As usual, a synthesis later emerges. Firstly the BBC has transformed itself under the challenge. The tycoons, particularly Val Parnell, urge that the BBC should contract out of the race for viewers, and look after cultural minorities: 'The BBC should never have copied commercials: now there isn't an alternative programme'. But the BBC is well aware that its future too depends on a popular, though very different, mandate—not from ratings, but from parliament, which must review its charter; and they have gradually lowered their sights to keep pace with commercial. In some respects the two sides are now almost indistinguishable; it has even been said that the BBC shows slightly more inches of leg per minute than commercial. The BBC likes to talk about 'Gresham's Law of Commercial TV—bad programmes drive out good', but they are not themselves invulnerable to that law. But in the important news-magazine programmes—Panorama, To-night, Monitor—the BBC has consistently beaten its competitors, not simply by being less conscious of ratings, but by maintaining the loyalty of serious commentators, and building up a tradition of serious journalism in which commercial programmes have so far largely failed. The corporate loyalty of the BBC remains strong, and horrified though Reith now is by the abandonment of his ideals, much of his austere and brooding spirit still hangs around the buildings.

And meanwhile, the character of the commercial companies

has been gradually changing. Sidney Bernstein likes to quote an old Hollywood saying: 'There was a time when you couldn't afford to be honest: but later you couldn't afford to be dishonest'. The fat years of TV profits are probably already over; the huge profits are steadily being nibbled away by the unions, the actors and the usual Parkinsonian tendencies; the tycoons are beginning to diversify their interests, and have sold out part of their holdings. By 1964 the contracts will come up for renewal, which will almost certainly limit their scope. At the time of writing (April 1962) the outcome of the Pilkington Committee is still unknown, but the mere presence of the committee has had some effect, inducing the companies to provide a flood of expensive highbrow programmes to impress it. The assumption (which seems implicit in Sir Robert Fraser's attitude) that there is no half-way between giving people what they want and what they ought to want, between the Benthamite and Platonic ideals, becomes less obvious as the BBC becomes more conscious of ratings, and the companies more conscious of parliament.

Out of its wild origins, from show business, bus business, box offices and stately homes, commercial TV will no doubt gradually throw up a new race of professional television managers: in twenty years' time the first fat years will seem as legendary as the old days of Hollywood. But the origins, no doubt, will still stamp the corporate characters, as Mond and McGowan stamped ICI, or Reith the BBC. To future historians it may seem surprising that a British government, between long speeches about the unique glories of the British traditions and cultural heritage, should have arranged that the most powerful medium of communication ever devised should be sub-contracted to groups bent on total commercialisation.

TELEVISION CIRCUS

Whoever runs it, the impact of television will continue. Britain is the second biggest TV market in the world, but while in America commercial TV rose out of an established jungle of commercial radio, salesman's attitudes, publicity machines and a vast film business, in Britain it has burst into a more tribal and placid territory with the suddenness of an invasion. This mobile column has barged through the middle of many old British institutions: it threatens to by-pass parliament by bringing major discussions straight to the viewer, so that politicians (even Macmillan[1]) bother

[1] *See* page 333.

more about the screen than about the back-benchers. It provides new scope for the Church to project discussions both serious and ridiculous (e.g., the Archbishop of York and Adam Faith). It has changed the whole pace of consumer buying, bringing salesmen into the drawing-room and regulating the movements of packets in supermarkets. It gives new scope for the love of pageantry, and the quasi-religious attitude to monarchy. It provides a huge new weapon of education and information. And it projects a classless, Americanised, competitive world, full of mid-Atlantic accents and sleek cars, into the remotest villages where TV aerials stick up with the regularity of chimneypots.

No doubt its influence is often exaggerated; TV has a fairytale quality, and a knack of draining subjects of their meaning, leaving the faces remembered, but not what they said. But its indirect, insidious power of projecting images, ways-of-life and associations of ideas is such that no institution can afford to ignore it. The keys to this new magical kingdom are essential for anyone concerned with salesmanship, politics or simply fame. TV already has its 'New Boy Net' of men who have mastered this publicity machine: as the Old Boy Net has its magic of antiquity, with the Palace in the background, so the New Boys have a new synthetic magic, which can turn nonentities into national heroes.

At the big studios outside London the ephemeral dream-world of television is carefully concocted by technicians and producers, in their factories of images and fame. Under the cameras dangling like bats from the roof, the disparate subjects assemble—an archbishop talking to a pop singer, a trade unionist talking to a Tory MP: they troop on and off in endless cavalcade, all mixed together —professors, jugglers, cabinet ministers, ventriloquists, dukes, chairmen, compères and diplomats—all punctuated by quick glimpses of detergents and toothpaste. On the magic screen people who have never met each other before chat away with Christian names, as if they jostled together every day in some inner world of power.

39

ANATOMY OF BRITAIN

Everything is always decided *somewhere else*.
Barbara Wootton

Things fall apart; the centre cannot hold,
Mere anarchy is loosed upon the world.
W. B. Yeats: ' *The Second Coming* '

HERE, at the end of a baffling journey, I will not try to give a broad assessment of Britain's problems, but simply to pull together some threads from thirty-eight chapters and to give some personal journalist's impressions: about the problems of the end of empire; the discrepancy between prestige and power; the elusive nature of 'The Establishment'; the deepening grooves of the professions; and the apparent lack of dynamic and stimulus in Britain today.

THE VICTORIANS

All through this book I have felt haunted by the Victorians, who invented so many of the institutions which we now work—regiments, public schools, civic universities, the professional civil service, political parties, the Pru: their vast and confident buildings and churches which we now so awkwardly inhabit were monuments to their sense of purpose. It is hardly surprising that, in twenty years since the war, Britain should have felt confused about her purpose—with those acres of red on the map dwindling, the mission of the war dissolving, and the whole imperial mythology of battleships, governors and generals gone for ever. Her ideologies, both conservative and socialist, have become confused. 'The trouble is', said one cabinet minister, 'we don't believe in *anything*: we don't believe in Communism, or in anti-Communism, or in free enterprise.'

Of all stages in a great country's history, the aftermath of Empire must be the hardest. At the back of many politicians' minds there remains a dread that Britain will become trapped in her past and that, in Sir Geoffrey Crowther's words, 'Britain will be to the twenty-first century what Spain was to the eighteenth'. So many of the institutions which we like to regard as timeless were, like Tower Bridge or KCMGs, devised by the Victorians for a specific and calculated purpose, as part of the great system of Empire. Men in their forties, like Macleod, can remember 'the day when at school a third or a quarter of the map was coloured red, and you did get some sort of consolation for being in this bright little, tight little island, and all the old jingo phrases, because of the very vastness of the empire, of which Britain was not only the head, but the owner'.[1]

Many politicians have stressed the new predicament: 'People don't often realise that the Victorian Age was only an interruption in British History', said Harold Macmillan: 'the trouble is that a lot of people look back to that time of stability'.[2] But for this unawareness, it seems to me, the government and its institutions are at least as much to blame as the governed. The civil service, the palace, the honours system, have all projected an apparently unchanged and permanent world; while Britain becomes again a competitive trading nation, the weight of tradition and prestige remains in an imperial context. Of all the ideas which the Victorians fostered, surely one of the most dangerous was permanence —whether of Britain's supremacy, of consols or of the 'permanent way'. While the sense of the future and the radicalism of the Victorians evaporated, the idea of permanence remained. Railways, family firms, coal mines or regiments all acquired the safe, unchanging character of a country estate.

In this misleading calm, the old pragmatic attitudes continue to be cherished; our outdated Victorian inventions are defended because they are '*there*', or because 'it's odd but it works'. In a country which was expanding steadily, acquiring an Empire by accident, developing vast new institutions, the old complacent empiricism was justifiable enough. The cotton industry, railways or Oxford colleges 'just growed', and perhaps were none the worse for it. But when the country has to change direction quickly, pruning its commitments and limiting the national effort to definite fields, bold decisions soon become essential and 'it's *there*' is no answer. A reluctance to analyse new rôles appears in many institutions, but most markedly in the two most influential. The Foreign Office fights shy of any long-term assessment of

[1] *See* p. 91.
[2] *See* p. 341.

Britain's foreign commitments; while the Treasury evades the basic question of 'in what sense should Britain still be a great power'?[1] The inherited network of British commitments, bases, and institutions, needs pruning as drastically as British Railways' branch lines; to remember past doctrines about the indispensability of Suez or Cyprus is to see how expensive the empiricism can be. The civil service, still contained in its 1870 structure, distrusts any attempt at 'long-think', and Whitehall is full of Snorris, wise men 'who had not the gift of foresight'.[2] The distrust, I suspect, stems not only from devoted pragmatism, but a certain subconscious dread of the future.

PAGEANTRY AND SECRECY

The dominating presence of the Victorians is enhanced by the traditional British habit of preferring to honour the old institutions, with their pageantry and rigmaroles, rather than the new more powerful ones. I have encountered in nearly every sphere the discrepancy between Britain as she likes to appear, and Britain as she is. The gap between pomp and power, between the 'dignified' and the 'efficient' parts, is an immemorial British trait, and an attractive safeguard against demagogy. It is reassuring to hear crowds applauding a royal procession or a Lord Mayor's show, and to know that the objects of their interest have scarcely any power. While the Court of the Bank of England assemble on their hundred-and-fifty-coloured carpet, a few shy under-secretaries in the Treasury cut the ground from under their feet. While heads of colleges process through the quadrangles, the University Grants Committee doles out the money in Belgrave Square. The Lords summon the Commons to their chamber, while the Commons deprive the Lords of their power. At the centre of the show stands the monarch, surrounded with every splendour except power.

The pageantry is picturesque, apparently harmless, and much envied and copied by other countries. Moreover, if pomp and power *do* come together (as Gaitskell pointed out) you are liable to have dictatorship. But after visiting the darker caves of government, I believe that this game has gone to ridiculous lengths. Whitehall loves to present an irrelevant façade, behind which the real machinery can work in secrecy (which is just as strong a

[1] *See* p. 274.
[2] C. P. Snow. *See* p. 242.

British tradition as pageantry). Some secrecy, no doubt, is essential to good government, but vast territories of British administration are totally uncharted, and much of the obscurity is devoted to concealing, not great state secrets, but petty squabbles, for instance about maps.[1] A Defence white paper, deciding how to spend more than a quarter of Britain's budget, emerges from the New Public Buildings, but who knows what were the arguments that preceded it, and what evidence is offered for parliament to latch on to? Industrial chairmen issue hollow annual reports which make a mockery of directors' responsibilities to shareholders (except, as with Courtaulds recently, when they suddenly need them).[2] While Lord Mayors, judges, bishops, the royal family and the noisier parliamentarians are all paraded in public, most of the real men of power who are actually shaping the future—men like Sir Robert Scott, Sir Richard Powell, Sir Keith Murray, Leslie Brown, George Cole, Sir Richard Hull—are hardly ever heard of.

No doubt there are dangers in letting light into these caves. The English inheritance of anonymous and selfless public service *is* a magnificent one, and civil servants are rightly terrified of public intrigue and showmanship—all the more so after watching their lords and masters. But there is a mean between total secrecy and total exposure, as French or American civil servants demonstrate. The public surely has the right to know something about how the central decisions are taken.

The Press, perhaps, are partly to blame; they have loved the old outward shows, revolving round the Budget and parliament's argy-bargy, and seem to have lost some of that intruding zeal which in the eighteenth century made journalists fight into parliament itself. And when they *do* penetrate Whitehall, the reasons for not uncovering (for instance) an incompetent official are usually overpowering; (he can't answer back; the Foreign Office would withdraw its co-operation; publicity, they say, would achieve the opposite to what is intended). But much more to blame for the prevailing secrecy is parliament, which likes to continue as if that 'continental nuisance, called bureaucracy' never existed, and delights in ancient and irrelevant procedures. If it is one of the parliament's main functions, as Bagehot maintained, to educate the public, then that education is now absurdly inadequate.

[1] *See* p. 276
[2] *See* p. 501

THEY

The idea of a few powerful people sitting round a table to fix Britain's future is one which many people fondle, as the fascination with the word 'Establishment' suggests. Britain's monarchic and aristocratic past encourages the idea of a few glittering drawing-rooms where all the key people gather together. Writers particularly, who are often not sure where they belong, have loved to describe 'the Great World' (Thackeray), 'The Thing' (Cobbett), or just 'They'. People love to imagine a set of concentric and narrowing circles, like a solar system, with the Prime Minister, the Governor of the Bank, the Lord Chancellor and the Editor of *The Times* in the middle. And this vision of a 'great world' helps to give dignity to the old professions.

There is much more support for this idea in Britain than in other countries. Memoirs are full of accounts of weekends where politicians, bankers, and diplomats settle the future together. Parliament still fosters the idea of a central amateur club, giving access to everyone else. The London clubs cultivate that image, and there are still London drawing-rooms—at Mrs. Ian Fleming's, Lady Pamela Berry's, Lady Antonia Fraser's—where astonishing juxtapositions suggest that They are after all one world—with Roy Thomson chatting to the Marquess of Salisbury, Hugh Gaitskell to John Wyndham. Television, too, with its cavalcade of Christian-name celebrities, gives the impression that there, just behind the screen, is the single, powerful province of They. And the Palace perpetuates a picture of a single society, with the Royal Enclosure separating the We from the They.

But this simple vision is a mirage. In the first place, most of the real rulers—including permanent secretaries, investment managers and corporation managers—are hardly ever asked on to television screens or into society drawing-rooms. In the second place the rulers are not at all close-knit or united. They are not so much in the centre of a solar system, as in a cluster of interlocking circles, each one largely preoccupied with its own professionalism and expertise, and touching others only at one edge—an image depicted symbolically on the end-papers of this book; they are not a single Establishment but a ring of Establishments, with slender connections. The frictions and balances between the different circles are the supreme safeguard of democracy. No one man can stand in the centre, for there is no centre.

In writing this book I have had a growing impression of having visited not a single country but a loose federation of institutions, each threatening, not to coalesce, but to conflict or break away. Their variety of character is rich and perplexing, and investigating them I have become all too well aware of the impossibility of describing the subtle unwritten laws of behaviour which distinguish one circle from another. Their substance is made up not so much by groups of powerful men with vested interests, as by vague inherited climates of loyalty, habit and techniques. (When *The Times*, for instance, has a main story forecasting the removal of Selwyn Lloyd from the Foreign Office, it turns out not to be a plot between the Editor and Mr. Butler, but a mild speculation by the political correspondent, transposed on to the main page for technical reasons.) This is what has always made the processes of pressurising and lobbying so difficult to analyse in Britain, for they do not often (except in a few bizarre cases like the Commercial TV lobby[1]) conform to the traditional radical's picture of powerful men pulling levers. The 'departmentalism' of civil servants, or the 'Shelliness' of Shell men is compounded not so much of hard round balls of material advantage, as of vague clouds of moods and feelings, casting shadows over each other, and very occasionally generating lighting.

The specialisation and complexity of modern organisations has made the clouds denser, and harder to see out of. Parliamentarians engrossed in their ceremonial by-play, dons 'crawling along the frontiers of knowledge with a hand-lens',[2] bishops engrossed in the revision of Canon Law, Treasury mandarins exchanging kid-glove phrases; in the regions where you might look for a broad view of the anatomy you are soon overwhelmed with intestinal problems. And while the Treasury is striving towards its own central planning, each circle is making its own plans, with very little reference to others. Universities, corporations, defence scientists, financiers, all map out their private pictures of the future, and for many of them the yearly ritual of the Budget has very little relevance: 'I cannot recall any of them' (the Budgets), said Lord Fleck, of ICI, 'that made any significant change in our approach to what we were thinking of doing'.[3]

In all large institutions, moreover, the ends become easily lost in the means. The smooth Rolls Royce of the civil service ('you know it's the best machine in the world, but you're not quite

[1] *See* chapter 38.
[2] Sir Eric Ashby, p. 204.
[3] *See* p. 448.

sure what to do with it'),[1] or the teams of bureaucrats in Shell, show how easily the elaborate machinery can become regarded (in Bagehot's words) as 'a grand and achieved result, not a working and changeable instrument'. Even at the top, the complexity of the bureaucracies is such that chairmen are preoccupied with nursemaid tasks, trying to keep their children happy, to bring on the younger generation, and to prevent their nurseries falling apart. 'Most of your time is spent in the engine room; only occasionally do you go up on the bridge.'[2] 'I'm concerned far more with inside problems than with outside ones', said John Loudon of Shell.[3] 'There is always a danger', said Lord Heyworth about Unilever, that 'the business might fly apart by centrifugal force'.[4]

And brooding over all these self-contained circles, sitting in every committee, is the ubiquitous figure of Muddle, for whose power and influence I have developed a growing respect. In many of the great dramas of our time—the battle for Courtaulds, the Central African crises, the Aluminium War, even Suez—Muddle seems to have played a decisive rôle. While the outsider imagines that top people live in a world of sharp issues, Lord Heyworth in Unilever explained 'I look upon myself as someone who is perpetually in a fog'.[5] And he is not alone up there.

Even the most central committee of all, the cabinet, does not seem to enjoy (to use Treasury language) quite the cohesion and unity that one might expect; the meetings themselves are more likely to be concerned with disagreements than agreements, and ministers are preoccupied with their own departmental battles. 'I'm always surprised', said one senior civil servant, 'how little politicians actually talk to each other': and the pressure of meetings and departments sets (as Gordon Walker wrote) 'a strict upper limit upon the extent of democratic planning'.[6] The buckle which the cabinet is supposed to provide between the legislature and the executive is under perpetual strain, and the theory of 'collective responsibility'—always a tricky one becomes increasingly lost in the conflicting interests of departments. ('There should be an improvement in arrangements to enable Ministers to discharge their collective responsibility' as the Plowden Report tactfully explained.)[7]

Radical people regard the idea of a small group of 'Them'

[1] R. A. Butler. *See p.* 228.
[2] *See p.* 490.   [3] *See p.* 434.   [4] *See p.* 444.
[5] *See p.* 492.   [6] *See p.* 144.   [7] *See p.* 143-5

operating under the cloak of a democracy as inherently sinister and threatening. But the alternative can often be much more alarming—that there might be no 'they' at all, and that those in positions of influence refuse to face up to their power. 'The difference between autocracy and democracy is not that the first provides leadership, while the second eliminates it (wrote Alan Bullock, defending Ernest Bevin's position in the 'T and G'): 'the true distinction is in the character of the leadership'.[1]

Within the bureaucratic seats of power—whether the Treasury, the Prudential, the Midland Bank, or Shell—the question in my mind 'Who Runs Britain?', soon seemed to be ground to dust in the machinery of committees, each one insisting that they are servants of the other. Decisions (as Barbara Wootton said) always seem to be taken *somewhere else*, and what looked from outside like a bold step turns out to be gradual shuffles by scores of vaguely grouped men. If you ask a corporation man 'who runs this place?' you will be met with mutterings about cybernetics, lines of communication or five hundred managers. If you ask a chairman what is his main problem, he will say 'finding successors'.[2] Who is responsible for an ugly new building? It will turn out to be owned by some insurance company, designed by a committee of unknown architects, employed by a property developer to produce the maximum floor-space for a faceless corporation.[3] Each group can, and does, disclaim responsibility; the shapelessness of the building seems to express the shapelessness of the 'irresponsible society'. This, surely, is the greater nightmare of a democracy —not that the government is full of sinister and all-powerful *eminences grises*, but that the will of the people dissolves in committees, with thousands of men muttering about their duty to 'those whom we serve'. The idea that insurance companies are merely trustees, or that civil servants are no more than servants cannot possibly be squared with their actual powers: but the evasive humility continues. When asked if he is a wielder of power the committee man will answer (as William Cooper wrote), *'that is not how it seems to him'*.[4]

But however faceless the institutions may appear, real people with real powers *can* run them, and behind the blank façade, the right decisive men in the right jobs, like Sir Norman Brook or Dr. Beeching, can still break through deadlocks, committees and

[1] Alan Bullock: *The Life and Times of Ernest Bevin* 1960. p. 206.
[2] For instances *see* pp. 372, 443.
[3] *See* p. 419-21.   [4] *See* p. 249.

W

muddle. I feel now much more convinced that despite the managerial revolution, a great deal still depends on two hundred men. ICI may appear to be a vast federation of boards and factories, run by a few hundred managers; but in a time of critical decision it is, for better or for worse, decisively run by Paul Chambers. In spite of the age of the common man, and the webs of committees and statistics, much of the history of our time has been forged by a handful of men, as different as Reith, Heyworth, Cousins and Norman Collins.

'All of us', said a barrister, 'are much more in grooves than we were', and the grooves cut through this book. It is true that managers in many respects have become more, not less, interchangeable, often indeed indistinguishable. Admirals, bishops, directors, have all become more alike, all tending to become house-trained committee-people, with a quiet de-personalised manner: they seem, as Lord Devlin said, like the same man playing different parts, 'all Gerald du Maurier in the end'.[1] Admirals (as Sir Caspar John said) are no longer 'men with black beards pacing the quarterdeck', but more like general managers of companies. Even a bomber pilot has become much more like a technologist, facing a battery of instruments. (Every profession, from the Bar to the Army, has lost some of its glamour and panache, and style, whether for furniture or barristers, has become more functional.) Diversification in industry[2] and the techniques of professional management have broken down much of the old mystiques about brewing, shipping or farming, so that a modern brewery boss, like Thompson of Ind Coope's, could equally well be running a chain store. And Treasury mandarins can apparently move quite easily from regulating taxation to running computers or steel-works.[3]

But these to-ings and fro-ings seem small compared to the great body of managers who spend their whole careers climbing up inside one great Leviathan, with little contact with anyone outside. The Whitehall mandarins switch from taxes to fish, but they remain within a single bureaucratic tradition; while in industry, the pyramids, pension rights, and organograms conspire to bind men with chains of gold to a single corporation.

In the past two great fields allowed individuals to prove them-

[1] *See* p. 156. [2] *See* p. 497. [3] *See* p. 286.

selves boldly, outside the conformism of bureaucracies. The first was the Empire, which provided a testing-ground for Britain's leaders, away from the world of 'it's not done'. Many of Britain's key figures—Sir Frank Lee in Nyasaland, George Cole in West Africa, John Loudon in Venezuela, Paul Chambers in India—had their first great opportunity on the frontiers of the Empire which helped to give them (I suspect) a decisiveness which they never afterwards lost. Industrial corporations still need their pioneers and frontiersmen, but they are more likely to be salesmen or technologists; and as 'regionalisation' progresses, so more administrators find themselves back in head office, treading on each others' toes.

But the greatest testing-ground was, of course, the war; and still, twenty years afterwards, British administration owes much to that colossal shake-up. It was then that Britain discovered its versatile dons, turned businessmen into civil servants, admen into propagandists, scientists into administrators, teachers into soldiers, businessmen into politicians. Most of the major figures in Britain today—Macmillan, Gaitskell, Lloyd, Wilson, Penney, Plowden—owed their first great breakthrough to that time, so that, after the war, Britain had a generation of young administrators to rival Kennedy's in youthfulness: Gaitskell, Chancellor of the Exchequer at 44, Harold Wilson, President of the Board of Trade at 31, or Sir Oliver Franks, Ambassador to Washington at 43.

Today presents a less stimulating spectacle: a cabinet of familiar figures, with younger men queueing outside; offices with bottlenecks of men in their fifties jostling each other, hoping perhaps to move to an Oxford college or an industrial firm; a queue of governors, returning from independent territories. Most of the spectacular young appointments—Christopher Soames (41) in the cabinet, Lord Cromer (43) at the Bank of England, David Ormsby-Gore (44) in Washington, Julian Amery (43) at the Air Ministry, belong to the network of families following page 34. The young 'whiz-kid' administrators, like Robert McNamara in America, or Franks and Gaitskell in the 1940's, are not much in evidence, yet it is hard to believe that Britain either lacks, or can afford to do without, such talents: 'Many mute, inglorious Franks's', wrote David Butler,[1] 'may be lying undiscovered in common rooms.' British leaders have not welcomed the 'New Frontiers' to take the place of the old frontiers of

[1] 'Too little change at the Top' *Daily Telegraph*, May 9, 1961.

W*

empire and war, and many of the jobs most vital for Britain's future—like vice-chancellorships of new universities or heads of nationalised industries—have been hawked around.

Youth itself has no special advantage; but a bold interchange of people from one sphere to another, before they become settled in one groove, is, it seems to me, an essential ingredient for reform and dynamic ideas. And as the grooves of the most central and complicated institutions, such as the Treasury or insurance companies, become deeper, so they become less and less able to see the problems of society as a whole.

Between my visits, I found myself playing with various classifications of top people—between the analytical and the practical, between the calmers-down and the rubbers-up, between the showmen and the mandarins, between those who enjoyed talking about their jobs (all politicians, many civil servants, Dr. Beeching, Jack Cotton, Harley Drayton) and those who didn't (most bankers, industrial chairmen, accountants). I was even tempted to divide top people simply into the short—(with Ernest Marples, Paul Chambers, Iain Macleod, Sir Frank Lee, Roy Thomson leading the team) and the tall (led by Harold Macmillan, Cecil King, Sir Norman Brook and all the dukes). But a genuine distinction, it seems to me, is between the open and closed minds—between the men whose thinking has been conditioned by the rules and atmosphere of a single institution, and those who see over the partitions, and adopt institutions to suit their new ends.

It is the charm and the danger of the old collegiate institutions, whether Oxbridge colleges, Inns of Court or Whitehall departments, that unless faced with a *visible* crisis they cultivate their privateness and pride. The stubborn independence of barristers, dons or scientists is the greatest safeguard of democracy, and to get them all into line would defy the most dictatorial government. But this fissiparity can have the most absurd results—like the squabbles of the Inns of Court, the jealousies of engineers,[1] or the scientists' arguments as to 'who drank the Nescafé'.[2] The war rubbed up (to use Butler's phrase) the whole surface of Whitehall, bringing in businessmen and dons, and the bonds that were then established (for instance Sir Frank Lee's contacts with businessmen) are still crucial. But the dons have sailed back to their 'medieval islands' and the Treasury has climbed back into its ivory tower; the 'Treasury stud list'—that cosy

[1] *See* p. 518.   [2] *See* p. 526.

circle of people considered acceptable for royal commissions, Government committees and boards—has its stage army of peers and public figures, often too old or too busy to apply much energy. Industrialists in mid-career do not emerge into Whitehall, and only by luck and Marples was Dr. Beeching unearthed from the inner caves of ICI.

AMATEURS

All this is the antithesis of the old English ideal of the amateur. In the House of Lords, in clubland, even at the Institute of Directors, you will hear people say 'we have chaps from every walk of life here, you know—there's nothing like *this* in America or Russia'. No English ideal is more attractive nor, it seems to me, more abused: the unwanted amateur has his apotheosis in the 'old boy nets' of insurance companies or joint stock banks, where boards of ex-generals, landowners or retired politicians are supposed to provide the 'all-round view', but more often merely block the view for the real managers. If the House of Lords were *really* a cross-section—led by the most distinguished scientists, managers, dons, accountants, lawyers—it could help to give the cross-fertilisation and access to professions which government lacks: but as it is, its most consistent expertise is about land, forestry or deer, and its amateur ideal has got stuck in the early nineteenth century—as if neither the industrial nor the bureaucratic revolutions had ever occurred.

The institution which should really provide the central meeting-place which one looks for is the House of Commons, and here, I believe, the betrayal of the amateur ideal is most serious: for parliament, the most precious and unique of all British institutions, has allowed larger and larger areas to disappear from its purview, until now it devotes most of its time to subjects on which the old-fashioned amateur can talk with confidence—about social reform, foreign and colonial affairs, taxation—while on questions of Treasury control, scientific spending or industrial organisation few members have anything interesting to say. The most effective of parliament's modern weapons, the select committees—which do provide insight into the workings of bureaucracies—remain astonishingly unpublicised and unread. In any country the problems of maintaining democratic control over a modern technological state are appalling: those huge seven-year defence projects which roll on under their own momentum are enough to baffle the most conscientious MP. Yet is is hard to believe that parliamentarians could not adapt their routine to give a more thorough surveillance, to hold up a broader mirror to the nation.

'The ordinary man in Great Britain', said Aneurin Bevan, attacking Eden's evasiveness about the Cairo conference in December 1943, 'has been spending his life for the last couple of generations in this will-o'-the-wisp pursuit of power, trying to get his hands on the levers of big policy, and trying to find out where it is, and how it was that his life was shaped for him by somebody else. We were convinced by our institutions and representative democracy that the House of Commons itself was that instrument, and that seat of power; but these Debates, and especially the speech of my Right Hon. Friend yesterday, convinced me that the House of Commons is becoming almost irrelevant.'

THE ESTABLISHMENT

Every developed country must have trouble preventing its interlocking circles from flying apart—what Khrushchev calls 'the decay of the sense of overriding purpose'. (We probably forget how hard Khrushchev has to work to keep *his* circles together.) Every country, to work at all, must have some 'power élite' of men who keep in touch with each other, and exchange inside information (as Lord Chandos puts it) like the croupier shuffling the cards.[1] The idea of a central nexus, shaking their heads and saying 'Well, mmm, perhaps' may be a radical's nightmare, but some kind of an inner group is essential. My own fear is not that the 'Establishment' in Britain is too close, but that it is not close enough, that the circles are overlapping less and less, and that one half of the ring has very little contact with the other half. In particular, the hereditary Establishment of interlocking families, which still has an infectious social and political influence on the Conservative party, banking and many industries, has lost touch with the new worlds of science, industrial management and technology, and yet tries to apply old amateur ideals into technical worlds where they won't fit.

The atmosphere of privilege which hangs round the Conservative party is not itself necessarily disastrous: politics and banking are dynastic businesses in most countries; not even the Churchills and Cecils can compete in scope with the Kennedys, and even

[1] *See* p. 20.

Khrushchev recognises the importance of sons-in-law. But the menace of the British Conservative nexus, it seems to me, lies in the fact that it has retreated into an isolated and defensive amateur world, which cherishes irrelevant aspects of the past and regards the activities of meritocrats and technocrats as a potential menace.

The contemporary obsession with 'Them' itself suggests a very serious failure of communication, whether among factory-workers talking about the 'Kremlin', or industrialists who see Whitehall as a solid phalanx of 'them': ('when deputations of businessmen come to see me', said one cabinet minister, 'they always seem to think of the Government as if it was something quite separate from themselves, for which they had no responsibility'). In every country, no doubt, outsiders are apt to have a complex about the power élite, and to anyone subject to persecution mania, 'they' provide the perfect bogy and the convenient new mythology. 'The conspiracy theory of society', wrote Professor Karl Popper,[1] 'is nothing but a kind of inverted theism, an inverted belief in gods whose whims and wills rule everything and look after everything. It comes from abandoning God and then saying "Who is in his place?".'

But although the 'conspiracy' theory is usually untenable, the corridors of Whitehall, with their secretive, collegiate traditions, easily give outsiders the appearance of a solid bastion, and lead scientists particularly to regard 'them', not without some reason, as a separate, arrogant breed. The resulting barrier, and the battles which rage across it (like the skirmishes between soldiers and civilians inside the War Office)[2] can do vast damage, and the isolation of the mandarins becomes more serious as Britain moves towards a programme of planning which needs above all a community of thought between politicians, civil servants and technocrats.

MALAISE

'The decay of the sense of overriding purpose' is no doubt a problem in all industrial countries as the circles become more complex and specialised. But when a country doesn't believe in anything, and is confused about its direction, the problem is obviously worse: 'Committees only get moving under the pressure of applied forces', as one scientist said, and the same seems to

---

[1] Karl Popper, 'Towards a Rational Theory of Tradition', *Rationalist Annual*, 1949.
[2] *See* p. 261.

happen with countries. The Victorians were pushed forward by a profound belief in progress and the imperial mission. In 1940 the applied forces of war brought together the scattered professions and tribes, and the common danger produced not only a burning radicalism but, paradoxically and wonderfully, an intense interest in the future. After the Fleming Report, the Beveridge Report, the White Paper on the Foreign Office, each with their insistence on social change and mobility, the post-war years have had a sense of tragic bathos. Radicalism seems less concerned with changing institutions than with a sense of doom from the H-bomb; the social ferment has subsided, the public schools have prospered as never before, and Oxford and Cambridge have refashioned their gilded cages. The professions have become more separate and self-absorbed, with less sense of belonging all to the same society: 'When I deliver lectures about the social responsibilities of science', said Sir Solly Zuckerman, 'the young scientists regard me as an old square'.[1] Without any special motives for change, the dons become more donnish, the Etonians more Etonian, the mandarins more mandarin, and Britain relapses into a strange new tribalism.

In the last year the sense of 'malaise', as Whitehall calls it, has become suddenly much more acute, leading some people to urge Britain's entry to the Common Market as the means of providing new stimulus.

'I think that most of us recognise that in a changing world, if we are not to be left behind and to drop out of the main stream of the world's life, we must be prepared to change and adapt our methods. All through history this has been one of the main sources of our strength.' So said Harold Macmillan, announcing the application to join the Common Market in July 1961.

'How can Britain look to other people if it continues to stagnate economically?' said Hugh Gaitskell in October 1961.[2] 'Visitors will still come and praise the behaviour of our policemen and will say half pityingly and half affectionately that we are easy-going, kindly, tolerant people with a great and glorious past whose only trouble is that they are stuck to it. They will no longer come to Britain for ideas about the future but only to study history. They will see that, somehow, the British have lost their dynamic, are sunk in complacency, are far too snobbish, and have carried on a pattern of social relationships that is disappearing elsewhere in the world.'

[1] *See* p. 520.   [2] *See* p. 99.

MONEY

'What would be the good if people were to say the British are nice people but they no longer have money?' said Dr. Per Jacobsson.[1] Towards the end of Britain's long Antonine Age, the ability to make money seemed often secondary to the administrative, regimental virtues which the public schools so succesfully fostered, and in the early 1900's the Empire provided a substitute for industrial success. It is difficult for Britain to realise now that her world influence depends on her economic strength (or to remember for instance that West Germany is giving as much aid to underdeveloped countries as Britain). After its long protection, and in the calm of old family firms, a large slice of British commerce has become astonishingly uncommercial, allowing the British to acquire what Paul Chambers calls 'a sentimental softness for inefficiency'.

A certain monotony of plot attends many of the post-war stories of take-overs and mergers; on the one side a stately board of titled and family directors, with perhaps a peer, a general or a courtier at the head; on the other a tough, un-English intruder, dedicated to maximisation of profits and selling up freeholds, and often appealing—a cad's trick—to the shareholders. One by one the stately edifices have been invaded—Harrods, Fortnum and Mason's, the *Sunday Times*,[2] British Aluminium:[3] only by a hair's breadth did Watneys and the Savoy escape the same fate. The battle for Courtaulds was more complicated: but part of it boils down to the different 'philosophies' of Sir John Hanbury Williams, (courtier, born in Windsor Castle, Director of the Bank of England), and Paul Chambers (aggressive, self-made, maximising, taxation expert). No doubt the battle between 'Old Freddies' and the upstarts is as old as money: the city has grown used to the rebels of one moment becoming the Establishment of the next.[1] And yet one suspects that the sharp polarity between the protective and the aggressive has become absurdly sharp: which is one to prefer, the stiff, protective world of the Old Freddies, or the ruthless maximising world of Charles Clore.

To many people, both extremes are equally unwelcome. Between protective monopoly and all-out exploitation there must be half-way houses. But Britain has been very unwilling to face up to the consequences and problems of free enterprise.

[1] *See* p. 368.   [2] *See* p. 119.   [3] *See* p. 383-92.

While the Labour Party has till recently regarded nationalisation as the panacea, the Conservatives (as Enoch Powell
complains) look askance at men like Charles Clore who push
competition to its logical limits, and their aristocrats, while skilful
at protecting their interests, have (with exceptions like Lord
Cowdray or the Duke of Bedford) continued to turn their backs on
aggressive trade. The background of country life, unchanging and
civilised, remains intact to mock the urban money-makers; the
stability and perspective of this old tradition protects British
businessmen from neurotic obsessions with money and ulcers. But
in the protected state of Britain in the last twenty years and more,
the attitudes of Old Freddies have managed to become ludicrously
unreal, and the city has lost a good deal of its 'rough and vulgar
structure'. With the result that exploitation of Britain's assets by
any vigorous transatlantic visitors such as Roy Thomson or
Garfield Weston, becomes something of a pushover ('there
must be something wrong with this country if I can make
money so easily out of it'). And while Conservatives have gone on
talking about 'all that's best in the British traditions' and 'our
typically British way of resolving problems of taste'[1] a large part of
the communications industry has been taken over by outfits no
more British than 'Rawhide'.

SURRENDER TO FACTS

It is hard to believe that the British people have lost that
capacity for change and realism that has been their most remarkable characteristic. 'The unconditional surrender to facts',
wrote Emerson of us, 'and the choice of means to reach their
ends, are as admirable as with ants and bees'.[2] Much of the
unreality of attitudes, I believe, stems from that long unchanging
time, from 1939 to 1957, when Britain in its outward shape seemed
insulated against change, and which was itself preceded by the
stagnation of the thirties. The social revolution of 1945, though
profound, took ten years to show its effects on spending. For
nearly twenty years London's skyline, broken by bomb damage,
remained almost unchanged. Newspapers rationed their newsprint.
The BBC was unchallenged. The joint-stock banks were 'driving
a very powerful car at twenty miles an hour'.[3] It was scarcely

---

[1] Lord Kilmuir. *See* p. 604.
[2] Emerson, *English Traits*, 1856.
[3] *See* p. 371.

surprising that, in that state of truce, people became less competitive minded, and sometimes mistook commercial enterprises for
feudal estates. Then, within two years, the credit squeeze ended,
skyscrapers rushed up, supermarkets spread over cities, newspapers became fatter or died, commercial television began making
millions, shops, airlines, even coal and banks had to fight for their
lives. After the big sleep many people welcomed any novelty; any
piece of Americanisation seemed an enterprising change, and any
thrusting tycoon, however irresponsible, was regarded as a
phenomenon. Only now is Britain becoming *visually* aware of
living in a state of perpetual and perilous change.

Within the last two years there have, I think, been considerable
rumblings and signs of change. The Treasury's Neddy—which
may eventually change the whole character of Whitehall—has
been established. The House of Lords has been threatened with
reform. Dr. Beeching has set to work on British Railways. Seven
new universities have been planned. Provincial cities have been
re-shaped. And a step has been taken towards Europe which
could alter the whole perspective of British institutions. In
surveying the more somnolent regions of industry and government, or the procession of ancient families into the Government,
I have had the feeling of observing, not a settled tradition, but a
desperate rearguard action against a more professional and less
complacent age. Among younger men in politics, banking, industrial management and trade unions, there is clearly a growing
impatience with the class-bound attitudes of their elders. And the
spectacular Liberal revival indicates a profound discontent with
the state of leadership.

But though the pace has changed, the direction is still confused and uncertain, made much more so by the apparent
necessity for Conservative leaders to say one thing and do another,
or the Treasury's fondness for concealing change as unchange.[1]
It may be that the Common Market can provide that stimulus and
sense of purpose which is so obviously absent: but dropping tariffs
is no substitute for leadership, and the real stimulus can only come
from inside the society and its leaders.

I have written this book with my mind on particulars, not on
generalities, and without the academic equipment of a social or
political theorist. But I have been trying nevertheless to sum up
in one paragraph what I have felt to be wrong with Britain's
leadership. Briefly it is that the old privileged values of aristocracy,

[1] *See* p. 204.

637

W**

public schools and Oxbridge which still dominate government today have failed to provide the stimulus, the purposive policies and the keen eye on the future which Britain is looking for, and must have. The old ethos was moulded by the success of an invincible imperial machine. Its style was to make big things seem small, exciting things boring, new things familiar: but in the unconfident context of today this bland depreciation—and the assumed superiority that goes with it—merely succeeds in dispelling enthusiasms, blunting curiosity and dulling experiment. The groove-outlook, the club-amateur outlook, the pragmatic outlook are all totally out of keeping with an age which suffers, unlike the Victorians', from an oppressive lack of innovation and zeal. The old fabric of the British governing class, while keeping its social and political hold, has failed to accommodate or analyse the vast forces of science, education or social change which (whether they like it or not) are changing the face of the country. The new and potentially exciting institutions which control large areas of the future—for instance nationalised industries, insurance companies, Redbrick universities—have grown up in a separate and unacknowledged sector, and the resulting rift has cut off the old from the new. Britain's malaise, I suspect, is not primarily a malaise of the ordinary people, but a malaise among the few thousand managers of our society who have failed to absorb and communicate new challenges and new ideas.

The British are still quite capable of surrendering to facts provided they are told them. But the institutions and the men who work them have, I believe, become dangerously out of touch with the public, insensitive to change, and wrapped up in their private rituals. As Bagehot wrote, in the words with which this book began, 'The characteristic danger of great nations, like the Romans or the English, which have a long history of continuous creation, is that they may at last fail from not comprehending the great institutions they have created.'

INDEX

644

649

653

654

657

658

660

661

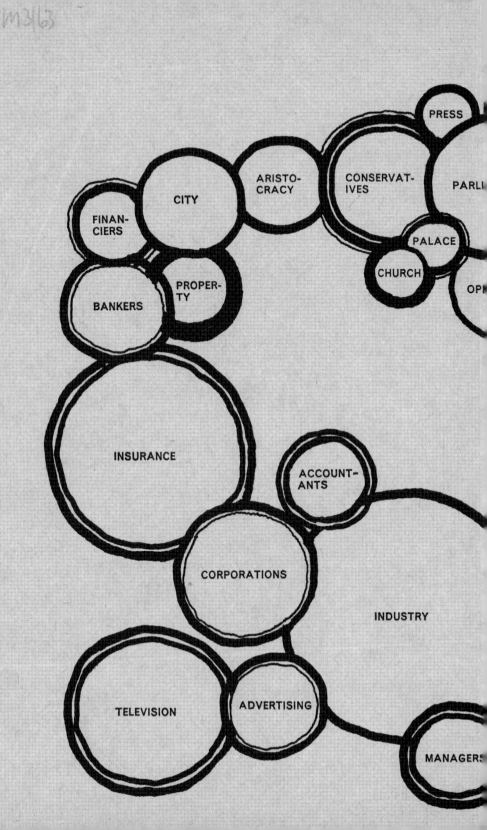